JOHN TAYLOR, TRAVELS AND TRAVELLING

John Taylor
Travels and Travelling
1616 – 1653

EDITED BY
John Chandler

THE HOBNOB PRESS

First published as *Travels through Stuart Britain: the Adventures of John Taylor, the Water Poet* in 1999 by Sutton Publishing.

This enlarged edition with additional material published in 2020 by The Hobnob Press,
8 Lock Warehouse, Severn Road,
Gloucester GL1 2GA
www.hobnobpress.co.uk

© John Chandler, 1999, 2020

The Author hereby asserts his moral rights to be identified as the Author of the Work.

All rights reserved. No part of this publication may be reproduced, stored in a retrieval system, or transmitted in any form or by any means, electronic, mechanical, photocopying, recording or otherwise, without the prior permission of the publisher and copyright holder.

British Library Cataloguing in Publication Data
A catalogue record for this book is available from the British Library

ISBN 978-1-906978-91-4

Typeset in Scala 11/14pt, with headings in Caslon Antique
Typesetting and origination by John Chandler

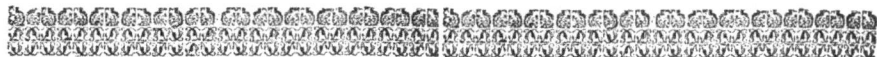

CONTENTS

Introduction vii
Bibliography xvi

TRAVELS

Three Weekes, Three Daies, and Three Houres Observations and Travel, from London to Hamburgh in Germanie (1616) 3

The Pennyles Pilgrimage (1618) 33

The Voyage in a Boat of Brown-Paper (1619) 85

Taylor his Travels. From the City of London in England, to the Citty of Prague in Bohemia (1620) 93

A Verry Merry Wherry-Ferry-Voyage: or Yorke for my Money (1622) 127

A New Discovery by Sea, with a Wherry from London to Salisbury (1623) 159

Taylor on Thame Isis (1631) 193

Part of this Summers Travels, or News from Hell, Hull, and Hallifax (1639) 215

John Taylors Last Voyage, and Adventure (1641) 249

Tailors Travels, from London, to the Isle of Wight (1648) 273

John Taylors Wandering, to see the Wonders of the West (1649)   287

A Late Weary, Merry Voyage, and Journey (1650)   309

A Short Relation of a Long Journey (1652)   327

The Certain Travailes of an Uncertain Journey (1653)   347

TRAVELLING

The Coaches Overthrow (c. 1636)   367

Taylors Travels and Circular Perambulation (1636)   373

The Honorable and Memorable Foundations (1636)   392

The Carriers Cosmographie (1637)   429

A Brief Director (c. 1642)   455

Index   463

INTRODUCTION

For every man would be a poet gladly,
Although he write and rime but badly, madly...

John Taylor came into my life about forty years ago when I was exploring the history of Salisbury. I discovered him tying up his wherry outside the King's Head in 1623, having proved – with four companions as crew – that it was possible to sail from London around the coast to Christchurch without drowning, and then to navigate the River Avon upstream from its mouth to the city. Not only that, but he could describe his voyage in swashbuckling verse, and – even more remarkably – he could persuade the mayor and council that they should set about improving their river for the city's prosperity. A larger than life character – why was he not better known?

And yet a century earlier an editor could write: 'The greater part of the reading public have heard many times of John Taylor, *The Water Poet*, and probably know a good deal about him'[1] That was no longer true. In the 1980s even professional historians, to whom Leland, Fiennes, Defoe and Cobbett were familiar friends, could only muster, 'oh yes, the water poet', when confronted with the name John Taylor, and became very vague when pressed to describe his work. The only study of him published last century up till then (so far as I was aware) was an eloquent and perceptive essay by Wallace Notestein, which appeared in 1956.[2]

By the time I set out about editing his travels for publication the obscurity had been lifted, by Bernard Capp's masterly biography and study of Taylor in all his facets,[3] and this became my essential and most illuminating point of reference throughout. My edition of the twelve

---

1 Taylor, 1888, p. 5
2 Notestein, 1956, pp. 169-208
3 Capp, 1994

journeys within Britain was published in 1999,[4] and after some years the book went out of print and the publisher went out of business. Meanwhile a great deal more was being written about Taylor. His pivotal role in the development of a minor genre – nonsense literature – was persuasively explored,[5] and the value of his journeys to the social historian was being recognized, for example in Felicity Heal's study of hospitality.[6] Major studies of the literature of travel during his period, by Andrew McRae, and of the means of travel, by Dorian Gerhold, have since been published, in both of which Taylor appeared as a significant figure.[7] Articles about specific works began to show up in academic periodicals, mostly by English scholars rather than historians, and I have included details of some of them in the bibliography which follows this introduction. A John Taylor conference took place in Cambridge in September 2017.

Meanwhile my work brought me to Gloucester, where Taylor originated, and I found myself living within view almost of the street where he was born, and walking daily past the site of the church where he would have been baptised. I became interested in his local connections and lectured to historical societies about 'the madcap adventures of a Gloucester boatman'. It seemed a good time to revisit my edition of the journeys.

This book includes the twelve journeys he made and reported on in Britain between 1618 and 1653, to which I have added his two overseas adventures, to Hamburg and Lower Saxony in 1616 and Prague in 1620. I have also included five pamphlets written between about 1636 and 1642 which shed interesting light on the business of travel and travellers at the period. Two concern inns and taverns, two are lists of carriers, and one is a brief poem complaining about coaches. The result is quite a substantial volume, although it comprises a relatively small proportion of Taylor's output through a writing career of more than forty years. Specialists can access facsimiles of all these works online, and will doubtless prefer to do so. The purpose of this edition is to bring an entertaining and important seventeenth-century author

4   Chandler, 1999
5   Malcolm, 1997
6   Heal, 1990, pp. 210-6
7   McRae, 2009; Gerhold, 2005

to a wider readership, especially to those interested in specific places and regions, in a handy and (I hope) trustworthy text, embellished with maps, annotations and an index.

***

Apart from a brief life by John Aubrey[8] most of what is known about Taylor comes from his own pen. He was born on St Bartholomew's Day, 24 August, 1578 in Gloucester, attended a school there without distinction, went off to London and became apprenticed on the Thames, was pressed for naval service, and from the late 1590s resumed his career as a waterman. This, under James I, became an overcrowded and rarely a lucrative calling but, like its modern counterpart, taxi-driving, afforded ample scope for conversation and (when trade was slack) private study. Taylor revelled in both.

There were other sources of employment too. From 1605 until 1613 and intermittently until 1617, he was employed as 'bottleman', a kind of excise officer who claimed for the governor of the Tower of London by ancient right a levy on wine imported through London. In 1613 he was made a 'King's' waterman, one of about forty officials who were responsible for ferrying members of the royal family and court. During the 1620s and 1630s he also became closely involved with the administration of his livery company, the Watermen. He lived at this period on the South Bank, Londoner's playground and red light district.

Ever a royalist and ridiculer of Puritanism, Taylor was in no doubt which cause to support in 1642. When war broke out he went with the court to Oxford, remained there administering traffic on the river until the king's defeat in 1646, and then returned to London in poverty. His days as a waterman were over, he was approaching seventy years old, dejected and destitute. He took up alehousekeeping with little success, and was buried in St Martin's-in-the-Fields on 5 December 1653. He may have starved to death.

Set beside this thumbnail biography of a man's modest rise and fall is John Taylor the writer. From 1612 until the weeks leading to his death he became a compulsive scribbler, in prose and verse, on every

[8]   Aubrey, 1898, vol. 2, pp. 252-3

imaginable subject. Today he would have been a journalist, and would probably have dabbled with chat shows and television documentaries. His writing earned him celebrity, hospitality and a better standard of living than a waterman might expect. He wrote for money, catching the public interest of the moment, and he organized the distribution and sale of his work himself. His most ambitious project (thus far) was to employ four printing presses to publish his collected works in 1630, a solid close-set folio, and a clear statement of his aspirations. During the civil war he found his ideal role, as pamphleteer of Royalist propaganda.

A browse through the 1630 corpus reveals the breadth of his canvas. There are sonnets, satires, histories of kings and queens, nonsense verse, squibs at other writers, journeys made for a wager or for subscribers, mock condemnations of vices, accounts of battles, murders, London during the plague, the cultivation of hemp, the habits of gluttons and whores. Closer inspection of these works demonstrates the vivacity of his much of his writing, his cleverness with puns, and a certain panache; but there is also an unevenness in quality, hack-work, and the smell of the lamp.

To Taylor, in fact, during his entire writing career of some forty years, are attributed more than two hundred works. Of these his fourteen journeys he saw as a group, and several times enumerated them towards the end. Although grouped together, the journeys are a mixed bag. Three of them were intended to promote inland navigation, to Salisbury (1623), on the Thames (1632) and around Gloucester (1641). One, the shortest, is sheer bravado (his paper boat adventure in 1619), and two are reportage, to Prague during the Bohemian wars (1620), and to the Isle of Wight on the eve of the regicide (1648). The remainder are travelogues, undertaken either near the beginning of his writing career, to Hamburg (1616), Scotland (1617) and York (1622), or right at the end (1649-53) when penury set the old man off on the road again, to the West Country, East Anglia, Wales and Sussex, in a desperate bid to emulate past successes. One other, and not the most successful, sees Taylor using travel writing as a vehicle for anecdote and contrived cleverness, as he darted between Leicester, Kings Lynn, Derbyshire, Halifax and Chester in 1639.

The lists of inns, taverns and carriers seem all to have been the product, if not of a single year (1636), at least over a short period, when Taylor was very much involved in the difficulties watermen faced in competition with other forms of travel. He was ideally equipped to produce such lists, since he had acquired substantial geographical knowledge, had access to the relevant reference sources of his day (including apparently the vintners' records), and was a streetwise Londoner who could engage with innkeepers and others possessed of the information he was trying to collect.

***

This is not the place to embark on a history of topographical and travel writing in Britain.[9] But it may be worthwhile to highlight some of the antecedents which influenced Taylor's efforts in this genre. The work of John Leland (c.1503-52), although not the first to write 'itineraries' or accounts of journeys in England and Wales, was enormously significant.[10] His descriptions of town and countryside during the 1530s and 1540s remained as manuscript notes after he became insane in 1547, but were heavily used by the next two generations of topographers (or chorographers as they styled themselves), notably William Camden (1551-1623). Taylor does not cite Leland (although he could have perused Leland's notes in the Bodleian Library during the 1640s), but he would have known of him through the work of Camden, and from William Harrison's (1534-93) topographical contributions to Raphael Holinshed's *Chronicles* (1577, 1586). Taylor refers to Holinshed, but his most important source for the history of specific places is Camden, whose *Britannia*, a chorographical description of the whole kingdom, was first published (in Latin) in 1586. Taylor had little Latin, so would have been acquainted with the work in the English translation (1610) by Philemon Holland of Coventry (1552-1637). He was on friendly terms with Holland, and stayed with him in 1618 on his way to Scotland.

Two other mentors are repeatedly cited. John Speed (c.1552-1629), the cartographer, published his *Theatre of the Empire of Great Britaine* in 1611, an atlas of all the English and Welsh counties, and with maps of Scotland and Ireland.[11] The atlas included brief chorographic

9 Cox, 1949; Moir, 1964; , Mendyk, 1989; McRae, 2009
10 Chandler, 1993; Carley, 2010, xxi-cv
11 Speed, 1988

descriptions, and Speed also compiled a history of Britain. The second was Michael Drayton (1563-1631), a versatile and established poet and dramatist, who drew heavily on Camden and Holinshed for his description of Britain in epic verse, *Poly-Olbion* (1612, 1622).

Leland and Harrison apart, all these authorities were older contemporaries of Taylor who were still active when he embarked on his writing career. They provided the academic and literary background to his topographical descriptions. But he owed as great a debt to writers in other fields, notably another member of Camden's and Drayton's generation, Thomas Nashe (1567-c.1601), who had died young. Nashe was a poet, entertainer and satirist, who moved in those same strata of London society which Taylor knew so intimately. He wrote a picaresque novel, *The Unfortunate Traveller* (1594); a satirical miscellany, *Lenten Stuffe* (1599; cf. Taylor's *Jack a Lent*) which included a chorographical description of Great Yarmouth, based on Camden, and to which Taylor alludes; and a battle of wits with another writer, *Pierce Penniless* (1592; cf. Taylor's *Penniles Pilgrimage*, and his controversy with Coryate). Nashe, one feels, was Taylor's role model.

Nashe, and later Taylor and others, were responding to a new appetite for travel literature, especially the exotic and unusual, which extended well beyond the educated classes, and which fed on Hakluyt's *Principall Navigations, Voiages and Discoveries of the English Nation* (1589-1600) at one level, and on the mass of chapbooks, ballads and other unsophisticated street literature at another. Journeys and adventures by 'ordinary' people came from the popular presses from the 1580s; the best known and most entertaining is William Kemp's *Nine Daies Wonder* (1600), describing a morris dance from London to Norwich. The most topical when Taylor took up his pen in c.1612 was Thomas Coryate's (c.1577-1617) description of his walk to Venice and back, published as *Coryats Crudities* (1611). Taylor felt that he could compete with Coryate on an equal footing, and made this abundantly clear by mocking and quarrelling with him in print.

And so we have the ingredients which, spiced with Taylor's own ebullient personality, make up the journeys presented here. Alongside the attempts at learned description there is plenty of knockabout foolery, yards of doggerel, muddle-headed moralizing, and worse. But Taylor's efforts should not be dismissed merely as some form of tabloid Leland, or

McGonagall's travels. For one thing he wandered very widely, reporting on what he saw throughout the British Isles; for another his travelling took place at a period when few other descriptions of Britain exist. A third point is that his writing is not artless. At his best, for instance on his way to York in 1622, he juxtaposes episodes of drama and farce, hostility and hospitality, serious information and anecdote, to keep the reader scudding along in his wherry. Most important of all, perhaps, he was the first to publish topography for and about everyman. His Britain is populated not only by noblemen, courtiers and bishops, as Leland's seems to be; on every page of Taylor we are introduced to fishermen, innkeepers or labourers as well. He seems to have had the knack of engaging everybody, and in his pages everybody is brought to life.

***

This is Taylor's book, not mine, and he of all people is quite capable of speaking for himself without interruption from me. Interruption has therefore been kept to a minimum. My principal aim in preparing this edition has been to provide a reliable text of the journeys and other travel-related pamphlets. I have tried, therefore, to present a text which is as faithful to the original publications as a modern reader would find comfortable. I have retained Taylor's punctuation, spelling (but substituting j for i, and v for u where appropriate), orthography of names and most of his abbreviations. I have, however, expanded the ampersand throughout, ignored Taylor's printers' use of italics (unless clearly employed for emphasis), and adopted modern conventions of capitalization. The typography and layout of the preliminary matter preceding most journeys, such as dedications, titles, and examples of the 'Taylor's Bills', are mine, not Taylor's, but I have not deviated from his words.

The six journeys included here which were made before 1630 were published twice during Taylor's lifetime,[12] first as separate tracts or pamphlets, and later reset in the 1630 collected works, production of which he oversaw. Although Taylor claimed in his subtitle to the collected works to have made corrections ('with sundry new additions,

12   The Prague journey was actually published twice, in 1620 and 1621, with significant changes, before the 1630 edition: see below, pp. 93, 95.

corrected, revised, and newly imprinted'), in fact the haste with which it was assembled appears to have introduced far more errors than it has removed. He admits as much in a prefatory poem to the collection, 'Errata, or faults to the reader'. Where there are discrepancies, therefore, I have followed the original edition, unless the 1630 reading is clearly a correction. Except for the most trivial differences, whenever I have preferred the 1630 edition to the original I have footnoted in italics the alternative. And when I have stuck to the original I have footnoted significant differences in the 1630 edition. Those journeys undertaken after 1630 do not, of course, occur in the collected edition, and none was published more than once during Taylor's lifetime. Obvious misprints are retained in the present text, followed by [sic], and where necessary clarification is provided by a footnote.

This is the full extent of the textual apparatus. But footnotes have also been used to convey other information. Taylor himself sometimes appended marginal notes, and these are reproduced as he wrote them, in quotation marks and followed by [Taylor]. My contribution to the footnotes has been to try to identify place-names, which I have given in the modern form and usually (in Britain) added the pre-1974 county; and to offer definitions of obscure and archaic vocabulary. I have also noted in a rather eclectic and unsystematic way (an approach of which Taylor, I think, would have approved) various matters which might interest or assist readers, including allusions to proverbs, quotations, Biblical and classical references, brief biographical details, historical and geographical explanations, and comparisons with Taylor's other works. Some places named in the lists of carriers and taverns cannot be identified with certainty.

To each journey I have prefixed a few words of introduction and a route map, in the conviction that, like me, many armchair travellers reading this book will not feel comfortable without a map. At the end is an index of persons and places.

True to the spirit of Taylor, who must have passed many a tedious mile ransacking his memory for rhyme or phrase, I am not ashamed to admit that much of my work on my previous edition was undertaken while travelling around England on public transport. This included journeys to the British Library and the Bodleian Library, Oxford, to examine originals and microfilms, and I should like to express my gratitude to the staff of both institutions. The availability on the internet (through Historical Texts, Early English Books Online) of facsimiles of Taylor's works has reduced the need for such excursions. I must also record my thanks to other libraries whose facilities I have used during the course of my research: the University Libraries of Bristol and London; the National Monuments Record Library, Swindon; public libraries in Bath and Wiltshire; and the Huntington Library, California, which for the previous edition kindly supplied a photocopy of *A Late Weary, Merry Voyage*. My debt to Bernard Capp's scholarship throughout (Capp, 1994) will be self-evident. For this enlarged edition research facilities made available to me by the University of the West of England (Bristol) and the University of London Institute of Historical Research are most gratefully acknowledged.

***

It is a peculiar, indeed an awesome, privilege which an editor enjoys, to befriend someone long dead, to try to enter their world and their mind, and then to link names on a title page. John Taylor, I hope that you would approve of this book, and that through it you will give others at least a modicum of the enjoyment which you have given me.

John Chandler
Gloucester
August 2020

> *Sixe things unto a traveller belongs,*
> *An asses back t' abide and beare all wrongs:*
> *A fishes tongue (mute) grudging speech forbearing.*
> *A harts quicke eare, all danger over-hearing,*
> *A dogs eyes, that must wake as they doe sleepe,*
> *And by such watch his corps from perill keepe.*
> *A swines sweet homely taste that must digest*
> *All fish, flesh, roots, fowle, foule and beastly drest:*
> *And last, he must have ever at his call*
> *A purse well linde with coyne to pay for all.*
> (below, p. 121)

BIBLIOGRAPHY

This bibliography includes works referenced in the introduction and some recent periodical literature influencing and reflecting the renewed interest in Taylor.

Aubrey, John, 1898, *Brief lives*, 2 vols., Oxford (edited by Andrew Clark)

Aune, M.G. 2020, 'Thomas Coryate versus John Taylor: the emergence of the early modern celebrity', *Cahiers Élisabéthains: a Journal of English Renaissance Studies*, vol. 101(1), pp. 85–104

Bradley, Katherine and Richard, 1982, 'William Bush - the flying boatman', *Berkshire Archaeological Journal*, vol. 71, pp. 57-70

Caldecott, J.B., 1940, 'John Taylor's tour of Sussex in 1653', *Sussex Archaeological Collections*, vol. 81, pp. 19-30

Capp, Bernard, 1994, *The world of John Taylor the Water-Poet, 1578-1653*, Oxford: Clarendon Press

Capp, Bernard, 2004, 'John Taylor [called the Water Poet], 1578-1653' in *Oxford Dictionary of National Biography* [online]

Carley, James P, (ed.) 2010, *John Leland, De viris illustribus, On famous men*, Oxford: Bodleian Library

Chandler, John (ed.) 1993, *John Leland's Itinerary: travels in Tudor England*, Stroud: Sutton

Chandler, John, 1995, 'John Taylor makes a voyage to Salisbury in 1623', *Hatcher Review* [Winchester], vol. 4 (no. 40), pp. 19-34

Chandler, John (ed.) 1999, *Travels through Stuart Britain: the adventures of John Taylor, the Water Poet*, Stroud: Sutton,

Cock, Emily, 2014, "Nonsence is Rebellion': John Taylor's *Nonsence upon Sence, or Sence, upon Nonsence* (1651–1654) and the English Civil War', *Ceræ: An Australasian Journal of Medieval and Early Modern Studies*, vol. 2, pp. 1-23

Cox, Edward G., 1949, *A reference guide to the literature of travel, vol. 3: Great Britain*, Seattle: Univ of Washington Press

Craik, Katharine, 2005, 'John Taylor's pot poetry', *Seventeenth Century*, vol. 20, pp. 185-203

Ellinghausen, Laurie, 2002, 'The individualist project of John Taylor, "the water poet"', *Ben Jonson Journal*, vol. 9, 147-69

Fall, Rebecca L., 2017, 'Popular nonsense according to John Taylor and Ben Jonson', *Studies in English Literature 1500-1900*, vol. 57 (1), pp. 87-110

Finlayson, J. Caitlin, 2017, 'John Taylor, the self-made poet, on merit and social mobility in mercantile London', *English Studies*, vol 98 (2), pp. 120-36
Gates, Joanne E., 2006, 'Travel and pseudo-translation in the self-promotional writings of John Taylor, water poet', in Di Biase, Carmine G. (ed.), *Travel and translation in the early modern period*, Amsterdam: Rodopi, pp. 267-80
Gerhold, Dorian, 2005, *Carriers and coachmasters: trade and travel before the turnpikes*, Chichester: Phillimore
Gerhold, Dorian, 2016, *London carriers and coaches 1637-1690*, Putney: Gerhold
Gregory, Johann, 2014, 'The publicity of John Taylor the water-poet: legitimating a social transgression', in Chiari, Sophie, and Palma, Hélène, *Transmission and transgression: cultural challenges in early modern England*, Aix-en-Provence: Presses Universitaires de Provence, pp. 139-52
Halasz, Alexandra, 2000, 'Pamphlet surplus: John Taylor and subscription publication', in Marotti, Arthur F. and Bristol, Michael D. (eds.), *Print, manuscript and performance: the changing relations of the media in early modern England*, Columbus: Ohio State University Press, pp. 90-102
Hartle, P.N., 2002, '"All his workes, sir": John Taylor's nonsense', *Neophilologus* vol. 86 pp.155–69
Heal, Felicity, 1990, *Hospitality in early modern England*, Oxford: Clarendon Press (Oxford Studies in Social History)
Hindley, Charles (ed.), 1872, *Works of John Taylor, the Water-Poet*
Januszczak, Waldemar, 2011, 'William Dobson: a portrait revealed', *Cassone: international online magazine of art and art books*, September 2011 [identifies Taylor as one subject of 'Portrait of an old and a younger man']
McRae, 2008, 'The literature of domestic travel in early modern England: the journeys of John Taylor', *Studies in Travel Writing*, vol. 12 (1), pp. 85-100
McRae, Andrew, 2009, *Literature and domestic travel in early modern England*, Cambridge University Press
Malcolm, Noel, 1997, *The origins of English nonsense*, London: Harper Collins
Mendyk, Stan A. E., 1989, *'Speculum Britanniae': regional study, antiquarianism, and science in Britain to 1700*, Toronto: University of Totonto Press
Moir, Esther, 1864, *The discovery of Britain: the English tourists 1540-1840*, London: Routledge
Notestein, Wallace, 1956, *Four worthies: John Chamberlain, Anne Clifford, John Taylor, Oliver Heywood*, London: Jonathan Cape
O'Callaghan, Michelle, 2007, *The English wits: literature and sociability in early modern England*, Cambridge University Press
Preiss, Richard, 2015, 'John Taylor, William Fennor, and the "Trial of Wit"', *Shakespeare Studies*, vol. 43, pp. 50-78
Rolfe, Kirsty, 2017, 'Probable pasts and possible futures', *Media History*, vol. 23 (2), pp. 159-76
Sanders, Julie, 2013, 'The *Pennyles Pilgrimage* of John Taylor: poverty, mobility

and performance in seventeenth-century literary circles', *Rural History*, vol. 24 (1), pp. 9–24

Semler, L.E., 2014, 'The Caroline grotesque in verse: Robert Herrick, Richard Flecknoe and John Taylor', *Yearbook of English Studies*, vol. 44, pp. 137-55

Speed, John, 1988, *The Counties of Britain: a Tudor atlas by John Speed*, London: Pavilion [facsimile, with introduction by Nigel Nicolson]

Taylor, John, 1630, *All the workes of John Taylor the Water-Poet. beeing sixty and three in number. collected into one volume by the author: with sundry new additions, corrected, revised, and newly imprinted*, London: James Boler (Scolar Press facsimile edition, 1973, with introduction by V.E. Neuberg)

Taylor, John, 1888, *Early prose and poetical works of John Taylor, the Water Poet...* London: Hamilton, Adams & Co.

TRAVELS

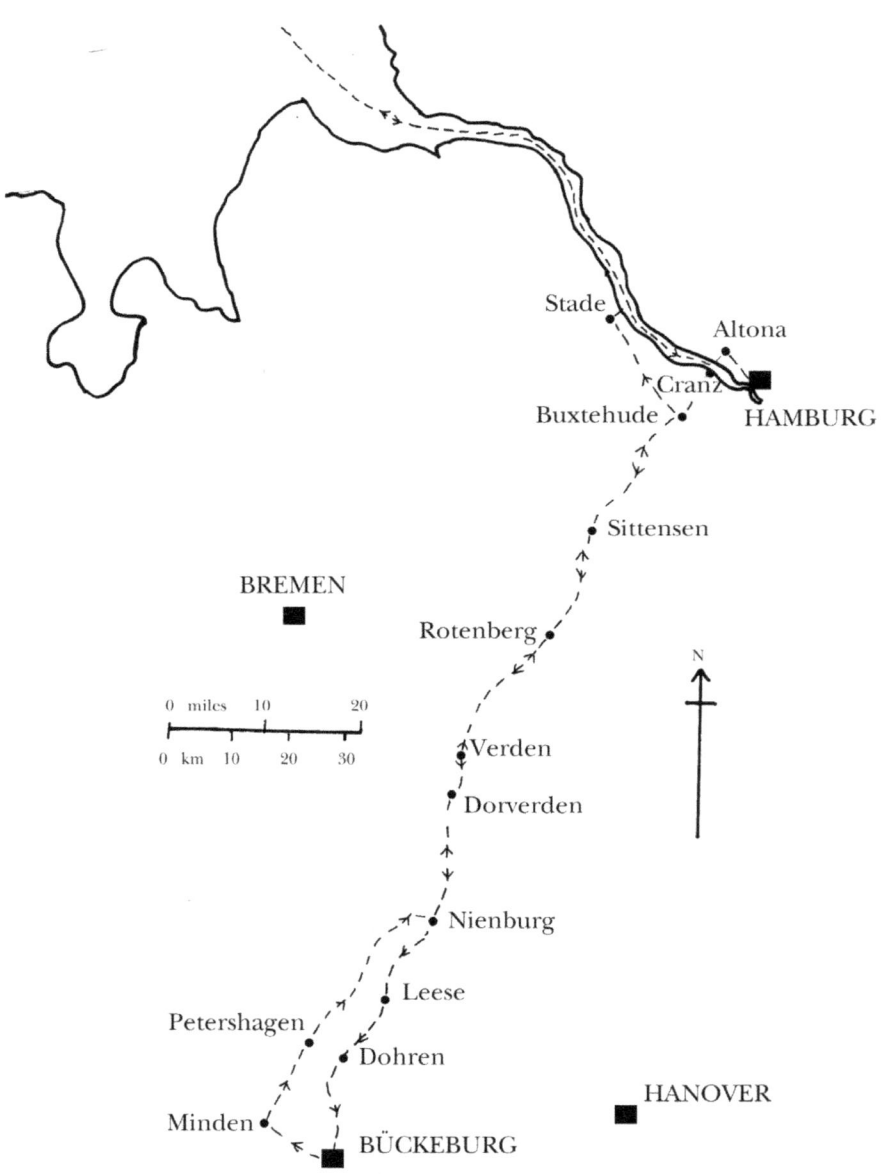

Three Weekes ... to Hamburgh

THREE WEEKES, THREE DAIES, AND THREE HOURES OBSERVATIONS AND TRAVEL, FROM LONDON TO HAMBURGH IN GERMANIE

*B*Y 1616, WHEN TAYLOR EMBARKED *on the first of his journeys a few days before his 38th birthday, he was already an established author, with a dozen and more pamphlets to his name on a variety of subjects, and all published within the previous four years. Three of his works lampooned the traveller Thomas Coryat, whose account of his journey across Europe to Italy and back,* Coryat's Crudities, *had scored a notable success when it appeared in print in 1611. Coryat by 1616 was off on an even more ambitious journey, to India, where he would die on his way back in December 1617, but in his absence Taylor felt he could take up his mantle, and capitalise on his success. In mock admiration he dedicated the account of his Hamburg journey to Coryat, but his false flattery was sincere to the extent that he imitated his rival's narrative prose and style. His official duties collecting excise duties were ending around this time, making possible his absence from London for a month or so.*

Taylor's choice of Hamburg as his destination may have been influenced by its close trading links with London, through the Merchant Adventurers, who had a headquarters there and from whom he could expect hospitality during his stay. But his purpose was also to visit a brother who was living in Bückeburg, a town in Lower Saxony 150km south-west of Hamburg near Minden. The name and circumstances of this brother are unknown, but a member of the ruling family whose seat was at Bückeburg had married a daughter of Lord Dudley the previous year, so he may have gone there in her service. The same brother accompanied Taylor to Prague four years later.

In most respects Taylor's account of his German adventure prefigures the later journeys, although (uniquely) we are spared long sequences of his doggerel verse. There are descriptive passages of churches and other buildings, including Hamburg's new fortifications then under construction; and the stages of his overland journeys from town to town are described. But Taylor is far more concerned to portray the customs and lifestyles of the local people he encounters, and to retell their anecdotes, hinting several times that these are traveller's tales and not necessarily true. His love of obscure and nonsense vocabulary is well seen in the sales pitch that he attributes to an itinerant medicine pedlar, all the sillier in that he claims that it has been translated for him by an interpreter. He is at pains not to conceal his disdain for foreigners generally and for Jews in particular. His unflattering depiction of the local peasants (he equates boors with boars) puts one in mind of the genre paintings of the Dutch masters. And he is no more respectful of catholic imagery. In one town he finds a wooden statue of St Peter and shakes hands with it, so that the arm breaks off – he takes it away with him as a talisman.

Apart from an enthusiasm for alcohol, which the English community in Hamburg clearly shared in large measure, Taylor (pandering no doubt to his targeted readership) shows an unhealthy interest in gruesome punishments. In Hamburg he witnesses and describes in detail the torture and execution of a murderer on the wheel. He then recounts with relish stories he has been told of other forms of capital punishment and instruments of torture. Taylor's Hamburg journey is not for the faint-hearted.

(17 August – 11 September 1616. Text derived from 1617 publication [copies BL c. 27 b. 32, and Folger Library copy online at Historical Texts]; a few variant readings have been taken from the 1630 reprint in All the workes . . .)

Three weekes, three daies, and three houres observations and travel, from London to Hamburgh in Germanie:[1] Amongst Jewes and Gentiles, with descriptions of townes and towers, castles and cittadels, artificiall gallowses, naturall hangmen: And dedicated for the present, to the absent Odcombian Knight Errant, Sr. Thomas Coriat, Great Brittaines Error, and the worlds Mirror. By John Taylor.

London, Printed by Edward Griffin, and are to be sold by George Gybbs at the signe of the Flower-deluce in Pauls Churchyard. 1617.

---

1 In the 1630 edition this heading is prefixed by another: Taylors Travels to Hamburgh in Germanie.

To the cosmographicall, geographicall describer, geometricall measurer; historiographicall calligraphicall relater and writer; enigmaticall, pragmaticall, dogmaticall observer, ingrosser, surveyer and eloquent Brittish Graecian Latinist, or Latine Graecian orator, the Odcombyan deambulator, perambulator, ambler, trotter, or un-tyred traveller, Sir Thomas Coriat, Knight of Troy, and one of the deerest darlings to the blind Goddesse Fortune.

Most worthy Sir, as Quintilian in his Apothegmes to the naked, learned Gimnosophists of Æthiopia,[1] very wittily saies, *Potanto Machyo corbatio monomosco kayturemon Lescus, Ollipufftingere whingo*, which is, knowledge is a main antithesis to ignorance, and paines and travell is the high way to experience. I being therefore well acquainted with the generous urbanity innated or rooted in your humanity, (in these daies of vanity,) I dedicate (out of my affability, debility, ability, imbecillity, facility, or agility,) this poore pamphlet to your nobility, in all servility and humility: not doubting but the fluent fecundity of your wisdomes profundity, in your heads rotundity, will conserve, reserve, preserve, and observe, what I and my industrious labors deserve. I do (out of mine owne cognition) averre and abett, that hee is senselesse that will assent, that the Fates did assigne, with their whole assistance, that any should aspire, to be an associate in any assembly, boldly to assimulate, assay, assault, or ascribe to any mortall but your selfe, superlative majority or transcendency for travels, observations, and oratorie. These things being revolved and ruminated, in the sagacitie or acutenesse of my Pericranion,[2] I imagined that no man under the cope was more worthy then your selfe to be a patronizing poplar to shelter my poore reed-like endevors. Howsoever in the preterlapsed occurrences there hath

---

1 Quintilian was a Roman orator, and collections of apophthegms (brief sayings by ancient philosophers) were attributed to various classical authors, including Aristotle and Plutarch, but not Quintilian. Ethiopian gymnosophists (ascetic sages) were described by the philosopher Apollonius of Tyana. The quotation is nonsense macaronic Latin, This opening is a display of mock erudition, aimed at ridiculing Coryate.
2 literally, the membrane which covers the surface of the skull, but used here grandiloquently for the mind.

beene an antagonisticall repugnancy betwixt us, yet I hope time and travell hath worne it thred-bare, or brought it to a most irrecoverable consumption; withall I know you are uncapable of inexpugnable malice, inveterate malignancy or emulation. I protest tongue-tide taciturnity should have imprisoned this worke in the lethargicall dungeon, or bottomlesse abisse of ever-sleeping oblivion, but that I am confident of your patronage and acceptance, which if it fall out (not according to any promerits of mine) but out of mine owne expectation of your matchles and unparalelld disposition, I shall heereafter sacrifice whole hecatombs[1] of invention both in prose and verse, at the shrine of your unfellowed and unfollowed vertues. So wishing more to see you then to heare from you, because writers want worke, and the presse is turned voluntarie through the scarcity of imployments, which I hope your presence will supply, I pray that Neptune, Aeolus, Tellus, Bacchus, and all the watery, windy, earthly, and drinking deities may be officious, auspicious, and delicious unto you, humbly imploring you to take in good part this my sophisticall, paradoxicall, submission, with a mentall reservation of my love and service, to sympathize or be equivalent to your kind liking and corroborated affecting.

He that hath a poore muse to trot in your service with all obsequious observance: John Taylor.

Three weekes, three daies, and three houres travels and observations. or, Taylors travels.

Upon[2] Saturday the 17. of August 1616. (after I had taken leave of some friends that would hardly give me leave to leave them) I was associated with five or six courteous comrades to the haven of Billingsgate, where I was no sooner come, but I was shipt in a wherry for the port of Gravesend, and having two women and three men in my company thither, we past the way away by telling tales by turnes. Where one of the women tooke upon her very logically to defend the honesty of brokers, and she maintained her paradoxicall arguments so pithily, as if her selfe like a

1   an ancient Greek sacrifice to the gods on a large scale, literally 100 oxen.
2   'Upon' only in 1630 edition. The 1617 publication begins 'Saturday . . .'.

desperate pawne had layen seaven yeares in lavender on sweetning in Long Lane, or amongst the dogged inhabitants of Houndsditch.[1] And one of the men replied that he thanked God he never had any need of them, whereupon I began to suspect him to be a crafty knave, because the proverbe saies, A crafty knave needs no broker,[2] and indeede after I had enquired what countriman he was, he told me he was a Welch man, and a justices clarke. I left him as I found him, hoping never to he troubled with his binding over, and withdrawing: and so landing at Graves-end, wee all went to the Christopher where wee tooke a Bachanalian farewell one of another, where I remained till the Munday following, awayting the comming downe of the ship that I was to be transported in. About the houre of three in the afternoone, with good hope we weighed anchor, and with a curteous tide and a gentle winde we sailed downe the river of Thames, as farre as the grand oyster haven of Quinborough,[3] where though our ship was not sea-sicke, yet shee cast, (anchor I meane.)

On the morrow, being Tuesday, wee weighed, and with the friendly breath of Zephirus, alias a westerne wind, our sailes being swolne, our ship called the Judith, who with her sterne cut the liquid mounting mountaines of Neptunes wavering territories, as nimbly as Hebrew Judith beheaded Holofernes,[4] so that by the bountifull favour of him that rules both windes and seas, on the Thursday following wee espied the coast of Freezeland, and the next day wee sailed by an iland called the Holy Land,[5] which may bee called the land of lobsters, or the countrie of crabs for the plentie of those kinde of crawling creatures that are taken there. But we, taking time by the fore-top, let no advantage slip, but with a merry gale, and a friendly floud, on the Friday wee sailed

---

1 The pawnbrokers and secondhand clothes dealers of Long Lane and Houndsditch were satirised by dramatists, although it was from them that their actors rented their costumes.
2 Anthony Nixon had written a pamphlet, *The Scourge of Corruption, or a Crafty Knave needs no Broker*, published in 1615.
3 Queenborough, on the Isle of Sheepey, which features later in the *Voyage in a Boat of Brown-Paper*, below pp. 89-90.
4 The story is told in the Old Testament Apocrypha book of *Judith*, and was a popular subject in renaissance and baroque art.
5 Heligoland.

up the River of Elve,¹ as farre as Stoad,² where we anchoured till the morrow, being Saturday, and the feast of S. Bartholmew the Apostle,³ we arived at a bleake alias, a towne an English mile from Hamburgh, called Altonagh,⁴ which is so called by the Hamburgers because it stands all-too-nigh them for their profit, beeing inhabited with divers tradesmen which doe hinder their freedome. I was no sooner landed there, but my company and my selfe went to a Dutch drinking-schoole, and having upsefreez'd⁵ foure pots of boone beere as yellow as gold, our host said we had foure shilling to betall, or to pay, which made me suspect it to bee a bawdy house by his large reckoning, till at last I understood that the shillings hee meant were but stivers,⁶ or three halfe pence a peece. So this terrible shot being discharged (which in the totall amounted to the sum of sixepence English,) we departed towards Hamburgh, where by the way I noted some 20. men, women, and children in divers places of Altonagh, all deformed, some with one eye, some with hare-lips, crooke backt, splay footed, halfe-nozed, or one blemish or other. I admiring at them, was told they were all Jewes,⁷ wherein I perceived the judgement of the high Judge of all, that had permitted nature to deforme their formes, whose gracelesse mindes were so much mishapen through want of grace.

But I being entred the city of Hamburgh on the Saturday, I was presently conducted to the English house,⁸ where I found a kinde host, an honest hostesse, good company, store of meat, more of drinke, a true tapster, and sweet lodging. And being at dinner, because I was a stranger, I was promoted to the chiefest place at the table, where to

1 Elbe.
2 Stade.
3 24 August.
4 Altona.
5 The expression occurs in plays of the period, and is conjectured to be a corruption of Dutch *op-zyn-fries*, 'in the Friesian fashion,'
6 a coin of small value circulating in the Low Countries.
7 Because of restrictions on Jews living in Hamburg, from 1611 a Jewish trading community developed in nearby Altona, which had previously been a fishing village.
8 The Hamburg headquarters of the Merchant Adventurers, the principal English cloth trading company with Germany.

observe an olde custome, every man did his best endevour to hauns[1] me for my welcome, which by interpretation is to give a man a loafe too much out of the brewers basket;[2] in which kinde of potshot,[3] our English are growne such stout proficients, that some of them dares bandy and contend with the Dutch their first teachers. But after they had hanced me as well as they could, and I pleas'd, they administred an oath to mee, in manner and forme as followeth; *Laying my hand on a full pot* I sweare by these contents, and all that is heerein contained, that by the courteous favour of these gentlemen, I doe find my selfe sufficiently hanced, and that henceforth ever I shall acknowledge it; and that whensoever I shall offerto be hanced again, I shall arme my selfe with the craft of a fox, the manners of a hogge, the wisdome of an asse, mixt with the civility of a beare. This was the forme of the oath, which as neere as I can shall be performed on my part; and heere is to be noted that the first word a nurse or a mother doth teach her children if they be males, is drinke, or beere: So that most of them are transformed to barrels, firkins, and kinderkins,[4] alwaies fraight with Hamburgh beere.

And though the city is not much more then halfe the bignes as London is within the walls, yet are there in it almost 800. brewhouses, and in one day there hath beene shipped away from thence, 337. brewings of beere, besides 13 or 14. brewings have been wrackt or stayed in the towne, as not sufficient to be bezelled[5] in the country.

The Saturday beeing thus past, and Sunday come, I went toward the English Church,[6] where I observed many shops open, buying and selling, chopping and changing of all maner of wares, with the streetes furnished with apples, peares, plums, nuts, grapes, or any thing else that an ordinary market can afford, as commonly as if the Sabbaoth were but a bare ceremony without a commandement. In which I note the

---

1 i.e. hance, to exalt (with drink), cf. enhance.
2 i.e to give him too much beer. A variant is included in John Ray's *Complete Collection of English Proverbs* (1670).
3 drunkenness.
4 A small barrell.
5 to waste or squander (in drink).
6 This was held in the English house; the resident preacher at this time was a puritan minister, John Wing.

Jewes in their execrable superstition, to be more devout and observant, then these pedlars in their profession; for on the Saturday (beeing the Jewes Sabaoth) they neglect all humane affares, and betake themselves irreligiously to their misbeleeving faithlesse religion.

The sermon being ended at the English Church, I walked in the afternoone with a friend of mine (an inhabitant of the towne) to see and to be seene, where at one of the gates was placed a strong guard of souldiers with muskets, pikes, halberts, and other warlike accoutrements. I asked the cause, and I was informed it was because of the building of certaine new mounts and bulwarks which were partly erected without the old wall: And when I perceived these fortifications, I was amazed, for it is almost incredible for the number of men and horses that are daily set on worke about it, besides the work it selfe is so great that it is past the credit of report, and as I suppose will proove most inexpugnable and invincible rampiers[1] to strengthen the towne on that side against the invasive attempts of the greatest monarke that should assaile them.[2]

But after much musing, walking further towards the fields, I espied foure or five pretty parcels of modesty goe very friendly into a counsell-house[3] by the wayes side, as we and thousands of people used to passe; they were handsome young girles of the age of 18. or 20. yeares a peece, and although they had a door to shut, yet they knowing their businesse to bee necessary and naturall, sate still in loving and neighbourly manner: so having traced a turne or two, wee returned into the towne againe, and entring a long garden within the walls, some of the townes-men were shooting for wagers at a marke with their muskets: some bowling: some at slide-thrift, or shovell-boord:[4] some dancing before a blinde fidler and his cowbellied, dropsie, durty drabb:[5] some

1 ramparts
2 Hamburg's ramparts (*Wallanlagen*) were designed by Dutch military engineer Johan van Valckenburgh and built between 1616 and 1625. Demolished in the 19th century their course is followed by the present *Wallring*.
3 a public lavatory. Taylor's pun on 'council house' (debating chamber) and 'counsell', which had implications of privacy or secrecy.
4 synonyms for shove ha'penny.
5 a dirty, immoral woman.

at one game, some at another, most of them drinking, and all of them drunke, that though it was a Sabboth, which should wholly be dedicated to God, yet by the abuse of these bursten-gutted bibbers, they made it an after-noone consecrated, or more truely execrated to the service of hell, and to the great amplification of the Devills kingdome.

When Christians dare Gods Sabboth to abuse,
They make themselves a scorne to Turkes and Jewes:
You stealing Barabasses[1] beastly race,
Rob God of glory, and your selves of grace.
Thinke on the supreame Judge who all things tries,
When Jewes in judgement shall against you rise,
Their feigned trueth, with fervent zeale they show,
The truth unfeign'd you know, yet will not know.
Then at the barre in new Jerusalem,[2]
It shall be harder much for you then them.

    But leaving them to their drunken designes, I return'd toward my lodging, where by the way I saw at the common jayle of the town, a great number of people were clustred together, I asked the cause of their concourse, and I was certified that there was a prisoner to be broken upon the wheele[3] the next day, and that these idle gazers did prease to gape upon him for want of better imployments, I being as inquisitive after novelties, as a traveller of my small experience might be, enquired earnestly the true cause of the next daies exeeution: my friend told me that the prisoner was a poore carpenter dwelling in the towne, who lately having stolne a goose, and plucking it within his doores, a little girle, (his daughter in law) went out of his house, and left the dore open, by which meanes, the owner of the goose passing by, espied the wretched theefe very diligently picking what hee before had beene stealing, to whom the owner said; Neighbour I now perceive which way my geese use to goe, but I will have you in question for them, and so away he

---

1 In Christian tradition, when given a choice by Pontius Pilate whether to crucify Jesus or Barabbas, the crowd chose Jesus, and Barabbas was released.
2 the gates of Heaven, described in the New Testament in *Revelations*, ch. 21.
3 The breaking wheel was a form of torture and execution used in many European countries.

went: the caitife[1] being thus reproved grew desperate, and his child comming into his house: ye yong whore, quoth hee, must ye leave my dore open for folkes to looke in upon me? and with that word, hee tooke a hatchet, and with a fatall cursed stroake, he clove the childes head: for the which murder hee was condemned and judged to be broaken alive upon the wheele. Close to the jayle I espied a house of free stone, round and flat roofed, and leaded, upon the which was erected the true picture of a most unmatchable hang-man;[2] and now I am entred into a discourse of this brave abject, or subject, you must understand that this fellow, is a merry, a mad and a subsidie hangman, to whom our Tyburne tatterdemallian,[3] or our Wapping windpipe-stretcher,[4] is but a raggamuffin, not woorth the hanging: for this teare-throat termagant is a fellow in folio, a commander of such great command, and of such greatnesse to command, that I never saw any that in that respect could countermand him: For his making is almost past description, no Saracens head seemes greater, and sure I thinke his braine-pan if it were emptied, (as I thinke hee hath not much braine in it,) would well containe halfe a bushell of mault, his shaggie haire and beard would stuffe a cusheon for Charons boate,[5] his imbost nose and embroydered face, would furnish a jeweller; his eies well dried, would make good tennis-balls, or shot for a small peece of ordinance, his yawning mouth would serve for a conniborrow,[6] and his two ragged rowes of teeth, for a stone wall, or a pale; then hath hee a necke like one of Hercules his pillars, with a windepipe, (or rather a beere pipe) as bigge as the boare of a demiculvering, or a wooden pumpe; through which conduit halfe a brewing of Hamburgh beere doth run downe into his unmeasurable paunch, wherein is more

[1] caitiff: a cowardly or despicable person.
[2] Hamburg's executioner at this period (1612-21), a man named Grave, was apparently mild-mannered and compassionate. There was, however, a young man of prodigiously large size living in the city, Jacob Damm, known as *Lewerenz sin Kind*, who is not known to have had any position of authority.
[3] a person wearing ragged clothing. Tyburn tree (near present-day Marble Arch) was the site of London'e public hangings.
[4] Execution Dock, Wapping, was where criminals sentenced by Admiralty courts were hanged, using a short rope which resulted in slow strangulation.
[5] In classical mythlogy Charon was the ferryman who rowed dead souls to Hades.
[6] rabbit hole.

midriff, guts and garbage then three tripe-wives could be able to utter before it stunke. His post-like legges were answerable to the rest of the great frame which they supported, and to conclude, Sir Bevis, Ascapart, Gogmagog, or our English Sir John Falstaff,[1] were but shrimpes to this bezzeling bombards longitude, latitude, altitude, and crassitude, for hee passes, and surpasses the whole Germane multitude.

And as he is great in corpulency, so is he powerfull in potency, for figuratively he hath spirituall resemblance of Romish authority, and in some sort hee is a kinde of demy-pope, for once a yeere in the dogge-daies[2] he sends out his men with bats in stead of buls, with full power from his greatnes to knocke downe all the curs without contradiction, whose masters or owners will not be at the charge to buy a pardon for them of his mightines, which pardon is more dureable then the popes of waxe or parchment, for his is made of a piece of the hide of an oxe, a horse, or such lasting stuffe, which with his stigmaticall stampe or seale is hanged about every dogs necke who is freed from his furie by the purchase of his pardon. And sure I am perswaded that these dogges are more sure of their lives with the hangmans pardon, then the poore besotted blinded papists are of their seduced soules from any pardon of the popes.

The priviledges of this graund haulter-master are many, as he hath the emptying of all the vaults or draughts in the city, which no doubt he gaines some favour by. Besides all oxen, kine, horses, hogs, dogs, or any such beasts, if they dye themselves, or if they be not like to live, the hang-man must knocke them on the heads, and have their skins: and whatsoever inhabitant in his jurisdiction doth any of these things aforesaid himselfe, is abhorred and accounted as a villaine without redemption. So that with hangings, headings, breakings, pardoning and killing of dogges, flaying of beasts, emptying vaults, and such privy commodities, his whole revenue sometimes amounts to 4. or 5. hundred pounds a yeere. And hee is held in that regard and estimation, that any man will converse and drinke with him, nay sometimes the lords of the towne will feast with him, and it is accounted no impeachment to their honours; for he is held in the ranke of a gentleman, (or a ranke gentleman) and he scornes

1   all legendary giants.
2   the hottest part of the year, July and August.

to bee clad in the cast weedes of executed offenders: No, he goes to the mercers, and hath his sattin, his velvet, or what stuffe he pleases, measured out by the yard or the ell, with his gould and silver lace, his silke stockings, laced spangled garters and roses, hat and feather, with foure or five brave villaines attending him in livery cloakes, who have stipendary meanes from his ignominious bounty.

Monday the 19. of August, about the houre of 12. at noone, the people of the towne in great multitudes flocked to the place of execution; which is halfe a mile English without the gates, built more like a sconce[1] then a gallowes, for it is walled and ditched about with a draw-bridge, and the prisoner came on foot with a divine with him, all the way exhorting him to repentance, and because death should not terrifie him, they had given him many rowses and carowses of wine and beere: for it is the custome there to make such poore wretches drunke, whereby they may be sencelesse eyther of Gods mercy or their owne miserie; but being prayed for by others, they themselves may die resolutely, or (to be feared) desperately.

But the prisoner beeing come to the place of death, hee was by the officers delivered to the hangman, who entring his strangling fortification with two graund hangmen more and their men, which were come from the city of Lubeck, and another towne, (which I cannot name) to assist their Hamburghian brother in this great and weighty worke: the draw-bridge was drawne up, and the prisoner mounted on a mount of earth, built high on purpose that the people without may see the execution a quarter of a mile round about: foure of the hangmans men takes each of them a small halter, and by the hands and the feet they hold the prisoner extended all abroad lying on his backe: then the arch-hangman, or the great master of this mighty busines tooke up a wheele, much about the bignesse of one of the fore wheeles of a coach: and first having put off his doublet, his hat, and being in his shirt as if he meant to play at tennis, he tooke the wheele, and set it on the edge, and turned it with one hand like a top or a whirigigg, then he tooke it by the spoaks, and lifting it up with a mighty stroke he beat one of the poore wretches leggs in peeces, (the bones I meane) at which he rored

---

[1] In this sense a small mound or earthwork supporting artillery used for defence.

grievously; then after a little pawse he breakes the other legg in the same manner, and consequently breakes his armes, and then he stroke foure or five maine blowes on his breast, and burst all his bulke and chest in shivers, lastly he smoate his necke, and missing, burst his chin and jawes to mammocks;[1] then hee tooke the broken mangled corps, and spreads it on the wheele, and thrusts a great post or pile into the nave or hole of the wheele, and then fixed the post into the earth some sixe foot deepe, being in height above the ground, some tenne or twelve foote, and there the carkasse must lye till it be consumed by all-consuming time, or ravening fowles.

This was the terrible manner of this horrid execution, and at this place are twenty posts with those wheeles, or peeces of wheeles, with heads of men nailed on the top of the posts, with a great spike driven through the skull. The severall kinds of torments which they inflict upon offenders in those parts, makes me to imagine our English hanging to be but a flea-biting.

Moreover, if any man in those parts are to be beheaded, the fashion is, that the prisoner kneeles downe, and being blinded with a napkin, one takes hold of the haire of the crowne of the head, holding the party upright, whilest the hangman with a backward blow with a sword will take the head from a mans shoulders so nimbly, and with such dexterity, that the owner of the head shall never misse the want of it. And if it be any mans fortune to be hanged for never so small a crime, though he be mounted whole, yet hee shall come downe in peeces, for he shall hang till every joynt and limbe drop one from another.

They have strange torments and varieties of deaths, according to the various nature of the offences that are committed: as for example, he that counterfets any princes coyne, and is prooved a coyner, his judgement is to be boyled to death in oyle, not throwne into the vessell all at once, but with a pully or a rope to bee hanged under the armepits, and let downe into the oyle by degrees: first the feete, and next the legs, and so to boyle his flesh from his bones alive. For those that set houses on fire wilfully, they are smoked to death, as first there is a pile or post fixed in the ground, and within an English ell[2] of the top of it is a peece

1 fragments.
2 45 inches, or 1¼ yards (about 1.14m).

of wood nailed crosse, wherepuon the offender is made fast sitting, then over the top of the post is whelmed a great tub of dry fat, which doth cover or overwhelme the prisoner as low as his middle. Then underneath the executioner hath wet straw, hay, stubble, or such kinde of stuffe, which is fired, but by reason it is wet and danke, it doth not burn but smoulder and smoake, which smoake ascends up into the tub where the prisoners head is, and not being able to speake, hee will heave up and downe with his belly, and people may perceive him in these torments to live three or foure hours.

Adultery there, if it bee prooved, is punished with death, as the losse of both the parties heads, if they be both married, or if not both, yet the married party must dye for it, and the other must endure some easier punishment, eyther by the purse or carkasse; which in the end proves little better then halfe a hanging.

But as after a tempest a calme is best welcome; so I imagine it not amisse after all this tragicall, harsh discourse, to sweeten the readers pallat with a few comicall reports which were related unto me, wherein, if I seeme fabulous, it must be remembred that I claime the priviledge of a traveller, who hath authority to report all that hee heares and sees, and more too. I was informed of a fellow that was hanged somewhat neere the high way, within a mile or two of Collein,[1] and the fashion being to hang him with a halter and a chaine, that when the haulter is rotten with the weather, the carkasse drops a butten hole lower into the chaine. Now it fortuned that this fellow was executed on a winters afternoone towards night, and being hanged, the chaine was shorter then the halter, by reason whereof hee was not strangled, but by the gamming[2] of the chaine which could not slip close to his necke, he hanged in great torments under the jawes, it happened that as soone as he was trust up, there fell a great storme of raine and winde, whereupon all the people ran away from the gallowes to shelter themselves. But night being come, and the moone shining bright, it chanced that a country boore, or a waggoner and his sonne with him were driving their empty waggon by the place where the fellow was hanged, who being not choaked, in the

---

1 probably Kolín, on the River Elbe, Czech Republic. This folktale is told at length by Robert Southey, in his *Collected Poems* (1837) as 'Roprecht the Robber', who derives it from Taylor's version, but locates it to Cologne.
2 i.e. jamming.

extremity of his paines did stirre his legges and writhe and crumple his body, which the waggoners sonne perceived, and said; Father looke, the man upon the gallowes doth moove: quoth the olde man he moves indeed, I pray thee let us make hast, and put the waggon under the gibbet,¹ to see if we can unhang and save him. This beeing said was quickely done, and the wretch halfe dead was laid in straw in the boores wagon, and carried home, where with good attendance he was in foure or five daies recovered to his health, but that he had a cricke in his necke, and the crampe in his jawes. The olde man was glad that he had done so good a deed, (as he thought) began to give the thiefe fatherly counsell, and told him that it was Gods great mercy towards him to make mee (quoth he) the instrument of thy deliverance, and therefore looke that thou make good use of this his gracious favour towards thee, and labour to redeeme the time thou hast mispent, get thee into some other princes countrey, where thy former crimes may not bring thee into the danger of the law againe, and there with honest industrious endevours get thy living.

The theefe seemed willing to entertaine these good admonitions, and thanked the boore and his sonne, telling them that the next morning he would be gone: and if ever his fortunes made him able, he promised to be so gratefull unto them that they should have cause to say their great curtesies were well bestowed upon him; but all his sugred sweet promises, were in the proofe but gall and wormwood in the performance: for this gracelesse caitiffe arose betimes in the morning, and drew on a paire of bootes and spurs which were the mans sonnes of the house, and slipping out of the dores, went to the stable and stole one of his kinde hosts best horses, and away rode hee. The man and his sonne, when they were up and missed the thiefe and the horse, were amazed at the ingratitude of the wretch, and withall speed his sonne and he rode severall waies in pursuit of him, and in briefe one of them tooke him, and brought him backe to their house againe, and when it was night they bound him, and laid him in their wagon (having deafe eares, and hardened hearts to all his intreaties) and away to the gallowes where they found him hanging, there they with the halter being a little

---

1   Strictly speaking not a gibbet, which encased a hanged corpse in a metal cage.

shortned, they left him. The next day the country people wondred to see him hanging there againe, for they had seene him hanged, and missed him gone, and now to be thus strangely and privately come againe in boots and spurs, whereas they remembered at his first hanging he had shoes and stockings, it made them muse what journey he had beene riding, and what a mad ghest he was to take the gallowes for his inne, or (as I suppose) for his end.

The rumour of this accident being bruited abroad, the people came far and neere to see him, all in generall wondring how these things should come to passe. At last, to cleere all doubts, proclamations were published with pardon, and a reward to any that could discover the truth, whereupon the old boore and sonne came in and related the whole circumstance of the matter.

At another place (the hangmans place being void) there were two of the bloud, (for it is to be noted that the succession of that office doth lineally descend from the father to the sonne, or to the next of the bloud) which were at strife for the possession of this high indignity. Now it happened that two men were to be beheaded at the same towne, and at the same time, and (to avoid suite in law for this great prerogative) it was concluded by the arbitrators, that each of these new hangmen should execute one of the prisoners, and hee that with greatest cunning and sleight could take the head from the body, should have the place, to this they all agreed, and the prisoners were brought forth, where one of the executioners did binde a red silke thred double about his prisoners necke, the threds beeing distant one from another onely the bredth of one thred, and he promised to cut off the head with a backward blow with a sword, betweene the threds. The other called his prisoner aside, and told him that if he would bee ruled by him, hee should have his life saved, and besides, (quoth he) I shall be sure to have the office. The prisoner was glad of the motion, and said he wold doe any thing upon these conditions, then said the hangman, when thou art on thy knees, and hast said thy prayers, and that I doe lift up my axe, (for I will use an axe) to strike thee, I will cry Hem, at which word doe thou rise and run away, (thou knowest none will stay thee if thou canst once escape after thou art delivered into my custody, it is the fashion of our countrie) and let me alone to shift to answer the matter. This being said, or whispered, the heads-man with the sword did cut off his prisoners head just betweene the threds as hee had said, which made all the people wonder at the steddinesse of his hand, and most of them judged that he was the man that was and would be fittest to make a mad hangman of.

But as one tale is good till another be told, and as there be three degrees of good, better, and best, so this last hangman did much exceed and ecclips the others cunning: For his prisoner being on his knees, and he lifting up his axe to give the fatall blow, Hem, said he (according to promise) whereupon the fellow arose and ran away, but when he had run[1] some seven or eight paces, the hangman threw the axe after him, and strooke his head smoothly from his shoulders: now for al this, who shall have the place is unknowne, for they are yet in law for it; and I doubt not but before the matter be ended, that the lawyers will make them exercise their owne trades upon themselves to end the controversie. This tale doth savour somwhat hyperbolicall, but I wish the reader to beleeve no more of the matter then I saw, and there is an end.

At another towne there stood an olde over-worne despised paire of gallowes, but yet not so old but they will last many a faire yeare with good usage, but the townsmen a little distance from them built another pair, in a more stately geometricall port and fashion, whereupon they were demanded why they would be at the charge to erect a new gallowes, having so sufficient an old one: they answered, that those old gallowes should serve to hang fugitives and strangers; but those new ones were built for them and their heires for ever. Thus much for hangmen, theeves, and gallowses.

Yet one thing more for theeves. In Hamburgh those that are not hanged for theft, are chained 2. or three together, and they must in that sort sixe or seaven yeares draw a dung-cart, and clense the streetes of the towne, and every one of those theeves for as many yeares as he is condemned to that slavery, so many bells he hath hanged at an iron above one of his shoulders, and every yeare a bell is taken off, till all are gone, and then he is a free-man againe, and I did see ten or twelve of these carts, and some of the theeves had seven bels, some 5. some 6. some one, but such a noyse they make, as if all the devils in hell were dancing the morrice.[2]

1 'run', 1630 edn; 'ran', 1617 edn.
2 A similar punishment was proposed to Charles II in the 1670s in an anonymous petition, but not implemented.

Hamburgh is a free city, not being subject to the Emperor, or any other Prince, but onely governed by 24 Burgomasters, whereof two are the chiefe, who are called Lords, and doe hold that dignity from their first election during their lives; The buildings are all of bricke, of one uniforme fashion, very lofty and stately, it is wonderfull populous, and the water with boates comes through most of the streetes of the towne.

Their churches are most gloriously set forth, as the most of them covered with copper, with very lofty spires, and within sides they are adorned with crucifixes, images and pictures, which they doe charily[1] keepe for ornaments, but not for idle or idoll adoration; In Saint Jacobs and in Saint Catherines churches, there is in one of them a pulpit of alabaster,[2] and in the other a paire of such organs,[3] which for worth and workemanship are unparalelld in Christendome, as most travellers doe relate.

The women there are no fashion-mongers, but they keepe in their degrees one continuall habite, as the richer sort doe weare a huicke,[4] which is a robe of cloth or stuffe plaited, and the upper part of it is gathered and sowed to a thing in the forme of an English potlid, with a tassell on the top, and so put upon the head, and the garment goes over her ruffe and face if she please, and so down to the ground, so that a man may meet his owne wife, and perhaps not know her from another woman.

They have no porters to beare burdens, but they have bigge burly-bon'd knaves with their wives that doe daily draw carts any whether up and downe the towne, with marchants goods or any other imployments: And it is reported that these cart-drawers are to see the rich men of the towne provided of milch-nurses for their children, which nurses they call by the name of Ams, so that if they doe want a nurse at any time, these fellowes are cursed, because they have not gotten wenches enough with childe to supply their wants.

1 sparingly.
2 The pulpit was new when Taylor saw it, made of alabaster, marble and sandstone in 1610.
3 Part of the organ, made in 1540, was incorporated into its replacement in 1670, which J.S Bach played. It was destroyed in 1943, but has been reconstructed.
4 huke is the usual spelling of this garment, accurately described here.

But if a man of any fashion doe chance to goe astray to a house of iniquity, the whilst he is in the house at his drudgery, another of the whores will go to the sherif (which they call the Rightheere[1]) and informe that such a man is in such a suspected howse; then is his comming forth narrowly watched, and hee is taken and brought before the Right-heere, and examined, where if he be a man of credit, he must, and will pay forty, fifty, or sixty Rex Dollors[2] before hee will have his reputation called in question. Of which money, the queane[3] that did inform shall have her reward.

A lawyer hath but a bad trade there, for any cause or controversie is tried and determined in three daies, Quirks, Quiddits, Demurs, Habeas Corposes, Sursararaes, Procedendoes,[4] or any such dilatory law-tricks are abolished, and not worth a button there.

But above all, I must not forget the rare actions and humours of a quacksalver[5] or mountebanke, or to speake more familiarly, a shadow of a skilfull chirurgian.[6] This fellow beeing clad in an ancient doublet of decayed satin, with a spruce leather jerkin with glasse buttons, the rest of his attire being correspondent, was mounted upon a scaffold, having shelves set with viols, gallipots, glasses, boxes, and such like stuffe, wherein as he said, were waters, oyles, unguents, emplasters, ellectuaries,[7] vomits, purges, and a world of never heard of drugs; and being mounted (as I said) he and his man begin to proclaime all their skill and more, having a great number of idle and ignorant gazers on, he began as followeth (as I was informed by my interpreter) for I understood not one worde he spake.)

I, Jacomo Compostella, practitioner in physicke, chyrurgery, and the mathematicks, being a man famous through Europe, Asia, Affricke and America, from the orientall exaltation of Titan,[8] to his occidentall

1 praetor.
2 the *reichsthaler* was from 1566 the standard silver coin of the Holy Roman Empire, in use across northern Europe.
3 whore.
4 Mostly these are approximations of terms for legal instruments and procedures, such as demurrer, certiorari and procedendo.
5 a medical impostor.
6 surgeon.
7 a sweetened medicine.
8 a name for the Greek sun god Helios.

declination, who for the testimony of my skill, and the rare cures that I have done, have these princes hands and seales; as first the great Cham of Tartaria,[1] in whose court, onely with this water, which is the Ellixar of Henbane diafracted in a diurnall of ingredients Hippocratonticke, Avicenian, and Catarackt, With this did I cure the great Dutchesse of Promulpho of the cramp in her tongue: and with this oyle did I restore the Emperor Gregory Evanowich of a convulsion in his pericranion. From thence I travelled through Slavonia, where I met with Mustapha Despot of Servia, who at that time was intolerably vexed with a Spasmus, so that it often drove him into a syncope with the violent obstructions of the conflagerating of his vaines. Onely with this precious unguent being the quintessence of Mugwort, with Auripigmenty terragrophicated in a limbecke[2] of christalline translucency, I recovered him to his former health, and for my reward I had a Barbary horse with rich caparisons, a Turkish semitar, a Persian robe, and 2000. Hungarian ducats.

Besides, here are the hands and seales of Potohamacke, Adelantado of Prozewgma, and of Gulch Flownderscurfe chiefe burgomaster of Belgrade, and of divers princes and estates, which to avoid tedious prolixity I omit. But good people if you or any other be troubled with apoplexies, palsies, cramps, lethargies, cataracks, quincies, tisicks, pleurisies, coghs, headaches, tertian, quartan, and quotidian agues, burning fevers, jawndizes, dropsies, collicks, Illiaca passio's,[3] the stone, the strangury, the poxe, plague, botches, biles, blanes, scabs, scurfs, mange, leprosies, cankers, megrimms, mumps, fluxes, meazels, murreins, gouts, consumptions, tooth-ache, ruptures, hernia aquosa,[4] hernia ventosa, hernia carnosa, or any other malladie, that dares afflict the body of man or woman, come and buy while you may have it for money, for I am sent for speedily to the Emperour of Trapezond[5] about affaires of great importance that highly concernes his royall person.

1 Although this title is genuine, most of the following personages, and some of the cures, though plausible, are the product of Taylor's fertile imagination.
2 i.e. alembic, a glass distilling vessel.
3 intestinal obstruction.
4 these and the following two hernias were all medieval terms for ruptures or swellings of the testicles.
5 a real place, a division of the Byzantine empire, but the last emperor had surrendered to the Ottomans in 1461.

Thus almost two houres did this fellow with embost words, and most laborious action, talke and sweat to the people, that understood no more what hee said, then hee himselfe understood himselfe. And I thinke his whole takings for simple compounds did amount in the totall to 9. pence sterling.

But leaving Hamburgh, (having gathered these few observations aforesaid) out of it I went August 28. and my first jaunt of my travels was by water, to a towne called Buckstahoo,[1] it is a little walled towne, and stands on the other side of the river, three miles (as they call it) from Hamburgh. The boate wee passed in is called an Iuar, not so good as a Graves-end barge, yet I thinke it bee as great, and the three miles longer then from London to Graves-end, for I am sure that we were going nine houres before we could be landed: Our passage cost us threepence a peece, and one thing I remember well, that the lazie water-men will sit still all (or the most part of) the way, whilest their passengers, (be they never so rich or poore, all is one to them, be they men or women) they must rowe by turnes, an houre or such a matter: and we landed in the night at a place called Crants,[2] where all the passengers were to goe to supper, but such diet we had that the proverbe was truely verified, God sent meat, and the Devill sent cookes;[3] for as there was no respect of persons in the boate, so all fellowes at the table, and all one[4] price, the palatine and the plebeian: our first messe was great platters of blacke broath, in shape like new tarre, and in tast cosen germane, to slut pottage; our second were dishes of eeeles, chop'd as small as hearbs, and the broth they were in as salt as brine: then had wee a boyled goose, with choake peares[5] and carrats, buried in a deepe dish; and when wee demanded what was to pay, it was but three pence a man, I mused at the cheapnesse of it, but afterward they came upon us with a fresh reckoning of five pence a man for beere, for they never count their meate and drinke together, but bring in severall[6] reckonings

---

1 Buxtehude.
2 Cranz.
3 first recorded in 1542, and included in Thomas Deloney's *Dictionary of Proverbs* (1574).
4 'one', 1630 edn; 'once', 1617 edn.
5 An astringent pear, but the name also of a metal instrument of torture.
6 separate.

for them: but the morning being come, we hired a boores wagon, to carry us to a place called Citizen;¹ three miles there, or 12. English miles from Buckstahoo: a little bald dorp it is, where we came about noone, and found such slender entertainment, that we had no cause to boast of our good cheere, or our hostesse cookery. We having refreshed our selves, and hyred a fresh wagon, away wee went two miles further to another dorp called Rodonburgh,² this village belongeth to the bishop of Rodonburgh, who hath a faire house there, stronglie walled and deepely ditched and moated about, very defensible, with draw-bridges and good ordinance. This bishop is a temporall lord, notwithstanding his spirituall title;³ and no doubt but the flesh prevailes above the spirit with him; So the bishops of Breame,⁴ Luningburgh,⁵ and divers other places in Germany, doe very charitably take the fleece, (for they themselves never looke to the flocke) by reason they use no ecclesiasticke function, but onely in name.

Being lodged at Rodonburgh, in a stately inne, where the host, hostesse, guests, cowes, horses, swine, lay all in one roome; yet I must confesse their beds to be very good, and their linnen sweet, but in those parts they use no coverlet, rugge or blanket, but a good featherbed undermost, with cleane sheetes, pillowes, and pillowbeares, and a nother featherbed uppermost, with a faire sheet above all, so that a mans lodging is like a womans lying in, all white.

August the 30. wee went from Rodonburgh, and about noone wee came to an olde walled towne, called Feirden,⁶ it hath two churches in it, and the hangmans statue very artificially carved in stone, and set on a high pillar, with a rod rampant in his hand, at this towne I met with sixe strangers, all travellers, where we went to dinner together all at one table, and every man opened his knapsack or budget with victualls; (for he that carries no meat with him, may fast by authority in most places

1   Sittensen.
2   Rotenburg an der Wüumme.
3   The prince-bishop of Verden had his castle at Rotenburg, but after Lutheranism prevailed in the diocese from 1558 he no longer had ecclesiastical control.
4   Bremen.
5   Lüneburg.
6   Verden an der Aller.

of that country) but to note the kindnes of these people one to another, some had bread and a boxe of salt butter, some had raw bacon, some had cheese, some had pickled herring, some dried beefe, and amongest the rest, I had brought three ribs of rost beefe, and other provision from Hamburgh: to conclude, wee drew all like fidlers, and fed (for the most part) like swine for every man eat what was his owne, and no man did proffer one bit of what he had to his neighbor, so he that had cheese must dine with cheese, for he that had meat would offer him none; I did cut every one a part of my rost beefe; which my guide told me they would not take well because it is not the fashion of the countrey: I tried, and found them very tractable to take any thing that was good, so that I perceived their modesty to take one from another, proceedes from their want of manners to offer. But dinner being done, away wee went over a bridge, in the midst whereof is a jynn, made in the likenesse of a great lanthorne, it is hanged on a turning gybbet, like a crane: so that it may be turned on the bridge, and over the river, as they shall please that have occasion to use it. It is bigge enough to hold two men, and it is for this purpose, if any one or more doe rob gardens or orchards, or cornefields, (if they be taken) he or they are put into this same whirligigge, or kickumbob,[1] and the gybbet being turned, the offender hangs in this cage over the river some 12 or 14 foot from the water, then there is a smal line made fast to the party some 5. or 6. fadome, and with a tricke which they have, the bottome of the cage drops out, and the thiefe fals sodenly into the water. I had not gone farre, but at the end of the bridge I saw an olde chappell, which in olde time they say was dedicated to St. Frodswicke,[2] which hath the day after S. Luke the Evangelist: I entring in, perceived it was a charitable chappell, for the dores and windowes were alwaies open, by reason there were none to shut, and it was a common receptacle for beggars and rogues. There was the image of our Lady, with a vaile over her, made (as I thinke) of a bakers bolter,[3] and Saint Peter houlding a candle to her. I cut a peece of her vaile, and taking Peter by the hand at my departure, the kind image (I know not upon what acquaintance) being loose handed, let me have his hand with mee,

1 A nonsense word for something without a name, akin to thingumajig.
2 St Frideswide (an English saint, associated with Oxford), whose feast day was 19 October.
3 A form of sieve for flour, made of a cylinder of cloth.

which being made of wood, by reason of ruinous antiquity, burst of in the handling: which two precious relickes I brought home with me to defend me and all my friends from sparrow blasting.[1]

From this place we were glad to travell on foot one dutch mile to a dorpe called Durfurne,[2] where we hired a boores waggon to a town called Neinburgh,[3] but we could not reach thither by 2 English miles, so that we were glad to lodge in a barne that night: On the morrow early, we arose and came to Nienburgh, which is a little walled town, belonging to that bishopricke from whence it is so named. There we staied 3. houres before wee could get a waggon, at last we were mounted to a dorpe called Leiz,[4] two dutch miles; I would have bargained with the boore to have carried us to Dorne,[5] which I bade my guide tell him it was but a mile further, a mile quoth the boore, indeed we call it no more, but it was measured with a dogge, and they threw in the taile and all to the bargaine; so to Leiz he carried us, and there we found a waggon of Dorne homeward bound, which made us ride the cheaper; but it was the longest mile that ever I rode or went, for surely it is as much as some ten of our miles in England. But having overcome it at last, from thence I tooke a fresh waggon to carry me two miles further to a town called Buckaburghe,[6] where I had, and have, I hope, a brother residing; to whom my journey was entended, and with whom my perambulation was at a period. This towne of Buckaburgh is wholely and solely belonging to the Graff or Grave of Shomburgh,[7] a prince of great command and eminence, absolute in his authority and power, not countermanded by the Emperour, or any other further then curtesie requires; and in a word, hee is one of the best accomplisht gentlemen in Europe for his person, port, and princely magnificence. He hath there to his inestimable charge, built the towne, with many goodly houses,

1 Being affected by some mysterious unseen force.
2 Dorverden.
3 Nienburg
4 Leese
5 Döhren
6 Bückeburg
7 Count Ernst of Schaumburg (1569 -1622). Schaumburg, in Lower Saxony, had been a medieval county in the Holy Roman Empire. Count Ernst made Bückeburg castle his residence and granted the town privileges in 1609; he built the church 1611-15. Church and castle, with its ornate chapel, survive.

streets, lanes, a strong wall, and a deepe ditch, all well furnished with munition and artillery, with a band of souldiers which he keepeth in continuall pay, allowing every man a doller a weeke, and double apparell every yeere. Besides, hee hath built a stately church, being above 120. steps to the roofe, with a faire paire of organes, a curious carved pulpit, and all other ornaments belonging to the same. His owne pallace may well be called an earthly paradice, which if I should run into the praise of the description of, I should bring my wits into an intricate labyrinth, that I should hardly find the way out: yet according to the imbecillity of my memory, I will onely touch a little at the shadow of it, and let the substance stand where it doth.

At the front or outward gate is a most stately arch, upon the top whereof is erected the image of Envy, (as great as a demy Colossus) betweene two dragons, all guilt with gold; before the gate is an iron grate to open and shut as it were of flowers or worke of embroydery, at which gate stands alwaies a court of guard, and a sentinell, and at the lower part of the arch is the Princes title or in capitall letters as followeth; ERNESTUS, DEI GRATIA, COMES HOLST, Scomburgh, Sternburgh, Etc.

After I was entred within the outward gate, I was shewed his stables, where I saw very faire and goodly horses, both for warre and other uses, amongst the rest there was one naturally spotted like a leopard, or panther, and is called by the name of leopard, a stately couragious beast, and so formed as if nature had laid all hir cunning aside, onely to compose that horse, and indeed I must acknowledge that hee was made for the service of some great prince, and not for any inferior person.

Passing further, I came to another court of guard, and over a draw-bridge, into the inner court, where on the right hand, I was conducted into the chappell, in which chappell, if it were possible that the hand of mortall men, (with artificiall workemanship) could visibly set forth the magnificent glory of the immortal Creator, then absolutely there it is, but beeing impossible so to doe, (as neere as I can) I will describe it; the pavement is all of blacke and gray marble, curiously wrought with chequer-worke, the seats and pues are carved wainscot of wonderfull cunning and workemanship: the roofe is adorned with the statues of angels and cherubins, many in number, all so richly guilded, as if gold were as plentifull as peauter, there could not be more liberality bestowed: besides there are a faire set of organs, with a brave sweete quire of queristers: so that when they sing, the lutes, viols, bandoraes, organs, recorders, sagbuts, and other musicall instruments, all strike up together, with such a glorious delicious harmony, as if the angelicall musicke of the spheares[1] were descended into that earthly tabernacle. The prince himselfe is a Protestant, very zealous in his prayer, and diligent in his attention to the preacher, who although I understood not, yet I perceived he was a good divine, who gravely and sincerely with reverence and eloquent elocution delivered the breade of life to the understanding auditors.

In this towne I stayd with my brother from Saturday the last of August, till the Thursday following which was the fifth of September. When I was conducted an English mile on my way by certaine of my countrey-men my lords musicians, where we dranke and parted, onely my brother and my guide brought mee that night to a strong walled town called Minden, which standeth on the river of Weazer,[2] and belongeth to the bishop of that see. On the morrow I walked to see the towne, where I bought 36. cheeses for eightpence, and a yard and halfe of pudding for five pence, which I brought into England for rarities. So about noone wee tooke a boat to passe downe the river, which boat is much longer than any westerne barge, but nothing neere so broad, it was halfe laden with lime and chalke, and by reason the winde blew hard, we were almost choaked with the flying and scattering of that dusty commodity. Besides the water was so shallow, that we ran a ground 3. or 4. times, and sometimes an houre, sometimes lesse before we could get a float againe: which made mee and my guide goe a shore at a village called Peterhaghen,[3] where we hired a waggon to Leize, where wee stayd all night, (being come into our olde way againe) where were a crew of strowling rogues and whores that tooke upon them the name of Aegyptians,[4] juglers and fortune-tellers,

---

1 The music of the spheres, or *musica universalis*, was a philosophical concept of the harmony between sun, moon and the planets derived from ancient Greece, but fundamental to the teaching of Johannes Kepler, whose *Harmonices Mundi* was published in 1619, and to other astronomers of the period.
2 Weser.
3 Petershagen.
4 Gypsies.

and indeede one of them helde the good-wife with a tale, the whilst another was picking her chest, and stole out ten dollors, which is fortie shillings, and she that talked with her, looked in her hand, and tolde her that if shee did not take great heede, she knew by her art that some mischance was neere her: which prooved true, for her money was gone the whilst her fortune was telling.

But I appoynted a waggon over night to bee ready by three of the clocke in the morning, when I arose and applyed my travell so hard by changing fresh waggons, so that that day I came as farre as Rodonburgh, which was nine dutch miles, where I stayd that night: The next day being Sunday the eighth of September, wee tooke waggon towards Buckstahoo, we had a mad merry boore, with an hundred totters about him; and now I thinke it fit a little to describe these boores,[1] their natures, habits, and unmannerly manners. In our English tongue the name bore or boore doth truely explane their swinish condition, for most of them are as full of humanity as a bacon-hogge, or a bore, and their wives as cleanely and courteous as sowes. For the most part of the men they are clad in thinne buckerom, unlined, barelegged and footed, neither band or scarce shirt, no woollen in the world about them, and thus will they runne through all weathers for money by the waggons side, and though no better apparrelled, yet all of them have houses, land, or manuall meanes to live by. The substantiall boores I did meet above 120. of them that Sunday, with every one an hatchet in his hand, I mused at it, and thought they had been going to fell wood that day, but my guide told me they were all going to church, and that in stead of cloakes they carried hatchets, and that it was the fashion of the country: whereupon it came to my mind, cloake, *quasi* cleave-oake, *ergo* the boores weare hatchets in steede of cloakes.

There are other fashion boores, who weare white linnen breeches as close as Irish trouzes, but so long, that they are turned up at the shooe in a role like a maides sleeves at the hand, but what these fellowes want in the bignesse of their hose, they have in dublets, for their sleeves are as big as breeches and the bodies great enough to hold a kinderkin of beere and a barrell of butter.

---

[1] Husbandmen or peasant small farmers. Taylor puns the German word with English boar, for pig.

The countey is very full of woods, and especially oakes, which they very seldome cut downe, because of the mast for their swine, which live there in great abundance. If any man bee slaine or murthered on the way, they use to set up a woodden crosse in the place, for a memoriall of the bloody fact committed there, and there were many of those woodden crosses in the way as I travelled.

They seldom have any robbery committed amongst them, but there is a murther with it, for their unmannerly manner is, to knocke out a mans braines first, or else to lurke behinde a tree, and shoot a man with a peece or a pistoll, and so make sure worke with the passenger,[1] and then search his pockets.

It is as dangerous to steale or kill an hare in some places there, as it is to rob a church or kill a man in England, and yet a two-penny matter will discharge the offender, for the best and the worst is but an halter; and I was enformed that an English marchant (not knowing the danger) as he was riding on the way, having a peece charged in his hand (as it is an ordinary weapon to travell with there) by chance hee espied an hare, and shot at her and killed her; but he was apprehended for it, and it was like to have cost him his life; but before he got out of the trouble, he was faine to use his best friends and meanes, (and pleading ignorance for his innocency) at last with the losse of a great deale of liberty, and five hundred pound in money, he was discharged: The reason of this strict course[2] is, because all the hares in the countrey doe belong to one lord or other, and being in abundance, they are killed by the owners appoyntment, and carried to the markets by cart-loads, and sold for the use of the honourable owners: and no boore or tenant that dwels in those parts where those hares are plenty, must keepe a dogge, except he pay five shillings a yeere to the lord, or else one of his fore-feet must be cut of that he may not hunt hares.[3]

A man is in almost as high promotion to bee a knave in England, as a knight in Germany, for there a gentleman is called a youngcurr,[4] and a knight is but a youngcurs man, so that you shall have a scurvy

1   i.e. traveller.
2   1630 edn; misspelled 'conrse' in 1617 edn.
3   Expeditation, the cutting of a dog's feet, was practised in medieval England in areas subject to forest law.
4   Junker, i.e. jung herr, 'young nobleman'.

squire command a knight to hold his stirrup, plucke off his boots, or any other unknightly peece of service: and verily I thinke there are an 100. severall princes, earles, bishops and other estates, that do every one keepe a mint, and in their owne names stampe money, gold, silver, and brasse, and amongst 23. two pences which I had of their brasse money (which they call grushes[1]) I had 13. severall[2] coynes.

Many more such worthy injunctions and honourable ordinances I observed, which are hardly worth pen and inke the describing, and therfore I omit them, and draw toward an end, for on the Wednesday morning[3] I was at an anchor at Stoad, and on the Friday night following I was (by Gods gracious assistance) landed at London. So that in three weeks and three dayes, I sailed from England to Hamburgh and backe again, staying in the countrey 17. dayes, and travelled 200. miles by land there: gathering like a busie bee all these honyed observations, some by sight, some by hearing, some by both, some by neither, and some by bare supposition.

FINIS.

[1] Groschen, small coins (originally of silver) issued by various states across northern Europe. cf English groat.
[2] Different.
[3] 11 September 1616.

The Pennyles Pilgrimage

THE PENNYLES PILGRIMAGE

*T*AYLOR'S LONGEST AND *most ambitious British journey was undertaken in 1618, two years after his Hamburg trip, and hard on the heels of the king's own expedition to Scotland in 1617, to which at Preston he alludes. Like Germany, Scotland to most Londoners was still a foreign country, and it seems to have been with genuine surprise that Taylor crossed the border to find the countryside much the same: '. . . I thought my selfe in England still', he exclaims. The differences become apparent only later, when crossing narrow mountain passes, lodging with Irish- [Gaelic-] speaking cottagers, and hunting with Scottish nobility in the wastes of Braemar. This unplanned adventure in the highlands, so alien to the world of a Thames waterman, prompts some of Taylor's best descriptive writing; but no less interesting is the seemingly miraculous coal-mine near Dunfermline which ran under the sea, and which warrants a long and entertaining account.*

The journey itself, as far as Edinburgh and back, is relatively uneventful, Taylor maintaining the interest by constantly reminding us of his pennyless condition (the result of a wager explained in the title), and thus his picaresque artfulness in cadging food and lodging. With minor deviations, to Sutton Coldfield and Manchester, his route follows the established thoroughfares (as mapped by Ogilby sixty years later), the Holyhead road via Coventry as far as Staffordshire, then the Carlisle road, and returning via Berwick, York and Stamford. A pattern emerges, to become a familiar feature in subsequent journeys, of 'buying' hospitality with the promise of a complimentary mention in the ensuing book; conversely harsh treatment, as at Daventry, is rewarded with abuse in print (which he was subsequently forced to retract). On his arrival in Edinburgh Taylor memorably collars a complete stranger, and at Newcastle on his return he is given a horse in payment for an old favour.

Taylor's artistry and popular appeal is seen in his ability to maintain the reader's interest, by switching from verse to prose and back, and by spicing his account with anecdote. So we learn of his narrow escape at Brechin from a nocturnal seductress, God's punishment on the Sabbath-breaking fishermen of Berwick, near starvation in the Azores years earlier, and the cannon at

Edinburgh Castle in which a child was conceived. Such was the stock-in-trade of the popular travelogue, which Taylor had learnt from Kempe and Coryate, and had himself used when describing gruesome executions in Hamburg two years earlier.

Prolonged travel for Taylor only became possible after 1616, as his contract to collect the 'Tower Bottles' was coming to an end. The Pennyless Pilgrimage was conceived as a business venture (albeit a high-risk one) as much as a publicity stunt. From his subsequent recriminatory pamphlet (A Kicksey-Winsey or a Lerry Come-Twang, 1619) we appear to be told (although Taylor is not always innocent of exaggeration) that the print run was 4,500, costing him nearly £60, but that of his 1,600 subscribers who had promised 5s. (£0.25) or more apiece, about half defaulted, presumably because they felt that Taylor had not fulfilled his wager (to travel pennyless) to the letter. Indeed the rather contrived ending, which seeks to explain why he had money with him at Islington on his return, suggests that they may have been justified. The success of the adventure, nevertheless, and the subsequent controversy, assured Taylor's celebrity, and pointed his course toward further exploits in similar vein.

[14th July - 15th October, 1618. Text derived from 1618 publication (copies BL G510 and Huntington C23784 69265 = STC microfilm 941), and 1630 All the Workes...]

To the truly Noble, and Right Honorable Lord, George Marquesse of Buckingham, Viscount Villeirs, Baron of Whaddon, Justice in Eyre of all his Majesties Forests, Parkes, and Chases beyond Trent, Master of the Horse to his Majesty, and one of the Gentlemen of his Highnesse Royall Bed-Chamber, Knight of the most Noble Order of the Garter, and one of his Majesties most Honorable Privie Councell of both the Kingdomes of England and Scotland.[1]

Right Honorable, and worthy honour'd Lord, as in my travailes, I was entertain'd, welcom'd, and reliev'd by many honourable lords,

---

[1] George Villiers (1592-1628) prominent politician and court favourite. His star was very much in the ascendant when this dedication was penned in 1618, having just received his marquisate.

worshipfull knights, esquires, gentlemen, and others, both in England, and Scotland. So now your lordships inclination hath incited, or invited my poore muse to shelter herselfe under the shadow of your honourable patronage, not that there is any worth at all in my sterill invention, but in all humilitie I acknowledge that it is onely your lordships acceptance, that is able to make this nothing, something, and withall engage me ever.

Your honours, in all observance: John Taylor.

To all my loving adventurers, by what name or title so ever, my generall salutation.

Reader, these travailes of mine into Scotland, were not undertaken, neither in imitation, or emulation of any man, but onely devised by my selfe, on purpose to make triall of my friends, both in this kingdome of England, and that of Scotland, and because I would be an eye-witnesse of divers things which I had heard of that country; and whereas many shallow-brain'd critickes, doe lay an aspersion on me, that I was set on by others, or that I did undergoe this project, either in malice, or mockage of Master Benjamin Jonson,[1] I vow by the faith of a Christian, that their imaginations are all wide, for he is a gentleman, to whom I am so much obliged for many undeserved courtesies that I have received from him, and from others by his favour, that I durst never to be so impudent or ingratefull, as either to suffer any mans perswasions, or mine owne instigation, to incite me, to make so bad a requitall, for so much goodnesse formerly received; so much for that, and now Reader, if you expect

That I should write of cities scituations,
Or that of countries I should make relations:
Of brooks, crooks,[2] nooks; of rivers, boorns[3] and rills,

---

1   Ben Jonson (c.1573-1637) poet and dramatist, who had travelled on foot to Edinburgh earlier in 1618. Taylor seems to have enjoyed friendly relations with him.
2   a crooked corner of ground.
3   i.e. bournes, streams.

Of mountaines, fountaines, castles, towers and hills,
Of shieres, and pieres, and memorable things,
Of lives and deaths of great commanding kings:
I touch not those, they not belong to mee,
But if such things as these you long to see,
Lay down my booke, and but vouchsafe to reede
The learned Camden, or laborious Speede.[1]

And so God speede you and me, whilst I rest
yours in all thankefulnes: Io: Taylor

The Pennyles Pilgrimage, or the money-lesse perambulation, of John Taylor, alias the Kings Majesties Water-Poet. How he travailed on foot, from London to Edenborough in Scotland, not carrying any money to or fro, neither begging, borrowing, or asking meate, drinke or lodging. With his description of his entertainment in all places of his journey, and a true report of the unmatchable hunting in the Brea of Marre and Badenoch in Scotland. With other observations, some serious and worthy of memory, and some merry and not hurtfull to be remembred. Lastly that (which is rare in a travailer) all is true.

List Lordings, list[2] (if you have lust to list)
I write not here a tale of had I wist:[3]
But you shall heare of travels, and relations,
Descriptions of strange (yet English) fashions.
And he that not beleeves what here is writ,
Let him (as I have done) make proofe of it.
The yeare of grace, accounted (as I weene)
One thousand, twice three hundred and eighteene,
And to relate all things in order duly,
'Twas Tuesday last; the foureteenth day of July,

---

[1] William Camden (1551-1623), historian, and John Speed (c.1552-1629), cartographer and historian, were Taylor's principal sources of topographical and historical information, to whose work he repeatedly refers the reader for more information.
[2] listen
[3] i.e. by hearsay

THE PENNYLES PILGRIMAGE

Saint Revels day,[1] the Almanacke will tell ye
The signe in Virgo was, or neere the belly:
The moone full three dayes old, the winde full south;
At these times I began this tricke of youth.
I speake not of the tide; for understand,
My legges I made my oares, and rowed by land,
Though in the morning I began to goe,
Good fellowes trooping, flock'd me so,
That make what hast I could, the sunne was set,
E're from the gates of London I could get.
At last I tooke my latest leave, thus late
At the Bell Inne, that's extra[2] Aldersgate.
There stoode a horse that my provant[3] should carie,
From that place to the end of my fegarie,[4]
My horse no horse, or mare, but guelded nagge,
That with good understanding bore my bagge:
And of good cariage he himselfe did show,
These things are ex'lent in a beast, you know.
There, in my knapsack, (to pay hungers fees)
I had good bacon, bisket, neates-tongue,[5] cheese,
With roses, barbaries, of each conserves,
And Mithridate,[6] that vigorous health preserves;
And I entreate you take these words for no-lyes,
I had good Aqua Vita, Rosa so-lies:[7]
With sweet Ambrosia, (the gods owne drinke)
Most ex'lent geere for mortalls, as I thinke.
Besides, I had both vineger and oyle,
That could a daring sawcie stomack foyle.

1 unexplained
2 outside
3 provisions
4 i.e. vagary, 'wandering'
5 ox-tongue
6 cures and remedies: barbaries are berberis; Mithridate was a cure-all medicine.
7 beverages with health-giving properties: ardent spirit; sundew (*Rosa solis*) cordial; perfumed or fruit drink

This foresaid Tuesday night 'twixt eight and nine,
Well rigg'd & ballac'd, both with beere and wine,
I stumbling forward, thus my jaunt begun,
And went that night as farre as Islington.
There did I finde (I dare affirme it bold)
A Maydenhdead of twenty five yeeres old,
But surely it was painted, like a whore,
And for a signe, or wonder, hang'd at' dore,
Which shewe, a Maidenhead, that's kept so long,
May be hang'd up, and yet sustaine no wrong.
There did my loving friendly host begin
To entertaine me freely to his inne:
And there my friends, and good associates,
Each one to mirth himselfe accommodates.
At well head both for welcome, and for cheere,
Having a good New tonne,[1] of good stale beere:
There did we trundle downe health, after health
(Which oftentimes impaires both health and wealth.)
Till every one had fill'd his mortall trunke,
And onely Nobody was three parts drunke.
The morrow next, Wednesday Saint Swithins day,[2]
From ancient Islington I tooke my way.
At Hollywell[3] I was inforc'd carrowse,
Ale high, and mightie, at the blinde-mans house.
But ther's a helpe to make amends for all,
That though the ale be great, the pots be small.
At High-gate hill to a strange house I went,
And saw the people were to eating bent,
I neither boorrow'd, crav'd, ask'd, begg'd or bought,
But most laborious with my teeth I wrought.
I did not this cause meate or drinke was scant,
But I did practise thus before my want;
Like to a tilter[4] that would winne the prize,

1 tun, or barrel
2 15th July
3 Holloway, north London; the inn was probably the Mother Red Cap
4 jouster

Before the day hee'le often exercise.
So I began to put in ure,[1] at first
These principles 'gainst hunger, and 'gainst thirst.
Close to the gate, there dwelt a worthy man,
That well could take his whiffe, and quaffe his canne,
Right Robin Good-fellow,[2] but humors evill,
Doe call him Robin Pluto, or the Devill.
But finding him a Devill, freely harted,
With friendly farewels I tooke leave and parted.
And as alongst I did my journey take,
I dranke at Broomes-well,[3] for pure fashions sake.
Two miles I travelled then without a bayte,
The Sarazens head at Whetstone[4] entring straight,
I found an host, might lead an host of men,
Exceeding fat, yet named Lean, and[5] Fen.
And though we make small reckoning of him heere,
Hee's knowne to be a very great man there.
There I tooke leave of all my company,
Bade all farewell, yet spake to No-body.
Good reader thinke not strange, what I compile,
For No-body was with me all this while.
And No-body did drinke, and winke, and scinke,[6]
And on occasion freely spent his chinke.[7]
If any one desire to know the man,
Walke, stumble, trundle, but in Barbican.
Ther's as good beere and ale as ever twang'd,[8]
And in that street kinde No-body is hang'd.
But leaving him unto his matchlesse fame,
I to St. Albanes in the evening came,

1 operation
2 Puck, a mischievous and sometimes malevolent sprite
3 Brownswell, Finchley Common, rebuilt in 1593
4 Middlesex, now part of Barnet
5 1630 (*Lean, ard*: 1618)
6 i.e. skink, 'to pour drink'
7 money
8 of a sharp taste, 'kicked'

Where Mr Taylor, at the Sarazens head,
Unask'd (unpaid for) me both lodg'd and fed.
The tapsters, hostlers, chamberlaines, and all,
Sav'd mee a labour, that I need not call,
The jugges were fild and fild, the cups went round,
And in a word great kindnes there I found,
For which both to my cosen, and his men,
Ile still be thankefull in word, deed, and pen.
Till Thursday morning there I made my stay,
And then I went plaine Dunstable high-way.
My very hart with drought me thought did shrinke,
I went twelve miles, and no one bad me drinke.
Which made me call to minde, that instant time,
That drunkennes was a most sinfull crime.
When Puddle-hill[1] I footed downe, and past
A mile from thence I found a hedge at last.
There stroke we sayle,[2] our bacon, cheese, and bread
We drew like fidlers,[3] and like farmers fed,
And whilst 2 houres we there did take our ease,
My nagge made shift to mump[4] greene pulse and pease.
Thus we our hungry stomacks did supply,
And dranke the water of a brooke hard by.
Away t'ward Hockley in the hole,[5] we make,
When straight a horsman did me over-take,
Who knew me, and would faine have given me coyne.
I said my bonds did me from coyne injoyne,
I thank'd and prayd him to put up his chinke,
And willingly I wisht it drownd in drinke.
Away rode he, but like an honest man,

1 west of Houghton Regis, Beds
2 i.e. struck sail, stopped
3 probably allusion to 'fiddlers fare', which should be meat, drink, and money
4 munch
5 Hockcliffe, Beds., so-called on Ogilby's map, 1675. Since Hockcliffe was a highwayman's retreat, this version of the name is presumably an allusion to Hockley-in-the-hole near Clerkenwell Green, London, which was notorious for bull-baiting and fighting.

I found at Hockley standing at the Swan,
A formall tapster, with a jugge and glasse,
Who did arest mee, I most willing was
To try the action, and straight put in bale,
My fees were paide before, with sixe-pence ale.
To quitt this kindnesse, I most willing am,
The man that paide for all, his name is Dam
At the Greenedragon, against Grayes-Inne gate,
He lives in good repute, and honest state.
I forward went in this my roaving race,
To Stony Stratford I toward night did pace,
My minde was fixed through the towne to passe,
To find some lodging in the Hay or Grasse,
But at the Queenes-Armes from the window there,
A comfortable[1] voyce I chaunc'd to heare,
Call Taylor, Taylor and be hang'd come hither,
I look'd for small intreaty and went thither,
There were some friends, which I was glad to see
Who knew my journey; lodg'd, and boorded me.
On Friday morne, as I would take my way,
My friendly host entreated me to stay,
Because it rain'd he tolde me I should have
Meate, drinke, and horse-meate[2] and not pay or crave.
I thank'd him, and for's love remaine his debter,
But if I live, I will requite him better.
(From Stony Stratford the way hard with stones)
Did founder me, and vexe me to the bones,
In blustring weather, both for winde and raine,
Through Tocetter[3] I trotted, with much paine,
Two miles from thence, we satt us downe and dynde,
Well bulwark'd by a hedge, from raine and winde
We having fed, away incontinent,[4]
With weary pace toward Daventry we went.

1 reassuring.
2 food for the horse.
3 Towcester, Northants.
4 without delay.

Foure miles short of it, one o're-tooke me there,
And tolde me he would leave a jugge of beere,
At Daventry at the Horse-shoe, for my use,
I thought it no good manners to refuse,
But thank'd him, for his kinde unasked gift,
Whilest I was lame as scarce a leg could lift,
Came limping after to that stony towne,
Whose hard streetes made me almost halt tight[1] downe.
There had my friend performed the words he saide,
And at the doore a jugge of liquor staide
The folkes were all informed, before I came,
How, and wherefore my journey I did frame,
Which caused mine hostesse from her doore come out,
(Having a great wart rampant on her snowt.)
The tapsters, hostlers, one another call,
The chamberlaines with admiration all,
Were fild with wonder, more then wonderfull,
As if some monster sent from the Mogull,[2]
Some elephant from Affricke, I had beene,
Or some strange beast from th' Amazonian queene.
As buzards, widgions, woodcocks, and such fowle,
Doe gaze and wonder at the broad-fac'd owle,
So did these brainelesse asses, all-amaz'd,
With admirable non sence talk'd and gaz'd.
They knew my state (although not tolde by me')
That I could scarcely goe, they all could see,
They dranke of my beere, that to me was given,
But gave me not a drop to make all eeven,
And that which in my minde was most amisse,
My hostesse she stood by and saw all this,
Had she but said, Come neere the house my friend,
For this day heere shall be your journeys end,
Then had she done the thing which did not,
And I in kinder wordes had paid the shot.[3]

1 *right*, 1630.
2 Rulers of the Islamic empire in India from 1526-1707.
3 recompensed

I doe intreat my friends, (as I have some)
If they to Daventry¹ doe chance to come,
That they will balke² that inne; or if by chaunce,
Or accident into that house they glaunce,
Kinde gentlemen, as they by you reape profit,
My hostesse care of me, pray tell her of it.
Yet doe not neither, lodge there when you will,
You for your money shall be welcome still.
From thence that night, although my bones were sore,
I made a shift to hobble seav'n miles more:
The way to Dunchurch, foule with dirt and mire,
Able, I thinke, both man and horse to tire.
On Dunsmore Heath,³ a hedge doth there enclose
Grounds, on the right hand, there I did repose.
Wits whetstone, want,⁴ there made us quickly learne,
With knives to cut down rushes, and greene fearne,
Of which we made a field-bed in the field,
Which sleepe, and rest, and much content did yeeld.
There with my mother earth, I thought it fit
To lodge, and yet no incest did commit:
My bed was curtain'd with good wholesome ayres,
And being weary, I went up no stayres:
The skie my canopy, bright Phaebe shinde,
Sweet bawling Zephirus⁵ breath'd gentle winde,
In heav'ns starre chamber I did lodge that night,
Tenne thousand starres, me to my bed did light;
There baracadoed⁶ with a banke lay wee
Below the lofty branches of a tree,

---

1   After objection from the landlord, Andrew Hilton, Taylor was subsequently forced to retract this injunction, in *A Kicksey-Winsey* (1619) and *The Scourge of Basenesse* (1624).
2   pass by.
3   Warwicks., south of Rugby.
4   allusion to a treatise on algebra by Robert Recorde, *The Whetstone of Witte* (1557).
5   the moon and the west wind.
6   barricaded

There my bed-fellowes and companions were,
My man, my horse, a bull, foure cowes, two steere:
But yet for all this most confused rowt,
We had no bed-staves,[1] yet we fell not out.
Thus nature, like an ancient free upholster,
Did furnish us with bedstead, bed, and bolster;
And the kinde skies, (for which high heav'n be thanked,)
Allow'd us a large covering and a blanket:
Aurora's[2] face gan light our lodging darke,
We arose and mounted, with the mounting larke,
Through plashes, puddles, thicke, thinne, wet and dry,
I travail'd to the citie Coventry.
There Maister Doctor Holland[3] caus'd me stay
The day of Saturne, and the Sabaoth day.
Most friendly welcome, he did me affoord,
I was so entertain'd at bed and boord,
Which as I dare not bragge how much it was,
I dare not be ingrate and let it passe,
But with thankes many I remember it
(In stead of his good deedes) in words and writ,
He us'd me like his sonne, more then a friend,
And he on Monday his commends did send
To Newhall, where a gentleman did dwell,
Who by his name is hight Sacheverell.[4]
The Tuesday Julyes one and twenteth day,
I to the citie Lichfield tooke my way,
At Sutton Coffill[5] with some friends I met,
And much adoe I had from thence to get,
There I was almost put unto my trumps,[6]

1 the slats of a bedstead.
2 dawn.
3 Philemon Holland (1552-1637), master of the free school at Coventry, and the translator of (among other Latin works) Camden's *Britannia* (1610).
4 Henry Sacheverell (d.1620) of New Hall, Sutton Coldfield.
5 Sutton Coldfield, Warwicks.
6 i.e. to play my trump cards, so to take desperate measures.

THE PENNYLES PILGRIMAGE

My horse shooes were worne as thinne as pumps;[1]
But noble Vulcan, a mad smuggy[2] smith,
All reparations me did furnish with.
The shooes were well remov'd, my palfrey shod,
And he referr'd the payment unto God.
I found a friend, when I to Lichfield came,
A joyner, and John Piddock is his name,
He made me welcome, for he knew my jaunt,
And he did furnish me with good provant:
He offred me some money, I refus'd it,
And so I tooke my leave, with thanks excus'd it.
That Wednesday I a weary way did passe,
Raine, winde, stones, dirt, and dabling[3] dewie grasse,
With here and there a pelting[4] scatter'd village,
Which yeelded me no charity, or pillage:
For all the day, nor yet the night that followed,
One drop of drinke I'm sure my gullet swallowed.
At night I came t'a stonie towne call'd Stone.
Where I knew none, nor was I knowne of none:
I therefore through the streetes held on my pace,
Some two miles farther to some resting place:
At last I spide a meddow newly mowde,
The hay was rotten, the ground halfe o're-flowde:
We made a breach,[5] and entred horse and man,
There our pavillion, we to pitch began,
Which we erected with greene broome and hay,
T'expell the colde, and keepe the raine away;
The skie all muffled in a cloud gan lowre,
And presently there fell a mighty showre,
Which without intermission downe did powre,
From tenne a night, untill the mornings foure.
We all that time close in our couch did lye,

1 a type of slipper.
2 grimy.
3 splashing.
4 worthless, contemptible.
5 broke in.

Which being well compacted, kept us dry.
The worst was, we did neither sup nor sleepe,
And so a temperate dyet we did keepe.
The morning all enroab'd in drisling fogges,
We being as ready as we had beene dogges:
We neede not stand upon long ready making,
But gaping, stretching, and our eares well shaking:
And for I found my host and hostesse kinde,
I like a true man[1] left my sheetes behinde.
That Thursday morne, my weary course I fram'd,
Unto a towne that is Newcastle[2] nam'd,
(Not that Newcastle standing upon Tine)
But this townes scituation doth confine
Neere Cheshiere, in the famous county Stafford,
And for their love, I owe them not a straw for't;
But now my versing Muse craves some repose,
And whilst she sleepes Ile spowt a little prose.

    In this towne of Newcastle, I overtooke an hostler, and I asked him what the next towne was called, that was in my way toward Lancaster, he holding the end of a riding rod in his mouth, as if it had been a fluit, piped me this answere, and said, Talke on the hill;[3] I asked him againe what hee said, Talke on the hill: I demaunded the third time, and the third time he answered me as he did before, Talke on the hill. I began to grow chollericke,[4] and asked him why hee could not talke, or tell mee my way as well there, as on the hill; at last I was resolved, that the next towne was foure miles off mee, and the name of it was, Talke on the hill. I had not travailed above two miles farther: but my last nights supper (which was as much as nothing) my mind being enformed of it by my stomacke, I made a vertue of necessity, and went to breakefast in the Sunne: I have fared better at three Sunnes many a time before now, in Aldersgate streete, Creeplegate,[5] and new Fishstreete, but here is the

1 honest; i.e. he did not pilfer the linen.
2 Newcastle under Lyme, Staffs.
3 Talke, Staffs., west of Kidsgrove.
4 angry.
5 Cripplegate.

oddes, at those Sunnes they will come upon a man with a taverne bill as sharp cutting as a Taylors bill of items: A watch-mans bill,[1] or a Welch-hooke[2] falls not halfe so heavy upon a man; besides, most of the vintners have the law in their owne hands, and have all their actions, cases, bills of debt, and such reckonings tried at their owne barres;[3] from whence there is no appeale. But leaving these impertinencies, in the materiall Sunne-shine, wee eate a substantiall dinner, and like miserable guestes wee did budget up the reversions.[4]

And now with sleepe, my Muse hath eas'd her braine,
I'le turne my stile from prose, to verse againe.
That which we could not have, we freely spar'd,
And wanting drinke, most soberly we far'd.
We had great store of fowle (but 'twas foule way)
And kindly every step entreates me stay,
The clammy clay sometimes my heeles would trip,
One foote went forward, th' other backe would slip.
This weary day, when I had almost past,
I came unto Sir Urian Legh's at last,[5]
At Adlington, neere Macksfield he doth dwell,[6]
Belov'd, respected, and reputed well.
Through his great love, my stay with him was fixt,
From Thursday night, till noone on Monday next,
At his owne table I did dayly eate;
Whereat may be suppos'd, did want no meate,
He would have giv'n me gold or silver either,
But I with many thankes, received neither.
And thus much without flatterie I dare sweare,
He is a knight beloved farre and neere.
First, he's beloved of his God above,
(which love, he loves to keepe, beyond all love)

1 the weapon carried by night watchmen. *bill*, 1630 (*blil*: 1618).
2 weapon shaped like a bill-hook.
3 pun on bar in a law-court, and bar in a tavern.
4 bagged up the leftovers (to take with them).
5 of Adlington, born *c*.1568, BA Oxford 1583.
6 Adlington Hall, Cheshire, between Macclesfield and Stockport.

Next with a wife and children he is blest,
Each having Gods feare planted in their brest.
With faire demaines,[1] revennue of good lands,
Hee's fairely blest by the Almighties hands.
And as hee's happy in these outward things,
So from his inward minde continuall springes
Fruits of devotion, deeds of piety,
Good hospitable workes of charity,
Just in his actions, constant in his word,
And one that wonne his honour with his sword.
Hee's no carranto, capr'ing,[2] carpet knight,[3]
But he knowes when, and how to speake or fight.
I cannot flatter him, say what I can,
Hee's every way a compleat gentleman.
I write not this, for what he did to me,
But what mine eares, and eyes did heare and see,
Nor doe I pen this to enlarge his fame,
But to make others imitate the same.
For like a trumpet were I pleasd to blow,
I would his worthy worth more amply show,
But I already feare have beene too bolde,
And crave his pardon, me excusd to holde.
Thankes to his sonnes and servants every one,
Both males and females all, excepting none.
To beare a letter he did me require,
Neere Manchester, unto a good esquire:
His kinsman Edmond Prestwitch,[4] he ordain'd,
That I at Manchester was entertain'd
Two nights, and one day, ere we thence could passe,
For men and horse, rost, boyl'd, and oates, and grasse:
This gentleman, not onely gave me harbor,[5]

1 demesnes, i.e. estates.
2 dancing a coranto or courante, a type of gliding dance.
3 one who gains a knighthood by favour at court, rather than by military prowess.
4 of Hulme, Manchester (c.1577-1629).
5 lodging.

But in the morning sent me to his barber,
Who lav'd,[1] and shav'd me, still I spard my purse,
Yet sure he left me many a haire the worse.
But in conclusion, when his worke was ended,
His glasse informd, my face was much amended.
And for the kindnesse he to me did show,
God grant his customers beards faster grow,
That though the time of yeare be deere or cheape,
From fruitfull faces hee may mowe and reape.
Then came a smith, with shoes, and tooth and nayle,
He searched my horse hooves, mending what did faile,
Yet this I note, my nagge, through stones and dirt,
Did shift shoes twice, ere I did shift one shirt:
Can these kind thinges be in oblivion hid?
No, Master Prestwitch, this and much more did,
His friendship did command, and freely gave
All before writ, and more then I durst crave.
But leaving him a little, I must tell,
How men of Manchester, did use me well,
Their loves they on the tenter-hookes did racke,[2]
Rost, boyld, bak'd, too too much, white, claret, sacke,
Nothing they thought too heavy or too hot,
Canne follow'd canne, and pot succeeded pot,
That what they could do, all they thought too little,
Striving in love the traveller to whittle.[3]
We went unto the house of one John Pinners,
(A man that lives amongst a crew of sinners)
And there eight severall[4] sorts of ale we had,
All able to make one starke drunke or mad.
But I with courage bravely flinched not,
And gave the towne leave to discharge the shot.[5]
We had at one time set upon the table,

1   washed.
2   here with the meaning 'stretched'.
3   intoxicate.
4   different.
5   to pay the reckoning.

Good ale of hisope,[1] 'twas no Esope fable:
Then had we ale of sage, and ale of malt,
And ale of worme-wood, that can make one halt,
With ale of rosemary, and bettony,
And two ales more, or else I needes must lye.
But to conclude this drinking alye tale,
We had a sort of ale, called scurvy ale.[2]
Thus all these men, at their owne charge and cost,
Did strive whose love might be expressed most.
And farther to declare their boundlesse loves,
They saw I wanted, and they gave me gloves,
In deed, and very deede, their loves were such,
That in their praise I cannot write too much;
They merit more then I have here compil'd,
I lodged at the Eagle and the Childe,
Whereas my hostesse, (a good aunciency woman)
Did entertaine me with respect, not common.
She caus'd my linnen, shirts, and bands[3] be washt,
And on my way she caus'd me be refresht,
She gave me twelve silke poyntes,[4] she gave me baken,
Which by me much refused, at last was taken,
In troath she prov'd a mother unto me,
For which, I evermore will thankfull be.
But when to minde these kindnesses I call,
Kinde Master Prestwitch author is of all,
And yet Sir Urian Leigh's good commendation,
Was the maine ground of this my recreation.
For both of them, there what I had, I had,
Or else my entertainment had bin bad.
O all you worthy men of Manchester,
(True bred blouds of the County Lancaster)
When I forget what you to me have done,
Then let me head-long to confusion runne.

1 hyssop, pun on Aesop.
2 medicated ale taken to prevent scurvy.
3 collars.
4 laces.

To noble Master Prestwitch I must give
Thankes, upon thankes, as long as I doe live,
His love was such, I ne're can pay the score,
He farre surpassed all that went before,
A horse and man he sent, with boundlesse bounty,
To bring me quite through Lancasters large county.
Which I well know is fifty miles at large,
And he defrayed all the cost and charge.
This unlook'd pleasure, was to me such pleasure,
That I can ne're expresse my thankes with measure.
So Mistresse Saracoale, hostesse kinde,
And Manchester with thankes I left behinde.
The Wednesday being Julyes twenty nine,
My journey I to Preston did confine,
All the day long it rayned but one showre,
Which from the morning to the eve'n did powre,
And I, before to Preston I could get,
Was sowsd, and pickeld both with raine and sweat.
But there I was supply'd with fire and food,
And any thing I wanted sweete and good.
There, at the Hinde, kinde Master Hinde mine host,
Kept a good table, bak'd and boyld, and rost,
There Wedensday, Thursday, Friday I did stay,
And hardly got from thence on Saturday.
Unto my lodging often did repaire,
Kinde Master Thomas Banister, the Mayor,
Who is of worship, and of good respect,
And in his charge discreet and circumspect.
For I protest to God I never saw,
A towne more wisely govern'd by the law.
They tolde me when my soveraigne there was last,[1]
That one mans rashnes, seem'd to give distast.
It griev'd them all, but when at last they found,
His Majesty was pleasd, their joyes were crown'd.

---

[1] James I stayed at Ashton Hall near Lancaster, on his journey from Scotland to London, August 1617.

He knew the fairest garden hath some weedes,[1]
He did accept their kinde intents, for deedes:
One man there was, that with his zeale too hot,
And furious hast, himselfe much over-shot.
But what man is so foolish, that desires
To get good fruit from thistles, thornes and bryers?
Thus much I thought good to demonstrate heere,
Because I saw how much they grieved were.
That any way, the least part of offence,
Should make them seeme offensive to their prince.
Thus three nights was I staide and lodg'd in Preston,
And saw nothing ridiculous to jest on,
Much cost and charge the mayor upon me spent,
And on my way two miles, with me he went,
There (by good chance) I did more friendship get,
The under Shriefe[2] of Lancashire, we met,
A gentleman that lov'd, and knew me well,
And one whose bounteous minde doth beare the bell.[3]
There, as if I had beene a noted thiefe,
The mayor delivered me unto the shriefe.
The shriefes authority did much prevaile,
He sent me unto one that kept the jayle.
Thus I perambulating, poore John Taylor,
Was giv'n from mayor to shriefe, from shriefe to jaylor,
The jaylor kept an inne, good beds, good cheere,
Where paying nothing, I found nothing deere:
For the under shriefe kinde Master Covill nam'd,
(A man for house-keeping renown'd and fam'd)
Did cause the towne of Lancaster afford
Me welcome, as if I had beene a Lord.
And 'tis reported, that for dayly bounty,
His mate[4] can scarce be found in all that county.

1 variant of a proverb first recorded 1579.
2 sheriff.
3 to be the foremost or best, from the bellwether, or leading sheep, which wore the bell.
4 like.

Th' extreames of mizer, or of prodigall
He shunnes, and lives discreete and liberall,
His wives minde, and his owne are one, so fixt,
That Argos eyes[1] could see no oddes betwixt,
And sure the difference, (if there diff'rence be)
Is who shall doe most good, or he, or she.
Poore folks reports, that for releeving them,
He and his wife, are each of them a jem;
At th'inne, and at his house two nights I staide,
And what was to be paid, I know he paide;
If nothing of their kindnesse I had wrote,
Ingratefull me the world might justly note:
Had I declar'd all I did heare and see,
For a great flatt'rer then I deem'd should be,
He and his wife, and modest daughter Besse,
With earth and heav'ns felicity, God blesse.
Two dayes a man of his at his command,
Did guide me to the midst of Westmerland,
And my conductor with a liberall fist,
To keepe me moyst, scarce any alehouse mist.
The fourth of August (weary, halt, and lame)
We in the darke, t'a towne call'd Sebder[2] came,
There Maister Borrowd, my kind honest host,
Upon me did bestow unasked cost.
The next day I held on my journey still,
Sixe miles unto a place call'd Carling hill,
[3]Where Maister Edmond Branthwaite doth recide,
Who made me welcome, with my man and guide.
Our entertainement, and our fare was such,
It might have satisfied our betters much;
Yet all too little was, his kinde heart thought,
And five miles on my way himselfe me brought,

1   In Greek mythology Argus had 100 eyes, and Juno set him to watch carefully anyone of whom she was jealous. *Argos* (1618), *Argus* (1630).
2   Sedbergh, West Riding.
3   Carlin Gill, West Riding, south-west of Sedbergh.

At Orton[1] he, I, and my man did dine,
With Maister Corney a good true divine,
And surely Maister Branthwait's well belov'd,
His firme integrity is much approv'd:
His good effects, doth make him still affected
Of God and good men, (with regard) respected.
He sent his man with me, o're dale and downe,
Who lodg'd, and borded me at Peereth[2] towne,
And such good cheere, and bedding there I had,
That nothing, (but my weary selfe) was bad;
There a fresh man, (I know not for whose sake)
With me a journey would to Carlile make;
But from that citie, about two miles wide,
Good Sir John Dalston lodg'd me and my guide.
Of all the gentlemen in England bounds,
His house is neerest to the Scottish grounds,[3]
And fame proclaimes him, farre and neere, aloud,
He's free from being covetous, or proud:
His sonne Sir George, most affable, and kinde,
His fathers image, both in forme and minde:
On Saturday to Carlile both did ride,
Where (by their loves and leaves) I did abide,
Where of good entertainement I found store,
From one that was the mayor the yeare before,
His name is Maister Adam Robinson,
I the last English friendship with him won.
He (gratis)[4] found a guide to bring me thorough,
From Carlile to the citie Edinborough:
This was a helpe, that was a helpe alone,
Of all my helps inferiour unto none.
Eight miles from Carlile runnes a little river,[5]

1   Westmorland, south-west of Appleby.
2   Penrith, Westmorland.
3   His seat was actually at Dalston, south-west of Carlisle.
4   'My thankes to Sir John and Sir George Dalstone, with Sir Henry Gurwin'. [Taylor]
5   River Sark, at Gretna.

Which Englands bounds, from Scotlands grounds doth sever.
Without horse, bridge, or boate, I o're did get[1]
On foote, I went yet scarce my shooes did wet.
I being come to this long look'd for land,
Did marke, remarke, note, renote, viewd and scand:
And I saw nothing that could change my will,
But that I thought my selfe in England still.
The kingdomes are so neerely joyn'd and fixt,
There scarcely went a paire of sheares betwixt;
There I saw skie above, and earth below,
And as in England, there the sunne did shew:
The hills with sheepe replete, with corne the dale,
And many a cottage yeelded good Scotch ale;[2]
This county (Anandale) in former times,
Was the curst climate[3] of rebellious crimes:
For Cumberland and it, both kingdomes border,
Were ever ordred, by their owne disorders,
Such sharking, shifting, cutting throates, and thieving,
Each taking pleasure, in the others grieving;
And many times he that had wealth to night,
Was by the morrow morning beggerd quite:
To many yeares this pell-mell[4] furie, lasted,
That all these borders were quite spoyl'd and wasted,
Confusion, hurly-burly raign'd and reveld,
The churches with the lowly ground were leveld;
All memorable monuments defac'd,
All places of defence o'rethrowne and rac'd.[5]
That who so then did in the borders dwell,
Liv'd little happier then those in hell.
But since the all-disposing God of heaven,

---

1 'Over Esk I waded.' [Taylor]
2 'The afore named knightes had given money to my guide, of which hee left some part at every ale-house.' [Taylor]
3 in general sense of 'region'.
4 derived from a game, an early form of croquet.
5 razed.

Hath these two kingdomes to one monarch given,[1]
Blest peace, and plenty on them both hath showr'd
Exile, and hanging hath the theeves devowr'd,
That now each subject may securely sleepe,
His sheepe, and neate,[2] the blacke the white doth keepe,
For now those crownes are both in one combinde,
Those former borders, that each one confinde,
Appeares to me (as I doe understand)
To be almost the center of the land,
This was a blessed heaven expounded riddle,
To thrust great kingdomes skirts into the middle.
Long may the instrumentall[3] cause survive
From him and his, succession still derive
True heires unto his vertues, and his throane,
That these two kingdomes ever may be one.
        This county of all Scotland is most poore,
By reason of the outrages before,
Yet mighty store of corne I saw there growe,
And as good grasse as ever man did mowe:
And as that day I twenty miles did passe,
I saw eleven hundred neat at grasse,
By which may be conjectur'd at the least,
That there was sustenance for man and beast.
And in the kingdome I have truly scand,
There's many worser parts, are better mand,
For in the time that theeving was in ure,[4]
The gentles fled to places more secure.
And left the poorer sort, t'abide the paine,
Whilest they could ne're finde time to turne againe.
That shire of gentlemen is scarce and dainty,[5]
Yet there's reliefe in great aboundance plenty,
Twixt it and England, little oddes I see,

1 James VI of Scotland became James I of England in 1603.
2 cattle
3 in the sense of 'effective'.
4 practice.
5 in the sense of 'rare'.

They eate, and live, and strong and able bee,
>So much in verse, and now Ile change my stile,
>And seriously I'le write in prose a while.

To the purpose then: my first nights lodging in Scotland was at a place called Mophot,[1] which they say is thirty miles from Carlile, but I suppose them to be longer then forty of such miles as are betwixt London and Saint Albanes, (but indeed the Scots doe allow almost as large measure of their miles, as they doe of their drinke, for an English gallon either of ale or wine, is but their quart, and one Scottish mile now and then may well stand for a mile and a halfe or two English) but howsoever short or long, I found that dayes journey the weariest that ever I footed; and at night being come to the towne, I found good ordinary countrey entertainment; my fare, and my lodging was sweete and good, and might have served a far better man then my selfe, although my selfe have had many times better: but this is to be noted, that though it rained not all the day, yet it was my fortune to be well wet twise, for I waded over a great river called Eske in the morning, somewhat more then foure miles distance from Carlile in England, and at night within two miles of my lodging, I was faine to wade over the River of Annan in Scotland, from which river the county of Annandale hath it's name. And whilst I waded on foote, my man was mounted on horse-backe, like the George without the Dragon. But the next morning, I arose and left Mophot behind me, and that day I travailed twenty one miles to a sory village called Blithe,[2] but I was blithe my selfe to come to any place of harbour or succour, for since I was borne, I never was so weary, or so neere being dead with extreame travell; I was founderd and refounderd[3] of all foure, and for my better comfort, I came so late, that I must lodge without doore all night, or else in a poore house where the good-wife lay in child-bed, her husband being from home, her owne servant mayd being her nurse. A creature naturally compacted and artificially adorned with incomparable homelines; but as thinges were I must either take or leave, and necessity made me enter, where we gat egges and ale by measure and by tale.[4]

1   Moffat, Dumfriesshire.
2   Blyth Bridge, Peeblesshire, north of Broughton; pun on blithe, 'cheerful'.
3   restored.
4   by number.

At last to bed I went, my man lying on the floore by me, where in the night, there were pidgeons did very bountifully mute[1] in his face: the day being no sooner come, and I having but fifteene miles to Edenborough, mounted upon my ten toes, and began first to hobble, and after to amble, and so being warme, I fell to pace by degrees; all the way passing through a most plentifull, and firtill[2] countrey for corne and cattle: and about two of the clocke in the afternoone that Wednesday, being the thirteenth of August, and the day of Clare the Virgin (the signe being in Virgo) the moone foure dayes olde, the winde at west, I came to take rest, at the wished, long expected, aunceint famous city of Edenborough, which I entred like Pierce penilesse,[3] altogether monyles, but I thanke God not friendlesse; for being there, for the time of my stay I might borrow, (if any man would lend) spend if I could get, begge if I had the impudence, and steale, if I durst adventure the price of a hanging, but my purpose was to house my horse, and to suffer him and my apparell to lye in durance,[4] or lavender in stead of litter, till such time as I could meete with some valiant friend that would desperately disburse.

Walking thus downe the street, (my body being tyred with travell, and my minde attyred with moody, muddy, moore-ditch melancholly) my contemplation did devoutly pray, that I might meete one or other to prey upon, being willing to take any slender acquaintance of any man whatsoever, viewing, and circumviewing[5] every mans face I met, as if I meant to draw his picture, but all my acquaintance was *Non est inventus*,[6] (pardon me Reader, that Latine is none of mine owne, I sweare by Priscians Paricranion,[7] an oath which I have ignorantly broken many times.) At last I resolv'd, that the next gentleman that I met withall, should be acquaintance whether he would or no, and presently fixing

1   defecate.
2   'most plentifull, and' omitted, 1630; 'firtill' i.e. fertile.
3   The hero of a Rabelaisian work by Thomas Nashe (1567-c.1601), *Pierce Penniless his Supplication to the Devil* (1592).
4   confinement.
5   looking around at.
6   Latin 'he has not been found'.
7   Priscian was a 6th-century Latin grammarian, whose work was influential during the middle ages. Pericranion refers to the skull. A favourite proverb, from Skelton (c.1525) onwards, was 'to break Priscian's head', meaning to ignore the rules of grammar.

THE PENNYLES PILGRIMAGE 59

mine eyes upon a gentleman-like object, I looked on him as if I would survay something through him, and make him my perspective: and hee much musing at my gazing, and I much gazing at his musing, at last hee crost the way and made toward me, and then I made downe the streete from him, leaving him to encounter with my man who came after me leading my horse, whome hee thus accosted. My friend (quoth hee) doth yonder gentleman, (meaning mee) know mee that he lookes so wistly[1] on me; Truely Sir, said my man I thinke not, but my master is a stranger come from London, and would gladly meete with some acquaintance to direct him where he may have lodging and horse-meate: presently the gentleman, (being of a generous disposition) over-tooke me with unexpected and undeserved courtesie, brought me to a lodging, and caused my horse to bee put into his owne stable, whilest we discoursing over a pinte of Spanish,[2] I related as much English to him as made him lend me ten shillings, (his name was Master John Maxwell) which money I am sure was the first that I handled after I came from out the walles of London: but having rested two houres and refreshed my selfe, the gentleman and I walked to see the citty, and the castle, which as my poore unable and unworthy pen can, I will truely describe.

The castle on a loftie rocke is so strongly grounded, bounded, and founded, that by force of man it can never bee confounded; the foundation and walles are unpenetrable, the rampiers[3] impregnable, the bulwarkes invincible, no way but one to it is or can be possible to be made passable. In a word, I have seene many straights[4] and fortresses, in Germany, the Netherlands, Spaine, and England, but they must all give place to this unconquered castle both for strength and scituation.

Amongst the many memorable thinges which I was shewed there, I noted especially a great peece of ordinance of iron, it is not for batterie, but it will serve to defend a breach, or to tosse balles of wilde-fire against any that should assaile or assault the castle; it lyes now dismounted. And it is so great within, that it was tolde mee that a childe was once gotten[5] there, but I to make tryall crept into it, lying on my

1 earnestly.
2 i.e. wine.
3 ramparts.
4 in the sense of 'confined place'.
5 conceived.

backe, and I am sure there was roome enough and spare for a greater then my selfe.

So leaving the castle, as it is both defencive against any opposition, and magnificke for lodging and receite,[1] I descended lower to the citty, wherein I observed the fairest and goodliest street that ever mine eyes beheld, for I did never see or heare of a streete of that length, (which is halfe an English mile from the castle to a faire port which they call the Neather-bow)[2] and from that port the streete which they call the Kenny-hate[3] is one quarter of a mile more: downe to the kings pallace, called Holy-rood-House, The buildings on each side of the way being all of squared stone, five, sixe, and seaven storyes high, and many bylanes and closes on each side of the way, wherein are gentlemens houses, much fairer then the buildings in the high streete, for in the High-street the marchants and tradesmen doe dwell, but the gentlemens mansions and goodliest houses are obscurely founded in the aforesaid lanes: the walles are eight or tenne foote thicke, exceeding strong, not built for a day, a weeke, or a month, or a yeare; but from antiquitie to posteritie, for many ages; There I found entertainment beyond my expectation or merite, and there is fish, flesh, bread and fruit, in such variety, that I thinke I may offencelesse call it superfluitie, or sacietie.[4] The worst was, that wine and ale was so scarce, and the people there such mizers of it, that every night before I went to bed, if any man had asked mee a civill question, all the wit in my head could not have made him a sober answer.

I was at his Majesties pallace, a stately and princely seate, wherein I saw a sumptuous Chappell most richly adorned, with all apurtenances belonging to so sacred a place, or so royall an owner. In the inner court, I saw the kings armes cunningly carved in stone, and fixed over a doore aloft on the wall, the red lyon being the crest, over which was written this inscription in Latine,

Nobis haec invicta miserunt, 106. proavi.

I enquired what the English of it was? it was told me as followeth, which I thought worthy to be recorded.

1 receiving guests.
2 Netherbow, Edinburgh's east gate, was demolished in 1764.
3 Canongate, the eastern continuation of High Street.
4 i.e. satiety, 'surfeit'.

106. fore-fathers have left this to us unconquered.
This is a worthy and a memorable motto, and I thinke few kingdomes or none in the world can truly write the like, that notwithstanding so many inroades, incursions, attempts, assaults, civill warres, and forraigne hostilities, bloodie battels, and mightie foughten fields, that maugre[1] the strength and pollicie of enemies, that royall crowne and scepter hath from one hundred and seaven descents, keepe[2] still unconquered, and by the power of the King of Kings (through the grace of the Prince of peace) is now left peacefully to our peacefull king, whom long in blessed peace, the God of peace defend and governe.

But once more, a word or two of Edinborough, although I have scarcely given it that due which belongs unto it, for their lofty and stately buildings, and for their faire and spacious streete, yet my minde perswades me that they in former ages that first founded that citie, did not so well in that they built it in so discommodious[3] a place; for the sea, and all navigable rivers, being the chiefe meanes for the enriching of townes and cities, by the reason of traffique with forraigne nations, with exportation, transportation, and receite of variety of marchantdizing; so this citie had it beene built but one mile lower on the sea side, I doubt not but it had long before this beene comparable to many a one of our greatest townes and cities in Europe, both for spaciousnesse of bounds, port, state, and riches. It is said that King James the fifth[4] (of famous memorie) did graciously offer to purchase for them, and to bestow upon them freely, certaine lowe and pleasant grounds a mile from them on the sea shore, with these conditions, that they should pull downe their citie, and build it in that more commodious place, but the citizens refused it: and so now it is like (for me) to stand where it doth, for I doubt such another proffer of removeall will not be presented to them, till two dayes after the faire.[5]

Now have with you for Leeth,[6] whereto I no sooner came, but I

1 in spite of.
2 kept (1630).
3 unsuitable
4 1512-1542.
5 proverbial for 'too late'. To come a day after the fair was a popular expression in the 16th century, but has Greek and Latin antecedents.
6 Leith, the port of Edinburgh.

was well entertained by Master Barnard Lindsay, one of the groomes of his Majesties bedchamber, hee knew my estate was not guilty, because I brought no guilt[1] with mee (more then my sinnes, and they would not passe for current there) hee therefore did replenish the vaustity[2] of my emptie purse, and discharged a peece at mee with two bullets of gold, each being in value worth eleven shillings white money:[3] and I was credibly informed that within the compasse of one yeare, there was shipped away from that onely port of Leeth, fourescore thousand boles[4] of wheate, oates, and barley, into Spaine, France, and other forraigne parts, and every bole containes the measure of foure English bushels, so that from Leeth onely hath beene transported three hundred and twenty thousand bushels of corne; besides some hath been shipped away from Saint Andrewes, from Dundee, Aberdeene, Disert, Kirkady, Kinghorne, Burnt-Iland,[5] Dunbar, and other portable[6] townes, which makes mee to wonder that a kingdome so populous as it is, should neverthelesse sell so much bread corne beyond the seas, and yet to have more then sufficient for themselves.

So I having viewed the haven and towne of Leeth, tooke a passage boate to see the new wondrous well, to which many a one that is not well, comes farre and neere in hope to be made well: indeede I did heare that it had done much good, and that it hath a rare operation to expell or kil divers maladies; as to provoke appetite, to helpe much for the avoyding of the gravell in the bladder, to cure sore eyes, and olde ulcers, with many other vertues which it hath, but I (through the mercy of God having no neede of it, did make no great inquisition what it had done, but for novelty I dranke of it, and I found the taste to be more pleasant then any other water, sweet almost as milke, yet as cleare as cristall, and I did observe that though a man did drinke a quart, a pottell,[7] or as much as his belly could containe, yet it never offended or lay heavie upon the

1 pun on gilt, 'money'.
2 emptiness
3 silver money.
4 boll, a measure, usually six bushels.
5 Dysart, Kirkcaldy, Kinghorn and Burntisland are adjacent ports in Fife, opposite Edinburgh.
6 to which boats may navigate.
7 half-gallon.

stomacke, no more then if one had dranke but a pint or a small quantity.

I went two miles from it to a towne called Burnt-Iland, where I found many of my especiall good friends, as Master Robert Hay, one of the groomes of his Maiesties Bed-chamber, Maister David Drummond, one of his Gentlemen Pentioners, Maister James Acmooty, one of the Groomes of the Privie Chamber, Captaine Murray, Sir Henry Witherington Knight, Captain Tyrie, and divers others: and there Master Hay, Maister Drummond, and the good olde Captaine Murray did very bountifully furnish mee with gold for my expences, but I being at dinner with those aforesaid gentlemen, as we were discoursing, there befell a strange accident,[1] which I thinke worth the relating.

I know not upon what occasion they began to talke of being at sea in former times, and I (amongst the rest) said I was at the taking of Cales,[2] whereto an English gentleman replied, that he was the next good voyage after at the Ilands:[3] I answered him that I was there also. He demanded in what ship I was? I tolde him in the Rainebowe of the Queene's why (quoth hee) doe you not know me? I was in the same ship, and my name is Witherington.

Sir, said I, I doe remember the name well, but by reason that it is neere two and twenty yeeres since I saw you, I may well forget the knowledge of you: Well, said hee, if you were in that ship, I pray you tell me some remarkable token that happened in the voyage: whereupon I tolde him two or three tokens which hee did know to be true. Nay then said I, I will tell you another which (perhaps) you have not forgotten; as our ship and the rest of the fleete did ride at anchor at the Ile of Flores[4] (one of the Isles of the Azores) there were some fourteene men and boyes of our ship, that for novelty would goe a shore, and see what fruit the iland did beare, and what entertainement it would yeeld us: so being landed, wee went up and downe and could finde nothing but stones, heath and mosse, and wee expected oranges, limonds, figges, muske-millions,[5] and potatoes: in the meane space the winde did blow so stiffe, and the sea was so extreame rough, that our ship-boate could

---

1 co-incidence.
2 Calais was recaptured after a naval engagement by the Spanish in 1596.
3 Azores expedition, 1597.
4 one of the Azores, west of the main group.
5 lemons... melons.

not come to the land to fetch us, for feare she should be beaten in pieces against the rockes: this continued five dayes, so that wee were all almost famished for want of foode: but at last (I squandring[1] up and downe) by the providence of God I happened into a cave or poore habitation, where I found fifteene loaves of bread, each of the quantity of a penny loafe in England, I having a valiant stomacke of the age of almost of a hundred and twenty houres breeding, fell too, and eate two loaves and never said grace: and as I was about to make a horse-loafe[2] of the third loafe, I did put twelve of them into my breeches, and my sleeves, and so went mumbling[3] out of the cave, leaning my backe against a tree, when upon the sodaine a gentleman came to me, and saide, friend, what are you eating, bread quoth I, for Gods sake said hee, give me some, with that I put my hand into my breeh, (beeing my best pantrey) and I gave him a loafe, which hee received with many thankes, and said that if ever hee could requite it hee would.

I had no sooner tolde this tale but Sr Henry Witherington did acknowledge himselfe to bee the man that I had given the loafe unto two and twenty yeeres before, where I found the proverbe true, that men have more priviledge then mountaines in meeting.[4]

In what great measure, hee did requite so small a courtesie, I will relate in this following discourse in my returne through Northumberland: So leaving my man at the towne of Burnt Iland, I tolde him, I would but goe to Sterling, and see the castle there, and withall to see my honourable friends the Earle of Marr, and Sir William Murray Knight, Lord of Abercarny, and that I would returne within two dayes at the most: But it fell out quite contrary; for it was five and thirtie dayes before I could get backe againe out of these noble mens company. The whole progresse of my travell with them, and the cause of my stay, I cannot with gratefulnesse omit; and thus it was.

A worthy gentleman named Master John Fenton, did bring mee on my way six miles to Dumfermling, where I was well entertained,

1 wandering.
2 horse-bread was made of beans and bran, and intended for horses. This may be an allusion to the proverb, as high as three horse-loaves.
3 munching.
4 variant of the proverb, friends may meet, but mountains never greet, first recorded in 1530.

and lodged at Master John Gibb his house, one of the Groomes of his Maiesties Bed-chamber, and I thinke the oldest servant the king hath: withall I was well entertained there by Master Crighton at his owne house, who went with mee, and shewed me the Queenes Palace;[1] (a delicate and a princely mansion) withall I saw the ruines of an aunciente and stately built abbey, with faire gardens, orchards, and medowes belonging to the palace: all which with faire and goodly revenues, by the suppression of the abbey, were annexed to the crowne. There also I saw a very faire church, which though it be now very large and spacious, yet it hath in former times been much larger. But I taking my leave of Dumfermling, would needs goe and see the truely noble knight Sir George Bruce, at a towne called the Cooras:[2] there hee made mee right welcome, both with varietie of fare, and discourse,[3] and after all, hee commaunded three of his men to direct mee to see his most admirable cole-mines; which (if man can or could worke wonders) is a wonder: for my selfe neither in any travels that I have been in, nor any history that I have read, or any discourse that I have heard, did never see, reade, or heare of any worke of man that might parallell or be equivalent with this unfellowed[4] and unmatchable worke: and though all I can say of it, cannot describe it according to the worthinesse of his vigilant industry, that was both the occasion, inventor, and maintainer of it: yet rather then the memory of so rare an enterprise, and so accomplisht a profit to the common-wealth shall bee raked and smothered in the dust of oblivion, I will give a little touch at the description of it, although I amongst writers, am like he that worst may, holds the candle.[5]

The mine hath two wayes into it, the one by sea and the other by land;[6] but a man may go into it by land, and returne the same way if

1 The guest house of Dunfermline Abbey, Fife, was reconstructed between 1590 and 1600 as a palace for Anne of Denmark, queen of James I.
2 Bruce built Culross Palace between 1597 and 1611 from the proceeds of the mining enterprise.
3 'and discourse' omitted, 1630.
4 unrivalled.
5 proverb, he that is worst may hold the candle, from c.1534, and in Shakespeare, *Romeo and Juliet*. Taylor chooses an appropriate analogy for a coal mine.
6 Bruce reopened Culross Abbey's coal mine, from 1575, and extended it under the sea. The lowest part of the mine was inundated in 1625.

he please, and so he may enter into it by sea, and by sea hee may come foorth of it: but I for varieties sake went in by sea, and out by land. Now men may object, how can a man goe into a mine, the entrance of it being in the sea, but that the sea will follow him, and so drown the mine. To which objection thus I answer, That at a low water, the sea being ebd away, and a great part of the sand bare; upon this same sand (beeing mixed with rockes and cragges) did the master of this great worke build a round circular frame of stone, very thicke, strong, and ioyned together with glutinous or bitunous[1] matter, so high withall, that the sea at the highest flood, or the greatest rage of storme or tempest, can neither dissolve the stones so well compacted in the building or yet overflowe the height of it. Within this round frame, (at all adventures) hee did set workemen to digge with mattockes, pickaxes, and other instruments fit for such purposes. They did digge more then[2] fourtie foot downe right, into and through a rocke. At last they found that which they expected, which was sea-cole,[3] they following the veine of the mine, did digge forward still: So that in the space of eight and twentie, or nine and twenty yeeaes, they have digged more then an English mile under the sea, that when men are at worke belowe, an hundred of the greatest shippes in Britaine may saile over their heads. Besides, the mine is most artificially cut like an arch or a vault all that great length, with many nookes and by-wayes in it:[4] and it is so made, that a man may walke upright in the most places, both in and out. Many poore people are there set on worke, which otherwise through the want of imployment would perish. But when I had seene the mine, and was come foorth of it againe; after my thankes given to Sir George Bruce, I tolde him, that if the plotters of the powder treason in England had seene this mine, that they (perhaps) would have attempted to have left the Parliament House, and have undermined the Thames, and so to have blowne up the barges and wherries, wherein the king, and all the estates of our kingdome were. Moreover, I said that I could affoord to turne tapster at London: so that I had but one quarter of a mile of his mine to make mee a celler, to keepe beere and bottle-ale in. But leaving these jestes in prose, I will relate a few verses that I made

1   i.e. bituminous, 'pitchy'.
2   'more then' omitted, 1630.
3   mined or mineral coal, as opposed to charcoal.
4   'in it' omitted, 1630.

merrily of this mine.

I that have wasted, months, weekes, dayes, & howers
In viewing kingdomes, countreys, townes, and towers,
Without all measure, measuring many paces,
And with my pen describing subdrie[1] places,
With few additions of my owne devizing,
(Because I have a smacke of Coriatizing.)[2]
Our Mandevill, Primaleon, Don Quixot,
Great Amadis, or Huon,[3] traveld not
As I have done, or beene where I have beene,
Or heard and seene, what I have heard and seene;
Nor Britaines Odcomb (zanye brave Ulissis)[4]
In all his ambling saw the like as this is.
I was in (would I could describe it well)
A darke, light, pleasant, profitable hell,
And as by water I was wasted in,
I thought that I in Charons boate[5] had bin:
But being at the entrance landed thus,
Three men there (in the stead of Cerberus)[6]
Convaid me in, in each ones hand a light
To guide us in that vault of endlesse night.
There young and old with glim'ring candles burning,
Digge, delve, and labour, turning and returning,
Some in a hole with baskets and with baggs,
Resembling furies, and infernall haggs:
There one like Tantall[7] feeding, and there one,

1 many, 1630.
2 a taste for describing the exotic, in the style of Thomas Coryate, who had died during a journey to India the previous year.
3 exotic travellers: Sir John Mandeville (d.1372?); Primaleon (not identified); Don Quixote, hero of Cervantes' romance; Amadis of Gaul, subject of a 15th-century Spanish romance; Huon of Bordeaux, subject of a 13th-century French romance.
4 Coryate (Britain's Ulysses) came from Odcombe, Somerset, near Yeovil.
5 in Greek mythology the ferryman to the underworld.
6 the dog which guarded the entrance to the underworld.
7 Tantalus was punished by being set in a lake, whose waters always receded

Like Sisiphus[1] he rowles the restlesse stone.
Yet all I saw was pleasure mixt with profit,
Which prov'd it to be no tormenting Tophet;[2]
For in this honest, worthy, harmelesse hell,
There ne'r did any damned Divell dwell:
And th' owner of it gaines by 't more true glory
Then Rome doth by fantastic Purgatory.
A long mile thus I past, downe, downe, steepe, steepe,
In deepenesse farre more deepe, then Neptunes deepe,
Whilst o're my head (in fourefould stories hye)
Was Earth, and Sea, and Ayre, and Sun, and Skie:
That had I dyed in that Cimerian[3] roome.
Foure elements had covered ore my tombe:
Thus farther than the bottome did I goe,
(And many Englishmen have not done so;)
Where mounting Porposes, and mountaine whales,
And regiments of fish with finnes and scales,
Twixt me and Heaven did freely glide and slide,
And where great ships may at an anchor ride:
Thus in by sea, and out by land I past,
And tooke my leave of good Sir George at last.

    The sea at certain places doth leake, or soake into the mine, which by the industry of Sir George Bruce, is all conveyd to one well neere the land; where hee hath a devise like a horsemill, that with three horses and a great chaine of iron, going downeward many fadomes, with thirty six buckets fastened to the chaine, of the which eighteene goes downe still to be filled, and eighteene ascends up to be emptied, which doe empty themselves (without any mans labour) into a trough that conveyes the water into the sea againe; by which meanes he saves his myne, which otherwise would be destroyed with the sea, when he tried to drink.

1 Sisyphus had perpetually to push a stone up a hill, which then rolled down again.
2 An Old Testament hell, where the Assyrian king would be destroyed by fire (2 Kings 23 verse 10; Isaiah 30 verse 33).
3 mythical land of constant mist and darkness.

beside he doth make every weeke ninety or an hundred tuns of salt, which doth serve part[1] of Scotland, some hee sends into England, and very much into Germany, all which shewes the painefull[2] industry with Gods blessings to such worthy endeavours : I must with many thankes remember his courtesie to mee, and lastly, how he sent his man to guide me ten miles on the way to Sterling, where by the way I saw the outside of a faire and stately house called Allaway,[3] belonging to the Earl of Marr, which by reason that his Honor was not there, I past by and went to Sterling, where I was entertained and lodged at one Master John Archibalds, where all my want was that I wanted roome to containe halfe the good cheere that I might have had there; hee had me into the castle, which in few words I doe compare to Windsor for scituation, much more than Windsor in strength, and somewhat lesse in greatnes : yet I dare affirme, that his Majesty hath not such another hall to any house that he hath neither in England nor Scotland, except Westminster Hall which is now no dwelling hall for a prince, being long since metamorphosed into a house for the law and the profits.[4]

This goodly hall was built by King James the fourth, that marryed King Henry the eights sister and after was slaine at Flodden field;[5] but it surpasses all the halls for dwelling houses that ever I saw, for length, breadth, height and strength of building, the castle is built upon a rocke very lofty, and much beyond Edenborough Castle in state and magnificence, and not much inferiour to it in strength, the roomes of it are lofty, with carved workes on the seelings, the doores of each roome beeing so high, that a man may ride upright on horsebacke into any chamber or lodging. There is also a goodly faire chappell, with cellers, stables, and all other necessary offices, all very stately and befitting the maiestie of a king.

1 *serve most part* (1630).
2 painstaking.
3 Alloa House, Clackmannanshire.
4 Parliament moved into Westminster Palace in 1512. Pun on 'the law and the prophets', a term for the books of the Old Testament.
5 James IV (1473-1513) married Margaret Tudor, and died at the battle of Flodden Field, Northumb., September 1513.

From Sterling I rode to Saint Johnston,[1] a fine towne it is, but it is much decayed, by reason of the want of his maiesties yearely comming to lodge there. There I lodged one night at an inne, the goodman of the house his name being Patrick Pettcarne, where my entertainement was with good cheere, good drinke,[2] good lodging, all too good to a bad weary guest. Mine host tolde mee that the Earle of Marr, and Sir William Murray of Abercarny were gone to the great hunting to the Brea of Marr;[3] but if I made haste I might perhaps finde them at a towne called Breekin,[4] or Breechin, two and thirty miles from Saint Johns Stone whereupon I tooke a guide to Breekin the next day, but before I came, my lord was gone from thence foure dayes.

Then I tooke another guide, which brought mee such strange wayes over mountaines and rockes, that I thinke my horse never went the like; and I am sure I never saw any wayes that might fellow them. I did goe through a country called Glaneske,[5] where passing by the side of a hill, so steepe as is the ridge of a house, where the way was rocky, and not above a yard broad in some places, so fearefull and horrid it was to looke downe into the bottome, for if either horse or man had slipt, he had fallen (without recovery) a good mile downe-right; but I thanke God, at night I came to a lodging in the Lard of Eggel's Land,[6] where I lay at an Irish[7] house, the folkes not being able to speake scarce any English, but I sup'd and went to bed, where I had not laine long, but I was enforced to rise, I was so stung with Irish musketaes,[8] a creature that hath sixe legs, and lives like a monster altogether upon mans flesh, they doe inhabite and breed most in sluttish houses, and this house was none of the cleanliest, the beast is much like a louse in England, both in shape and nature; in a word they were to me the A. and the Z. the Prologue and the Epilogue, the first and the last that I had in all my travells from Edenborough; and had not this highland Irish house helped mee at a

1 former name for Perth.
2 'good drinke' omitted, 1630.
3 Braemar, area of the Grampians.
4 Brechin.
5 Glen Esk, valley running north from Brechin.
6 perhaps Ecclesgreig, north of Montrose.
7 Gaelic.
8 mosquitoes, used loosely for biting insects.

pinch, I should have sworne that all Scotland had not beene so kind as to have bestowed a louse[1] upon me: but with a shift[2] that I had, I shifted off my caniballs, and was never more troubled with them.

The next day I travelled over an exceeding high mountaine, called mount Skeene,[3] where I found the valley very warme before I went up it; but when I came to the top of it, my teeth beganne to daunce in my head with colde, like virginall jackes;[4] and withall, a most familiar[5] mist embraced mee round, that I could not see thrice my length any way: withall, it yeelded so friendly a deaw, that it did moysten through all my clothes: Where the old proverbe of a Scottish miste[6] was verified, in wetting mee to the skinne. Up and downe, I thinke this hill is sixe miles, the way so uneven, stonie, and full of bogges, quagmires, and long heath, that a dogge with three legs will outrunne a horse with foure: for doe what we could, wee were foure houres before we could passe it.

Thus with extreame travell, ascending and descending, mounting and alighting, I came at night to the place where I would bee, in the Brea of Marr, which is a large countie, all composed of such mountaines, that Shooters Hill, Gads Hill, Highgate Hill, Hampsted hill, Birdlip hill, or Malverne hilles,[7] are but mole-hilles in comparison, or like a liver, or a gizard under a capons wing, in respect of the altitude of their toppes, or perpendicularitie of their bottomes.[8] There I saw Mount Benawne,[9] with a furr'd mist upon his snowie head in stead of a nightcap: (for you must understand, that the oldest man alive never saw but the snow was on the top of divers of those hilles, both in summer, as well as in winter.) There did I finde the truely Noble and Right Honourable Lords John Erskin Earle of Marr, James Stuart Earle of Murray, George Gordon Earle of Engye, sonne and heire to the Marquesse of Huntley, James Erskin, Earle of Bughan, and John Lord Erskin, sonne and heire to the

1 something worthless.
2 shirt or nightshirt.
3 perhaps Mount Keen, south of Ballater.
4 the jacks carry the quills which pluck the virginall strings.
5 closely embracing.
6 Proverb, found from 1589.
7 Taylor chooses four hills near London, and two (Birdlip and Malvern) visible from his birthplace, Gloucester.
8 valleys, here meaning valley sides.
9 perhaps Ben Avon, north of Braemar village.

Earle of Marr, and their Countesses, with my much honoured, and my best assured and approoved friend, Sir William Murray knight, of Abercarnye, and hundred of other knights, esquires, and their followers; all and every man in generall in one habit, as if Licurgus[1] had beene there and made lawes of equalitie: For once in the yeare, which is the whole moneth of August, and sometimes part of September; many of the nobilitie and gentry of the kingdome (for their pleasure) doe come into these high-land countreyes to hunt, where they doe all conforme themselves to the habit of the high-land men, who for the most part speake nothing but Irish; and in former time were those people which were called the Red-shankes:[2] Their habite is shooes with but one sole apiece; stockings (which they call short hose) made of a warme stuffe of divers colours, which they call Tartane: as for breeches, many of them, nor their forefathers never wore any, but a jerkin of the same stuffe that their hose is of, their garters beeing bands or wreathes of hay or straw, with a plead about their shoulders, which is a mantle of divers colours, much finer and lighter stuffe then their hose, with blew flat caps on their heads, a handkerchiefe knit with two knots about their neckes: and thus are they attyred. Now their weapons are long bowes, and forked arrowes, swords and targets, harquebusses,[3] muskets, durks[4] and Loquhabor Axes.[5] With these armes I found many of them armed for the hunting. As for their attire, any man of what degree soever that comes amongst them, must not disdaine to weare it: for if they doe, then they will disdaine to hunt, or willingly to bring in their dogges: but if men bee kinde unto them, and bee in their habit; then are they conquered with kindnesse, and the sport will be plentifull. This was the reason that I found so many noblemen and gentlemen in those shapes. But to proceed to the hunting.

My good Lord of Marr having put me into that shape, I rode with him from his house, where I saw the ruines of an olde castle, called

1   Lycurgus, king of the Greek city of Sparta (9th century BC), who framed a new code of laws and constitutions.
2   Name commonly given to Gaelic Scots in the 16th and 17th centuries, on account of their bare legs.
3   i.e. arquebus, a type of handgun.
4   a Highland dagger.
5   i.e. Lochaber-axes, a type of long-handled halberd.

the Castle of Kindroghit.[1] It was built by King Malcolm Canmore[2] (for a hunting house[3]) who raigned in Scotland when Edward the Confessor, Harold, and Norman William raigned in England: I speake of it, because it was the last house that I saw in those parts; for I was the space of twelve dayes after, before I saw either house, corne field, or habitation for any creature, but deere, wilde horses, wolves, and such like creatures, which made mee doubt that I should never have seene a house againe.

Thus the first day wee traveld eight miles, where there were small cottages built on purpose to lodge in, which they call Lonquhards,[4] I thanke my good Lord Erskin, he commanded that I should always bee lodged in his lodging, the kitchin being always on the side of a banke, many kettles and pots boyling, and many spits turning and winding, with great variety of cheere: as venison bak't, sodden, rost, and stu'de beefe, mutton, goates, kid, hares, fresh salmon, pidgeons, hens, capons, chickins, partridge, moorecoots, heathcocks, caperkellies, and termagants;[5] good ale, sacke, white and claret, tent (or allegant)[6] with most potent Aqua vitae.[7]

All these, and more then these wee had continually, in superfluous aboundance, caught by faulconers, foulers, and fishers, and brought by my lords tenants and purveyers to victuall our campe, which consisted of fourteene or fifteene hundred men and horses; the manner of the hunting is this. Five or six hundred men doe rise early in the morning, and they doe disperse themselves divers wayes, and seven, eight or tenne miles compasse they doe bring or chase in the deere in many heards, (two, three, or foure hundred in a heard) to such or such a place as the noblemen shall appoint them; then when day is come, the lords and gentlemen of their companies, doe ride or goe to the said places, sometimes wading up to the middles through bournes and rivers: and then they being come to the place, doe lye downe on

1 perhaps Kindrochet Lodge, west of Blair Atholl.
2 Malcolm III (1031-93).
3 'horse', 1618, presumably in error.
4 temporary cottages or sheilings.
5 ptarmigans.
6 Spanish wine.
7 spirits.

the ground, till those foresaid scouts which are called the Tinckhell,[1] do bring downe the deere: But as the proverbe sayes of a bad cooke, so these Tinckhell men doe lick their owne fingers;[2] for besides their bowes and arrowes which they carry with them, wee can heare now and then a harguebuse or a musquet goe off, which they doe seldome discharge in vaine: Then after wee had stayed three houres or thereabouts, wee might perceive the deere appeare on the hills round about us, (their heads making a shew like a wood) which being followed close by the Tinkhell, are chased downe into the valley where wee lay; then all the valley on each side being way-laid with a hundred couple of strong Irish grey-hounds, they are let loose as occasion serves upon the heard of deere, that with dogges, gunnes, arrowes, durks, and daggers, in the space of two houres, fourescore fat deere were slaine, which after are disposed of some one way and some another, twenty or thirty miles, and more then enough left for us to make merry withall at our Rendevouze. I liked the sport so well, that I made these two sonnets following.

Why should I wast invention to endite,
Ovidian fictions,[3] or Olympian games?
My misty Muse enlightened with more light,
To a more noble pitch her ayme she frames.
I must relate to my great Master James,
The Calydonian annuall peacefull warre;
How noble mindes doe eternize their fames,
By martiall meeting in the Brea of Marr:
How thousand gallant spirits came neere and farre,
With swords and targets, arrowes, bowes, and gunnes,
That all the troope to men of judgement, are
The god of warres great never conquered sonnes.
The sport is manly, yet none bleed but beasts,
And last, the victor on the vanquisht feasts.

1   i.e. tinchel, the 'circle' of deer hunters.
2   proverbial, recorded from c.1510, meaning that cooks generally help themselves to some of the food, as 'perks'. The 1630 reading is *'like'* for *'lick'*.
3   Ovid, Latin poet, whose works in English translation were influential in spreading knowledge of classical mythology.

If sport like this can on the mountaines be,
Where Phoebus flames[1] can never melt the snow:
Then let who list delight in vales below,
Skie-kissing mountaine pleasures are for me:
What braver object can mans eyesight see,
Then noble, worshipfull, and worthy wights,[2]
As if they were prepard for sundry fights,
Yet all in sweet society agree:
Through heather, mosse, 'mongst frogs, and bogs, and fogs,
Mongst craggy cliffes, and thunder battered hills,
Hares, hindes, buckes, roes are chas'd by men and dogs,
Where two howres hunting fourescore fat deere killes.
Low lands, your sports are low as is your seate,
The high-land games and minds, are high and greate.

    Beeing come to our lodgings, there was such baking, boyling, rosting, and stewing, as if Cooke Ruffian[3] had beene there to have scalded the Devill in his feathers: and after supper a fire of firrewood as high as an indifferent may-pole: for I assure you, that the Earle of Marr will give any man that is his friend, for thankes, as many firre trees (that are as good as any shippes mastes in England) as are worth (if they were in any place neere the Thames, or any other portable river) the best earledome in England or Scotland either: For I dare affirme hee hath as many growing there, as would serve for mastes (from this time to the end of the world) for all the shippes, carackes,[4] hoyes, galleyes, boates, drumlers, barkes, and water-craftes, that are now, or can bee in the world these fourtie yeares.

    This sounds like a lie to an unbeleever; but I and many thousands doe knowe that I speake within the compasse of truth: for indeede (the more is the pitie) they doe grow so farre from any passage of water,

---

1 a name for Apollo, the sun-god.
2 people.
3 Cook-Ruffian (perhaps from Ruffin, a fiend) occurs in 1565 as responsible for spoiling food by cooking it badly. The proverb, in the form given by Taylor, is recorded again in 1670.
4 carrack, a large ship; hoy, a one-decked sloop; drumbler, a small fast vessel; bark, a three-masted vessel. The terms can be used loosely, and overlap.

and withall in such rockie mountaines, that no way to convey them is possible to bee passable either with boate, horse, or cart.

Thus having spent certaine dayes in hunting in the Brea of Marr, wee went to the next countie called Bagenoch,[1] belonging to the Earle of Engye, where having such sport and entertainement as wee formerly had; after foure or five dayes pastime, wee tooke leave of hunting for that yeare; and tooke our journey toward a strong house of the Earles, called Ruthen[2] in Bagenoch, where my Lord of Engye and his noble countesse (being daughter to the Earle of Argile) did give us most noble welcome three dayes.

From thence wee went to a place called Ballo Castle,[3] a faire and stately house; a worthie gentleman beeing the owner of it, called the Lard of Graunt; his wife beeing a gentlewoman honourably descended, being sister to the right Honouable Earle of Atholl, and to Sir Patricke Murray knight; shee beeing both inwardly and outwardly plentifully adorned with the guifts of grace and nature: so that our cheere was more then sufficient; and yet much lesse then they could affoord us. There staied there foure dayes, foure earles, one lord, divers knights and gentlemen, and their servants, footemen and horses; and every meale foure long tables furnished with all varieties: Our first and second course beeing threescore dishes at one boord; and after that always a banquet: and there if I had not forsworne wine till I came to Edinbrough, I thinke I had there dranke my last.

The fifth day with much adoe wee gate from thence to Tarnaway,[4] a goodly house of the Earle of Murrayes, where that right honourable lord and his ladie did welcome us foure dayes more. There was good cheere in all varietie, with somewhat more then plentie for advantage: for indeed the countie of Murray[5] is the most pleasantest, and plentifullest countrey in all Scotland; being plaine land, that a coach may bee driven more then foure and thirtie myles one way in it, all alongst by the sea-coast.

1 Badenoch, area of upper Speyside, around Dalwhinnie and Kingussie.
2 Ruthven, south of Kingussie.
3 Balloch, east of Inverness.
4 Darnaway Castle, south-west of Forres.
5 Morayshire.

From thence I went to Elgen[1] in Murray, an auncient citie, where there stood a faire and beautifull church with three steeples, the walles of it and the steeples all yet standing; but the roofe, windowes, and many marble monuments and toombes of honourable and worthie personages all broken and defaced: this was done in the time when ruine bare rule, and Knox[2] knock'd downe churches.

From Elgen we went to the Bishop of Murray his house which is called Spinye,[3] or Spinaye. A reverend gentleman hee is, of the noble name of Dowglasse,[4] where wee were very well welcomed, as befitted the honour of himselfe and his guests.

From thence wee departed to the Lord Marquesse of Huntleyes,[5] to a sumptuous house of his, named the Bogg of Geethe,[6] where our entertainement was like himselfe, free, bountifull and honourable. There (after two dayes stay) with much entreatie and earnest suite, I gate leave of the lords to depart towards Edinbrough: the noble marquesse, the Earles of Marr, Murray, Engie, Bughan, and the Lord Erskin; all these, I thanke them, gave me gold to defray my charges in my journey.

So after five and thirtie dayes hunting and travell, I returning, past by another stately mansion of the lord marquesses, called Stroboggy,[7] and so over Carny mount[8] to Breckin, where a wench that was borne deafe and dumbe came into my chamber at mid-night (I beeing asleepe) and shee opening the bed, would faine have lodged with mee: But had I beene a Sardanapalus,[9] or a Heliogobalus,[10] I thinke that either the great travell over the mountaines had tamed me; or if not, her beautie could never have mooved me. The best parts of her were, that her breath was as sweet as

---

1   Elgin.
2   John Knox (1505-72) architect of the Scottish reformation.
3   Spinye, north of Elgin.
4   Alexander Douglas, bishop of Moray 1611-23.
5   George Gordon (c.1563-1642), created 1st marquess of Huntley in 1599
6   Keith, Banffshire.
7   Huntly Castle, Huntly, Aberdeenshire. George Gordon rebuilt his palace there on the site of Strathbogie Peel.
8   Cairn o' Mount, Kincardineshire, north of Fettercairn.
9   Assyrian king, who ruled from 668 BC. A notorious philanderer, according to classical historians.
10 Roman emperor, 218-22 AD, with a similar reputation. *Heliogabalus* (1630).

sugar-carrion,[1] being very well shouldered[2] beneath the waste; and as my hostesse tolde mee the next morning, that shee had changed her maidenhead for the price of a bastard not long before. But howsoever, shee made such a hideous noyse, that I started out of my sleepe, and thought that the Devill had beene there: but I no sooner knewe who it was, but I arose, and thrust my dumbe beast out of my chamber; and for want of a locke or a latch, I staked up my doore with a great chaire.

Thus having escaped one of the seven deadly sinnes at Breekin, I departed from thence to a towne called Forfard;[3] and from thence to Dundee, and so to Kinghorne,[4] Burnt Iland, and so to Edinbrough, where I stayed eight dayes, to recover my selfe of falles and bruises which I received in my travell in the high-land mountainous hunting. Great welcome I had shewed mee all my stay at Edinbrough, by many worthy gentlemen, namely, olde Master George Todrigg, Master Henry Levingston, Master James Henderson, Master John Maxwell, and a number of others, who suffered me to want no wine or good cheere, as may be imagined.

Now the day before I came from Edinbrough, I went to Leeth, where I found my long approved and assured good friend Master Benjamin Johnson, at one Master John Stuarts house: I thanke him for his great kindnesse towards mee: for at my taking leave of him, hee gave mee a piece of golde of two and twentie shillings to drinke his health in England. And withall, willed mee to remember his kind commendations to all his friendes: So with a friendly farewell, I left him, as well, as I hope never to see him in a worse estate: for hee is amongst noble-men and gentlemen that knowes his true worth, and their owne honours, where with much respective love hee is worthily entertained.

So leaving Leeth, I return'd to Edinbrough, and within the port or gate, called the Netherbowe, I discharged my pockets of all the money I had: and as I came pennilesse within the walles of that citie at my first comming thither; so now at my departing from thence, I came

1 sugar-candian, i.e. sugar-candy, has been suggested as an emendation. But in view of 'well-shouldered...' and the dumb maid making a hideous noise, perhaps this should just be regarded as nonsense. See also p. 117, note 2.
2 Nonsense?
3 Forfar.
4 Kinghorn, east of Burntisland.

moneylesse out of it againe; having in my company to convey mee out, certaine gentlemen, amongst the which was Master James Acherson, Laird of Gasford, a gentleman that brought mee to his house, where with great entertainement hee and his good wife did welcome me.

On the morrowe he sent one of his men to bring mee to a place, called Adam,[1] to Master John Acmootye his house, one of the groomes of his majesties bed-chamber; where with him, and his two brethren, Master Alexander, and Master James Acmootye, I found both cheere and welcome not inferiour to any that I had had in any former place.

Amongst our viands that wee had there, I must not forget the Soleand Goose,[2] a most delicate fowle, which breedes in great aboundance in a little rocke called the Basse, which stands two miles into the sea. It is very good flesh, but it is eaten in the forme as wee eate oysters, standing at a side-boord, a little before dinner, unsanctified without grace; and after it is eaten, it must be well liquored with two or three good rowses[3] of sherrie or canarie sacke.[4] The lord or owner of the Basse doth profite at the least two hundred pound yearely by those geese; the Basse it selfe being of a great height, and neere three quarters of a mile in compasse, all fully replenished with wildfowle, having but one small entrance into it, with a house, a garden, and a chappell in it; and on the toppe of it a well of pure fresh water.

From Adam, Master John and Master James Acmootye went to the towne of Dunbarr with mee, where tenne Scottish pintes of wine were consumed and brought to nothing for a farewell: there at Master James Baylies house I tooke leave, and Master James Acmootye comming for England, said, that if I would ride with him, that neither I nor my horse should want betwixt that place and London. Now I having no money or meanes for travell, beganne at once to examine my manners, and my want: at last my want perswaded my manners to accept of this worthy gentlemans undeserved courtesie. So that night he brought mee to a place called Coberspath,[5] where wee lodged at an inne, the like of which

1 Haddington.
2 The gannet (*Sula bassana*), known as the solan goose, although not a true goose. Bass Rock, off North Berwick.
3 draughts.
4 dry wine from the Canary Islands.
5 Cockburnspath, south-east of Dunbar.

I dare say, is not in any of his Majesties dominions. And for to shewe my thankfulnesse to Master William Arnet and his wife, the owners thereof, I must a little[1] explaine their bountifull entertainement of guests, which is this:

Suppose tenne, fifteene, or twentie men and horses come to lodge at their house, the men shall have flesh, tame and wild-fowle, fish, with all varietie of good cheere, good lodging, and welcome; and the horses shall want neither hay or provender: and in the morning at their departure the reckoning is just nothing. This is this worthy gentlemans use, his chiefe delight beeing onely to give strangers entertainement *gratis*: And I am sure, that in Scotland beyond Edinbrough, I have beene at houses like castles for building; the master of the house his beaver[2] being his blew bonnet, one that will weare no other shirts, but of the flaxe that growes in his owne ground; and of his wives, daughters, or servants spinning; that hath his stockings, hose, and jerkin of the wooll of his owne sheepes backes; that never (by his pride of apparell) caused mercer, draper, silke-man, embroyderer, or haberdasher to breake and turne bankerupt: and yet this plaine home-spunne fellow keepes and maintaines thirtie, fourtie, fiftie servants or perhaps more, every day releeving three or fourescore poore people at his gate; and besides all this, can give noble entertainement for foure or five dayes together to five or sixe earles and lords, besides knights, gentlemen and their followers, if they be three or foure hundred men and horse of them, where they shall not onely feed but feast, and not feast but banquet, this is a man that desires to know nothing so much as his duty to God and his king whose greatest cares are to practise the works of piety, charity, and hospitality: hee never studies the consuming art of fashionlesse fashions, hee never tries his strength to beare foure or five hundred acres on his backe at once, his legges are always at liberty, not being fettered with golden garters, and manacled with artificiall roses, whose weight (sometime) is the last reliques of some decayed lordship: Many of these worthy house-keepers there are in Scotland, amongst some of them I was entertained; from whence I did truely gather these aforesaid observations.

So leaving Coberspath, we rode to Barwicke,[3] where the worthy

1 'a little' omitted, 1630.
2 felt hat.
3 Berwick on Tweed, Northumb.

old soldier and ancient knight, Sir William Bowyer, made me welcome, but contrary to his will, we lodged at an inne, where Master James Acmooty paid all charges: but at Barwicke there was a grievous chance hapned, which I think not fit the relation to be omitted.

In the River of Tweed, which runnes by Barwicke, are taken by fishermen that dwell there, infinite numbers of fresh salmons, so that many housholds and families are relieved by the profit of that fishing; but (how long since I know not) there was an order that no man or boy whatsoever should fish upon a Sunday: This order continued long amongst them, till some eight or nine weekes before Michaelmas last, on a Sunday, the salmons plaid in such great aboundance in the river, that some of the fishermen (contrary to Gods law and their owne order) tooke boates and nettes and fished, and caught neere[1] three hundred salmons; but from that time untill Michaelmas day that I was there which was nine weekes, and heard the report of it, and saw the poore peoples miserable lamentations, they had not seene one salmon in the river; and some of them were in despaire that they should never see any more there; affirming it to be Gods judgement upon them for the prophanation of the Saboth.

The thirtieth of September we rode from Barwicke to Belford, from Belford to Anwick,[2] the next day from Anwick to Newcastle, where I found the noble knight, Sir Henry Witherington; who, because I would have no gold nor silver, gave mee a bay mare, in requitall of a loafe of bread that I had given him two and twenty yeares before, at the Iland of Flores, of the which I have spoken before. I overtook at Newcastle a great many of my worthy friends, which were all comming for London, namely, Maister Robert Hay, and Maister David Drummond, where I was welcomed at Maister Nicholas Tempests house. From Newcastle I rode with those gentlemen to Durham, to Darington,[3] to Northallerton, and to Topcliffe in Yorkshire, where I tooke my leave of them, and would needs try my pennilesse fortunes by my selfe, and see the citty of Yorke, where I was lodged at my right worshipfull good friends, Maister Doctor Hudson one of his Majesties chaplaines, who went with me, and shewed me the goodly minster

1 'neere' omitted, 1630.
2 Alnwick, Northumb.
3 Darlington, Co. Durham.

church there, and the most admirable, rare- wrought, unfellowed[1] chapter house.

From Yorke I rode to Doncaster, where my horses were well fed at the Beare, but my selfe found out the honourable knight, Sir Robert Anstruther at his father in lawes, the truely noble Sir Robert Swifts house, hee being then high Sheriffe of Yorkeshire, where with their good ladies, and the right Honourable the Lord Sanquhar, I was stayed two nights and one day, Sir Robert Anstruther (I thanke him) not only paying for my two horses meat, but at my departure, hee gave mee a letter to Newarke upon Trent, twenty eight miles in my way, where Master George Atkinson mine host made me as welcome as if I had been a French lord, and what was to bee paid, as I cal'd for nothing, I paid as much; and left the reckoning with many thankes to Sir Robert Anstruther.

So leaving Newarke, with another gentleman that overtooke mee, wee came at night to Stamford, to the signe of the Virginitie (or the Maydenhead) where I delivered a letter from the Lord Sanquhar; which caused Master Bates and his wife, being the master and mistresse of the house, to make mee and the gentleman that was with mee great cheare for nothing.

From Stamford the next day wee rode to Huntington,[2] where wee lodged at the post-masters house, at the signe of the Crowne; his name is Riggs. Hee was informed who I was, and wherefore I undertooke this my pennilesse progresse: wherefore hee came up into our chamber, and sup'd with us, and very bountifully called for three quarts of wine and sugar, and foure jugges of beere. Hee did drinke and beginne healths like a horse-leech,[3] and swallowed downe his cuppes without feeling, as if he had had the dropsie, or nine pound of spunge in his maw. In a word, as he is a poste, hee drank poste,[4] striving and calling by all meanes to make the reckoning great, or to make us men of great reckoning. But in his payment hee was tyred like a jade,[5] leaving the gentleman that was with mee to discharge the terrible shott, or else one of my horses

1 unrivalled.
2 Huntingdon.
3 insatiable blood-sucker.
4 with great speed.
5 a worthless horse.

must have laine in pawne for his superfluous calling, and unmannerly intrusion.

But leaving him, I left Huntington, and rode on the Sunday to Puckeridge,[1] where Master Holland at the Faulkon, (mine olde acquaintance) and my loving and aunciente hoste gave mee, my friend, my man, and our horses excellent good cheere, and welcome, and I paid him with, not a penie of money.

The next day I came to London, and obscurely comming within Moore-gate, I went to a house and borrowed money: and so I stole backe againe to Islington, to the sign of the Mayden-head, staying till Wednesday that my friendes came to meete me, who knewe no other, but that Wednesday was my first comming; where with all love I was entertained with much good cheere: and after supper wee had a play of the life and death of Guy of Warwicke, plaied by the Right Honourable the Earle of Darbie his men.[2] And so on the Thursday morning beeing the fifteenth of October, I came home to my house in London.

THE EPILOGUE TO ALL MY ADVENTURERS AND OTHERS.

Thus did I neither spend, or begge, or aske,
By any course, direct, or indirectly:
But in each tittle[3] I perform'd my taske,
According to my bill most circumspectly.
I vow to God I have done Scotland wrong,
(And (justly) gainst me it may bring an action)
I have not given't that right which doth belong,
For which I am halfe guilty of detraction:
Yet had I wrote all things that there I saw,
Misjudging censures would suppose I flatter,
And so my name I should in question draw,
Where asses bray, and prattling pies[4] do chatter:

1 Herts., between Buntingford and Ware.
2 Probably *The Tragical History of Guy Earl of Warwick*, an anonymous play (1593), later revised (1620). The second company of the Earl of Derby's men were active 1594-1618.
3 detail.
4 magpies.

Yet (arm'd with truth) I publish with my pen,
That there th' Almighty doth his blessings heape,
In such aboundant food for beasts and men;
That I ne're saw more plenty or more cheape:
Thus what mine eyes did see, I do beleeve;
And what I do beleeve, I know is true:
And what is true unto your hands I give,
That what I give may be beleev'd of you.
But as for him that sayes I lye or dote,[1]
I doe returne, and turne the lye in's throat.
    Thus gentlemen, amongst you take my ware,
    You share my thankes, and I your moneyes share.

Yours in all observance and gratefulnesse, ever to be commanded, John Taylor.

FINIS.

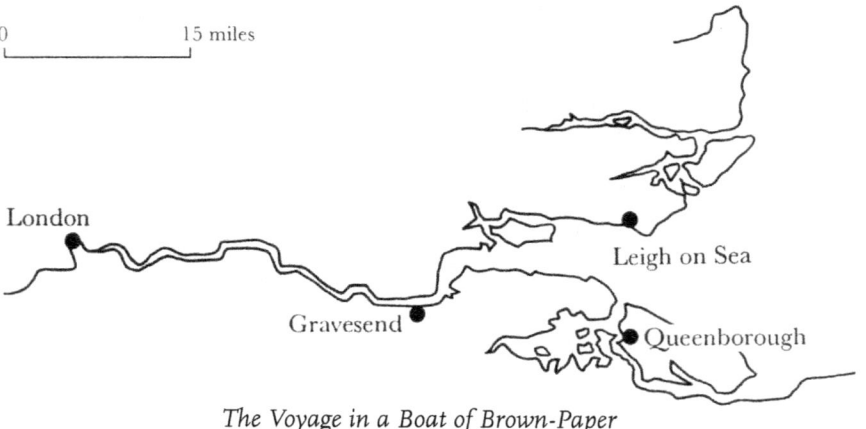

The Voyage in a Boat of Brown-Paper

1   talk nonsense.

THE PRAISE OF HEMP-SEED. WITH THE VOYAGE OF MR. ROGER BIRD AND THE WRITER HEREOF, IN A BOAT OF BROWN-PAPER, FROM LONDON TO QUINBOROUGH IN KENT...

*T*HE *VOYAGE IN A BOAT OF BROWN-PAPER* has been described (Malcolm, 1997, p. 22) as almost a 'nonsense journey', comparable with Kempe's Nine Days' Wonder. A closer parallel is perhaps the travels in 1607 of Mr Bush, 'in which hee past by ayre, land, and water: from Lamborne, a place in Bark-shire, to the Custome house Key in London' (Bradley, 1982). This involved winching a wheeled boat to the top of Lambourn church tower, prior to trundling across the downs to the Thames at Streatley.

Taylor's stunt was undertaken from Saturday 24th to Monday 26th July 1619, by when he had tired of pursuing defaulting subscribers to his Scottish journey. The idea was perhaps Roger Bird's, a vintner who accompanied him, and the date was probably chosen because St James (whose feast fell on the Sunday) was a fisherman. Taylor made the boat, in which neither metal nor wood were permitted. The construction was of brown paper, and the oars were made of dried fish bound to canes with pack-thread. While these ingredients were ludicrous, another, inflated bullocks' bladders, was eminently sensible, and these were to prove their salvation. It is not clear that the navigators had any idea of their destination, nor the likely duration of their voyage, but in the event they attracted (according to Taylor) a vast audience, spent two nights afloat (after a fashion) and eventually (and in time for the annual feast) made landfall at Queenborough on the Isle of Sheppey, some forty miles downstream from London.

This is the briefest of Taylor's journeys and the silliest, and his account of it was too slight to stand alone as a publication. He incorporated it into a larger work, The Praise of Hempseed, which treats at length the uses of hemp and flax, including of course as rope, nets and sails for mariners, but also when worn out as rags for making paper. In his mind, however, it always formed part of his canon of 'vagaries', to be recounted thirty years later as one of his achievements; Queenborough, in his view, owed what fame it had to his visit there in a paper boat.

[24th - 26th July 1619. Text derived from 1620 publication (copy BL c.30 d.25), and 1630 All the Workes...]

A VOYAGE IN A PAPER-BOAT FROM LONDON TO QUINBOROUGH.[1]

I therefore to conclude, this much will note
How I of paper lately made a boat,
And how in forme of paper I did row
From London unto Quinborough[2] Ile show.
I and a vintner (Roger Bird by name)
(A man whom fortune never yet could tame)
Took ship upon the vigill of Saint James,[3]
And boldly venter'd downe the River Thames,
Laving[4] and cutting through each raging billow,
(In such a boat which never had a fellow)[5]
Having no kinde of mettle or no wood
To helpe us either in our ebbe, or flood:
For as our boat was paper, so our oares
Were stock-fish,[6] caught neere to the island shores.
Stock-fishes unbeaten, bound fast to two canes with pack-thread.
Thus being oar'd and shipt away we went.
Driving 'twixt Essex calves, and sheepe of Kent:
Our boat a female vessell gan to leake

1 this line omitted in 1620 edn.
2 Queenborough, on the Isle of Sheppey, Kent.
3 24th July.
4 perhaps 'streaming along', with the association of 'bathing'.
5 equal.
6 unsalted dried fish. 'Stock-fishes unbeaten, bound fast to two canes with pack-threed' (Taylor).

Being as female vessels are, most weake,[1]
Yet was she able (which did grieve me sore),
To drowne Hodge[2] Bird, and I and forty more.
The water to the paper being got,
In one halfe houre our boat began to rot:
The Thames (most lib'rall) fil'd her to the halves,
Whilst Hodge and I sat liquor'd to the calves.
In which extremity I thought it fit
To put in use a stratagem of wit,
Which was, eight bullocks bladders we had bought
Puft stifly full with winde, bound fast and tought,[3]
Which on our boat within the tide we ti'de,
Of each side foure, upon the outward side.
The water still rose higher by degrees,
In three miles going, almost to our knees.
Our rotten bottom all to tatters fell,
And left our boat as bottomlesse as hell.
And had not bladders borne us stifly up,
We there had tasted of deaths fatall cup.

And now (to make some sport) Ile make it knowne
By whose strong breath my bladders all were blowne.
One by a cheverell conscienc'd usurer,[4]
Another by a drunken bag piper,
The third a whore, the fourth a pander blew,
The fift a cutpurse, of the cursed crew,
The sixt, a post-knight[5] that for five groats gaine
Would sweare and for foure groats forsweare't againe.
The seaventh was an informer, one that can
By informations begger many a man.

---

1 Proverb derived from Biblical injunction (1 Peter 3 verse 7) that husbands should honour their wives, as woman is the weaker vessel.
2 abbreviation of Roger.
3 i.e. taut.
4 with a conscience like kid-leather, hence pliable and flexible.
5 knight of the post, one who derives a living by false accusations.

The eight was blowne up by a swearing royster,[1]
That would cut throats as soone as eate an oyster.[2]
We being in our watry businesse bound,
And with these wicked winds encompass'd round,
For why such breaths as those, it fortunes ever,
They end with hanging, but with drowning never;
And sure the bladders bore us up so tight,
As if they had said, Gallowes claime thy right.[3]
This was the cause that made us seeke about,
To finde these light Tiburnian[4] vapours out.
We could have had of honest men good store,
As watermen, and smiths, and many more,
But that we knew it must be hanging breath,
That must preserve us from a drowning death.[5]
Yet much we fear'd the graves our end would be
Before we could the towne of Gravesend see:
Our boat drunke deepely with her dropsie thirst,
And quafft as if she would her bladders burst,
Whilst we within six inches of the brim
(Full of salt water) downe (halfe sunck) did swim.
Thousands of people all the shores did hide,
And thousands more did meet us in the tide
With scullers, oares, with ship-boats, and with barges
To gaze on us, they put themselves to charges.

Thus did we drive, and drive the time away,
Till pitchy night, had driven away the day:
The sun unto the under world was fled:
The moone was loath to rise, and kept her bed,

---

1   reveller.
2   Taylor adds after this line the following note: 'We had more winds then the compasse, for we had eight severall winds in our bladders, and the 32 of the compasse, in all 40'.
3   Proverbial, first recorded c.1592, meaning that the gallows will claim its own at last.
4   pertaining to Tyburn (Marylebone), the place of execution by hanging.
5   Taylor adds after this line the following: 'Carefully and descreetly provided'.

VOYAGE IN A BOAT OF BROWN-PAPER

The starres did twinckle, but the Ebon[1] clouds
Their light, our sight, obscures and overshrowds.
The tossing billowes made our boat to caper,
Our paper forme scarce being forme of paper,
The water foure mile broade, no oares to row,
Night darke, and where we were we did not know.
And thus 'twixt doubt and feare, hope and despaire
I fell to worke, and Roger Bird to praier.
And as the surges up and downe did heave us,
He cride most fervently, good Lord receive us.
I praid as much, but I did worke and pray,
And he did all he could to pray and play.
Thus three houres darkling I did puzzell and toile
Sows'd and well pickl'd, chafe and muzzell and moile,[2]
Drencht with the swaffing waves, and stewd in sweat,
Scarce able with a cane our boat to set,[3]
At last (by Gods great mercy and his might)
The morning gan to chase away the night.
Aurora made us soone perceive and see
We were three miles below the towne of Lee,[4]
And as the morning more and more did cleare,
The sight of Quinbrough castle did appeare.
That was the famous moumentall marke,
To which we striv'd to bring our rotten barke:
The onely ayme of our intents and scope,
The ancker that brought Roger to the hope.[5]
Thus we from Satturday at evening tide,
Till Monday morne did on the water bide,[6]

---

1 black as ebony.
2 various words for fretting and working ineffectively.
3 to propel the boat (by rowing).
4 Leigh-on-Sea, Essex, now a district of Southend.
5 'Hope we have as anchor of the soul' (Hebrews 6 verse 19). Hope also means a haven or inlet. Taylor adds after this line the following note: 'He dwelleth now at the Hope on the Banck-side'.
6 Taylor adds after this line (1620 ed. only) the following note: 'A dry-house had bin worth the having then'.

In rotten paper and in boistrous weather,
Darke nights, through wet, and toyled altogether.
But being come to Quinbrough and aland,
I tooke my fellow Roger by the hand,
And both of us ere we two steps did goe
Gave thankes to God that had preserv'd us so:
Confessing that his mercy us protected
When as we least deserv'd and lesse expected.
The Mayor of Quinborough in love affords
To entertaine us, as we had beene lords;
It is a yearely feast kept by the Mayor,
And thousand people thither doth repair,
From townes and villages that's neere about,
And 'twas our luck to come in all this rout.
I'th'streete, bread, beere, and oysters is their meat,
Which freely, friendly, shot-free[1] all do eat.
But Hodge and I were men of ranck and note,
We to the Mayor gave our adventrous boat;
The which (to glorifie that towne of Kent)
He meant to hang up for a monument.
He to his house invited us to dine,
Where we had cheare on cheare, and wine on wine,
And drinke, and fill, and drinke, and drinke and fill,
With welcome upon welcome, welcome still.

But whilst we at our dinners thus were merry,
The country people tore our tatter'd wherry
In mammocks[2] peecemeale, in a thousand scraps,
Wearing the reliques in their hats and caps.
That never traytors corps[3] could more be scatter'd
By greedy ravens, then our poore boat was tatter'd;
Which when the Mayor did know, he presently
Tooke patient what he could not remedy.
The next day we with thankes left Quinbroghs coast

1 free from payment or punishment, similar to scot-free.
2 scraps or torn fragments.
3 the punishment for high treason was to be hanged, drawn, and quartered.

And hied us home on horse-backe all in post.
Thus Master Birds strange voyage was begun,
With greater danger was his money won.
And those that doe his coyne from him detaine
(Which he did win with perill and much paine)
Let them not thinke that e're 'twill doe them good,
But eate their marrow, and consume their blood.
The worme of conscience gnaw them every day
That have the meanes, and not the will to pay.
Those that are poore, and cannot, let them be
Both from the debt and malediction free.[1]
...

[1] The poem then continues with remarks about the Thames, and a general conclusion about hempseed.

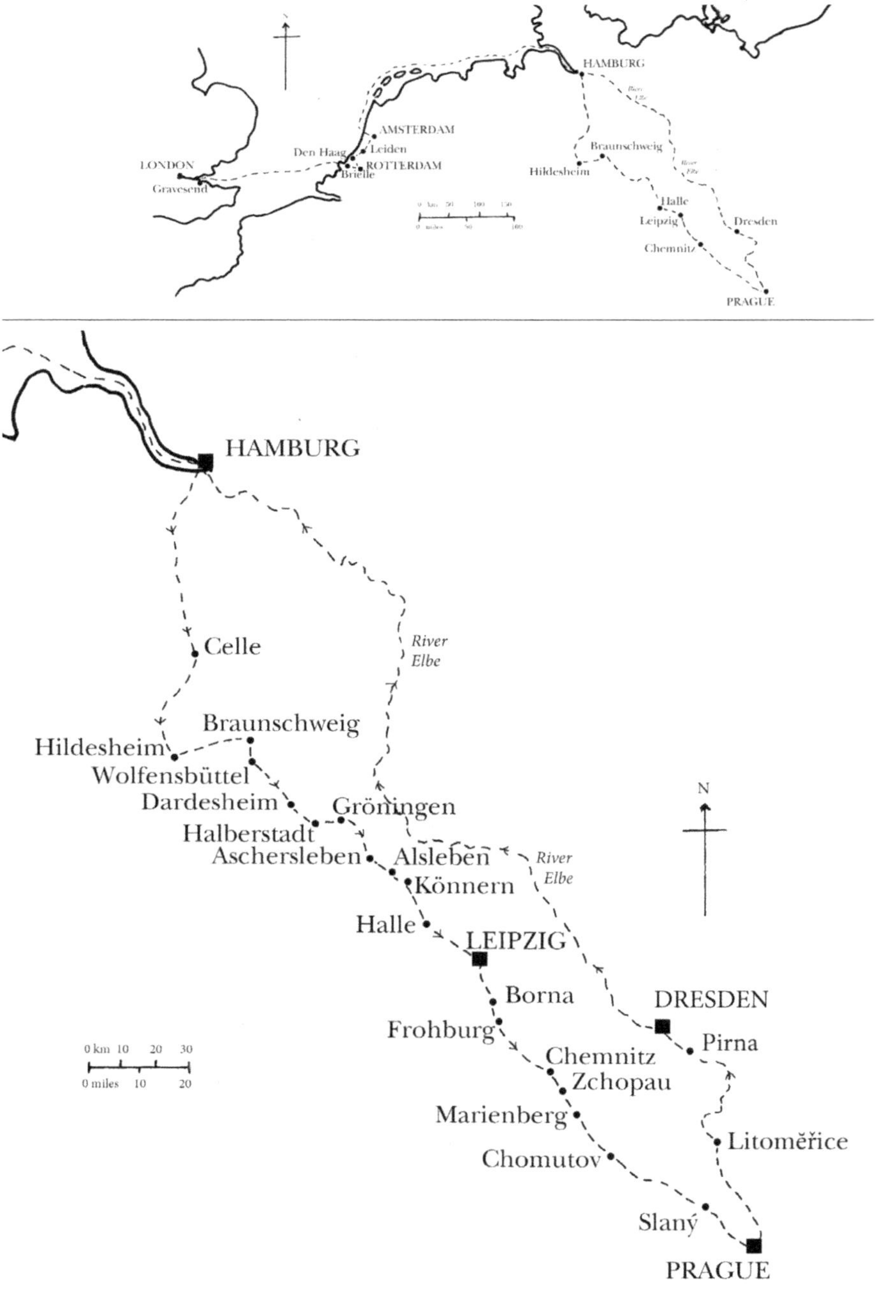

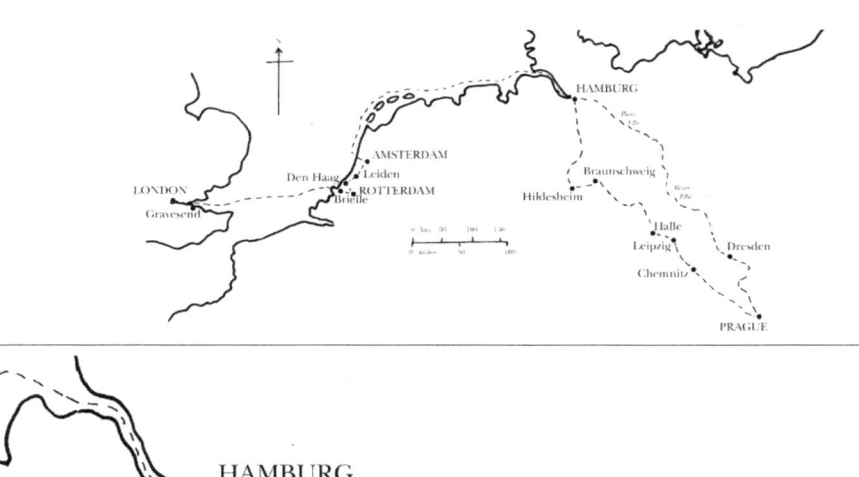

Taylor his Travels ... to Prague in Bohemia

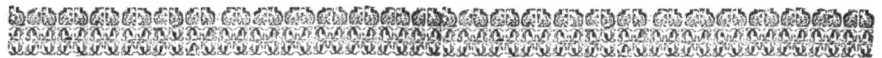

TAYLOR HIS TRAVELS. FROM THE CITTY OF LONDON IN ENGLAND, TO THE CITTY OF PRAGUE IN BOHEMIA

*T*HE MOST CHALLENGING *and furthest of Taylor's journeys, his travels to Prague took him eleven weeks to accomplish, 4 August to 28 October 1620. His account exists in three versions. The first seems to have been printed rapidly after his return ('hurld' from the press is not perhaps an exaggeration) and includes a long, interesting but entirely irrelevant account of his arrest in Gravesend before the journey was properly under way. He edited this out of a second edition, dated 1621, which had become necessary because his optimism and enthusiasm for Bohemia's cause in the opening salvos of the Thirty Years' War had been overtaken by news of King Frederick's crushing defeat at the Battle of the White Mountain in November 1620 and his subsequent exile. Taylor's response was to add a coda cautioning against accepting unfounded rumours as truth – 'fake news'! The 1621 version was reprinted with minor alterations in the 1630 collected edition.*

Four years since his Hamburg adventure Taylor visited the city a second time, and again one purpose seems to have been to see his brother, whom he met this time near Braunschweig (Brunswick) whence they travelled to Prague together, along with a fellow waterman, Tilbury. But with the prospect of a flourishing writing career, which included his traveller's tales, Taylor now adopted the mantle of a foreign correspondent, reporting on the warring principalities of Germany and Bohemia which marked the first phase of the Thirty Years' War. Between 1618 and 1623 the conflict was waged between supporters of the Catholic Holy Roman Emperor, especially the states of southern Germany, and protestant Bohemia and northern Germany. The English (and Scottish) king, James I, was father-in-law of Frederick V, king of Bohemia, through the marriage of his daughter, Elizabeth Stuart, to Frederick in 1613; and her fate became the rallying call for thousands of volunteer English and Scottish troops to fight in the protestant cause. Bohemia in 1620 was therefore a topic of great interest and conversation in Taylor's London, and the account of his journey was intended to describe the living conditions and atmosphere of its capital, Prague, under the reign of Frederick and Elizabeth. To bestow authenticity on his report he describes how he held their youngest son, Prince Rupert, in his arms (and – in typical Taylor fashion – made off with his baby-shoes as a souvenir).

At one level, therefore, this pamphlet was propaganda for the ill-fated Bohemian cause, and was one of several that Taylor penned around the same time. In this respect it resembles his 1648 journey to the Isle of Wight to see the imprisoned Charles I on behalf of the royalist cause. But it is also an adventure story, fraught with discomfort and danger. After the Gravesend episode he sailed for Rotterdam and then Hamburg, and travelled overland to Hildesheim. This leg of the journey, which took him five weeks (including three in Hamburg), he skirts over in a few lines, but then describes in some detail the notable buildings of Hildesheim, Wolfenbüttel and Gröningen. After Leipzig travelling became more precarious, through mountainous woodland infested with robbers who when caught were executed in barbarous fashion (we are not spared the details). Eventually Prague was reached, where they remained three weeks. The city, crowded with an influx of refugees from the war, and with a large Jewish population, was nevertheless amply provided for with good, cheap food, and its citizens ostentatiously paraded their wealth. Conditions in the army were good, and the large British contingent were in good spirits.

For the return journey Taylor resorted to his preferred mode of travel. The River Elbe, a day-and-a-half's journey by coach from Prague, flows all the way to Hamburg, so that Taylor and his fellows purchased a boat and he and Tilbury managed to sail it without reported mishap almost 600 miles downriver in 12 days. Allowing for exaggeration this does appear to have been quite an achievement, explained away by Taylor – 'we being both his Maiesties watermen'. Of the voyage he says little, but about the lousy accommodation and food on the way he gives more detail. A further ten days' wait with the English merchants in Hamburg ensued before they found a ship to bring them home.

After the Prague adventure Taylor confined himself to describing places in Britain. But he was now a seasoned traveller, and had learnt the art of travel, as true perhaps in the 21st as in the 17th century: 'Which made mee call to minde six severall principalls, that doe belong to a traveller, as patience, silence, warinesse, watchfulnesse, a good stomacke, and a purse well monied; for if he want any one of these, (perhaps) the other five will never bring him to his journies end.'

[The 2nd ed. 1621 (Folger copy, on STC microfilm 669) has been preferred, with additional material from 1st ed. 1620 (Huntington copy, on STC microfilm), and 1630 collected edition included. Passages in the 1st ed. excluded from the 2nd are enclosed in {}; passages added to the 2nd ed. are enclosed in <>.]

Taylor his travels. from the citty of London in England, to the citty of Prague in Bohemia. The manner of his abode there three weekes, his observations there, and his returne from thence: How he past 600 miles downe the river of Elve, through Bohemia, Saxony, Anhalt, the Bishoprick of Magdeburge, Brandenberge, Hamburgh, and so to England. With many relations worthy of note. {By John Taylor.} <The second edition, corrected and much enlarged, with diverse things that were in the first impression omitted.>

London Printed by Nicholas Okes, for Henry Gosson, and are to be sold by Edward Wright. {1620} <1621>

Reader take this in your way.

A pamphlet (Reader,) from the presse is hurld,
That hath not many fellowes in the world:
The maner's comon, though the matter's shallow,
And 'tis all true, which makes it want a fellow.[1]

And because I would not have you either guld of your mony, or deceived in expectation, I pray you take notice of my plaine dealing; for I have not given my booke a swelling bumbasted title, of a promising inside of newes; therefore if you looke for any such matter from hence, take this warning; hold fast your mony, and lay the booke downe; yet if you do buy it (I dare presume) you shall find somewhat in it worth part of your mony; the troth is that I did chiefely write it, because I am of much

---

1   it has no equivalent.

acquaintance, and cannot passe the streets, but I am continually stayed by one or other, to know what newes, so that sometimes I am foure houres before I can go the length of too paire of butts,[1] where such nonsence or sencelesse questions are propounded to me, that calles many seeming wise mens wisedoms in question, drawing aside the curtaines of their understanding, and laying their ignorance wide open. First John Easie takes me, and holds mee fast by the fist halfe an houre; and will needes torture some newes out of me from Spinola,[2] whom I was never neere by 500 miles; for hee is in the Pallatinate country, and I was in Bohemia. I am no sooner eased of him, but Gregory Gandergoose, an alderman of Gotham[3] catches me by the goll,[4] demanding if Bohemia bee a great towne, and whether there be any meate in it, and whether the last fleet of shipps be arived there: his mouth being stopt, a third examines mee boldly, what newes from Vienna, where the emperours army is, what the Duke of Bavaria doth, what is become of Count Buquoy,[5] how fares all the Englishmen; Where lies the King of Bohemiaes forces, what Bethlem Gabor[6] doth, what tydings of Dampeier,[7] and such a tempest of inquisition, that it almost shakes my patience in pieces. To ease my selfe of all which, I was inforced to set pen to paper, and let this poore pamphlet (my herald or nuntius)[8] travell and talke, whilst I take my ease with silence. {Thus much I dare affirme, that whosoever he or they bee; that do scatter any scandalous speeches against the plenty in Bohemia of all manner of needfull things for the sustenance of man and beasts, (of

1 archery butts, on which the target was placed, or from which the archer fired at the target, were often constructed in pairs about 100m apart.
2 The Genoan nobleman Ambrogio Spinola led the Spanish campaign to conquer the German Palatinate, fighting in the Rhineland area during the first phase of the Thirty Years War, 1620-2.
3 Gotham, near Nottingham, was proverbially inhabited by simpletons and fools.
4 i.e. 'gullet', throat.
5 Charles Bonaventure de Longueval, Count of Bucquoy, commanded the imperial forces defending Vienna and was killed in action in 1621.
6 Gabriel Bethlen (d. 1629), Prince of Transylvania, king-elect of Hungary 1620-1.
7 Henry Duvall, Count of Dampier, was Bucquoy's lieutenant, and was shot by Bethlen's troops in 1620.
8 Latin for messenger.

the which there is more aboundance then ever I saw in any place else) or whatsoever they bee that report any ill successe on the kings party, this little booke, and I the author doth proclaime and prove them false lyers, and they are to be suspected, for coyning such falshoods, as no well-willers to the Bohemian prosperity. One thing I must entreate the readers patience in reading one hundred lines: wherein, I have kept a filthy stirre about a beastly fellow, who was (at my going from England, a piece of a Graves-end[1] constable) at which time hee did me such wrong, as might have drawne my life in question; for hee falsly sayd that I would have fired[2] their towne. I did promise him a jerke[3] or two of my penne at my returne; which now I have performed, (not out of any mallice, but because I would bee as good as my word with him.) Thus craving you...} <Thus much I dare avow of it, that Bohemia is the most plentiful countrey that mine eyes ever beheld, for the abundance of sustenance for man and beast: and howsoever it hath pleased God to dispose of the affaires there, the ill successe cannot justly be imputed either to want of pay, meat, munition or resolution. But leaving these things, with their proceedings to the Almighties protection, I crave you...> ...to reade if you like, and like as you list: leaving you a book much like a pratling gossip, full of many words to small purpose. Yours, as you are mine, John Taylor.

Taylors travels from the citty of London in England, to the citty of Prague in Bohemia.

I come from Bohem, yet no newes I bring,
Of businesse 'twixt the Keysar[4] and the King:
My Muse dares not ascend the lofty staires
Of state, or write of princes great affaires.
And as for newes of battailes, or of war,
Were England from Bohemia thrice as far:
Yet we do know (or seeme to know) more heere

1 Gravesend, a town in Kent, on the Thames about 20 miles downstream from London.
2 set fire to.
3 a stroke, but in this sense a witty or cutting speech.
4 Kaiser (Caesar) was a title adopted by the Holy Roman Emperors.

Then was, is, or will ever be knowne there.
At ordinaries,[1] and at barbers-shoppes,
There tydings vented[2] are, as thicke as hoppes,
How many thousands such a day were slaine,
What men of note were in the battell ta'ne,[3]
When, where, and how the bloody fight begun,
And how such sconces,[4] and such townes were won;
How so and so the armies bravely met,
And which side glorious victory did get:
The month, the weeke, the day, the very houre,
And time, they did oppose each others power,
These things in England prating fooles do chatter,
When all Bohemia knowes of no such matter.
For all this summer, that is gone and past,
Untill the first day of October last,[5]
The armies never did together meete,
Nor scarce their eye sight did each other greete:
The fault is neither in the foote or horse,
Of the right valiant brave Bohemian force,
From place to place they dayly seeke the foe,
They march, and remarch, watch, ward, ride, run, go,
And grieving so to waste the time away,
Thirst for the hazard of a glorious day.
But still the enemy doth play bopeepe,[6]
And thinks it best in a whole skin to sleepe,
For neither martiall policy, or might,
Or any meanes can draw the foe to fight:
And now and then they conquer, spoyle and pillage,

---

[1] taverns and eating-houses, where fixed-price meals were served.
[2] sold.
[3] taken.
[4] a mound, part of a fortification.
[5] probably a reference to the capture by Spinola of Bacharach, a small town on the Rhine between Mainz and Koblenz, on 1 Oct. 1620.
[6] an alternative name for the children's hiding and discovering game peekabo; it is referred to by Shakespeare in *King Lear*.

Some few thatcht houses, or some pelting¹ village;
And to their trenches run away againe,
Where they like foxes in their holes remaine,
Thinking by lingring out the warres in length,
To weaken and decay the Beamish² strength.
This is the newes, which now I meane to booke,
He that will needes have more, must needes goe looke;
{Thus leaving warres, and matters of high state,
To those that dare, and knowes how to relate,
I'le onely write, how I past heere and there,
And what I have observed everywhere.
I'le truely write what I have heard and eyed,
And those that will not so be satisfied,
I (as I meet them) will some tales devise,
And fill their eares (by word of mouth) with lies:

The month that beares a mighty emp'rours name,
(Augustus hight) I passed downe the streame,
Friday the fourth, just sixteene hundred twenty
Full moone, the signe in Piscis, that time went I;
The next day being Saturday, a day,
Which all Great Brittaine well remember may,
When all with thankes doe annually combine,
Unto th' Almighty majesty divine,
Because that day, in a most happy season,
Our Soveragne was preserv'd from Gouries treason;³
Therefore to churches people do repaire,
And offer sacrifice of praise and praire,
With bells and bonfires, every towne addressing,
And to our gracious King their loves expressing,

---

1   paltry or insignificant.
2   i.e Böhmische, German for Bohemian.
3   The Gowrie conspiracy, probably an attempt to kidnap James VI (of Scotland, subsequently James I of England), took place on 5 August 1600 at Perth, and resulted in the death of its perpetrator, John Ruthven, 3rd Earl of Gowrie. The king's deliverance was commemorated annually, although with some scepticism about the authenticity of his account of the conspiracy.

On that day, when in every nooke and angle,
Faggots and bavins[1] smoak'd, and bells did jangle:
Onely at Graves-end, (why I cannot tell,)
There was no sparke of fire, or sound of bell,
Their steeple, (like an instrument unstrung,)
Seem'd (as I wish all scolds) without a tong,
Their bonfires colder then the greatest frost,
Or chiller then their charities (almost,)
Which I perceiving, sayd I much did muse,
That Graves-end did forget the thankfull use,
Which all the townes in England did observe;
And cause I did the King of Brittaine serve.
I and my fellow, for our maisters sake,
Would (neere the waters side) a bonfire make;
With that a Scotch man, Tompson by his name,
Bestowed foure faggots to increase the flame,
At which (to kindle all) a Graves-end baker,
Bestowed his bavine, and was our partaker:
We eighteene foote from any house retir'd,
Where we a jury of good faggots fir'd;
But ere the flame, or scarce the smoake began,
There came the fearefull shaddow of a man,
The ghost or image of a constable,
Whose frantick actions (downeright dunce-stable,)[2]
Arm'd out of France and Spaine, with Bacchus bounty:[3]
(Of which ther's plenty in the Kentish county,)
His adle coxcomb with tobaco puff'd
His guts with ale full bumbasted and stuff'd,
And though halfe blind, yet in a looking glasse,
He could perceive the figure of an asse;
And as his slavering chapps non-sence did stutter,
His breath (like to a jakes)[4] a sent did utter,
His leggs indenting scarcely could beare up,

1   bundles of firewood or kindling wood.
2   presumably a pun on Dunstable, Beds.
3   i.e. drunk, Bacchus being the Greek god of wine.
4   lavatory.

His drunken trunk (o're charg'd with many a cup.)
This riff raff rubbish, that could scarcely stand,
(Having a staffe of office in his hand,)
Came to us as our fire began to smother,
Throwing some faggots one way, some another,
And in the Kings name did first breake the peace,
Commanding that our bonfire should succease.
The Scotchman angry at this rudnes done,
The scattered faggots, he againe layd on:
Which made the demy constable[1] go to him,
And punch him on the brest, and outrage do him;
At which a cuffe or twaine were given, or lent,
About the eares, (which neither did content.)
But then to heare how fearefull the asse braid,
With what a hideous noyse he houl'd for aid,
That all the ale in Graves-end, in one houre,
Turn'd either good, bad, strong, small, sweete, or soure:
And then a kennell of incarnate[2] currs,
Hang'd on poore Thomson, like so many burrs;
Haling him up the dirty streetes, all foule,
(Like divells pulling a condemned soule.)
The jaylor (like the grand dev'll) gladly sees,
And with an itching hope of fines and fees,
Thinking the constable, and his sweete selfe,
Might drinke and quaffe with that ill gotten pelfe;[3]
For why such hounds as these, may if they will,
Under the shew of good, turne good to ill;
And with authority the peace first breake,
With lordly domineering o're the weake,
Committing (oft) they care not whom or why,
So they may exercise themselves thereby,
And with the jaylor share both fee and fine,

1 parish constables, were also called petty constables, 'demy' here implying half or part.
2 literally, 'made of flesh', but in a pejorative sense probably a reference to the expression 'Devil incarnate'.
3 ill-gotten gains.

Drowning their damned gaine in smoake and wine:
Thus hirelings constables, and jaylors may,
Abuse the kings leige people night and day,
I say they may, I say not they do so,
And they know best if they do so or no,
They hal'd poore Thomson all along the streete,
Tearing him that the ground scarce touch'd his feete,
Which he perceiving, did request them cease
Their rudenes, vowing he would go in peace,
He would with quietnesse goe where they would,
And prayed them from his throate to loose their hold.
Some of the townesmen did intreat them there,
That they their barbarous basenes woud forbeare,
But all entreaty was like oyle to fire,
Not quench'd; but more enflam'd the scurvy squire.
Then they afresh began to hale and teare,
(Like mungrell mastifes, on a little beare,)
Leaving kind Tompson neither foote or fist,
Nor any limb or member to resist,
Who being thus opprest with ods and might,
Most valiant with his teeth, began to bite,
Some by the fingers, others by the thumbs,
He fang'd within the circuit of his gummes;
Great pitty 'twas his chaps did never close,
On the halfe constables, cheekes, eares, or nose;
His service had deserv'd reward to have,
If he had mark'd the peasant for a knave:
Yet all that labour had away bin throwne,
Through towne and country he's already knowne;
His prisoner, he did beate, and spurn'd and kick'd,
He search'd his pockets, (I'le not say he pick'd)
And finding (as he sayd) no mony there,
To heare how then the bellwether[1] did sweare,
And almost tearing Tompson into quarters,

---

[1] trendsetter, derived from the leading sheep of a flock, which therefore had a bell placed around its neck.

Bound both his hands behind him with his garters,
And after in their rude robustious rage,
Tide both his feete, and cast him in the cage,
There all night he remained in lowsie litter,
Which for the constable had bin much fitter,
Or for some vagabond (that's sprung from Caine,)[1]
Some rogue or runagate,[2] should there have laine,
And not a gentleman that's well descended,
That did no hurt, nor any harme intended:
But for a bonfire in fit time and place,
To be abus'd and us'd thus beastly base.
There did I leave him till the morrow day,
And how he scap'd their hands I cannot say.
This piece of officer, this nasty patch,[3]
(Whose understanding sleepes out many a watch)
Ran like a towne bull, roring up and downe,
Saying that we had meant to fire the towne;
And thus the divell his maister did devise,
To bolster out his late abuse with lies;
So all the streete downe as I past along,
The people all about me in a throng,
Calling me villaine, traytor, rogue and thiefe,
Saying that I to fire their towne was cheife.
I bore the wrongs as patient as I might,
Vowing my pen should ease me when I write;
Like to a grumbling cur, that sleepes on hay,
Eates none himselfe, drives other beasts away.
So this base fellow would not once expresse,
Unto his prince, a subjects joyfulnesse,
But cause we did attempt it (as you see)
H' imprison'd Thompson, and thus slandered me.
Thus having eas'd my much incensed muse,
I crave the reader this one fault excuse,

---

1 Descendants of Cain were cursed by God, often a term for those indulging in the occult.
2 deserter.
3 a fool or clown; derived from the name of Cardinal Wolsey's jester.

For having urg'd his patience all this time,
With such a scurvy subject, and worse rime;
And thou Graves-endian officer take this,
And thanke thy selfe, for all that written is,
'Tis not against the towne this tale I tell
(For sure there doth some honest people dwell,)
But against thee, thou fiend in shape of man,
By whom this beastly outrage first began,
Which I could do no lesse, but let thee know,
And pay thee truely what I long did owe,
And now all's even betwixt thou and I,
Then farrewell and be hang'd, that's twice God buy.

The first letters of his names are R.L and his full name being anagramatiz'd is *A Trobeler*, a ?[1] he was to mee, and so I feare he hath beene to my reader.}

<And this is all that was, when I came thence,
Not knowing what will, or hath hapned since.
Thus leaving warres and matters of high state,
To those that dares, and knowes how to relate,
I'le onely write how I past here and there,
And what I have observed every where,
I'le truly write what I have heard and eyed,
And those that will not so be satisfied,
I (as I meete them) will some tales devise,
And fill their eares (by word of mouth) with lies:
At Gravesend, whilst I lay there for a winde:
A constable did use me much unkinde:
I vowed I would requite his lewd transgression,
And I performd it in my first impression.
Enough's enough, with him I had a bout,
And now in charity I leave him out.>

      Sunday the 6. of August we set sayle from Graves-end, and

---

[1] presumably his name was Robert Lea.

with various windes, some large and some scarce, we happily past the seas, and sayled up the River of Maze,[1] by the Brill,[2] and on the Wednesday following I arived at Roterdam in Holland, at which time the worthy regiment of the right honorable Colonell Sir Horace Veare,[3] and the two noble Earles, of Essex, and Oxford departed from thence in marshall equipage towards the Palatinate country, whose heroick and magnanimous endevors I beseech the Lord of Hoasts, and God of battels to direct and blesse.

The same day I went to the Hage,[4] and from thence to Leiden, where I lodged all night, and the morrow being Thursday the 30. of August, I sayled from Leyden, to Amsterdam, where I saw many things worthy the noting, but because they are so neare and frequent to many of our nation, I omit to relate them, to avoid tediousnes: but on the Friday at night I got passage from thence toward Hambrogh, in a small hoy,[5] in the which we were wether-beaten, at sea three daies and nights before we arived there.

Saturday the eight of September I left Hambrogh, and beeing carried day and night in waggons, on the Munday night following, I came to an ancient towne called Heldesheim,[6] it standeth in Brunswick land, and yet it belongeth to the Bishop of Collin, where I did observe in their Doome Kirke, or Cathedrall Church, a crowne[7] of silver 80. foot in compasse, hanged up in the body of the church, in the circuit of which crowne were placed 160 wax candles, the which on festivall dayes, or at the celebration of some high ceremonyes are lighted, to lighten their darknesse, or their ignorance chuse you whether.

Moreover, there I saw a silver bell in their steeple, of sixe hundred and thirty pound weight, and the leades of their steeple, shining and sparkling with the sun beames, they did affirme to mee, to bee gold, the

1 Maas.
2 Brielle or Brill, historic port at the mouth of the Maas.
3 Horace Vere, later Baron Vere of Tilbury (1565-1635), military commander sent by James I to support the protestant cause at the beginning of the Thirty Years War. He had left Gravesend on 22 July.
4 Den Haag, or The Hague.
5 a trading vessel or barge.
6 Hildesheim, city in Lower Saxony.
7 St Mary's cathedral, Hildesheim, retains four *coronae*, or wheel chandeliers.

truth of which I am doubtfull of.[1]

In this towne I staied foure dayes, and on Fryday the 14. of September, I went sixe dutch miles[2] to the strong towne of Brunswick,[3] where by reason of my short stay, which was but two houres, I observed nothing worthy of memory, but their triple walls and double ditches, their artillery and fortifications, which they thinke to be impregnable: besides there I saw an old house[4] of the Duke of Brunswick, with the statue of a golden lion,[5] of a great bignesse, standing aloft upon a pillar, with the broken walles and houses, which the Dukes cannon hath left there sixe yeares since, as tokens and badges of his fury, and their rebellion.[6]

From thence on the morrow I went one dutch mile further, to an ancient towne called Wolfunbuttle,[7] where the Duke of Brunswick keepes his court, in the which I and my fellow could get no further admittance, then over a bridge into his outtermost, or base court, for his souldiers seeing us with swords and pistols, were fearefull, belike, that we would have taken the fortresse from them, and therefore, though wee were but two Englishmen, yet they durst not let us enter, which made me call to remembrance the frequent and daily egresse and regresse, that all people and nations have to his Majesties royal court of Great Britaine, where none that are of any good fashion or aspect, are debard entrance: when those inferior princes houses are guarded with hungry halberdiers and reverend rusty bil-men, with a brace or two of hot shots; so that their pallaces are more like prisons then the free and noble courts of commanding potentates.

After two dayes entertainment at Wolfunbuttle with an English merchant residing there, of good fame and credit named Maister

---

1 The cathedral, including steeple and most bells, was destroyed during World War II, but has been reconstructed.
2 sometimes defined as one hour's walking, or about 5km.
3 Braunschweig, a major historic city in Lower Saxony
4 *Burg Dankwarderode*, rebuilt in the 19th century.
5 The bronze Brunswick lion, or *Burglöwe*, cast in 1166.
6 Frederick Ulrich became duke of Brunswick-Wolfenbüttel in 1613, but was not recognised by the city, and in 1615 waged war on it.
7 Wolfenbüttel, residence of the Brunswick rulers from 1432.

Thomas Sackville,[1] I with my brother,[2] my fellow Tilbery, and another man in my company departed from thence on foote, onward on our journey towards Bohemia, in which travell, what occurences hapned, and what things of note I saw, were as followeth.

Passing with many weary steps, through the townes of Rosondink, Remling, Soclem, Hessen, Darsam, and Halverstadt,[3] (which is all in Brunswick land,) but this towne of Halverstadt belongs to a bishop so styled, who is Duke Christian brother to the now Duke of Brunswick,[4] a long dutch mile,[5] (or almost six English) is a small towne or a Bleck called Groning,[6] belonging to the Duke, in the which place I observed two things worthy of remembrance:

First a most stately pallace built with a beautifull chappell,[7] so adorned with the images and formes of angells, and cherubins, with such exquisitnesse of arts best industry of carving, graving, guilding, painting, glasing, and paving, with such superexcellent workmanship of organes, pulpit, and font, that for curiosity and admirable rarenesse, all the buildings, and fabricks that ever I beheld, must give it preheminence. I confesse that Henry the seavenths chappell at Westminster,[8] Kings Colledge chappell in Cambridge, and Christs Church in Canterbury,[9] are beyond it in height and workmanship of stone: for indeed this chappell is most of wood gipps, and plaster of Parris; but it is so gilded as if it had bin made in the golden age, when gold was esteemed as drosse, so that

1   Sackville was a comic actor and playwright who entered the household of the Duke of Brunswick, and then settled in Wolfenbüttel as a respected merchant.
2   This brother in 1616 was living in Bückeburg, some 80km west of Braunschweig, when Taylor visited him during his Hamburg journey. See p. 26.
3   These places, now Gross Denkte, Remlingen, Semmenstedt, Hessen and Dardesheim, all lie along the direct route south-east from Wolfenbüttel to Halberstadt.
4   Christian the Younger (1599-1626), bishop and titular duke.
5   computed as one hour's walking, around 5km.
6   Gröningen, in Saxony-Anhalt (not to be confused with the Dutch city).
7   Probably St Vitus's priory church. The priory buildings were converted at the reformation to a residence for the dukes of Brunswick, and Christian was born there. The palace does not survive.
8   The Lady Chapel of Westminster Abbey, London.
9   Canterbury Cathedral.

a man had need to weare a vaile over his dazeling eyes, or else he can hardly looke upon it.

The carving and painting seeme to out-go the arts of Pigmalion, Apelles, or Praxiteles;[1] the paving of chequered blacke and white marble, and the windowes glassed with christall: but all this great cost and shew is very little to the honor of God, the propagation of the Gospell, or the edification of the ignorant. For in the[2] chappell of ease, there is no service. If the painted pulpit could preach, the dumbe images might (perhaps) have a sermon now and then; for scarce at any time there comes any body into the chappell, but a fellow that shewes the beauty of it for two pence or three pence a piece.

In the same house, in a place or celler built of purpose, is a great tonne or vessell of wood, that was 7 yeares in making and hath used to be filled with Rhenish wine: it is said to be twise as bigge as the vessell at Heidelberge,[3] and the hoopes of it are twelve inches thicke, and the staves or boards of it being as much: I went up to the top of it with a ladder of 18. steps, he that keepes it saith it will hold 160. tonnes. My fellow Tilbery did creepe in at the tap hole, it is in length thirty two foot, and in bredth acrosse 19, and verily I thinke that bable cost more money the making, then would have built a good ship, or founded an almes house for 6 poore people.

This is the tub of tubs, tub of tubs hall,
Who n'ere had fellow yet, nor ever shall;
O had Diogenes[4] but had this ton,
He would have[5] thought that he more roome had won
Then Alexanders conquests, or the bounds
Of the vast Ocean, and the solid grounds.

1 Pygmalion was a sculptor in Greek legend; Apelles was a painter from Kos, ancient Greece; and Praxiteles an ancient Athenian sculptor.
2 *this*: 1630 edn.
3 Thomas Coryat had described the vessell at Heidelberg in great detail, and this paragraph, which is modelled on his description, seems to be an attempt to outdo him in exaggeration.
4 Diogenes the Cynic, Greek philosopher, was renowned for living in a large jar, or barrell.
5 *had*: 1621 edn.

Or had Cornelius but this tub, to drench
His clients that had practis'd too much French,[1]
A thousand hogsheads then would haunt his firkin,[2]
And Mistris Minks[3] recover her lost mirkin.[4]
This mighty caske great Bacchus us'd to stride,
When he to drunkards hall did often ride.
And in this barrell he did keepe his court,
Bathing himselfe in Rhenish for disport.
But now these eight yeares it hath dry bin kept;
In it the wine-god hath nor pist or wept;
That now the chappell, and the caske combine,
One hath no preaching, t'other hath no wine.
And now the use they put it to is this,
'Tis shew'd for money, as the chappell is.

From Groning wee travelled to a towne called Ashers Leaven, to Ashleaven, to Kinderne, to Hall,[5] and so to Leipzig, which is one of the chiefest townes in Saxony, being famous for a yearely mart[6] that is yearely held there, whereto merchants and other people from the most part of Christendom have annuall concourse: in this town we staid two dayes, and taking our leave then of some English merchants, who used us kindly, we there would have hired a coach or waggon to Prague; but all the Saxon coach-men and carters were afraid to looke upon any part of Bohemia, because their Duke is a profest enemy in armes against the King of Beame,[7] so that we were forced to hire a fellow with a wheelebarrow two dayes to carry our cloaks, swords, guns, pistols, and other apparell and luggage which were our necessaries, to a towne called

---

1 The Cornelian (or Mother Cornelius's) tub was a sweating treatment for venereal (French) disease. The name may derive from a physician, Henry Cornelius Agrippa (1496-1535) who advoated medical hot baths.
2 a small cask for wine or beer.
3 slang expression, used by Marlowe and Nashe, for an immoral woman.
4 a cosmetic vaginal wig.
5 Aschersleben, Alsleben, Könnern, Halle.
6 What is now Leipzig Trade Fair began in the 12th century, but by Taylor's time there were three annual fairs of international importance.
7 i.e. Bohemia.

Boorne, to Froburge, and so to another town called Penigh,[1] where we cashierd our one wheeld coach, and hired a cart with two, which carried both us and our baggage to Chemnizt another towne in Saxony, from whence to a place called Shop,[2] wee were faine to be our owne sumpter[3] horses, walking on foot to the last towne in Saxony, called Marienberg. From thence passing up and downe inaccessable mountaines, we came to a wood, which parts Bohemia from Saxony on the west, which wood is called by the people of those parts the Beamer Wolts or Wolt,[4] and is in breadth ten English miles, and in length further then I know how to describe truely: but thus much of it I dare affirme, that it is a naturall impregnable wall to the kingdome of Bohem, which kingdome is all incompast round with woods and mountaines, so that there is no passage on that side of it, for any army to enter into it with munition and artillery, all the wayes being uneven, and the mountaine tops all boggs, mosses, and quagmires, that great ordinance or any heavy cariage either of horse, cart or waggon, will sinke and be lost. Besides, there are numbers past numbering of firre trees, many standing, and such store fallen of themselves, that any passage might easily be stopped by laying them crosse the way. And of all my journey, the travell through that dismall wood was the most heavy unto mee, for the trees grew so thicke, and so high, that the sunne was obscured, and the day seemed night; in some places the way paved with swimming[5] trees two miles together on the tops of hills, which now and then I slipping besides, sunke to the middle in a quagmire.

When wee had thus footed it and travelled past the hills and woods, (being at the least 4 houres toyle) and that wee might looke downe the mountaines, into the fruitfull land of Bohem, never did sight more rejoyce us, the lower hills being all full of vineyards, and the vallies, corne and pasture; not an English mile distance, but a village every way; and twenty, thirty, or forty reecks[6] or stacks of corne which their barnes cannot hold, in the space of every houres journy: in a word, every thing

1   Borna, Fröhburg and Penny.
2   Zchopau.
3   a beast of burden.
4   Erzgebirge, Krusné Horgy.
5   probably in the sense of 'wavering', i.e. swaying in the wind.
6   ricks.

that belonged to the use and commodity of man, was and is there, and al the delightfull objects to satisfie evey sense is there abundantly, so that nature seemed to make that country her storehouse or granary, for there is nothing wanting except mens gratitude to God for such blessings.

The first night wee lodged there at a pretty towne called Comoda,[1] which towne by negligence and occasion of fire had fifty houses burnt two dayes before our comming thither, it being eleven dutch miles from Prague. There we hired a wagon 7 dutch miles to a towne called Slowne,[2] from whence we walked on foot along 16. English miles to Prague, which long looked for city wee could not see untill we came within an houres travell of it: within halfe a dutch mile is a fearefull place, being frequented with inhumane and barbarous murderers, that assault travellers, first shooting and murdering them, and after searching their pockets, where if they have mony or not, all is one, it is but so many slaine: for these villaines have a wood, and a deepe valley[3] to shelter themselves in, that they are hardly taken afterwards; but if they chance at any time to be but apprehended, they are racked and tortured to make them confesse, and afterwards their executions are very terrible. But (I thanke God) wee past that place, and many other as dangerous as that, where some were robbed and murdered (as report told us) both before us, behind us, and on each side: and we saw in our journey above seaven score gallowses and wheeles, where theeves were hanged some fresh, and some halfe rotten, and the carkasses of murtherers, broken limb after limb on the wheeles; and yet it was our happinesse only to see the dead villaines, and escape the living.

I came into Prague on Thursday the seaventh of September, whther if I had come but the Friday before, I had seene a most fearefull execution of two notorious offenders; the manner how, with their faults, as it was truely related to mee by English gentlemen that saw it, I thinke it not much impertinent to relate.

The one of them being taken, apprehended and racked, for ripping up a live a woman with child, and for taking the infant out of her body, did sowe a living puppye into her belly, all which he confessed

1 Chomutov.
2 Slany.
3 presumably Divoká Šárka, a dramatic gorge in rugged and wooded countryside north-west of Prague.

hee did to make properties for witchcraft: and being further tortured, hee confessed when and where he had committed 35. murthers more: the other in respect of him was but a petty offender, for he in all his life time had murdered but 14. For the which execrable facts, their deserved executions were as followeth: First, they were brought out of the jayle naked from the girdle upward; and so being bound fast on high in a cart, that the spectators might see them; then the hangman having a panne of coales neere him, with red hot pincers nipped off the nipple of one brest: then he tooke a knife and gives him a slash or cut downe the backe on one side, from the shoulder to the waste, and presently gave him such another slash, three inches from the first; then on the top he cut the slashes into one, and presently taking pincers, tooke hold of the crosse cut, and tore him downe lke a girse[1] below the middle, letting it hang downe behind him like a belt: after which he tooke his burning pincers, and pluck'd off the tops of his fingers of one hand: then passing to another part of the towne, his other nipple was plucked off, the other side of his back so cut and mangled, (which they call by the name of rimming, (if it had beene riming, I would never have written but in prose) his other fingers nipped off; then passing further, all his toes were nipped off with the burning pincers; after which hee was enforced to come out of the cart, and goe on foote up a steepe hill to the gallowes, where he was broken with a wheele alive one bone after another, beginning at his legs and ending with his neck, and last of all, quartered and laid on the wheele, on a high post, till crowes, ravens, or consuming time consume him.

This was the manner of both their executions, but I speake but of the greatest murtherer particularly, because it is reported, that all these torments never made him once to change countenance, or to make any signe or action of griefe, to call to God for mercy, or to entreat the people to pray for him; but as if he had beene a senselesse stocke or stone, he did most scornefully, and as it were in disdaine abide it; whilest the other villaine did crye, rore, and make lamentation, calling upon God often. The difference was not much in their lives, and manner of their deaths, but I am perswaded the odds was great in their dying.

The city of Prague is almost circular or round, being divided in

---

1 a saddle-girth, a leather strap fastened around a horse to secure a saddle

the midle by the River of Moldove,[1] over which is a faire stone bridge,[2] of 600. of my paces over, and at each end a strong gate of stone:[3] there is said to bee in it of churches and chappells, 150. for there are great numbers of Catholiques, who have many chappells dedicated to sundry Saints, and I was there at foure severall sorts of divine exercises, viz. at good sermons with the Protestants, at masse with the Papists, at a Lutherans preaching and at the Jewes synagogue, three of which I saw and heard for curiosity, and the other for edification.

The Jewes in Prague are in such great numbers,[4] that they are thought to be of men, women and children, betwixt 50. or 60000. who do all live by brocage and usury upon the Christians, and are very rich in money and jewells, so that a man may see tenne or twelve together of them, that are accounted worth 20. 30 or 40000. l.' a piece; and yet the slaves go so miserably attired, that 15. of them are not worth the hanging[5] for their whole ward-robes.

The castle where the king and queene[6] doe keepe their court, is magnificent and sumptuous in building, strongly situated and fortified by nature and art, beeing founded on a high hill, so that at pleasure it keepes the town in command, and it is much more spacious in rooms for receipts in gardens and orchards then twice the bounds of the Towre of London.[7] I was in it daily the space of 20. dayes, and saw it royally graced with the presence of a gracious king and queene, who were honorably

1 Moldau is the German name for the river Vltava, which flows through Prague.
2 Charles Bridge, begun in 1357, connects the castle area and old town of Prague across the Vltava. It has 16 arches and is 516m long.
3 The existing bridge towers are medieval, but the statuary for which the bridge is famous dates from after Taylor's time.
4 Taylor is correct in noting the large Jewish population, which had flourished in Prague since the 1560s, but exaggerates the total, in fact probably about 7,000.
5 The expression occurs in Shakespeare *Cymbeline* (act 1, scene 6), first performed in 1611.
6 Frederick V, 'the winter king', whose queen was Elizabeth Stuart, daughter of James I. His reign as king of Bohemia was very brief, 1619-20, and ended with his abdication following the battle of the White Mountain in November 1620, two months after Taylor's visit,
7 Prague Castle claims to be the largest medieval castle in the world.

attended by a gallant courtly traine of lords and ladies, and gentles, of Britaines, the high Dutch and Bohemians, and where was free and bountifull entertainment to strangers in abundance: I must ever humbly and thankfully acknowledge the Queens Majesties goodnesse towards me, whose undeserved favors and gracious bounty were helpfull unto me, both there and in my tedious journey homeward. Moreover there I saw (and had in mine armes) the King and Queens yongest son, Prince Robert,[1] who was borne there on the 16. of December last which is there[2] S. Johns day in Christmas, a goodly child as ever I saw of that age, whom with the rest I pray God to blesse, to his glory and his parents joy and comfort.

There (for a token) I did thinke it meet,
To take the shooes from off this prince his feet:
I doe not say I stole, but I did take,
And whilst I live Ile keepe them for his sake:
Long may his Grace live to be stylde a man,
And then Ile steale his boots too if I can.
The shoes were upright shoes, and so was he
That wore them, from all harme upright and free:
He usde them for their use, and not for pride,
He never wrong'd them, or ne're trode aside.
Lambskin they were, as white as innocence,
(True patternes[3] for the foot-steps of a Prince,)
And time will come (as I do hope in God)
He that in childhood with these shooes was shod,
Shall with his manly feete once trample downe,
All Antichristian foes to his renowne.

The city of Prague hath in it (by reason of the wars) thrice the number of its[4] owne inhabitants, and yet for all that, victuals are in such

---

1 Prince Rupert of the Rhine, Duke of Cumberland, (1619-82), royalist general during the English civil wars.
2 Bohemia adopted the Gregorian calendar in 1584, therefore St John's day, 27 December, was celebrated on 16 December.
3 Pun on 'pattern' and 'patten', a protective overshoe resembling a clog.
4 *it*: 1621 edn.

great plenty, that sixe men cannot eate three halfe penny worth of bread, and I did buy in the market a fat goose well roast for the value of nine pence English, and I and my brother have dined there at a cookes with good roasted meate, bread and beere, so that we have bin satisfied and left, for the value of five pence: a good turky there may bee bought for two shillings, and for fresh fish I never saw such store, for in one market day I have known in Prague 2000. carps, besides other fishes, which carps in London, are five shilling a piece, and there they were for eight pence, or ten pence at the most, so that one of their fresh fish markets heere were worth at the least five or 600. pounds, and as for all other manner of wilde foule, they are there in satiety, besides, their fruits are in such abundance, that I bought a basket of grapes of the quantity of halfe a pecke for a penny and farthing, and a hatfull of faire peaches for as much, pickled cowcumbers[1] I have bought a pecke for three pence, and muskmelons,[2] there hath beene cast five or sixe carts load of them in one day to their hogs.

As concerning the dyet that is in the kings armyes I could never yet heare any man complaine of want, but that it is more plentifull then in the city, the greatest scarcity hath bin to some sicke souldiers, who being not able to march with the leaguers[3] (by reason of their weaknesse) they have bin left amongst the Boores, or husbandmen in the next villages, where their languages not understood, their succour hath beene but small, but for all this in the campe hath ever bin a continuall cheapenesse of all things, the king most duely paying his souldiers at the end of every month, having in his great leguer under the conduct of the Princes of Hollock and Anhalt,[4] of foot and horse 43000, and at the least of carts and waggons to carry provision and baggage for the army, to the number of 18000. In his little leaguer under the leading of Count Mansfelt[5] there are of foote and horse 7000. besides carts and waggons for carriage, and yet for these great numbers of men and beastes, there is food in all abundance.

1 The usual spelling of 'cucumber' in the 17th century
2 Most culinary melons are variants of the muskmelon species.
3 Military camps, and those soldiers involved in them.
4 Hollock was probably the Prince of Hohenlohe; and Christian I, Prince of Anhalt-Bernburg
5 Count Ernst of Mansfeld.

In the campe with Grave Mansfelt is the Brittane regiment under their Colonell Sir Andrew Gray Knight,[1] and in Prague I met with many worthy gentlemen and souldiers, which were there sicke, as the worthy Captaine Bushel Lieuetenant Grimes, Lieuetenant Langworth, Ancient Galbreath, Ancient Vandenbrooke, Master Whitney, Master Blundel, and others, all which did most courteously entertain me, unto whom I must ever rest thankful, and they doe affirme that now it hath pleased God to grant their souldiers recovery, that they doe hope every Britaine souldier doth retaine more good spirit, then three enemies of what nation soever.

Thus having shewed part of the best things in Bohemia, the court and city of Prague, it shall not be amisse if I relate a little merily, of some things there tolerable, some intolerable, some naught, and some worse then naught: for as every rose hath a prickle, and every bee a sting, so no earthly kingdome hath such perfection of goodnesse but it may be justly taxed with imperfections.

Prague is a famous, ancient, Kingly seat,
In scituation and in state compleat,
Rich in abundance of the earths best treasure,
Proud and high minded, beyond bounds or measure:
In architecture stately, in attire
Bezonians[2] and Plebeians do aspire,
To be apparel'd with the stately port
Of worship, honor, or the royall court:
There coaches and caroches[3] are so rife,
They do attend on every trades-mans wife,
Whose husbands are but in a meane regard,
And get their living by the ell or yard,
How ever their estates may be defended,
Their wives like demy ladies are attended.
I there a chimney-sweepers wife have seene,
Habillimented like the Diamond Queene,

1 Scottish military commander, who organised and led the British troops sent by James I to support Frederick V.
2 beggar or scoundrel.
3 luxurious coach or carriage used in towns.

Most gaudy garish, as a fine maidmarrian,[1]
With breath as sweet as any sugar carrion,[2]
With sattin cloak, lin'd through with budge[3] or sable,
Or cunny[4] furre, (or what her purse is able)
With velvet hood, with tiffanies,[5] and purles,
Rebatoes, frizlings, and with powdred curles,[6]
And (lest her hue or sent should be attainted),
She's antidoted, well perfum'd, and painted,
She's fur'd she's fring'd, she's lac'd, and at her wast
She's with a massy chaine of silver brac'd,
She's yellow starch'd, she's ruff'd, and cuff'd, and muff'd,
She's ring'd, she's braceleted, she's richly tuff'd,
Her petticoate good silke, as can be bought,
Her smocke about the taile lac'd round and wrought,
Her gadding legs are finely Spanish booted,
The whilst her husband like a slave all sooted,
Lookes like a courtier to infernall Pluto,
And knowes himselfe to be a base cornuto.[7]
Then since a man that lives by chimney sweepe,
His wife so gaudy richly clad doth keepe,
Thinke then but how a merchants wife may goe,
Or how a burgamaisters wife doth show:
There (by a kinde of topsie turvy use,)
The women weare the boots, the men the shooes,
I know not if't be profit, or else pride,
But sure they're oftner ridden then they ride:
These females seeme to be most valiant there,
Their painting shewes they do no colours feare

---

1 The Queen of the May in morris dances, usually a man dressed as a woman.
2 This oxymoron is hardly found apart from in Taylor's writings. If not nonsense, it seems to mean foul-breathed, cf his attempted seducer during the Edinburgh journey, p. 78.
3 lamb's wool.
4 rabbit
5 thin muslins.
6 various refinements to her costume and her hair.
7 cuckold, a husband cheated by his wife.

Most art-like plaistring natures imperfections,
With sublimated, white and red complexions:
So much for pride I have observed there,
Their other faults are almost everywhere.

Thus having staid in Prague almost 3. weekes, I returned from thence homeward, on Tuesday the 26. of September, having in my company three gentlemen, a widow (and foure small children) whose husband being an Englishman, and the kings brewer for beere, deceased, and was buried there in Prague whilest I was there: the good desolate woman having received reward after seaven yeares service there and at Heidelberg, being desirous to retire to her country (England) came with us, with my brother and my fellow Tilbery. We tooke two coaches at the castle of Prague, and in a day and halfe, we were carried seaven dutch miles, to a town in Bohemia, (standing on the River Elve) called Leutmeritz,[1] at which towne we all layd our moneyes together, and bought a boate of 48. foote in length, and not 3. foote in bredth, and because we did not know the river, wee hired a Bohemian waterman to guide us 15. dutch miles, to the towne of Dreason[2] in Saxony. But 4 miles short of that towne, which was the first towne in the Saxon countrey, called Pirne,[3] where we were staied 5 houres without the gates, till such time as the Burgamaster wold be pleased to examin us: in the meane space our waterman (not daring to abide the terrible triall of examination, because the Duke of Saxon was in armes against the king of Beame)[4] hee ranne away, and left us to bring the boate downe the river 600. English miles our selves to Hamburgh.

But now to close up all, I will relate what rare dyet, excellent cookery, and sweet lodging we had in our journey in Germany: first for our comfort, after very hard getting of house-roome, our lodgings were every night in straw, where lying together well littered, we honestly alwayes left our sheets behinde us: then at our suppers at a table square, and so broad, that two men can hardly shake hands over it, we being some twelve about it. Our first dish being a raw cabbadge, of the quantity

1 Litomerice, on the River Elbe.
2 Dresden.
3 Pirna.
4 Bohemia.

of halfe a pecke,[1] cut and chopped small, with the fat of resty[2] bacon powred upon it in stead of oyle, which dish must be emptied before we could get any more: Our second dish perhaps a pecke of boild apples and honey, the apples being boiled skins, stalkes, cores and all. Thirdly 100. gudgeons, newly taken perhaps, yet as salt as if they had beene three yeares pickled, or twice at the East Indies, boyled with scales, guts, and all, and buried in ginger like saw dust: a fresh pike as salt as brine, boyled in flat milke, with a pound of garlicke. This was the manner of the most part of our dyet: and if we did aske them why they did salt their meat so unreasonably, there answere was, that their beere could not bee consumed, except their meate were salted extraordinarily.

In many places where we came to lye,
We lodg'd like swine together in a stye:
The marchant and the begger, rich and poore,
All lodg'd alike upon our mother floore.
The man, the ram, bull, bore, asse, horse, and plow,
His wife, his maid, his ewe, his cow, his sow,
His cart, his colt, his mare, his geese, his guests,
Dogs, bitches, calves, cocks, hens, men, fowles & beasts,
All in one roome our lodging we must take,
And all alike in straw must sleepe or wake,
The gallant that's all scarfe,[3] and foole, and feather,
The tinker, and the pedler all together,
Gill Turntripe, and Jone Ugly, (filthy hags)
Embroder'd over with lice, scabs, and rags,
These beastly queanes[4] their carcasses would lay
With Bettrice, that might be the Queene of May.
No striving for the pillow or the sheet,
The beds head no man knowing from the feet;
Our feathers, straw, oates, barly, wheat, or rye,
Where we all us'd to lye, or else I lye,
And after of our coverlet or blanquet,

1 *becke*: 1621 edn.
2 stale or rancid; Taylor appears to be describing sauerkraut.
3 perhaps a variant of 'scaff', to scrounge.
4 whores.

Our bed-fellowes (the beastes) did make a banquet:
And who so scornes such lodging or such fare,
The fields and fasting shall be all their share.>

If a man doe finde fault or seeme distasted with their beastly diet, he is in danger to be thrust out of doores, and take up his lodging in the streetes: and in the conclusion when supper or dinner is ended, then comes mine host, or his leather lip'd Froe,[1] with a sawcy[2] reckoning of what they please, which sounds in our eares like a harsh epilogue after a bad play; for what they say wee must pay, their words are irrevocable (like the ancient kings of Persia)[3] and we must not question or aske how, and how it can bee so much, but pay them their demand without grumbling to halfe a farthing.

Which made mee call to minde sixe severall principalls, that doe belong to a traveller, as patience, silence, warinesse, watchfulnesse, a good stomacke, and a purse well monied; for if he want any one of these, (perhaps) the other five will never bring him to his journies end. A mans patience must be such, that (though he be a barron) he must beare all abuses, either in words, lodging, dyet, or almost any thing, though offered from or by a sowter,[4] tinker, or a merchant of tripes and turneps: his silence must be, that though he heare and understand himselfe wronged, yet he must be as dumbe as a gudgeon or a whitingmop:[5] and though his mouth be shut, his warinesse must bee such, that his eares must ever be open, to listen and over-heare all dangers that may bee complotted against him, his watchfulnesse must be so, that he must seldome sleepe with both his eyes at once, lest his throat be cut before he wake againe. But for his stomacke, hee must eate grasse with a horse, and draffe[6] with the hogges, for hee that cannot eate pickl'd herring broth, and dirty puddings, shall many times fast by authority, and goe

1 *frau*, German for woman or wife.
2 impertinent.
3 An Old Testament reference, Daniel, ch. 6 , verse. 8: 'Now, O king, establish the decree, and signe the writing, that it be not changed, according to the law of the Medes & Persians, which altereth not.'
4 cobbler (Latin *sutor*).
5 a young whiting.
6 dregs, or pigswill.

to bed without his supper: and last of all, he must have Fortunatus or a prince his purse,[1] that must be (like a drunkards dagger) ever drawne, to pay bountifully for such wash and graines, as his valiant stomacke hath overcome, conquered and devoured. But of this a little in verse:

Sixe things unto a traveller belongs,
An asses back t' abide and beare all wrongs:
A fishes tongue (mute) grudging speech forbearing.
A harts quicke eare, all danger over-hearing,
A dogs eyes, that must wake as they doe sleepe,
And by such watch his corps from perill keepe.
A swines sweet homely taste that must digest
All fish, flesh, roots, fowle, foule and beastly drest:
And last, he must have ever at his call
A purse well linde with coyne to pay for all.

With this kinde of lodging and dyet, and with tedious labour sometimes night and day, wee came in 14. daies 607. miles from Prague in Bohemia, to Hambrogh on the hither skirts of Germany, the river having above 1000. shelves and sands, and 800. ilands, so that a man cannot see on which side of them to go, there being 240. milles chained in boates on the first streame, and a number numberlesse of oakes and other trees sunke with the violence of the river, and sometimes fogs and mists that we could not see a boates length from us: besides great rocks and stones that were fallen into the water, that any or many of these impediments do often overthrow boats and drowne passengers; yet I, and my fellow Tilbery (we being both his Maiesties watermen) did by Gods assistance safely escape them all, and brought our selves, as is afore said, to Hambrogh, where being winde bound[2] 10. dayes, I thanke the English merchants,[3] I was well welcomed, untill at last it pleased God, the winde came faire, I tooke ship, and after nine dayes and nights of various weather (I give praise to the Almighty) I safely came home to

1 Fortunatus was a German fairy-tale character whose purse was inexhaustible, featured in a 1599 play by Thomas Dekker.
2 They could not sail because of unfavourable winds.
3 Taylor had made their acquaintance and enjoyed their hospitality in 1616.

my house in London, on Saturday the 28. of October,[1] 1620.

Thus what the preface of my booke did say,
I have perform'd as much, just every way:
I promist that my muse no newes did bring,
And she hath kept my word in every thing.
I bade you keepe your money, and not buy
This booke, and gave you honest reasons why,
But since you bought it, grieve not at the cost,
There's something worth your noting, al's not lost.
For I relate of hils, and dales, and downes, ...>

{You that have bought this, grieve not at the cost,
Ther's something worth your noting, al's not lost,
First halfe a constable is well bumbasted,
If there were nothing else, your coynes not wasted,
Then I relate of hills, and dales, and downes, ...}

Of churches, chappels, pallaces, and townes,
And then to make amends (although but small)
I tell a tale of a great tub withall,
With many a gallowse, jibbit, and a wheele,
Where murd'rers bones are broke from head to heele:
To Prague the highway, which way, how, and whither,
How many miles from thence, how many thither,>
How rich Bohemia is in wealth and food,
Of all things which for man or beast is good.
How in the court at Prague (a princely place),
A gracious queene vouchsafed me to grace,
How with the Prince Rupertus I did play,
And for remembrance brought his shooes away.
How I in Germany had dirty diet,
And beastly lodging, yet must take all quiet:>
How on the sixteenth day[2] of September last,

---

1 October in 1621 edn., September in 1630 edn.
2 *day*: omitted, 1621 edn.

King Frederick to his royall army past,
How fifty thousand were in armes araid,
Of the kings force, beside th' Hungarian aid,

Then though no newes of state may here be had,
The best is I know not of any bad.
Thus in October I left all things well,
But what hath chanced since I cannot tell:
Although I travel'd, I will not aspire,
To be (in print) a base recorded lier.
Betwixt a Jesuit and a witch[1] (I wot)
In hell (of late) a bastard was begot,
Cal'd Rumor,[2] having neither hue, or forme
Of man, beast, fish, fowle, nor of creeping worme,
Nor any substance or substantiall shape,
Yet is (in imitation) truthes ape.
It is the onely tell-tale prating post,
That hourely carries newes from coast to coast,
More swifter then an arrow from a bow,
And tells more tales then truth shall ever know.
It is so vigilant, that in two daies
It carries tydings twenty thousand waies,
The hackneies[3] that doe beare it are mens tongues,
And every where attend on it in throngs:
If any where good happy newes it brings,
It seemes as if it flew with leaden wings,
But with bad newes it spurs amaine outright,
More swift then is a falcon in her flight.
And oftentimes the wicked Elfe will swell,
That every inch she tells will be an ell.
It may be true that (by the chance of war)

---

1 Jesuits and witches were widely identified by Protestant writers as subversive enemies of reformed religion and of England itself.
2 Elaborate metaphorical descriptions of Rumour (*Fama*) by classical authors, such as Virgil in *Aeneid* book 4, were taken up in the 17th century by writers including Francis Bacon.
3 Hackney coaches for hire operated in London from the 1620s. See p. 367.

Bohemia hath receiv'd a blow, or scar,[1]
But ere it shall receive a mortall wound,
I hope confusion shall their foes confound.
Wars are not like confections sweetly candied,
But rather like to balls at tennis bandied,
Whereas the victory, is as the ball,
In faults, in hazzards,[2] in the chase, in all.
Then if Bohemia hath receiv'd a cuffe.
'Twill be requited with a counterbuffe.
That they who seeme to vaunt or flourish most,
May have small stomacke to prate, brag, or boast,
This late ill newes for ought that I do know,
Perhaps may be compar'd to Scoggins[3] crow:
Most part devis'd and amplifi'd, by those
Who are Great Britaine and Bohemiaes foes.
I can drinke ale or wine, and write and prate,
And let alone such matters of high state,
I had much rather let my muse be mute,
Then write to helpe the hangman to my sute.
God gripes all earthly kingdomes in his fist,
And will dispose them, how, and where he list,
And be things as he please, I wish all good
Unto my soveraigne and his royall bloud.
David had many troubles with King Saul,
But he obtain'd his kingdome after all:
When man is weakest, God is strongest ever,
And those that trust in him, he leaves them never:
To him therefore, that is he King of Kings,

---

1   A reference to the Battle of the White Mountain, 8 November 1620, in which the Bohemian forces were defeated, and in consequence Frederick went into exile and his short-lived reign came to an end.
2   In real tennis the hazard was the receiver's end of the court.
3   Scoggin was jester to Edward IV and his name was attached to a jest-book published in editions in 1613 and 1626, though compiled earlier. In the 1626 edition Scoggin, to test whether his wife was a gossip, told her that he had baked a crow. She passed on the story and eventually he was credited with baking 21 crows, and his health was prayed for in church.

I leave th' events of all these doubtfull things.
No bringer of strange tales I meane to be,
Nor Ile beleeve none that are told to me.>

{And how Bohemia strongly can oppose,
And cuffe and curry all their daring foes.
Then though no newes of state, may heere be had,
I know heer's something will make good men glad,
No bringer of strange tales I meane to be,
Nor Ile beleeve none that are told to me.}
FINIS

A Verry Merry Wherry Ferry Voyage: or Yorke for my Money

A VERRY MERRY WHERRY-FERRY-VOYAGE: OR YORKE FOR MY MONEY

A VERY MERRY WHERRY-FERRY-VOYAGE, *the 1622 expedition to York, is written entirely in verse, and extends to some 850 lines. As a poem it occasionally rises above the jogging doggerel which Taylor seems to have possessed in inexhaustible supply. Indeed, a tranquil passage by sunset and starlight on a calm Norfolk sea off Blakeney provided inspiration for lines which Robert Herrick might not have felt ashamed to put his name to. There is artistry too in the placing of this sea interlude, since it offers a calm aftermath to the knockabout pantomime of Taylor's arrest at Cromer.*

York, which Taylor had visited before on his return from Scotland in 1618, was to be his destination, but this time he undertook the journey in an old wherry. It was partly a business trip, since he carried for resale in the north a trunk full of the pamphlets which he had steadily been writing and publishing during the previous decade. This time there is no mention of sponsorship, in the form of 'Taylor's bills' subscribing to the account of the journey which he intended to write.

The voyage took Taylor and four accomplices by sea around the East Anglian coast from London, by Harwich and Yarmouth to Boston, and then by rivers and waterways to Lincoln, Hull and York. At York the boat was sold, and they hired horses for the return journey (which is scarcely mentioned) overland. York, Yarmouth and Lincoln are briefly described, but almost exactly half the poem is devoted to the contrasting treatment which the expedition received at two east coast communities, Cromer and Hull. At Cromer they were arrested as suspected pirates by incompetent and scared (in Taylor's view) petty officialdom; eventually the local magistrates rescued them, but not before their boat had been maliciously damaged. The mayor and aldermen of Hull adopted an entirely different attitude, feasting them and regarding them as celebrities. In return Taylor pens a long and interesting account of the town's virtues, the quality of its government, its excellent water supply and defences. So complimentary is his verdict that he feels the need to defend himself from the charge, '... that I partiall in my writings were, Because they made me welcome, and good cheere'. Here is Taylor in his prime, enjoying his success and confident in his opinions and abilities.

[25th July - after 10th August, 1622. Text derived from 1622 publication (copy BL c.30 b.28); some readings taken from the 1630 collected edition All the Workes...*]*

A Verry Merry Wherry-Ferry-Voyage: or Yorke for my money: sometimes perilous, sometimes quarrellous, performed with a paire of oares, by sea from London, by John Taylor, and Job Pennell. and written by J.T.

London: Imprinted by Edw: All de 1622

As much happinesse as may bee wished, attend the two hopefull, impes[1] of gentility and learning, Mr Richard and George Halton.[2]

You forward payre, in towardly designes,
To you I send these sowsde salt-water lines:
Accept, reade, laugh, and breath, and to't againe,
And still my muse, and I, shall yours remaine
     John Taylor

PROLOGUE.
I now intend a voyage heere to write,
From London unto Yorke, helpe to indite,
Great Neptune! lend thy ayde to me, who past
Through thy tempestuous waves with many a blast.
And then I'le true describe the townes, and men,
And manners, as I went and came agen.

---

1 here in sense of 'scions, offspring of a noble house'.
2 *Hatton,* 1630.

A VERY MERRY WHERRY-FERRY-VOYAGE. OR, YORKE FOR MY MONEY.

The yeare which I doe call as others doe,
    Full 1600. adding twenty two:[1]
    The month of July that's for ever fam'd,
(Because 'twas so by Julius Caesar[2] nam'd,)
Just when six dayes, and to each day a night,
The dogged dog-dayes[3] had began to bite,
On that day which doth blest remembrance bring,
The name of an apostle, and our king,
On that remarkeable good day, Saint James,[4]
I undertooke my voyage downe the Thames.
The signe in Cancer,[5] or the ribs and brest,
And Eeolus[6] blewe sweetly west southwest.
Then after many farewels, cups and glasses,
(Which oftentimes hath made men worse then asses)
About the waste or navell[7] of the day,
Not being dry or drunke, I went my way.
Our wherry somewhat olde, or strucke[8] in age,
That had endur'd neere 4. yeares pilgrimage,
And caryed honest people, whores, and thieves,
Some sergeants, bayliffes, and some under-shrieves,[9]
And now at last it was her lot to be
Th' advent'rous bonny barke to carry me.
But as an olde whores beauty being gone

1 'The yeere of our Lord.' [Taylor]
2 'July was so-nam'd by Caesar.' [Taylor]
3 'The dogdayes were 6. dayes entred.' [Taylor] July and August, when Sirius was believed to augment the sun's heat (a favourite allusion of Taylor's).
4 St James's day, 25th July.
5 'I observe signes, windes, tides, dayes, houres, times, scituations and manners.' [Taylor]
6 in Greek mythology, Aeolus was ruler of the winds. *Aeolus*, 1630.
7 'Noone if you'd take it so.' [Taylor]
8 i.e. stricken, afflicted with.
9 'Boats are like barbars, chayres, hackneyes, or whores: common to all estates.' [Taylor]

Hides Natures wracke, with artlike painting on:
So I with colours finely did repaire
My boats defaults, and made her fresh and faire.
Thus being furnish'd with good wine and beere,
And bread and meate (to banish hungers feare)
With sayles, with ancker, cables, sculs and oares,
With carde[1] and compasse, to know seas and shores,
With lanthorne, candle, tinder-box and match,
And with good courage, to worke, ward, and watch,
Well man'd, well ship'd, well victual'd, wel appointed,
Well in good health, well timberd and well joynted:
All wholly well, and yet not halfe fox'd[2] well,
Twixt Kent, and Essex, we to Gravesend fell.
There I had welcome of my friendly host,
(A Gravesend trencher, and a Gravesend tost)
Good meate and lodging at an easie rate,
And rose betimes although I lay downe late.
Bright Lucifer[3] the messenger of day,
His burnisht twinkling splendour did display:
Rose cheek'd Aurora hid her blushing face,
She spying Phoebus[4] comming gave him place.
Whilst Zephirus, and Auster,[5] mix'd together,
Breath'd gently, as fore-boding pleasant weather.
Old Neptune had his daughter Thames supplide,
With ample measure of a flowing tide,
But Thames supposde it was but borrowed goods,
And with her ebbes, payde Neptune backe his floods.
Then at the time of this auspicious dawning,
I rowz'd my men, who scrubbing, stretching, yawning,
Arose, left Gravesend, rowing downe the streame,
And neere to Lee,[6] wee to an ancker came.

1 chart.
2 drunk.
3 the morning star.
4 the goddess of the dawn, and the sun god.
5 west wind and south wind.
6 Leigh-on-Sea, Essex, near Southend.

Because the sands were bare, and water lowe,
We rested there, till it two houres did flowe:
And then to travell went our galley foyst,[1]
Our ancker quickly weigh'd, our sayle soone[2] hoyst,
Where thirty miles we past, a mile from shore,
The water two foote deepe,[3] or little more.
Thus past we on the brave East Saxon[4] coast,
From 3. at morne, till 2. at noone almost,
By Shobury, Wakering, Fowlenesse, Tittingham,[5]
And then wee into deeper water came.
There is a crooked bay runnes winding farre,
To Maulden, Esterford, and Colchester,[6]
Which cause 'twas much about, (to ease mens paine)
I left the land, and put into the mayne.
With speed, the crooked way to scape and passe,
I made out straight[7] for Frinton and the Nasse.[8]
But being 3. leagues then from any land,
And holding of our maine sheate in my hand,
We did espy a coleblacke cloud to rise,
Fore-runner of some tempest from the skies;
Scarce had we sayl'd a hundred times our length,
But that the winde began to gather strength:
Stiffe Eolus with Neptune went to cuffes:
With huffes, and puffes, and angry counter-buffes,
From boyst'rous gusts, they fell to fearefull flawes,[9]
Whilest we 'twixt winde and water, neere Death's jawes,
Tost like a corke upon the mounting maine,

1 barge or light galley, propelled by oars and sails.
2 *up*, 1630.
3 'These flat sands are called the Spits.' [Taylor]
4 i.e. Essex.
5 Shoeburyness, Great Wakering, Foulness, Tillingham, all Essex, east of Southend.
6 Maldon is on the Blackwater, Colchester on the Colne; Esterford is perhaps connected with Good Easter and High Easter, west of Chelmsford.
7 *strait*, 1630.
8 the Naze, south of Harwich.
9 blows.

Up with a whiffe, and straight way downe againe,
At which we in our mindes much troubled were,
And said, God blesse us all, what wethers heere?
For (in a worde) the seas so high did growe,
That ships were forc'd to strike their topsailes lowe:
Meane time (before the winde) wee scudded brave,
Much like a ducke, on top of every wave.
But nothing violent is permanent,
And in short space away the tempest went.
So farewell it; and you that readers be,
Suppose it was no welcome guest to me:
My company and I, it much perplext,
And let it come when I send for it next.
But leaving jesting, thankes to God I give,
Twas through his mercy wee did scape and live.
And though these things with mirth I doe expresse,
Yet still I thinke on God with thankefulnes.
Thus ceast the storme and weather gan to smile,
And we row'd neere the shoare of Horsey Ile.
Then did illustrious Titan[1] seeme[2] to steepe
His chariot in the westerne ocean deepe:
We saw the farre spent day, withdraw his light,
And made for Harwich, where we lay all night.
There did I finde an hostesse with a tongue,
As nimble as it had on gimmols[3] hung:
Twill never tyre, though it continuall toyl'd,
And went as yare,[4] as if it had bin oyl'd:
All's one for that, for ought which I perceive,
It is a fault which all our mothers have:
And is so firmely grafted in the sexe,
That hee's an asse that seemes thereat to vexe.
Apolloes beames began to guild the hils,

---

1 the sun (Sol/ Helios was a Titan).
2 *gin* [i.e. begin], 1630.
3 hinges, especially rings designed to act as hinges.
4 ready for action.

And west southwest the winde the welkin[1] fils,
When I left Harwich, and along we row'd
Against a smooth calme flood that stifly flow'd,
By Bawdsey Haven, and by Orford Nasse,
And so by Aldbrough[2] we at last did passe.
By Lestoffe[3] we to Yarmouth made our way,
Our third dayes travell being Saturday,
There did I see a towne well fortifide,
Well govern'd, with all Natures wants supplide,
The scituation in a wholesome ayre,
The buildings (for the most part) sumptuous, faire,
The people courteous, and industrious, and
With labour makes the sea inrich the land.
Besides (for aught[4] I know) this one thing more,
The towne can scarcely yeeld a man a whore:
It is renownd for fishing farre and neere,
And sure in Britaine it hath not a peere.[5]
But noble Nash[6] thy fame shall live alwayes,
Thy witty pamphlet, the red herrings praise[7]
Hath done great Yarmouth much renowned right,
And put my artlesse muse to silence[8] quite:
On Sunday we a learned sermon had,
Taught to confirme the good, reforme the bad;
Acquaintance in the towne I scarce had any,
And sought for none, in feare to finde too many,
Much kindnesse to me by mine host was done,

1 firmament.
2 Aldeburgh, Suffolk.
3 Lowestoft, Suffolk.
4 *ought*, 1630.
5 'It hath not a fellow in England for fishing.' [Taylor] The asterisk on which this footnote should depend is missing, but it is presumably intended to gloss these lines.
6 Thomas Nashe (1567-c.1601) wrote *Nashe's Lenten Stuff* (1598) which included a description of Great Yarmouth (based partly on Camden), woven into a play called The Praise of Red Herring. See next note.
7 'A booke called The Praise of the red herring.' [Taylor]
8 *silent*, 1630.

(A marriner[1] nam'd William Richardson)
Besides mine hostesse gave to me at last
A cheese, with which at sea we brake our fast,
The guift was round, and had no end indeede,
But yet we made an end of it with speede:
My thanks surmounts her bounty, all men fees
My gratitudes in print: But where's the cheese?
So on the Munday, betwixt one and twaine,
I tooke my leave, and put to sea againe.
Down Yarmouth Roade[2] we row'd with cutting speed,
(The wind all quiet, armes must doe the deed)
Along by Castor,[3] and sea-bord'ring townes,
Whose cliffes and shores abide sterne Neptunes frownes,
Sometimes a mile from land, and sometimes two,
(As depthes or sands permitted us to do)
Till drawing toward night, we did perceave
The wind at east, and seas began to heave:
The rowling billowes all in fury roares
And tumbled us, we scarce could use our oares:
Thus on a lee shore[4] darknesse gan to come,
The sea grew high, the winds gan hisse and hum:
The foaming curled waves the shore did beate,
(As if the ocean would all Norfolke eate)
To keepe at sea, was dangerous I did thinke,
To goe to land I stood in doubt to sinke:
Thus landing, or not landing (I suppos'd)
We were in perill[5] round about inclos'd;
At last to rowe to shore I thought it best,
'Mongst many evils, thinking that the least:
My men all pleas'd to doe as I command,
Did turne the boates head opposite to land,
And with the highest wave that I could spie,

1   'And a ship carpenter.' [Taylor]
2   anchorage offshore from Great Yarmouth.
3   Caister-on-Sea, north of Yarmouth.
4   shore on the sheltered side, away from the wind.
5   'We were in a puzzell.' [Taylor]

I bad them row to shore immediatly.
When straite[1] we all leap'd over-boord in hast,
Some to the knees, and some up to the waste,
Where suddainly t'wixt owle-light[2] and the darke,
We pluck'd the boat beyond high water marke.
And thus halfe sowsde, halfe stewd, with sea and sweat,
We land at Cromer towne, halfe dry, halfe wet.
But we supposing all was safe and well,
In shunning[3] Silla, on Caribdis[4] fell:
For why some women, and some children there
That saw us land, were all possest with feare:
And much amaz'd, ranne crying up and downe,
That enemies were come to take the towne.
Some said that we were pyrats, some said theeves,
And what the women saies, the men beleeves.
With that foure constables did quickly call,
Your ayde! to armes you men of Cromer all!
Then straitway forty men with rusty bills,
Some arm'd in ale, all of approved skills,
Devided into foure stout regiments,
To guard the towne from dangerous events;
Brave Captaine Pescod did the vantguard lead,
And Captaine Clarke the rereward governed,
Whilst Captaine Wiseman, and hot Captaine Kimble,[5]
Were in the mayne battalia fierce and nimble:
One with his squadron watch'd me all the night,
Least[6] from my lodging I should take my flight:
A second (like a man of speciall[7] note)

1 *straight*, 1630.
2 dusk.
3 'We were like flounders alive in a frying-pan, that leap'd into the fire to save themselves.' [Taylor]
4 i.e. Scylla and Charybdis, two treacherous rocks flanking the strait between Italy and Sicily.
5 'These were the names of the cumbersome Cromorian constables.' [Taylor]
6 1630 (*Least*, 1622).
7 *simple*, 1630.

Did by the sea side all night watch my boate,
The other two, to make their names renownd,
Did guard the towne, and bravely walke the rownd.
And thus my boat, my selfe, and all my men,
Were stoutly guarded, and regarded then:
For they were all so full with feare possest,
That without mirth it cannot be exprest.
My invention doth curvet,[1] my muse doth caper,
My pen doth daunce out lines upon the paper,
And in a word, I am as full of mirth,
As mighty men are at their first sonnes birth.
Me thinkes Moriscoes[2] are within my braines,
And Heyes,[3] and Antiques[4] run through all my vaines:
Heigh, to the tune of Trenchmoore[5] I could write
The valient men of Cromers sad affright:
As sheepe doe feare the wolfe, or geese the fox,
So all amazed[6] were these sencelesse blockes:
That had the towne beene fir'd, it is a doubt,
But that the women there had pist it out,
And from the men reek'd such a fearefull sent,
That people three miles[7] thence mus'd what it meant,
And he the truth that narrowly had sifted,
Had found the constables, had need t'have shifted.[8]
They did examine me, I answer'd than
I was John Taylor, and a waterman,
And that my honest fellow Job and I,
Were servants to King James his Majstie,
How we to Yorke, upon a mart[9] were bound,

1 leap or frolic, like a horse.
2 morris dances.
3 type of country dance, a reel.
4 antics, grotesque dances.
5 boisterous country dance.
6 terror-struck.
7 'People did come thither 3. or 4. miles about, to know what the matter was.' [Taylor]
8 changed their clothes.
9 a trading deal.

And that we landed, fearing to be drownd:
When all this would not satisfie the crew,
I freely op'd my trunke, and bad them view,
I shew'd them bookes, of chronicles and kings,
Some prose, some verse, and idle sonnettings,
I shewed them all my letters to the full:
Some to Yorkes archbishop, and some to Hull,
But had the twelve apostles sure beene there
My witnesses, I had beene ne'r[1] the neere.
And let me use all oathes that I could use,
They still were harder of beliefe then Jewes.
They wanted faith, and had resolv'd before,
Not to believe what e're we said or swore.
They said the world was full of much deceit,
And that my letters might be counterfeit:[2]
Besides, there's one thing bred the more dislike,
Because mine host was knowne a Catholike.
These things concurring, people came in clusters,
And multitudes within my lodging musters,
That I was almost wooried[3] unto death,
In danger to be stifled with their breath.
And had mine host toooke pence a peece[4] of those
Who came to gaze on me, I doe suppose,
No Jack an Apes, Baboone, or Crocodile[5]
'Ere got more money in so small a while.[6]
Besides, the pesants did this one thing more,
They call'd and dranke foure shillings on my score:
And like unmanner'd mungrells went their way,

1 1630 (*nere*, 1622). 'I had as good to have said nothing.' [Taylor]
2 'Diligent officers.' [Taylor]
3 in sense of 'pestered'.
4 *apiece*, 1630.
5 performing animals exhibited for profit. A jackanapes was originally a monkey imported from Naples.
6 'The dancing on the ropes, or a puppet play, had come short of his takings, accounting time for time.' [Taylor]

Not spending aught, but leaving me to pay.[1]
This was the houshold businesse: in meane space
Some rascals ran unto my boate apace,
And turn'd and tumbled her, like men of Goteham,[2]
Quite topsie turvy upward with her bottome,
Vowing they would in tatters piece-meale teare
The cursed pyrates boate, that bred their feare;
And I am sure, their madnesse (to my harme)
Tore a boord out, much longer than mine arme.
And they so bruis'd, and split our wherry, that
She leak'd, we cast out water with a hat.
Now let men judge, upon these[3] truthes revealing,
If Turkws or Mores could use more barbarous dealing;
Or whether it be fit I should not write
Their envie, foolish feare, and mad despight.[4]
What may wise men conceive, when they shall note,
That five unarm'd men, in a wherry boate,
Nought to defend, or to offend with stripes[5]
But one old sword,[6] and two tobacco pipes,
And that of constables a murnivall,[7]
Men, women, children, all in generall,
And that they all should be so valiant, wise,
To feare we would a market towne surprise!
In all that's writ, I vow I am no lyer,
I muse the beacons were not set on fire.
The dreadfull names of Talbot, or of Drake,[8]
Ne'r made the foes of England more to quake
Then I made Cromer; for their feare and dolour,

---

1 'This was more then I could willingly afford.' [Taylor]
2 Gotham, Notts., whose inhabitants were proverbially stupid. *Gotham*, 1630.
3 *this*, 1630.
4 malicious contempt.
5 blows.
6 'And the sword was rusty with salt-water, that it had need of a quarters warning ere it would come out.' [Taylor]
7 in cards, a set of four aces or other picture cards.
8 John Talbot, earl of Shrewsbury (d.1453), and Sir Francis Drake (d.1596).

Each man might smell out by his neighbours collor.[1]
At last, the joyfull morning did approach,
And Sol began to mount his flaming coach,
Then did I thinke my purgatory done,
And rose betimes intending to be gone;
But holla, stay, 'twas otherwayes, with me
The messe[2] of constables were shrunke to three:
Sweet Mr Pescods double diligence
Had horst himselfe, to beare intelligence
to Justices of Peace within the land,
What dangerous businesse there was now in hand,
There was I forc'd to tarry all the while,
Till some said he rode foure and twenty mile,
In seeking men of worship, peace, and quorum,[3]
Most wisely to declare strange newes before um.
And whatsoever tales he did recite,
I'm sure he caus'd Sir Austine Palgrave, knight,
And Mr. Robert Kempe a Justice there
Come[4] before me, to know how matters were.
As conference 'twixt them and I did passe,
They quickly understood me, what I was:
And though they knew me not in prose and lookes,
They had read of me in my verse, and bookes;
My businesses account I there did make,
And I and all my company did take,
The lawfull oath of our alleageance then,
By which we were beleev'd for honest men.
In duty, and in all humility
I doe acknowledge the kinde courtesie
Of those two gentlemen: for they did see,
How much the people were deceiv'd in me.
They gave me coyne, and wine, and suger too,
And did as much as lay in them to doe

1 'A brave sent.' [Taylor]
2 in two senses: troop, and muddle.
3 a body of justices.
4 *Came*, 1630.

To finde them that my boate had torne and rent,
And so to give them worthy punishment.
Besides Sir Austin Palgrave[1] bade me this,
To goe but foure miles, where his dwelling is,[2]
And I and all my company should there
Finde friendly welcome, mix'd with other cheare.
I gave them thankes, and so I'le give them still,
And did accept their cheere in their goodwill.
Then 3. a clocke at afternoone and past,
I was discharg'd from Cromer at the last.
But for men shall not thinke that enviously
Against this towne I let my lines to flye:
And that I doe not lye, or scoffe, or fable,
For them I wil write something charitable.
It is an ancient market towne that stands
Upon a lofty cliffe of mouldring sands:
The sea against the cliffes doth dayly beate,
And every tide into the land doth eate,
The towne is poore, unable by expence,
Against the raging sea to make defence:
And every day it eateth further in,
Still wasting, washing downe the sand doth win,
That if some course be not tane[3] speedily,
The towne's in danger in the sea to lye.
A goodly church stands on these brittle grounds,[4]
Not many fairer in Great Britaines bounds:
And if the sea shall swallow't, as some feare,
Tis not ten thousand pounds the like could reare.
No Christian can behold it but with griefe,
And with my heart I wish them quicke reliefe.
So farewell Cromer, I have spoke for thee,

---

1 'He would have had us to have stayed 3. or foure dayes with him.' [Taylor]
2 probably North Barningham Hall, north-west of Aylsham, a seat of the Palgraves.
3 taken.
4 Cromer church survives, its tower the tallest of any Norfolk parish church. A Victorian chancel has replaced one demolished by gunpowder in 1681.

Though thou didst much unkindly deale with me.
And honest marriners, I thanke you there,
Laboriously you in your armes did beare
My boat for me three furlongs at the least,
When as the tyde of ebb was so decreast,
You waded, and you launch'd her quite a floate,[1]
And on your backes you bore us to our boate.
Th' unkindnes that I had before, it come
Because the constables were troublesome:
Long'd to be busie, would be men of action,
Whose labours was their travels[2] satisfaction,
Who all were borne when wit was out of towne,
And therefore got but little of their owne:
So farewell Pescod, Wiseman, Kimble, Clarke,[3]
Foure sonnes of Ignorance (or much more darke)
You made me loose a day of brave calme weather.
So once againe farewell, fare ill together.
Then longst the Norfolke coast we rowde outright
To Blakeney,[4] when we saw the comming night,
The burning eye of day began to winke,
And into Thetis lap his beames to shrinke:
And as he went stain'd the departed skie,
With red, blew, purple, and vermillion dye.
Till all our hemispere laments his lack,
And mourning night puts on a robe of blacke,
Bespangled diversly with golden sparkes,
Some moveable, some sea-mens fixed markes.
The milky way that blest Astrea[5] went,
When as she left this earthly continent,
Shew'd like a christall cawsey[6] to the thrones

---

1 *afloate*, 1630.
2 i.e. travails, 'labours'.
3 'They long'd for imployment, and rather then be idle, would be ill occupied.' [Taylor]
4 *Blackney*, 1630. i.e. Blakeney, Norfolk.
5 the star-maiden, who fled from the wickedness of earth to become a star.
6 causeway.

Of Jove and Saturne, pav'd with precious stones.
Old Occeanus, Neptune, Innachus,
And two and thirty huffecapt Eeolus,[1]
Had all tane truce and were in league combin'd,
No billowes foaming, or no breath of winde;
The solid earth, the ayre, the ocean deepe
Seem'd as the whole world had bin fast asleepe.
In such a pleasant even as this came I
To Blackney, with my ship and company:
Whereas I found my entertainment good
For welcome, drinking, lodging, and for food.
The morrow when Latonaes[2] sunne gan rise,
And with his light illumines mortall eyes:
When cockes did crow, and lambes did bleat and blea,
I mounted from my couch, and put to sea.
Like glasse the oceans face was smooth and calme,
The gentle ayre breath'd like Arabian balme:[3]
Gusts, stormes and flawes, lay sleeping in their celles
Whilest with much labour we row'd o're the Welles.[4]
This was our[5] greatest day[6] of worke indeed,
And it behoov'd us much, to make much speed,
For why before that day did quite expire
We past the dangerous Wash, to Lincolnshire.
And there in 3. houres space and little more
We row'd to Boston, from the Norfolke shore:
Which by report of people that dwell there,
Is six and twenty mile or very neere.
The way unknowne, and we no pilate[7] had,

1 Inachus was a son of Oceanus; the 32 swaggering winds blew from all points of the compass. *Innachus* 'The god of rivers, springs, brookes, foords [floods, 1630], and fountaines.' [Taylor]
2 Latona was the mother of Apollo, identified with the sun-god.
3 Taylor probably means the balm of Gilead, referred to in Jeremiah 8 verse 22.
4 Wells-next-the-Sea, Norfolk.
5 *the*, 1630.
6 'We rowed above 100. miles that day.' [Taylor]
7 *pilot*, 1630.

Flats, sands, and shoales; and tides all raging mad,
Which sands our passage many times denide,
And put us sometimes[1] 3. or foure miles wide,
Besides the flood runs there, with such great force,
That I imagine it out-runnes a horse:
And with a head some 4. foot high, that rores,
It on the sodaine swels and beats the shores.
It tumbled us a ground upon the sands,
And all that wee could doe with wit, or hands,
Could not resist it, but we were in doubt
It would have beaten our boates bottome out.
It hath lesse mercy then beare, wolfe, or tyger,
And in those countries it is call'd the Hyger.[2]
We much were unacquainted with those fashions,
And much it troubled us with sundry passions:
We thought the shore we never should recover,
And look'd still when our boate would tumble over.
But He that made all with his word of might,
Brought us to Boston, where we lodg'd all night.
The morrow morning, when the sunne gan peepe.
I wak'd and rub'd mine eyes, and shak'd off sleepe,
And understanding that the river went,[3]
From Boston, up to Lincolne, and to Trent,
To Humber, Owse, and Yorke, and (taking paine)
We need not come in sight of sea againe,
I lik'd the motion, and made hast away
To Lincolne,[4] which was 50. mile, that day.
Which citty in the 3. King Edwards raigne,
Was th' onely staple, for this kingdomes gaine
For leather, lead, and wooll, and then was seene
Five times ten churches there, but now fifteene,

1 'Sands lying crookedly in our way, making us goe 3. or foure miles about at lowe water.' [Taylor]
2 Eagre, a strong tide rushing up an estuary. 'It is so called in Mr. Draytons second part of Polyalbion, in his treatise of Humber.' [Taylor]
3 the River Witham flows from Lincoln through Boston to the sea.
4 following lines derived from Camden, etc.

A brave cathedrall church there now doth stand,
That scarcely hath a fellow in this land:
Tis for a Godly use, a goodly frame,
And beares the blessed Virgin Maryes name.
The towne is ancient, and by course of Fate,
Through warrs, and time, defac'd and ruinate,
But monarchies, and empires, kingdomes, crownes,
Have rose or fell, as Fortune smiles or frownes:
And townes, and citties, have their portions had
Of time-tost variations, good and bad.
There is a proverbe, part of which is this,
They say that Lincolne was, and London is.[1]
From thence we past a ditch of weedes and mud,
Which they doe (falsely) there call Forcedike Flood:[2]
For I'l be sworne, no flood I could finde there,
But dirt and filth which scarce my boate would beare,
'Tis 8. miles long, and there our paines was such.
As all our travell did not seeme so much,
My men did wade, and drawe the boate like horses,
And scarce could tugge her on with all our forces:
Moyl'd,[3] toyl'd, myr'd, tyr'd, still lab'ring, ever doing,
Yet were we 9. long houres that 8. miles going.
At last when as the day was wellnigh spent,
We gat from Forcedikes floodles flood to Trent.
Ev'n as the windowes of the day did shut,
Downe Trents swift streame to Gainsborough we put,
There did we rest untill the morning starre,
The joyfull doores of dawning did un-barre:
To Humbers churlish streames, our course we fram'd,

1 'Lincoln was, London is, and York shall be,' first recorded 1588.
2 Fossdyke. 'It is a passage cut thorow the land eight miles from Lincolne into Trent, but through either the peoples poverty or negligence, it is growne up with weedes, and mudde, so that in the summer it is in many places almost dry.' [Taylor] Of Roman construction, it was scoured from 1121, but fell into poor condition until improvement under an act of 1671.
3 laboured.

So nam'd, for drowning of a king so nam'd.[1]
And there the swift ebbe tide ranne in such sort,
The winde at east, the waves brake thicke and short,
That in some doubts, it me began to strike,
For in my life, I ne're had seene the like.
My way was up to Yorke, but my intent
Was contrary, for from the fall of Trent
I fifteene mile[2] went downewards east northeast,
When as my way was upward west southwest,
And as against the winde we madly venter,[3]
The waves like pirates boord our boate and enter,
But though they came in fury, and amaine
Like thieves we cast them over-boord againe.
This conflict lasted two houres to the full,
Untill we gat to Kingstone upon Hull:
For to that towne I had a proved friend,
That letters did and commendations send
By me unto the worthy maiestrate,
The maior, and some of's brethren, in that state.
Besides I had some letters, of like charge
From my good friend, the master of the barge
Unto some friends of his, that they would there sort, short,
Give me Hull cheese,[4] and welcome and good cheere.
Sunday at Mr Maiors much cheere and wine
Where as the Hall did in the parlour dine,[5]
At night with one that had bin shrieve[6] I sup'd
Well entertain'd I was, and halfe well cup'd:
On Monday noone, I was invited than

1 Humber, according to Geoffrey of Monmouth, was king of the Huns, who invaded Britain c.1000 BC, but fled in defeat and was drowned in the river.
2 'I went fifteene mile out of Trent downe Humber on purpose to see Hull, when my way was quite contrary.' [Taylor]
3 venture.
4 'Hull cheese, is much like a loafe out of a brewers basket, it is composed of two simples, mault and water, in one compound; and is cousin germane to the mightiest ale in England.' [Taylor]
5 presumably a proverb, but not traced.
6 sheriff.

To a grave justicer, an alderman,
And there such cheere as earth and waters yeeld,
Shew'd like a harvest in a plentious feild.
Another I must thanke for his goodwill,
For he prest on to bid we welcome still.
There is a captaine of good life and fame
And, God with us,[1] I oft have call'd his name.
He welcom'd me, as I had bin his fellow,
Lent me his silken colours, blacke and yellow,
Which to our mast made fast, wee with a drum
Did keepe, till we to Yorke in triumph come.
Thankes to my loving host and hostesse pease
There at mine inne, each night I tooke mine ease:
And there I gat a cantle[2] of Hull cheese
One evening late, I thanke thee Macabees.[3]
Kinde Roger Parker, many thankes to thee,
Thou shewedst much undeserved love to me,
Layd my boat safe, spent time, coyne and endeavour,
And mad'st my money counted copper ever.
But as at feasts, the first course being past,
Men doe reserve their dainties till the last,
So my most thankes I ever whilest I live
Will to the mayor, and his bretheren give,
But most of all, to shut up all together
I give him thankes that did commend me thither,[4]
Their loves (like Humber) over-flow'd the bankes,
And though I ebbe in worth, I'le flowe in thankes.
Thus leaving off the men, now of the towne
Some thinges which I observ'd I'le heere set downe:
And partly to declare it's praise and worth,
It is the onely bulwarke of the north.

---

1 'The meaning of those marks are only knowne to the townsmen there.' [Taylor]
2 slice.
3 'An ingenuous man named Machabeus.' [Taylor]
4 'Mr J.J.' [Taylor]

All other townes for strength to it may strike,[1]
And all the northerne parts have not the like,
The people from the sea much wealth have wonne,
Each man doth live as he were Neptunes sonne.
Th' antiquity thereof a man may reede
In Reverend Cambdens workes, and painfull Speede:
How in King Edwards raigne first of that name
Then called Wike.[2] Then did they Kingston frame,
And then the townesmen cut a river[3] there,
An exc'lent haven, a defence or peere:
Built with excessive charge, to save it from
Fierce Humbers raging, that each tide doth come.
From time to time, more greatnes still it gain'd,
Till lately when the eight King Henry raign'd,
He made it greater, by his oft resort,
And many times kept there his royall court,
He wall'd it well, built battlements, and gates,
And (more with honour to augment their states)
He built two blockhouses, and castle strong
To guard the towne from all invasive wrong.
He gave them much munition, swords, shafts, bowes,
And brazen ordnance, as the world well knowes,
Which guns he gave them for the townes defence,
But were in 88.[4] all borrowed thence,
With promise they againe should be sent backe,
But the performance ever hath bin slacke.
Now in this yron age, their guns I see,
Are mettle like the age, and yron be:
And glad they would be if they could obtaine,
To change that mettle, for their owne againe.
Foure well built gates, with bolts, and lockes, and barres

1 salute.
2 Wyke upon Hull was enlarged c.1293 and renamed Kingston.
3 'The River of Hull is 20. miles in length, cut with mens labour, to the infinite commodity of the countrey.' [Taylor] Meaux Abbey, according to chroniclers, in the 13th century diverted the river into a new channel.
4 presumably in 1588, for defence against the Spanish Armada.

For ornament or strength, in peace or warres:
Besides to keepe their foes the further out,
They can drowne all the land[1] 3. miles about.
Tis plentifully serv'd with flesh and fish,
As cheape, as reasonable men can wish.
And thus by Gods grace, and mans industry,
Dame Nature, or mens art doth it supply.
Some 10. yeares since fresh water there was scant,
But with much cost they have supply'd that want;
By a most exc'lent water-worke[2] that's made,
And to the towne in pipes it is convay'd,
Wrought with most artificiall engines, and
Perform'd by th' art of the industrious hand
Of Mr. William Maltby,[3] Gentleman,
So that each man of note there alwayes can
But turne a cocke within his house, and still
They have fresh-water alwayes at their will,
This have they all unto their great content,
For which they each doe pay a yearely rent.
There is a proverbe, and a prayer withall,
That we may not to three strange places fall:
From Hull, from Hallifax, from Hell, 'tis thus,
From all these three Good Lord deliver us.[4]
This praying proverb's meaning to set downe,
Men doe not wish deliverance from the towne:
The townes nam'd Kingstone, Huls the furious river
And from Hulls dangers, I say, Lord deliver.
At Hallifax,[5] the law so sharpe doth deale,

1 This was done by cutting the sea-defence banks along the Humber.
2 The scheme was begun in 1613, and remained partly a private enterprise until 1765.
3 A Londoner, one of the three original proprietors of the waterworks. 'He built another faire water-worke at Yorke, of free-stone, which doth the city exceeding service.' [Taylor] *Maultby*, 1630.
4 Proverb incorporated by Taylor into the title of his 1639 journey, pp. 215-47. It may have begun as a vagrant's mock prayer, and 'Hell and' may be a corruption of Elland, a chapelry of Halifax.
5 Beheading could result from a felony worth thirteen pence half-penny or

That whoso more then 13. pence doth steale,
They have a Jynn that wondrous quicke and well,
Sends thieves all headlesse unto Heav'n or Hell.
From Hell each man sayes, Lord deliver me,[1]
Because from Hell can no redemption be:
Men may escape from Hull and Hallifax,
But sure in Hell there is a heavier tax,
Let each one for themselves in this agree,
And pray, from Hell good Lord deliver me.
The proverbe and the prayer expounded plaine,
Now to the orders of the towne againe:
I thinke it merites praise for government,
More then all townes in Britaines continent,
As first their charity doth much appeare,
They for the poore have so provided[2] there,
That if a man should walke from morne till night,
He shall not see one begger; nor a mite[3]
Or any thing shall be demaunded ever,
But every one there doth their best endevour
To make the idle worke, and to relieve
Those that are olde and past, or sicknes grieve.
All poore mens children have a house most fit[4]
Whereas they sowe, and spin, and card, and knit,
Where all of them have something still to doe,
As their capacities will reach unto,
So that no idle person, olde or young
Within the towne doth harbour or belong.
It yearely costs five hundred pounds besides,
To fence the towne, from Hull and Humbers tides,

more, according to Harrison. The engine of execution is described in *Part of this Summers Travels*, pp. 234-5.
1 Part of the Litany in the Book of Common Prayer.
2 'Marke, for all is true.' [Taylor]
3 a very small coin, less than a farthing.
4 Charity Hall, the corporation workhouse in Whitefriargate. It was first recorded in 1594.

For stakes, for bavins,[1] timber, stones, and piles,
All which are brought by water many miles,
For workmens labour, and a world of things
Which on the towne excessive charges brings.
All which with perill, industry and sweat,
They from the bowels of the ocean get.
They have a Bridewell,[2] and an exc'lent skill
To make some people worke against their will:
And there they have their lodging and their meate,
Cleane whips, and every thing exceeding neate,
And thus with faire or foule meanes alwayes, they
Give idle persons little time to play.
Besides, for every sea or marine cause
They have a house of Trinity,[3] whose lawes
And orders doe confirme, or else reforme
That which is right, or that which wrongs deforme.
It is a comely built well ordred place,
But that which most of all the house doth grace,
Are roomes for widdowes who are olde and poore,
And have bin wives to marriners before.
They are for house-roome, foode, or lodging, or
For firing,[4] Christianly provided for,
And as some dye, some doe their places win,
As one goes out, another doth come in.
Should I in all things give the towne it's due,
Some fooles would say I flatter'd, writ[5] untrue:
Or that I partiall in my writings were,
Because they made me welcome, and good cheere:
But for all those that have such thoughts of mee,

1 faggots of brushwood.
2 Hull gaol, sometimes known as the Guildhall Tower, stood in Market Place next to the Guildhall. It was demolished c.1790.
3 Important charitable foundation, established 1369, which became a shipman's guild and harbour authority. The almshouses were rebuilt in 1752.
4 fuel.
5 *spake*, 1630.

I rather wish that them I hang'd may see,
Then that they justly could report, that I
Did rime for victuals, hunger to supply.
Or that my Muse, or working braines should beate,
To flatter, fawne, or lye, for drinke or meate:
Let trencher-poets[1] scrape, for such base vailes,[2]
I'le take an oare in hand when writing failes;
And 'twixt the boate and pen, I make no doubt,
But I shall shift to picke a living out,
Without base flatt'ry, or false coyned words
To mowldy madames, or unworthy lords;
Or whatsoe're degree, or townes, or nations
I ever did, and still will scorne such fashions.
Hearesay,[3] sometimes upon a lye may light,
But what I see and know, I dare to write.
Mine eyes did view before my pen set downe,
These things that I have written of this towne.
A new built custome-house, a faire towne hall,
For solemne meetings, or a festivall:
A maior, twelve aldermen, one shriefe, recorder,
A towne-clarke, altogether in one order,
And uniformity doe governe so,
They neede not flatter friend, or feare a foe,
A sword, a cap of maintainance, a mace
Great, and well guilt, to doe the towne more grace:
Are borne before the maior, and aldermen,
And on festivities, or high dayes then
Those maiestrates their scarlet gownes doe weare,
And have six sergeants to attend each yeare.
Now let men say what towne in England is,
That truly can compare it selfe with this:
For scituation, strength and government,
For charity, for plenty, for content,
For state? and one thing more I there was told,

1 poets who write for a patron in order to be invited to dine at his table.
2 perquisites.
3 'I write not by heare-say.' [Taylor]

Not one recusant, all the towne doth hold,
Nor (as they say) there's not a Puritan,
Or any nose-wise foole Precissian,[1]
But great and small, with one consent and will,
Obay his Majesties injunctions still.
They say that once therein two sisters dwelt,
Which inwardly the prick of conscience felt,
They came to London (having wherewithall)
To buy two Bybles, all Canonicall,
Th' Apocripha[2] did put them in some doubt,
And therefore both their bookes were bound without,
Except those two, I ne're did heare of any
At Hull, though many places have too many.
But as one scabbed sheepe[3] a flock may marre,
So there's one man, whose nose did stand a jarre:
Talk'd very scurvily, and look'd ascue,
Because I in a worthy townes-mans pue
Was plac'd at Church, when (God knowes I ne're thought
To sit there, I was by the owner brought.
This squire of low degree, displeased than,
Said, I at most was but a water-man.
And that they such great kindnesse setting forth,
Made more a'th flesh,[4] then e're the broth was worth:
Which I confesse, but yet I answere make,
'Twas more then I with manners could forsake:
He sure is some high minded Pharisie,
Or else infected with their heresie,
And must be set downe in their catalogues,
They lov'd the highest seates in sinagogues.

1 a conceited Puritan.
2 The books of the Apocrypha were included in the 1611 Authorized Version of the Bible, but were disliked by Puritans, who declared them not to be inspired scripture in 1646-7.
3 A popular medieval and later proverb, first recorded in the satires of the Roman poet Juvenal.
4 Apparently a variant of the proverb (not recorded until 1628), ill flesh never made good broth.

And so (perhaps) doth he, for aught I know
He may be mounted when I sit below:
But let him not a water-man despise,
For from the water he himselfe did rise,
And windes and water both on him have smil'd
Else, the great marchant he had ne're beene stil'd:
His character I finely will contrive,
He's scornfull proud, and tatling[1] talkative:
A great ingrosser[2] of strange speech and newes,
And one that would sit in the highest pues,
But bate an ace,[3] he'le hardly winne the game,
And if I list, I could rake out[4] his name.
Thanks Mr Maior, for my bacon gammon,
Thankes Roger Parker for my small fresh sammon,
'Twas ex'lent good, and more the truth to tell ye,
Boyl'd with a fine plum-pudding in the belly.
The sixth of August, well accompanide
With best of townes-men to the waters side,
There did I take my leave, and to my ship
I with my drum and colours quickly skip.
The one did dub a dub and rumble,[5] brave
The ensigne in the ayre did play and wave:
I launch'd, supposing all things had beene done,
Bownce, from the block-house, quoth a roaring gun.
And waving hats on both sides, with content
I cride Adiew, adiew, and thence we went.
Up Humbers flood that then amaine did swell,
Windes calme, and water quiet as a well:
We rowed to Owse, with all our force and might,

1 *talking*, 1630.
2 profiteering monopolist.
3 make a very slight adjustment. The expression was sometimes used to convey incredulity.
4 'But I was ever better with forks to scatter, then with rakes to gather, therefore I would not have the townes-men to mistake chalke for cheese, or Robert for Richard.' [Taylor]
5 onomatopoeia for drum-beating.

To Cawood[1] where we well were lodg'd all night.
The morrow, when as Phoebus gan to smile,
I forwards set to Yorke eight little mile:
But two miles short of Yorke I landed than,
To see that reverend metropolitan,[2]
That watchfull shepheard, that with care doth keepe,
Th' infernall wolfe, from Heav'ns supernall sheepe:
The painefull[3] preacher, that most free almes-giver,
That though he live long, is too short a liver:
That man, whose age the poore doe all lament,
All knowing, when his pilgrimage is spent,
When earth to earth returnes, as Natures debter,
They feare the proverbe, seldome comes the better.
His doctrine and example, speake his due,
And what all people sayes, must needes be true.
In duty I most humbly thanke his grace,
He at his table made me have a place,
And meate and drinke, and gold he gave me there,
Whilst all my crue it'h hall were fill'd with cheere:
So having din'd, from thence we quickly past
Through Owse strong bridge, to Yorke faire citie last,
Our drowning scap'd, more danger was ensuing,
'Twas size time there, and hanging was a brewing;
But had our faults beene ne're so capitall,
We at the vintners barre[4] durst answere all.
Then to the good Lord Maior I went, and told
What labour, and what dangers manifold,
My fellow and my selfe had past at seas,
And if it might his noble lordship please,
The boat that did from London thither swim
With us, in duty we would give to him.

1 north-west of Selby, where the archbishops of York had a palace.
2 'At Bishopsthorpe, wher the right reverend father in God, Toby Mathew archbishop of Yorke, his grace, did make mee welcome.' [Taylor] Tobias Matthew (1546-1628), archbishop of York from 1606.
3 painstaking.
4 equivalent, in a tavern or wineshop, of a modern pub bar.

His lordship pawsing, with a reverend hum,
My friend (quoth he) to morrow morning come,
In the meane space I'le of the matter thinke,
And so he bad me to goe neere and drinke.
I dranke a cup of clarret and some beere,
And sure (for aught I know) he keepes[1] good cheere.
I gave his lordship in red guilded leather,
A well bound booke of all my workes together,
Which he did take.[2]
There in the citie were some men of note,
That gladly would give money for our boat:
But all this while good manners bad us stay,
To have my good Lord Maiors yea, or nay.
But after long demurring of the matter,[3]
He well was pleas'd to see her on the water,
And then my men rowde halfe an houre or more,
Whilst he stood viewing her upon the shore.
They bore his lordships children in her there,
And many others, as she well could beare.
At which his honour was exceeding merry,
Saying it was a pretty nimble wherry:
But when my men had taken all this paines,
Into their eyes they might have put their gaines.
Unto his shop he did perambulate,[4]
And there amongst his barres of iron sate.
I ask'd him if he would our boat forgoe,
Or have her, and his lordship answer'd, no.
I tooke him at his word, and said God buye,
And gladly with my boate away went I.

1   'There is some oddes betweene keeping and spending.' [Taylor]
2   'Heere I make a full point, for I received not a point in exchange.' [Taylor]
3   'I thought it my duty (being wee had come a dangerous voyage) to offer our boat to the chiefe maiestrate. For why should not my boat be as good a monument, as Tom Coriats everlasting overtrampling land-conquering shooes, thought I?' [Taylor] Coryate nailed up his buskins in Odcombe church porch.
4   'And forgat to say, I thank you good fellowes.' [Taylor]

I sold the boat, as I suppos'd most meete,
To honest Mr. Kayes;[1] in Cunny streete:[2]
He entertain'd me well, for which I thanke him,
And gratefully amongst my friends I'le ranke him.
My kinde remembrance here I put in paper,
To worthy Mr. Hemsworth there, a draper,
Amongst the rest he's one that I must thanke,
With his good wife, and honest brother Franke.
Now for the citie:[3] 'Tis of state and port,
Where emperors and kings have kept their court,
989. yeare, the foundation
Was layde, before our Saviours incarnation,
By Ebrank[4] who a temple there did reare,
And plac'd a Flammin[5] to Diana there,
But when King Lucius here the scepter swayde,
The idols levell with the ground were layde,
Then Eleutherius, Romes high bishop plac'd,
An Archbishop at Yorke, with tytles grac'd.
Then after Christ, 627.
Was Edwin[6] baptiz'd by the grace of heaven,
He pluck'd the Minster downe, that then was wood,
And made it stone, a deede both great and good.
The citie oft hath knowne the chaunce of warres,
Of cruell forraigne, and of home-bred jarres.
And those that further please thereof to read,
May turne the volumes of great Hollinshead.
'Tis large, 'tis pleasant and magnificent,
The Norths most fertile famous ornament:[7]

1 'A substantiall worthy citizen, who hath beene shriefe of Yorke, and now keeps the George in Cunny Streete.' [Taylor]
2 Coney Street stills exists, but it formerly included Spurriergate and Lendal.
3 Taylor gives Holinshed as his authority; much of the legendary material originates with Geoffrey of Monmouth.
4 'Ebrank was the 5. K. of Britaine after Brute.' [Taylor]
5 'An ArchFlammin which was as an idolatrous high priest to Diana.' [Taylor]
6 'Edwin and his whole family were baptized on Easter day the 12. of Aprill 627 ['6 7', 1630].' [Taylor]
7 'Yorkshire the greatest shire in England, and 308 miles about. Speed.'

'Tis rich and populous, and hath indeede
No want of any thing to serve their neede,
Abundance doth that noble citie make
Much abler to bestow, then neede to take.
So farewell Yorke, the tenth of August then
Away came I for London with my men.
To dinner I to Pomfret[1] quickly rode,
Where good hote venson stay'd for my abode,
I thanke the worshipfull George Shillito,
He fill'd my men and me, and let us goe.
There did I well view over twice or thrice,
A strong, a faire, and aunceint edifice:[2]
Reedifide, where it was ruin' d most,
At th' high and hopefull Prince of Wales[3] his cost.
I saw the roome where Exton[4] and his rowt
Of traytours, royall Richards[5] braines beat out:
And if that king did strive so many blowes,
As hacks and hewes upon one pillar showes,
There are one hundred slashes, he withstood,
Before the villaines shed his kingly blood.
From Pomfret then, unto my noble friend,
Sir Robert Swift[6] at Doncaster we wend,
An ancient knight, of a most generous spirit,
Who made me welcome farre beyond my merit.

    [Taylor]. There is no textual mark to show on what line this footnote depends.
1 Pontefract, West Riding.
2 'Pomfret Castle.' [Taylor] There is no textual mark to show on what line this footnote depends. Pontefract Castle underwent three sieges during the civil war, and was slighted in 1649.
3 'Prince Charles.' [Taylor]
4 'Sir Peirce of Exton knight.' [Taylor] Richard II died in confinement at Pontefract in 1400, but probably not at the violent hands of the legendary Sir Piers of Exton.
5 'King Richard the second murdered there.' [Taylor] There is no textual mark to show on what line this footnote depends.
6 of Streethorpe (now Edenthorpe), north-east of Doncaster, royal official in Hatfield Chase, and perhaps the Robert Swift (1568-1625) who was high sheriff of Yorkshire.

From thence by Newarke, I to Stamford past,
And so in time to London at the last.
Where[1] friends and neighbours, all with loving harts,
Did welcome me with pottles,[2] pintes, and quarts.
Which made my Muse more glib, and blyth to tell
This story of my voyage. So farewell.

An Epilogue.

Thus have I brought to end a worke of paine,
I wish it may requite me with some gaine:
For well I wote[3] the dangers where I ventered,
No full bag'd man[4] would ever durst have entered:
But having further shores for to discover
Hereafter, now my pen doth here give over.

FINIS.

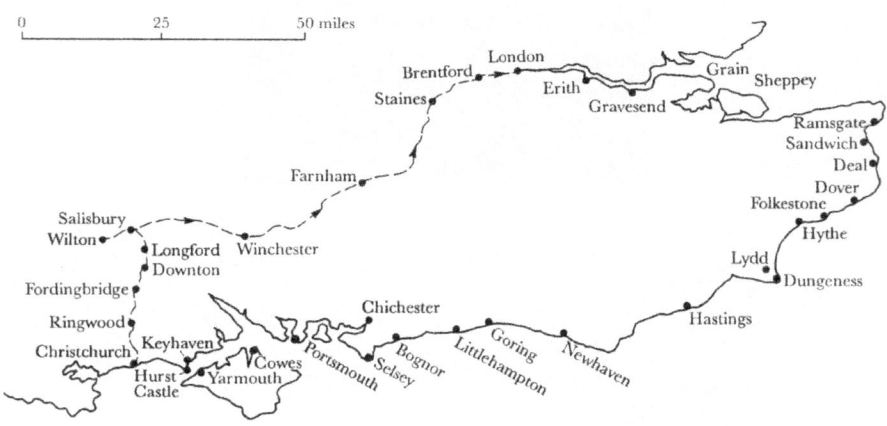

A New Discovery by Sea ... to Salisbury

1 *With*, 1630.
2 half-gallons.
3 knew.
4 presumably 'with full bags', therefore wealthy.

A NEW DISCOVERY BY SEA, WITH A WHERRY FROM LONDON TO SALISBURY

A NEW DISCOVERY BY SEA, the following (1623) summer's expedition to Salisbury, has many affinities with the York voyage. The journey was undertaken in a wherry, containing Taylor and four crew (including two Salisbury natives, Gregory Bastable and Thomas Estman), sailing at first around the coast, and then by river. There were dangerous storms, a repetition of the Cromer incident (at Goring, now part of Worthing) when they were arrested on suspicion of piracy, and, by contrast, there were occasions when Taylor was allowed to hob-nob with his betters, naval officers at Portsmouth, with Sir Edward Gorges at Longford Castle, and with the civic fathers of Salisbury. At Salisbury, just as at York, the boat is disposed of, and the adventurers' return journey by road is cursorily disposed of in a few lines, with merely a few disparaging lines about Salisbury's rival, Winchester (Taylor knew how to ingratiate himself with his chosen audience)!

Like the York trip, too, this was not a sponsorship journey, but it had a serious purpose. It had been suggested by Bastable, who clearly shared Taylor's advocacy of water over land travel. In the whole of England, the argument is here advanced, 'there is not any one towne or citie which hath a navigable river at it, that is poore, nor scarce any that are rich which want a river with the benefits of boates'. Salisbury, formerly a major city but now beset by economic and social difficulties, lay on an important river (the Christchurch Avon) which could readily, in Taylor's and Estman's view, be made navigable, and so restore Salisbury's fortunes. By demonstrating that the river could be navigated, and by highlighting the obstructions, Taylor felt that he might persuade the mayor and aldermen to initiate an improvement scheme.

In addition to describing the journey itself, therefore, the pamphlet includes a long lecture-cum-sermon, phrased (however distasteful Taylor found it to write) to appeal to the Puritan ruling elite in Salisbury, about the potential benefits of river navigation. It is an illuminating contribution to a debate about urban decay, social upheaval and inland trade in Jacobean

England, which struck a chord at Salisbury, and which Taylor was to repeat eighteen years later, in 1641, when visiting his native Gloucester.

As we have come to expect in Taylor's writing, alongside the serious purpose there are some side-shows. The account of this voyage is unusually full in describing the Thames below London. The pillar at 'Cuckolds Haven', he noticed as he sailed past, was out of repair, and he spends fifty lines of verse on and around a favourite subject, cuckoldry. He must have written this passage during the journey, because on his return he found that it was obsolete -- Greenwich benefactors had repaired the pillar during his absence. The gardens of Wilton House held a particular attraction for him (he was to visit and describe them again towards the end of his life, during his 1649 journey, p. 307). So taken is he with the skill of their architect, Adrian Gilbert, that he composes a sonnet about them and anagrams on Gilbert's name. There is also a comic episode in the shallows off Sandwich, where the crew encounter a merman, whom Taylor addresses with high-falutin classical oratory, only to discover that he is a Kentish fisherman looking for whelks.

After being feted at Salisbury Taylor returned to London to discover that he was believed drowned at sea, to the relief of those who still owed him money. He reissued his 'kicksey-winsey' against the debtors, titling it The Scourge of Basenesse; *in it he vowed never again to chance his life, 'adventuring any more dangerous voyages to sea, with wherries, or any extraordinary meanes'. It was one promise which he was to keep. The remaining journeys were all by road or river.*

[28th July - 23rd August, 1623. Text derived from 1623 publication (copy Bodleian Arch. A I.20 = STC microfilm 1118), some readings taken from 1630 All the Workes...*]*

A New Discovery by Sea, with a wherry from London to Salisbury. or
A voyage to the West,
The worst, or the best.
That e're was exprest.
      By John Taylor

London, Printed by Edw: Allde for the author. 1623.

To the nobilitie, gentrie, and communaltie, who are inhabitants, or well-willers to the welfare of the citie of Salisbury, and county of Wiltshire.

Right honourable, worshipfull, and loving country-men, I have named my booke and voyage, The Worst, or the Best, which I ever undertooke and finished, and it lyes in your pleasures, to make it which you please; I am sure for toyle, travaile, and danger, as yet I never had a worse, or a more difficult passage, which the ensuing discourse will truly testifie; yet all those perils past I shall accompt as pleasures, if my infallible reasons may move or perswade you to cleere your river, and make it navigable from the sea to your citie; I have in part touched what the proffit and commodities of it will be unto you, and I have briefly shewed the inconveniences which you have through the want of it: I have also declared, that the maine intent or scope of my comming unto you with a wherry; was, to see what lets or impediments were the hinderances unto so good and beneficiall a worke. All which I have (according to my simple survey, and weake capacity) set downe, which with the merrines of my most hazardous sea-progresse, I humbly dedicate to your noble, worshipfull and worthy acceptances, ever acknowledging[1] my selfe and my labour in your services to be commanded in all dutie. John Taylor.

A DISCOVERY BY SEA, FROM LONDON TO SALISBURY.

As our accompt in almanacks agree,
The yeare cal'd sixteen hundred twenty three:
That Julyes twenty eight, two houres past dinner,
We with our wherry, and five men within her,
Along the christall Thames did cut and curry,[2]
Betwixt the counties, Middlesex and Surry:
Whilst thousands gaz'd, we past the bridge with wo'der,
Where fooles and wise men goe above and under.
We thus our voyage bravely did begin
Downe by S. Katherines,[3] where the priest fell in,

1 1630 (*acknowledgling*, 1623).
2 scurry.
3 Royal Foundation of St Katherine's Hospital, and St Katherine's Stairs, east of the Tower of London.

By Wapping, where as hang'd drownd pirats dye;[1]
(Or else such rats,[2] I thinke as would eate pie.)
And passing further, I at first observ'd
That Cuckolds-Haven[3] was but badly serv'd,
For there old Tyme, had such confusion wrought,
That of that ancient place remained nought.
No monumentall memorable horne,
Or tree or poste, which hath those trophees born,
Was left, whereby posteritie may know
Where theire forefathers crests did growe,[4] or show.
Which put into a maze[5] my musing Muse,
Both at the worlds neglect, and times abuse,
That that stout pillar, to oblivions pit
Should fall, whereon *Plus ultra* might be writ,[6]
That such a marke of reverend note should lye
Forgot, and hid, in blacke obscurity,
Especially, when men of every sort
Of countries, cities, warlike campes or court,
Unto that tree are plaintiffs or defendants,
Whose loves,[7] or feares, are fellowes, or atendants:
Of all estates, this haven hath some partakers
By lot, some cuckolds, and some cuckold-makers.
And can they all so much forgetfull be

1 Pirates were hanged at the low-water mark at Wapping and their bodies left for three tides to flow over them.
2 'Any rat that eates pye, is a pyrat.' [Taylor]
3 'When I past down the river, there was not any post or horne there, but since it is most worthily repaired.' [Taylor] Cuckold's Point, below Rotherhithe church on the south bank at the beginning of Limehouse Reach. It was so called from a tradition that King John seduced a miller's wife there, and recompensed him by granting an annual 'horn fair'.
4 One explanation for the attribution of horns to cuckolds is that the spurs of castrated cocks were grafted to their excised combs, where they grew. Hence the implication that a cuckold must be sexually defective.
5 bewilderment.
6 Latin, literally 'more beyond'. *Ne plus ultra* 'so far and no further' was the royal motto of Spain, but *Ne* was removed after the discovery of America.
7 'All estates or degrees doe either love or feare this haven.' [Taylor]

Unto that ancient, and renowned tree,
That hath so many ages stood erected,
And by such store of patrones beene protected,
And now ingloriously to lye unseene
As if it were not, or had never beene?
Is lechery wax'd scarce, is bawdery scant,
Is there of whores, or cuckolds any want?
Are whore-masters decaide, are all bawdes dead,
Are panders, pimps, and apple-squires,[1] all fled?
No surely, for the surgeons can declare
That Venus warres, more hot then Marses are.
Why then, for shame this worthy port maintaine,
Let's have our tree, and hornes set up againe:
That passengers[2] may shew obedience to it,
In putting off their hats, and homage doe it.
Let not the cornucopiaes[3] of our land,
Unsightly and unseene neglected stand:
I know it were in vaine for me to call,
That you should raise some famous hospitall,
Some free-schole, or some almeshouse for the poore,
That might encrease good deeds and ope heav'ns dore
'Tis no taxation great, or no collection
Which I doe speake of, for this great erection,
For if it were, mens goodnesses, I know,
Would prove exceeding barren, dull, and slow:
A post and hornes,[4] will build it firme and stable,
Which charge to beare, there's many a begger able;
The place is ancient, of respect most famous,
The want of due regard to it doth shame us,
For Cuckolds Haven, my request is still,
And so I leave the reader to his will.
But holla Muse, no longer be offended,
'Tis worthily repair'd, and bravely mended,

1 prostitute's attendants.
2 passers-by.
3 horns of plenty, pun on the abundance of cuckold's horns.
4 a pair of horns were still fixed on the column there as late as 1840.

For which great meritorious worke, my pen
Shall give the glory unto Greenwich[1] men.
It was their onely cost, they were the actors
Without the helpe of other benefactors,
For which my pen their praises here adornes,
As they have beautified the hav'n with hornes.
From thence to Debtford[2] we amaine were driven,
Whereas an anker unto me was given
With parting pintes, and quarts for our farewell
We tooke our leaves, and so to Greenwich fell.
There shaking hands, adiews, and drinkings store
We tooke our ship againe, and left the shore.
Then downe to Erith, 'gainst the tyde we went
Next London, greatest mayor towne in Kent
Or Christendome, and I aprove it can,
That there the mayor was a waterman,
Who governes, rules, and reignes sufficiently,
And was the image of authority:
With him we had cheap reck'nings and good cheere,
And nothing but his friendship we thought deare.
But thence we rows'd our selves and cast off sleepe
before the day-light did begin to peepe.
The tyde by Gravesend swiftly did us bring
Before the mounting larke began to sing,
And e're we came to Lee,[3] with speedy pace
The sun gan rise with most suspicious face,
Of soule foreboding weather, purple, red,
His radient tincture, east, northeast o'respread,
And as our oares thus downe the river pul'd,
Oft with a fowling-peece[4] the gulls we gull'd,
For why, the master gunner[5] of our ship,

1   *Greenwitch*, 1630.
2   Deptford, Kent, now London.
3   Leigh on Sea, Essex, near Southend.
4   gun for killing wildfowl.
5   'His name is Arthur Bray, a waterman of Lambeth, and a good markman.' [Taylor]

Let no occasion or advantage slip,
But charg'd and discharg'd, shot, and shot againe,
And scarce in twenty times shot once in vaine.
Foule was the weather, yet thus much Ile say
If 't had beene faire, fowle was our food that day.
Thus downe alongst the spacious coast of Kent
By Grane, and Sheppeies Ilands[1] downe we went,
We past the Nowre-head, and the sandie shore
Untill we came to th' east end of the Nowre,[2]
At last by Ramsgates peere we stiffly rowed
The winde and tyde, against us blowed and flowed,
Till neere unto the haven where Sandwich[3] stands,
We were enclosed with most dangerous sands.
There were we sowsd and slabberd,[4] wash'd and dash'd,
And gravell'd, that it made us halfe abash'd:[5]
We look'd and pry'd, and stared round about
From our apparant perils to get out,
For with a staffe, as we the depth did sound,
Foure miles from land, we almost were on ground.
At last (unlook'd for) on our larboord[6] side
A thing turmoyling in the sea we spide,
Like to a meareman;[7] wading as he did
All in the sea his neather parts were hid,
Whose brawney limbes, and rough neglected beard
And grim aspect, made halfe of us afeard,
And as he unto us his course did make
I courage tooke, and thus to him I spake.
Man, monster, fiend or fish, what e're[8] thou be

1 Isles of Grain and Sheppey, Kent.
2 The Nore is the sandbank at the Thames estuary between the Isle of Sheppey and the Essex coast at Shoeburyness.
3 *Sandwitch*, 1630.
4 slobbered, became thoroughly wet.
5 'We were five men and two of us were afraid two were not afraid, and I was halfe afraid.' [Taylor]
6 left hand side.
7 merman, male equivalent of a mermaid.
8 *what-e'r*, 1630.

That travelst here in Neptunes monarchy,
I charge thee by his dreadfull three-tin'd mace
Thou hurt not me or mine, in any case,
And if thou be'st produc'd of mortall kinde
Shew us some course, how we the way may finde
To deeper water, from these sands so shallow,
In which[1] thou seest our ship thus wash and wallow.
With that (he shrugging up his shoulders strong)
Spake (like a Christian) in the Kentish tongue,
Quoth he, Kinde sir, I am a fisherman
Who many yeares my living thus have wan
By wading in these sandy troublous[2] waters
For shrimps, wilks,[3] cockles, and such usefull matters,
And I will lead you, (with a course I'le keepe)
From out these dangerous shallowes to the deepe.
Then (by the nose) along he led our boate
Till (past the flatts)[4] our barke did bravely floate,
Our sea-horse, that had drawne us thus at large
I gave two groates unto, and did discharge.
Then in an houre and a halfe,[5] or little more,
We throgh the Downes[6] at Deale went safe on shore.
There did our hostesse dresse[7] the fowle we kill'd,
With which our hungry stomacks well we fill'd,
The morrow being Wednesday (breake of day)
We towards Dover took our weary way:
The churlish windes awak'd the seas high fury,
Which made us glad to land there, I assure yee.
Blinde Fortune did so happily contrive,
That we (as sound as bells) did safe arive

---

1 1630 (*I which*, 1623).
2 1630 (*troblous*, 1623).
3 whelks.
4 shallows.
5 1630 (*and a halfe*, 1623).
6 The Downs referred to the sea within the Goodwin Sands, off the Kent coast, and opposite Deal.
7 cook.

At Dover, where a man did ready stand
To give me entertainment by the hand.
A man of mettle, marke and note, long since
He graced was to lodge a gratious prince,
And now his speeches sum, and scope and pith
Is Jack and Tom, each one his cosin Smith,
That if with pleasant talke you please to warme ye
He is an host, much better then an army,
A goodly man, well fed, and corpulent
Fill'd like a bag-pudding[1] with good content,
A right good fellow, free of cap and legge,
Of complement, as full as any egge:
To speake of him, I know it is of folly,
He is a mortall foe to melancholly.
Mirth is his life and trade, and I thinke very
That he was got[2] when all the world was merry:
Health upon health, he doubled and redoubled,
Till his, and mine, and all our braines were troubled,
Unto our absent betters there we dranke;
Whom we are bound to love, they not to thank,
By us mine host could no great proffit reape
Our meate and lodging, was so good and cheape,
That to his praise thus much Ile truly tell,
He us'd us kindely every way and well.
And though my lines before are merry writ,
Whereere I meet him Ile acknowledge it.
To see the castle there I did desire,
And up the hill I softly did aspire,
Whereas it stands, impregnable in strength
Large in circumference, heigth, bredth, and length,
Built on a fertile plat[3] of ground, that they
Have yearely growing twenty loads of hay,
Great ordnance store, pasture for kine[4] and horses,

1 pudding boiled in a bag.
2 conceived.
3 plot of ground.
4 cattle.

That be it[1] well with truth and courage man'd,
Munition, victuall'd, then it can withstand
The powers of twenty Tamberlaines[2] (the Great)
Till in the end with shame they would retreat.
Tis govern'd by a grave and prudent Lord,[3]
Whose justice doth to each their right afford,
Whose worth (within the castle, and without)
The five ports, and the country all about,
The people with much love, doe still recite,
Because he makes the wrongers render right.
The kindnesse I received there was such,
That my remembrance cannot be too much.
I saw a gun thrice eight foot length of brasse,
And in a wheele I saw a comely asse
(Dance like a dogge) that's turning of a spit,
And draw as it were from the infernall pit,
(Whose deepe abisse is perpendicular)
One hundred fathome[4] (or well neere as farre)
So christaline, so cleere, and coole a water,
That will in summer make a mans teeth chatter,
And when to see it up, I there had stood,
I dranke thereof, and found it sweet and good.
So farewell castle, Dover, Dover peere,
Farewell Host Bradshaw,[5] thanks for my good cheere.
My bonny barke to sea was bound againe;
On Thursday morne, we launchd into the maine,
By Folstone,[6] and by Sangates[7] ancient castle,
Against the rugged waves, we tugge and wrastle

---

1 *That it be*, 1630.
2 Timur the Lame (1336-1405) was a Tartar warrior and emperor, whose mighty conquering exploits achieved epic fame.
3 'The right Ho: the Lo: Zouch, Lord Warden of the Cinque ports.' [Taylor] Edward la Zouche (c.1556-1625) was a patron of poets, including Ben Jonson.
4 In fact 380 ft. deep.
5 *Oast Bradshaw*, 1630.
6 Folkestone, Kent.
7 Sandgate, now the western suburb of Folkestone.

By Hyde, by Rumney, and by Rumney Marsh,
The tyde against us, and the winde blew harsh,
'Twixt Eolus and Neptune[1] was such strife,
That I n're felt worse weather in my life.
Tost and retost, retost and tost againe;
With rumbling, tumbling, on the rowling maine,
The boystrous breaking billowes curled locks
Impetuously did beate against the rockes,
The winde much like a horse whose wind is broke,
Blew thicke and short, that we were like to choake,
As it outragiously the billowes shaves
The gusts (like dust) blowne from the bryny waves,
And thus the windes and seas robustious gods
Fell by the eares[2] starke mad, at furious ods.
Our slender ship, turmoyld 'twixt shores and seas,
Aloft or lowe, as stormes and flawes[3] did please:
Sometimes upon a foaming mountaines top,
Whose heigth did seeme the heav'ns to underprop,
When straight to such profunditie she fell
As if she div'd into the deepest Hell,
The clowdes like ripe apostumes[4] burst and showr'd,
Their mattery watery substance, headlong powr'd;
Yet though all things were mutable and fickle
They all agreed to souse us in a pickle,
Of waters fresh and salt, from seas and skye,
Which[5] with our sweat joynd in triplicitie,
That looking each on other, there we saw
We neither were halfe stewd, nor yet halfe rawe,
But neither hot or cold, good flesh or fishes
For caniballs, we had beene ex'lent[6] dishes.
Bright Phoebus hid his golden head with feare,

1   figuratively of wind and wave.
2   began to fight.
3   gusts.
4   abscesses.
5   1630 (*Wihch*, 1623).
6   1630 (*ex'lents*, 1623).

Not daring to behold the dangers there,
Whilst in that straight or exigent[1] we stand,
We see and wish to land, yet durst not land,
Like rowling hills the billowes beate and roare
Against the melancholly beachie shore,
That if we landed, neither strength or wit
Could save our boate from being sunke or split.
To keepe the sea, sterne puffing Eols breath
Did threaten still to blow us all to death,
The waves amaine (unbid) oft boorded us,
Whilst we almost three houres beleaguerd thus
On every side with danger and distresse
Resolv'd to runne on shore at Dengie Nesse.[2]
There stands[3] some thirteene cottages together,
To shelter fishermen from winde and weather,
And there some people were as I suposd,
Although the dores and windowes all were closd:
I neere the land, into the sea soone leapt
To see what people those same houses kept,
I knockd and cald, at each, from house to house,
But found no forme of mankinde, man or mouse.[4]
This newes all sad, and comfortlesse and cold
Unto my company I straightwaies told,
Assuring them the best way I did thinke
Was to hale up the boate, although she sinke.
Resolved thus, we altogether please
To put her head to shore, her sterne to seas,
They leaping overboord amidst the billowes
We pluck'd her up (unsunke) like stout tall fellowes.
Thus being wet, from top to toe we strip'd
(except our shirts) and up and downe we skip'd,
Till winde and sunne our wants did well supply
And made our outsides, and our insides drie.

1   pressing need.
2   Dungeness, Kent.
3   *stand*, 1630.
4   'No dwelling within neere three miles of those cottages.' [Taylor]

Two miles from thence, a ragged town[1] there stood,
To which I went to buy some drinke and food:
Where kindely over reckon'd, well misus'd
Was, and with much courtesie abusde.
Mine hostess[2] did account it for no trouble,
For single fare to make my paiment double:
Yet did her minde and mine agree together
That I (once gone) would never more come thither.
The cabbins where our boate lay safe and well,
Belong'd to men which in this towne did dwell:
And one of them (I thanke him) lent us then
The key to o'pe his hospitable den,
A brazen kettle, and a pewter dish,
To serve our needs, and dresse our flesh and fish,
Then from the butchers we bought lambe and sheep
Beere from the alehouse, and a broome to sweepe
Our cottage, that for want of use was musty,
And most extreamly rusty-fusty-dusty.
There, two dayes space, we roast, and boyle, and broyle
And toyle, and moyle,[3] and keepe a noble coyle,[4]
For onely we kept open house alone,
And he that wanted beefe might have a stone.[5]
Our Grandam Earth (with beds) did al befriend us
And bountifully all our lengthes did lend us,
That laughing, or else lying downe[6] did make
Our backs and sides sore, and our ribs to ake.
On Saturday the windes did seeme to cease,
And brawling seas began to hold their peace,
When we (like tenants) beggerly and poore,
Decreed to leave the key beneath the doore,

---

1 'The towns name is Lydd, two miles from Rumney in Kent.' [Taylor]
2 *oastesse*, 1630.
3 labour.
4 i.e. coil, in the sense of 'bustle'.
5 cf. Matthew 7, verse 9, '... if his son ask bread, will he give him a stone?'
6 'Our beds were cables and ropes, every feather at the least 20. fatham long.' [Taylor]

But that our land-lord did that shift prevent
Who came in pudding time,[1] and tooke his rent,
And as the sunne, was from the ocean peeping
We launch'd to sea againe, and left house-keeping.
When presently we saw the drisling skyes
Gan powt and lowre,[2] and windes and seas gan rise,
Who each on other playd their parts so wilde
As if they meant not to be reconcilde,
The whilst we leape upon those liquid hills
Where porposes did shew their finns and gills,
Whilst we like various Fortunes tennis ball
At every stroake, were in the hazzard[3] all.
And thus by Rye, and Winchelsey[4] we past
By Fairleigh,[5] and those rockie cliffs at last.
Some two miles short of Hastings, we perceiv'd
The lee shore dangerous, and the billowes heav'd,
Which made us land (to scape the seas distresse)
Within a harbour,[6] almost harbourlesse,
(We give God thankes) amongst the rocks we hit,
Yet were we neither wash'd or sunk, or split.
Within a cottage nigh there dwels a weaver
Who entertain'd us, as the like was never,
No meat, no drinke, no lodging (but the floore)
No stoole to sit, no locke unto the doore,
No straw to make us litter in the night,
Nor any candlesticke to hold the light,
To which the owner bid us welcome still,
Good entertainment, though our cheare was ill.
The morrow when the sun with flushed face

---

1   literally, and figuratively, meaning a time when one is in luck. Pudding was traditionally served first, thus one had come in time for dinner.
2   began to pout and frown.
3   in tennis, the side of the court into which the ball is played.
4   'I walk'd to Winchelsey, where I thanke my couzin Mr. Collins, the mayor there, he made me kindely welcome.' [Taylor]
5   Fairlight, Sussex, east of Hastings. *Fairlegh*, 1630.
6   presumably near Ore.

In his diurnall[1] course began to trace,
The winde exceeding stiffe and strong and tough,
The seas outragious, and extreamely rough,
Our boate laid safe upon the Beachy sand
Whilst we to Hastings went or walk'd by land.
Much (to that towne) my thankfulnesse is bound,
Such undeserved kindnesse there I found.
Three nights we lay there, and three daies we spent
Most freely welcom'd, with much merriment.
Kinde Mr Mayor[2] his love above the rest;
Me and my crew, he did both feed and feast,
He sent us gold, and came himselfe to us;
My thankes are these, because his love was thus.
Mine host and hostesse Clayton both I thanke[3]
And all good fellowes there, I found so francke,[4]
That what they had, or what could there be got
They neither thought too heavy or too hot.
The windes and seas continued still their course
Inveterate seem'd their rage, untam'd their force,
Yet were we loath to linger and delay:
But once againe to venture and away.
Thus desperatly resolvd, twixt hope and doubt
Halfe sunke with launching, madly we went out,
At twelve a clocke[5] at noone, and by sun set
To Miching, or New Haven,[6] we did get.
There almost sunke (to save our boat at last)
Our selves into the shallow seas we cast:
And pluck'd her into safety to remaine
Till Friday that we put to sea againe.

1 daily.
2 'The mayors name was Mr. Richard Boyse, a gentleman whose laudable life, and honest government is much beloved and aprov'd.' [Taylor]
3 *thus I thanke*, 1630.
4 in sense of open.
5 1630 (*clorke*, 1623).
6 Miching or Meeching was the former name of Newhaven, used until the course of the Ouse was straightened in the 16th century.

Then mongst our old acquaintance (storms and flaws)
At every stroake neere deaths devouring jawes:
The weary daye we past through many feares,
And land at last quite sunke ore head and eares.
All dropping drie, like five poore rats halfe drownd
From succour farre, we halde the boate on ground:
Cast out our water, whilst we bravely drop'd,
And up and downe to drie ourselves we hop'd.
Thus we our weary pilgrimage did weare,
Expecting for the weather calme and cleare:
But stormes, flawes, windes, seas, tooke no minutes[1]
Continuall fiercely blowing, west southwest.
A towne call'd Goreing,[2] stood neere two miles wide
To which we went, and had our wants supplide:
There we reliev'd our selves (with good compassion)
With meate and lodging of the homely fashion.
To bed we went in hope of rest and ease,
But all beleaguer'd with an host of fleas:
Who in their furie nip'd and skip'd so hotly,
That all our skins were almost turn'd to motly.
The bloudy fight endur'd at least six houres,
When we (opprest with their encreasing powres)
Were glad to yeeld the honour of the day
Unto our foes, and rise and runne away.
The night before, a constable[3] there came,
Who ask'd my trade, my dwelling, and my name:
My businesse, and a troope of questions more,
And wherefore we did land upon that shore?
To whom I fram'd my answers true, and fit
(According to his plenteous want of wit)
But were my words all true, or if I lyde,
With neither I could get him satisfide.
He ask'd if we were pyrates? We said no,
(As if we had, we would have told him so.)

1 probably 'underwent no diminution'.
2 Goring, Sussex, now part of Worthing.
3 Asterisked in both 1623 and 1630 editions, but no note glosses it.

He said that lords sometimes would enterprise
T'escape, and leave the kingdome in disguise:
But I assur'd him on my honest word,
That I was no disguised knight or lord,
He told me then that I must goe sixe miles
T' a Justice there, Sir John, or else Sir Giles:
I told him I was loath to goe so farre,
And he tolde me, he would my journey barre.
Thus what with fleas, and with the severall prates[1]
Of th' officer, and his ass-ociates,[2]
We arose to goe, but fortune bad us stay:
The constable had stolne our oares away,
And borne them thence a quarter of a mile,
Quite through a lane, beyond a gate and stile,
And hid them there, to hinder my depart,
For which I wish'd him hang'd with all my hart.
A plowman (for us) found our oares againe,
Within a field well fill'd with barly graine:
Then madly gladly out to sea we thrust,
Gainst windes and stormes, and many a churlish gust:
By Kingston chappell, and by Rushington,
By little Hampton, and by Midleton,
To Bognors[3] fearefull rockes, which hidden lie
Two miles into the sea, some wet, some drie,
There we suppos'd our danger most of all,
If we on those remorcelesse rockes should fall,
But by th'Almighties mercy, and his might,
We row'd to Selsey, where we stay'd all night.
There, our necessity could have no law,
For want of beds we made good use of straw,
Till Sol, that olde continuall travailer[4]

1 1630 (*prat*, 1623).
2 *ass-sociats*, 1630.
3 Kingston (near Ferring, not Kingston by Sea near Shoreham: the church was lost to the sea); Rustington, Middleton on Sea; Bognor Regis. *Middleton*, 1630.
4 *traveller*, 1630.

From Thetis lap, gan mount his flaming car.
The weather kept it's course, and blow'd, and rag'd,
Without appearance it would e're be swag'd,[1]
Whilst we did passe those hills, and dales, and downes,
That had devour'd great ships, and swallow'd towns.
Thus after sixe or five houres toyle at least,
We past along by Wittering, West and East,
Upon the lee shore still the winde full south,
We came neere Chichesters faire havens mouth.
And being then halfe sunk, and all through wet,
More fear'd then hurt, we did the haven get.
Thus in that harbour we our course did frame
To Portsmouth, where on Monday morne we came.
Then to the Royall fleete we row'd abord,
Where much good welcome they did us afford.
To the Lord Generall,[2] first my thanks shall be,
His bounty did appeare in gold to me,
And every one abord the Prince[3] I found,
In sted of want, to make their loves abound,
Captaine Penrudduck there amongst the rest,
His love and bounty was to us exprest,
Which to requite, my thankfulnes I'le showe,
And that I'le ever pay, and ever owe.
On Tuesday morning we with maine and might,
From Portsmouth crost unto the Ile of Wight:
By Cowes stout castle, we to Yarmouth hasted,
And still the windes and seas fierce fury lasted.
On Wedn'sday we to Hursts strong castle[4] crost,
Most dangerously sowsd, turmoyl'd and tost:
Good harbour there we found, and nothing deere,

1 assuaged.
2 Francis Manners, 6th earl of Rutland (1578-1632).
3 warship built in 1610, and in service until 1666; named after Henry, prince of Wales (James I's eldest son).
4 Hurst Castle, a Henrician defence on a spit of land projecting from Hampshire into the Solent.

I thank kinde M. Figge,[1] the porter there,
He shew'd us there a castle of defence
Most usefull, of a round circumference:
Of such command, that none can passe those seas
Unsunk, or spoil'd, except the castle please.
On Thursday we, our boat row'd, pull'd and hal'd
Unto a place which is Key Haven[2] call'd.
The winde still blowing, and the sea so high,
As if the lofty waves would kisse the skie,
That many times I wish'd with all my hart,
My selfe, my boat, and crewe, all in a cart;
Or any where to keepe us safe and dry,
The weather raged so outragiously.
For sure I thinke the memory of man
(Since windes and seas to blowe or flowe began)
Cannot remember so stormy weather
In such continuance, held so long together
For ten long weekes ere that, tis manifest,
The winde had blowne at sowth or west southwest,
And rais'd the seas: to shew each others power,
That all this space (calme weather) not one hower,
That whether we did goe by sunne or moone,
At any time, at midnight, or at noone:
If we did launch,[3] or if to land we set,
We still were sure to be halfe sunk, and wet.
Thus toyling of our weary time away,
That Thursday was our last long look'd for day:
For having past, with perill, and much paine,
And plow'd, and furrow'd, o're the dangerous[4] maine,
O're depths, and flats, and many a ragged rock,
We came to Christ-Church[5] hav'n at five a clock.
Thus God, in mercy, his just judgement sparing

1 'Mathew Figge, a right good fellow.' [Taylor]
2 south-west of Lymington, Hants.
3 *launce*, 1630.
4 1630 (*dangeroas*, 1623).
5 Christchurch, Hants.

(Gainst our presumption, over bold, and daring)
Who made us see his wonders in the deepe,
And that his power alone aloft did keepe,
Our weather-beaten boate above the waves,
Each moment gaping to be all our graves.
We sinking scap'd, then not to us, to Him
Be all the glory, for he caus'd us swim.
And for his mercy was so much extended
On me (whose temptings, had so farre offended)
Let me be made the scorne and scoffe of men,
If ever I attempt the like agen.
My love, my duty, and my thankfulnesse,
To Sir George Hastings[1] I must here expresse:
His deedes to me, I must requite in words,
No other payment, poore mens state affords.
With fruitlesse words, I pay him for his cost,
With thanks to Mr. Templeman mine host.
So leaving Christ-Church, and the haven there,
With such good friends as made us welcome cheere:
Some serious matter now I must compile,
And thus from verse to prose I change my stile.

God, who of his infinite wisedome made man, of his unmeasurable[2] mercy redeemed him, of his boundlesse bounty, immense power, and eternall eye of watchfull providence releeves, guards, and conserves him; It is necessary, that every man seriously consider and ponder these things, and in token of obedience and thankfulnesse say with David:[3] What shall I render, and the man having thus searched considerately, the causer of his being, then let him againe meditate for what cause[4] hee hath a being: indeede it may be objected that almost every thing hath a being, as stones have being, trees, hearbs, and plants, have being and life: Beasts. fowles, and fishes, have being, life, and sence: but to man is given a Being, life, sence, and reason, and after a mortall an immortall

1 Second son of the 4th earl of Huntingdon, a landowner in Christchurch.
2 *unmeasured*, 1630.
3 Psalm 116 verse 12.
4 'Men should consider why God hath given them a being in this life.' [Taylor]

ever-being; this consideration will make a man know that hee hath little part of himselfe, which hee may justly call his owne: his body is Gods, he made it; his soule is his, who bought it; his goods are but lent him, by him that will one day call him to a reckoning, for the well or ill disposing of them: so that man having nothing but what he hath received, and received nothing but what is to be imployed in the service of God, and consequently his Prince and Countrey, it is plainely to be perceived, that every man hath, the least share[1] or portion of himselfe to boast of.

I have written this preamble, not onely to enforme such as know not these things already; but also to such whose knowledge is, as it were fallen into a dead sleepe; who doe live as though there were no other being then here, and that their life and being was ordained onely of themselves, neither God, Prince, or Countrey, having no share or portion of them or of what they call theirs. But oh you inhabitants of Salisburie, I hope there are no such crawling cankerwormes,[2] or common-wealth caterpillers amongst you. Nay, I am assured of the contrary, that there are many, who (with religious piety, open hands, and relenting hearts) doe acknowledge that your goods are but lent in trust unto you,[3] and doe patiently beare the over-burthensome relieving of many hundreds of poore wretches, which (were it not for your charity) would perish in your streetes.

This being entred into my consideration, that your citie is so much overcharged[4] with poore, as having in three parishes neere 3000[5] besides decayed men a great many, and that those fewe which are of the wealthier sort, are continually overpressed with sustaining the wants of the needy, the citie being as it were at the last gaspe, the poore being like Pharaohs[6] leane kine, even ready to eate up the fat ones: I have made bold to write this treatise ensuing, both to entreat a constant perseverence in those who have begun to doe good workes, and an encouragement or animating of all others, who as yet seeme slowe in

---

1 'No man is owner of himselfe.' [Taylor]
2 synonym for caterpillar.
3 1630 (*yon*, 1623).
4 'Here is an honest course set downe for the inriching of your rich, and the relieving of your poore.' [Taylor]
5 Not a wild exaggeration; a local estimate in 1626 suggested 2,700.
6 Genesis 41 verse 20.

these good proceedings. And if any thing here written by me, be either impertinent, extravagant, rude, harsh, or over bold, I humbly entreate you to impute it rather to my want of judgement, learning, and capacity, then to any presumption, or want of love and duty to the citie and cause, which is hereafter handled.

It is sufficiently knowne that my intent and purpose at this time, was not to make any profit to my selfe upon any adventure (as it is deemed by many) by my passage from London to Salisbury with a wherry, but I was entreated by a waterman[1] which was borne in Salisbury, that I would beare him company for the discovery of the sands, flats, depthes, shoales, mills, and weares, which are impediments and lets, whereby the river is not navigable from Christ- Church, or the sea to Salisbury. Which after many dangerous gusts, and tempestuous stormes at sea, (which I have recited in verse before) it pleased God that at the last we entred the river, which in my opinion is as good a river, and with some charge may be made as passable as the River of Thames is upwards from Brentford to Windsor, or beyond it; the shallow places in it are not many, the mills neede not be removed, and as for the weares, no doubt but they may with conscience be compounded for.[2] By which meanes of navigation, the whole city and countrey would be relieved, loyterers turned into labourers, penurie into plenty, to the glory of God, the dignity and reputation of your citie, and the perpetuall worthy memory of all benefactors, and well-willers unto so noble a worke.

If you will but examine your owne knowledges, you shall finde that in the whole dominion of England, there is not any one towne or citie which hath a navigable river at it, that is poore, nor scarce any that are rich which want a river with the benefits of boates: The towne of Kingston upon Hull in Yorkshire, the river there was cut out of Humber, by mens labours 20. miles[3] up into the countrey, and what the wealth and estate of that towne is, (by the onely benefit of that

---

1 'His name is Gregory Bastable, and his ordinary place where he plyes, or attends his labour, is at the Temple, and there also plyes Thomas Estman another Wiltshire man, which went with me.' [Taylor]
2 compensated for.
3 Meaux Abbey in the 13th century diverted the course of the River Hull. Taylor had discovered this on the previous journey, p. 147, note 3.

river) it is not unknowne to thousands: but you men of Sarum[1] may see what a commodity navigation is, neerer hand; there is your neighbour Southampton on the one side, and your deere friend Poole on the other, are a payre of hansome looking-glasses for you, where you may see your want in their abundance, and your negligence in their industry.

God hath placed your being in a fertile soyle, in a fruitfull valley, environed round with corne, and as it were continually besieged with plenty: whilst you within (having so many poore amongst you) are rather lookers upon happinesse then enjoyers: moreover (by Gods appointment) Nature hath saved you the labour of cutting a river, for I thinke you have one there as olde as your citie ready made to your hands, if you will bee but industrious to amend those impediments in it, I dare undertake to be one of the 3. or 4. men which shall bring or carrie 16. or 20. tunnes of goods betwixt the sea and your citie; Now, with extreame toyle of men, horses and carts, your wood is brought to you 18. or 20. miles, whereby the poore which cannot reach the high prices of your fewell, are enforced to steale or starve in the winter, so that all your neere adjoyning woods are continually spoyled by them: which faults by the benefit of the river would be reformed, for the new Forrest standeth so neere to the water, that it is but cut the wood and put it into a boate, which shall bring as much to your citie as 20. carts, and fourescore horses: besides, by this river you might draw to you a trade of sea-coale,[2] which would enrich you, and helpe the plaine and inland townes and villages where no wood growes. And for the exportation of your corne from port to port, within our owne countrey, as it is well knowne what abundance of your barley is continually made into mault amongst you: which if you had cariage for it, might be brewed into beere, wherewith you might serve divers places with your beere, which is now served with your mault: besides cariages of brickes, tyles, stones, charcoales, and other necessaries, which is now carried at deere rates by horse or carts, which now you send in carts, or on horses backes, to Southampton, to Bristow,[3] and to many other places: so that the deerenesse of the cariages eates up all your commodities and profit, which discommodity may be avoyded, if your river be cleansed: and what man can tell what good in time may redownd to your citie from

1 abbreviated and alternative name for Salisbury.
2 coal brought by sea (i.e. mined), as opposed to charcoal.
3 Bristol.

the sea, by forraigne goods, which may be brought into Christ-Church haven by shipping? nor can it be truly imagined, what new and usefull profitable businesses may arise in time by this meanes.

Our forefathers and auncestors did in their lives time in former ages doe many worthy and memorable workes, but for all their industrie and cost, they did not (or could not) doe all; but as there was much done to our hands, so there was much left for us to doe, and very fitting it was that it should be so: for it is against common sence and reason our fathers should toyle in good workes like drudges, and wee spend our times loytring like drones: no, what they did was for our imitation. And withall, that wee should be leaders of our posterities by our examples into laudable endevours, as our progenitours hath before shewed us: we are their sonnes and offspring, wee have their shapes and figures, wee beare their names, we possesse their goods, we inherit their lands; we have materials of stones, timber, iron, and such necessaries which they had, (if not in greater abundance) and having all these, let us withall have their willing and liberall hearts, and there is no question to be made, but that our River of Avon will quickly be cleansed to the honest enriching of the rich, and the charitable relieving of the poore.

I am assured that there are many good men in the citie and county[1] of Wiltshire, and others of worth and good respect in this kingdome, who would willingly and bountifully assist this good work: but (like gossips neere a stile) they stand straining curtesie who shal go first: or the mice in the fable,[2] not one will adventure to hang the bell about the cats neck. So that if one good man would begin, it would be (like a health drank to some beloved prince at a great feast) pledged most heartily, and by Gods grace effected most happily.

You have already begun a charitable worke amongst you, I meane your common towne brew-house,[3] the profit of which you entend shall be wholy imployed for the supply of the poore and impotents which live in your citie: from which sort of people (being such a multitude) the brewers there have found their best custome: for no doubt but the meanest begger amongst you, is (in some sort) more valiant then the

1 1630 (*country*, 1623).
2 Popular fable, first recorded by Langland in *Piers Plowman*, c.1370.
3 the scheme, much as Taylor describes it, had only been agreed two months earlier, and was not yet implemented.

richest man: because the one dares to spend all he hath at the alehouse, so dares not the other; for the poore man drinks stifly to drive care away, and hath nothing to loose, and the rich man drinks moderatly, because he must beare a brain to look to what he hath. And of all trades in the world a brewer is the load-stone,[1] which drawes the customs of all functions unto it. It is the marke or upshot[2] of every mans ayme, and the bottomlesse whirlepoole that swallowes up the profits of rich and poore. The brewers art (like a wilde kestrell or unmand[3] hawke) flies at all games; or like a butlers box[4] at Christmasse, it is sure to win, whosoever looses: In a word, it rules and raignes (in some sort) as Augustus Caesar did, for it taxeth the whole earth.[5] Your innes and alehouses are brookes and rivers, and their clyents are small rills and springs, who all (very dutifully) doe pay their tributes to the boundlesse ocean of the brewhouse. For all the world knowes, that if men and women did drinke no more then sufficed Nature, or if it were but a little extraordinary now and then upon occasion, or by chance as you may terme it; if drinking were used in any reason, or any reason used in drinking, I pray yee what would become of the brewer then? Surely wee doe live in an age wherein the seaven deadly sinnes[6] are every mans trade and living. Pride is the maintainer of thousands, which would else perish; as mercers, taylers, embroyders,[7] silk-men, cutters, drawers, sempsters, laundresses, of which functions there are millions which would starve but for Madame Pride with her changeable fashions. Leachery, what a continuall crop of profit it yeelds, appeares by the gallant thriving, and

1 a magnet used as a compass.
2 the last shot in an archery match.
3 'uncontrolled by man'.
4 at Christmas dice-players put a portion of their winnings into a box for the butler; thus whatever the outcome of the game the butler was bound to be a winner.
5 Luke 2, verse 1.
6 'Some make a profit of quarelling, some picke their lyvings out of contentions and debate, some thrive and grow fat by gluttonie: many are bravely maintained by bribery, theft, cheating, roguery, and villany: but put all these together, and joyne to them all sorts of people else, and they all in generall are drinkers, and consequently the brewers clients and customers.' [Taylor]
7 *embroydrers*, 1630.

gawdy outsides of many he and she, private and publike sinners, both in citie and suburbs. Covetousnesse is embroidered with extortion, and warmely lined and furred with oppression. And though it be a devill, yet it is most idolatrously adored, honoured, and worshipped, by those simple sheepe-headed fooles, whom it hath undone and beggered. I could speake of other vices, how profitable they are to a commonwealth; but my invention is thirsty, and must have one carouse more at the brewhouse, who (as I take it) hath a greater share then any, in the gaines, which spring from the worlds abuses: for pride is maintained by the humble, yet one kinde of pride doth live and profit by another: leachery is supported by the cursed swarme of bawdes, panders, pimps, applesquires, whores, and knaves; and so every sinne lives and thrives by the members, agents, ministers, and clyents, which doe belong unto them: but drunkennesse playes at all; all trades, all qualities, all functions and callings can be drunke extemporie, not[1] at any great feast, or but at every ordinary[2] dinner or supper almost, when men are well satisfied with sufficiency, that then the mysterie of quaffing begins, with healths to many an unworthy person (who perhaps) would not give the price of the reckoning to save all them from hanging (which make themselves sicke with drinking such unthankfull healths) I my selfe have oftentimes dined or sup'd at a great mans boord, and when I have risen, the servants of the house have inforc'd me into the seller or buttry, where (in the way of kindenesse) they will make a mans belly like a sowse-tub,[3] and inforce me to drinke as if they had a commission under the devills great seale to murder men with drinking, with such a deale of complementall oratory,[4] *As, off with your cup, winde up your bottome,* Up with your taplash, and many more eloquent phrases, which Tully[5] or Demosthenes[6] never heard of; that in conclusion I am perswaded three dayes fasting would have beene more healthfull to me, then two houres feeding and swilling in that manner.

1 casually, unpremeditated. *ex tempore*: note, 1630.
2 a fixed-charge meal.
3 pickling-tub.
4 slang exhortations to drink up: 'winde' is a verb not a noun; 'taplash' is dregs. The 1630 edition has *lap* instead of *cup*.
5 Cicero, Roman orator and philosopher.
6 Greek orator.

If any man hang, drowne, stabbe, or by any violent meanes make away his life, the goods and lands of any such person, is forfeite[1] to the use of the King: and I see no reason but those which kill themselves with drinking, should be in the same estate, and be buryed in the highwayes, with a stake[2] drove through them: And if I had but a graunt of this suite, I would not doubt but that in seaven yeeres (if my charity would but agree with my wealth) I might erect almes-houses, free-schooles, mend highwaies, and make bridges; for I dare sweare, that a number (almost numberlesse) have confessed upon their death-beds, that at such and such a time, in such and such a place, they dranke so much which made them surfeit, of which surfeit they languished and dyed.[3] The maine benefit of these superfluous and man-slaughtering expences comes to the brewer, so that if a brewer be in any office, I hold him to be a very ingratefull man if he punish a drunkard: for every stiffe pot-valiant drunkard is a post, beame, or piller which holds up the brew-house: for as the barke is to the tree,[4] so is a good drinker to a brewer.

But you men of Salisbury, wisely perceiving how much evill to your citie, hath come by the abuse of good drinke, you would now worke by contraries, to drawe good for your poore out of these forepassed[5] and present evils: To drawe evill out of good, is devillish, but to worke or extract goodnesse out of what is evill is godly, and worthy to be pursued. The abuse of good drinke, and excessive drinking hath made many beggers amongst you, to the inriching of a few brewers, and now you would turne the world off from the barrels, as I would off from the coach-wheeles,[6] that the benefit of your new built towne brew-house might relieve many of those poore amongst you, who have formerly beene impoverished by the inriching of your towne-brewers. It is no doubt but they will oppose this good worke of yours, as the image-makers in Ephesus did Paul,

---

1 *are forfeite*, 1630. Suicide was regarded as a felony, self-murder, and a felon's goods were forfeit to the crown.
2 this remained the practice until 1823.
3 'Let these lines be considered if I lye or not.' [Taylor]
4 proverb, as near as the bark to the tree, recorded from 1580.
5 previous.
6 Taylor's pamphlet opposing the introduction of coaches, *The World runs on Wheels*, was published in 1623, the same year as this journey.

when hee preached against their idolatrous worshipping Diana;¹ but be not you discouraged: for Nehemiah (in time) did build the Temple, although Sanballat² and many other³ did oppose him: for as your intents are pious, so no doubt but God will make your events prosperous.

Now to turne from beere and ale to faire water, (your river I meane) which if it be clensed, then with the profit of your towne-brewhouse, and the commodity of the river, I thinke there will be scarce a begger or a loyterer to be found amongst you: I have written enough before concerning the benefit of it, and to encourage such as seeme slow towards so good a worke, which had it beenee in the Low-Countries, the industrious Dutch would not so long have neglected so beneficiall a blessing, witnesse their aboundance of navigable rivers, and ditches, which with the onely labour of men they have cut, and in most places, where never God or Nature made any river; and lately there is a river made navigable to St. Yeades⁴ in Huntington-shire, wherein stood seaven mills, as impediments in the way. And now the citie of Canterbury are cleering their river that boates may passe to and fro betwixt them and Sandwich haven: the like is also in hand at Leedes in Yorkeshire; Now, if neither former or present examples can move you, if your owne wants cannot inforce you, if assured proffit cannot perswade you, but that you will still be neglective and stupid, then am I sorry that I have written so much, to so little purpose, but my hopes are otherwaies; if all blinde, lame, and covetous excuses be laid aside, then those who are willing will be more willing, and those who are slacke or backward, will in some reasonable manner drawe forward: And there is the mouth of an uncharitable obiection which I must needs stop, which is an old one, and onely spoken by old men; for (say they) we are aged and stricken in yeares, and if we should lay out our moneys, or be at charges for the river, by the course of nature we shall not live to enjoy any proffit to requite our costs: this excuse is worse then Heathenish, and therefore it ill becomes a Christian; for as I wrote before, man was not created,

---

1 Acts 19, verses 23-41.
2 Sanballat's opposition to Nehemiah is the main theme of Nehemiah 2-6.
3 'Tobyah, Arabians, Amonites.' [Taylor]
4 The Ouse was made navigable from St Ives to St Neots during the 1620s; either town may be masquerading under this aberrant form of the place-name.

or had either the goods of minde, body, or Fortune bestowed on him by his Maker, but that he should have the least part of them himselfe, his God, Prince and Countrie, claiming (as their due) almost all which every man hath. The oldest man will purchase land, which is subiect to barrennesse, and many inconveniences, he will buy and build houses,, which are in danger of fire, and divers other casualties, he will adventure upon wares or goods at high prises, which to his losse may fall to lowe rates; he will bargaine for cattell and sheepe, who are incident to many diseases, as the rot, the murraine, and divers the like, and all this will he doe in hope to raise his state, and leave his heires rich; at his death perhaps (when hee can keepe his goods no longer, when in spight of his heart he must leave all) he will give a few gownes, and a little money to pious uses, a groce or two of penny loaves, and there's an end of him, so that there remaines no more memory of him.

But this good worke of your river is not subiect to barrennesse or sterilitie, but contrarily it will be a continuall harvest of plenty, it is not in danger of being consumed, or wasted, but it is assured of a perpetuall encrease. The names and memories of contributors towards it, shall be conserved in venerable and laudable remembrance, to the eternizing of their fames, the honour of their posterities, and the good example of succeeding times to imitate. Therefore you men of Salisbury, I entreate you in this case to be good to your selves. Or else you may say hereafter, If we had beene industrious we had beene happy: if we had not beene covetous, wee had beene rich.

Now, to returne to my travels and entertainements: as I passed up the river at the least 2000. swans like so many pilots swam in the deepest places before me, and shewed me the way: When I came to the towne of Ringwood (14 miles short of Salisburie) I there met with his Maiesties trumpeters, and there my fellows Mr. Thomas Underhill, and Mr. Richard Stocke, Mr. Thomas Ramsey, Mr. Randall Lloyd, with others, which I name not, did walke on the banke and gave me two most excelent[1] flourishes with their trumpets, for the which I thanke them in print, and by word of mouth. At last I came to a towne called Forthing Bridge,[2] where (not many dayes before) a grievous mischance hapned,

---

1 *two excellent*, 1630.
2 Fordingbridge, Hants.

for two men being swimming or washing in the river, a butcher passing over the bridge (with a mastiffe dogge with him) did cast a stone into the water and say a Duck, at which the dog leapd into the river and seasd upon one of the men and kild him, and the butcher leaping in after thinking to save the man, was also slaine by his owne dog, the third man also hardly escaping, but was likewise bitten by him.

From thence I passed further, to a place called Hale, where we were welcommed by the Right Worshipfull Sir Thomas Penrudduck Knight,[1] whom we carried there in our boate, and who I am assured will be a forward and a liberall benefactor towards cleering of the river.

So passing on our course by the villages of Burgate, Breamer, Chartford,[2] Downton and Stonelye,[3] we came at last to Langfoord,[4] where we were well entertained by the Right Honourable the Lord Edward Gorge,[5] (Lord barron of Dundalke, and Captaine of his Maiesties strong and defencible[6] castle of Hurst, in Hantshire) to whom in love and duty we profferd the gift of our tattered, windshaken and weatherbeaten boate, which (after our being at Salisbury, being but two miles from thence) his Lordship accepted. And though he knew she was almost unserviceable, yet his noble bounty was such, that he rewarded us with the price of a new boate. I had some conference with his honour concerning the impediments and clensing of the river, and I know he is most forwardly and worthily affected towards it, and no doubt if it be pursued, that then he will doe that which shall become a gentleman of his honourable calling and ranke.

So on the same Friday at night we came to Salisbury where we brought our boate through Fisherton Bridge, on the west side of the citie, taking our lodging at the signe of the Kings head[7] there, with mine host Richard Estman, whose brother Thomas, was one of

1   of Hale, c.1578-1637.
2   Breamore and Charford, Hants.
3   *Stonely*, 1630. Standlynch, Wilts., north of Downton.
4   Longford Castle, south-east of Salisbury.
5   Edward Gorges, c.1583-c.1650, created baron Dundalk in 1620. Longford Castle was built for his father, 1578-91.
6   *his strong and Ma'ties defencible*, 1630.
7   by Fisherton Bridge, demolished late-19th century; its replacement retains the name.

the watermen which came in the boate thither from London: on the morrow I with my company footed it two miles to Wilton, where at the Right Honourable the Earle of Pembrooks,[1] my Lord Chamberlaines house, I was most freely (and beyond my worth and merit) kindely welcommed, by the Right Worshipfull Sir Thomas Morgan Knight, with whom I dined, and by whose command I was shewed all or the most part of the admirable contrived roomes, in that excellent, and well built house, which roomes were all richly adorned with costly and sumptuous hangings; his Maiestie some few dayes before having dined there with most magnificent entertainment, as did expresse the love of so noble a house-keeper for so royall a guest: upon the sight of which house with the furniture, I wrote these following verses.

If wholsome ayre, earth, woods, and pleasant springs
Are elements, whereby a house is grac'd:
If strong and stately built, contentment brings,
Such is the house of Wilton, and so plac'd.
There Nature, Art, Art-Nature hath embrac'd;
Without, within, belowe, aloft compleate:
Delight and state, are there so enterlac'd
With rich content, which makes all good, and great
The hangings there, with histories repleate
Divine, profane, and morrall pleasures giving
With worke so lively, exquisite, and neate,
As if mans art, made mortall creatures living.
In briefe, there all things are compos'd so well,
Beyond my pen to write, or tongue to tell.

Then was I shewed a most faire and large armorie, with all manner of provision and furniture,[2] for pike, shot, bills, halberts, javelins, with other weapons and munition, which for goodnesse, number, and well-keeping, is not second to any noblemans in England: Afterwards I went to the stables,[3] and saw my lords great horses, whom I saw such and so good, that what my untutour'd pen cannot sufficiently commend,

1   William Herbert (1580-1630), 3rd earl of Pembroke.
2   1630 (*furnitue*, 1623).
3   The stables at this period adjoined Washern Grange, south-east of the house.

I am forced with silence to overpasse. But amongst the rest, the paines and industrie of an ancient gentleman Mr. Adrian Gilbert,[1] must not be forgotten, for there hath he (much to my lords cost and his owne paines) used such a deale of intricate setting, grafting, planting, inocculating,[2] rayling, hedging, plashing,[3] turning, winding, and returning circular, trianguler, quadranguler, orbiculer,[4] ovall, and every way curiously and chargeably conceited: There hath he made walkes, hedges, and arbours, of all manner of most delicate fruit trees, planting and placing them in such admirable artlike fashions, resembling both divine and morrall remembrances, as three arbours standing in a triangle, having each a recourse to a greater arbour in the midst, resembleth three in one, and one in three: and he hath there planted certain walkes and arbours all with fruit trees,[5] so pleasing and ravishing to the sense, that he calls it Paradise, in which he plaies the part of a true Adamist,[6] continually toyling and tilling. Moreover, he hath made his walkes most rarely round and spacious, one walke without another, (as the rindes of an onion are greatest without, and lesse towards the center) and withall, the hedges betwixt each walke are so thickly set, that one cannot see thorow from the one walke, who walkes in the other: that in conclusion, the worke seemes endlesse,[7] and I thinke that in England it is not to be fellowed,[8] or will in hast be followed. And in love which I beare to the memory of so industrious and ingenious a gentleman, I have written these following annagrams.

Adryan Gilbert, annagarams. Art redily began A breeding tryal.

1 Aubrey described him in *Brief Lives*, as an excellent chemist, 'operator' to the countess of Pembroke, a man of great parts, but the greatest buffoon in England.
2 a technique of grafting.
3 interweaving branches, as in hedge-laying.
4 circular or spherical.
5 'Not a tree stands there, but it beares one good fruit or other.' [Taylor]
6 Genesis 3, verse 17.
7 'A round worke is endlesse, having no end. I touch not the matchlesse adioyning wood and walkes of Rowlington here, whose praises co'sists in it selfe, my pen being insufficient.' [Taylor]
8 rivalled.

Art redily began a breeding tryal,
When she inspir'd this worthy gentleman:
For Natures eye, of him tooke full espiall,
And taught him Art, Art readily began,
That though Dame Nature, was his tuteresse, he,
Out-workes her, as his workes apparent be.

For Nature brings but earth, and seeds and plants,
Which Art, like taylers, cuts and puts in fashion:
As Nature rudely doth supply our wants,
Art is deformed Natures reformation.
So adryan Gilbert mendeth Natures features
By Art, that what she makes, doth seem his creatures.

Thus with my humble thankes to Sir Thomas Morgan, and my kinde remembrance to all the rest of my lords servants there, my legges and my labouring lynes returne againe to Salisbury, and from the next day (being Sunday) to Langford to my Lord Gorge his house, with whom I dined, and left my humble thanks for the reckoning. In briefe, my fruitlesse and worthy lip-labour, mixt with a deale of ayrie, and non substantiall matter I gave his lordship, and the like requitall I bestowed on the right worshipfull M. Thomas Squibb, mayor of Sarum, with M. Banes, M. John Ivy, M. Windover,[1] with all the rest; and more then thankes, and a gratefull remembrance of their honourable, worshipfull, and friendly favours, I know they expect not, and lesse then such a common duty as gratitude I must not, or cannot pay. To shut up all in few words, I know his maiesties pious inclination is so ample, that he will be graciously pleased with any of your laudable endevours for your welfare and commodity, if you take good and speedy advice, then no doubt but the effects will be according to your honest intendments.

So farewell, Salisbury, till we meete againe, which I hope will be one day: in the meane space I pray thee take this poore pamphlet as a loving pledge of my returne. Me thinks I see already, men, horses, carts, mattocks, shovels, spades, wheelebarrowes, handbarrowes, and baskets

---

1   Squibb, Robert Banes, John Ivie and William Windover were all prominent members of Salisbury's governing Puritan administration.

at worke for the clearing of your river: But if my thoughts doe deceive me, and my expectation faile, I shall ever hereafter give small credit to their intelligence. So once more, Salisbury I wish thee thankfully well to fare.

On Thursday the 21. of August I tooke Winchester in my way homewards; where I saw an ancient citie, like a body without a soule: and I know not the reason of it, but for aught which I perceived, there were almost as many parishes[1] as people. I lodged at the signe of the Cock, being recommended to the host of the house, by a token from Salisbury, but mine host dyed the night before I came, and I being weary, had more minde to goe to bed then to follow him so long a journey, to doe my messuage, or deliver any commendations: but the whole citie seemed almost as dead as mine host, and it may be they were all at harvest worke: but I am sure I walked from the one end of it to the other, and saw not 30. people of all sorts: So that I thinke if a man should goe to Winchester for a goose,[2] he might lose his labour, for a trader cannot live there, by venting such commodities.

On Friday I gallopp'd a foote pace one and twenty miles, from Winchester to Farneham; where I and one of my company hired a couple of Hampshiere jenets,[3] with seaven legs, and three eyes betwixt them, upon whom wee hobled seaventeene miles, to Stanes, whence on Saturday the 23. of August we footed it to Brentfoord, and boated it to London.

1 Winchester had about 57 parish churches in the 12th century, although the number declined thereafter.
2 a Winchester goose was a prostitute, and a venereal disease. Taylor treated the subject at length in *Taylors Goose* (1621).
3 i.e. jennet or gennet, a small horse. Farnham is actually in Surrey.

TAYLOR ON THAME ISIS

Taylor on Thame Isis, which was published in 1632 but describes a journey undertaken the previous year, stands alone among the canon of Taylor's travels. The 1630s were the mid-point and also the high-point of his writing career, following the publication of the collected works in 1630 and before the catastrophe of the civil wars. During the 1630s he wrote reportage, reissued earlier works, busied himself with propaganda on behalf of the Watermen's Company, of which he was a senior and sometimes respected figure; and in 1636 he embarked on a new phase of utilitarian publications, which included directories of inns and carriers. But he did not return to travelling in the old style until 1639.

Taylor on Thame Isis is a hybrid, and its background has been described by Capp (1994, pp. 30-1). As a royal waterman Taylor served in August 1631 among the crew taking a commission of privy councillors by barge to survey the Thames from Oxford to Staines with a view to improving navigation. The death of Dudley Carleton in March 1632, to whose memory the pamphlet is dedicated, deprived the scheme of its principal champion, and Taylor, who had naturally been taking notes throughout the voyage, published

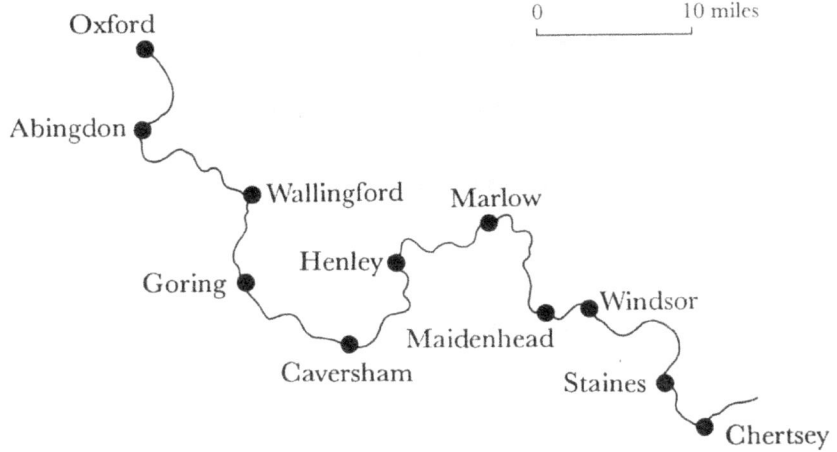

Taylor on Thame Isis

his own account as a way of 'kick-starting' the project again. In this he was only partly successful.

The pamphlet falls into two distinct sections, as well as an introduction and a peroration. The first section, which does not describe a journey, is an account of the origin and course of the Thames and all its tributaries in a logical geographical order. This was the technique pioneered by William Harrison in his contributions on the topography of Britain to Raphael Holinshed's influential Chronicles, 1577 and 1587; it was subsequently taken up in Michael Drayton's epic poem, Poly-Olbion, 1622. Taylor acknowledges in his introduction his debt to both works.

The second section describes the voyage from Oxford to Staines, noting the specific obstructions such as weirs, locks out of repair and sunken trees. In their very different styles it mirrors John Leland's Latin poem Cygnea Cantio, of 1546, which described the progress of a swan along the river from Oxford to Greenwich. But Taylor enlivens what could be a dull catalogue by inserting two interludes, a long description of a medicinal spring near Wallingford, and an enthusiastic account of dinner with Judge Whitlock at Henley. The newly discovered spring, described as 'a mungrill spaw' and apparently no longer identifiable, is particularly interesting. Taylor takes account of similar healing waters elsewhere, near Burntisland during the 1618 Scottish tour, and St Winifred's Well near Flint in 1652. Here beside the Thames his scepticism is unbridled. The water, it is claimed, cures everything (except lack of money) -- deafness, apoplexy, fractures, measles, even the loss of virginity. Visitors break their skulls on purpose in order to have them mended by the magic liquid. It also has a curious effect on writers, by making them exaggerate its properties!

[(August, 1631). Text derived from 1632 publication (copy BL c.30 b.36)]

Taylor on Thame Isis: or the description of the two famous rivers of Thame and Isis, who being conjoyned or combined together, are called Thamisis, or Thames. With all the flats, shoares, shelves, sands, weares, stops, rivers, brooks, bournes, streames, rills, rivolets, streamelets, creeks, and whatsoever helps the said rivers have, from their springs or heads, to their falls into the ocean. As also a discovery of the hinderances which doe impeach the passage of boats and barges, betwixt the famous University of Oxford, and the City of London. London, printed by John Haviland. 1632.

To the Right Honourable Lords, Thomas Earle of Arundell and Surrey,[1] Earle Marshall of England: Edward Lord Viscount Wimbleton:[2] Henry Lord Viscount Fawlkland:[3] and Sir Thomas Edmonds, Knight, Treasurer of the Kings Houshold:[4] Lords of his Majesties most honourable Privy Councell, and Commissioners[5] for the navigation and fishing of the famous Rivers of Thames and Medway.

Right noble lords, with sorrow I beheld,
That which to write my duty hath compel'd,
And (from my pen) the Thames flow'd to the presse,
From thence it ebbes to you to finde redresse.
My honourable Lord of Dorchester,[6]
He truly noted in particular,
Dame Isis wrongs, and Thames great injuries,
For they were sad persepctives to his eyes,
And had his Lordship liv'd his meaning was
To make the river passable, to passe.
For then with noble care and diligence
He view'd the helps, and the impediments,
Which aid, or hinder passage up and downe,
Twixt Oxford city, and brave Windsor towne;
Yet as I sometimes row'd and sometimes steer'd,
I view'd where well, where ill the way appeard;
And here I have describ'd the way we went,
Commixing truth with honest merriment,
My threed-bare wit a mad wooll gathering goes,
To shew the things in verse I saw in prose;
And (honourable peeres) I humbly crave,
My artlesse lines may your acceptance have,

1 Thomas Howard, 2nd earl of Arundel and Surrey (1586-1646).
2 Sir Edward Cecil (1572-1638), viscount Wimbledon from 1626, governor of Portsmouth, 1630-8.
3 Sir Henry Cary (d.1633), viscount Falkland from 1620.
4 or Edmondes (c.1563-1639), diplomat and Royalist MP.
5 The royal commission was established in 1630 to improve Thames navigation, but foundered in 1632 upon Carleton's death.
6 Sir Dudley Carleton (1573-1632), viscount Dorchester, the work's dedicatee.

Wishing each fault remov'd (which stands unfit)
As soone as you can reade what I have writ,
Desiring God to give you high content
Here, and hereafter glory permanent.

Humbly devoted with his best endevours to all your honourable personages, JOHN TAYLOR.

To the memory of the truly noble deceased, DUDLEY CARLETON, Lord Viscount Dorchester, principall Secretary of State to his Majestie of Great Britaine.

If he be blest that is of noble bloud,
And being made great, is both great and good,
Who is a Christian every way compleat,
Who holds it better to be good than great,
Whose life was guided with good conscience,
Whose end was saving faith and penitence,
These blessings noble Dorchester were thine,
And these have made thee 'immortall and divine.

To any body.

I that ne're tasted the Castalian fount,[1]
Or came in ken of the Thessalian Mount;[2]
I that could ne're attaine to wet my lips,
With Tempes liquour,[3] or sweet Aganipps,[4]
Who never yet have so much favour won,
To purchase one carrowse from Helicon,
Who with good poets dare compare no way
But one, which is in being poore as they;

---

1 On Mount Parnassus, Greece, and sacred to Apollo and the Muses.
2 In northern Greece, associated with Apollo.
3 River Peneus flows through Tempe valley in Thessaly, where Apollo purified himself.
4 Aganippe was a fountain at the foot of Mount Helicon, Greece, which inspired those who drank its water.

And having never seene the Muses hill,
Am plentifully stor'd with want of skill,
Then fount, or mount, nor sacred treble trine,[1]
Are no assistants in this worke of mine:
But ancient Isis current chrystall spring
Inspires my braine, and I her praises sing,
And Tame with Isis[2] joynes his pearely streames,
Whose combination are my ample theames;
Though (for the most part) in the tracts I tread,
Of learned Camden,[3] Speed,[4] and Hollinshead,[5]
And Draytons painfull Polyolbyon,[6]
Whose fame shall live, despight oblivion,
These are the guides I follow, with pretence
T' abbreviate and extract their quint-essence;
Nor can it be to them disparagement,
That I come after in the wayes they went,
For they of former writers followers be,
I follow them, and some may follow me;
And man to man a president is made
In art or science, mysterie or trade,
As they before these rivers bounds did show,
Here I come after with my pen and row.

TAYLOR ON THAME ISIS.

Our patron Phoebus,[7] whose sweet influence,

1 'three threes', i.e. the nine Muses.
2 Taylor derives the name Thames from the conjunction of the rivers Thame (largely in Oxon.) and Isis (the upper reaches of the Thames around Oxford). The confluence is at Dorchester on Thames, Oxon.
3 William Camden, author of *Britannia*, Taylor's principal source of historical information.
4 John Speed, cartographer and historian.
5 Raphael Holinshed (d.1580?), chronicler; the topographical portions of his *Chronicle* were actually written by William Harrison (1534-93).
6 Michael Drayton (1563-1631), poet, who wrote an epic poem on English topography, *Poly-Olbion* (completed 1622). Painfull means painstaking.
7 the sun.

Doth quicken all our reason, life and sense,
Tis he makes grasse to grow, and rivers spring,
He makes both my songs, subject, and me sing;
His beames the waters doe extenuate
To vapours, and those vapours elevate
Into the middle region, where they tumble,
And melt, and then descend and are made humble,
Moystning the face of many a spacious hill,
Where soaking deepe the hollow vaults they fill,
Where into rivers they againe breake out,
So nature in a circle runnes about.
Large downes doe treasure up great store of raine,
Whose bowels vent it[1] in the vales againe:
No place in England could a treasure keepe,
Thames to maintaine, but Coteswould[2] (queene of sheepe.)
In Glostershire (my dearest mother earth)
From whose faire city[3] I derive my birth,
Are Coteswould hills, and in the farthest cliffe
Of all those hils of Isis head is chiefe:
Schollers from Gloster that to Oxford ride
The truth of my assertion oft have tride;
On their right hand neare Cubberley[4] they passe,
Two wells as sweet as milke, as cleare as glasse,
Whence Isis first doth pedegree derive,
Those two are able there two mills to drive.
At Burton on the water,[5] south from Stow
Upon the Would,[6] great vaines of waters flow
To Burford, and to Witney, and along
Till they make meadowes large, and Isis strong.
The famous River Isis hath her spring

1 discharge.
2 the Cotswolds, a hilly region of Gloucestershire and neighbouring counties.
3 Gloucester, also spelled Gloster.
4 Coberley, near Cheltenham, Glos., the source of the Churn, a Thames tributary.
5 Bourton on the Water, Glos., on the Windrush, lies south of Stow on the Wold
6 'Corruptly called Stow the old.' [Taylor]

Neare Tetbury, and downe along doth bring
(As hand-maids) to attend her progresse, Churne,
Colne, Windrush, Yenload,[1] Leech, whose windings turne,
And meads, and pastures trims, bedecks, and dresses,
Like an unvaluable chaine of ESSES.
After releese of many a ducke and goose,
At Saint Johns bridge they make their rendevous,
And there like robbers crossing London way,
Bid many a bare-foot Welshman[2] wade or stay.
Close under Oxford one of Englands eyes,
Chiefe of the chiefest universities,
From Banbury desirous to adde knowledge
To zeale, and to be taught in Magdalen College,[3]
The River Charwell doth to Isis runne,
And beares her company to Abington,[4]
Whil'st very neare that towne on Barkshire side,
The River Ock doth into Isis glide;
These fountaines and fish-breeding rivolets,
(The countries nurses, nourishers, and teats,)
Attend Dame Isis downe to Dorchester,
Neare which her lovely Tame doth meet with her,
There Tame his Isis doth embrace and kisse,
Both joyn'd in one, cal'd Tame or Tame Isis,
Isis like Salmacis becomes with Tame
Hermaphrodite[5] in nature and in name.
Tame doth derive his spring or pedegree
Near Mesworth[6] in the vale of Aylsbury,
From whence he many miles with strange meanders,
To finde his lovely Isis slowly wanders,

1 River Evenlode, a Thames tributary.
2 This Thames crossing, below Lechlade, lay on the main road from Cirencester to London, and was much used by Welsh drovers.
3 The River Cherwell flows beside this Oxford college.
4 Abingdon, Berks.
5 In Greek mythology the nymph of Salmacis fountain, near Halicarnassus, embraced Hermaphroditus, and their bodies became united.
6 Marsworth, Bucks., near Tring.

Through fertile lands a quiet course he keepes,
Till southward under Whately[1] bridge he creepes,
And (like a pilgrim) travels all alone,
No brooke or river waiting him upon,
Onely three namelesse rivolets and two springs,
Which very privately their tribute brings,
Bewailing Isis absence, and his fate,
Poore Tame all heavie and disconsolate,
Unnavigable, scorn'd, despis'd, disgrac'd,
Having in vaine so many paces pac'd;
Despairing and quite desperate with these harmes,
He hurles himselfe unwares in Isis armes;
Nor closer can the barke be to the tree,
Than their infoldings and embracings be;
They rise and fall together, and they are
In want and plenty to have equall share;
And Tame with Isis will be both one river,
Till in the Ocean they their names deliver.
At Wallingford and Pangbourne, two small rils,
Their homages to Thamisis instils.
The more the river runnes, the more tis spreading,
Till in it's course it falls as low as Reading,
Where Kennet kindly comes with force and source,
To aid and helpe Thamisis in their course.
The head of Kennet is neare Ramsbury,[2]
Passing to Hungerford by Newbury.
The River Anborne[3] out of Hampshire flies,
To Kennet with some namelesse small supplies
Of pettie rills, which passing here and there,
Who to repeat, teadious and needlesse were.
To Sunning[4] and by Bisham Thames descends
To Marlow (called great) from whence it wends;

1   Wheatley, Oxon., east of Oxford.
2   East of Marlborough, Wilts. In fact the River Kennet rises much further
    north-west, above Wroughton, Wilts.
3   Enborne. It defines the boundary between Hants. and Berks. south of Newbury.
4   Sonning, Berks., near Reading.

Whereas a little rill from Wickham towne,[1]
To wait upon the Thames comes gliding downe;
Then pleasantly the river takes free way
To Topley[2] hills, by Maidenhead and Bray,
Till it to Windsor and to Stanes doth win,
And there the River Colne comes gliding in:
Colne hath its head or spring in Hartfordshire,
At Abbots Langley, or else very neere,
With some small petty rils and rivolets,
By Colbrooke[3] unto Stanes and Thames it gets,
The river Wey, with divers namelesse springs
Neare Chertsey, unto Thames their service brings.
Wey (beyond Guilford)[4] help'd with creeks and crooks,
At last at Oatlands towards Sunbury lookes,
And there a little rill, (scarce worth a line)
In Middlesex doth with the Thames combine.
Neare Reygate[5] towne the river Mole is found,
Bearing its course, runs (Mole-like) under ground;
But rising up by Notbury[6] againe,
At Molsey[7] it the Thames doth entertaine.
From Ewell towne the river Brent makes haste,
Who by the Thames is lovingly embrac'd:
Next which is Chiswicke towne, and Hammersmith,
It entertaines a rill, or little frith,
And after that below, neare Wandsworth mill,
Comes in another brooke or namelesse rill;
Thus I the river bring, and it brings me
From their first springs to London bridge you see.
Now from the bridg below descend I must,
Till Thames it selfe doth in the ocean thrust,

1 High Wycombe, Bucks.
2 Taplow, Bucks.
3 Colnbrook, Bucks., near Slough.
4 Guildford, Surrey.
5 Reigate, Surrey.
6 Norbury, near Croydon.
7 East and West Molesey, near Walton on Thames, London.

And if my paines to good men prove a pleasure,
My gaine's beyond my merit, beyond measure,
Of watermen, men scarce can finde a slower,
Yet hey, to Gravesend hoe and somewhat lower.
Brave London Bridge claimes right preheminence
For strength, and architects magnificence,
To be true None-such,[1] for no eye beheld
A bridge which it each way hath paralleld.
The arches (Tame and Isis) shadie bowres,
Through which both East and West in twice twelve houres
Twice Neptune greets it flowing from the Maine,
And twice the river sends it backe againe,
And as the flouds or ebbes encrease or falls,
They through the arches murmure madrigals,
Whil'st th' eddies divers wayes doth turne and trace,
Tame doth with Isis dance the wilde goose chace,[2]
From this rare matchlesse piece of workmanship,
I with the tide of ebbe must quickly slip,
And downe into the River Lea I hie,
That parts Midsaxon from East Saxony.[3]
Which river fals from Ware to Walthamstow,
And downe by Layton[4] unto Stratford Bow,
Some call it Lea, but Camden calls it Stowre,
And neare Blackwall it in the Thames doth powre,
Next Rodeing[5] is (a brooke or river small)
Which foord from Berking[6] into Thames doth fall.
From Havering, Burntwood and from Ockingdon,
Three little rils into the Thames do run,
Th'are namelesse, or scarce worth the nomination.

---

1 unique, but probably also an allusion to Nonsuch Palace, a Royal Tudor mansion in Surrey.
2 originally a race in which one horse had to follow accurately the wavering course of another, used figuratively in Shakespeare, *Romeo and Juliet*.
3 The Lea divides Middlesex and Essex.
4 Leyton, east London.
5 River Roding, which rises near Bishop's Stortford, Essex.
6 Barking, Essex.

And so on Essex side I end my station.
And now I'le crosse into the county Kent
To note what rivers from her bound are sent,
To wait upon the mighty bigswolne[1] Thames,
Who now is grown the prince of Brittains streams.
By Bromley glides the river Ravensburne
To Deptford downe with many a wandring turne,
The river Darrent[2] is the next and last,
Which downe by Dartford into Thames is cast.
And thus from Glocester shire neare Tetbury
And Buckingham shire close by Aylsbury,
I have brought Isis and her partner Tame
With twenty seven helpes losing each their name,
Who spend themselves to make the Thames grow great,
Till (below Lee) it lose both name and seat,
Through many countries as these waters passe,
They make the pastures fructifie in grasse:
Cattell grow fat, and cheese and butter cheape,
Hey in abundance, corne by stricke[3] and heape,
Beasts breed, and fish increase, fowles multiply,
It brings wood, cole, and timber plenteously:
It beares the lame and weake, makes fat the leane,
And keepes whole townes and countries sweet and cleane;
Wer't not for Thames (as heavens high hand doth blesse it)
We neither could have fish, or fire to dresse[4] it,
The very brewers would be at a fault,
And buy their water dearer than their mault,
And had they malt and water at desire,
What shift (a Gods name)[5] would they make for fire?
There's many a seaman, many a navigator,
Watermen, fishers, bargemen on this water,
Themselves and families beyond compare,

1 big-swollen.
2 River Darent, which rises near Westerham, Kent.
3 a bundle, usually applied to hemp or flax before heckling.
4 cook.
5 'What expedient (in God's name)...'

In number more than hundred thousands are,
Who doe their prince and country often serve,
And wer't not for this river might goe sterve;[1]
And for the good to England it hath done,
Shall it to spoyle and ruine be let runne?
Shall private persons for their gainfull use,
Ingrosse[2] the water and the land abuse,
Shall that which God and nature gives us free,
For use and profit in community,
Be barr'd from men, and damb'd up as in Thames.
(A shamelesse avarice surpassing shames;)
I speake not of the rivers bounds below,
Whereas the tides perpetuall ebbe and flow,
Nor is the river wanting much repaire,
Within the bounds of Londons honour'd maior,
Which limits all are cleare from stakes and piles,
Beyond Stanes bridge (thats more than forty miles)
But I (from Oxford) downe to Stanes will slide,
And tell the rivers wrongs which I espide,
Not doubting but good mindes their powers will lend,
T' endevour these abuses to amend:
Therefore I pray the readers to dispence,
And pardon my abrupt intelligence.
From Oxford two miles Ifley[3] distant is,
And there a new turne pike doth stand amisse,
Another stands at Stanford,[4] below that,
Weeds, shelves, and shoales all waterlesse and flat;
At Newnham[5] locke there's plac'd a fishing weare,
A gravell hill too high, scarce water there;
At Abington the shoales are worse and worse,
That Swift[6] ditch seemes to be the better course,

---

1   starve.
2   monopolise for one's own profit.
3   Iffley, a suburb of Oxford.
4   Sandford on Thames, south of Oxford.
5   Nuneham Courtenay, Oxon.
6   Now called the Back Water, it leaves the Thames above Abingdon and rejoins

Below which towne neare Sutton there are left
Piles that almost our barges bottome cleft;
Then Sutton locks are great impediments,
The waters fall with such great violence,
Thence downe to Cullom,[1] streame runs quicke and quicker,
Yet we rub'd twice a ground for want of liquor.
The weare of Carpenter's sans fault I thinke,
But yet neare Witnum[2] towne a tree did sinke,
Whereas by fortune we our barge did hit,
And by misfortune there a board was split;
At Clifton[3] there are rocks, and sands, and flats,
Which made us wade, and wet like drowned rats,
The passage bare, the water often gone,
And rocks smooth worne, doe pave it like free stone.
From Clifton downe to Wallingford we fleet,
Where (for annoyance) piles are plac'd unmeet;
From thence our oares did downe the river draw,
Untill we came unto a mungrill spaw,[4]
A bath, a spring, a fountaine, or a rill,
That issues from the bowels of a hill,
A hill it may be tearm'd or demie[5] mountaine,
From out whose entralls springs this new-found fountaine,
Whose water (cleare as chrystall, sweet as hony,)
Cures all diseases (except want of mony,)
It helpes the palsey, cramp, or apoplexie,
Scab, scurfe, or scald,[6] or dropsie if it vex yee,

---

    it at Culham, forming Andersey Island. The main navigable stream until 1790.
1 Culham, Oxon., south of Abingdon.
2 Long Wittenham, Oxon.
3 Clifton Hampden, Oxon.
4 'hyprid spa (spring)'. The location is unknown, but was probably near The Springs, a large Victorian house south of Mongewell (hence mungrill), in North Stoke, near Crowmarsh Gifford, Oxon.
5 half-.
6 complaints causing flaking skin: scald may be for scall (scabby skin), rather than scald (burnt skin).

The plurisie, the lethargie, strangury,[1]
It cures the cataracke, and the stone assure yee;
The head-ach, megrim,[2] canker, or the mumps,
Mange, murrians, meazles, melancholy dumps,
It is of vertue, vigor, and of force
To drive all malladies from man or horse;
Help'd of a Tertian ague[3] I saw one,
(Weake, and not worth the ground he went upon)
Who drank the water mingled with the clay,
And presently the ague ran away;
It cures an old sore, or a bruised blow,
It made the deafe to heare, the lame to goe;
One dumbe came thither, and straightway disputed,
And on the trees are crutches executed;
To heale greene wounds[4] it hath such soveraigne power,
It cur'd a broken pate in halfe an houre,
Which sconce[5] was crack'd on purpose to th' intent,
To try the vertue of the element.
If any man imagine I doe lie,
Let him go thither, breake his pate and trie.
Some say crack'd maidenheads[6] are there new sodered,
I'm sure the hill with beggers is embroidered,
And all those beggers are with little cost,
With lice and scabs embroidered and embost;
And as it were the well of Aristotle,[7]
The water is farre fetch'd in many a bottle,
The clay mixt with the liquour kils the cornes,
Ah could it cure some cuckolds of their hornes,[8]

1 painful retention of the urine.
2 the English word for the affliction now generally known by its French equivalent, migraine.
3 a fever which returns on alternate days.
4 a recent wound, or one which has not healed.
5 the crown of the head.
6 virginity restored by repairing (soldering) the hymen.
7 the proverb 'truth lies at the bottom of a well', was attributed to various Greek philosophers.
8 cuckolds (husbands of unfaithful wives) were derisively said to be

It would have patients out of every climat,
More than my patience could endure to rime at,
And had it but the vertue to surcease[1]
Some clamorous tongues, and make them hold their peace,
Thousands of husbands would their wives send thither;
Apothecaries I lament your lots,
Your medcines now will mould in gallipots,[2]
Your drugges with barbarous names unbought will lie,
And waste and languish in obscurity,
Twill begger all the quacksalvers[3] outright,
And all our mountebanks[4] are undone quite,
But whats become of me? can any tell?
Good reader helpe me out of this strange well;
I with my pen its praise did meane to touch,
And it (I feare) hath made me write too much,
Which if I have, let your constructions be,
Blame the strange working waters and not me:
But he that sayes that I doe over-doe,
Let him goe thither and hee'le doe so to;
So farewell, Well, well fare thou, still excell,
Increase in operation, Well farewell.
Beneath the fountaine, next is Cleave[5] locks fall,
And neare to that a locke men Goring call,
But having past the locke at Gorings there,
At Master Coltons house we had good cheare,
With hearty welcome, but 'twas for his sake
That did this hopefull businesse undertake,
Yet with our hearty thanks we thanke them all,
That din'd us lke a solemne festivall.

    distinguishable by imaginary horns which they wore on their heads. To insult a cuckold the fist was shaken at him, with first and fourth fingers extended, like horns.
1 put a stop to.
2 glazed medicine jars.
3 bogus medical practitioners.
4 charlatan or quack doctors.
5 Cleeve, Oxon, near Goring.

From thence to Harts locke[1] downward we descended,
And next to Whitchurch locke which must be mended,
Because the waters turne so swift and various,
And gainst our wils to dangerous courses carry us:
Next there's a weare, that if it had its right,
Should be well lib'd,[2] or else removed quite;
Below that Maple Ducham[3] locke appeares,
Where stands three faulty and untoward weares;
Then neare the bridge of Caversham there is
One Welbecks weare, fit to be mov'd I wis;
As past the locke at Caversham we row,
We found the river very foule below,
With weeds and hills of mud and gravell choak'd,
That with our oares and staves we thrust and poak'd.
Next Breaches weare near Sunning naught doth lie,
And Sunning locke the groundsill[4] is too high,
Besides two gin-holes[5] that are very bad
And Sunning bridge much need of mending had;
Haules weare doth almost crosse the river all,
Making the passage straight and very small,
How can that man be counted a good liver
That for his private use will stop a river?
Shiplocke,[6] or Cottrels locke stand very neare,
Not from that farre is Elmes his fishing weare,
Whereas the rivers case is altered well,
For Master Ployden neare that place doth dwell;
Marsh locke is plac'd a little above Henly,
And there the Thames is kept indifferent cleanly,
And here at Henley once in fifteene yeares,
A river stranger in the street appeares,

1 south-west of Lower Basildon, Berks.
2 castrated, i.e. cut through.
3 Mapledurham, Oxon., north of Reading.
4 foundation or threshold.
5 the gin was presumably the winch used to haul boats through the flash-lock, and the holes were part of this apparatus.
6 Shiplake, Oxon, south of Henley

Whose cesterne in the woods his wealth doth gather,
In that long space, and cannot get it rather,
But gotten out of high-way-flouds, and leaves,
As Dutchmen keepe the drops of their house-eves.
The cesterne fils and then the wals breake downe,
And send their stowage unto Henley towne,
Another fifteene yeares the wals repaire,
And fill the place with raine or thawed ayre,
And being so replenisht in that space,
It runnes (rub rub) close by the bowling place.
Neare Henley (some three quarters of a mile)
A little Ile digresse and change my stile.
Should I forget the good Judge Whitlocks[1] love,
Unmanner'd and ungratefull I should prove,
It was about the time (as I remember)
In August, some five dayes before September)
We landed neare the noble judges harbour,
(With stomacks sharpe as razour of a barber)
The time was short, we neither toyd nor trifled,
The kitchin, pantry, pastry strait we rifled;
The celler and the buttery both we forrag'd,
By which brave booty we were much encourag'd,
Sacke and good claret drawne from tierce and punchion,[2]
That serv'd one whole day, and two evenings nunchion;[3]
Our bread as good as ever baker sifted,
Our wine (rare wine) as ere to mouth was lifted,
And in our businesse (though we all were hasty)
We did surprize an excellent venson pasty,
We there did save the labour of inviters;
Whole joynts of mutton prov'd us good sheepe-biters,[4]
Our beere was bravely boyl'd and strongly malted,

---

1 Sir James Whitelocke (1570-1632), eminent lawyer. The house was Fawley Court, Bucks.
2 two sizes of wine cask.
3 snack or light meal.
4 originally dogs which worried sheep, but with various slang meanings by the 17th century, including shifty or thieving fellows, and womanisers.

Our pidgeon pie was pepper'd well and salted,
Most tender chickins, pullet, and a capon,
We (in our fury) did commit a rape on;
A mighty scarlet lobster last we seased,
And so with these acchats[1] our minds were eased,
But that which made our viands taste the better,
Was welcome, which made each of us a debter;
And long may he and his survive and flourish,[2]
That did poore travellers so kindly nourish,
These lines are writ in duty to expresse
Our love, our duty, and our thankfulnesse.
From thence we hi'd us with the streame and wind,
And in the barge at noone we bravely din'd,
And as our meat our gratefull minds did move,
We dranke Judge Whitlocks health to shew our love.
Then came we to a locke call'd Hambleton,[3]
Whereas the streame a handsome course doth runne;
Next Mednam[4] weare doth speedy mending lacke,
It puts the Thames, and Thames puts it to wracke,
And neare Frogge-mill[5] two paltry stops there are,
That in the river take too great a share;
Newlocke at Harley,[6] and a weare below,
Almost a stop, (fit to be clear'd I know;)
Then Temple locke,[7] 'bove Bisham church there is,
Beneath which is a weare somewhat amisse,
Then Marlow locke is worst I must confesse,
The water is so pinch'd with shallownesse,
Beneath which is a weare should be defac'd,

1 provisions, especially items purchased rather than made at home.
2 In fact Whitelocke died on 22 June 1632 (the year this pamphlet was published) and his house was severely damaged ten years later during the civil war.
3 Hambleden, Bucks., north of Henley.
4 Medmenham, Bucks.
5 Frogmill Farm, west of Hurley.
6 Hurley, Berks.
7 at Temple Mill, between Hurley and Bisham.

And Cottrels weare of Cookham be displac'd.
A weare doth to one Holdernesse belong,
Which doth the river most injurious wrong,
Neare which a spring runs from the chalkie hills,
The which (not long agoe) did drive two mills,
A stop 'gainst Toplow[1] Warren much doth spread
Next Bolters lock,[2] (a mile from Maydenhead.)
Thus have I past the locks, now weares and stops,
From thence as farre as Stanes mine inkhorne drops.
'Bove Maidenhead bridge a stop and one beneath,
Which both to be amended I bequeath;
Against Bray church, and Bray mill, stand three more,
Indifferent bad as any were before;
A stop at Water Oakley naught doth lie,
At Rudles poole the gravell hills too high,
The water turnes so short, and runnes so quicke,
That oft the barges there a ground doe stricke;
Neare Boveney church a dangerous stop is found,
On which five passengers[3] were lately drown'd;
Below the bridge at Windsor (passing thus)
Some needlesse piles stand very perillous:
Neare Eaton College is a stop and weare,
Whose absence well the river may forbeare;
A stop, a weare, a dangerous sunke tree,
Not farre from Datchet Ferry are all three;
A gravell bed, two stops and stakes beside,
Against and neare Old Windsor church we spide,
With two stops more we saw neare Ankerwike,[4]
And neare my Lord Maiors stone[5] we saw the like,

1 Taplow, Bucks.
2 Boulter's Lock, Bucks., north of Maidenhead.
3 usually 'passers-by' or 'travellers' at this period, rather than 'persons being conveyed'.
4 Ankerwycke Priory, Bucks., north of Runnymede.
5 This marked the upstream limit of the City of London's jurisdiction over the Thames, and stood close to St Mary's church, Staines. Its successor survives in the nearby recreation ground.

Besides an aight[1] or island there we found,
Hedg'd farre into the streame to gaine more ground;
From Stanes we past to Lallum guls,[2] most shallow,
Whereas five barges fast aground did wallow;
And such a trowling[3] current there did set,
That we were vildly[4] puzzled by to get;
Tumbling 'twixt Middlesex and Surrey land,
We came where Chertseyes crooked bridge doth stand,
Which sure was made all by left-handed men,
The like of it was never in my ken;
Wiw waw to Oakam ward, kim kam, kiwwaw,[5]
That through it men can hardly set or row,
That's the last fault I found that merits note,
And down from thence we merrily did flote.
Thus have I shew'd Thames wrongs in generall,
And wish they may be mov'd, or mended all;
And who can but with pity here behold[6]
These multitudes of mischiefes manifold?
Shall Thames be barr'd its course with stops and locks,
With mils, and hils, with gravell beds, and rocks:
With weares, and weeds, and forced ilands made,
To spoile a publike for a private trade?
Shame fall the doers, and Almighties blessing
Be heap'd upon their heads that seeke redressing.
Were such a businesse to be done in Flanders
Or Holland mongst the industrious Netherlanders;
They to deepe passages would turne our hils,
To windmils they would change our watermils.

1   ait or eyot, an island in the river.
2   Laleham, Middlesex, south of Staines. A gull in this sense means a channel made by the stream.
3   i.e. trolling, 'rolling' or 'streaming'.
4   variant of vilely, presumably here meaning 'wretchedly', or merely to intensify the adjective.
5   The wooden bridge was often in poor condition, and in 1630 the inhabitants of Chertsey had petitioned the king to repair it. Kim-kam means crooked or awry; the rest is probably nonsense inspired by kim-kam.
6   this passage, with variations, is re-used to end a later journey, pp. 269-71.

All helpes unto this river they would ayd,
And all impediments should be destroyed;
Our vagabonds (the wandering brood of Caine,)[1]
They would enforce those runnagates[2] take paine,
Whereby much profit quickly would accrue,
(For labour robs the hangman of his due.)
In common reason, all men must agree
That if the river were made cleane and free,
One barge, with eight poore mens industrious paines,
Would carry more than forty carts or waines.
And every waine to draw them horses five,
And each two men or boyes to guide or drive,
Charge of an hunded horse and 80. men
With eight mens labour would be served then,
Thus men would be employed, and horse preserv'd,
And all the countrey at cheape rates be serv'd.
T'is said the Dutchmen taught us drinke and swill,[3]
I'm sure we goe beyond them in that skill,
I wish (as we exceed them in what's bad,)
That we some portion of their goodnesse had:
Then should this worthy worke be soone begun,
And with successeful expedition done:
Which I despaire not of, but humbly plead,
That God his blessings will increase and spread
On them that love this work, and on their heires,
Their goods and chattels, and on all that's theirs:
I wish them blest externall, and internall,
And in the end with happinesse eternall.

FINIS.

---

[1] God cursed Cain: '... a fugitive and a vagabond shalt thou be in the earth' (Genesis 4 verse 12).
[2] archaic for renegades, turncoats.
[3] Perhaps referring to a proverb recorded in 1659: The Dutchman drinketh pure wine in the morning, at noon wine without water, in the evening as it comes from the butt.

News from Hell, Hull, and Hallifax

PART OF THIS SUMMERS TRAVELS, OR NEWS FROM HELL, HULL, AND HALLIFAX

Part of this Summers Travels marks a return to the Taylor of the *Pennyles Pilgrimage*, more than twenty years earlier. *Indeed, some of the places visited in 1618 on his way to Scotland, or in 1622 on his way to York, such as Coventry, Manchester and Hull, and York itself, are revisited now. There seems to be no high ideal, beyond entertaining his readers, making a profit, and perhaps exercising itchy feet. As a journey it cannot be counted a success. There is no destination and no itinerary. Drawn out on the map Taylor's wanderings seem aimless, as if he has lost his way. Even the title emphasizes that travelling is only part of the story, and the route has been contrived to take in Hell (in the guise of the Devil's Ars a Peak), Hull and Halifax.*

So where was Taylor going in 1639? With the world beginning to turn upside-down it is hard to say what his plan, if plan he had, might have been. In the earlier journeys anecdote and incident had spiced the drudgery of travel. But by now he had cultivated his reputation as a dapper raconteur: 'facetious and diverting company; and for stories and lively telling them, few could out-doe him,' recalled John Aubrey, who met him at Oxford in 1643, and guessed that he was 'then neer 50' -- in fact he was 65. And so perhaps Taylor felt now that the 'many pleasant passages' of his sub-title were what mattered, and the journey merely a framework from which to hang the jokes and fine writing.

At this level Part of this Summer's Travels *still works tolerably well. The description of the Halifax 'engine' when read aloud to an audience holds their attention, with the sobering sting in its tail; John Tilly's will, the Dadlington geese, and the miserly, suicidal Norfolk farmer, are still amusing, though the diabolical 'jerks' seem tediously contrived. Much more important are Taylor's detailed descriptions of specific places, such as Leicester's archaeological remains, Leeds parish church, and the belvedere at Wharncliffe. But life could not be so carefree for much longer.*

[16th July - 20th September, 1639. Text derived from 1639 publication (copy Bodleian Wood 155 (2) = STC microfilm 1498)]

Part of this Summers Travels, or news from Hell, Hull, and Hallifax, from York, Linne, Leicester, Chester, Coventry, Lichfield, Nottingham, and the Divells Ars a Peake. With many pleasant passages, worthy your observation and reading. By John Taylor. Imprinted by J.O.

A few words of direction to the reader.

I have not written every place in that order, as is set downe in the title of this pamphlet, but of such places as I travelled unto, I have truly related the passages, and the time, both when, where, why, and how I went, came and perform'd it. If any man aske wherefore this book is good, or how it may be any way usefull, I answer that it is foure wayes commodious: First, it is profitable, for it will direct a man the high-wayes of crossing divers countries from place to place, which no other book shews, as from Leicester to Linne[1] in Norfolke, from Linne to Kingstone, upon Hull in Yorkeshire, from Hull to Yorke, thence to Hallifax, to Chester, Darby, Nottingham, Coventry, Lichfield, and the Devils Ars a Peake:[2] all these wayes are herein described; secondly, there are some monuments of antiquitie are mentioned, which greater authours have omitted; thirdly, there are some passages of delightfull mirth and recreation. And lastly, all is true, or else you have the authours leave to travell as hee hath done, and doe your best and worst to prove him a liar.

Passages and entertainments from London to Leicester, with some observations of the said town and shire.

Upon Saint Swithin's day, I noted well,
The wind was calme, nor any rain then fell,
Which faire day (as old sawes saith) doth portend,
That heav'n to earth, will plenteous harvest send.[3]

1 King's Lynn, Norfolk.
2 Peak Cavern, Castleton, Derbs., see below.
3 Rainfall on the feast of St Swithun's translation, 15th July, was believed to

The morrow being Julies sixteenth day,
In my progression I began my way.
I need not to relate the towns that lie
Just in my way, (as I road through or by)
Onely at Mims,[1] a Cockney boasting bragger
In mirth, did aske the women for Belswagger,[2]
But strait the females, like the Furies fell,
Did curse, scold, raile, cast dirt, and stones pell mell,[3]
But we betook us nimbly to our spurs,
And left them calling us rogues, knaves, and curs;
With other pretty names, which I discern'd
They from their old fore-mothers well had learn'd.
The reason why they are with rage inflam'd,
When as they heare Belswagger nam'd,.
Is (as report doth say) there dwelt a squire,
Who was so full of love, (or lusts desire)
That with his fair tongue, Hippocritick-hood,[4]
(By slanderous[5] people 'twas misunderstood)
The women were so fruitfull, that they were
All got with childe, in compasse of one yeare,
And that squires name, they say, Belswagger was,
And from that tale, the lying jeere doth passe,
Wherefore the women there will chide and swagger,[6]
If any man do aske them for Belswagger.
Thence past I on my journy unto Hockly,[7]
Whereas I saw a drunkard like a block lye,
There I alighted at the sanguine Lion,[8]
Where I had meat, drink, and a bed to lie on.

    predict forty more days of rain.
1 South Mimms, Herts.
2 obsolete term for a swaggering gallant, or pimp.
3 game resembling croquet, with balls (pell), hoops and mallet (mell).
4 hypocrisy, in sense of deceit.
5 probably in the earlier sense of 'shameful, disgraceful'.
6 in the sense 'quarrel, grumble'.
7 Hockliffe, Beds., near Leighton Buzzard.
8 i.e. Red Lion.

The next day I road stately to Northampton,
And all the way my horse most proudly stampt on,
On Thursday, trotting, galloping and ambling,
There, at the blue Boare I was welcome than
Unto my brother Miles, a downright man,
Plain dealing, free from flattery, fraud or feare,
Who hath liv'd long with reputation there,
He's old and honest, valiant, courteous, free:
(I write not this for making much of me)
But they that doubts on't, let them go and try
And if he be a changling, say I lie.
That house King Richard lodg'd in,[1] his last night,
Before he did the field of Bosworth fight,
And there's a room, a king to entertain,
The like is not in Leister town again,
Th' Assizes then were there, some causes tride,
And law did there the corps and souls divide,
Of two offenders, one had with a knife
Stabd his contracted love, and reav'd[2] her life,
Tother, a wench that had stolne *some* poor rayment,
And fir'd the house, deserv'd the hangmans payment.
King Leir a temple did to Janus reare,
And plac'd a Flamine in't, there doth appeare[3]
The arched ovens foure yards thick at least,
Wherein they heathen sacrifices drest;
Like as the Jews in their idolatry,
Offered their sonnes and daughters impiously,
To Moloch, Nisroch, Ashtaroth, and Ball;[4]

1 One of Leicester's principal inns, demolished 1836. The tradition that Richard III stayed there was well-known.
2 robbed.
3 Geoffrey of Monmouth linked a Celtic figure Llyr with Leicester, and his legend was repeated by Holinshed and others (and used of course by Shakespeare). The underground chamber, supposedly a temple of Janus (the Roman divine gatekeeper), and probably remains of the Roman town, was known in the middle ages. A flamen was a Roman priest.
4 pagan gods of the Old Testament. Ball is more commonly spelled Baal.

And to those devillish gods adore and fall,
So people here, when warre or peace they sought;
They offrings unto Janus temple brought;
This was eight hundred forty and foure yeare
Before our Saviou's birth, built by King Leire,
Long after Etheldred,[1] (the Mercian king)
A happy and a Christian change did bring
The temple raz'd, the Flamine he defac'd,
And there a Christian bishops sea he plac'd,
Which lasted but few yeares, for then this land
Was seven-fold yoaked, beneath 7 kings command
And those kings still were in perpetuall wars
That England was quite spoyl'd with endless jars,[2]
And in those garboyles[3] Leister had her share,
Spoil'd, rifled, ransack'd, robd, and left most bare,
Till Edelfred,[4] with great magnificence,
Repair'd and wall'd it strongly for defence.
Then did it flourish long in wealth and state,
Till second Henry it did ruinate:
He in out-ragious fury fir'd the town,
Diswall'd it quite, and cast the castle down,[5]
So nothing but some ruines doth appeare,
Whereby men may perceive that such things were.
Thus Leister fell, from state superlative,
Her fifty churches[6] all consum'd to five.
Yet it is faire and spacious at this day,
And East, West, North, and South 'tis every way
Above a mile in length, so that no doubt,

---

1 Ethelred, king of Mercia 674-704. There were bishops of Leicester from 679-c.880.
2 clashes, conflicts.
3 i.e. garboils, 'disorders, uproars'.
4 Ethelfleda (d. 918?), daughter of King Alfred, and known as 'lady of the Mercians'.
5 In c.1173-6, following the Earl of Leicester's rebellion.
6 Leicester had six churches in 1086, and never more than 11 or 12, including monastic foundations.

The town's in circuit six large miles about.
Henry first Duke of Lancaster in war,
In peace, or bounty, a bright blazing star
For buildings in this city is renown'd,
Which as time rais'd, time did again confound.
Yet one large fabrick there doth still abide,
Whereby the good Dukes name is dignifide,
And that's an hospitall or bead-house,[1] where
One hundred and ten men are harbour'd there,
From perishing through want, still to defend
Those aged men untill the world shall end.
Twice every day a chaplain doth repair
To them; and unto God sends prayse and prayer,
And nurses are allow'd to dresse[2] their meat,
To make their beds, to wash, and keep them neat:
For which they thankefull be to God alone
Who rais'd such means to ease the poor man's mone.
Good Henry Earle of Huntingdon[3] (renown'd)
A free schoole did erect there, from the ground,
With means (though meane) for mayntenance endow'd
Two ushers, and one schoolmaster allow'd,
They teach young lads, such rules as do belong,
To reade the English and the Latine tongue,
And when their knowledge is with hope discernd,
They in the Greek may learn, and be more learn'd.

But to relate something in prose of this ancient towne of Leicester, in the time of nine weeks, which I abode there to and fro, I observed such a civill government and decency, which is not in many places to be found or equallized.

First, I noted the peace, tranquillity, and unity which the people live in, under the rule and command of the maior and his brethren, to

---

1 i.e. almshouse. Newark Hospital was established in 1330 by Henry, earl of Lancaster, and enlarged by his son, Henry, first duke of Lancaster (d. 1361).
2 cook.
3 Henry Hastings, 3rd earl of Huntingdon, reorganized in c.1564-73 the free grammar school founded by Thomas Wigston (d. 1537).

whose authority and power (under the king) the inhabitants do willingly obay.

Secondly, the clergy (or ministry) are learned, diligent and painfull;[1] and both clergie and layity, are conformable to the orders and discipline of the Church of England, and I did not heare of any one, residing there, that is, either schismatically opinioned with dogmaticall whimseyes, or Amster-damnable fopperies.[2]

Thirdly, they are so charitable, and carefull in providing for the relief of the poore and needy, that a man must go seek where to bestow his almes, for there is not any one (that I could see) that begg'd in the whole town.

Fourthly, the streets are so well paved, and kept so clean from dunghils, filth, or soyle, that in the wettest or fowlest weather, a man may go all over the towne in a paire of slippers, and never wet his feet.

Lastly, the people are generally so loving one to another, that the lawyers want work, and so honest that the apparitors[3] are idle, and those few drunkards which they have, are very civill and faire condition'd.

Certain other observations.

There is a faire library, and a well founded almes-house within the town, also two gaoles, two houses of correction, and for mad and frantick[4] people. Also it is reported,[5] that when King Richard the Third went from Leicester, to fight the battaile neer Bosworth, that then there was a man of mean calling (some say he was a weaver, and some say a plough-wright by his trade) hee had a spirit of divination or prophecie, of whom the tyrant King Richard demanded some questions, what the event of that dayes fight might be to him, to whom the other (most bluntly answered, Marke my words King Richard, that as thou dost ride out of the towne of Leicester, this morning thou shalt hit thy right foot

1 painstaking.
2 Taylor frequently alludes to Amsterdam as a Puritan stronghold.
3 court officials.
4 violently insane.
5 Another version has a wise woman foretelling that where he struck his spur on Bow Bridge, there should his head be broken. Bow Bridge was later known as King Richard's Bridge in consequence.

against a stone, and as thou returnest thou shalt knock thy head against the same: which proved true, for as he road, he did strike against the corner of a wall his foot, and after hee was slain in the field, hee was stript, and his body layd crosse behind a man on hors-back, (like a calfe) and in that vile and ignominious manner, as they brought his corps back to Leicester, his head did knocke against the aforesaid wall or stone, which place I saw there; also I went eight miles to see Redmore field,[1] where the king fell, which is a moorish[2] kinde of ground, altogether unfruitfull, and the water doth seem red, which some foolish people do suppose to be the staine of King Richard's bloud, but it is onely the colour of the red earth that makes the water seeme so, and the ground close adjoyning is very fertile for corne and pasturage, but in the lower parts it is boggy and moory: by nature, and not either barren or bloudy by any reason of the kings death.

Another observation is concerning the alteration of the measures of miles,[3] and good sufficient pots or jugs of drink, but the further I travelled northward, the more the miles were lengthened and the pots shrunke and curtald;[4] but indeed, what the liquor wanted in measure it had in strength: the power of it being of such potencie, that it would fox a dry traveller, before he had half quencht his thirst.

In this county of Leicester, I observed a piece of extream justice, executed upon three geese, which was thus.

At a village called Dadlington, eight miles from Leicester, there dwels a gentlewoman a kinswoman of mine, who the last Trinity tearm 1639, was at London, about some businesse in law, which much concern'd her: and in her absence, the pinder[5] of Dadlington, finding three of her geese innocently grazing upon the common, for to shew the full power, force, vertue, and marrow of his office and authority, drave the geese into the pound or pindfold, and because they could procure no bayle for their release, nor sureties for their true imprisonment, hee put

---

1   Redmoor Plain, south of Market Bosworth, Leics.
2   wasteland or marsh.
3   In 1635, when the postal service was reorganized. Taylor refers to this again at the end of a later journey, see p. 308, note 1.
4   i.e. curtailed, 'cut short'.
5   parish official responsible for impounding stray animals.

all their three necks into a horslock,[1] which engine or neck-fetter was so strait, close, and pinching, that the geese were all strangled: Now the question is whether Willy, Tilly,[2] (the pinder so silly) were the cause of their deaths, or whether the geese did desperately cast away themselves: all which I humbly refer to the discretion of the jury.

But some readers may muse why I do write so much of Leicester, in this little book; the reason is that I lay there from the 17 of July, to the 20 of August, which was five weekes, but in the mean space I rode to Coventry, and return'd in a day to Leicester again, of Coventry I have little to say, but that it is a faire, famous, sweet, and ancient city, so walled about with such strength and neatnesse, as no city in England may compare with it: in the wals (at severall places) are 13 gates and posterns whereby to enter, and issue too and from the city: and on the wals are 18 strong defensible towers, which do also beautifie it: in the city is a faire and delicate crosse, which is for structure, beauty, and workmanship, by many men accounted unmatchable in this kingdome: although my selfe with some others, do suppose, that of Abington[3] in Berkeshire will match it, and I am sure the crosse in Cheapside at London doth farre out-passe it. I have bin at this city foure times, and have written of it before,[4] and therefore at this time (my stay being so short there) I have but little to say, onely this that some are of opinion, that at the first it was called Coventry, from the French word Trey Covent,[5] because there were founded three covents, for three severall orders of friers, namely, the Franciscan Friers, the Augustine Friers, and the Dominicans: It matters not much who erected the said foundations and covents, but it is certain, that the renowned King Henry the Eighth did suppresse and demolish them, whose memories now is almost quite buried in their owne ruins. Coventry is a county of it selfe;[6] it hath been grac'd

1 a shackle for a horse's leg, also used generally to mean a padlock.
2 Probably nonsense, influenced by willy-nilly ('whether willing or not') and tilly-vally (an explanation of impatience).
3 Abingdon, Berks.
4 above, p. 44, and later, pp. 332-3.
5 Coventry probably means 'tree of a man named Cofa'; the name was in use before friaries were established. Coventry has Benedictine and Carthusian monasteries, and Carmelite and Franciscan friaries.
6 This privilege was secured in 1451.

and dignified much by the grants and priviledges given to it by former kings, as King Edward the Third and King Henry the Sixt; the major's[1] name (at my being there, was Master Thomas Forrest a vintener) and Master Thomas Phineas sword-bearer there dyed at the beginning of the sessions (much about the time of my being there) he was a man of that comely bulk and corpulency, that his coffin was a full yard wide at the shoulders, and it is said, that in his life time hee could have been (at one meale) the consumption of a large shoulder of mutton; but he and his good stomack being both deceast, I left Coventry, because it was Sessions time, and returned to my randevouze at Leister.

The eleventh day of August I road from Leister to Nottingham, where I lodged at the signe of the Princes Arms; but I was wel entertained at the house of the Right Worshipfull Sir Thomas Hutchinson, Knight, himselfe and his good lady made mee welcome, and did expresse their bounty to mee in good cheere and money: for the which I am heartily thankfull.

The towne of Nottingham is seated on a hill, which hill is almost of one stony rocke, or a soft kinde of penetrable sandy stone; it hath very faire buildings, many large streetes, and a spacious market place: a great number of the inhabitants (especially the poorer sort) doe dwell in vaults, holes, or caves, which are cut and digged out of, (or within) the rocke; so that if a man be destitute of a house, it is but to goe to Nottingham, and with a mattock, a shovell, a crow[2] of iron, a chizell, and mallet, and such instruments, he may play the mole, the cunny,[3] or the pioner,[4] and worke himselfe a hole, or a burrow, for him and his family: Where, over their heads the grasse and pasture growes, and beasts do feed; faire orchards and gardens are their coverings, and cowes are milkt upon the tops of their houses. I was much befriended by Master Palmer the jaylor there, for he went with me, and shewed me the (sometimes) strong and defencible castle, but now much ruined: yet still there are many faire and sumptuous roomes in reasonable reparation and estate. On the lofty battlements of the said castle, there is a most spacious

---

1 i.e. mayor's.
2 i.e. a crow-bar.
3 rabbit.
4 pioneers were originally an advance guard of soldiers who dug trenches and prepared the way for the army.

prospect round about: for from thence I could see the most stately castle of Belvoyre or Bever Castle,[1] which doth (as it selfe) belong to the Right Honourable the Earle of Rutland: and nearer hand, within three miles, I saw the ancient town of Gotham,[2] famous for the seven sages (or wise men) who are fabulously reported to live there in former ages.

In the aforesaid castle of Nottingham, I was shewed divers strange wonderfull vaults, cut or hewen out of the rocke, whereof one is said to be the place where David King of Scots[3] was detained many years in captivity: where the said king, with his owne hands (without any other instrument than the nayles of his fingers) did with the said tooles engrave and claw out the forme of our Saviours life, death, and passion; which worke is there to bee seene upon the walls.

Also there is another vault or passage through the rocke, whereby men may descend or ascend out, or into the castle; which vault is called Mortimers Hole,[4] through which hole (as report goes) the great Roger Mortimer, Earle of Wigmor, and Lord of Wallingford, had egresse and regresse to the queene, wife to King Edward the Second, or the infortunate Edward of Carnarvan.

Thus having seene as much of Nottingham towne and castle as is related; on the twelfth of August, I road to the ancient towne of Darby: On the thirteenth of August I left Darby,[5] with an intent to retire to Leister; but after I had road halfe a mile, I met with an acquaintance of mine, who was travailing towards the Peake in Darby shire, to a towne called Wirksworth, and from thence to Chesterfield, I returned with him. The country is very mountainous, and many lead mines are found thereabouts: the best and most richest is called Dove Gany,[6]

1 Belvoir Castle, Leics., west of Grantham, and about 16 miles from Nottingham.
2 village south of Nottingham proverbial since the middle ages for the stupidity (or feigned stupidity) of its inhabitants.
3 David II (David Bruce, 1324-71) invaded England and was captured 1346, released 1357. The present castle was built 1674-9.
4 Roger de Mortimer (c.1287-1330) was paramour of Edward II's queen, Isabella; he was captured by her son, Edward III, at Nottingham Castle, and executed at Tyburn for procuring the murder of Edward II.
5 Derby.
6 Dove Gang mine was opened c.1632, and by 1652 was said to extend from Cromford Moor to Middleton Moor, Derbs., north of Wirksworth.

within a mile or little more of Wirksworth (corruptly called Wortsworth:) and two miles from thence are most dangerous wayes, stony, craggy, with inaccessible hils and mountains: the grounds there are lawfull (as they told me) for any man to dig or mine in for lead, be they of what condition soever: for the laws of mining is, that those that will adventure their labours shall have all the profits, paying the tenth part to the lord or landlord, of all the lead which they get. If it happen that they take pains, a yeare or two in sundry places to finde a myne if their fortune be so hard to finde none (as it often falls out so) they do work all that while for nothing, and finde themselves as they are able, and in the end their toyle and labour is all lost: but if they doe hit upon a good myne that doth hold out, and yield plentifully, then they may quickly enrich themselves (if they be good husbands.)[1] I was told of a poore thatcher that left his trade, and venturing his time and pains, he found so rich a lead myne, that he would turn gentleman, and he kept men in liveries, living at the rate of the expence of 100 pound a week; so that he supposing that leaden, golden world would never be ended, took no care to save any thing, but after a while, the myne failed, and hee spent that little which hee had left in digging for more, could finde none, so that for a conclusion, he forsook the Peake, and turnd thatcher again.

That part of the Peak, which is called the Devils Ars,[2] is at or neere a towne named Castleton, or Castle Towne, so stiled from an ancient ruined castle[3] on a hill, at the end of the town; It is 30 miles from Darby, the castle stands on the top of a hill, and under it is a cliff or riffe[4] in the said hill, which is as wide at the entrance as three barn doores, but being entred in it is enclosed again so narrow, that a man must stoop to passe further, but after that straight passage is past, there is rooms of incredible and wonderfull greatnesse, with strange and intricate turnings and windings, which no man can see without great store of lights, and by reason that those things are naturall, and formed without any art or labour of man, and withall so dismall horrid, darke, and hideous, that place is called the Devils Ars a Peak, at or upon which

1 i.e. managers.
2 Peak Cavern, Castleton. The name, in a form meaning 'Peak's arse' is recorded in 1086, but in the form Divillsarse not before 1630.
3 Peveril Castle.
4 rift.

I have (accordirig to my promise) given three jerks[1] with my pen, at the latter end of this book.

From thence I returned towards Leicester 30 miles, on the 15 of August, and lodged at a market towne called Narbury,[2] and the next day I came all tyred and weary (both man and beast to Leicester) and on the 20 day, I took my journey 64 miles into Norfolke, to the famous town of Linne, and three miles from thence, at a village called Wooton,[3] I was there well welcomed by Master Richard Miles (to whom I am and must be thankfull brother in law) whose loving kindnesse to me was shewed in such extraordinary manner, which because I cannot expresse, I will remayn gratefull with silence.

Concerning Linne, it is an excellent sea-town and strong port, it is gravely and peaceably governed by a major, 12 aldermen, and a recorder. It hath been honored by divers, but chiefly by King John 440 yeares since, and by King Henry the Third, the first gave them a faire gilt cup, which is there to be seene, as a witnesse of his royall liberality: and whoso will know more of Linne, let them goe thither and look the records of the town, or else let them read Master Camdens Britania, or the painfull labours of Master John Speed. The troth is, mine hoast Noble, was a noble hoast to me, at whose house, my brothers kindred and friends, gave me a friendly farewell. On Tuesday the 27 of August, from Linne to Boston in Lincolnshire 24 miles, where I dined with the right worshipfull Sir Anthony Thomas knight, from Boston I road 14 miles to Horn Castle, where I lodg'd the 28 of August. But I crave pardon of the reader, for I had almost forgotten a merry passage[4] or two which hapned in Norfolke, not farre from Linne: and thus it was.

At a place called Priors Thorns, neere to two towns, namely, Northbery and Sapham,[5] there dwelt a man named Frier, who was rich in substance, but very poore and miserable in his conditions: belike hee had read or heard of a play that was written 40 years since by Master

1 strokes or lashes.
2 Narborough, Leics.
3 North Wootton, Norfolk, north of King's Lynn. Taylor returns there in 1650, below, p. 324.
4 here in the sense 'occurrence, incident'.
5 probably Narborough and Swaffham, Norfolk, 10 and 15 miles south-east of King's Lynn.

Benjamin Johnson, the play is extant, and is called Every man out of his Humour,[1] in which play was acted and personated a mizerly farmer, that had much corne in his barnes, and did expect a scant or barren harvest, that through want and scarcity hee might sell his corne at what deare rates hee pleased, but (contrary to his wicked hopes) the harvest proved abundantly plentifull, wherefore hee being in an extraordinary merry or mad veine, put himselfe to the charge of the buying of a two penny halter, and went into his barn as secretly as he could, and puttirig the halter about his neck with a riding knot, he fastned the other end to a beam, and most neatly hang'd himself: But (as ill luck would have it) his man presently came into the barne, and espyde his master so bravely mounted, the unlucky knave drew his knife and cut the halter, crying out for help as lowde as he could, rubbing and chafing his master with all care and diligence to recover him to life again; at the last he awak'd out of his traunce and fetch'd a deep groan, began to stare and look about him; and taking the end of the cut halter in his hand, his first words to his man was, Sirrah, who did cut this, O Master (said the fellow) it was I that did it, and I thank God that I came in good time to doe it, and I pray you to take God in your minde, and never more to hazard your soule and body in such a wicked manner: to which good counsell of the poor fellow, the caitiffe[2] replyde, Sirrah, if you would be medling (like a sawcy busie rogue) you might have untyde it, that it might have serv'd another time, such an unthrifty rascall as thou will never be worth such a halter, it cost me two pence, and I will abate[3] the price of it in thy quarters wages. And when the quarter day came, hee did abate the said two pence, for the which the fellow would dwell no longer with him, but went and got him another service: This was acted really and lately at the place aforesaid, in imitation of that part in the play, of Every man out of his Humour.

After the said Frier had some hogs which were like to die with the murrain, which hogs he killed and powdred,[4] and his wife, children, and family, as many as did eat of the porke, fell sick and dyed all: for the

1 In act 3 of *Every man out of his humour* (performed 1599, published 1600) Sordido hangs himself with a halter and is cut down by five rustics.
2 a despicable person.
3 deduct.
4 salted.

which the slave deserv'd a hanging, and a hangman, but hee yet lives for some worse purpose.

Concerning a paire of brewers, and a piece of justice. Another short Norfolk tale is not impertinent. There was one Master Fen a brewer at Fensham,[1] and one Master Francis Dix a brewer at Sapharn,[2] this Dix was riding in the countrey amongst his customers (the inkeepers and victuallers) and he call'd for a pot of ale or beere as he road by; (now that ale-house was a customer to Fen, as soon as Dix had drank, hee asked who brewed that drink, to whom the hoastesse sayd, that Master Fen of Fensham brewed it; well said Dix, I dare lay a wager, that I will give my mare but a peck of mault, and she shall pisse better drink than this: at the last these words came to Fens hearing, for the which disparagement, he sued Dix, and recovered from him twenty pound damage besides cost, at the Assizes last at Norwich 1639. And now to returne to the narration of my travels, from whence I have digrest, since I lodg'd at Horne Castle in Lincolneshire.

From thence, on the 18 of August, I road 30 miles to Barton upon Humber, and the next day (being Friday) I tooke a boat for my selfe, my squire, and my two palfreyes,[3] down to Hull, or Kingstone upon Hull, the strength and scituation of which towne I have formerly written of: and I had no new thing there whereof to make any new relation: let it suffice, that it is absolutely accounted the strongest and most defensible town in the kingdome of England, and for good government inferiour to none: I might speak somewhat of their good fellowship; but my book would swell big with it, therefore I will pay them with thinking and thanking of them, both my old friends and new acquaintance all in generall.

The 31 of August I left Hull, and road to Holden[4] 16 miles, and on the morrow I road to Cowood Castle,[5] to see the most Reverend Doctor Neale,[6] the Lord Archbishop of Yorke his Grace, whom in all humility I do acknowledge my self much bound in duty daily to pray for, and remember him with unfained reverend thankfulnesse, not only for

1 Fincham, Norfolk, east of Downham Market.
2 Swaffham, Norfolk.
3 saddle-horses.
4 Howden, East Riding.
5 Cawood, West Riding, near Selby, residence of the archbishops of York.
6 Richard Neile (1562-1640), archbishop of York from 1631.

the undeserved favours and bounty which his Grace extended towards mee now, but for many other former approvements of his Graces love and liberality, when his Grace liv'd neere mee at Winchester House.[1] At dinner with his Grace, I had the happinesse to renew my acquaintance with the noble and worthy Knight Sir Francis Wortley,[2] who most courteously invited and commanded me to visit him in my journey, of which more followeth.

My humble thanks rememberd to the right worthy worshipfull Knight, Sir Paul Neale, with his fair and vertuous lady, as also my gratefull remembrance to all my lords gentlemen and servants, to whose loves and for whose friendships I shall ever acknowledge my selfe an ingaged debter.

Thus having past the Sunday with my Lords Grace, and those other before named gentlemen, on Munday the second of September, I took my breakfast and my leave both of Cowood, and road to Yorke, where I visited the worthy Knight (my old acquaintance) Sir Arthur Ingram,[3] with whom I thank his worship, I dined, and also had some other token of his love and bounty, for the which I remayn thankfull.

Of Yorke I have but little to say, though it be a great, a faire, and the second city in England, built 989 years before our Saviours birth, by Ebrank[4] king of this land, from whom the city is called Eboracensis, this Ebrank is said to have 21 wives, by whom he had twenty sons, and 70 daughters: he raigned here when as King Solomon raigned in Jerusalem; hee overran France, he builded Alclaid, or Dumbritton[5] in Scotland, hee founded York, hee erected a temple there, and therein plac'd a Flamine to Diana: but after (in King Lucius time) Elutherius pull'd downe the said idolatrous wooden temple, and displac'd the Flamine, and caused the minster to be built in that magnificent manner of free stone, placing

1 Neile had previously been bishop of Winchester, 1628-31, when Winchester House (on the south bank) would have been his London residence.
2 Wortley (1591-1652) was a poet, friend of Ben Jonson, and a prominent Royalist in the civil war.
3 Ingram (d.1642) was a financier and courtier, whom Taylor had befriended in London, probably during the 1620s. He was subsequently MP for York.
4 Taylor described Ebrank, the fifth legendary ruler after Brutus, in similar terms, in his *A Memorial of all the English Monarchs* (1622). The source is Geoffrey of Monmouth, via Holinshed.
5 Dumbarton.

there an Archbishop; Severus the Roman Emperour dyed there, and also there dyed the Emperour Flavius Valerius Constantius (which some call Chlorus) those that will know more of York, let them reade chronicles and larger volumes.

The Lord Major of Yorke was (at my being there, one Sir Roger Jaques, knight, a gentleman of approved wisdom and government: my self did not stay three houres, and myne hoast Master Corney at the Talbot, told mee all the news which I heard there, which was a fellow, that (amongst other offenders) was the first that was hang'd, and the last that was cut down, and being put into the grave or pit, with his fellows, when the earth was cast upon them, he began to stir and recover life, and was return'd to the gaole, is now there living, and able to report truly what hanging is, Probatum est.[1]

From Yorke I rode after dinner to Tadcaster, and so to a place called Kidell,[2] where at a poore ale-house I was glad of entertainment, and had the company of a tinker who made pretty music with his Banbury kettledrum,[3] there was also with him two drovers and 35 hogs, which were to be driven on the morrow seven miles further to Leeds market, this good lodging and company, I past the night with all, and on the morrow I rode to the town of Leeds; of which towne I must say somewhat. This town is (for the bignesse of it) one the most populous towns in England, it hath in it above 12000 people, and having but one church there,[4] it was not halfe capable to receive so great a congregation, they were extremly thronged and dangerously crowded (especially in the heat of summer, or sultry contagious weather) that the most part of the people were inforc'd either to go two or three miles severall ways to other village churches, or else to stay at home and want the hearing of Gods word, and the meanes of their salvation. The care and consideration of these grievances entred into the pious minde of one Master John Harrison,[5] gentleman there, (now living) so that God opened his heart,

---

1 Latin: 'it has been proved'.
2 Kiddal Hall and Kiddal Lane End, West Riding, east of Leeds.
3 Proverbially tinkers from Banbury try to put things right, but make them worse.
4 St Peter's, demolished and replaced, c.1838.
5 Harrison (1579-1656) built St John's church, New Briggate, 1632-4 in Perpendicular style. Taylor's account of him is well informed.

that of his owne proper costs he caused a church to be built, (though it have but the name of a chappell) which is so large, that it will contain 4000 people, it is so neatly compacted and framed, with exquisite art of carving and masonry, with painting, gilding, polishing, embellishing, and adorning, with a most stately roofe, a fair lofty tower or steeple, a sweet ring of bels; besides the admirable and costly joyners and carvers workmanship in the font, pulpit, pewes, chancell, communion boord, and all other things and ornaments for the decent adornment of such a house consecrated and dedicated to the service of God. I do absolutely affirme, that neither the church or the founder hath any fellows[1] to be found.

This chappell is called by the name of Saint John Evangelist, it hath a faire churchyard for burials, well and strongly walled about, and at the west end of the church-yard, the said gentleman hath founded a fair almse-house, and therein placed 21 poore aged people; also hee hath founded and finished a faire school-house for the instruction of youth, and a fine sweet street hee hath built on both sides in a uniforme and faire manner, with houses: the rents whereof are for the mayntenance of the almes-houses, the schoole, and reparations of the church to the end of the world. And I leave this worthy founder to God for a blessing, and to the world for imitation.

From Leeds I went to Wakefield, where if the valiant Pinder[2] had been living, I would have play'd Don Quixot's part,[3] and challenged him; but being it was so happy that he was dead, I past the town in peace to Barnsley, and so to Wortley,[4] to Sir Francis Wortleyes ancient house. The entertainment which himselfe, his good lady, and his most faire and hopefull daughter gave mee there, as I never did or can deserve, so I never shall be able to requite, to talke of'meat, drinke, money, and free welcome for horse and man, it were but a meer foolery for me to

---

1 counterparts or rivals.
2 George a Green, a folk hero who rivalled and later accompanied Robin Hood in daring exploits, and who was celebrated in plays and chapbooks. He was renowned for his strength in combat.
3 Cervantes' tale of Don Quixote, published 1605/15, was rapidly translated into English, and Taylor several times alludes to it, placing himself in the role of Quixote.
4 south-east of Penistone, West Riding.

begin, because then I should run myself into a labyrinth, out of which I should hardly finde the way: Therefore to his worship, my humble thanks remembred, and everlasting happinesse wished, both to him and all that is his. Yet I cannot forbeare to write a little of the further favour of this noble knight. Upon the fourteenth of Septernber afternoon, he took horse with mee, and his lady and daughter in their coach, with some other servants on horseback; where three miles we rode over rocks and cloud-kissing mountains, one of them is so high, that (in a cleere day) a man may from the top thereof see both the minsters or cathedrall churches, Yorke and Lincolne, neere 60 miles off us; and as it is to be supposed, That when the Devill did looke over Lincolne,[1] as the proverbe is) that hee stood upon that mountaine) or neer it: Sir Francis brought me to a lodge, the place is called Wharncliffe,[2] where the keeper dwels, who is his man, and keeps all this woody, rocky, stony, vast wildernesse under him, for there are many deere there, and the keeper were an asse if he would want venison, having so good a master.

Close to the said lodge, is a stone in burthen at the least 100 cart loads, the top of it is foure square (by nature) and about 12 yards compasse, it hath three seats in the forme of chaires, made by art (as it were in the front of the rocke) wherein three persons may easily sit, and have a view and goodly prospect over large woods, towns, corn-fields, fruitfull and pleasant pastures, valleyes, rivers, deere, neat,[3] sheep, and all things needful for the life of man: contayned in thousands of acres and all (or the better part, belonging to that noble knights ancestors, and himself. Behinde the stone is a large inscription ingraven, where in an old character is described the ancient memory of the Wortleys (the progenitors to Sir Francis now living) for some hundreds of yeares, who were lords and owners of the said lands and demaynes which hee now holds as their right heire. About a bow shoot from thence (by the descent of many rungs of a ladder) his worship brought mee to a cave or vault in a rocke, wherein was a table with seats, and turfe cushions round, and in

---

1 The Devil looking over Lincoln is proverbial for a stern critic, referring either to the Lincoln Imp (a carving in Lincoln Cathedral) or another at Lincoln College, Oxford.
2 Wharncliffe Crags, a high point along the road from Sheffield to Huddersfield.
3 cattle.

a hole in the same rock, was three barrels of nappy liquour,[1] thither the keeper brought a good red deere pye, cold roast mutton, and an excellent shooing-horn of hang'd Martimas biefe:[2] which cheer no man living would thinke such a place could afford: so after some merry passages and repast, we returned home.

On the fifth of September, I hired a guide, and rode to Hallifax 16 miles, the ways were so rocky, stony, boggy and mountaynous, that it was a days journey to ride so short a way. At Hallifax I saw the fatall engine,[3] wherewith they do behead pilfering thieves, which Sir Francis Wortley told me was set upon this occasion following.

This towne of Hallifax hath (for time out of minde) liv'd and subsisted by the rich and laudable trade of cloathing, and oftentimes their cloathes were stolne from the tenterhooks,[4] (or tenters) whereupon the king (then raigning) upon their humble suite had priviledge granted to the town for ever: that if a thiefe were taken, either of these three ways, which is, hand-napping, back-bearing, or tongue-telling, that is, either about to steale, or carrying it away, or confessing, that then the party offending (after triall by a jury of townsmen) if the goods, be it cloth, cattell, or whatsoever is valuable, is judg'd to have their heads struck off with the said engine, without any assize or sessions. Now the engine is two high pieces of timber, an ell[5] or yard asunder, fixed and closed on the top, with a crosse piece like a gallowse; in the inner sides of the two standing pieces are two gutters, and on the top (or crosse piece is a pulley through which they do put a small line or rope, and fastning it to another heavyer piece of wood of 100 weight (in which they doe fix the sharp-edge-toole) then they doe pull or hoyst up the said weight, and the stolne goods is brought to the place of execution with the malefactor; now one end of the rope is made fast to a pinne or stake, which being cut, the engine fals so ponderously and speedily, that it severs the head from the body in a moment, but there is no man will

1   strong ale.
2   an appetizer or 'starter'. The beef would have been salted the previous November, and so become very strong.
3   This primeval guillotine was used about fifty times c.1550-1650. Its base and steps survive as an ancient monument in Gibbet Street.
4   used to stretch fulled cloth on tenters or tentering racks after fulling.
5   a measure, usually 3 ft. 9 ins., or slightly over 1 metre.

or must cut the line, but the owner of the stolne goods, which if he do, hee hath all again: if he will not cut it, then he must lose all, and it is employed to some charitable uses; by which means the thiefe escapes; and this is Hallifax law.

The sixt day I left Hallifax, and road over such wayes as are past comparison or amending, for when I werrt downe the lofty mountaine called Blackstone Edge, I thought my selfe with my boy and horses had been in the land of Breakneck,[1] it was so steep and tedious, yet I recovered 12. miles to Rochdale, and then I found smooth way to Manchester, and to Sandy Lane end[2] 13 miles: and to Chester 14 miles, which was the furthest place of my tedious travell.

For my short stay at Chester (which was but one day and two nights, I had good and friendly entertainment, of many gentlemen, to whom I must rest thankfull, especially to the worshipfull Master Alderman Edwards, and to Master Wright and his wife. It was my fortune to see and rejoyce at the sight of the Noble, Right Honorable Earle and Knight of the Renowned Order of Saint George, William Earle of Darby:[3] And although I have no relation to his lordship or acquaintance with him, yet for the reverend respect which I doe owe and beare to nobility, it did me good to see so grave and honourable a peere.

The city of Chester, is of ancient erection and fame, it was the royall seat of kings, and there are yet some ruines left of the memorable pallace of King Edgar,[4] to which mansion the said king was rowed in a barge by eight captives (or tributary kings from Saint Johns) on the River of Dee, which river there is spoyled and impeached[5] by a bank of stones all over it, onely for the employment of a mil or two, which river other ways would be both passable and profitable to the whole country, for many miles, for the carriage of goods in boats and barks. Chester itself is a fair city four square, well walled, with an old ruin'd castle, which hath beene a strong fabrick, but now a gaole, the streets are spacious,

1 precipitous hills, likely to break one's neck; perhaps a reference also to the Welsh county of Brecknock.
2 probably Sandiway, in Weaveham parish, Cheshire.
3 William Stanley, 15th earl of Derby (1561-1642).
4 In 973 Edgar received the submission of kings from Scotland and Wales, who rowed him along the River Dee from his palace at Farndon to Chester
5 impeded.

the buildings sumptuous, and so contrived,[1] that four or five men may walk in the most parts of a breast, dry from the injury of raine, or any falling weather: it is gravely and peaceably governed by a major and his 12 brethren, it hath foure gates and three posterns, goodly churches, and chiefly painfull and learned preachers. And so much for Chester.

Onely a merry tale, of a late true businesse which hapned there; There dwelt a bricklayer, a good workman (but a good husband) whose name was John Tilly, who had the good hap to spend all that he got in his lifetime, except two sonnes and one daughter: and being sicke and in his death-bed, there came a poore neighbour to visit him, whom he desired to make or write his last will and testament; the poor man (having ink and paper) asked him what hee should write?

Quoth honest John Tittle, my estate is but little, but I pray thee write thus:

Imprimis, I give and bequeath to my wife (for her solace and comfort) my little dog, for it is a pretty nimble active curre, and wil make her some sport which may delight her, and put the grief of my death out of her sad remembrance.

Item, I give and bequeath to my eldest sonne John, all my working tools belonging to my trade of bricklaying, which as hee may use, may be as available to him, as they have beene to me, and this is the summe of my will.

His youngest sonne standing by, sayd, Father, have you nothing to give mee? Yes sonne (quoth hee) I had almost forgotten thee, but I will leave thee somewhat.

Item, I give and bequeath to my sonne George seven foot of ground under the gallowse.

Good father take comfort (said George) for my hope is that you will recover, and live to enjoy that legacie your selfe.

Then the daughter pray'd him to give her somewhat whereby she might remember his fatherly love, Yes, quoth he, I pray write.

Item, I give and bequeath to my onely daughter a whores conditions and qualities, which as shee may use them, she may live in such estate and fame that she may be mistaken for a gentlewoman.

---

[1] a reference to the Rows, or penticed walkways, which survive at Chester.

Lastly, I doe make and ordaine my neighbour here, my full executor: and for his paines for writing my will, I do give him and his heires male for ever, an old shooing-horn.

The ninth of September I turn'd my back upon Chester, (almost without taking leave) and road 15 miles to Nantwich, the tenth I rode to Stone and to Lichfield, 32 miles.

Of the ancient town of Lichfield I can say nothing (by reason of my short stay) onely there is a faire and curious old cathedrall church or minster.

And the towne hath that priviledge[1] (as mine hoast told me) that they can draw and hang one another, and never trouble any other judge, assize or sessions.

The eleventh I rode to Faseley, Abersom,[2] Hinckley and Dadlington, eighteen miles, where all weary and almost worne out with age and travell, I rested untill Saturday the fourteenth of September, and then rode eight miles to my brother Miles, at my old welcome lodging at Leicester.

Newes from Hell, with a short description of the Hell at Westminster.

Not from that Hell where souls tormented lye
In endlesse death, and yet shall never die,
Where gnashing cold, commixt with flames still burning,
Where's entrance free, but never back returning:
Where nought but horrour, fiends, and torments dwell;
I bring no news from that accursed Hell;
Yet mine own merits are of such low price,
To barre me from Celestiall Paradise,
And sinke me in that horrid lake infernall,
But that my hope and faith is fixt supernall,
The Hell I write of is well known to be
A place of pleasure, and for all men free,

---

1 Lichfield was created a county in its own right by charter of 1553, with its own sheriff.
2 Fazeley, Staffs., Atherstone, Warwicks.

Where wretched ghosts are not in torments stayd,
For all the pains upon the purse is laid.
To finde this Hell you need not travell farre,
'Tis understood the high Exchequer Barre
At Westminster, and those who thither venter,
Do not give Cerberus[1] a sop to enter,
For Charons fury,[2] you need never feare it,
(Although ten thousand do land somwhat neer it)
Within this Hell is good content and quiet,
Good entertainment, various sorts of diet,
Tables a score at once, in sundry places,
Where hungry mouthes fall to, and say short graces,
And then (in some sort) I may parallell
This earthly Hell, with the infernall Hell.
Hot sweltring vapours, pots, and cauldrons boyling,
Great vehement fires, with roasting, stewing, broyling;
The cooks and scullions, all be smear'd and smoak'd,
And in their masters grease well stew'd and soak'd,
And had the Devill a stomack unto it,
The cook himselfe is not the rawest bit.
Like as th' infernall Hell doth entertain
All commers, so this Hell doth riot refrain
To give free welcome unto every one
If money fayle not, there's excepted none.
This Hell is govern'd by a worthy duke
That Pluto like, his under fiends rebuke,
There the tormenting tapster is control'd,
If courteously he nick[3] not (as he should)
He must attend at every knock and rap,
His reverend jugge deckt with a frothy cap,
He fils and empts, and empts and fils again
Like Sisyphus,[4] he toyles, but not so vain,

---

1 Mythical dog which guarded the entrance to the underworld.
2 the ferryman who conveyed the dead to Hades.
3 trick.
4 see p. 68, note 1

Like Danaus¹ daughters, taking up, and spilling,
He's always emptying, and he's never filling.
Thither the counsellour for comfort comes
To rince his toyling tongue, and wash his gums,
The client having Tityus² empty maw
(His guts tormented with the vulture law)
He comming to this Hell may finde reliefe,
Of comfortable Plum broath and roast biefe.
There, for your solace you may feed upon
Whole seas of pottage, hot as Phlegeton,³
And midst those seas, by art, the cooks hath laid
Small iles of mutton, which you may invade
With stomack, knife and spoon, or tooth and naile,⁴
With these, the victory you cannot faile.
Therefore this earthly Hell is easier farre,
Then where the miserable damned are,
There's no redemption from that black abisse,
And here regresse, as well as egresse is,
Therefore they falsly do mistake the story,
To call this Hell, which is but Purgatory,
For here's no thraldome,⁵ from this place you may
Get present freedome, if the shot you pay.

Here followeth three satyricall lashes or jerks, given with the pen of the authour, at or upon the Devil's Ars a Peak.

Pens, are most dangerous tools, more sharp by ods
Then swords, and cut more keene then whips or rods;
Therefore (most high and mighty Duke of Dis)⁶

---

1 The 50 daughters of Danaus were punished in Hades by being compelled continually to pour water into a sieve.
2 A mythical giant, whose punishment for offending the gods was to be stretched out on the ground while two vultures ate his liver.
3 A river in the underworld which flowed with fire, not water.
4 by biting and scratching, a proverb first recorded in 1533
5 servitude or bondage.
6 Dis means the underworld, and Taylor then assembles a variety of synonyms

Commander where the Lake Avernus is,
Great Lord of Limbo, Styx, and Phlegeton,
Of Tartarus, Gehenna, Acheron,
Most potent Monarch of black Erebus,
Prince of the triple-headed Cerberus,
Sole Emperour of Darknesse, and dark works,
Master of hereticks, infidels and Turks,
Arch-flammin of hot Tophets smouldring flames,
King of Cocytus, and th' infernall streams,
Earle of all errors, and chief dominator
Of all sins done, by earth, ayre, land, or water,
Viscount, and Baron of large Barathrum,
Since I have liv'd to come so neare your bum,
As is your wicked worships Ars a Peake,
Though some men think my muse is all too weake;
I with my pen doe meane to yerke and ferke[1] ye,
And (as I promis'd) with three jerkes will jerke ye.
I know that many fooles will jeere and frumpe,[2]
That I durst come so neare the Divells rumpe,
And lash with my poore penne satyricall,
This great Don Diego Diabolicall:
But I would have him and his friends to know,
I jeere him not, for all his bug-bare[3] show:
'Tis knowne that he, and all that him attend,
To any poet never was a friend:
And therefore now I daring him oppose,
And jerke his hellish majesty in prose.

Although you (great master of the perpetuall hot-house) Don sel de Lucifer, have on the earth in all places and countries many multitudes of damnable sonnes, friends, and servants, to oppose mee and take

and allusions from classical mythology.
1 strike and push.
2 mock.
3 bear-shaped hobgoblin supposed to devour children, and therefore used as a threat.

your part, yet I being come so neer your podex,¹ must jerk your breech with my Satyre Pendragonly² goose quill, you know that reproofe is as ill taken as correction by the ungracious, Therefore although you are so bad that you are quite past any mending, yet your gracelesse Majesty may be lawfully touch'd by reprehending; you have been a cheater ever since the Creation, and in that art of coozening, you first cheated your selfe of everlasting happinesse, and gained thereby perpetuall perdition, and ever since you have play'd hocus pocus,³ and with your tricks, sleights, and jugling legerdemayne,⁴ done your best to draw all the whole race of mankinde after you into your kingdome of Cimerian tenebrositie;⁵ you taught our first parents infidelity, pride, disobedience and lying, which qualities of theirs are so naturally descended to us, that (by your industrious instigation) we do continually shew (by our lives and conversations) of what house wee came. By their example of believing too much in you, we are growne incredulous in things which most concerns our better and best of being, and wee are so inur'd and practisde in lying, (by your inspiration being the father of lyes) that wee are doubtfull to believe one another. And yet (like the Cretans)⁶ with long use and custome, wee doe many times believe our own lyes to be true.

May it please your infernall Hell-hood to take into your execrable consideration, that you were the first inventer of the most ignoble science of offence, you taught Caine the Imbrocado,⁷ and shewed him how to murder his brother, and from that time to this, the art of murdering, killing, and cutting throats hath beene universally and perfectly learned and practised. You have beene the inventer of all manner of destroying

1   Latin 'anus'.
2   term used for a winged dragon, also a tyrannical ruler. Taylor is probably referring to the dragon standard carried by Uther, the celtic prince, into battle (related by Geoffrey of Monmouth).
3   originally the start of a macaronic imprecation used by conjurors (like abracadabra), perhaps parodying words of the Latin mass ('Hoc est Corpus...')
4   sleight-of-hand.
5   The Cimmerii were a tribe who lived in the far west and, according to Homer, were continually enveloped in misty darkness.
6   According to St Paul, quoting Epimenides, the Cretans are always liars (Titus 1, verse 12)
7   in fencing, a thrust over the arm.

weapons, from the high degree of the Welsh-hook,[1] to the lower descent of the Taylors bodkin;[2] and in these later times you (with the helpe of a frier)[3] have devisde a burning, smouldring, most hellish and undefencible mischief that murders men by heaps, and (with a powder) can blow whole kingdomes into the firmament; and for the innumerable engines that are daily used and cast for such uses, your most high and imperiall malediction have declared your selfe an excellent artist, from the double cannon to the elder gun-mines, counter-mines, petards, granadoes, fire-works, wild-fire, and the Devill and all doe continually seek and worke the destruction of miserable mankinde. You are a great traveller, and will take the paines to compasse the whole earth to finde a just man, on purpose to doe him a mischiefe, but for a crew of common drunkards, rascals, bawds and whores, you know you need not wet your foot to seek them, they are your own already, and by your good will, you would fill Hell so full, that Heaven should have but a few.

And so let that passe for one and the first jerke.

Secondly, you know that there is but one narrow way to happinesse, and many wayes to your Zona Torrida, Frigida,[4] (for all those large wayes doe meet in one at the last, and bring poore soules into your pestiferous pursnet)[5] some go by the way of Sodome, to finde out your most damnable mansion, some by the way of incest, some by adultery, some by fornication (for they say you are the Master of the Honourable and Worshipfull Company and Brotherhood of the Fornicators) in which regard you are a great friend to parators and panders.[6] You

---

1 a weapon shaped like a bill-hook.
2 The original meaning of bodkin is dagger, later transferred to the pin used by tailors.
3 Roger Bacon (c.1214-94), a Franciscan friar and scholar, was popularly credited with inventing gunpowder. The Gunpowder Plot of 1605 is presumably alluded to in the phrase, 'whole kingdomes into the firmament'.
4 In ancient and medieval cosmography the world was divided into burning (*zona torrida*), freezing (*zona frigida*) and temperate zones.
5 bag-shaped net closed at the neck by a draw-string.
6 panders procure sexual favours for others; parators = apparitors, court officials, but the sexual innuendo is unclear.

shew'd Cham¹ the way how to deride his father, by which example a company of Chammists, have ever since practised not onely to mock, scoff, and abuse their naturall parents, but also to contemne, raile and revile against kings and princes, who are the royall fathers of terrestriall government, and further to despise, slight, and libell against the most reverend fathers, the stewards and painfull dispensers of the spirituall food of eternity; you directed Corah² and his complices the high rodeway to murmur; Achitophel to give wicked counsell, and Absolon³ to rebel and usurpe; you shewed Joab⁴ the way to treachery, Achan to steale, Jobs wife to abuse her husband, from whom the most part of women (like apt schollers) are very expert in that kinde of miserable mystery. You put Gehezi into the high-way of taking a bribe, and it is too well known what a wicked number of followers he hath had of all degrees, from the scepter to the swain, from the black gown to the buckrum bag. You directed Nabal (who anagrammatized or lead backward is Laban) to be as churlish as a hog, from whom miserable Dives hath perfectly learn'd the way to true misery, you taught Nimrod⁵ the way to tyrannize, and enclose and encroach upon land and territories, which hath beene the bounding, mounding, and curtalling of commons. The raysing of ambition, pride, voluptuousnesse, and such earthly vertues of accursed greatnesse, and to the Almighty making of beggers. You tye fast the rich mans purse, and let loose the poore mans curse, you instructed Pharaoh, Senacherib, and Rabsheka in the way of blasphemy, and from those Hellish presidents their wickednesse is daily impiously imitated, Shimei was one of your anathema profound schollers, and from you hee learn'd to curse the Lords anointed extempore: once (as I have read) you were so addicted to peace and unity that you made Herod and Pilate friends, who were hatefull enemies, but afterwards your hypocrisie was

1 Ham, son of Noah, who saw his father's nakedness, and whose descendants were cursed (Genesis 9, verses 22-5).
2 Korah set himself up against Moses, and murmured against Aaron (Numbers 16, verse 11).
3 Ahithophel betrayed David and turned to Absalom (2 Samuel 17)
4 Taylor lists various Old Testament traitors and malefactors.
5 Nimrod, the mighty hunter, expanded his territory and founded cities (Genesis 10 verses 8-12). Taylor compares him with the Tudor enclosers of common land.

found, that it was your plot to destroy innocence: you made Demas to forsake the truth, and embrace the world (your wicked sister:) you have never been unprovided of a kennell of whores, queans,[1] and concubines, to tempt and draw the wisest men to folly, and for him that is most strong (in his owne opinion) you have alwayes one darling sinne or other to fit his disposition, constitution, inclination, or humour, that like a Dalilah shall weaken him, or quite overthrow him.

And this shall suffice for the second jerke.

Thirdly and lastly, you know that your end draws nigh, and therefore now you rave, rage, and are more mad than ever you were, you know that after Doomsday, that you shall have no more power over mortals, then you shall be for ever chain'd in your denne like a dogge in a kennell; and therefore now you with all double diligence, doe endevour to doe your best to doe your worst, and as much as in you lyeth, you draw us from bad to worse, and from worse to worst. The hypocrite (by your intcitement) doth vizard[2] all his villany, with the maske or veile of vertue; hee follows the steps of Ananias and Saphira[3] to a haire, hee with his sower looke shrowds a lofty mind. You have scatterd pride into as many shapes as Proteus,[4] so that a proud fashion hunter (if either money or credit will furnish him) will transforme himselfe into as many formes as you can do; our roarers (who by your pestiferous favour are stiled the damn'd crue) are so given to most unhallowed meditation, that they lie a bed almost till dinner time to study new oaths, to vent at this ordinary,[5] at bowls, cock-fighting, horse-race, whore-house, or any other place of gentleman like or noble exercise; and as you have taught them to sweare without feare, so they doe often forsweare without shame: although sometimes they hazzard their eares, as they doe their souls. You set bad

---

1   women of ill-repute.
2   to wear a mask, and therefore conceal.
3   both died after colluding to defraud the apostles of the full proceeds of a piece of land (Acts 5, verses 1-11)
4   In classical mythology, the old man of the sea, a prophet who kept changing shape in order to prevent anyone forcing him to prophesy the future.
5   a fixed-price supper at an eating-house.

projectors[1] (and unprofitable) a work, as thick as crab-lyce[2] or caterpillers, and it is no doubt but you will deale so justly with them, that you will pay them their wages, and after you have set them agog (with a vengeance) to doe injury with a mischiefe. You are so skilfull in physicke, that you have made too many believe that the losse of a mayden-head is an approved and speedy medicine for the green sicknesse.[3] Poets, painters (and some few courtiers) you have so well taught that they can flatter most artificially with pen, picture, and by word of mouth.

It is long of you that what ever the choplin and the chaplin hath, yet the thin-cheek'd chiplin[4] hath nothing at all. I know a poore curate that comes and goes a mile every Sunday, be it winter or summer, all manner of weathers, sometimes wet to the skin, and preaches once a week (on Sundays) for bare five pound a yeare, the tythe being valued at sixty pound per annum, so that the miserable stipend or hireling wages will hardly buy wood to make a fire for him when hee comes home to dry him, when hee is through wet. This is your worke (Monsieur Diabola) for it is your inspiration to put such wrangling spirits into impropriatours,[5] that for the not paying of a tenth pudding or a tythe egge the law must take his course. You have brought the schismaticall separatist to be as unconformable as your selfe, for (like you) they cannot bide the crosse or the signe of it (if it be not upon money) and you have made them as unmannerly as your selfe, for they will not move a hat, or bow a knee at the name of our Saviour, and they are wax'd as slovenly as you can make them, for they hate clean linnen, and all order, neatnesse and decency in the church; And you have long practiz'd a politick slight, which is, that when a reverend pastor is painfully and carefully preaching to his audience, instructing them how to avoid your snares and traps; then you are so angry and impatient when you are told of your faults, and heare your damnable devices laid open, that you could afford to pull the preacher out of the pulpit by the eares, or to teare him in pieces, but that hee is so happy that you have no power over

1 speculators, used in a pejorative sense.
2 parasitical insects which infest the pubic hair.
3 chlorosis, a form of anaemia once prevalent in adolescent girls.
4 Nonsense inspired by chaplain. Choplin presumably refers to a fat cleric, chiplin to the thin curate.
5 laymen who were entitled to the profits (e.g. tithes) of a benefice

him: your inveterate malice being limited, curb'd, and snaffled by an unresistable high and omnipotent power, and hee very well understands and knowes in whose service he is, and whose embassage[1] he delivers, and therefore is so valiant that he neither feares or cares a rush for you; which your imperiall malevolence perceiving, you have another trick for him, which is to lull the people asleep, (of which number many times the best of the parish are some), by which means you do debarre them of what they should heare, and in the mean time, the preacher speaks to the bare walls. And I am perswaded that is against your will, that there is any good preacher living, and seeing they do live (in despight of you) and that by their care and industry they doe now and then violently plucke a soule from you, in revenge thereof you chiefly seek their confusion, either by war, slander, or starving them through want of means. Yet this much may be spoken as one of your good parts, which is, that you were never known to be drunke, and though you never walke uprightly, yet you never stumbled, you were never so fox'd but you knew the way home (and the troth is, you are so bold, that you would make every place your home.) The court, the city, the country, the pallace, the castle, the cottage, and the church and all, you are so audacious either to enter them by force, or else to insinuate and sneak into them by craft and subtilty. And though you are no drunkard, yet you doe love the whole rabble of them so well, that you are unwillling to lose one of them all, but my hope is better. For if they leave it and mend their manners as they should do, the Devill the one of them you are like to have. You have the art to make great scholler to learne retrograde, for if a man be never so good a grammarian, and hath Greek and Latine as perfect as Homer or Virgil, yet (if he be married) you doe too often teach his wife the way to reade him backward, like an Hebrician, and though he be never so well skild in learned volumes, and the seven liberall arts, yet shee puts him againe into his horn-book.[2] You have so much devotion in you, that you doe assist those brethren that doe pray zealously, that they may be disobedient with a safe conscience, and you make them so stout and valiant that some of them are more able to doe more service in a white sheet then the honestest man in a whole shire can doe. You know that

1   the business of an ambassador.
2   The Hebrew language is written and read from right to left. Hornbooks were teaching aids for children.

the projector would be an honest man if hee did not keep company with himselfe, therefore you might do somwhat to be talk'd off, if you would separate him. It is a scurvy fashion of your devising, that wisemen in russet,[1] must reverence and stand bare to silken fools; but to conclude, you have gotten such a freedome that you have a finger in all trades, and an oare in every mans boat, nor was there ever any bad thought, word, or deed, imagined, spoken, or committed since the Creation, but you were at the middle and both ends of it; and I do remember that I have read how once you bragged,[2] boasted and promised to give all the kingdomes of the world to be worshipped, and afterwards you were in that poore roguish case, that you were faine to aske leave to take possession of a silly hog. In which manner of vain-glorious ostentation, bragging and boasting, the most part of men are expert, and to promise much, and performe nothing, is so easie a lesson of your teaching, that many great men are more ready and perfit[3] in it then in their Pater Noster. And now you grand master of mischief, you may trusse up your hose,[4] for at this time my pen is worn blunt, my inkhorn dry and my selfe weary with jerking, where correction is in pain, and no possibility of no amendment.

Thus after the expence of much money, and ten weeks time, having ridden 645 miles (of sundry measures and sizes) all weary and almost monylesse, I returned to London on Friday the twentieth of September, 1639. FINIS.

1 coarse, homespun cloth.
2 Biblical references to the temptation of Christ in the wilderness (Matthew 4, verses 8-10, etc.) and the Gadarene swine (Matthew 8, verses 28-34 etc.).
3 perfect.
4 i.e. to tie the points or laces of the hose to the doublet, the equivalent of 'to pull your trousers up' after the three lashes to the arse.

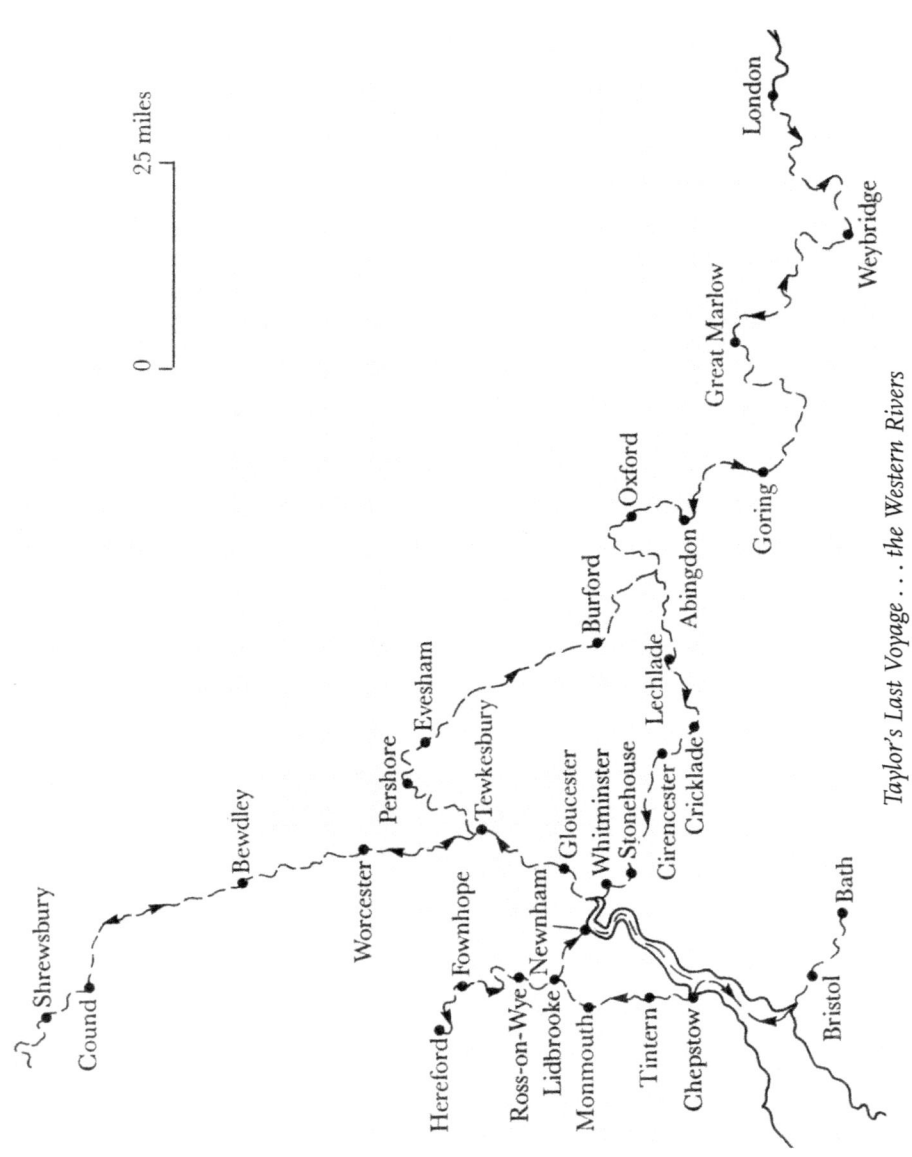

JOHN TAYLORS LAST VOYAGE, AND ADVENTURE, PERFORMED FROM THE TWENTIETH OF JULY LAST 1641. TO THE TENTH OF SEPTEMBER FOLLOWING

*J*OHN TAYLOR'S LAST VOYAGE, *so-called (another five were to follow), took place in the summer of 1641, in the teeth of gathering war-clouds which he for the most part studiously ignored. It has nothing in common with the frivolous and carefree jaunt of two years earlier, but its theme is closely related to those of the Salisbury voyage in 1623 and the Thames survey of 1632. Indeed he revises and reuses the concluding poem of the latter to round off this new work. As the most celebrated and articulate waterman in the kingdom, and a seasoned traveller, he probably felt uniquely placed to influence policy on fostering navigable rivers to improve the inland trade. He therefore set out on what now would be called a feasibility study, to explore by boat the state of five major rivers: the Thames above Oxford, the Severn between Bristol and Shrewsbury, the Wye from its mouth at Chepstow up to Hereford, and the Bristol and Stratford Avons.*

Like his 1632 study of the Thames he catalogued specific problems which he encountered during the journey, and offered suggestions for their solution. He also noted where canals might be dug to connect river systems, and pondered the advantage to trade of such improvements. He was by no means the first to suggest linking the Thames and Severn by a cut in the Cirencester–Malmesbury–Stroud area (an idea eventually achieved some 150 years later), but he had a particular motive in suggesting it. Just as in 1623 he had advised Salisbury that it ignored its river at its economic peril, so now he was spurred to rescue his native Gloucester from decline by making it the hub of a network of navigable and interconnecting waterways. Having completed his account of the journey he devotes several pages to a prospectus extolling Gloucester's potential.

This is an earnest work which commands our respect. It shows Taylor as a thoughtful and pragmatic campaigner. There is little whimsical diversion in it (although it was written for subscribers to 'Taylors bills'), but it is by no means devoid of good writing. One of his introductory sentences, beginning: 'My selfe bearing a naturall affection to portable rivers...' is as good an example of sturdy Jacobean prose as one could wish to find. This follows a strikingly egalitarian sentiment expressed in verse, with lines such as: 'Yet sure me thinkes the water should be free | For passage, for all men of each degree.' A year later Taylor would be embroiled in the Royalist cause, such matters as river improvement set firmly on one side. There is just a hint of the impending calamity, right at the end of this piece. A paragraph is set aside for ridiculing Puritans, and ends: 'Good Lord, in thy mercy looke upon us, and give us true peace and unity, both in Church and Commonwealth.' It was a vain hope.

[20th July - 10th September, 1641. Text derived from 1641 publication (copy BL Thomason E1100.(3)]

John Taylors last voyage, and adventure, performed from the twentieth of July last 1641. to the tenth of September following.

In which time he past, with a scullers boate from the citie of London, to the cities and townes of Oxford, Gloucester, Shrewesbury Bristoll, Bathe, Monmouth and Hereford.

The manner of his passages and entertainement to and fro, truly described, with a short touch of some wandring and some fixed scismatiques, such as are Brownists, Anabaptists, Famalies, Humorists and foolists, which the authour found in many places of his voyage and journey. by John Taylor.

Printed at London by F.L. for John Taylor, and may be had at the shoppe of Thomas Bates in the Old Baily. 1641.

To his friend Mr. John Tayler, on his voyage and journey.

If true affection doth your muse inspire
To'th honor'd welfare of your native place,
Then set your hand to now I you desire;
The time is now, when you may do us grace.

The subject sure is large, if you thinke of it
You are not bounded, but you may at ease
Survey, collect the good the honour profit
Of trade, of citie, countrey, rivers, seaes.
It may provoke some yet not thought upon
To raise the ruines of this decayed place;
To prosecute this hopefull worke begun
And leave some honour to our after race.

From ancient Monmouth Geffery tooke his name,
So Henry did from Huntington[1] likewise;
Why may not Glouceter ad to Taylors fame,
Since that from thence his birth and name did rise.

Gloucester this 3 of August, 1641. Yours to command
Henry Ellis.[2]

John Taylor water-poet anagramme: Loapety-Troian roweth.[3]

Strange newes! There is arrived at our key;
A wandring poet alwaies in his way;
Whose wilfull errors makes him thus to vaunt,
Aeneas-like, I came from Troyonvant.[4]

1 Geoffrey of Monmouth (d.1154), and Henry of Huntingdon (d.1155) were influential medieval chroniclers and historians.
2 A Gloucester merchant of this name endowed a charity in his will (1647).
3 Short dedicatory poems inspired by making an anagram of the subject's name were popular among Taylor's milieu. Taylor had included a collection of his own in *The Nipping and Snipping of Abuses*, 1614; and composed one at Wilton during his Salisbury journey, 1623; see pp. 190-1.
4 In Greek and Roman mythology Aeneas, the Trojan hero, journeyed to Italy and became regarded as the ancestor of the Romans. London (Troyonvant, supposed home of the Romano-British tribe the Trinovantes) was equated

I rowed in rivers sometimes checkt by milles,
Steer'd under bridges, and came over hilles.
The oares of pleasure and of profit brought
This water-poet hither in his boat;
And hence he must, but yet he will I trow
To the Brittaines[1] rather than the Latines row:
English will serve him rightly to rehearse
His crooked travells in good prose or verse.
When as the winds of fancy cease to blow him,
If he have watermen to row or tow him;
Expect relations, I beleeve in fyne
The poets waterworkes will goe in wine,
And all his dry-land passages appeare
With casuall events both here and there.
Now I doe wish he may accomplsh it
Without expence of any thing but wit.

Gloucester 3. August. 1641. Yours Jo. Dorney.[2]

John Taylors last voyage, and adventure performed from the twentieth of July last 1641. to the tenth of September following.

Of famous rivers, brooks, bournes, rills, and springs,
   Of deepes and shallowes my invention sings,
   Of rocks impenetrable, fourds and mills
Of stopps, and weares, shelves, sands, and mighty hills
Of navigable passages (neglected)
Of rivers spoyl'd, men begger'd and deiected.
Of Tame, of Isis, Seaverne, Wye and Teme
Lugge, Loden, Doyre, and Monnoes[3] pearly streame,

---

    with Troy, so the grandiose imagery is of Taylor, a latter-day Aeneas, leaving London to found a dynasty based on Gloucester

1   Unlike Camden, Taylor writes in English, not Latin.
2   Town clerk of Gloucester, who was to become prominent in town government during the civil war, on the Parliament side.
3   now Thame, Isis, Severn, Wye, Teme (a tributary of the Severn), Lugg, Ladon, Dore and Monnow (all tributaries of the Wye).

Of these, of more then these, and of their uses,
And of their miserable strange abuses.
I truely treate, that men may note and see
What blessings navigable rivers bee,
And how that thousands are debar'd those blessings,
By few mens avaritious hard oppressings.
I also shew how those faults may be mended
And no man have just cause to be offended.
And with a paire of oares (for that intent)
I once from London unto Lincolne went,
Whereas a passage seven miles was cut thorowe
From Lincolne into Trent, and to Gainsborowe;[1]
That way I past, and into Humber past
To Hull, from thence to Owse, and Yorke at last,
Another voyage to the west, againe
I (with a wherry) past the raging maine
From London to the Isle of Wight and thence
To Salisbury (with time and coynes expence)
Since when our gratious soveraigne did ordaine
The Viscount Dorchester[2] to take the paine
To view what wrongs the River Thames did beare
I served then, and every stoppe and weare
And all impediments, I found I writ
And (hoping for amendment) printed it.
For care was taken, and true industrie
That from faire Oxfords University
To London I annottomiz'd[3] the flood
And shew'd it's qualities both bad and good.
Promise was made, Thames wrongs should bee reform'd
And some small helps were speedily perform'd
But yet not halfe is done that then was spoken
(All promises are either kept or broken)
For as a monument, of our disgraces
The rivers too too fowle in many places.

1   Gainsborough, Lincs.
2   Dudley Carleton, see p. 195, note 6
3   anatomize, in the sense of examining the constituent parts.

I have describ'd heere many an injury
In three great Rivers, Severne, Thames, and Wye)
Besides two Rivers Avon, one makes speede
To Bristol, (and doth make it rich indeede.)
And would Bathe cure[1] that rivers great amisse
That city would be richer then it is,
But each man to himselfe beares private love[2]
And no man will the generall griefe remove.
The other Avon ruines[3] *[sic]* past Gloster west
From Bristols Avon fifty miles at least,
It glides to Stretford[4] towne from Coventry
And into Severne falls at Tewxbury.[5]
Of rivers, many writers well have done
Grave Camden, Draytons *Polyolbyon*,
And painefull Speede, doth in his mappes declare[6]
Where all these brookes and waters were and are,
But yet not any one have sought (but I)
To finde their wrongs, and shew some remedy.
I shew the meane neglect of navigation
For few mens profit, publique lamentation.
To encrease some five or six mens treasury
Whiles twenty thousand lives in misery,
From shore to shore brave rivers are dam'd so
That not a woodden dish hath roome to go,
no not a hand breadth, but that all is stop'd
And from the poore man all reliefe is stop'd.
It is the goodnesse of our God to give
To us foure Elements, whereby we live:
Those Elements, Fire, Water, Ayre are nam' d
And Earth (of which althings are made and fram'd,
And all those blessings, the great God of Heaven

1 An allusion to the curative properties of Bath water.
2 self-interest.
3 misprint for *runnes*.
4 Stratford on Avon, Warwicks.
5 Tewkesbury, Glos.
6 Taylor's sources of historical information: see notes on p. 197

(Some more, some lesse to every man hath given.
By ayre and breath (and breath no man buy
Ayre serves all creatures in community)
And though earth yeeld materialls for the fire,
Which many a sonne (by right) holds from his sire,
Yet sure me thinkes the water should be free
For passage, for all men of each degree.
And though the rivers in proportions are
Shar'd thine, or mine, or this or that mans share
Yet sure, where God gives water, boates to beare
It should not be stop'd up, with mill or weare.
And now my meaning plainer to disclose,
A little while I'le turne my verse to prose.

As Raine from the Firmament is drawne from the Sea, and other waters and vapours of the Earth, and Ayre, by the vigour of the Sunne, whereby rivers spring and overflow grasse, groves, fruits encrease, fishes multiplie, beasts and cattell breede and waxe fat, corne plentifull, butter and cheese in abundance, and all other blessings for the life of man or beast is nourished with milke of heaven (as raine may justly be called) So navigable rivers are the cherishing veines of the body[1] of every countrey, kingdome, and nation: And as the veines of man doth distill supporting sustinence, to every part and member of his body; so doe passable rivers convey all manner of commodities from place to place, to the benefit of all and every place in every countrey and teritorie.

    My selfe bearing a naturall affection to portable[2] rivers, and a setled inclination and desire of the preservation and use of them, did for the same intent especially lately passe with a small scullers boate into five great rivers of this kingdome; for the which intent, (to beare charges)[3] I procured divers[4] of my friends to subscribe to severall bills, for them to pay me some severall small summes of money, upon my

---

1 William Harvey had published his discovery of the circulation of the blood a few years earlier, in 1628.
2 occasionally used, as here, to mean 'capable of carrying' (i.e. navigable) rather than 'capable of being carried'.
3 i.e. to pay my expenses.
4 various.

delivery to each of them a booke at my returne of the passages and entertainements which I had in my journey; which booke this is, which you are now reading, and how I past out and came back againe, with many occurrences that happened I have truely related as followeth.

On the twentieth day of July last, 1641. (the second day of the dogged Dogdayes[1] (I with my two men and a brace of boyes were embarqued with a scullers boate first from London, and within halfe a quarter of an houre after, I past from my house neare the Beares Colledge[2] on the Banckside, I tooke leave of some friends, and had a flagge advanced as a token of my publike departure; but some enemies gave out that I was runne away, who I doe know (since my returne,) to be a crew of malicious vermin, (that still being the most auntient name of their captaine and leader,) on the day afforesaid with many stops, stayes, and taking leaves, wee gat to Oatlands at night, and lodged at Weybridge at the signe of the sixe Ankers. The next day, being wendnesday I strived against the streame as farre as Great Marlow, in Buckinghamshire, where I lodg'd at the signe of the Crowne. Thurseday the 22. of July, I past (with much toyle) from Marlow to Goring; and the next day I came to Abington. If it be demanded why I was so may[3] [sic] dayes in passing 130 miles, I answer that the river (by reason of a great drought) wanted water in may places, so that wee were forc'd to wade, and leade or hale[4] the boate divers times, and moreover we did pull the said boate over or thorough 14. locks, besides many other impediments, which hindred our passage.

As farre as above Stanes (which is forty miles by water from London, the River Thames is by the care and providence of the Lord Mayor well conserved and kept from impediments of stops, weares, sand beds and other hindrances of passages of eyther boates or barges, and from Stanes to the furthest part almost there is no stoppage (but only weares, which weares have lockes to open and shut for the passing to and fro of all manner of vessells (passable thorough from London to

---

1 July and August, when Sirius, the dog-star, appeared close to the sun, and was believed to augment its heat-giving properties. A favourite expression of Taylor's.
2 Facetiously for the Bear Gardens and baiting ring on Bankside.
3 misprint for *many*.
4 i.e. haul.

Oxford; betwixt which cities the barges doe draw up nineteene of those lockes with engines (like capstanes) which are called crabbs.[1] I doe relate this heare, because the reader may by that which followeth understand, that though weares be necessary in rivers, yet they ought not to stop up all passages, but to suffer lockes to be opened and shut as Thames hath.

Thursday the twenty seaven, I passed with my boate from Abington[2] to Oxford, where I was well entertained with good cheere and worshipfull company at University Colledge; The next day I passed to a place called Bablack Hive (or Hithe.)[3] And on Thursday the twenty nine, I passed by Lechlad,[4] and came to Creeklad;[5] This towne of Creeklad is five miles distant by land from Ciciter,[6] but it is easier to row sixtie miles by water on the River of Thames, then it is to passe betweene those two townes, for there are so many milles, fords and shallowes with stops, and other impediments that a whole daies hard labour with my selfe and foure more could neyther by toyle or art get but to a mill of one Master Hortones at a place called Suddington,[7] a mile short of Ciciter, so that according to land measure we went but foure miles in a long dayes travell. The last of July I left Suddington Mill, with the honest welcome of the miller and his wife, and with much a doe for want of water I gatt to Ciciter, where the river was so dry that it would beare my boate no further; at the hither end of that towne there stands a great barne belonging to one Cooke, of whom I hired a waine, wherein I put my boate my selfe and my men, boyes, and luggage; this waine did in lesse then five houres draw me from the River Isis neere Ciciter, to a brooke called Stroud, which booke [sic] hath it's head or spring in Bessley Hundred neere Misserden[8] in Cotswould in Glostershire, (Stowd and Churne might be cut into one, and so Severne and Thames might be made almost joyned friends) are within 4. miles of Churne, which hath

1 pound locks were not in general use; the more primitive flash-locks required the boat to be winched against the flow through hatches temporarily opened for the purpose. The winch was known as a crab.
2 Abingdon, Berks.
3 Bablock Hithe, Oxon, south of Eynsham.
4 Lechlade, Glos.
5 Cricklade, Wilts.
6 Cirencester, Glos.
7 Siddington, Glos., south of Cirencester.
8 The Stroudwater rises near Miserden in Bisley hundred.

its first spring nere Coberley,[1] 7. miles from Glocester and falles into Isis about Laechlad, so that 4 miles cutting in the land betwixt Churne and Stroud, would be a meanes to make passages from Thames to Severne, to Wye, to both the Rivers of Avon in England, and to one River of Avon in Monmouthshire, which falles into the River of Uske neere Carlion[2] in Wales. By which meanes goods might be conveyed by water too and from London, in rivers at cheape rates without danger, almost to half the countyes in England and Wales. But there is a devill or two called sloth and covetuousnesse, that are the bane of all good endeavours and laudable actions, but more of this shall be said hereafter.

I being uncarted (with my boate) at a place called Stonehouse, in the afforesaid brooke called Stroud, with passing and wading, with haling over high bankes at fulling milles (where there are many) with plucking over suncke trees, over and under strange bridges of wood and stone, and in some places the brooke was scarce as broad as my boate, I being oftentimes impeached[3] with the bowghes and branches of willowes and alder trees, which grew so thicke, hanging over and into the brooke, so that the day light or sunne could scarce peepe through the branches, that in many places all passages were stop'd; so that I was sometimes forced to cut and hew out my way with a hatchett; with this miserable toyle all the day I gat at night to a mill called Froombridge Mill,[4] whereas (for our comfort) was neither victualing house, meate, drinke or lodging, but that a good gentlewoman, one Mistris Bowser, there did comiserare[5] our wants, and though she were not accustomed to victuall or lodge travellers, yet the rarety of our boate, and strangenes of my adventure moved her so farre that shee at an easie rate did furnish us with good dyet, my selfe with a bed in an out-house, and my men and boyes with a sweet new mowed and new made hayloft.

I am much ingaged[6] to a gentleman (one Master John Stephens,) whose worthy father Nathaniell Stephans Esquire) is one of the knights of the shire for the county of Glocester, in this honorable and high court

1   south of Cheltenham, described on p. 198.
2   Caerleon, Mon., near Newport.
3   impeded.
4   Fromebridge Mill, Glos., east of Frampton on Severn.
5   The reading could be *comiserare*; perhaps a misprint for *comiserate*.
6   obliged.

of Parliament. To this house at Estingron[1] (corruptly called Eston) I was invited from the mill with my company, where we both at dinner and supper had welcome and good entertainement on Sunday the first of August. I doe further acknowledge my gratitude to Master Mew the minister there, both for his spirituall paines taking, twice the said Saboth, and and [sic] also[2] I thanke him for other courtesies which hee bestowed on me.

Munday the second of August I tooke my leave at Froombridge Mill, and (falling to our old worke againe of haleing and draweing from mill to mill, and from one hindrance to another, I came at last to Whitmister,[3] where after I had plucked my boate over, I with my Murnivall[4] of followers were stayed at the command of a worthy gentleman named Master Thomas Lloyd, to whose house neere there[5] we went upon small intreaty, whence my sudden entertainement was so freely generous as might have beseemed the perso' of a good knight or esquire. The said gentleman went with me to the brookes mouth, and saw me entred into the River of Severne, where (with thankes) I tooke my leave of him, and in two or three howers space I swom up the Severne to the ancient citie of Glocester, where I was borne, and where by reason of almost fifty yeares absence I was scarce knowne. But the right worshipfull Thomas Hill Esquire, Mayor of Glocester gave me noble entertainement, and invited mee and my servants to his house: the next day at dinner, and afterwards about three in the afternoone, he came to the key at the river side, where I entred my boate and tooke leave of him, & went to Tewxbury being (some twelve miles by water that night, the fourth of August I past by the citie of Worcester up the river to Bewdley, where I lodged at the signe of the Pyde Bull; The third of August, I went from Bewdley (being an extreame rainy day) and that night approaching I saw a faire house[6] belonging to a knight named Sir William Whitmore, thither I went and demanded of some of his

---

1 Eastington, Glos.
2 *and and also* is printed in error.
3 Whitminster, Glos.
4 a mournival, in card-playing a set of four aces or other picture cards, used figuratively of his four companions.
5 Whitminster (or Wheatenhurst) House.
6 A predecessor of the present Apley Hall, near Bridgnorth.

servants whether lodging might bee had for money, where a poore man did answer, that if I would but crosse the river with him, and goe but halfe a mile up a hill, I should have the best entertainement his poore cottage could afford, and necessity having no law, I accepted willingly;

And surely that faire house I last spake of, was of a strange operation, for I was wet to the skinne when I went thither, and in lesse then halfe a quarter of an houre I came away as dry as ever I was in my life; this is a misterie or a riddle, for I saw not the butler.[1]

The sixt of August I past thorough many sharpe streames, fords, and shallowes to a place called Coond-lane-end,[2] where I lodged at a smiths, it being the one and only house there

The seventh of August (being Saterdy) I arived at Shrosebury,[3] where I tooke harbour at one Luckmans house upon the lower bridge, in the afternoone I went to the Major Thomas Wingfield Esquire, he bad me welcom (but had no leasure to bid me drinke,) but he came from the Towne Hall with me to my lodging, and saw mee in my boate, and afterwards with his hand and seale of his office, tooke his leave dryly of me. But Master Thomas Jones, an alderman there, that had borne the office of a bayliffe there, sixe times before Shrewesbury was a mayor towne, and (as I was informed hee was the first mayor of that place,[4] and he hath also beene high Sheriffe of the County of Salop (or Shropshire) that gentleman invited mee to dine with him on munday the ninth of August, where there was no want of good company, fish, flesh, foule, venison, wine, and welcom.

That afternoone I left Shewesbury, and returned downe the river twelve miles by water to Coonde-lane-end, where I lodged at my old hosts the smiths house.

The tenth of August I came to the citie of Worcester, where the right worshipfull William Norris Esquire, Mayor there made me extraordinarily welcome, giving his testimoniall under his hand and seale of Mayoraltie, that I was there with my boate.

1 Presumably a proverb, though not traced.
2 Coundlane, Salop, south-east of Shrewsbury.
3 Shrewsbury, Salop.
4 Thomas Jones, an immensely rich merchant, was Shrewsbury's first mayor, in 1638; his house, Jones's Mansion, stood at the foot of Wyle Cop, and was demolished in 1829.

Wendnesday the eleventh of August I returned to Gloucester, where I was well entertained at a venison feast, by the right worshipfull Master Mayor and his Bretheren. And presently (after dinner) I tooke boate and left Gloucester, and past downe the river 12. miles to a place called Gatcombe,[1] there I stayed while such time as the tyde would serve me towards Brystow,[2] (which was about midnight,) But one Master Hooper that dwells there, being a very good seaman, did give me good instructions and directions to avoyde many dangers in that nightly passage, besides I followed the tract of a boate laden with fruit which was bound for Bristow, so that after all nights labour amongst rockes and perrilous deepes, whirling gulfes and violent streames, about the breake of day, on Friday the 13 of August, I came to Kingroad, and staying there a while for the flood, I past up that River of Avon at Hungroad by Crockhampill,[3] and by nine of the clock in the forenoone I came to the rich and famous city of Bristoll.

My entertainement there I will set downe in briefe, which was by the right worshipfull John Taylor Esquier Mayor, a gentleman endowed (by the bounty of Heaven) both with right and left hand blessings, on Sunday the fifteenth of August my selfe and followers were his invited guests twice: and the next day hee gave mee a certificate under hand and seale of my arivall at that citie, and at my taking leave of him (he knowing that travell was chargeable) did discharge a peece at me,[4] and I unfearefull of the shott, did put it up most thankefully; my humble thankes to my cosin Master Thomas Taylor at the Marsh[5] there, whose friendship and favour I cannot requit or forget.

On the sixteenth of August I departed from Bristoll, towards the citie of Bath, which is ten miles distant by land, and neere seventeene by water, which with passing by water over foure or five milles and weares, I attained to, at which citie of Bathe I stayed two nights, being

1 near Blakeney, Glos., on the Dean side of the estuary.
2 Bristol.
3 King Road is an anchorage in the Severn estuary opposite Avonmouth, Hung Road is in the Avon next to Pill (formerly Crockern Pill) on the Somerset bank.
4 a favourite pun, meaning 'gave me a coin' rather than 'fired at me'.
5 probably St Phillip's Marsh, a suburb around Bristol Castle.

welcome to the right worshipfull Master Mathew Clift mayor,[1] with good entertainement from him and some other townesmen, I tooke his hand and seale of Mayoraltie for my certificate, and so returned to Bristoll againe on wednesday the eighteenth of August.

The nineteenth of August, at midnight I left Bristoll, and with the tyde past downe the river into Kingroad, where I lay at the Hole mouth (as they call it) till the flood came, and day light beginning to appeare, with the same tyde I past the broad water twelve miles to the River of Wye in Monmouth shire; that day I past by Cheapstow,[2] by the old Abbey of Tinterne, and to litle Tinterne[3] where I lay all that night, in a very cleanely wholsome welch English alehouse. The twenty one I came to Monmouth (the shire towne of that countrey) where one Master William Guilliam) did give me such entertainement at his house (on Sunday the twenty two of August,) as I am bound gratefully to remember.

Munday the twenty three of August, I left Monmouth, and (with a whole dayes labour by water) according to the miles by land) I got not a foote of ground; for at night when I came to a place called Lidbrooke,[4] I was twelve miles from Hereford, and I was but twelve miles from the said citie when I was in the morning at the towne of Mounmouth, this doth shew that the River of Wye doth runne a littie [sic] crooked from Lidbrooke. I went (on Saint Bartholomewes day)[5] to the towne of Rosse,[6] where I lodged nere Wilton Bridge there: and on the twentie five I went to Foane Hope;[7] and the twenty six day about tenne of the clocke I gat to the citie of Hereford, which was the last place and the end of my painefull travell, joruney, voyage, perambulation, and peregrination, or what you please to call it; at Hereford I was invited to three severall places to dine on the Friday, and I being not able to satisfie them all, gave them all the slippe, the three places were Edmond Ashton Esquire

---

1 Clift was a leading Puritan in Bath, with whom Taylor can have had little sympathy. He received a less cordial welcome when he returned to Bath nine years later: see p. 293.
2 Chepstow, Mon.
3 Tintern Parva, north of Tintern Abbey, Mon.
4 Lower Lydbrook, Glos., north of Coleford.
5 24th August (Taylor's 63rd birthday).
6 Ross on Wye, Herefs.
7 Fownhope, Herefs., south-east of Hereford.

Mayor, the second the vicars at the minster or colledge;[1] thirdly, at a taverne with diverse gentlemen, but I having gotten the mayors hand and seale, because I could not please all, left all, and stole away like a true man, leaving my thankes for Master Mayor, and Master Phillip Traherne, with all the rest, for their kindnesse to me the day before.

At my being at Hereford I was in a quandary or browne studdy,[2] whether it were best to sell my boat, and returne to London by land, or else to bring the boate home againe either by land or water, or both, or how I could: at last I determined and resolved to bring the monumentall vessell backe againe, which I did as followeth.

On friday the 27. of August I passed downe the River of Wye to a place called Inckson Weare,[3] where, with great entertainement and welcom I was lodged and my men also at the house of one Master Aperley, dwelling there, to whom (for many) favours I doe acknowledge my selfe to bee extraordinarily beholding. And on the Saterday I came to Lidbrook to my former hoste Master Mosse, where understanding and knowing the passage down Wye and up Severne to be very long and dangerous (especially if stormye weather should arise, the boate being split, torne and shaken that she did leake very much) these things considered, and that I was within five miles of Severne by land to Newnham, and that by water thither there was no lesse than 50 miles, I hired a wayne frow[4] [sic] Lidbrook to Newnham. And on Munday the 30. of August I past up Severne, by Glocester (and working all night) came in the morning betimes to Tewxbury, into another river called Avon, which by the great charge and industry of Master Sands is made navigable, many miles up into the countrey. Tuseday the 31 of August I came to a market towne in Worcestershire called Pershore. On the first of September I came to the auncient towne of Evesholm (corruptly called Esham)[5] and seeing that river to bee further and further out of my way home, I hired another wayne from Esham to Burford, where I found a crooked brooke called Windrush, in which brooke (after one

---

1 The college of the vicars choral forms part of the cathedral precinct.
2 serious or gloomy uncertainty.
3 Presumably Ingestone, near Foy, Herefs., in a meander of the Wye north of Ross.
4 misprint for *from*.
5 Evesham, Worcs.

nights lodging) with my appendixes having taken each of us a Burford bait,[1] we passed many strange letts and hindrances into the River of Isis or Thames: Againe at Newbridge 12. or 14. miles from Oxford by water. By which university I past to Abingdon. The fourth of September, where I stayed till Wednesday the eight day: from thence was I with my boate at home on the Friday following And thus in lesse then twenty dayes labour 1200. miles were past to and fro in most hard, difficult and many dangerous passages, for the which I give God most humble and hearty prayse and thankes; and now I crave the readers patlence [sic] a little whilst I briefely treate of a few things that may bee profitable as well as pleasant.

I have before related of certaine stops, milles, and wares that doe hinder the passages of boates of Thames and Isis, now I will treate a little of the abuses and uses of other rivers.

As for the River of Severne, it is almost as much abus'd as us'd, for an instance, there are coale-mines neere it, and by the benefit of that river, mane a hundred family is served with sufficient fewell at cheape rates, but some of those cole-mines doe yeeld neere 1000 tunnes of rubbish yearely, which by reason of the neerenesse of the river is all washed into it, and makes so many shallowes, that in time Severne will bee quite choaked up, and all passage stopped, but of that river more at the conclusion.

Avon River, that serveth Bristoll would also be made to serve Bathe, and many other parts and places, if lockes were made at west Hanham weare, and at Kenisham,[2] (with 4. or 5. places more) for the river doth offer Gods blessing to the peoples mouthes, if they would but open their lippes to receive them.

The River Wye is debard of all passages with boates, by 7. weares, 2. of them are Monmouth Weare, and Wilton Weare,[3] the other 5. are Inkson Weare, Carow,[4] Founehope, Hancocks[5] and Bondnam[6]

1 a heady brew to make one drunk, referred to by Taylor in his *Catalogue of Taverns*, 1636 (see p. 426), and later by Fuller.
2 Keynsham, Som.
3 immediately west of Ross on Wye.
4 perhaps Carey, near Ballingham, west of Brockhampton.
5 perhaps Hadnock, east of Monmouth.
6 possibly Baynham, in Welsh Bicknor, south-east of Goodrich.

Weare, these seven weares (like the seven deadly sinnes) doe dam up all goodnesse that should come from Monmouth to Hereford by water, and if the yron milles[1] in the forrest of Deane doe eate up all the wood there (as it hath already done reasonably well and ill) within these few yeares, if the passages be stopt with weares that coales cannot be carried by water to Hereford and many other places, it is to be feared that many rich men will bee glad to blow their fingers ends in the winter through want of fiering, and numbers of poore will perish with extreame cold; the complaints and cryes are grievous already; which if I had not heard and seene I would not have beleeved: and 7. lockes at those weares would helpe all and hinder nobody, or else onely two lockes would doe much good, the one at Monmouth Weare, and the other at Wilton, which is but eight miles from Hereford, and good way by land, for the carriage of any thing that might be brought by water.

For the other Kiver [sic] Avon, it comes from beyond the city of Coventry, and running by the townes of Stretford, Evesholme, and Pershore, it falles into Severne at Tewxbury, so that Gloucestershire (my native countrey) is encompast round with navigable rivers, of which citie and countrey I will speake a little for countries sake, but most of all for love I beare to truth and charity.

Records and histories[2] doe make true relation of the antiquity of the citie of Gloucester, that it was built by Arviragus (a Brittaine king) in the time of Claudius Tiberius Caesar, The said Claudius being the Roman emperour, and commander of the whole world; in whose raigne our blessed Saviour suffered; King Arviragus and Lucius (the first Christian king doe lye there buried: when the Saxons had the rule and domination here in the raigne of Uter Pendragon and the renowned worthy King Arthur, that city and county had a duke, a bishop, and a major; above 1100 yeares past, their names were Edell, Eldadus, and Eldor, the shire is divided in 33. hundreds, of which the citie it selfe is one, and two hundreds more named Kings Burton and Dunstone, with 30. townes and villages are annexed to the said citie; which is all under the commande of the major and his brethren. It hath beene anciently famous for the trade of merchandising, (now altogether decayed, the

1 The king's ironworks, the most important of the early blast furnaces in Dean, were erected in 1612-13.
2 This account is derived largely from Camden's *Britannia* (1610 edn.)

more is the pitty) King Henry the third was crowned there the 28. of October 1216, there hath been many Dukes and Earles of Glocester since the Norman Conquest, as first Robert fitz Hamon, second William de Mondevill, third Robert de Millent, which Robert was taken prisoner and was exchanged for King Stephen, the said king being then taken prisoner by Maude the Empresse) the fourth Earle of Glocester, was William sonne to the said Robert, and Lord of Glamorgan, was buried at Kinsham 1183. John (who was afterwards King of England) was the third *[sic]* Earle of Glocester, the Sixt was Almerick Mountfort, buried at Keinsham. Sixt Geoffery de mandevile, he was slaine at a tilting or tournament 1216. The 7. was Gilbert di Clare 1230. The 8. Richard de Clare 1262. The 9. Gilbert de Clare, the second of that name 1295. all these three were buried at Tewxbury. Richard de Mount hermer was the 10. Earle 1323. Gilbert de Clare (the son of Gilbert the second) was the 11. Earle, was slaine at Sherbin in Scotland, and buried at Tewxbury 1313. Hugh de Audley the 12 Earle dyed 1347. buried at Tunbridge. Thomas of Woodstock, the son of K. Edward the third, Duke of Glocester, was murthered at Callice 1397. Thomas Spencer the 13 Earle, was beheaded at Bristow 1400. Humphrey Plantagenet, the fourth son of K. Edward the fourth (who was called the good Duke Humphrey) was murthered, buried at S. Albons 1440. Richard Duke of Glocester (afterwards King of England) was slaine at the battle of Bosworth, and buried at Leicester, 1485. Henry of Oatlands the fourth sonne to our Soveraigne Lord King Charels, was borne at Oatlands in Surey on wednesday the eight of July 1640, now Duke of Glocester, whom God blesse. And so much (though much more might be said for the honour of Glocester and Glocestershire.

That commerce and trade is the strength and sinnewes of the common wealth, the chiefe and onely subsistance of cities and corporations, it is apparently evident. And the greatest honour and glory of kingdomes, and the reasons why severall meanes there are that brings wealth and honour to a citie, all of them put together in one ballance, and the trade of merchandising in the other, it shall overprize[1] them al, upon it alone hangs and depends almost all other trades, it brings great wealth and honour to all places where it is prosecuted with successe.

---

1   to surpass in value; but perhaps a misprint for *overpoize* [*overpoise*], which would bear the precise meaning of 'outweigh'.

Witnesse that of Leogorne,[1] which within this 30. or 40. yeares was but a poore fishing towne which by that trade alone is now the greatest mart of the Medeterenian Seas. As likewise the Low-countries, although they cannot build a ship, but must fetch the materials from 6. severall kingdomes, yet they build and have more ships then all Christendome besides, and have not any thing almost of a naturall staple commodity to deale upon, yet by that trade alone they have ingrossed the greatest part of the trade, of the Christian world to the'selves; and some of them (if they please) may be gaineful in the trade of merchandising there. Now that the citie of Glocester is scituated in as convenient a place as any other within this kingdome, the reasons following shall demonstrate. First the said citie hath beene an auncient port towne, graced and infranchesed with priviledges as ample as London, or any other citie or towne within this kingdom, and dignified with the title of the 3. son of the Kings, and hath beene famous in former ages for the trade of merchandizing now altogether decayed; And is likewise situated in as rich a soyle as any in this kingdome, whose markets are alwaies stored with abundance and varieties of all commodities that the kingdome of England affords, incident to the life and being of man. And it is likewise situated in as convenient a place for any trade of merchandizing being upon the famous River of Severne, then which there is not any more miles navigable within this kingdome, and also the River of Avon being made navigable within foure miles of Warwick which standeth in the heart and center of the said kingdome, having both the said rivers, the advantage of all opportunities both for exportation and importation of all goods and commodities whatsoever into and from at least a third part of the said kingdome, and which parts vents[2] as many forraine commodities and yeelds as many varieties of commodities as any other part of the said kingdome doth. And which said parts cannot bee served by or from any other parts, then by the said rivers unlesse they will fetch and bring their commodities over the land three or foure score miles at a great charge, which cannot be conceived they will doe, if it may be brought home to their doores by water; the said citie having by speciall grant under the Great Seale, a spatious and convenient key

1   Leghorn, now Livorno, the Italian port near Pisa.
2   sells or trades in.

or wharfe built of stone neare the Kings Custome-house upon the said river, at which key or wharfe the sea doth in its due course continually ebbe and flow for the bringing in and out of ships, and other boates of convenient burthen, so that a ship of a hundred and fifty tunne, or thereabouts, may at every tide come to Gatcombe, which is but 12 miles from Gloucester, and there lye secure, and the River of Wye runneth into the Severne tenne miles above Kingrode, where ships of two or three hundred tunnes may lye secure and safe.

And I have observed, that the trade that Bristoll driveth up to the city of Gloucester: and beyond it, in small barkes hoighes and trowes,[1] is at the least two hundred tunnes of all commodities, every spring,[2] which is every fortnight or lesse. And it is conceived and more then probable, that if the said trade of merchandizing were settled within the said city of Gloucester, (as heretofore it hath beene) that neither the trades men of the said city of Gloucester, nor others that live three or foure score miles above it, will goe downe to Bristoll, and may have their commodities in Gloucester, for divers reasons and inconveniences that may thereby happen.

At first it saveth threescoure miles riding in a dirty countrey, next the ventring[3] of their goods from Bristoll to Gloucester by water, sometimes cast away, sometimes (the spring not serving) they are benept,[4] and so cannot have their commodities to serve their turne, but usually much abused by trow-men, so that many that live up the river beyond Gloucester, are thereby greatly discouraged, and doe many times buy their commoditys at London, Souththampton, Hull, and Chester, and so bring it home by land three or fourescore miles at a great charge, which if the trade were settled at Gloucester they would not doe, for which reasons aforesaid and many other that might be alledged, it hath caused divers men well skilled and versed in the said trade of merchandizing, much to wonder that the said trade hath beene so long neglected, many of which hath concluded that the said city of Gloucester with the said key and havens, and the Kings custome house thereunto, doe lye as convenient for the said trade of merchandizing, as any other

1 varieties of river craft.
2 the highest tides, which occur after full and new moon.
3 risking.
4 beneaped, i.e. left aground by the neap tides.

city or towne within this kingdom, and might drive the greatest trade of any other (London only excepted.) For this city of Gloucester, stands almost within (or neere) the center of this kingdome, and for exportation and importation, of all native and forraigne commodities (by reason of the riches of the soyle) and commodiousnesse of the adiacent rivers, it is comparable to any place, except the metropolis London. The village of Galcombe [sic] being at first built for the trade of Gloucester, (most commodious.) Now forasmuch as it may be objected, that the River of Seavern is dangerous, I must confesse it is so to those that know it not; and through want of practise (whereby experience showeth) but to those that know it, noe danger at all. For there is not one barge in twenty that hath beene cast away, but it hath been by the owners covetousnes in loding too deep, or venturing too rash upo' the tide, for feare they should be be [sic] kept,[1] and so loose the spring, all which with a certaine trade up and downe the river might wisely be prevented; All other difficulties that can or may be alledged, are of small consequence to hinder, if men of meanes and ingenious spirits doe undertake it. The reason aforesaid hath induced some men well affected to the publike good, and welfarre of this city, to endeavour a beginning of this most honourable action, and were they seconded with that incouragement from others, which if they were as willing, as every way able, both with their place and meanes, The necessity of this cause so earnestly requiring it, the necessity of this cause (I say) so greatly moveing it, there is no doubt but by the blessing of the Almighty, and that in a short time it might raise the ruines of the decayed trade of this city, so much complained of by all, and make it as honourable as now it is contemptible, which is and shal be the deadly prayers and desires of him, who presenteth this; Hoping that no churlish Naball, mallicious Sanballat, corrupted Tobiah, proud Haman, unmercifull Dives,[2] or any of the deadly sinnes, can or shall hinder so good a worke.

For who can (but with pittie) here behold
These multitudes of mischiefes manifold,
Shall rivers thus be barr'd with stops and locks,

1 probably a misprint for *be benept*, see previous note.
2 Four Old Testament miscreants, and Dives, uncharitable wealth personified in the parable of Dives and Lazarus, Luke 16, verses 19-31.

With mills, and hills, with gravels beds, and rocks:
With weares, and weedes, and forced islands made,
To spoyle a publique for a private trade?
Shame fall the doers, and th'Almighties blessing
Be heap'd upon their heads that seeke redressing.
Were such a businesse to be done in Flanders
Or Holland mongst the industrious Netherlanders,
They to deepe passages would turne our hils,
To windmills they would change our watermils.
All helps unto these rivers they would ayd,
And all impediments shall be destroyed:
Our vagabonds (the wandring brood of Caine,)
They would inforce those runnagates take paine,
Whereby much profit quickly would accrue,
(For labour robs the hangman of his due.)
In common reason, all men must agre:
That if these rivers were made cleane and free,
One barge, with eight poore mens industrious paines,
Would carry more than forty carts or waines.
And every waine to draw them horses five,
And each two men or boye, to guide or drive.
Charge of an hundred horse and eighty men
With eight mens labour would be served then,
Thus man would be imployd, and horse preserv'd,
And all the countrey at cheape rates be serv'd.
'Tis said the Dutchmen taught us drinke and swill,
I'm sure we goe beyond them in that skill,
I wish (as we exceede them in what's bad,)
That we some portion of their goodnesse had:
Then should this worthy worke be soone begun,
And with successefull expedition done?
Which I dispaire not of, but humbly plead,
That God his blessings will increase and spread
On them that love this worke, and on their heires,
Their goods and chattels, and on all that's theirs?
I wish them blest externall, and internall,

And in the end with happinesse eternall.[1]

In the most part of my journey, I came to few places but their was to be found plenty of beggers, or doggmaticall, scismaticall, full of beggerly rudiments, as the apostle saith, Galathians 4.[2] Opinionated divers wayes; and every one would have his owne fancy, to stand for his religion; for they all differ one from another, yet all joyne against that which they have beene baptized and brought up in; In one place there is a blind old woman, and she repeates, and interprets: in another a pavier, and he will take upon him to mend the way. Then their is a strange fellow (a baker,) one light loafe and he will new bolt, fist, knead, and mould relligion. In another a quondam brewers clearke, (would fame be a priest) and preaches most wonderfully in a mault house, besides a zealous sowgelder, that professeth most desperate doctrine, Good Lord in thy mercy looke upon us, and give us true peace and unity, both in Church and Commonwealth.

FINIS.

1   reused from the end of the Thames journey, pp. 212-13.
2   Galatians 4 verse 9: '... how turn ye again to the weak and beggarly elements...'

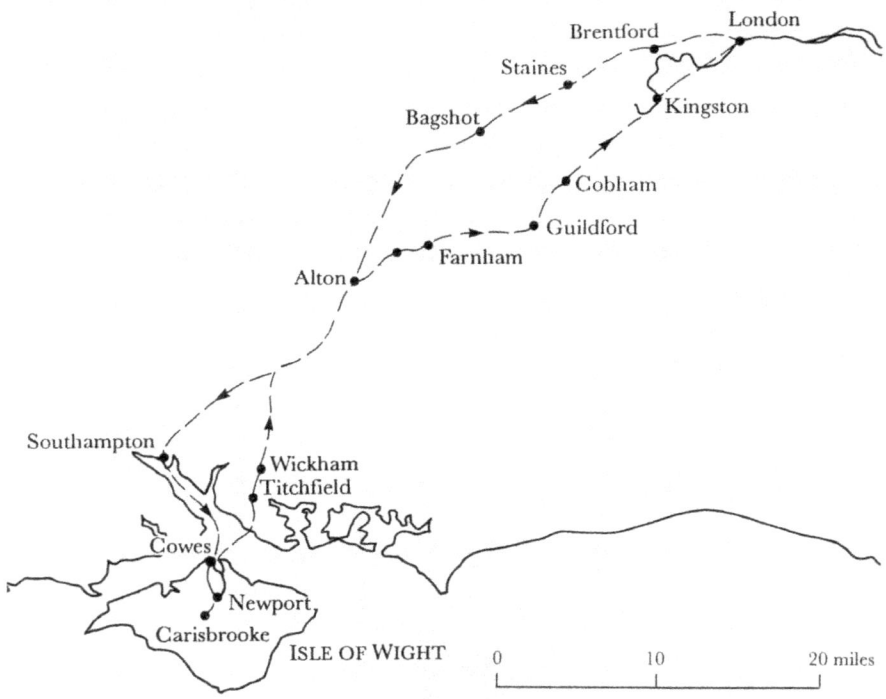

Tailors Travels, from London to the Isle of Wight

TAILORS TRAVELS, FROM LONDON, TO THE ISLE OF WIGHT: WITH HIS RETURNE, AND OCCASION OF HIS JOURNEY.

*T*AILORS TRAVELS, FROM LONDON TO THE ISLE OF WIGHT, *set the seal on the most turbulent period of Taylor's life, and of the nation during his lifetime. In early 1643, after threats and attempts on his life, he fled London and made his way to court at Oxford, where he spent the first civil war (to 1646) as a water-bailiff controlling traffic on the Isis. He also wrote Royalist propaganda. The cause lost he returned to London, and by 1647, in abject penury, he was running an alehouse near Covent Garden. The failure of the second civil war in 1648 saw the king under arrest at Carisbrooke Castle, and in October Taylor resolved to visit him.*

This is the most highly-charged of Taylor's journeys. We see him operating as a journalist, reporting events and negotiations on the Isle of Wight up to the day of his departure, and carrying the news back to London. We see him too, no longer a cynic with regard to quack remedies, as Royalist pamphleteer, cataloguing (almost as hagiography) the miraculous cures of those resorting to 'touch for the king's evil' (traditionally physical contact with the reigning monarch was a cure for scrofula). We learn too that his personal reason for the journey was his desperate poverty -- a desperation that would send him out on the road four times more. Finally we see that he has not lost his sense of humour. Approaching Newport on horseback he and a maid are thrown into the mud when their horse loses its footing. It was their guide's fault for misleading them, and he is rewarded with one of Taylor's most graphic and comprehensive curses, extending to twenty lines of 'riff raff rime'.

[19th Oct. - 13th Nov. 1648. Text derived from 1648 publication (copy BL 10368 b.23)]

Tailors travels, from London, to the Isle of Wight: with his returne, and occasion of his journey.

The occasion why I undertooke this insulary journey or voyage from one island to another, was for three respects: First, I had a great importunate desire to see my Gracious Soveraigne afflicted Lord and Master: Secondly, I travelled with an intent to get some silver in this iron age, (for pleasure and profit should be the reward of honest and harmelesse paines taking.) Before I began this high and mighty perambulation, I did put forth many bills to divers and sundry friends, to pay me some small sums of that pretious thing called money, at my returne; the purport, purpose, pretence, signification, meaning, or marrow-bone of the bill, were these following words.

When John Taylor hath beene from London to the Isle of Wight, and returned againe, and that at his returne, he doe give or cause to be given to me, a booke or pamphlet of true newes and relations of passages at the island, and to and fro in his journey; I doe promise to give to him or his assignes, the summe of what I please in lawfull money of England, provided that the sayd summe be not under 6 pence.

Now at my returne, if all my customers doe pay me according to the bill then am I exceedingly deceived; but if none of them doe pay me, then I am meerely couzened; and now begins the story.

Printed at the authors charge, and are no where to be sold, 1648.

This pamphlet is not stuft with triviall bables,[1]
Or vaine prodigious undisgested[2] fables:
This is no Mercury[3] (with scoffs, and jeeres)
To raise debate, and set us by the eares,
As if poore England had not yet endur'd

1   i.e. babbles, 'prattle'.
2   undigested.
3   printed newsheets of propaganda which were issued by both sides during the civil war.

Sufficient plagues, but she must be assur'd,
By new, new, newes, of new frights, and new foes,
And future mischiefes worse than present woes:
I bring no tidings of such consequence,
To breed feares, jealousies, or give offence,
Nor am I fraught with wonders, wounds, and scarres,
Or any thing relating to the warres:
It is so writ that no man can accuse
Me of detraction, scandall, or abuse;
My lines are all from feare and horror free,
And here and there as true as true may be:
Yea much more true, I may be bound to sweare
Then many bookes have beene this twice foure yeare,
Or any Mercury writ heretofore,
Or old Currantoes,[1] in the daies of yore.
Then stroke your beards, or wipe your mouthes (at least,)
And read, and heare what I have here exprest.

The next succeeding month unto September,
October was this yeare, (as I remember)
Without the charge of proxey or atturney,
My selfe in proper person[2] tooke this journey:[3]
Two gentlewomen (by two maides attended)
Accompanied me till my travells ended.
We tooke one coach, two coach-men, and foure horses,
And merrily from London made our courses:
We wheel'd the top of th' heavy hill, call'd Holborne,
(Up which hath been full many a sinfull soule borne:)[4]
And so along we jolted past Saint Gileses,
Which place from Brainford,[5] six (or neere) seven miles is.

---

1   i.e. corantos, propaganda news-sheets similar to mercuries.
2   archaic expression, translating *in propria persona*, simply meaning 'in person'.
3   'I set forth on Thursday the 19. of Octob.' [Taylor]
4   'We hired the Southamton coach which comes weekly to the Rose near Holborne Bridge.' [Taylor] Holborn led to Tyburn, the former name of Marylebone, where hangings took place.
5   Brentford, Middlesex.

To Stanes that night at five a clock we coasted,
Where (at the Bush)[1] we had bak'd, boyl'd, and roasted.
Bright Sols illustrious rayes, the day adorning,
We past Bagshot and Bawwaw,[2] Friday morning;
That night we lodg'd at the White Hart at Alton,
And had good meate, a table with a salt on:
Next morne w' arose, with blushing cheek'd Aurora;[3]
The wayes were faire but not so faire as Flora:
For Flora was a Goddesse, and a woman,
And (like the high wayes) was to all men common:[4]
Our horses, with the coach, which we went into,
Did hurry us amaine through thick and thine to
With fiery speede, the foaming bits they champt on,
And brought us to the Dolphin at Southampton.
There found I friendship more then I expected
Or did deserve, so much to be respected:
The gentlewomen both their husbands met there;
The moone was mounted, and the sun was set there;
And after two houres time, or some such matter
We turn'd our coach t' a boat, and swam by water;
My entertainement was good wine and welcome,
The cups most kindly unto me pell mell come;
Southamptons Governour, much love did show me,
He was my old acquaintance, and did know me:
He gave me' s passe, to passe me to the Island
And I tooke boate, and left him on the dry land;
It was as bright a mooneshine night, I say
As ever man saw in a summers day;
Thus with a fore winde, and faire Cintha's light,[5]

1 'The signe of the Bush.' [Taylor]
2 conceivably Blackwater, Hants, near Camberley.
3 'The dawning.' [Taylor]
4 'Flora was a beautifull courtezan in Rome, who gat great treasure by the prostitution of her body, which wealth she gave to the common treasury, for which they did esteeme her a goddes, and the goddes of Flowers, and built a temple to her.' [Taylor]
5 Cynthia was a name given to Artemis, the Greek moon goddess.

In foure houres time we came to the Isle of Wight:
We past Cowes Castle, and into the towne went,
Wher some short time we wandring up and downe went;
Thus being favour'd by men, windes and weathers,
At Cowes I landed, and lodg'd at the Feathers:
The Isle of Wight contain'd a Wight of Waigh then,
And on that Wight of Waight, I came to wait then.[1]
Long live he blest internall, and externall.
And blest be England in his love paternall,
To guide and guard him, grace and power supernall,
Defend him from all trecherous traps infernall:
In imitation of him let us learne all
To live so heer that we may live eternall:
And thou, whose mercy nere can be exhausted,
In thy compassion thinke on England wasted:
The sword of wrath that's drawne is justly thine,
The sinnes that made thee draw it forth are mine:
Jonas the storme did to himselfe apply;[2]
Let each say so now, each man say tis I.
And now my story briefely Ile compose,
From harsh hard rugged rime, to smooth fac'd prose.

And thus have I truly, and merrily told the passages and relations, how I came to the royall captiving Isle of Wight. Now it followes requisitely, that I certifie you of some occurrences, and accidents there. It is to be noted, that the gentlemen with their wives, having such faire, and speedy passage from Southampton to the Island, that at the towne called Cowes they had two horses, which they left with their maides with me till the morning, for me to bring by land to Newport where His Majesty was: they with their wives tooke a small boat, about midnight, having the tide with them to carry them that Saturday night (or neere Sunday) 3 miles up by water to Newport: so they left me.

---

1 pun on the island's name, wight meaning person, and waight, a variant spelling of weight. Wight of waight therefore means person of substance, the king.
2 The storm was quelled by throwing Jonah into the sea (Jonah 1 verses 12-16).

All the fagge end of the Saturday night, and part of Sunday morning, I had the happinesse to be John amongst the maides,[1] for we honestly lay in 2 beds in one chamber, but I would have no man so mad to imagine that we lay all three both together.

Sunday the 22. of October we arose with the sun, betweene the houres of the careles number of 6 and 7 (he is carelesse that sets all at 6 and 7)[2] we quickly made our selves as fine as could be, in hope to see fine folkes, and fine things at Court, and so we mounted our palfreys: (the hostler of the Princes Armes at Cowes, being hired to be our guide) who did ride before one maid, and my selfe before the other, and so (by consequence) both the maides were behinde us.

The hostler that should have guided me, guided himselfe, riding before me, and leaving me behinde him sometimes a flight shoot or two; for he had many advantages of me; first he had the stronger horse, secondly he had the lighter carriage (for the maide behinde him was like Lent, light, leane, and lank) but my female male was like Shrove-Tuesday, fat, fair, plump, well fed, and weighty; thirdly he had two spurres, and a switch, of all which necessaries I was destitute, and without switch or spurre my horse would not goe.

And now a dirty tale I meane to tell:
Ile shew you what befell, and how I fell.

My ungodly guide being much before me, within a mile of Newport, I came to a boggy-quagmire miry, rotten, filthy, dirty, slow, through, over, or into which I must passe; I not knowing the way, called alowd to the guide to come back to direct me, which he did; but I having no switch or spurre (for correction) the horse would obey no direction; so that at last the guide said there was no danger, but that I might ride through it anywhere.

Then I with kicking set my heeles to horse,
Advent'ring to ride through it force perforce:

1 proverb recorded as Jack among the maids in 1785, meaning a 'gallant or ladies' man'.
2 The proverb then meant careless rather than confused, and was used by Chaucer and Shakespeare. It probably originates in a form of dice game.

My guides misguiding made me much the bolder,
The horse fell in, quite plung'd up to the shoulder.
I forward fell, and backward fell the maid,
Man, maide, and horse in curious pickle laid,
And never eare did heare, or eye did see
Such a pair-royall faire triplicity.[1]
The danger past, we each on other gaping;
Not angry, or well pleas'd, we fell to scraping:
Sometimes we fretted, and our lips did bite,
And somtimes (at our selves) we laught out right.
I scrapt my selfe, the maide, the hostler drest,
The horse lookt on, uncurried like a beast.
Thus we to Newport came in gay attire,
Embrodred over all with dirt and mire:
And thus from Cowes we tumbled in the slowes,[2]
Man, maide, and horse, moil'd[3] like three beastly sowes:
'Twas my base guide that put me in this trim,
For which abuse Ile have a bout with him:
The Divell misleades us all, we plainely see,
And that same stinking hostler misled me.
      For which:
First in a knaves skinne I will wrap him hot,
Which he shall alwaies weare until it rot:
My prayer for him shall be this execration,
Let him be nasty in his occupation:
Oh let his provender be ever musty,
His hay be most distastfull, foule, and dusty:
His pease, and beanes, and oates most odious fusty,
And's curry combe (for want of use) be rusty:
This musty, dusty, fusty, rusty, crusty,
Shall plague the knave that was to me untrusty.
In urine, and beasts ordure let him toile:
Soile be his trade, yet nere be lord oth' soile.

[1] In card games such as cribbage a pair-royal denotes three cards of the same denomination.
[2] i.e. slough, a muddy hollow or marsh.
[3] bedaubed and defiled.

Let boot haling be most part of his living:
Let guests be sparing to him in their giving:
Under his rack let him in tortures lye,
And (in his manger) let him stinke and dye:
And let the preaching cobler at Blackwall[1]
Be 3 houres prating at his funerall:
Let him be grav'd in his owne element:
Let litter, and horse dung be his monument.
But leaving riff raff rime,[2] Ile turne my stile,
To some more serious businesse in the Isle.
Thus having overpast this foule disaster,
I went to see my suffring soveraigne master:
Which sight to me was all my earthly blisse,
He gave me straight his royall hand to kisse,
Which grac'd me much in all the publique sights
Of commons, gentles, and brave lords and knights.

His Majesty, with an heroick an unconquered patience, conquers his unmatchable afflictions, and with Christian constancy, expects a happy deliverance out of all his troubles. His greatest griefe is the calamity of his people, and kingdomes, and his chiefest endeavours (on earth) is to settle them in peace and happinesse; for which end he is twice every day (with his meniall servants) upon his knees, in publique prayers to his God, besides his frequent, and pious cogitations, and ejaculations; and it is not to be doubted but the prayers, and humble petitions of His Majesty (with those of his loyall subjects) do asend the Throne of Grace, from whence (by the Almightyes mercy) strong and firme faith assures him of peace, pardon, and the fruition of future happinesse.

And for infallible testimonies against all ignorant, malicious, detracting, mis-believing heretiques, schismatiques, and sectaries to

---

1 possibly referring to Captain John Smith, a cobbler who left Blackwall (in east London) in 1606 as one of the first settlers in Virginia. He was captured, but rescued by the native princess Pocahontas. He returned to London and died in 1631.
2 riff raff used in the specialist sense, applied to verse, of rude, noisy, or crudely alliterative.

assure those buzards[1] of incredulity, that the gracious, favourable, and preserving hand of God is with His Majesty, whereby he hath been a blessed instrument, (not onely in his former curing the griefe, or disease called the evill)[2] but since he came into this island, he hath cured many, of whom so cured, there are 6 or 7 most remarkable, which I will relate as followeth.

1. At a towne called Winburne, (or Wimborne) in Dorcetshire, there dwels an ancient woman, the wife to a clothier (whose name I could not know by enquiry;) For testimony of the truth of this, there is one John Newbery, a cloth-worker, who dwels in Newport in the streete called Castle Holt, this man did come over the water with her, and did see her lame, and cured.[3] this woman had a long time been so lame that she could not goe, and she hearing that the King was lodg'd in Carisbrook Castle in the Isle of Wight, she was perswaded in her minde that His Majesty could cure her, in which beliefe she made towards the Island, and with horse or cart, or both, or otherwaies, she was brought to Hurst Castle in Hampshire by land, from whence she was carried into a boat in mens armes, which boat brought her to Newport, from whence she was carried a mile to Carisbrook, where His Majesty did touch her, and her lamenesse ceased in three dayes space, so that with thankes to God, and prayers for the King, she departed from the Island, and went home 20. miles on foot. This was before the treaty began,[4] much about the midst of August last.

2. Mistresse Elizabeth Steevens of Durley in Hampshire, came from her home to Winchester, and from thence to the Island to His Majesty to be cured of the evill, whereof she had been blinde of one eye 16. daies and could not open her eye by any meanes, and after the King had touched her, her eye opened and she saw immediatly, with a clear and perfect sight. This was about the seventh of October.

3. Elizabeth Gage of Southampton (being 3 yeares of age) was

---

1 slang for worthless or ignorant people.
2 scrofula, a form of tuberculosis, was known as the king's evil, because from Saxon times to the 18th century it was believed that touching by the monarch would effect a cure.
3 This sentence is a marginal note in the original.
4 treaty here means negotiation, which began between Charles and Parliament at Newport in September.

exceeding lame, and in great paine, she came to his Majesty, and he touched her, whereby (through Gods blessing) she was presently cured.

4. Joane Mathewes, aged 15. yeares, a braziers daughter one William Mathewes, dwelling in Newport in the Isle of Wight, she had been long time painefully lame, and had been at the Bathe,[1] and used many medicines in vaine; she came to the King on Thursday the 19. of October, He toucht her, and she had present ease, and every day shee goes better then other: myselfe saw her and spake with her, and I left her able to go reasonable well.

5. A souldier in Calshot Castle in Hampshire, had 2. sore issues in his thighes, to which he did frequently apply medicines which eased him, but cured him not: This man went to the Island to His Majesty, who did touch him, and he did after that use his former medicines, which were wont to give him ease, but then the said application did most grievously vex and torment him; so that he was perswaded to forbeare to use the said oyles, emplasters, and unguents, and then he was suddenly cured.

6. Mistresse Elizabeth Paine of Bristoll was blinde, and such a rhewmatick defluxion[2] did dayly fall from her eyes, which did wet two or three large hancherchiefes every day; she came to the King on Sunday last, the 5. of this November, His Majesty did touch her eyes, the rhewme ceased; so that she went away presently with a cleere and perfect sight; and two houres after she came to the King againe, and gave him thanks upon her knees; His Majesty bade her give thanks to God; so she with giving God praise, and prayers for the King, went from the Island to Bristoll with exceeding joy for her recovery.

7. Margaret Heyden, aged 73. yeares, dwelling in Newport in Chayne lane, was not able to stir but as she was lifted from bed to chaire, and from chaire to bed, touched by His Majesty, and cured, so that with one crutch she did goe about her house, and drew 5 or 6. pots of ale for me, and my company.

These things (me thinkes) should move the mindes of some unmannerly Levellers[3] to esteeme his Majesty as one that is not to he

---

1 i.e. Bath, Som., usually then known as the Bath.
2 a discharge of fluid.
3 a democratic republican movement within the Parliamentary army and supporters.

ranked or filed with common men.

Concerning any newes of businesse at the Treaty, there is so much made of it at London, that there is little (or none at all) at the Court; this is certaine, that from the 21. of October, till the first of November, (being 11. dayes) there was no debating or treating at all: for Sir Peter Killegrew was all that time from the Island to the Parliament at Westminster, and till his returne with orders and directions, all things were silent, however the London Mercuries, and Moderate Occurrances[1] did not faile to set forth newes (of their owne making) every weeke.

All that I can relate, is, that Sir Peter came to the King on Tuesday night, the last of October, and the next day (being the *quondam* All Saints)[2] His Majesty, with the Commissioners began to treate, where it was agreed that the Presbyterian Governement in the Church should continue three yeares, that the Booke of Common Prayer should be discontinued, and not used publickly: That no masse should be tollerated to be sayd in the kingdomes of England and Ireland, or in the principallity of Wales: These matters of high consequence being concluded and agreed, there is great hope of speedy restauration[3] of His Majesty to his just rights, and a blessed peace for the Church, people, and kingdomes.

I came from the Island on Tuesday the 7. of November, and landed at a place called Hell Head,[4] from thence I came 3 miles to Titchfield, on Wednesday I came 4 miles to Wickham, Thursday to Warnford, (7. miles) Fryday I footed it 17. miles to Alton, and to Farnham, Saturday to Guilford, and to Cobham 18. miles, and Sunday 6 miles to Kingston, and on Munday the 13. of November, I came to London 10. miles.

And as I have written, merrily, truely, and impartially; so I must conclude accordingly without flattery, concerning the Governour of the

---

1   another name for propaganda newssheets.
2   1st November, quondam 'formerly' because feast days were no longer observed.
3   These hopes were ill-founded. Cromwell and Fairfax rejected Charles's terms, and transferred him to Hurst Castle, from where he was brought to trial and execution the following January (1649).
4   Hill Head, Hants., near Lee-on-the-Solent.

Isle of Wight, Colonel Hammond:[1] the plaine truth is, that my selfe (with many others) did hate him so much, that he was very seldome or never prayed for; the reasons and motives which possest most men with this mistaking and misapplyed inveterate mallice, was upon the flying, lying reports, that the Governour had behaved himselfe most coursly ridged,[2] and barbarously unrespective to His Majesty: The false weekely pamphlets and pamphleteers (being inspired by their father the Divell) were not ashamed to publish in print, that the Governour had proceeded so far in incivility, as to immure or wall His Majesty in a small close[3] roome, under many bolts, bars, grates, locks and keyes, and debarred him the comforts of his soule, and of the scociety of men; and further it was often printed (by severall lying villaines) that the sayd Governour Hammond, did strike the King on the face, and gave him a black eye: These reports being invented by the Devills imps[4] (the firebrands of contention) printed and published by needy, greedy knaves and varlets, and believed by too many fooles and foolish Gotehamists[5] (amongst which number, I with much simplicity was one;) and as by oath and duty I am bound to serve, love, and honour my soveraigne lord and master; so (on the contrary) my selfe with all true and loyall subjects had no cause to be well affected to any man that should dare to affront His Majesty with such transcendent base indignities.

But to give the world satisfaction of the truth; it is certaine that all those aspersions and rumours against the Governour, are most odious, scandalous, and malicious lies: for (according to the trust reposed in him) he hath always carried himselfe with such deportment, and humblenesse of dutifull service to His Majesty, that he hath gained much love and favour from his soveraigne, and such good regard from all knowing men, as belongs to a gentleman of his place and quallity.

1 Robert Hammond (1621-54), distinguished Parliamentary soldier, as governor of the Isle of Wight held Charles I from Nov. 1647 - Nov. 1648.
2 i.e. rigid, in sense of inflexible and severe.
3 i.e. closed or enclosed.
4 often applied to the servants or familiars who were supposed to accompany witches.
5 natives of Gotham, Notts., who were proverbial for their stupidity.

And therefore Reader understand and note,
Who ever sayes I lye, he lies in's throate.

Blest Englands joy (the King) will come er'e long.
Praise God, make bonefires, swing the bells, ding dong.
And let him never beare a Christians name,
Whose trade and pleasure is in blood and flame
Of his deare countrey, and rip, rend, and teare
His mothers womb, that such a brat did beare.

FINIS

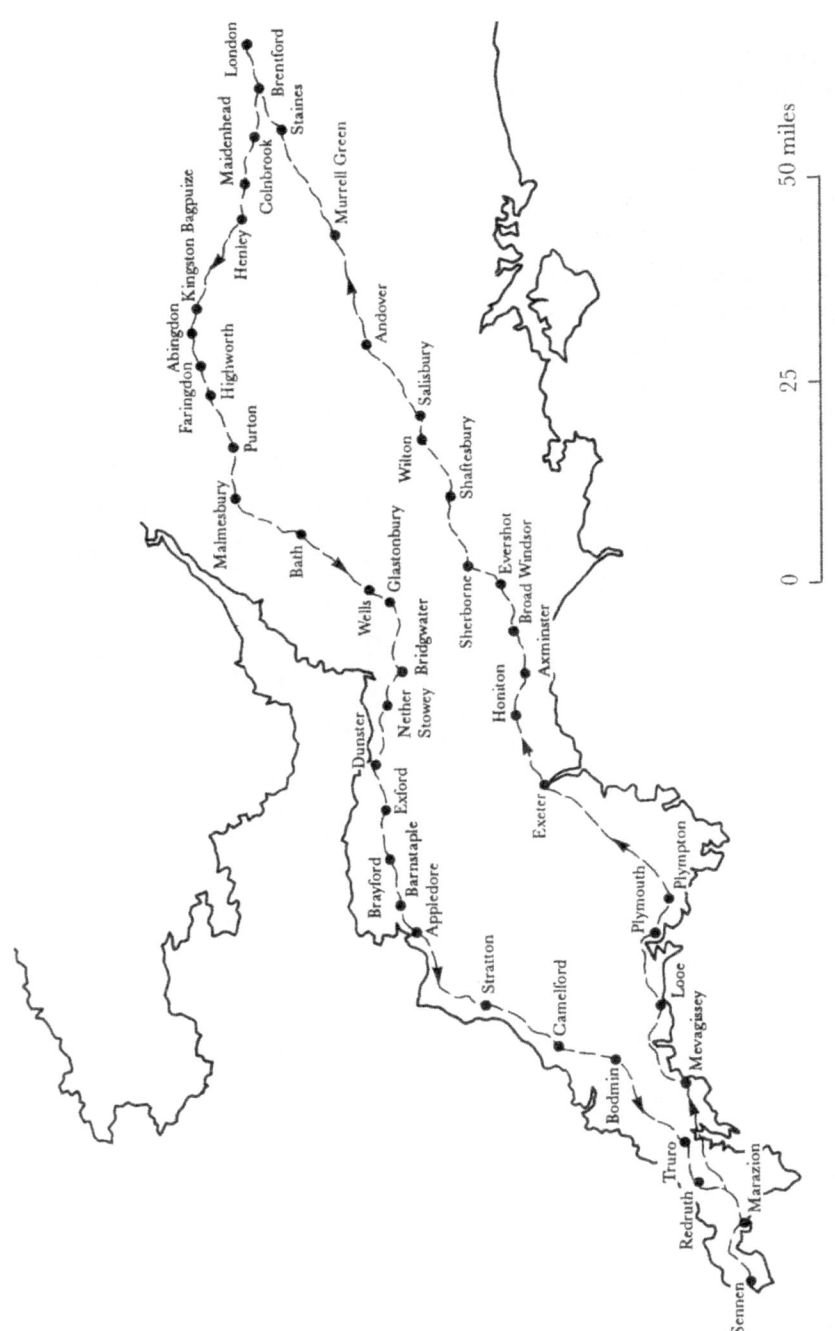

Wandering, to see the Wonders of the West

JOHN TAYLORS WANDERING, TO SEE THE WONDERS OF THE WEST

JOHN TAYLOR'S WANDERING, recording his journey to Land's End and back in the summer of 1649, marks a return to the style of travel-writing which Taylor had used to best effect in the Pennyles Pilgrimage *more than thirty years earlier. Pennyless once more (but by circumstance now, not choice) Taylor issues his 'bill' and is gratified to secure nearly 3,000 subscribers to the projected work – his reputation has not suffered through time and strife. Such confidence was rewarded with one of his finest productions, a well-defined journey which throws up incident and adventure at every turn, witty and clever without the contrived joke-telling of a decade before, the production of a self-assured author, comfortable within the modest parameters which he has set himself. It provides an instructive contrast with John Leland's very similar itinerary of over one hundred years earlier.*

After reciting the 'Taylors bill' the work begins in verse with a (borrowed) flourish, but quickly tires of rhyming. 'And now me thinkes a little prose may be relished amongst friends...' In prose it resolutely stays for all but a few lines until the clever peroration. Some of the incident is timeless – there can be few more amusing descriptions of poor innkeeping in English literature than that endured by Taylor at Nether Stowey (the premises are still in business, incidentally). There is a Rabelaisian quality about the Cornish pilchard calculation, which ends with queasiness, and 'a wambling in the gizzard'. There is the traveller's perennial misfortunes, being asked to pay (Salisbury Cathedral), or being snubbed (Bath), or refused accommodation (Mevagissey), or cheated over transport (Honiton), or a splinter in the breeches (Bridgwater).

But there also stalks the aftermath of war. The good fellowship which Taylor enjoys is almost always from Royalist gentry. He is frightened to go near Pendennis Castle for fear of being regarded a spy, and at Plymouth, where he does visit a Royalist prisoner, he is careful that their conversation is overheard. The damage to towns and buildings inflicted by the conflict, at Faringdon, Wells and Exeter, for instance, is noted with anger and regret. Such eye-witness descriptions, and those of St Michael's Mount, Glastonbury, and Wilton House, are historically significant, and deserve to be better known.

Taylor's caution was well-founded. Upon his return to London he was arrested on suspicion of spying for the Royalist cause. Although he was soon released, all his 'Taylors bills' were confiscated, and without them his chance of reward was lost.

[21st June - 4th Aug. 1649. Text derived from 1649 publication (copy BL Thomason E573 (12)

John Taylors Wandering, to see the wonders of the West. How he travelled neere 600. miles, from London to the Mount in Cornwall, and beyond the Mount, to the Lands end, and home againe. Dedicated to all his loving friends, and free minded benefactors.

In these dangerous dayes[1] for rich men, and miserable times for the poore servants of the late King, (whereof I was one, 45. yeers to his Royall Father and Himself, I thought it needful to take some course to make use of some friends, and devise a painfull[2] way for my subsistence; which was the journey I have past, and this booke heere present; for which purpose I gave out many of these following bills, to which neere 3000. gentlemen and others, have kindly subscribed, to give me a reasonable reward.

Printed in the yeere 1649.

The Bil of John Taylor, or a Taylors Bill, without either Imprimis, or Items.[3]

Old, lame and poor, by mad contentions beggerd,

1   Charles I was executed on 30th January 1649.
2   laborious.
3   Latin for 'firstly', and 'likewise'. The first item on a list, such as an account or inventory, generally began *Imprimis*; subsequent entries began *Item*...

And round about with miseries beleaguerd:
Too many masters made me masterlesse,
Too many wrongs have made me monylesse,
Helples, and hopeles, and remedilesse,
And every way encompast with distresse.
To ease my griefes I have one trick of wit,
(If you that read will set your hands to it:)
Which is, when I do give you good account
From London unto Cornewals Michaels Mount,
Of all my journey, and what news I found
In ayre, or sea above, or under ground;
When I do give you truths of this in print,
How I did travell, gravell,[1] dust, durt, flint,
My entertainment, where twas good, where ill,
Then (in good mony) give me what you will,
Your, nams and dwellings, write that I may find you,
And I shal (with my book) seek, find, and minde you,
      with humble thankes.

Seven times at sea I servd Eliza Queen,[2]
Since when, I thrice in Germany have been.[3]
Once in Bohemia twixt earth, sea, and sky.
And once to Scotland, and the mountains high:
Then unto Quinbrough, in a paper boat,
Then next (from London) I to Yorke did float
With a small paire of oares (or little wherry)
And in like sort from London to Salsberry.
Next that my man and I did ride our steedes
To Leicester, Lin, Hull, Hallifax and Leedes,
Ore lofty mountains, wher the winds blew bleak,
To Chester, Darby, and Devils arse a peak.

1 perhaps for 'grovell'.
2 Taylor served in the navy during the 1590s.
3 To Hamburg in 1616, and through Germany to Bohemia in 1620, journeys described on pp. 3-31, 93-125; the third visit was probably at about the same time, and may have also included Antwerp.

Then with a scullers boat to Cicester,[1]
From thence (up Seaverns flood) to Glocester,
To Worster, and the town of Shrewsbery,
From thence to Bristoll, and to Bath I fly;
These are no fictions, or false idle tales,
I passe from Bathe to the River Wye in Wales:
Then Hereford did me well entertain,
From whence I home came in my boat again.
Last (to the King) at the Isle of Wight I went,
Since when my best content, is discontent:
Thus having traveld North, and South, and East,
I meane to end my travels with the West.

Taylors Westerne Voyage to the Mount.

Tis a mad world (my masters) and in sadnes
I travail'd madly in these dayes of madnes:[2]
Eight yeares a frenzy did this land molest,
The ninth year seem'd to be much like the rest,
My selfe (with age, griefe, wrongs, and wants opprest,
With troubles more then patience could disgest)[3]
Amongst those isles, I chose the least and best,
Which was to take this journey to the West:
And sure it is an argument most fit,
T'was he who hath a portion of small wit
As I have, and good store of friends, 'twere sloth
And foolery, not to make use of both.
My wit was worne threadbare, halfe naked, poore,
And I, with it, went wool-gath'ring[4] for more.

---

1 Cirencester, Glos.
2 As a proverb the expression can be traced back to 1603. It was used by Nicholas Breton as the title of a dialogue in 1635. Nevertheless this phrase alone (incorrectly punctuated) earned Taylor his place in the *Oxford Dictionary of Quotations*, 2nd ed., 1953. cf. Shakespeare, *King John* (1591): 'Mad world! mad kings! mad composition!'
3 variant of 'digest'.
4 literally 'to gather wool caught in bushes', but figuratively from the

This long walke (first and last) I undertooke
On purpose to get money by my booke:
My friends (I know) will pay me for my paine,
And I will never trouble them againe.[1]
Six hundred miles, I (very neere) have footed,
And all that time was neither sho'd or booted;
But in light buskins [2]I perform'd this travell
O're hill and dale, through dust, dirt, flint, and gravell.
And now no more words I in vaine will scatter,
But come unto the marrow of the matter.
My reader must not her suppose that I
Will write a treatise of geography:
Or that I meane to make exact relations
Of cities, townes, or countries scituations;
Such men as those, I turne them o're to reade
The learned Cambden,[3] or the painefull Speed.
And now (good reader) I my muse do tune,
I London left, the twenty one of June:
To Brainford,[4] Colebrooke,[5] Maidenhead and Henly,
I past (the weather faire, the high wayes cleanely)
To Abington,[6] where foure dayes I remain'd,
By friends and kinsfolkes kindely entertain'd:
Thankes to my nephew John, with all the rest,
To whom that time I was a costly guest.

And now me thinkes a little prose may be relished amongst friends; I left Abington on Wednesday the 27. of June, and (for the ease of my purse) I gave 2s. 6d. for the hire of the skelliton or anatomy of a beast to carry

---

Elizabethan period, 'to day-dream or indulge in wandering fancies'.
1 Taylor did trouble them again, but perhaps not through his own fault (see above).
2 a type of long boot, but perhaps also an echo of the old dispute with Coryate, who had travelled in buskins.
3 William Camden's *Britannia*, the source of many of Taylor's historical statements.
4 Brentford, outer London, former Middlesex.
5 Colnbrook, Bucks., near Slough.
6 Abingdon, Berks.

me ten miles to Farington;[1] the thing I was mounted on was neither horse, mare, or gelding, it was all spirit, with very little (or no flesh.) It was none of your pursy foggy jades,[2] and amongst horsemen it might have past for a light horse, too much worke, and too little meate,[3] made him as gaunt as a greyhound: Thus (mounted like Don Quixot)[4] I entred Farington, but worse guests[5] then I had been there since these troubles; for the kings party burnt one part of the towne, and the Parliaments fired the rest, so that between them there was a good hansome market towne turned into ashes and rubbidge:[6] It begins to bud and spring out againe, for heere and there a pritty house peepes up: so that it will in short time be rebuilt, and Phaenix like (out of it's owne cinders) be revived and reneued to a more pleasing and beautifull prospect.

From Farington I footed it foure miles to Hiworth,[7] (a market towne) and from thence to Purton seaven miles more, where I lodged, there was nothing remarkable in all that dayes travels; but that in the morning a church at a village called Kingston,[8] (five miles from Abington) having no steeple; but the church at Purton (where I lay all night) had two steeples;[9] but I was certified that the minister that had two steeples, had but one benefice, and he that had none, had two, by which meanes the reckoning was even betwixt them, for what the one had, the other had not.

The 28. of June, I betook me to my feete an houre and halfe before the sunne could shew his face in Somersetshire, and for one

---

1 Faringdon or Great Faringdon, Berks.
2 corpulent, puffed-up, worn-out horses.
3 food generally.
4 Cervantes's hero, whose adventures (written 1605-12) appeared in English translation, 1612-20, and had a profound influence on literature. Quixote imagined that his broken-down old horse was Bucephalus, the unrivalled charger of Alexander the Great.
5 Faringdon was repeatedly fought over 1644-6, and much of the town was destroyed by fire during the siege of Faringdon House, 1646.
6 rubbish.
7 Highworth, Wilts.
8 presumably Kingston Bagpuize, Berks., but its tower had been rebuilt in 1603.
9 Purton church still has two steeples. The second benefice attached to Kingston Bagpuize was nearby Fyfield; both formed part of the endowment of St John's College, Oxford.

shilling I hired an old drunkard to guide me eight long miles to the towne of Malmsbury, where all worthy remembrance was, that I found an ancient towne, an old castle,[1] and new ale; from thence I hired a horse for 2s. seaven miles, and footed it seaven miles more that day to the famous, renowned, ancient, little pritty city of Bathe; I lodged in the mayors house: But his worship was as ignorant as my selfe, for he being a baker, had let halfe his house to a victualler: so he sold bread without, and I bought drinke within: The next day I had notice where I was, wherefore I went to his stall or shop window, and told him what I was, and that I was he who came nine yeares agoe[2] from London, to that city with a small scullers boate; Mr. Mayor was pleased to entertaine me most kindely (with both his hands in his pocket)[3] and like a man of few words, forbore to say wellcome to towne; so wee parting dryly I left him in his shop, Lord Baron of the Brown Loaves, and Master of the Rolls[4] (in that place:) but there is no doubt but the man may live a faire age, and dye in his bed, if he escape the unfortunate destiny of Pharoahs baker.[5]

Friday 29. of June, I had the luck twice to have not one dry thread about me, (being wet to the very skin) and yet my cloathes were as dry as a bone: the reason is, that I was in the Bathe, and my cloathes out.

June 30. I travelled fifteene miles to the towne of Wells, where I stayd but little, and found as little matter of observation, but that these holy, prophane days, and blessed execrable times of troublesome tranquility, have spoyled and defaced[6] one of the goodliest and magnificent cathedrall churches in the Christian world: But such pious workes as polution[7] and abusing of churches, wee neede not goe

1 Malmesbury had a medieval castle and town walls; the town was garrisoned 1642-6.
2 The earlier visit to Bath is recorded above, pp. 261-2
3 in contrast to the usual meaning of 'dipping one's hands in one's pockets', signifying generosity, the mayor kept his hands and money firmly in his pockets.
4 As principal justice in Bath the mayor would have been responsible for the civic records, hence *custos rotulorum*, or master of the rolls. One of Taylor's better puns.
5 who was hanged, according to Joseph's prophecy (Genesis 40, verse 22).
6 Wells Cathedral had been damaged early in the civil war, in August 1642.
7 used in its specific sense of profaning a sacred place.

amongst Turkes[1] for proofes; for though Peters at Westminster[2] hath scaped reasonable cleanely, yet Pauls in London[3] hath layen out of order, in ordure a battenning.[4]

The same day I went foure miles further to the ancient towne of Glastonbury, there I saw the ruines of an abby, which was one of the statelyest and most sumptuous structures in England or Europe: there remaines yet the ruined walls of a chappell built in memory of Joseph of Arimathea (who as it is recorded by authentique historians)[5] did first convert this land from paganisme to Christianity: And wee have great neede of another good Joseph to come amongst us, to doe as much for us now. But there is no memoriall of any place where that good old man was buried: the abby was walled more then a mile about, with a wall of free-stone, as faire as London wall; it is very probable that King Arthur (our English worthy) was there sepulchred; for there I saw some stones of marble,[6] of which I placed the broken pieces together: I read these words in Latin,

Hic jacet Guineverus Regina, Uxores, etc.

Queene Guinever was wife to the great Arthur, and she being buried there, it is to be conjectured that his bones were not layd far from her.

Mr. Camden, doth quote the ancient historian, William of Malmsbury, to write these words following concerning Glastenbury.

That it was the first land of God in England, the first land of saints in England, the beginning and fountaine of all religion in England, the tombe of saints, the mother of saints, the church founded and built by the Lords disciples.

---

1 used generally in the sense of anyone behaving in a barbarian or anti-Christian way.
2 Westminster Abbey.
3 Old St Paul's was soon to be destroyed in the great fire, 1666.
4 a contrived pun: ordure ('dung') was spread on soil to improve ('batten') it.
5 the legend first occurs in a 13th-century revision of William of Malmesbury's history of Glastonbury Abbey.
6 The monks of Glastonbury claimed to have found the tombs of Arthur and Guinevere in 1191, and Camden published an illustration of a lead cross which mentioned *Artorius rex*. But Taylor seems to have found something different.

I saw a branch or slip[1] of the hawthorne tree[2] that did beare blossomes every yeare (when all other trees were frost-bitten, and seemed dead:) this tree onely, on Christmas day, the day of our blessed Saviours birth; this tree did (in its kinde) shew its joy in comemoration of the nativity of the redeemer of unkinde mankinde: There are all the inhabitants in the towne will verifie it, and thousands in England and other countries will affirme that it is no fable: The souldiers being over zealous did cut it downe in pure devotion; but a vintner dwelling in the towne did save a great slip or branch of it, and placed or set it in his garden, and he with others did tell me that the same doth likewise bloome on the 25. day of December, yearely; I saw the sayd branch, and it was ten foote high, greene, and flourishing; I did take a dead sprigge from it, wherewith I made two or three tobacco stoppers,[3] which I brought to London; my humble thankes to Mr. Brooke, with (his good sister) for they entertained me freely; so that the towne of Glastonbury was not one penny the richer for any expences of mine.

Monday the second of July, I went to Bridgewater ten miles, where all that was worthy of note was, that neare the towne, at a stile I had a great disaster; for a shagge[4] or splinter of the stile tooke hold of my one and onely breeches, and tore them in that extreme unmercifull, unmannerly manner, that for shame and modesties sake I was faine to put them off, and goe breechlesse into the towne, where I found a botching[5] threepenny taylor, who did patch me up with such reparations as made me not ashamed to put my breeches on againe, and trot five miles further to a ragged market towne called Neather-Stoy, where extreame weary, I tooke up my lodging, at a signe and no signe, which formerly was the Rose and Crowne;[6] but Roses are withered, and Crownes are obscured, as the signe was.

1 cutting.
2 the Christmas hawthorn is recorded in a poem of 1520, but is not known to have been linked with Joseph of Arimathea (as it still is) until 1677. Taylor does not connect the two stories.
3 used for pushing down tobacco in the bowl of the pipe while smoking.
4 perhaps a misprint for *snagge,* 'a sharp projection' (OED).
5 'repairing' rather than manufacturing, probably not at this date implying poor workmanship.
6 Nether Stowey, Somerset. The Rose and Crown, in St Mary's Street, is still an inn

Surely that day was a mad, sad, glad, auspicious, unlucky day to me, worse then an ominous, Childermas,[1] or a dogged byting dog-day;[2] for the hostesse was out of towne, mine host was very sufficiently drunke, the house most delicately deckt with exquisite artificiall, and naturall sluttery, the roome besprinckled and strewed with the excrements of pigs and children; the wall and sielings were adorned and hanged with rare spiders tapistry, or cobweb lawne;[3] the smoake was so palpable and perspicuous, that I could scarce see any thing else, and yet I could scarce see that, it so blinded me with rheum a signe of weeping;[4] besides all this, the odorifferous and contagious perfume of that house was able to outvie all the millainers[5] in Christendome or Somersetshire.

I being thus embellished, or encompassed with these most unmatchable varieties; but to comfort me compleatly, mine host swing'd off[6] halfe a pot to me, bad me be merry, and asked me if I would have any powdred beefe and carrets to supper; I told him yes, with all my heart; but I being weary of the house, I went and sate three houres in the street, where mine host often did visit me with most delightfull and hydropicall [7]non-sense; at last, 7 of the clock was struck, and I went into the house to see if supper were ready; but I found small comfort there, for the fire was out, no beefe to be boyled, mine host fast asleep, the maid attending the hogs, and my hungry selfe halfe starv'd with expectation; I awaked mine host, and asked him where the beefe was, he told me that he had none, and desired me to be contented with egges fryed with parsly; I prayed him to shew me my chamber, which he did; the chamber was sutable[8] to the rest of the house; there I stayd till neere 9 a clock, expecting fry'd

---

1   28th December, which commemorated Herod's massacre of the innocents.
2   the hottest days of the year, during July and August, when Sirius, the Dog star, rises with the sun.
3   a type of fine linen.
4   moisture or mucus, and may refer to tears.
5   dealers in fancy goods, especially clothing accessories (originally from Milan), had a reputation for drawing attention to their wares by perfuming themselves. 'He was perfumed like a milliner' (Shakespeare *Henry IV part 1*).
6   i.e. *swinged*, 'drink'. The landlord drinks Taylor's health, but appears not to have offered him a drink.
7   i.e. dropsical, in the figurative sense of having an insatiable thirst.
8   in accordance with.

egges, when mine host came to me with an empty answer, there were no egges to be had, so at the last I purchased a piece of bread and butter, and to bed, and then began my further torments; for thinking to take a little rest, I was furiously assualted by an Ethiopian army[1] of fleas, and do verily believe that I layd so manfully about me that I made more then 500 *mortuus est*:[2] they were so wel grown that as I took 'em I gave 'em no quarter, but rub'd 'em between my finger and my thumbe, and they were so plumpe and mellow, that they would squash to pieces like yong boyled pease: But all these troubles I patiently past by, making no more account of them, then of so many flea-bytings. For my further delight, my chamber-pot seemed to be lined within with crimson plush,[3] or shag'd scarlet bayes,[4] it had scaped a scowring time out of minde, it was sut'd with antiquity, and withall it had a monumentall savour; and this pisse-pot was another of my best contentments.

At last, wearinesse and watching, began to inforce sleep upon me, so that (in spight of the fleas teeth) I began to winke, when suddenly, three children began to cry, and for an hours space I was kept waking, which made mee fall to the slaughter againe. The children being hush'd asleep, the game began afresh amongst the dogs, for the cry was up, and the bawling currs took the word one from the other, all the towne over; and the dogs had no sooner done, but the day break appeared, and the hogs began to cry out for their breakfast: so I arose, and travelled (almost sleeping) 10. miles that day; which was to a towne called Dunstar,[5] where upon a lofty hill stands a strong castle, it had then a garrison in it; I must confesse I was free there,

> From nasty roomes, that never felt broomes,
> From excrements, and all bad sents,
> From childrens bawling, and caterwawling,
> From grunting of hogs, and barking of dogs,
> And from byting of fleas, there I found ease.

1 probably just signifying black or swarthy.
2 Latin for 'he (or it) is dead'. Taylor is thinking of a list of names, against some of which this annotation has been placed.
3 soft velvet-like cloth.
4 tufted baize.
5 Dunster, Somerset.

The fourth of July, I travelled to Exfourd[1] (so named) because it stands near the head, or spring of the River Ex, which runs downe from north to south neere 40 miles to the city of Exeter, and to Exmouth, where it delivers it selfe into the Ocean, and from thence to Brayfourd,[2] (another fourd which runs into the River of Ex, as the people told me; but I finde it not so in the map,) that dayes journey was sixteene miles, a teadious weary way for a crazy,[3] old, lame, bad, foundered footman, I am sure I found it so; for when I came to my lodging I had more minde to eate then to fight, and a better stomack to a bed then a supper.

The fifth of July, I walked but seven miles to Barnstable, a very fine sweete towne, so cleane and neate, that in the worse of weather, a man may walke the streets, and never foule shooe or boote; there I stayd till the next day noone, being well and well-comely entertained by one Mr. John Downes, who gave me fidlers fare,[4] meate, drinke and money, for which I heartily thanked him: From thence I past by water five miles to Aplear.[5]

July the sixt (being Friday) I paced it ten miles to a place named Ferry Crosse,[6] in the parish of Allington, and the seven day I turned my back upon Devonshire, having gone that day fifteene miles to the first market towne in Cornewall (on the north-side of the county) named Stratten.[7]

Cornewall is the *Cornucopia*,[8] the compleate and repleate horne of abundance for high churlish hills, and affable courteous people; they are loving to requite a kindenesse, placable to remit a wrong, and hardy to retort injuries; the countrey hath its share of huge stones, mighty rocks, noble, free, gentlemen, bountifull housekeepers, strong, and

1   Exford, Somerset, south of Porlock.
2   Brayford, Devon, north of South Molton.
3   here used in the sense of frail or broken-down.
4   the proverb, first recorded in 1586, is that meat, drink, and money were fiddler's fare.
5   Appledore, Devon, north of Bideford.
6   Fairy Cross, on the main road south-west of Bideford.
7   Stratton, Cornwall, inland from Bude.
8   the shape of Cornwall and its name lend themselves to association with Latin *cornu* ('horn'), and therefore with the classical image of the horn of plenty, cornucopia.

stout men, handsome, beautifull women, and (for any that I know) there is not one Cornish cuckold to be found in the whole county: In briefe they are in most plentifull manner happy in the abundance of right and left hand blessings.[1]

It is a wonder that such rugged mountains to produce such fertility of corn, and cattle; for if the happy dayes and times of peace were once settled, Cornewall might compare with any county in England, for quantity of all necessaries needfull, and quallity of persons.

The ninth of July I left Stratten, and ambled twenty miles to the towne of Camelfourd,[2] and to a village called Blistland,[3] and there I was taken for the man I was not; for they suspected me to be a bringer of writs and processe to serve upon some gentlemen, and to bring men into trouble: But with much adoe I scaped a beating, by beating into their beliefes that I was no such creature.

July the tenth, I came to Bodman,[4] (a market town) and from thence the same day to a village called St. Enedor,[5] a part of which parish is called Penhall,[6] there at a smiths house was good lodging, better cheare, and best drinke; the smith was lame, his wife was faire and handsome, where if I could have acted the part of Mars, there might have been played the comedy of Vulcan and Venus:[7] that dayes travell was eighteen miles.

July eleaventh, I progressed to Truro, another market towne, which is the Lord Roberts[8] his land; there I bought a fish called a Breame for three pence, it would have served foure men; after dinner I went

---

1 cf Genesis ch. 48, verse 14: 'And Israel stretched out his right hand, and laid it upon Ephraim's head, who was the younger, and his left hand upon Manasseh's head . . .'
2 Camelford.
3 Blisland, north of Bodmin.
4 Bodmin.
5 St Enoder, between Truro and Newquay.
6 Penhale, Fraddon.
7 In Greek and Roman mythology the lame god of fire and smithing, Hephaestus or Vulcan, was cuckolded by his wife, Aphrodite or Venus. She and her lover Aries, or Mars, were caught by the sun god in an invisible net, and exposed to ridicule among the gods. No English comedy with this title is recorded.
8 John, Lord Robartes of Lanhydrock (1604-85), a prominent Puritan.

eight miles further to a towne called Redruith,[1] in all that dayes travells eighteen miles, I saw nothing strange to me but a few Cornish Dawes (or Choughs)[2] with red bills, and legs: They saluted me upon the wing, just in the language of our Jack Dawes about London, Ka, Ka.

The twelfth of July, I came within two miles of Saint Michaels Mount, to an ancient house called by the name of Trimineague:[3] it hath been, and is the birth place of worthy families, of the noble name of the Godolphins: The right owner and possessour of it now is Francis Godolphin, Esquire, a gentleman endowed with piety, humanity, affability and ability; he hath a heart charitable, a minde bountifull, and a hand liberall; he hath (deservedly) the cordiall love of all the county, and would have the enjoyments of earthly contentments, if once these discontented times were quieted: Seaven dayes I stayed with him, in which time he was pleased to send a kinsman of his (Mr. Anthony Godolphin) with me to see the Mount, which I thus describe. It is about a mile in compasse at the foote, and it rises 700 paces very steepe to the top, it is in forme like a great haycock or reeke, or much like a mounteere;[4] on the top or piramis[5] of it, is a fine church called Saint Michaels, the sayd church is now for no other use but a well stored magazine with ammunition, from whence (for a relique of remembrance) I brought halfe a yard of Saint Michaels Mounts monumentall match: I went to the top of the church tower seventy steps higher, and in my comming downe I viewed the bells (which were five in number) being faire and handsome, they cannot be rung, because the crack rope souldiers[6] have broke all the bell-ropes, insomuch as for any more ringing there, the bells being ropelesse, the people are hopelesse.

To speake the truth of this so much talked of famous mount; it is lofty, rocky, innaccessible, impregnable not to be taken, or kept, nor worth the taking or keeping: It is a barren stony little wen or wart, that with men, amunition, and victualls is able to defend it selfe; but it

1 Redruth
2 A member of the crow family, and the emblem of Cornwall, where it frequents cliffs.
3 Treveneague, north-east of Marazion.
4 rick... mountain.
5 pyramid.
6 the soldiers are worthy of a hanging, i.e. of cracking or straining a rope.

hath not the sea and land to friend, there is an enemy called hunger (or famine) that will conquer mounts and mountaines:[1] It can do no service to the seaward, for the water is so shallow, that no ship can saile within shot of it, and for land service the towne of Market Jew,[2] stands better for defence: The Mount is an island, and no island, twice in every 24 houres: for when the sea is up, boates must be used to go to it, but upon the ebbe, troopers may ride to it forty in ranck: Market Jew is about two flight shoote of it, the mayor whereof (one Mr. William Mabb) caused me to dine with him, for which I returne him a few printed thanks.

In the Mount I saw a craggy rugged seat, of rocky upholstery, which the old fabulous rumour calls St. Michaels Chayre:[3] and a well[4] I saw there, which twice in 24. howres is fresh water, and salt water. This Mount had a garrison within it, which made the country people to grumble without it; yet the soldiers are pretty civill: and one Captaine Geary did courteously regard and drink with me at the maiors house at Market Jew. From thence I returned to Mr. Godolphins, and he did perswade mee to see the Lands end, fourteen miles further; for which journey on the 16. day of July, he did lend me 2. horses, with his kinsman to ride with me, where (for his sake) I was welcome by the way, with a good dinner, at one Mr. Levales house, from whence I rode, and went as far as I could ride, goe, or creepe, for rockes and sea: and there I saw the Island of Silly,[5] with other smaller islands, which are sayd to be 16. or 17. in number. The mayne island is held for the Prince, by one Captaine (or as some say, a knight) called Sir John Greenvill;[6] it is very strong, with a good safe harbour, and as it is reported there, hath a good fleet of ships in it: some doe call it a second Argiere,[7] for there cannot a ship or vessell passe by it, but they doe make out upon them, whereby they have great riches, with all necessaries: it was 8. leagues at least from me, insomuch that I could but onely see it

1 a common proverb, from c.1350, usually in the form, hunger breaks stone walls.
2 Marazion, east of Penzance.
3 Inside the beacon on top of the medieval chapel.
4 Now known as Giant's Well, it is recorded by Leland as 'a fair spring in the mount', and was given a redoubt to defend it during the civil war.
5 Scilly Isles, west of Cornwall.
6 Sir John Grenville (1628-1701), later earl of Bath, Royalist commander, held the Scilly Isles 1649-51.
7 Algiers, north Africa, a notorious base for Barbary pirates.

dimly, and 2. ships I perceyved that lay at road (perdue)¹ to give notice (as I conjectured) of the appearance of any shipping that sayled within their ken:² I did cut my name 4. inches deep in a small patch of earth amongst the rockes, at the Lands end, and I am sure no man can go thither and set his name or foot, halfe a foot before me.

The same day I returned to one Mr. Jones his house a mile thence, in the farthest western parish of the county of Cornwall, called Sevin;³ there I had good entertainment all night, by the gentlemans and his wives free welcome, which was out of their owne curteous disposition; but chiefly for Mr. Godolphins sake, to whom at Trimiweagow I returned, on the 17. of July, where I rested one day: and on the 18. day I tooke my leave, having received 7. dayes hospitality in plenty, with many other curtesies in money and other necessaries which I wanted; besides hee sent his kinsman with mee to direct mee the way to another Francis Godolphin of Godolphin house.⁴ That gentleman is the chiefe of that noble name; his house a stately ancient pallace, and my chear and welcome at dinner, most freely bountifull. After dinner hee walked with me, where (in my way) I saw his mines of tin, and a house where his workemen were refining and melting of tin, which is a rich commodity. So at my taking leave of him, hee put ten shillings in my hand, which came to me in an acceptable time.⁵

From thence I jog'd 3. miles further, to a house called Clowance in the parish of Crowen,⁶ where dwells one Mr. John Sentabin, he is sonne in law to the first Godolphin I came to, whose daughter he marryed (a vertuous and beautifull gentlewoman) where I tooke a welcome, a supper and a bed, till the next morning, being July 19. he sent a man with me eight miles to a sister of his, named Mrs. Gertrude, to her I was so welcome, that after I thought she had been weary of me, she would faine have had me to stay two dayes more, which I (with thankes refusing) she lent me a mare (and a man to bring her

1 anchored out of sight.
2 field of vision.
3 Sennen.
4 between Helston and Hayle.
5 Biblical expression, Psalm 69 verse 13.
6 Crowan, near Camborne.

home againe) which mare I roade to a towne called Penny com quick,[1] within a mile of Pendennis Castle,[2] which castle I looked on a far off, but I durst not attempt to offer to go into it, for feares and jealousies might have mistaken me for a spy; for at all places of garison, there is very strict examinations of persons, and at every townes end, in all the sea townes of part of Cornewall, Devonshire, Dorsetshire, and every shire, no traveller could passe without catechizing words: As what is your name, whence came you, where dwell you, whither go you, what is your businesse, and wherefore came you hither? Now he that cannot answer these particular demands punctually, is to be had before Governours, Captaines, Commanders, Mayors, or Constables, where if a man doe chance to be suffered to passe freely from them, yet it is a hazard of the losse of a travellers liberty by either their unbeliefe or mispision,[3] and at the best it is a hinderance to a mans journey and losse of time.

These considerations made me doubtfull to presume to looke into Pendennis Castle, or any other garrison or place of defence: This castle is seated very high, and it stands very defensive for the famous haven of Faymouth (one of the best harbours for shipping in the world:) it was built by King Henry the eight, it is impregnable, and as long as it is well manned, amunitioned, and victualled, it is thought to be invincible, and theres an end of that poynt.

That day I past a ferry called King Harries Passage[4] (but why it is so named few men knowe) there I lodged at the ferry mans house, and the next morning being 21 of July, I travelled twelve miles to a fisher towne called Mevageasie;[5] that towne hath in it two tavernes, and six alehouses, to every one of which I went for lodging, and not any one would harbour me, then I sought for a constable to helpe me, but no constable was to be found; the people all wondring at me, as if I had been some strange beast, or monster brought out of Affrica; at which most incivill

---

1 There are places of this name in St Allen parish, north of Truro, and in Devon, now part of Plymouth, but neither is appropriate here.
2 Strong castle established by Henry VIII on a peninsula east of Falmouth.
3 misprision, in the sense of misunderstanding.
4 Ferry across the Truro River south of Truro, giving access to Roseland peninsula.
5 Mevagissey.

and barbarous useage, I began to be angry, and I perceiving that no body cared for my anger, I discreetely went into the house where I first demanded lodging; where the hostes being very willing to give me the courteous entertainement of Jack Drum,[1] commanded me very kindely to get me out of dores, for there was no roome for me to lodge in. I told her that I would honestly pay for what I tooke, and that if I could not have a bed, yet I was sure of a house over my head, and that I would not out till the morning: with that a yong saucy knave told me that if I would not go out, he would throw me out, at which words my choller grew high, my indignation hot, and my fury fiery, so that I arose from a bench, went to my youth, and dared to the combate; whereat the hostesse (with feare and trembling) desired me to be quiet, and I should have a bed, at which words my wrath was appeased, and my ire asswaged.

But straite wayes another storme seemed to appeare; for an ancient gentleman came suddenly out of another roome (who had heard all the former friendly passages,) and hee told mee that I should not lodge there, for though I had sought and not found a constable, yet I should know that I had found a Justice of Peace before I sought him; and that he would see me safely lodged: I was somewhat amazed[2] at his words, and answered him, Let him doe his pleasure, for I submitted my selfe to his disposall.

To which he replyde, That I should go but halfe a mile with him to his house, which I did, and there his good wife and he did entertayne me courteously, with such fare and lodging, as might have accommodated any gentleman of more worth and better quality than one that had been ten times in degree before me: there I stayd the Saturday and all the Sunday, where I found more Protestant Religion in 2. dayes, then I had in 5. yeers before. The gentlemans name is Mr. John Carew,[3] a gentleman of noble and ancient descent, and a worthy Justice of the Peace in those parts.

---

1 proverbial for a rough reception. *Jack Drum's Entertainment* was a play by John Marston (1601).
2 alarmed or bewildered.
3 of Penwarne, Mevagissey. Taylor was perhaps unaware that Carew's nephew (d.1660) was a regicide, having been appointed one of Charles I's judges, and signed his execution warrant.

I was certified,[1] that in that little town of Mevagesey, there are 44. fisher boats, which doe fish for pilchards, that every boat hath 6. men, and that every 2. boats have one net between them: they doe call the 2. boats a seine; so there are 22. seines, and 22. nets: every Cornish bushell is in measure 2. bushels and a halfe of our measure at London: every 2. boates (or seine) doe spend 250. bushels of salt (Cornish measure) to salt pilchards only; every seine do use 100. hogsheads to pickle the sayd pilchards in yearly. So that this one little towne, doth spend by Gods blessing, and the meanes of those small fishes, every year,

Of salt, 22 times 350 Cornish bushells, which is in the number of our bushells, 14000, 350.

Of hogsheads, or caske, 2200.

Of men for 44 boats, 6 men for each, 264.

These men with their families (being many in number) are all maintained by pilchard catching; but this is not all, for there are other greater townes in that county, which doe every one of them use the same trade of fishing, with more and greater numbers of men, boats, net, caske, and much more quantity of salt; some of the other townes are St. Keverne, Foye,[2] Loo, with others which I cannot recite.

This infinite number of pilchards, being salted and put up in caske, are bought a maine by the Spanish, French, Dutch, Italian, and other merchants, and by them they are either eaten or sold, and transported to many other people and nations: And now I hope I have filled my readers bellies with pilchards, without cloying or offending their stomacks; if any one be queasie, or doe feele a wambling in the gizzard;[3] let them call for a cup of sack,[4] drinke it, and pay for it.

The 23 of July, I came to Foye, and to Loo (or Low) twenty miles; this towne of Loo, is divided in two parts, or two townes together,[5] two mayors, two churches, two governours, and more then two religions; all that I can say of either of the Looes, is, that there was souldiers and swordmen, strong beere and dagger ale, land flesh and sea fish in plenty.

1 Carew's father Richard (1555-1620) was a topographer, whose *Survey of Cornwall* (1602) describes pilchard fishing at length.
2 Fowey.
3 queasiness in the stomach.
4 *vin sec*, dry wine such as Madeira or Canary.
5 East and West Looe.

On the 24. of July, I turned my back upon Cornewall, and went from Loo to Plimouth[1] in Devonshire, twelve miles: At Plimouth I stayd not two houres, the towne was too full of suspitions to hold me: There I saw Colonel William Leg,[2] a prisoner in the towerhouse, or guild hall. I spake to him (being on the one side of the way in a window, and he on the other) in a low whispering voice that every one might heare what we sayd; I wished him health and liberty, and so left him in thraldome;[3] There was two stationers did make me very welcome for two or three houres; their names were Thomas Ratcliffe and William Weekes, they gave me smoake and drinke in Plimouth, for which I requite them in paper and inck at London.

That afternoone I left Plimouth, and went foure miles further, to Plimpton,[4] and on the morrow (being Saint James his day)[5] I hired a horse forty miles to Exeter, where I was two dayes entertained at mine owne cost, with some charges that burgomasters and bookesellers underwent: I can say little of Exeter, but that it is a faire sweete city, a goodly cathedrall church (not yet quite spoyled or stabled) and it had large suburbs, with long streets, and many fine dwellings till this mad fire of contention turned all to ruines, rubbidge,[6] cinders, ashes, and fume.

Two houres before Phoebus[7] appeared in our hemisphere, I was on footback from Exeter to Honiton, the 27. of July, there I had a nights lodging, and dyet of such a homely fashion, as I have no occasion to boast of; there I hired a horse (which proved to be a blinde mare) she had two wens as big as clusters of grapes hung over both her eyes, and five or six wens on her shoulders and flanks, all which beautifull ornaments I could not perceive or see till I had road the beast foure mile, (for I was mounted before the breake of day;) but when I saw the comelynesse of

1 Plymouth, Devon.
2 William Legge (c.1609-1670) was a prominent Royalist commander, who was imprisoned from May 1648 at Arundel, and from 1649-51 or later, at Exeter (and according to this evidence at Plymouth).
3 captivity.
4 Plympton, Devon.
5 25th July.
6 rubbish.
7 the sun.

the beast, betweene shame and anger I was almost mad at the rogue that owned her; and being neere to a market towne called Axmister,[1] I dismounted, and footed eight miles to Broad Winsor[2] in Dorsetshire, where I was better horst eight miles further to Evershot, and then I paced on foote eight miles further to the towne of Sherbourne,[3] that dayes travell was 31 mile.

The 31 of July, I went from Sherbourne to Shaftsbury,[4] and so to Wilton, and Salisbury, 31 mile: At Wilton[5] I saw the Earle of Pembrokes magnificent and sumptuous building and repairing of such a stately fabrick, that for strength, beauty, forme, state, glazing, painting, gilding, carving, pollishing, embellishing and adorning: It may be a pallace for the greatest king in Christendome: the springs, and fishponds, the garden, the walkes, the fare artificiall rocks and fountaines, the ponds with fish on the house top, the strange figures and fashions of the water workes, the numerous, innumerable varieties of fruits and flowers; yea all, and every thing that may make an earthly Paradice, is there to be seene, felt, heard, or understood, (which because I understand not) I shut up all with this, there is inestimable cost, exquisite art and artists, most exceeding good work and workemen, onely one thing (that is quite out of fashion almost every where) is used there, which is good and just payment.

From Wilton, to Salisbury two miles, there I sleeped out the later end of the whole moneth of July. I had a desire to go into the church there (one of the fairest in England) but now the playes be downe,[6] there was no sights to be seen without money, which though I could have payd, yet for two reasons I would not; the one was because I had oftentimes seene that church in former times, when Gods service was sayd there, and the second cause why I would not be guilty of simony,[7] and with corrupting mammon enter or intrude into the house of God.

The first of August, I footed to Andover, fifteene old miles, and

---

1 Axminster, Devon.
2 Broadwindsor, Dorset.
3 Sherborne, Dorset.
4 Shaftesbury, Dorset.
5 Described at length during his Salisbury journey in 1623, pp. 190-1.
6 Theatres were officially closed in 1642.
7 trading in religious privilege.

eighteene new ones, (of the Posts late measuring:)[1] The next day to Morrell Greene,[2] 24 miles, the third day to Stanes,[3] eighteene miles, and the fourth of August fifteene miles to London: My journey being in all 546 miles, which I went and came in six weekes, and lay still and rested twelve dayes in severall places on weeke dayes, besides six Sundayes: But all this was nothing to me, being a youth of threescore and ten, with a lame leg and a halfe, and there is an end of the story.

Like to the stone of Sisiphus.[4] I roule
From place to place, through weather faire and foule,
And yet I every day must wander still
To vent[5] my bookes, and gather friends good will;
I must confesse this worke is frivalowse,
And he that (for it) daignes to give a lowse,[6]
Doth give as much for't as 'tis worth, I know;
Yet meerly merily I this jaunt did goe
In imitation of a mighty king,
Whose warlike acts, good fellowes often sing,
The King of France[7] and twenty thousand men,
Went up the hill, and so came downe agen.
So I this travell past, with cost and paine,
And (as I wisely went) came home againe.
      FINIS.

1 The postal service was reorganized in 1635 and for the first time private letters were carried at a charge based on mileage. This required the setting up of measured stages.
2 Murrell Green, near Hook, Hants.
3 Staines, Middlesex.
4 In Greek mythology his punishment in the afterworld was continually to roll a stone to the top of a hill, whence it always rolled down again.
5 sell.
6 proverbially a louse was considered worthless.
7 Popular 17th-century song, thought to commemorate an episode in 1610. Its continued currency influenced the more familiar 'Grand old Duke of York'.

A LATE WEARY, MERRY VOYAGE, AND JOURNEY

A LATE WEARY, MERRY VOYAGE, Taylor's 1650 journey to East Anglia, comes as a disappointment after the vitality of his west-country jaunt. Lameness and old age were afflicting him now as much as poverty, and it was only with great reluctance that he took to the road again. The vague 'Taylors bill' was hardly calculated to whet potential readers' appetites, rather to appeal to their charitable good nature. He decided to travel around East Anglia, by boat as far as Ipswich and then overland, perhaps in order to spend his 72nd birthday (on August 24th) with a cousin and his wife near Norwich. From there he continued to other relatives near King's Lynn, and then to Cambridge for Stourbridge Fair. But at Cambridge he was tempted to accept a lift back towards London, and missed the fair.

The jejune pamphlet reflects Taylor's weariness. He jogs along generally in verse, sometimes struggling to contrive rhymes, until he reaches Oxnead in north Norfolk, where he switches to prose. The first 120 lines of verse are general moralising, about travel, his old age, and the injustice inflicted on him after his west-country journey. Then he sets off, interspersing his account with fulsome thanks to hosts along the way, and historical descriptions (paraphrased from Camden) of Ipswich, Norwich and King's Lynn. He is still a welcome and appreciative guest, kindly entertained wherever he goes, and made much of. Indeed the generous hospitality shown him is one of the most striking features of this journey: a minister roasts a tithe pig to share with him; a 'little antient man', a widower, invites him to spend the night in his bed; and at Lynn he is feasted on fish, duck and oysters. Everything is free, and Taylor repays his benefactors in the only way open to him: 'In all this time I never wanted drinke, | And for their drinke, I give 'em thanks in inke'.

[14th August - 10th September, 1650. Text derived from 1650 publication (copy Huntington RB 56026)]

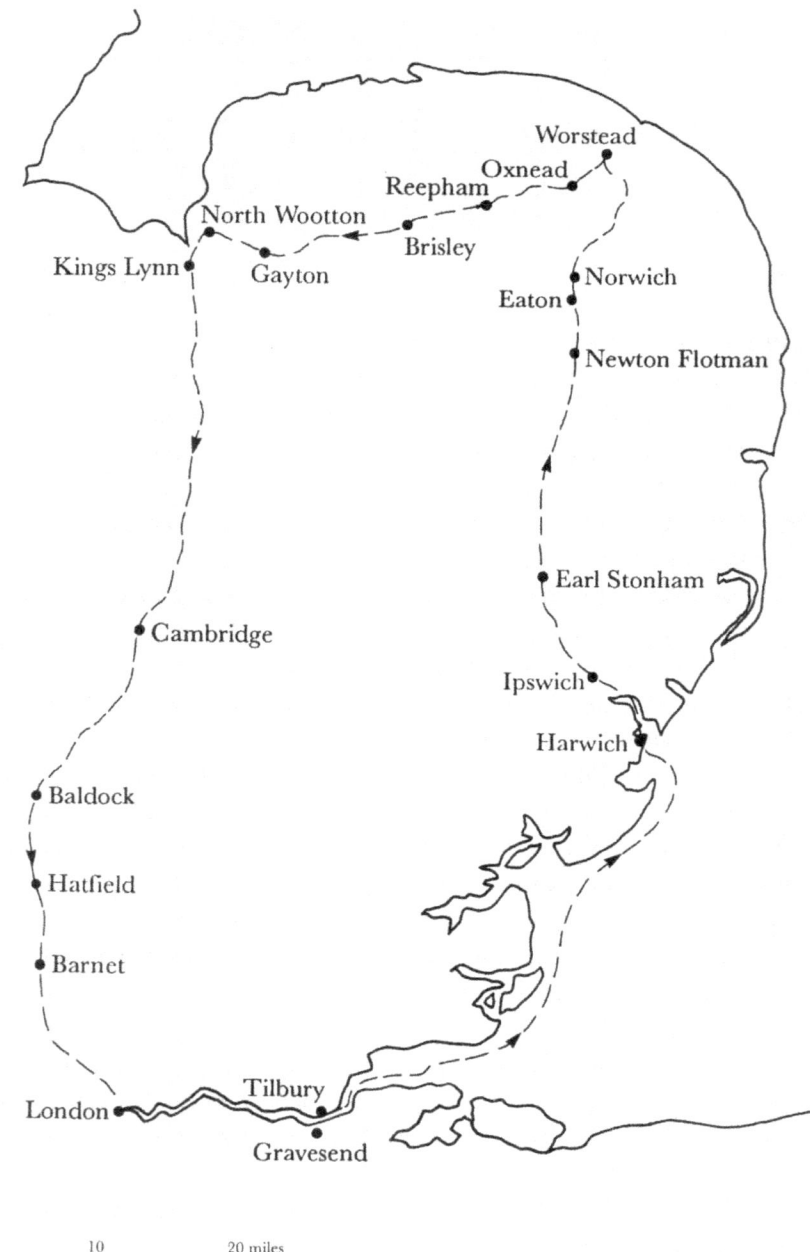

A Late Weary, Merry Voyage

A late weary, merry voyage

A late weary, merry voyage, and journey: or, John Taylor's moneth's travells, By sea and land, from London to Gravesend, to Harwich, to Ipswich, to Norwich, to Linne, to Cambridge, and from thence to London: Performed and written on purpose to please his friends, and to pleasure himselfe in these unpleasant and necessitated times. Printed in the yeare, 1650.

To the judicious, or ignorant reader, the author sends this loving advertisement.

Gentlemen and Yeomen: Let mee entreat you not to use my booke as you doe your oysters, (which you open in the middle) it is not so handsome entring into a house through a window, or the backside,[1] as it is in the front or fore-doore: He's no good courtier that salutes a faire lady behinde, nor can that reader finde the true sense of any book or pamphlet that begins at *Finis:* It is a prepostrous kinde of feeding for a man to eate his cheese before his rostmeat, and after that to sup up his broath. So much for introduction and instruction. I thanke my dictionary, I am furnished with as much broken Latine as declares my perambulating condition; *Vado,* bids mee to go, *Vadens,* commands mee to bee going, and *Vagus,* puts mee in minde of wandring, but *quo Gentium fugiam,* to what place or corner of the world shall I go or flye to, there lies the question: To stay at home I was in a starving condition, and to go from home, I was in a dillemma or wavering betwixt hope and diffidence, to what place, whither, to whom, why, wherefore, and how my resolution was constantly inconstant, and my determinations so slippery, that I could finde no steadfast footing in my minde, which wayes to bend my course: But considering that I had made eleven vagaries,[2] voyages, and journies before; and that one fling more would make my labours a douzen (much like the twelve labours of Hercules in number, though farre unequall in quantity, quallity, weight, and measure) To make my uncertaine travells a compleate jury, I framed this following humorous bill, which I gave to divers persons of sundry functions, callings, dispositions, and humours.

1 rear yard.
2 ramblings.

Anno Domini, 1650. Whereas John Taylor doth intend to make a progresse this summer (hee knowes not when, or whither) to see some friends in the countrey, (hee knowes not who,) being certaine that his journey and entertainments will bee (hee knowes not how;) and that hee purposeth to returne again to London (hee knowes not what time;) and that hee intends to write a relation of his perambulations (hee knowes wherefore:) That when hee doth give mee (or cause to bee delivered to mee) the said relations aforesaid, that then I will freely give to him for the same, in good English money, the summe of somewhat; though neither my selfe, or hee, knowes how much or little, that somewhat may bee: To the which engagement I have subscribed my name and dwelling: where, if at his returne, hee doe kindly finde mee, hee shall friendly feele mee.

To this unfellowed[1] matchlesse bill, there are many men that have subscribed to pay mee money for this booke at my returne. I thanke God I am not so light of beliefe as to believe that they will all pay mee; nor will I dispaire, but that some are as willing to pay as they were to subscribe. The countries that I have footed, have been fruitfull, plenteous, with abundance of most good things (except newes and cuckolds) but such stuffe as my observations collected, I ambled to distribute to delight my friends, to please mine enemies, and pleasure my selfe. John Taylor.

A late weary, merry voyage, etc.

Time was, this land was sick of peace and wealth,
And war, and poverty must give her health:
Grave Reformation, physick did apply,
And Mars himselfe us'd much phlebotomy;[2]
I will not say our land was full of witches
To charm us to contemn our peace and riches;
But my beliefe is fix'd, my thoughts are pich'd;
One halfe were witches, th' other halfe bewitch'd.
Stern War hath let us bloodith' master vaine,
And many a pursie[3] purse did purge and draine.

1 unmatched.
2 blood-letting.
3 swollen.

Thus Plenty made us proud, and War doth show
How good Peace was, and how our selves to know.
Affliction is the line, the hooke the net
To catch us from the world, they new beget
Our soules to Heav'n, and by a gratious birth
Lifts up our mindes to slight this sordid earth.
And I doe wish all sects, strifes, contradictions,
Would make such use of England's sad afflictions.

And now a short discourse of travelling
Of travellers, and of my wandering:
The sun's a traveller (and a great one to)
In twice twelve houres, he round the world doth goe;
The moone surrounds us in her changing spheare,
Three hundred sixty and five times a yeare.
But yet the thoughts of man more quick doth run
Then flashing lightning, or the moone or sun.
My restlesse thoughts can in a moment leape
To heaven, and thence to the infernall deepe.
To Europe, Asia, and America,
To the orient Indies, to hot Affrica;
The summer, autumne, winter, and the spring
Are in perpetuall motion, travelling.
And though my thoughts (like other men's are vaine,
Winds, seas, nor stormes, my thinking can restraine.
At travellers, let no man carpe or cavill,
Our mothers (at our births) were all in travell.
And from our birth unto our buriall,
In divers functions we do travell all.
The footman's feet, the statesman's working braine,
In travell, labour, and continuall paine
Do spend themselves, and all their courses bend
For private ends (to no end) till they end.
The lawyer travells, his tongue (swift with sleight)
Sells his words deare, by measure, tale,[1] and weight:

---

1 reckoning.

And those that buy them deare, do often find
They paid well for good words, but words are winde.
All men are born to travell, each man must
With paine and travell, turn unto his dust:
Then happy is the man that can go right,
Who doth his paths with David's lanthorne light.¹
And all my life time it hath been my fate
To be a traveller legitimate:
From head to heele, by either land or sea
I am a traveller, right *Cape a Pea*.²
Now Clothoe,³ my poor vitall thread hath spunne,
And Lachesis, her reeling work's near done:
Now Atropos is ready with her knife
To cut the uncertaine feeble twist of life;
Now in my autumne, or my fall o'th leafe
Halfe dead, halfe living, halfe blinde, lame, halfe deafe,
Now all these five halves can not make one whole
(From m' head unto my body bearing sole)
Now at this time, with brains, and feet, and pen,
I am an old new traveller agen.
'Tis not the greatnes of Golia's⁴ can
Perswade me to be lesser then a man:
She's cal'd a ship, whose burthen's⁵ but foure score,
And one thats fifteen hundred is no more.
Though *Folio* be our learned vollums, yet
Decimo sexto, may expresse some wit.⁶
A generous minde respects the poor man's mite,
'Tis said, a larke is better than a kite.⁷

---

1   1 Kings 15 verses 4-5.
2   from top to toe.
3   the three Fates, who determine the time of death.
4   Goliath, the Philistine giant killed by David, 1 Samuel 17 verse 50.
5   burden.
6   paper sizes: grand literature is printed in folio volumes, insignificant stuff in small volumes, whose pages have been folded to one-sixteenth (16mo or decimo-sexto) of their original size.
7   'For a leg of a larke is better than is the body of a kyght' J. Heywood, 1546.

Nor would I have the reader to mistake,
That odious bold comparisons I make:
Pamphlets must not compare with reverend writings
Of theologues, or historians grave enditings.
The owle must not as high as th' eagle flee,
Yet owles are fowles, as well as eagles bee.
So I, that am poor, weak, *Aquatticus*,[1]
A traveller, and poet *Minnimus*,[2]
The honour, wholly, humbly I ascribe
T' the worthies of most sacred Levie's tribe,[3]
And the learn'd servants of the triple Trine,[4]
Whose verses make mortallity divine:
Your genius high illuminations are
Transcending mine, as Titan[5] doth a starre;
Yet your refulgence doth not blinde me so,
But that my silly glowormes light doth glow.
I scribble, and I walke, I walke and scribble,
I give and take jests, bull, and clinch,[6] and quibble.
Amongst good poets I have plaid at *Crambo*,
And I have found mens words and deedes not *Ambo*.[7]
The last yeare (sixteen hundred forty nine)[8]
I went to Cornewall, and some foes of mine
Did certifie a lye, malitiously,
That I was subtle, and a dangerous spye;
And did with travell, and a faign'd pretence
With th' enemy have some intelligence.

1 reference to his sobriquet, the water poet.
2 least of all.
3 one of the tribes of Israel, whose members performed the lesser services in the temple.
4 three threes, referring to the nine muses.
5 used poetically of the sun-god, Helios. Titan, the largest moon of Saturn, was not discovered until 1655.
6 mock, and pun.
7 Crambo is a rhyming game, ambo is Latin for both, here presumably implying that words and deeds are not the same.
8 the journey described above does not refer to this imprisonment, which occurred after his return.

For which three dayes in prison I was closed,
With sleepe reposed, and my minde composed:
I knew my conscience clear, and well disposed,
By truths my accusations were opposed,
And I (not found the man I was supposed)
Without a fee or fine, on me imposed,
And unto misery and want exposed
(Not guilty found) from prison I was losed.
But if I had a thought, or bad intent
When I from London, into Cornwall went,
Against the army, state, or Parliament,
Let torments both my soule and corps torment.
No man can blame me much that I have grumbled,
That I, for no cause was thus tos'd and tumbled;
And that I never could m' accuser see,
My books and bills took, and detain'd from me:
The books declar'd my journy too and fro,
The bills, were names of men, and where to go
To finde the men, to pay me for my pain,
My losse of those, made all my labour vain;
And for that losse, I once more try my friends,
Hope tells me, time will make me some amends.
False fortunes frownes, makes me not fear or shrink,
And evill fall on him that ill doth think.[1]

My muse shall now sing, though she be no singer,
For (reader with thee) I'le no longer linger:
My brain enthusiastick holds it meet
To make the feet of verse, tell how my feet
Did travell gauling gravell, and surbated,[2]
Sometimes by day, sometimes by night belated.
To write my acts my selfe, as 'tis most fit,
Caesar himselfe his Commentaries writ:[3]

---

[1] The common proverb, translating the motto of the Order of the Garter, *Honi soit qui mal y pense.*
[2] made footsore.
[3] Julius Caesar wrote accounts of his own war exploits, *De Bello Civilo* and *De*

And solid Johnson made his muse his cock
To crow his savoury voyage up Fleet Dock:[1]
So I do hold it worthy imitation,
To follow them, and write mine own relation.
The fourteenth day of August, London, London
I left, O what hath many a mother's son don?[2]
What hath the mad and furious sword and gun don?
But klll'd some, made some rich, and some are undon.
That I may say of London, what a town ist,
There lives the Seeker, Dipper, and the Brownist:
There's roome for Ranters, and alas how apt ist
To harbour the ungovern'd Annabaptist?
Th'ast plaid thy game home, like a cunning gamester,
Thou more religions hast, then hath dam'd Amster.[3]
I downe the Thames the day aforesaid went,
(On one side Essex, on the other Kent)
Untill at last, to Gravesend I was borne,
And lodg'd in Milton,[4] at the plenteous Home.
That Home, was Cornucopia unto mee
Two dayes meat, drinke, and lodging, quarter free.[5]
From thence unto a private house I went,
And there (with small charge, and much discontent)
Foure dayes I stay'd, and every tide did watch

Bello Gallico.

1. Ben Jonson's *Volpone* (1605-6), which includes crow and raven figures and scenes of imprisonment, was produced in the light of the playwright's own imprisonment in 1605. Jonson's poem 'On the famous voyage' was written about 1610.
2. 'This kinde of verse or rime, is hard to make, and when they are made they are not worth any thing, especially when they are in the hands of an ignorant reader.' [Taylor]
3. The multitude of Puritan and dissenting sects; Amsterdam was a hotbed of dissent, and many Puritans in England were refugees from, or had links with, the Low Countries.
4. now a district of Gravesend.
5. 'I thank a baker. I thank John Brasserton the master of a tilt-boat there for my foure dayes entertainement.' [Taylor]

To have some ship, or hoigh,¹ boat, barke, or katch,
To carry me to Norfolk or some place
Where I might foot it, and jog on my race.
In all this time I never wanted² drinke,
And for their drinke, I give 'em thanks in inke:
No otherwayes my thanks I can expresse,
But verbally, and with the pen and presse.

The twentieth day of August, Kent and I
Tooke leave, and to the Fort of Tilberry³
I past, and ere I there an houre had bin,
A lucky ship of Ipswich tooke me in.
She quickly spread abroad her canvas wings,
The whistling winde in shrowdes and taklin sings:
That next day following, near the houre eleven
We came t' an anchor safe in Harwich haven:
My thanks unto the master I must utter,
He's owner of the ship, his sirname's Butter:
His ship and selfe both nam'd the Jonathan,
And I have seldome found a kinder man.
My fare was as he far'd, and well he far'd,
And (in his cabbin) I my lodging shar'd;
For which he would not take one mite⁴ of mee,
Thus was my passage, meat, and lodging free:
For which I would requite him, if I could,
And till I can, let him take what I would.

From Harwich harbour, with the winde and tide,
In a small boat, we up to Ipswich slide:
At the White Horse, I there was entertain'd
So well (for nothing) that they nothing gain'd.
For which among my worthy friends I ranke them,
Kind Master Atkins, and his wife, I thanke them.

1 hoy, a type of boat rigged as a sloop.
2 lacked.
3 Tilbury, Essex.
4 a coin of less value than a farthing.

Ipswich, is the chiefe towne of the county of Suffolke, it hath twelve parish churches in it: There hath been more in former times, it may bee called a city for the large bounds and extent of it: It is from the north to the south a large mile in breadth, and from east to west it is two miles in length: our famous infortunate Cardinall, Thomas Wolsey was borne there, where hee had caused to bee layd the foundation of a magnificent stately colledge, the ruines whereof are now scarce to be found; but in memory of his birth and birth place, there hee built a large and strong shambles (for butchers to sell, and others to buy flesh) the like of it is not in England; the towne hath been walled strongly, but spoyled and demollished by the Danes, was (nor is like to bee) ever repaired; it is governed by two bayliffes, and ten portmen, who doe weare scarlet gownes when occasion is, their common counsell (being many) are very substantiall men, read more in Mr. Cambden or Mr. Speed.[1]

August the two and twentieth, thence went I
Eight miles to Stanhum,[2] and lodg'd at the Pye.
The next day, was an extream rainy Friday,
Wet (through my cloaths) unto my skin, or hyde, a
Tedious and weary journy twenty miles,
Bedabbled, dirty, clambring many stiles,
I came at night unto a town call'd Newton,[3]
And there I had a dry house, and wet sute on.
On Saturday (the day call'd Bartholomew)
I rose, and trampled through the mire and dew;
My tyred feet the rotten highway beat on
Unto a village, or a bridge call'd Eaton:[4]
There at the Lyon (red as any stammell)[5]
Is harbour good, for man, or horse, or cammell:
There dwels my cousin Wil Hart, and's good wife Bridgid

---

1 The accounts of Ipswich, Norwich and King's Lynn rely heavily on William Camden's *Britannia*.
2 Earl Stonham, Little Stonham and Stonham Aspal are Suffolk villages near Stowmarket.
3 Newton Flotman, Norfolk, south of Norwich.
4 a district of Norwich.
5 a type of woollen cloth, usually dyed red.

By them two nights, I was well fed and lidged.[1]
I stayd with them the Saturday and Sunday,
And he with me to Norwich went on Munday:
There did my cousin Hart, prove more kind hearted,
And there we merry were, shooke hands and parted.
One Master Edward Martin there doth dwell,
Who both divine bookes, and prophane doth sell:
We (till that time) ne'er saw each others face,
Yet there he freely kept me three dayes space;
From Monday untill Thursday morning there
He thought no cost too heavy, or too deere:
He brought me out of town: a mile at least,
And there I freed him from a troublous guest.

Norwich, is a famous ancient city, built many yeares before the Norman conquest; it had a strong castle in it double ditched, out of the ruins or corruption of the castle, a jayle (or goale) was engendred, to which use it is now put: It was spoyled by Hugh Bigot Earl of Norfolk, in the raign of K. Henry the second, and a greater mischief befell the city in King Henry the third's time, for the citizens (in a tumultuous fury) spoyled it with fire, and withal burnt the goodly priory church, which afterwards they were caused to rebuild in a fairer manner. Lastly, Norwich was won and fired by Ket and his army of rebels, since when it hath been well repaired, and in a flourishing condition; the wals of the city are of more circuit or bounds then the wals of London: But it is to be considered, there are pasture grounds, gardens, and waste lands (not built upon) more then half the ground within the walls; it hath 12. gates to issue in and out 12. severall wayes, whereby it may be conceived that it is large in circuit, (for London hath not so many) there are 30. faire parish churches, there were five more, but they are ruined before these present troubles; the goodly cathedrall is much defaced in these late times of reformation. It was governed by 2 bayliffs, till King Edward the fourth impowred them to chuse a mayor, and gave priviledges to them, and charters of honorable and memorable regard: The Low Dutch (or Netherland nation) being frighted from their country by the cruelty of

---

1 i.e. lodged, a desperate attempt to cobble a rhyme for Bridgid.

the Duke D' Alva, who was Livetenant Govemour there under the King of Spaine, (who for his tyranny the people called Duke Diabola) they fled in multitudes into England, and thousands of them came to Norwich, where they have so thrived, and withall much inriched the city, that it is thought there are 10000. weavers, spinners, and other artificers, dayly imployed for the making of sundry sorts of sayes, with other stuffs innumerable, either for wearing or ornaments; to adorne houses with hangings, carpets, or curtaines, of innumerable sorts, colours, varieties, and more hard names than any apothecary hath upon his boxes or gallypots,[1] and so much for Norwich, with my further thanks to Mr. Edward Martin, with Mr. Richard Thacker, Mr. Vowte, *cum multis aliis, omnium gathrum, all ta mall.*[2]

    The county of Norfolk hath in some parts found a strange alteration, since the last yeare, 1649. in the price of hay, for it is fallen from 4s. 4d. the hundred weight, to one groat the hundred; this I thought worthy of relating to shew the fertility of the soyle, by the Almighties blessings.

Angust [sic] the nine and twentieth I went forth
From Norwich city ten miles further north,
To Worsted;[3] well wet, with a heavenly shower,
Mine hostesse entertain'd me, to her power;
Although the weather frown'd, she did not lower,
Her lookes were sweet, but yet her ale was sower.
My lodging good, my reck'ning was not deare,
For ten pence, supper, bed, and breakfast there.
I arose as soone as day began to show,
And (two miles thence) did unto Honing go;
There, to the minister I welcome was,
And merrily one day and night did pass:
And there we made a shift that Fryday night
To eate a well fed, fat tith pig outright.
Next day I Honing left, and did begin
To crosse the north of Norfolk, towards Lyn:

1 glazed medicine jars.
2 'with many others, altogether...' nonsense Latin.
3 Worstead near North Walsham, which gave its name to the cloth.

That day I chanc'd a gallant house to finde
A master bountifull, and servants kinde:
I need not tell my reader where, or who,
The name of Oxnet,[1] all doth plainly show.

Sir William Paston:[2] there I found and spake with the Apelles[3] of our age, Mr. Edward Peirce[4] painter, and Mr. John Stone[5] was there, whose rare arts are most exquisitly manifested both in painting, limming, and cunning carved statues in stone.

That Saturday I went t' a towne call'd Reepham,
And as amongst great sinners, I the chiefe am:
I grieve to see the churches there demollish'd,
Sects plenty, and true piety abollish'd.

This town of Repham (or Reepham) hath three faire churches, were standing in one church-yard, it is sayd they were built by three sisters; one of them hath beene long decayed and fallen to the ground, onely the tower stands faire and strong; the other two churches do serve four parishes, and I could hear no more but three bels on Sunday there: So that the reckoning is one church-yard, three bels, two churches, three steeples, foure parishes, and one broken church for lumber.

    The second of September (being Monday) I left Reepham, and travelled 18. miles to a village called Gayton; but by the way (at a place called Brissley)[6] I was told of a holy sister, who by falling back, had risen forward, to the increase of the faithfull: she being reproved falling and rising, sayd it was pure zeale that pricked her on, and that it was done with a brother, he and she, and every one being bound to do for, and

1 Oxnead Hall, near Aylsham. Most of the house visited by Taylor was demolished during the 18th century.
2 antiquary, of a famous family, created baronet 1642, died 1663.
3 famous Greek painter, 4th century BC, from Asia Minor.
4 the elder, decorative painter, died c.1670.
5 son of the famous stonemason, Nicholas Stone (died 1647), who succeeded to his father's business at Long Acre, and was thus Taylor's neighbour. Stone died in 1667.
6 Brisley, between Fakenham and Dereham.

with one another, and I hearing of her kindnesse bestowed this short epigram on her.

Hath lust defil'd her purenesse, never match'd?
No 'twas deceit, she hath been cunny-catch'd:[1]
It was a rule, she learned of her mother,
That 'twas no sin to couple with a brother.

But to return again where I left: at Gayton there are 2 playn ale-houses, and one wine ale-house; these houses were distant one from the other a furlong, or two flight shoot: at the first house (where the wine was) there were fellows swaggering, and ready to draw their fists, there I would not lodge; at the second I would have lodged, but could not, their beds were all taken up; at the third the doors were lock'd and the windows shut, no body at home, the folkes not come home from harvest worke; forward I knew not whether, and backward I would not goe, and to stand still there was cold comfort for an old weary traveller, there being no harbour, but a wild common, nor any company to passe the time withall but 3 or 4 flocks of geese; in this extremity I espy'd an old-old, very old,[2] neat handed little antient man, to him I went, and told him that I would have lodged at that house, but it was shut up; quoth he the folkes will come home by and by, but I doe not know whether they have any lodging or no, and sure me think you be a clean man, and tis pitty you should lye on the common, if you will goe home and lye with me, I am an old widdower, and one bed shall hold us both.

I thankfully embraced his courteous offer, and went with him, where I sup'd and log'd well, and would take nothing of me; his name is Sampson Warrington, in remembrance of whose kindnes I have written this thankfull expession [sic].

I was told there of a precise holy ma' in those parts, who sent his man unto a pasture ground to see his horse, the fellow went, and brought word to his master that his horse was dead, dead quoth hee, how

---

1 cony-catched, cheated, from cony (rabbit) but here perhaps with obscene overtones. The term was popularized by Robert Greene in the title of a pamphlet (1591).
2 Taylor was fond of this expression, and used it in the title of his biography of Thomas Parr.

dar'st thou tell me my horse is dead? the fellow answered, I pray you be not angry, sure I am that if he be not dead, that he is either deceased, or changed his life; well sayd the master, if my horse be departed, I have lost a good one, for he was so sure of his feet, that I would have put my life into his hands.

Tuesday September 3. I went 4 miles to a village called North-Wooton, 3 miles from Linn,[1] there I was much beholding to my kinsman Mr. John Clark, he gave me large and free welcome, for which to him with his good wife, my gratitude is manifested; also my thankes to Mr. Swift.

Wednesday I went to Linn, where a good old joviall lad named John Scarborow entertained mee sumptuously (for my cozen John Clark's sake) and also he was somewhat the kinder to me, because he had often heard of me, besides of his own disposition is free from discourtesie to strangers, I thank him for my fresh fish, my duck, or mallard, my lodging, ale, and oysters, with the appurtenances. etc.
Linn was much honoured by King John for their loyalty, for which that king gave them his owne sword, and a faire gilt bole, which they keep as honorable memorialls to this day: it is a faire large strong sea towne, it is now a garison, the river that the sea doth flow thereinto, disperseth it self into many branches, for the commodious enriching of divers shires, counties, townes, and places, as Rutlandshire, Huntingdonshire, Cambridge, and Cambridgeshire, the Isle of Ely, etc. those rivers doe carry and re-carry all maner of goods and merchandise, so that Linn with all those countreys are furnished with more sea-coales then doe come up the River of Thames, wood being so scarce that the rich might blow their nailes,[2] and the poore would bee starved in the winter for want of firing in all those counties, if the rivers were not.

Thursday the 5. of September I left Linn, and tooke an open passage boat, being bedewed all day and night, and almost all the Fryday with raine without ceasing, so that, on Fryday I came to Cambridge sufficiently pickled: there I tooke up my lodging at the signe of the Rose (one of the best innes) where I thank Mr. Brian and his wife (my old acquaintance) I had good cheere and lodging *gratis* and welcome; I tooke

---

1 King's Lynn, Norfolk.
2 warm their hands by blowing on them.

notice of the colledges, they stand as fair and stately as ever, and (for any thing that I know) there may be as much learning as ever was, but I saw but few schollars or gowne men.

On Saturday the 7. of September, I was determined to see Sturbridge Faire,[1] but by fortune I espyed an empty cart returning towards London 17 miles to a towne call'd Baldock; by which means I left Cambridge without taking my leave of Mr. Brian, for which I crave his and his Wives pardon.

That day I was uncarted at Baldock, and footed it 7 miles more to Steevenedge,[2] there (at the Faulcon) I stayd Saturday and Sunday, and on Monday I travelled to Hatfield, and to Barnet 17 miles, wher I was discreetly wet and dirty, and took up my lodging at the Bell with a silent clapper. The next day (being Tuesday) I came home to my house wet and weary in Phoenix Alley, at the signe of the Crowne, near the Globe Taverne, about the middle of Long-Acre or Covent Garden.

Thus having touch'd no state, or state affaires,
Or mentioned men that sit in honour's chaires:
I dare declare him of a base conditition [sic],
That of my lines or travels hath suspition.
I formerly have falsely been accus'd,
And therefore now I hope to be excus'd.
This time I travell'd (for my lives preserving)
To get some money, to prevent a starving:
And every one that for my booke doth pay me,
Doth love me, lodge me, feed me, and aray me.
With feet and pen, my walke and worke is done,
And (Caesar like) the conquest I have won:
And though I never shall have Caesar's fame,
Yet I did see, I came, and overcame.[3]

FINIS.

1 This was held at Casterton on the outskirts of Cambridge in early September, and was graphically described by Defoe seventy years later. He claimed that it was the largest fair in the world.
2 Stevenage, Herts.
3 allusion to Caesar's boast, as recorded by Suetonius, *Veni, vidi, vici*.

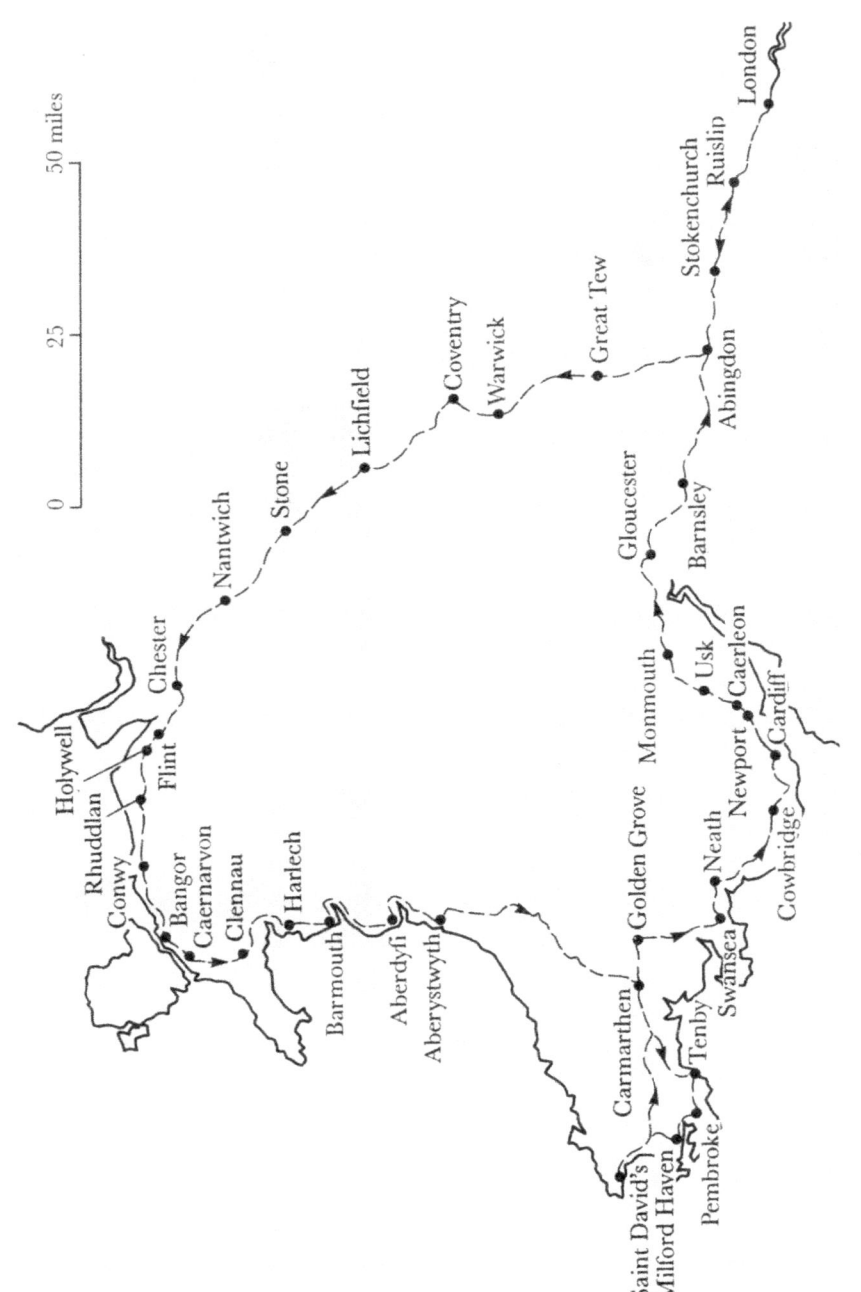

A Short Relation of a Long Journey

A SHORT RELATION OF A LONG JOURNEY

A Short Relation of a Long Journey, *an ambitious expedition of nearly 600 miles to and around Wales, was undertaken by Taylor in the summer of 1652, during the course of which he celebrated his 74th birthday. He travels alone, apart from his horse, Dun, of whom he speaks with affection, and about whose welfare he takes great pains. From Taylor's description of this skeletal 2 mph. beast, he appears to have been in about the same physical condition as his master. For Taylor is now, 'of strength bereft, | With one right leg, and one lame left leg left,' so that by the time that they reach Chester from London he urgently seeks medical attention from an Italian physician. Mentally, however, Taylor seems to be in excellent spirits, and his account of this journey has much more in common with his Cornish jaunt of three years earlier, than with the East Anglian slog which intervened. From Chester the plan seems to be roughly to follow the coastline around north, west and south Wales, arriving eventually at Gloucester, and so back to London. The whole journey takes eight weeks.*

The resulting account fits the pattern established by these late journeys. After the 'Taylors bill' the work begins in verse, and we are transported briskly (after over-imbibing at Warwick) as far as Chester. Thereafter most of the descriptions are in prose. We hear of the poverty and destruction apparent in north and mid-Wales towns, such as Flint, Harlech and Aberystwyth, which is contrasted with the abundance of cheap provisions at Carmarthen. There is the usual eulogy of generous hosts and their houses, such as the Vaughans of Golden Grove near Carmarthen, and a rumbustious denunciation of a household near Swansea where hospitality is denied. There are reminders of the late wars when, at Caernarvon, Taylor is detained at the garrisoned castle; and in his description of St David's cathedral, which has put off, 'the dull and heavy coat of peacefull lead, which was metamorphosed into warlike bullets'. The Puritans of Barnsley in Gloucestershire, whom he encounters on the way home, are contrasted with the irreligious Welsh, who play stool-ball (cricket) and other games in churchyards on Sundays. St Winifred's Well near Flint warrants a detailed description, and we are treated to an anecdote about a narrow escape from drowning. As usual Taylor falls in the mire somewhere along the way.

This time there is no moralizing or crusading. Taylor is simply an elderly tourist, an insatiable traveller who writes because he must, and accepts favours where he can, but who suspects that his travelling days are nearly over.

[13th July - 7th Sept. 1652. Text derived from 1st ed., 1652 (BL E.1432.2). Only pp.1-27 of this pamphlet have been transcribed. The remainder (pp.28-48) consists of an abbreviation by Taylor of works on Welsh history by Humphrey Lloyd and others; see p. 329, note 1]

A Short Relation of a long journey, made round or ovall by encompassing the principalitie of Wales, from London, through and by the counties of Middlesex and Buckingham, Berks, Oxonia, Warwick, Stafford, Chester, Flint, Denbigh, Anglesey, Carnarvan, Merioneth, Cardigan, Pembrooke, Caermarden, Glamorgan, Monmouth, Glocester, etc.

This painfull circuit began on Tuesday the 13 of July last, 1652. and was ended (or both ends brought together) on Tuesday the 7. of September following, being near 600. miles.

Whereunto is annexed an epitome of the famous history of Wales.

Performed by the riding, going, crawling, running, and writing of John Taylor, dwelling at the sign of the Poets Head, in Phenix Ally, near the midle of Long Aker or Covent Garden. [added in manuscript on BL copy: 'March 26 1653'.]

To all my honourable, worshipfull, and honest friends, that have subscribed to this folowing bill; I humbly desire them to read it againe, and consider the contents of it, and content mee accordingly.

A Taylors Bill, with few or no items: by or for John Taylor.

Now in the seventy fourth yeare of mine age,

I take an English and Welsh pilgrimage:
From London first I bend my course to Chester,
And humbly I to all men am requester;
That when I have past over hills and dales,
And compast with my travels famous Wales,
That when to you that I a book do give,
Relating how I did subsist and live,
With all my passages both here and there,
And of my entertainment every where.
Write but your names and dwellings in this bill,
I'le finde you, for the book give what you will.
Twelve voyages and journies I have past,
And now my age sayes this may be my last.
My travels story shall most pleasant be
To you that read, though painfull unto me.

In this bill I did promise to give to my friends (subscribers) a true relation of my journey, and entertainment, (which I have done) and I do give to them more then I promised, which is a briefe Chronicle of Wales,[1] (which I did not mention in my bill) I know there are foure or five sorts of adventurers with me in this wearisome journey, some of them have payd me already (before I went) and their paine is past: If all the rest do pay me (being near 3000) I am deceived; If none doe pay me I am miserably cousened: For those that have payd, or can and will pay, I thanke them; for such as would if they could, or will when they can, I wish them ability to performe their wills for their owne sakes, and mine both: But for those that are able to reward me and will not, I will not curse them, though I feare they are almost past praying for.

A Short Relation of a Long Journy, etc.

A traveller that loves to see strange lands,
May be a man or not a man of 's hands:
But yet 'tis very requisite and meet,

---

[1] Appended to this journey (and not reproduced in this edition) is 'Cambria Brittania: or, a short abreviation of the history, and chronicles of Wales', by John Taylor based on the work of Humphrey Lloyd and David Powell.

He should be furnish'd with good brains and feet;
For he that wants legs, feet, and brains, and wit,
To be a traveller is most unfit:
And such am I by age of strength bereft,
With one right leg, and one lame left leg left.
Beggers on their backs their brats[1] do reare;
But I my issue[2] in my leg do beare:
I dresse it often and impatiently
It lies and cries not, though it make me cry;
Yet I dare challenge Scottish Jock or Jackey,
Or any light-heel'd nimble footed lackey,
To travell such a jaunt as I have done,
With th' right leg going, and the left leg run:
Or if I please, the case I'le alter so,
To make the worst leg run, the best to goe.
And sure my heart was stout, men may suppose,
To venture travell with such legs as those.
But there be some few that do understand,
'Tis merry walking with a horse in hand.
Such was my lot, I had a stately courser,[3]
None courser quality'd, and for a worser,
There's neither Halifax, or Hull, nor Hell,
That for good parts my horse can parallel;
He was a beast, had heated been and cheated,
Too much hard over rid and under meated,[4]
That he as gaunt as any greyhound was,
And for a horses skelliton might passe:
You might have told his ribs, he was so thin,
And seen his heart and guts, but for his skin;
He was not pursie foggy,[5] cloy'd with greace,
And like his rider lov'd rest, ease, and peace:
Dun was, and is the dumb beast, and was done,

1   pun on brat, 'child' and brat, 'coarse coat worn by beggars'.
2   pun on issue, 'offspring' and issue, 'discharge'.
3   a swift horse.
4   fed.
5   synonyms, both mean corpulent or puffed-up.

E're I begun, or he with me begun.
He had a black list, from the mane to taile,
Which is a colour that doth seldome faile:
To change of paces he had been inur'd,
But yet not one t'endure, or be endur'd;
His trot would fling a dagger out ot'h sheath,
Or jolt a man to death, or out of breath.
His ambling was invisible to me,
From such smooth easie garbs his feet were free:
His common pace in sun-shine or in showre,
Was (as he pleas'd) about two mile an houre.
I never yet could put him in a sweat,
For he was never free, but at his meat.
Thus John upon Dun's back, were both Dun John,[1]
And thus the tedious way we wandred on.
Now to proceed in order duly, truly,
I London left the thirteenth day of July:
The wayes as faire as man could well desire,
'Cause I had none to draw Dun out o'th mire:
I fifteen miles (to Rislip)[2] that day went,
Baited at Edgworth,[3] to give Dun content;
There[4] my acquaintance, of good fame and worth,
Did welcome me: the next day I set forth,
With boots, sans spurs, with whip, and switch of burch,
I got on, twenty miles to Stoken Church:[5]
The fifteenth day, S. Swithin, I and Dun,
Did shuffle sixteen miles to Abington;[6]
There till the Tuesday following I abode,
From thence I sixteen miles to great Tue[7] rode,
There at the Swan mine host was free and kind,

1 pun on Don Juan, the profligate hero.
2 Ruislip, outer London, formerly Middlesex.
3 archaic spelling of Edgware, outer London, formerly Middlesex.
4 i.e. Ruislip (Edgware would have been visited on the way to Ruislip).
5 Stokenchurch, Bucks.
6 Abingdon, Berks.
7 Great Tew, Oxon, near Chipping Norton.

He had but one eye, tother side was blinde;
But surely he a right good-fellow was,
And there one night my Dun did eat good grass.
On July's twenty one from Tue I went,
And unto Warwick strait my course I bent,
There did I find another signe o'th Swan,
Mine hostesse kind, mine host a gentile man,
And for your love to me, good Master Venner,
With humble thanks I am your praises penner.
My gratitude to Master Jacob Harmer,
His drapers shop could never make me warmer,
Then high and mighty Warwick's drink did there,
It made my brains to caper and careere,
It was of such invincible strong force,
To knock me (in five miles) twice from my horse:
And sure I think the drink was certainly
Infused with the conqu'ring ghost of Guy.[1]
On July's two and twentieth day I came
Unto an ancient house call'd Hunningham,
There were two ladies of good worth and fame,
Whom for some reasons I forbeare to name:
Their son and grandson (John) I'le not forget,
He's nobly minded as a baronet;
Foure dayes they kept me with exceeding cheere,
And gave me silver because travels deare.
From thence my journey 5 miles I pursue,
To Coventry, most famous for true blew;[2]
There the faire crosse[3] of ancient high renown
Stands firme, though other crosses all are down.
'Tis a dry city, and dry let it be,
'Twas not made dryer one small drop for me:
Like a camelion[4] there I brake my fast,

[1] Guy of Warwick, romantic hero, and legendary ancestor of the earls of Warwick.
[2] Coventry was famous for its blue cloth, just as Lincoln was for its green.
[3] Coventry Cross was built in 1543 and demolished in 1771.
[4] chameleons were believed to feed on air.

And thence I twenty miles to Lichfield past;
There at the George I took my lodging up,
I well was lodg'd, and well did sup and cup,
When there by chance, I cast my wandring ey on
The ruin'd church,[1] with griefe I thought on Sion:
I sigh'd to see that sad confusion,
Like th' Hebrews by the Brook of Babylon.[2]
On July's twenty seventh I rode alone
Full sixteen miles unto a town call'd Stone.
Next day to Nantwich sixteen long miles more,
From thence to Chester near the Cambrian shore:
There was my welcome in such noble fashion,
Of which in prose I'le make some briefe relation.

My lodging at Chester was in the Watergate street, at the sign of the Feathers, I lay on a feather-bed, and in the same house I met with two brothers of mine acquaintance thirty years, they brought me to the chamber of a reverend Italian physition, named Vincent Lancelles he was more than 80 yeares of age, yet of a very able body, and vigorous constitution: The yong mens names were Thomas Morrine and Francis Morrine, the people were pleased (out of their ignorance, or in small wit) to call the old gentleman a mountebank;[3] but I am sure he was deservedly well reputed and reported of, for many malladies and diseases which hee cured, whereof divers were judged incurable: He helped such as were grieved for three severall considerations.

    First, hee cured the rich, for as much as hee could get.

    Secondly, hee healed the meaner sort for what they could spare, or were willing to part withall.

    Thirdly, hee cured the poor for Gods sake, and gave them mony and other reliefe, as I my selfe (with thankfull experience) must ever acknowledge: For he looked upon my lame leg, and applyed such medicine, as did not only ease me, but I am in hope will cure me, the griefe being nothing but a blast of lightning and thunder, or planet

---

1 Lichfield Cathedral was badly damaged during the civil war.
2 Psalm 137, verse 1: By the waters of Babylon we sat down and wept; when we remembered thee, O Sion.
3 a quack or charlatan.

stroke,[1] which I received nine years past at Oxford.

For a further courtesie, when I was taking my leave of Chester, I demanded what I had to pay for lodging, dyet, and horse-meat, mine host sayd, that all was fully payd and satisfied by the good old physition. My humble thanks remembred to Captain Vincent Corbet, but more especially to Captain John Whitworth at Chester.

On Fryday the 30. of July, I rode (and footed it) ten miles to Flint (which is the shire town of Flint-shire) and surely war hath made it miserable, the sometimes famous castle there, in which Richard the second of that name, King of England was surprised by Henry of Bullinbrook,[2] is now almost buried in it's own ruins, and the town is so spoiled, that it may truely be said of it, that they never had any market (in the memory of man) they have no sadler, taylor, weaver, brewer, baker, botcher, or button-maker; they have not so much as a signe of an ale-house, so that I was doubtfull of a lodging, but (by good hap) I hapned into the house of one Mr. Edward Griffith, where I had good meat and lodging for me and my dumb Dun beast, for very reasonable consideration, and this (me thinks) is a pitifull discription of a shire town.

Saturday, the last of July, I left Flint, and went three miles to Holy-well, of which place I must speak somewhat materially: About the length of a furlong, down a very steep hill, is a well (full of wonder and admiration) it comes from a spring not far from Rudland[3] Castle; it is and hath been many hundred yeares knowne by the name of Holy-well, but it is more commonly and of most antiquity called Saint Winifrids Well, in memory of the pious and chaste virgin Winifrid,[4] who was there beheaded for refusing to yield her chastity to the furious lust of a pagan prince; in that very place where her bloud was shed, this spring sprang up; from it doth issue so forceible a stream, that within a hundred yards of it, it drives certain mils, and some do say that nine corn mils and fulling mils are driven with the stream of that spring: It hath a fair

---

1 various disorders, including epilepsy and paralysis, were attributed to the malignant aspects of the planets; those afflicted were said to be planet-struck
2 King Henry IV.
3 Rhuddlan.
4 also known as Gwenfrewi, 7th-century saint beheaded by Caradoc. The building around the well was the work of Henry VII's mother, who sought a cure there.

chappell erected over it called Saint Winifrids Chappell, which is now much defaced by the injury of these late wars: The well is compassed about with a fine wall of free stone, the wall hath eight angles or corners, and at every angle is a fair stone piller, whereon the west end of the chappell is supported. In two severall places of the wall, there are neat stone staires to go into the water that comes from the well, for it is to be noted that the well it selfe doth continually work and bubble with extream violence, like a boiling cauldron or furnace, and within the wall, or into the well very few do enter: The water is christalline, sweet, and medicinable, it is frequented daily by many people of rich and poore, of all diseases, amongst which great store of folkes are cured, divers are eased, but none made the worse. The hill descending is plentifully furnished (on both sides of the way) with beggers of all ages, sexes, conditions, sorts and sizes, many of them are impotent, but all are impudent, and richly embrodered all over with such hexameter[1] poudred ermins (or vermin) as are called lice in England.

  Monday, the second of August, when the day begun, I mounted my Dun, having hired a little boy (to direct me in the way) that could speak no English, and for lack of an interpreter, we travelled speachless eight miles, to Rudland, where is an old ruined winde and war-shaken castle; from that town, after my horse, and the boy, and my selfe had dined with hay, oats, and barraw causs,[2] we hors't and footed it twelve miles further, to a fine strong walled towne, named Aberconwy; there I lodged at the house of one Mr. Spencer (an English man) he is post-master there, and there my entertainment was good, and my reckoning reasonable: There is a good defensive castle which I would have seen, but because there was a garrison, I was loath to give occasion of offence, or be much inquisitive.

The next day when the clock strook two and fowre,
I mounted Dun, Dun mounted Penmen Mawre;[3]
And if I do not take my aime amisse,
That lofty mountain seems the skies to kisse:

1 although nearly always used of poetry the word literally means 'of six measures or feet', so 'six-footed' is Taylor's punning meaning.
2 Welsh *bara a caws* 'bread and cheese'.
3 Penmaen-mawr.

But there are other hils accounted higher,
Whose lofty tops I had no mind t' aspire:
As Snowdon, and the tall Plinnillimon,[1]
Which I no stomack had to tread upon.
Merioneth mountains, and shire Cardigan
To travell over, will tire horse and man:
I, to Bewmaris[2] came that day and din'd,
Where I the good Lord Buckley,[3] thought to find:
But he to speak with me had no intent,
Dry I came into's house, dry out I went.
I left Bewmaris, and to Bangor trac'd it,
Ther's a brave church, but time and war defac'd it:
For love and mony I was welcome thither,
'Tis merry meeting when they come together.

Thus having travelled from Aberconwy to Beumorris and to Bangor, Tuesday 3. August, which in all they are pleased to call 14 miles, but most of the Welsh miles are large London measure, not any one of them but hath a hand bredth or small cantle[4] at each end, by which means, what they want in broadness, they have it in length; besides the ascending and descending almost impassable mountains, and break-neck stony ways, doth make such travellers as my selfe, judge that they were no misers in measuring their miles; besides, the land is courser then it is in most parts about London, which makes them to afford the larger measure: for course broad-cloath is not at the rate of velvet or satten.

Wednesday the 4. of August I rode 8 miles from Bangor to Carnarvan, where I thought to have seen a town and a castle, or a castle and a town; but I saw both to be one, and one to be both; for indeed a man can hardly divide them in judgement or apprehension; and I have seen many gallant fabricks and fortifications, but for compactness and compleatness of Caernarvon, I never yet saw a parallell. And it is by art and nature so sited and seated, that it stands impregnable, and if it be well mand, victualled, and ammunitioned, it is invincible, except fraud

1 Plynlimon or Pumlumon, mountain near Llanidloes.
2 Beaumaris, Anglesey.
3 Thomas Bulkeley (d. 1659) of Baron Hill by Beaumaris.
4 the raised rear part of a saddle, here meaning an extra piece.

or famine do assault, or conspire against it.

I was 5. hours in Caernarvon, and when I thought that I had taken my leave for ever of it, then was I meerly deceived; for when I was a mile on my way, a trooper came galloping after me, and enforced me back to be examined by Colonell Thomas Mason, (the governour there) who after a few words, when hee heard my name, and knew my occasions, he used me so respectively and bountifully, that (at his charge) I stayd all night, and by the means of him, and one Mr. Lloyd, (a Justice of Peace there) I was furnished with a guide, and something else to bear charges for one weeks travaile; for which curtesies, if I were not thankfull, I were worth the hanging for being ingratefull.

The 5. of August I went 12. miles, to a place called Climenie,[1] where the noble Sure John Owen[2] did, with liberall welcome, entertain me.

The 6. day I rode to a town called Harleck,[3] which stands on a high barren mountaine, very uneasie for the ascending into, by reason of the steep and uneeven stony way; this town had neither hay, grass, oats, or any relief for a horse: there stands a strong castle, but the town is all spoild, and almost inhabitable[4] by the late lamentable troubles.

So I left that towne (for fear of starving my horse) and came to a place called Bermoth,[5] (12. miles that day, as narrow as 20.) That place was so plentifully furnished with want of provision, that it was able to famish 100. men and horses: I procured a brace of boyes to goe two miles to cut grasse for my Dun, for which I gave them two groats; for my selfe and guide, I purchased a hen boyld with bacon, as yellow as the cowslip, or gold noble.[6] My course lodging there, was at the homely house of one John Thomson, a Lancashire English man.

Saturday the 7. of August, I horst, footed, (and crawling upon all 4.) 10. slender miles to Aberdovy, which was the last lodging that I had in Merionethshire, where was the best entertainment for men, but almost as bad as the worst for horses in all Merionethshire.

1 Clenennau near Dolbenmaen.
2 royalist commander, died 1666.
3 Harlech.
4 here 'uninhabitable', the opposite of the usual meaning, is intended.
5 Barmouth.
6 gold coin, one-third of a pound.

August 9. I gat into Cardiganshire, to a miserable market town called Aberistwith,[1] where before the late troubles, there stood a strong castle, which being blown up, fell down, and many fair houses (with a defensible thick wall about the town) are transformed into confused heaps of unnecessary rubbidge: within foure miles of this town, are the silver mines, which were honorable and profitable, as long as my good friend Thomas Bushell Esquire, had the managing of them, who was most industrious in the work, and withall by his noble demeanour, and affable deportment, deservedly gain'd the generall love and affection of all the countrey, of all degrees of people: but since he hath left that important imployment, the mines are neglected.

From Aberistwith, I went to the house of Sir Richard Price,[2] knight and baronet, where my entertainment was freely welcome, with some expression of further curtesies at my departure, for which I humbly thank the noble knight, not forgetting my gratefull remembrance to Mr. Thomas Evans there: that whole dayes journey being 9. miles.

Tuesday the 10. of August, having hired a guide, for I that knew neither the intricate wayes, nor could speake any of the language, was necessitated to have guides from place to place, and it being harvest time, I was forced to pay exceeding deare for guiding; so that some dayes I payd 2s. sometimes 3. besides bearing their charges of meat and drinke and lodging; for it is to bee understood that those kind of labouring people had rather reap hard all the day for six pence, then to go ten or twelve miles easily on foot for two shillings. That day, after sixteen miles travell, I came to the house of an ancient worthy and hospitable gentleman, named Sure Walter Lloyd,[3] he was noble in bountifull house-keeping, and in his generositie, caused his horse to be saddled, and the next day hee rode three miles to Conway,[4] and shewd me the way to Caermarden,[5] which they do call 18 small miles, but I had rather ride 30 of such miles as are in many parts of England; the way continually hilly, or mountainous and stony, insomuch that I was forced to alight and walke 30 times, and when the sun was near setting, I having foure long miles to go, and

1 Aberystwyth.
2 or Pryse (d. 1651) of Plas Gogerddan, inland from Aberystwyth.
3 prominent royalist (died c.1662) of Llanfair Clydogau near Lampeter.
4 perhaps Cwmann, near Lampeter.
5 Carmarthen.

knew no part of the way, was resolved to take my lodging in a reeke[1] of oats in the field, to which purpose, as I rode out of the stony way towards my field-chamber, my horse and I found a softer bed, for we were both in a bog, or quagmire, and at that time I had much ado to draw myselfe out of the dirt, or my poore weary Dun out if the mire.[2]

I being in this hard strait, having night (of Gods sending,) owl-light to guide me, no tongue to aske a question, the way unknown, or uneven; I held it my best course to grope in the hard stony way againe, which having found, after a quarter of an houres melancholy paces) a horsman of Wales, that could speak English, overtook me and brought me to Caermarden, where I found good and free entertainment at the house of one Mistris Oakley.

Caermarden, the shire town of Caermardenshire, is a good large town, with a defencible strong castle, and a reasonable haven for small barks and boats, which formerly was for the use of good ships, but now it is much impedimented with shelvs, sands, and other annoyances: It is said that Merlyn the prophet was born there; it is one of the plentifullest townes that ever I set foot in, for very fair egs are cheaper then small pears; for, as near as I can remember, I will set down at what rates victuals was there.

Butter, as good as the world affords, two pence halfe penny, or three pence the pound.

A salmon two foot and a halfe long, twelve pence.

Biefe, three halfe pence the pound.

Oysters, a penny the hundred.

Egs, twelve for a penny.

Peares, six for a penny.

And all manner of fish and flesh at such low prices, that a little money will buy much, for there is nothing scarce, dear, or hard to come by, but tobacco pipes.

My humble thanks to the governour there, to William Guinn of Talliaris,[3] Esquire; to Sure Henry Vaughan; and to all the rest, with the good woman mine hostess.

1   rick.
2   Dun in the mire was a medieval Christmas game, which gave rise to a proverb meaning that things were deadlocked.
3   Taliaris near Llandeilo.

Concerning Pembrookshire, the people do speak English in it almost generally, and therefore they call it little England beyond Wales, it being the farthest south and west county in the whole Principality: The shire town, Pembrook,[1] hath been in better estate, for as it is now, some houses down, some standing, and many without inhabitants; the castle there hath been strong, large, stately, and impregnable, able to hold out any enemy, except hunger, it being founded upon a lofty rock, gives a brave prospect a far off: Tenby towne and castle being somewhat near, or eight miles from it, seems to be more usefull and considerable. My thanks to Mistris Powell at the Hart there.

Tenby hath a good castle and a haven, but in respect of Milford Haven, all the havens under the heavens are inconsiderable, for it is of such length , bredth, and depth, that 1000. ships may ride safely in it in all weathers, and by reason of the hills that do inclose it, and the windings and turnings of the haven from one poynt of land to another, it is conjectured that 1500 ships may ride there, and not scarce one of them can see another. The haven hath in it 16 creekes, 5 bayes, and 13 rodes,[2] of large capacity, and all these are known by severall[3] names.

The goodly church of S. Davids hath beene forced lately to put off the dull and heavy coat of peacefull lead, which was metamorphosed into warlike bullets. In that church lies interred Edmund Earle of Richmond,[4] father to King Henry the seventh, for whose sake his grandson (K. Henry the eight) did spare it from defacing, when hee spared not much that belonged to the church.

Thus having gone and riden many miles, with too many turning and winding mountains, stony turning waies, forward, backward, sidewaies, circular, and semicircular, upon the 17. of August I rode to the house of the right honourable, Richard Vaughan Earle of Karbery,[5] at a place called Golden Grove;[6] and surely that house, with the faire fields, woods, walks, and pleasant scituation, may not onely be rightly called the

1 Pembroke.
2 anchorages.
3 separate or different.
4 Edmund Tudor (c.1430-56), created Earl of Richmond, 1452/3.
5 royalist commander (c.1600-86), created Earl of Carbery (Ireland). Alice Egerton, daughter of the 1st Earl of Bridgwater, was his third wife.
6 south-west of Llandeilo.

Golden Grove, but it may without fiction be justly stiled the Cambrian Paradise, and Elizium of Wales; but that which grac'd it totally, was the nobleness, and affable presence and deportment of the Earle, with his faire and vertuous new married Countess, the beautifull Lady Alice, or Alicia, daughter to the right honourable the late Earle of Bridgwater, deceased: I humbly thank them both, for they were pleased to honour me so much, that I supp'd with them, at which time a gentleman came in, who being sate, did relate a strange discourse of a violent rain which fell on the mountains in part of Radnorshire, and into Glomorganshire;[1] the story was, as near as I can remember, as followeth:

That on Saturday the 17. of July last, 1652. there fell a sudden showre of rain in the counties aforesaid, as if an ocean had flowed from the clouds to overwhelm and drown the mountains, it poured down with such violent impetuositie, that it tumbled down divers houses of stone that stood in the way of it; it drowned many cattell and sheep, bore all before it as it ran, therefore a poore man with his son and daughter forsook their house, and the father and son climed up into a tree for their safety, in the mean time the merciless waters took hold of the poore maid, and most furiously bare her away, down between two mountains, rolling and hurling her against many great stones, till at last it threw her near the side of the stream, and her hair and hair-lace being loose, it catched hold of a stump of an old thorn bush, by which means she was stayed, being almost dead; but as she lay in this misery, she saw a sad and lamentable sight, for the water had fiercely unrooted the tree, and bore it down the streame, with her father and brother, who were both unfortunately drowned: the maid, as I was certified, is like to live and recover.

My humble thanks to the good yong hopefull Lord Vaughan, and to all the rest of the noble olive branches of that most worthy tree of honour, their father, not omitting or yet forgetting my gratitude to Mr. Steward there, withall the rest of the gentlemen and servants attendant, with my love to Mr. Thomas Ryve, unknown, and so Golden Grove farewell.

The 18. of August, I hired a guide who brought me to Swansey[2] (16 well stretch'd Welch mountainous miles) where I was cordially

---

1 Glamorganshire.
2 Swansea

welcome to an ancient worthy gentleman, Walter Thomas Esquire, for whose love and liberality I am much obliged to him and the good gentlewoman his wife; he staid me till the next day after diner, and then sent his man with me a mile to his sons house, named William Thomas Esquire: There, as soone as I had rewarded my guide he slip'd from me, leaving me to the mercy of the house, where I found neither mercy nor manners; for the good gentleman and his wife were both rode from home; and though there were people old enough, and big enough, yet there was not one kind enough, or good enough to do me the least kind of courtesie or friendship; they did not so much as bid me come into the house, or offer me a cup of drink; they all scornfully wondred at me, like so many buzzards and woodcocks about an owle, there was a shotten[1] thin scul'd shallow brain'd simpleton fellow, that answered me, that he was a stranger there, but I believed him not, by reason of his familiarity with the rest of the folks, there was also a single-soal'd[2] gentlewoman, of the last edition,[3] who would vouchsafe me not one poor glance of her eye-beams, to whom I said as followeth.

Fair gentlewoman, I was sent hither by the father of the gentleman of this house, to whom I have a letter from a gentleman of his familiar acquaintance; I am sure that the owner of this place is famed and reported to be a man endowed with all affability and courtesie to strangers as is every way accommodating to a gentleman of worth and quality; and that if I were but a meer stranger to him, yet his generosity would not suffer me to be harbourless, but by reason of his fathers sending his servant with me, and a friends letter, I sayd that if Mr. Thomas had been at home I should be better entertained.

To which Mrs. Fumpkins[4] looking scornfully, ascue over her shoulders, answered me with (it may be so) then most uncurteous mistris, quoth I, I doubt I must bee necessitated to take up my lodging in the field: To which the said ungentle gentlewoman (with her posteriors, or butt end towards me) gave me a finall answer, that I might if I would.

Whereupon I was enraged and mounted my Dun, and in a friendly maner I tooke my leave, saying, that I would wander further

1 emaciated.
2 of little value, like a shoe with a single thickness of material in the sole.
3 old-fashioned.
4 probably a nonsense diminutive from dialect 'fump', an ill-tempered person.

and try my fortune, and that if my stay at that house, that night, would save either Mr. Shallow-pate, or Mrs. Jullock[1] from hanging, that I would rather lie, and venture all hazards that are incident to horse, man, or traveller, then to be beholding to such unmanerly mungrils.

Thus desperately I shaked them off, that would not take me on, and riding I knew not whither, with a wide wild heath under me, and a wider firmament above me. I roade at adventure,[2] betwixt light and darkness, about a mile, when luckily a gentleman overtook mee, and after a little talk of my distresse and travail, he bad me be of good chear, for he would bring me to a lodging and entertainment; in which promise he was better then his word, for hee brought mee to a pretty market towne called Neath, where he spent his money upon me; for which kindness I thank him. But one Doctour (as they call him) Rice Jones, (or Doctor Merriman) came and supt with mee, and very kindly payd all the reckoning. That dayes journey being but 6 miles sterling.

The 19. of August I hired a guide for 3s. (16 miles) to a place called Penline,[3] where somtime stood a strong castle, which is now ruined; adjoyning to it, or in the place of it, is a fair house, belonging to Anthony Turberville Esquire, where although the gentleman was from home, the good gentlewoman, his wife, did with hospitable and noble kindnesse, bid me welcome.

Fryday, the 20. of August, I rode a mile to an ancient town, named Coobridge,[4] from whence I scrambled two miles further to Llanstrithyott,[5] where the noble gentleman Sure John Awbrey, with his vertuous lady kept me three dayes, in the mean space I rode two miles to the house of the ancient and honorable knight, Sir Thomas Lewis at Penmark, to whom and his good lady, I humbly dedicate my gratitude: The same day after dinner, I returned back to Llanstrithyott, which was to me a second Golden Grove, or Welch Paradice, for building, scituation, wholsome ayre, pleasure and plenty, for my free entertainment there, with the noble expression of the gentlemans bounty at my departure, I heartily do wish to him and his, with all the rest of my honorable and

1 perhaps suggested by jollock, slang for 'fat' or 'hearty'.
2 aimlessly, randomly.
3 Penllyn, west of Cowbridge.
4 Cowbridge.
5 Llantrithyd, east of Cowbridge.

noble, worshipfull and friendly benefactors, true peace and happinesse, internall, externall, and eternall.

Monday, the 23. of August, I rode eight miles to the good town of Cardiffe, where I was welcome to Mr. Aaron Price, the town clark there, with whom I dined, at his cost and my perrill, after dinner he directed me two miles further, to a place called Llanrumney, where a right true bred generous gentleman, Thomas Morgan Esquire, gave me such loving and liberall entertainment, for which I cannot be so thankfull as the merit of it requires.

Tuesday, being both Saint Bartholomews Day, my birth day, the 24, of the month, and the very next day before Wednesday, I arose betimes, and travelled to a town called Newport, and from thence to Carbean, and lastly to Uske, in all 15 well measu'd Welsh Monmouthshire miles: at Uske I lodg'd at an inne, the house of one Master Powell.

The 25. of August I rode but 12 miles, by an unlook'd for accident, I found Bartholomew Faire at Monmouth, a hundred miles from Smithfield; there I stayed two nights upon the large reckoning of nothing to pay, for which I humbly thank my hospitable host, and hostess, Master Reignald Rowse and his good wife.

Monmouth, the shire town of Monmouthshire, was the last Welsh ground that I left behind me: August 27. I came to Glocester, where though I was born there, very few did know me; I was almost as ignorant as he that knew no body: my lodging there was at the signe of the George, at the house of my namesake, Master John Taylor, from whence on Saturday the 28. I rode 16. miles to Barnsley.

Of all the places in England and Wales that I have travelled to, this village of Barnsley doth most strictly observe the Lords day, or Sunday, for little children are not suffered to walke or play: and two women who had beene at church both before and after noone, did but walke into the fields for their recreation, and they were put to their choice, either to pay sixpence apiece (for prophane walking,) or to be laid one houre in the stocks; and the pievish willfull women (though they were able enough to pay) to save their money and jest out the matter, lay both by the heeles merrily one houre.

There is no such zeale in many places and parishes in Wales; for they have neither service, prayer, sermon, minister, or preacher, nor any church door opened at all, so that people do exercise and edifie in the church-yard, at the lawfull and laudable games of trap,[1] catt,[2] stool-ball,[3] racket, etc. on Sundayes.

From Barnsley on Monday the 30. of August, I rode 30 miles to Abington, from thence, etc. to London, where I brought both ends together on Tuesday the 7. of September.

Those that are desirous to know more of Wales, let them either travell for it as I have done, or read Mr. Camdens Brittania, or Mr. Speeds laborious history, and their geographicall maps and descriptions will give them more ample, or contenting satisfaction.

[1] trap-ball, a game involving a hollowed bat and a ball.
[2] tip-cat, in which a tapering piece of wood is struck.
[3] a precursor of cricket.

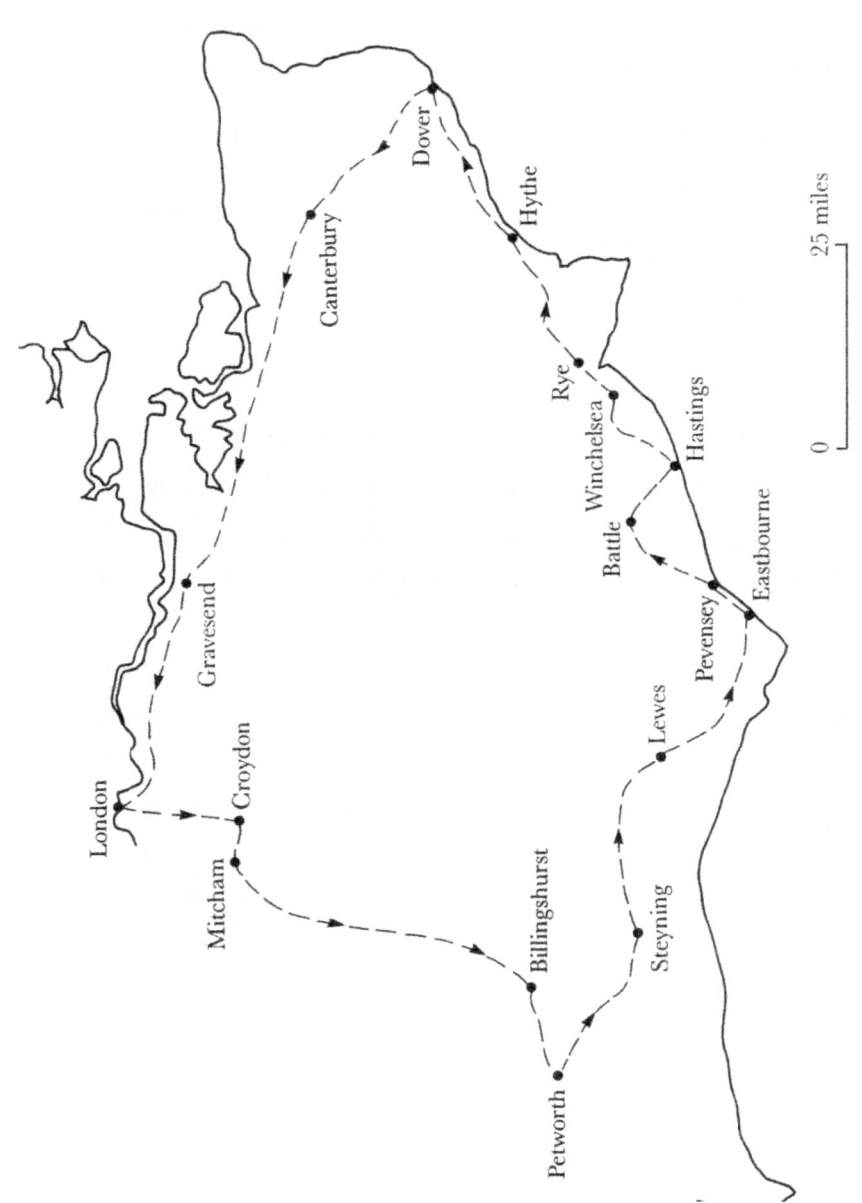

THE CERTAIN TRAVAILES OF AN UNCERTAIN JOURNEY

*T*HE CERTAIN TRAVAILES OF AN UNCERTAIN JOURNEY *may not have been published during Taylor's lifetime. He completed the journey in September 1653, and was buried at St Martin's in the Fields, near his London alehouse, on 5th December. The British Library copy bears date on its title page 17 Feb: 1653 [i.e. 1654]. If the claim is true (cited by Capp, 1994, p. 162) that want of money had made him die, then we can only regret that his traveller's wit at the end carried insufficient premium to save him. The postscript addressed to his subscribers predicts his death, and perhaps did not long precede it: 'I have made use of many friends before | Age tels me now I shall do so no more'.*

But this is not the journey of a man about to climb into his deathbed, nor of one whose intellectual abilities and capacity for enjoying life were on the wane. Less strenuous than his Welsh expedition of the previous year, he must nevertheless have covered between 200 and 300 miles on horseback, through Surrey, Sussex and Kent, and turned out over 400 lines of verse during the space of a few weeks (this is the first all-verse journey since York in 1622). 'Need makes the old wife trot', he remarks. The first third of the work, preceding the journey proper, is an old man's contemplation of the nature of travel, imagination and self-understanding, the journey of life, and his own misfortunes since the civil war. Then we are transported to West Sussex, to Billingshurst and Petworth, beneath the South Downs to Lewes, and eastward through the coastal towns as far as Dover, and then Canterbury, before returning rapidly to London in a day and a half.

Taylor offers the usual fare: good fellowship at various houses and inns (notably at Eastbourne, where he was introduced to a remarkable beer called Rug); his customary ridiculing of puritans, by punning the Rye preacher's name (Jeakes) with the colloquial word for a privy (jakes); and his irrepressible flashes of wit, such as his observation on the beaten down inn sign, the Kings Arms, at Billingshurst ('For armes are of no use without a head'). He tells us how to eat a wheatear, he discourses on the history of Lewes and the battle of Hastings, and he records the painted hangings on the wall of his bedroom at Rye. In the title of his poem he tells us that he undertook the journey, 'for no other purpose but to pleasure himself, and to please his friends in the first place'. It is hard not to believe him.

[9th August - 3rd September 1653. Text derived from 1st ed., 1653, (BL E.1434.1). Only pp.1-23 of this pamphlet have been transcribed. The remainder (pp.25-9) consist of a postscript on Sussex and Kent 'borrowed out of Mr. Speed'.]

The Certain Travailes of an uncertain Journey, begun on Tuesday the 9. of August, and ended on Saturday the 3. of September following, 1653.

Wherein the readers may take notice, that the authors purpose was to travell, and write this following relation, for no other intent or purpose, but to pleasure himself, and to please his friends in the first place.
By JOHN TAYLOR, at the signe of the Poets Head, in Phoeniz Alley, near the Globe Tavern, in the middle of Long-Acre, nigh the Covent-Garden.
Those twelve following lines I gave to divers gentlemen and friends, before I went, and as they have kindly subscribed to my bill, I do humbly expect their courteous acceptation of this booke.

A merry bill of an uncertaine journey, to bee performed by John Taylor, by land, with his Aqua Musa.[1]

To all my friends, and courteous gentlemen,
Know, that my journey is, I know not when:
Unto the parts I goe, I know not where,
Or of my entertainement far or neare;
Thus neither knowing when, or where, or whether,
Begun, or done, or both ends brought together,
When I this unknowne walke have put in print,

---

1   water muse, referring to his sobriquet 'water-poet'.

Each man to's pocket, put your fingers in't,
And, for my booke then give me what you list,[1]
To which end, to this bill, take pen in fist,
And write your names and habitations down,
I'le finde you when againe I come to towne.

The certainty of the uncertaine travels of John Taylor, performed in this yeere 1653.

Tis laudable to read well pen'd relations
Of foreign countries, and their situations,
That by the judgement of the eie and brain
Some knowledge to discourse we may attain.
For histories, and learn'd cosmographers,[2]
And diligent acute geographers;
One hath survay'd celestiall lofty sphears,
How all the planets run in their carriers:[3]
The stars, the signes, and every influence
In every heavenly orbs circumference,
And were it not for high astronomy
(Whose lofty painfull steps have scal'd the sky)
For times and seasons we might grope and seek,
Not knowing yeers, or quarters, month, or week,
Or houres, or minutes, nor the Sabbath day,
Nor when to eat, or sleep, or debts to pay.
Millions of people would this knowledge lack
Except directed from the almanack.
Thus art, (with pains and travell of the mind)
Taught mean capacities, these things to find.
He travels far that goes beyond the moone,
Or thinks this skill may be attayned soone.
Their overweening thoughts flie high and quick

---

1 please.
2 those who studied the world and its place within the universe, but commonly used by those who wrote descriptions of places, topographers..
3 careers, in its primary meaning of 'courses'.

But such mad fooles are only lunatick.[1]
Geographers have travel'd land and seas
Each coast, and opposite Antipodes;
And the description of all lands and parts
Described are, in severall maps and charts.
The sun and moon have seldom shewd their faces
On any empire, kingdom, place, or places,
Which travellers have not viewd and survayd,
And by rare geographique art displayd.
By either sea or land, by night or day,
Geography hath chalk'd us out the way:
That with maps, compas, and indifferent weather
True men or thieves may travell any whither.
And thus through thick and thin, ways hard or soft,
Thousand and thousand miles I travel'd oft.
Some men do travell in their contemplations,
In reading histories and strange relations:
Some few do travell in the wayes divine,
Some wander wildly with the Muses nine;
For every man would be a poet gladly,
Although he write and rime but badly madly.
Sometimes the wits and tongues do, most unfit,
Travell, when tongues do run before the wit.
But if they both keep company together,
Delight and profit is in both, or eyther.
Discretion gravely goes a gentle pace,
When speech, a gallop, runs a heedles race:
Mans earthly portion's travell, paine, and care,
(Of which I make a shift[2] to get my share.)
Some do disdain, and hold it in high scorn
To know thatcht cottages where they were born
Some crosse the sea to see strange lands unknown
And heer, like strangers, do not know their own.
Their own, 'tis fit work for a golden pen

---

1 insanity termed lunatic was believed to be affected by the phases of the moon.
2 to make an effort.

To write the names down of such knowing men:
Should ech on[1] know and have his own, 'twere rare
Right[2] owners wold be rich, and knaves stark bare.
Hee's counted wise, with the Italians,[3]
That knows his own wife from another mans.
But hee's more wise that knows himselfe to be
Fraile, mortall, and a map of misery.
But wisest he, that patient takes his lot,
And use the world as if he us'd it not.
Some seem to know most, yet know almost nothing,
For man, in knowledge, is a very slow thing.
Nosce teipsum,[4] Know thy selfe, and then
Each one will know himselfe the worst of men.
Many of forreign travels boast and vant,[5]
When they, of England, are most ignorant.
But yeerly I survey my country native,
And, 'mongst 6. cases, live upon the dative.[6]
I travell hard, and for my lifes supply,
I every yeere receive a subsidie.
(Or else to come more neer unto the sence)
'Tis fit to call it a benevolence.
Thus (travelling) a toyling trade I drive,
By reason of mine age, neer seventy five:
It is my earthly portion and my lot,
(The proverb says, *Need makes the old wife trot*.)[7]
Seven times at sea[8] I serv'd Elizabeth,
And 2. kings forty five yeers, untill death
Of both my royall masters quite bereft me,

1 one.
2 rightful.
3 perhaps a variant of the proverb, 'Italians are wise before the deed...'
4 'know thyself', Latin version of the Greek proverb '*gnothi seauton*', reported by the Latin satirist Juvenal.
5 i.e. vaunt, brag.
6 In Latin grammar nouns have six cases, the dative generally implying 'to' or 'for'.
7 proverb first recorded in the 13th century.
8 Taylor served in the navy during the 1590s.

That nothing now but age and want is left me.
This makes me travell, and my friends to trie,
Else I might (like my fellowes) sterve and die.
Had the last state, had consciences so tender
To think on Oxford siedge, with that surrender,
Had they kept articles and covenants,
In some sort, then they had releev'd our wants.
But they were in the land of promise borne,
Perform'd, and paid us nothing, but their scorn.
Camelion like[1] we had Ayre, Words, and Wind,
With these three empty dishes oft we din'd.
And with light suppers, and such breaking fast,
With meagre famine, many breath'd their last.
we nere bare arms, but houshold servants menial
We waited, if 'twere sin, it was but veniall.[2]
These thirteen yeers no wages I could get,
Which makes me thus to try my friends and wit.
Unto the Kings Revenews great Committee
We oft petitiond, and implor'd their pitty;
And first and last, we gave petitions plenty,
I'm sure, in number, neer two hundred twenty.
Two thousand books and bils then printed were,
Wherein our woes and wants wee did declare:
Lord Fairfax[3] was himselfe Lord Generall then,
He pitied us (poor miserable men;)
And he in person, more then one time went
And told our griefes unto the Parliament.
Besides, for us, to them he letters wrot,
For all which, only, promises we got.
I will not curse those men, but this I say,
If need and want afflict them, I doe pray
They may be comforted, and fed, and clad
With promises, as we from them have had.

---

1   It was believed that chameleons fed on air.
2   excusable.
3   Thomas, 3rd baron Fairfax (1612-71), parliamentary general.

Th' yeer sixteen hundred fifty, with 3. added,
Old Tib[1] my mare, and I, a journy gadded:
I London left, the 9. day I remember
Of August, neer 3. weeks before September.
In 4. houres riding post I got to Croydon,
And so hath many a man, and many a boy done.
There was the George a horseback day and night,
And there I, from my mares back did alight.
At Water there wine was, but that's a riddle,
At Croydon, you may know both ends and middle.[2]
To Micham,[3] from my way full 3. miles wide,
A gentleman, I thank him, was my guide.
Holland my sheets, and Holland was mine host,
My entertainment good for little cost.
August the tenth, my bonny beast and I,
From Surrey traveld to South Saxony,
Now called Sussex, where at Bellinshurst[4]
Six dayes I felt no hunger, cold, or thirst.
There at a sign, and no sign but a frame,
Twas the Kings arms, but shatering shot and flame
Did beat them down, as useles, of small stead,
For armes are of no use without a head.[5]
Mine host was mighty good, and great withall,
And, amongst hosts, may be a generall.
Hee's friendly, curteous, although big and burly,
A right good fellow, no way proud or surly.
Six nights at Bellinshurst I freely stayd,
And all the charge of mare and man was payd
By a gentleman, to name whom Ile refrain,
Whose love, my thankfull mind shall stil retain.
Thus in one week I rode post 30. mile,

1 originally a shortened or pet form of Isabel.
2 Perhaps a reference to a scheme to supply London with water from the River Wandle at Croydon, which failed in 1610 because of local opposition.
3 Mitcham, outer London, former Surrey.
4 Billingshurst, West Sussex.
5 the execution of Charles I had occurred four years earlier.

And neither man or mare tyr'd all that while.
A reverend preacher[1] preach'd on Sunday twice
Directing souls to th' Heavenly Paradice.
And if we could but do as he did say,
His doctrine told us all the ready way.
Thus Billinshurst thy bounty I extoll,
Thou feastedst me in body and in soule.
There was rare musick, sweet and gentile ayres,
For undeserved favours, I am theirs.
My love to Mr. Fist, and to mine host,
But love and thanks T.H. deserveth most.
From Billinshurst, August the sixteenth day,
I took my leave, before I took my way.
The way indifferent good, the welkin smiles,[2]
I rode to Petworth, 7. good Sussex miles.
To set forth Petworth, its worth more worth is,
Then I am worth, or worthy; but know this,
Northumberland the noble,[3] there doth dwell,
Whoe good housekeeping, few lords parallell.
There honourable bounty is exprest,
With daily charity to th' poor distrest.
I speak not this for any thing I got
Of that great lord, I felt or saw him not:
For had I seen him, my beliefe is such,
I should have felt and found his bounties tutch:[4]
But I, for my part, never was so rude
To flatter, fawn, or basely to intrude,
Yet I declare him liberall, honourable,
And there I din'd well, at his stewards table.
Thanks Mr. Williams there, the cook exact
By his good friendship there, I nothing lackd.
Thanks to my hostesse kind, good Mrs. Martin,

1   Probably Nathaniel Hilton (d.1655), vicar of Billingshurst.
2   fair weather.
3   Algernon Percy, 10th earl of Northumberland (1602-68), mediator during the civil war.
4   i.e. touch.

who welcom'd me with good whit wine a quart in.
And last of all, but not at all the least,
I was kind Mr. Barnards[1] costly guest:
To me he shew'd his bounty from the mint,
For which I give him heer my thanks in print.
He payd the chinque,[2] and freely gave me drink,
And I returne my gratitude with inke.
August the 18. twelve long miles to Stenning[3]
I rode, and nothing saw there worth the kenning,[4]
But that mine host there was a joviall wight,[5]
My hostess fat and fair; a goodly sight:
The signe the Chequer, eighteen pence to pay;
My mare eat mortal meat, good oats and hay.
Twelve miles from Stenning I jogd on to Lewes,
And there I found no beggars, scolds, or shrews;
Lewes hath no bayliff, mayor, or magistrate,
For every one there lives in quiet state:
They quarrell not for wagging of a straw,[6]
For each man is unto himselfe a law;
They need no bridle (like the horse or mule)
Where every one himselfe can wisely rule.
At the terrestriall Star[7] (a glistring signe)
I lodg'd, and found good diet, and good wine;
Mine host and hostess courteous, free, and kind,
And there I sip'd and sup'd, but seldom din'd:
Lewes is an ancient town, as may be seen
In Cambden,[8] page three hundred and thirteen:
Twelve men they chuse, the most substantiallest,

1 perhaps John Barnard, a Petworth tallow-chandler, who issued a token in 1660.
2 chink, slang for money.
3 Steyning, West Sussex.
4 viewing.
5 person.
6 a trifle, alluding to a medieval proverb, 'to be angry at the wagging of a straw'.
7 One of the principal inns of Lewes, on the site of the town hall.
8 William Camden's *Britannia*.

Most rich and wise, to govern all the rest;
And out of that discreet and honest dozen,
Two (as it were) high constables are chosen:
These have no pow'r themselves to hang or draw,
Or on offendors to inflict the law;
But to a Justice of the Peace, or Coram[1]
They bring the parties, and their cause before am.
From Friday unto Friday I did stay,
But in the mean time I did take my way
Five miles to Torring[2] where my old friend there,
The parson welcom'd me with country cheer;
His name is John, or honest Master Rice,[3]
Six meals he meated me, and lodgd me thrice.
He preachd on Sunday, Augusts twenty one,
Two sermons, tending to salvation:
His doctrine's good, and he himselfe doth frame
To live in conversation like the same.
I thank him, and his wife and family,
For making of so much (too much) of me:
Thus when he could no longer me retaine,
With love and thanks, I rode to Lewes againe.
This town contains six churches, and at least
It is a mile in length from west to east:
A strong and spacious castle there hath been,
As by its moldred ruines may be seene.
Thence 12 miles I was on my female beast born,
T' an unknown feast born, at a towne cal'd East Bourne;[4]
I at an inne alighted, and found there
Unlook'd for welcome, and good Sussex cheer:
Sir Thomas Dike, Sir Thomas Parker, knights,[5]

---

1   legal Latin for 'in the presence of', so to be brought before coram means, 'to be hauled up before the magistrate'.
2   Tarring Neville, East Sussex.
3   John Rice, rector 1641/2 - 1654/5, although he had apparently been ejected in 1648.
4   Eastbourne, East Sussex.
5   Dike was of Horeham; Parker, of Ratton, was lord of the manor of Eastbourne.

With kinde esquires, whose names and epithites
I mention not, because I know them not;
But to them all my thanks is unforgot,
For undeserv'd, unlook'd for, and unthought,
From the' my purse and person both were fraught;
This was on Augusts twenty sixt, a Friday,
Near dog dayes end,[1] a very fair and drie day.
The next day, and the next I felt the bounty
Of the high Sheriff of Sussex[2] famous county;
He entertain'd me Saturday and Sunday,
And would have kept me 20 dayes past Monday.
There was a high and mighty drink call'd Rug,[3]
Sure since the reigne of great King Gorbodug[4]
Was never such a rare infus'd confection,
Injection, operation, and ejection,
Are Hogen Mogen[5] Rugs, great influences
To provoke sleep, and stupifie the sences.
No cold can ever pierce his flesh or skin
Of him who is well lin'd with Rug within:
Rug is a lord beyond the rules of law;
It conquers hunger in the greedy maw:
And (in a word) of all the drinks potable,
Rug is most puisant,[6] potent, notable.
Rug was the capitall commander there,
And his Lievtenant Generall was strong beere.

1 Sirius, the Dog star, rises with the sun in July and August, and was believed to augment the sun's heat.
2 William Wilson, who had assisted with the escape of Charles II after the battle of Worcester.
3 Taylor appears to be the only authority to mention this drink. The Dutch phrase used to describe it has been thought to suggest that it included 'Hollands', a spirit widely smuggled into this area, and so was a kind of gin punch.
4 In Taylor's *A Memoriall of all the English monarchs...*, derived from the Brut, Gorbodug's dates are given as 559-496 BC, and he was supposedly buried at York.
5 high and mighty, derived from a Dutch expression.
6 powerful.

Wine plenteous both in bottles and in flaggons.
whose stre'gth would quel S. George and 20 draggo's
But Asshuerus Laws[1] were there inrol'd,
No man was forc'd to drink more than he would.
There was good Will, good Wills son, and good Willia'
As free as was the Emp'rour Maximilian:[2]
Beasts, fowls and fish, from earth, and sea and ayre
Unto the Table, well cook'd, did repair,
There were rare birds I never saw before
The like of them, I think to see no more:
Th' are called wheat ears,[3] less then lark or sparrow,
Wel roasted, in the mouth they tast like marrow.
When once tis in the teeth it is involv'd,
Bones, flesh, and all, is lushiously dissolv'd.
The name of wheat ears, on them is ycleap'd,[4]
Because they come when wheat is yeerly reap'd.
Six weeks,[5] or therabouts, they are catch'd there,
And are welnigh 11. months, God knows where.
My humble gratitude is heer exprest
To Mr. Sheriffe, and his beloved best;
His kindnes joind with hers, and hers with his,
Doth merit my unfaigned thankfulnes.
Unto my cozen Thomas Taylor there
My love remembred, and for my samphiere[6]
He promis'd me, I thank't him thrice before,
And when I have it, I will thank him more.
Twelve miles on Augusts 9. and 20. day,

---

1   At Ahasuerus's feast the drinking was according to the law, that none did compel... (Esther 1, verse 8).
2   Maximilian I (1573-1651), elector of Bavaria from 1623.
3   Taylor seems to have been among the first to connect this bird with wheat. Older forms of the name describe its colouring, 'white-arse'.
4   yclept 'called', a medieval word revived by Elizabethan writers.
5   Wheatears were numerous on the downs around Eastbourne between the end of July and mid-September, when they were snared in vast numbers by shepherds.
6   samphire, edible plant which grows on sea-cliffs.

From Bourne to Battell,[1] 4. miles on my way
At Pemsey[2] doth a ruin'd castle stand,
And there the Norman Conqueror did land.
Since his invading power arived there,
'Tis now 500, 60, and 6. yeere.
Eight miles from thence, the battel fierce was strook[3]
Where bloud of 70000, like a brook,
Or rather I may say like Sanguin rivers
Which down hills, it impetuously delivers
Into the vales: and where that bloud was spilt
The Conqueror caus'd an abbey to be built
Of stately structure, and what it hath been,
By great extended ruines may be seen.
When Norman forces England overcame,
From bloudy Battell, Battell had its name.
This abbey now is kept, by right and due,
By the Honourable Viscount Montague.[4]
That lord repair'd some part magnificent,
And ther's good house kept, when hees resident.
That noble lord is, in account most famous,
Though many miserable lords doe shame us.
At th' Empereall crest, or Eagle spred,
My selfe and mare, were stabled, lodg'd and fed.
About the reckoning I did not contend,
My friend T.H. paid all, and ther's an end.
August the thirtith, I rode on to Hastings,
Wher was relief for men of severall tastings,
Or sundry pallats, put them altogether,
Or relisht appetites, take all or neither.
At Hastings I staid not, but hastily
I ambled 6. miles unto Winchelsey:
Which hath been counted in the dayes of yore,[5]

1   Battle, East Sussex.
2   Pevensey, East Sussex.
3   Battle of Hastings, 1066.
4   Francis, viscount Montague (1610-82), prominent royalist.
5   Old Winchelsea was engulfed in the 13th century by the sea, and was

(Untill the seas contended with the shore)
A famous sea town, rich in merchandise,
But buried in the ocean now it lies,
A castle stands i'th sands,[1] enduring flawes,[2]
Gusts, tempests, storms, and times devouring jaws:
In twice twelve hours, 'tis twice embraced round
In th' arms of Neptune, seeming to be drownd:
And when the flouds are eb'd into the main,
Three miles in sands 'tis compast round again.
In Winchelsey that now is I could ken
Nothing worth observation of my pen.
Two miles from thence, upon a hill, stands Rye,
And there I, at the Star, did lodge and lie:
More ods there is 'twixt singing songs and crying
Then was betwixt my lodging, and my lying.
I lodg'd by night, and I did lie by day,
And as upon a bed I musing lay,
The chamber hang'd with painted cloth,[3] I found
My selfe with sentences beleaguerd round.
There was philosophy and history,
Poetry aenigmatick mystery.
I know not what the town in wealth may be,
But sure, I on that chambers walls did see
More wit then al the town had, and more worth
Then my unlearned muse can well set forth.
I will not hold my reader in dilemma,
Thus truly, lying, I transcribed them a'.

No flower so fresh, but frost may it deface,

    abandoned c.1280 in favour of New Winchelsea, built on a new site on higher ground.
1   No castle was built at Winchelsea, but Taylor may perhaps have seen vestiges of a hermitage destroyed in 1536.
2   squalls.
3   This painted hanging is usually associated with the Mermaid Inn, and no Star is recorded.

None sits so fast, but hee may lose his place:[1]
Tis Concord keeps a realme in stable stay,
But Discord brings all kingdomes to decay.
No subject ought (for any kinde of cause)
Resist his prince, but yeeld him to the lawes.
Sure God is just, whose stroake, delayed long,
Doth light at last, with paine more sharp, and strong
Time never was, nor n'ere I thinke shall be,
That Truth (unshent)[2] might speake, in all things free.

This is the sum, the marrow and the pith
My lying chamber was adorned with:
And 'tis supposed, those lines written there
Have in that roome bin, more then 40 yeare.
Now, Reader take this notice more of Rye,
'Tis worth remembring, and I'le tell you why:
If to unloade your bellies, Nature drive ye,
In all the towne you'le scarcely finde a privie.
For as our sectaries, in tubbs preach heere,
They make (Sir Reverence) Reverend Jakeses there,
Of pulpets of prophanity, and these
When they are full, are empti'd in the seas.[3]
My fare was good at Rye, my reck'ning small,
I thanke my noble friend, that payd for all,
Neere unto Rye, 2 dirty ferryes bee
So muddy, that they mir'de my mare and mee:
I past them, and on *ultima Augusti*,[4]
well meated, mounted, man and beast both lusty;
I cross'd or'e Gulford[5] ferry, and I went

---

1 'No flower is so freshe, but frost can it deface: |No man so sure in any seate but he maye leese his place.' From *A Hundreth Sundrie Flowres*, by George Gascoigne (1573).
2 uninjured.
3 'Jakes' was slang for a privy. The pun is on the name of Samuel Jeakes, a Puritan and Presbyterian from a prominent Rye family.
4 31st August.
5 East Guldeford, East Sussex.

From Rye in Sussex unto Hide[1] in Kent;
Septembers first day, Sol, with golden eye
Gilt Neptune with celestiall alchymie:
With sovereign splendor, kissing medows green,
And mantled hills tops were coruscant[2] seen.
When Phoebus[3] mounted was in glorious pride,
I mounted too, and rode away from Hide.
Still as I past through sea towns first and last,
I did enquire how businesses had past.
The people said that guns did bounce and thump,
Betwixt our English ships, and Dutch Van Trump.[4]
At Rumney,[5] and at Hide, they were in sight,
Folks heard the drums to beat, and saw the fight.
Thus, little was the newes from sea or shore,
Our weekly news books[6] will tel 3. times more.
From Hide to Dover, and to Canterbury
Full 25. miles, dirty, wet and weary,
I took my lodging up, and down I lay
Till Friday came, Septembers second day.
Then with the Lamb I arose, and with the Lark
I got to Gravesend when 'twas almost dark;
But I mistake, from sleep I rowz'd my head,
And rose with th' Lark, but went with Lamb to bed.
On th' way I was not vext with gates or stiles,
But three and thirty dirty Kentish miles,
With washing dashing ways, and rain wel sous'd,
It made my mare and I glad to be hous'd:
The signe was Welsh his pie-bald english Bull;
I there was welcome empty, welcome full:

1 Hythe, Kent
2 sparkling.
3 the sun.
4 Admiral Martin van Tromp was defeated twice by English ships off Dover, 29th May 1652 and 13th February 1653.
5 Romney.
6 these, the fore-runners of the national newspapers, had proliferated from c.1620, and especially during the civil war.

But at the high and mighty Gravesend Whale,
I found most potent admirable ale,
'Tis second to no drink, but East-Bourne Rug,
Put it in pot or flaggon, can or jug;
You'le finde it is the grand ale, and you'l grant,
That 'tis ale parramount, predominant:
'Twas given me by a friend; but let him end
With hanging, that loves ale more then his frie'd
From Gravesend (Satruday Septembers third)
I rode without spurs, as I had been spurr'd:
I came to London when the clock struck one;
And so my journey and my booke is
DONE.

Amongst the Muses where the number nine is,
The learned poets end their works with *Finis:*
But when unlearned I have volumes pen'd,
Finis is Latine, English Done's an End.[1]

To all my friends that have subscribed their names and dwellings to my bill.

According as you pay, or pay me not;
So is my lucky or unlucky lot:
I have made use of many friends before
Age tels me now I shall do so no more.
Some friends I have, and some small share of wit,
And want hath forc'd me to use them, and it.
I, in my best of wishes will include
Their kindnesse, and my humble gratitude.

FINIS

---

[1] Taylor adds at this point a short postscript, 'of some parts of Sussex and Kent that I travelled, which I have borrowed out of Mr, Speed.' This has not been transcribed.

TRAVELLING

THE COACHES OVERTHROW

*T*HIS UNDATED BALLAD, *printed partly in black letter on a double sheet in two columns with two woodcuts, is attributed to Taylor. It celebrates a royal proclamation made in January 1636 which severely curtailed the operation of 'Hackney' coaches for public hire in London, on account of the traffic congestion that they were causing since they had begun to proliferate a few years earlier. In 1634 the London watermen petitioned the king to limit their use to north–south journeys, because when they took passengers east–west they were competing with and undercutting the service provided by the Thames wherries.*[1] *Taylor's antagonism to coaches, understandable from such a champion of water travel, was longstanding. He expressed it in a long polemic in 1623,* The World Runnes on Wheeles, *which was adorned with a woodcut of a globe-shaped coach pulled by a devil and a whore. That work contributes little to the literature of travel and is not reprinted here; the sentiments recur in several of Taylor's works.*

(Text derived from the imperfect British Library copy, reproduced in STC 2nd ed 5451, and online at Historical Texts. It was transcribed (apparently from the same British Library copy) and published with minor discrepancies by J.P. Collier, in A Book of Roxburghe Ballads *(1847), 291-7.)*

The Coaches Overthrow. or, A Joviall Exaltation of divers tradesmen, and others, for the suppression of troublesome Hackney Coaches.
To the tune of, Old King Harry.[2]

---

1 W.T. Jackman, *Development of Transportation in Modern England* (3rd edn., 1966) 115-18. The text of the king's proclamation is printed in J. Rushworth, *Historical Collections*, pt. 2, vol. 2 (1721), 316.
2 The following lines were quoted by Charles Mackay, *The Thames and its Tributaries* (1840), 151:
Old King Harry was fond of canary,
    Fond of good victuals and sack was he;
But more than canary did old king Harry
    Love a sly joke, with his hey derry dee!

As I pass'd by this other day,
where sacke and clarret spring;
I heard a mad crew by the way,
that lowd did laugh and sing,
High downe, dery dery downe,
with the Hackney coaches downe;
Tis cry'd aloud
They make such a crowd,
Men cannot passe the towne.

The boyes that brew strong ale, and care
not how the world doth swing;
So bonny, blith, and jouiall are,
their lives are drinke and sing,
Hey downe, dery dery downe,
With the Hackney coaches downe,
To make them roome,
They may freely come,
And liquor the thirsty towne.

The collier he's a sack of mirth,
and though as black as soote,
Yet still he tunes, and whistles forth,
And this is all the note.
Heigh downe, dery dery downe,
With the Hackney coaches downe:
They long made fooles
Of poore carry-coales,
But now must leave the towne.

The carriers of euery shire,
are as from cares immune:
So joviall is this packe horse quire,[1]

      Hey down! Ho down! Derry down dee!
(Canary was a fortified wine imported from the Canary Islands)
1   At this period carriers generally used packhorses rather than waggons.

and this is all their tune.
Hey downe, dery dery downe,
With the Hackney coaches downe,
Farewell, adew,
To the jumping crew,
For they must leave the towne.

Although the carman[1] had a cold,
he strein'd his March-bird voice,
And with the best a part did hold
to sing and to rejoyce.
Heigh downe, dery dery downe,
with the Hackney coaches downe:
The carmens cars,
And the merchants wares
May passe along the towne.

The very slugs[2] did pipe for joy,
that coachmen hence should hye,
And that the coaches must away
a mellowing up to lye.
Hey downe, dery dery downe,
With the Hackney coach-men downe,
Passe they their scope,
As round as a rope,
Wee'l jogge them forth of towne.
Permouters,[3] and the informes,
that oft offences hatch;
In all our times the money-wormes,
and they are for the catch.
Heigh downe, dery dery downe,
With the Hackney coaches downe,

1   carmen were licensed carters of goods, who plied for hire in London and had their own city company.
2   slow sailing vessels
3   *Sic*, but promoters (i.e. speculators) must be meant. Promoters and informers proliferated under the Stuart kings, and were widely despised.

For these restraints,
Will with complaints.
Fill all the noisy towne.¹

The second part
To the same tune.

The world no more shall run on wheels,
with coach-men as't has done;
But they must take them to their heeles,
and try how they can run.
Heigh downe, dery dery downe,
with the Hackney coaches downe:
Wee thought they'd burst,
Their pride since first
Swell'd so within the Towne.

The Sedan² does (like Atlas) hope
to carry heaven pick-pack:
And likewise since he has such scope
to beare the towne at's back.
Heigh downe, dery dery downe,
with the Hackney coach-men downe:
Arise Sedan,
Thou shalt be the man
To beare us about the towne.

I love Sedans cause they doe plod,
and amble every where,
Which prancers are with leather shod,

---

1   Most of this line has been cropped from the only available copy. Collier, who must have used this copy, conjectured these words. 'Fill all' can be reconstructed from the cropped copy, and 'towne' is the likely rhyme, but the preceding adjective 'noisy' is only a suggestion.
2   Sedan chairs had been introduced to London in 1634 by Sir Sanders Duncombe, and he was given exclusive right by the king to operate them for 14 years:

THE COACHES OVERTHROW

and neere[1] disturbe the eare.
Heigh downe, dery dery downe,
with the Hackney coaches downe:
Their jumpings make
The pavement shake,
Their noyse doth mad the towne.

The elder brother shall take place,
the youngest brother rise:
The middle brothers out of grace,
and every tradesman cryes.
Heigh downe, dery dery downe,
with the Hackney coaches downe,
'Twould save much hurt,
Spare dust, and durt,
Were they cleane out of towne.

The sick, the weake, the lame also,
a coach for ease might beg:
When they on foot might lightly goe,
that are as right's my leg.
Heigh downe, dery dery downe,
with the Hackney coaches downe:
Let's foot it out,
Ere the yeare comes about,
Twill save us many a crowne.

What though we trip ore boots and shoes,
twill ease the prise of leather:
We shall get twice, what once we loose,
when they doe fall together.
Heigh downe, dery dery downe,
with the Hackney coaches downe;
Though one trade fall,
Yet in generall,

[1]   i.e. never

Tis a good to all the towne.

Tis an undoing unto none
that a profession use:
Tis good for all, not hurt to one,
considering the abuse.
Then heigh downe, dery dery downe,
with the Hackney coaches downe:
Tis so decreed
By a Royall Deed,[1]
To make't a happy towne.

Coach-makers may use many trades,
and get enough of meanes:
And coach-men may turne off their jades,[2]
and helpe to draine the fens.
Heigh downe, dery dery downe,
with the Hackney coaches downe:
The sythe, and flayle,
Cart, and plow-tayle
Doe want them out of towne.

But to conclude, tis true, I heare
they'l soone be out of fashion,
Tis thought, they very likely are
to have a long vacation.
Heigh downe, dery dery downe,
with the Hackney coaches downe:
Their terme's neere done,
And shall be begun
No more in London towne.

FINIS.
London Printed for Francis Grove

1   The royal proclamation of 19 January 1636 restricting the use of Hackney coaches (see introduction above).
2   Inferior or worn-out horses.

TAYLORS TRAVELS AND CIRCULAR PERAMBULATION

*A*FTER TAKING PART *in the 1631 survey of the Thames and publishing his account the following year, Taylor did not undertake and describe another journey until 1639. Following the appearance of his collected works in 1630 he had (or at least considered that he had) become a respected figure in society and something of a celebrity. One highlight of these years was a commission to write and arrange the 1634 Lord Mayor of London's pageant; another concern was to promote the causes of the Watermen's Company, as seen in his verbal attacks on Hackney coaches. Reportage and journalistic pieces continued to flow from his pen, but he also maintained his interest in travel, hospitality and inland trade.*

Three publications appeared in 1636-7 which resulted from what, in modern parlance, could be described as an enormous 'pub crawl'. The title of this, the first, gives the impression that it is literally a journey – a perambulation around the inns, taverns and alehouses of London and Westminster – although in fact it comprises a list of their signs and locations arranged by letter of the alphabet. It is not strictly alphabetical, and it is inconsistent – the White Horse in Lombard Street is listed under H, for instance, the White Horse in Nicholas Shambles under W. It is also incomplete, as a further 37 establishments were added to the next pamphlet. To adorn what would otherwise have been a mere list, Taylor cleverly prefaces his perambulation by rearranging it by topic and by signs of the zodiac, as well as discoursing on the history and respectability of the wine trade. Although he acknowledges John Stow and Edmund Howes as sources for some of this information, it seems likely that much was derived from information recorded and supplied by the Vintners Company, to whom he dedicated the work. Throughout the list which follows he intersperses epigrams, but these are trite and conventional, and do not describe specific inns – they have been omitted from this edition.

Having perambulated London and Westminster, Taylor set his sights further afield, to ten counties surrounding the capital, and these are the subject of his Honorable and Memorable Foundations . . ., *published in the same year and regarded as the second part of the present work. His research must also have informed the* Carrier's Cosmographie (1637), *a more significant work.*

Taken together, the three pamphlets are important source material for travel in Taylor's period, and emphasise the interdependence of innkeeping and carrying in their various forms.

TAYLORS TRAVELS AND CIRCULAR PERAMBULATION, through, and by more then thirty times twelve signes of the zodiack, of the famous cities of London and Westminster. With the honour and worthinesse of the vine, the vintage, the wine, and the vintoner; with an alphabeticall description, of all the taverne signes in the cities, suburbs, and liberties aforesaid, and significant epigrams upon the said severall signes. Written by JOHN TAYLOR. LONDON, Printed by A. M. 1636.

THE PREFACE TO the READER. Gentlemen and others (of what sex, estate, condition, calling, degree, Quallitie, art, mistery, craft, trade, science, function, or occupation soever) greeting and friendly salutations. First, I most humbly and thankefully remember my thankes to all such as have formerly taken my labours in such good part, as I have felt their liking in their loving bounty. Secondly, I doe expresse my gratitude to as many as have accepted my bookes at my hands, although some of them have not, and many of them could not requite mee. And thirdly, I doe request as many as doe receive this small pamphlet to take into their consideration, that I doe expect they shall pay mee for it. I am sure there hath beene within these 30. yeares[1] more then 200. impressions of bookes in my name; for though I have not written above 80. yet some of them hath been printed 10. or 12. times over, 1500. or 2000. every time. Amongst which number of pamphlets, I am sure, that (first and last) I have given freely for nothing (never expecting any thing but thankes) above 30000. Bookes, (besides those that I have beene rewarded for:) But so it is now (my good friends) that age, and some charge urging me to make triall of your loves, onely for this one small toy or trifle; and though it may seeme a trifle to you, it was a travell[2] to me in the collecting and writing: all which, with my selfe, I leave to be considered upon your receiving of the second part, which I am at as busie as a bee; always remaining yours heere and there or any where JOHN TAYLOR.

1 An exaggeration, as the earliest of his publications dates from 1612, only 24 years previously.
2 i.e. travail, in the sense of work.

TAYLORS TRAVELS through more then thirtie times twelve signes.

As the sunne, in his celestiall progresse, doth with perpetuall motion passe through the twelve signes of the zodiack, and every yeare doth beguirt the large circumference of his heavenly spheare; yet it is to be noted, that twelve signes only, and no more but twelve, are each one in his monethly course, the places of his perambulation, and circular travell.

And as a zany[1] or counterfeit, will (for sports sake) in a pleasant way, imitate an active nimble tumbler in his feates of activity, so I, in Imitation of the sunne, have in one moneth progress'd through London, Westminster, with the suburbs, and the burrough of Southwarke; not as the sunne doth through twelve, but neer thirtie times twelve signes.

I have found Aries and Taurus in Rams and Rams-head, Buls, and Bul-heads; for Gemini I have made shift with the signe of Adam and Eve in Tothill-street at Westminster, with all other double signes, as Rose and Crowne, Castle and Miter, the Man in the Moone, the Crosse-Keyes, or any such signes wherein two severall things are depicted, they serve mee in my course for Gemini.

Cancer (or the crab) was hardest for me to find out; nor did I much search for it; for in my horizon it appeared not, except in the crabbed frowne of a womans face, or in the rump or later end of a deare reckoning.

For Leo, I have found more then a den of Lyons, Or, Argent, and Gules, alias, Golden, White and Red.

Virgo, or the Maiden-head signe, was hard, or scarce to bee found neer a taverne-bush; but at last, Bush-lane afforded me one, which is as the Phaenix of Arabia, alone, there being no more of that signe within the hemispheare of the citie.

Libra was generally metamophosed in every taverne, from weights to measures, except at the bar, where gold was weighed to a graine; it is said that Astrea,[2] or Justice, fled from the earth, and was turned into the

1   A clown performing in the commedia dell'arte.
2   In Greek mythology Astrea was a celestial virgin who fled from earth to become the constellation Virgo, which was associated with Libra, and

equall, or Septembers equinoctiall signe of Libra.

The signe Scorpio (or the serpent) I conjecture to be transformed into greene Dragons; which signe I have often past through in my peregrination.

For Sagitarius, I was forced to make use of the signe of the Archer, neer Finsbury-fields, or Grubstreet end.

Capricornus, is said to be a signe in the heavenly Firmament, containing twenty stars; but if the Goat in West-smithfield had not furnished me, I had beene quite destitute of entertainment at Capricorne.

The signe of the Fountaine was my flowing (and sometimes overflowing) Aquarius.

In stead of Pisces, I was glad to make my Journey to the Dolphin and Mermaids.

Thus having declared my painefull passage through twelve sorts of signes, I proceed further to speake of some other signes.

A catalogue of such signes, as the author hath past by and through.

I have past by and through Ursa Major, at the Bridge-foot in Southwarke, and I have visited Ursa Minor, in more places then one; I have found the Dog-dayes[1] in the depth of winter, both at Westminster, and elsewhere. I have beene in conjunction neer the Dragons tayle. I have plaid the Man in the Moone; I have passed through a bakers dozen[2] of Suns, besides the seven Stars, for my further perambulation, through and by Angels, Kings and Queenes Heads, Crownes, Ankers, Antelops, Cities, Bels, Castles, Bores, Crosses, Crossekeyes, Cats and Cardinals, Hats, Eagles, Fleeces, Faulcons, Chequers, Hoops, Cranes, Christopher and Dunston, Globes, Griphons, Saint John, George and Gartar, Field-gate, Turnstile, and Flowerdelice, Harts, Hornes, Harrowes, and Horshooes, Katherine Wheele, Grashopper, Lambe, Kings, Queenes, and Princes Armes, Saint Martin, Mouth and Miter, Pauls-head, Bishops-head, Nags-heads, Pye,[3]

---

    therefore with justice.
1   The height of summer, a favourite expression of Taylor's.
2   Thirteen, a precaution by bakers against prosecution for selling underweight bread.
3   Magpie.

Pelican, Plow and Peacock, a navie of Ships, a brood of Swans, sweet Roses, kind Salutations, Tractable Tuns, an honest Shepheard, a Windmill, good Wrastlers, a faire Vineyard, a plentifull Vintage, and three tavernes onely with bushes without a thiefe.[1] All which, you that have leisure may find, and when you have found, you may read at your pleasure.

Furthermore, it is to be noted, that as in the firmament there are not so many fixed, as wandring stars:[2] and oftentimes the most part (or all of them) are darkned and involved round with clouds, vapours, mists, and fogs; so that they are obscured from our sight. So in this lower circle of my passage, I have found suns, moones and stars, in their bright and shining lustre (as it were to day) but upon the sudden some of my suns have been eclipsed, with a cloud of debts; bad customers (or small custome) hath brought some of my moones from the full, to an unrecoverable wane; too much beliefe in bad paymasters hath obscured, now and then a star; and many other of my lesser stars have beene too often shipwrack'd, with running on a rocke of chaulk, or too much scoring.

Amongst all these changes and mutabilities, I would have the reader to note, that all those signes which are in this following book nominated, were at the writing hereof in preterpluperfect[3] being, shining and adorning our terrestriall hemisphaere with most hopefull, resplendent, refulgent, and translucent luster. But if any planetary influence hath with malevolent aspect, cast a fog of obscurity, or perpetuall extinction upon any of my signes, let no man blame mee (the author) for I plead not guilty, either to the retrogradation, or declination of any of them; for I have, and do love all the worthy company of vintoners; that I desire they may ever be like the latter end of a scriveners bond (In full force and vertue.)

The antiquity of wine is recorded memorably by sacred and prophane historians, and vines have been planted, and vineyards allowed here in England by the permission of the Emperour Probus,[4] at such time

---

1. Perhaps a reference to Aristophanes, *Wasps*, 'one bush cannot hide two thieves'. A bush, or broom, used to sweep yeast from a the surface of a brew, was commonly used as a sign by drinking establishments.
2. planets.
3. The pluperfect (or preterpluperfect) tense denoted that an action was finished, generally denoted in English by the word 'had' before the verb.
4. Emperor 276-82 AD. He was said to have employed soldiers, in times of peace, to plant vines in Roman provinces to boost their economies.

as the Romanes had the government here. And there was a record (and I thinke is yet) in Windsor Castle, of an yearly account of the charges for the planting vines in the little parke there; and of the making of wines in many places of this land; and that grapes grew so plenteously, that some of the wines served for the Kings houshold, the rest were sold for the King's profit: and that the tythe of those vines and wines were paid to the abbot of Walthamstow, who was then parson of Old and New Winsor:[1] and in the raigne of King John, wine was so plenty, that it was sold for twenty shillings the tun, which is but one penny the gallon: and it was so cheape in the fifteenth yeare of King Henry the Seventh, that (much of it being brought out of France) it was given to the mariners (for their fraight) that brought it.

Wee are commonly entertain'd with wine at christenings, weddings, and burials, so that wine ushers us into the world, and kindly accompanies us all our life, and after death brings us to our graves. Thousands of people doe live by it, as the planters of vines, the keepers of vineyards, wine-merchants, vintoners, mariners, coopers, lightermen, wharfengers, shipwrights, carpenters, goldsmithes, pewterers, and carmen: besides, the great charge of cranedge and selleridge; and which is not to be forgotten, customes and imposts.

Thus much shall suffise to speake of wine. Now for the honor of vintoners, I find there have been many worthy and honorable men of them; for in anno, 1271, the fifty six yeare of the raigne of King Henry the third, one John Adrian, vintoner, was Lord Maior of London. In the eighth yeare of King Edward the third's raigne, 1334, one Reignold at the Conduit was Lord Maior: In the fifteenth yeare of the same King, one John of Oxford was Lord Maior. In the one and thirty yeare of Edward the third, 1356, Sir Henry Picard, vintoner, was Lord Maior; who for a perpetuall honorable memory of this cities worthinesse; and for a brooch, Jewell, or famous ornament to the Right Worshipfull Company of Vintoners, the said Sir Henry Picard did feast foure kings in one day with most sumptuous magnificence, namely, Edward the third, King of England, John, King of France, David, King of Scotland, and William, King of Cypress, with Edward the Black Prince of Wales, the Daulphin

---

[1] Waltham abbey appropriated the churches of Old and New Windsor in 1189, and was therefore entitled to the tithes, including from 1232 tithes from the royal garden.

of France, with many other princes, dukes and peeres, as may be read in Stowes and Howes Chronicle,[1] and in the Survay of London.[2] In the yeare 1558, Sir John Stody, vintoner, was Lord Maior of London. In the yeare 1395, the nineteenth yeare of King Richard the second, Sir William Moore, vintoner, was likewise in that honorable office. In the nineteenth yeare of the raigne of King Henry the eight, 1527, Sir James Spencer, vintoner, was Lord Maior of London. And in the yeare 1594, in the five and thirty yeare of the raigne of Queene Elizabeth, Sir Cuthbert Buckle, vintoner, did nobly serve in that honorable office of London's Maioralty. Besides, I find that in the seventeenth yeare of Queene Elizabeth, Master Henry Prannell, vintoner, was one of the sheriffes of London.

As concerning pious and charitable works done by this famous company, and by their wives, or widdowes, he that list's to read the Survay of London, shall find the memorable records of (not onely those before named) but of Master Stephen Skidmore, Master Richard Jacob, Mistris Sibbella Jacob, with many others which for brevities sake, I omit.

And thus I dedicate my selfe and this my labour to that right worthy, and ample company, requesting them, and as many as loves them, to take nothing in ill part, because I know there was not any thing ill meant. And now I proceed to my alphabeticall and epigrammaticall peregrination.

A
Angell in Long Aker.
Angell in Shoreditch.
Angell at the Tower Gate.
Angell neere the Gatehouse at Westminster.
Anker in West Smithfield.
Anker in East Smithfield.
Anker and Ship in the Minories.
Anker in St. Olaves, at Bermondsey street end.
Adam and Eve at Westminster in Tuthill street.
Antelop in West Smithfield.

[1] Edmund Howes in 1618 published an abridgement of John Stow's *English Chronicle*.
[2] by John Stow, published in 1598.

Andrewes Crosse in Fetter lane neer Holborn.
Antwerp behind the Royall Exchange
Archer neere Finsbery Fields, or Grub-street end.

B.
Bishops-head in Chancery Lane.
Bell within Temple Barr.
Bell without Bishopsgate
Bell in Saint Nicholas Lane, through into Canning street.
Bell at Saint Thomas in Southwarke
Bell at Westminster in Kings street.
Bell in Distar Lane
Bell in Newgate Market
Bell Savadge
Bell in the Strand.
Bull head in Towerstreet
Bull head in East-smithfield
Bull head in Cheapeside
Bull head in the Borough of Southwarke
Bull head without Bishopsgate.
Bull-blacke in the Pallace at Westminster
Bull-blacke in the Burrough of Southwarke
Bull-red in Thames street neere Coleharbour
Bull-red in Saint Iohns street.
Beare in the Pallace at Westminster
Beare and Dolphin in Tower street
Beare neere Fleetbridge
Beare at the Bridgefoote in the Borough of Southwarke.
Bores head in West-Smithfield
Bores head behind the Exchange
Bores head in East-Cheape
Bores head at Criplegate
Bores head in Old Fishstreet.

C.
Crowne in West-Smithfield.
Castle without Newgate

Castle in Paternoster Row
Castle in Cornehill
Castle neere Pauls Chaine
Castle behind Saint Clements neere the Strand
Castle in Fleetstreet
Castle in Bredstreet
Castle in Woodstreet
Castle in White Chapple.
Crosse White in Whitecrosse street
Crosse Red in Redcrosse streete
Crosse Taverne neere Charing Crosse.
Crosse Keyes in Bedford Berry, alias, Covent Garden
Crosse Keyes in the Strand, neere Yorke, or Buckingham house
Crosse Keyes in Holbourne.
Cat in Long Lane.
Cardinals Hatt without Newgate
Cardinalls Hatt in Cornehill.
Chequer in White Chappell
Chequer in the Strand.
The Christopher at Clearkenwell, at Turnebull street end.
The Coopers hoope in Leadenhal street neere Limestreet.
The Crane at Hoxton in the Parish of St Leonards Shoreditch.
3 Cranes in the Vintage
3 Cranes in the Powltry
3 Cranes in the Strand neere the Savoy Gate
3 Cranes in the Old Bayly
3 Cranes in Chancery Lane
3 Cranes in Saint Olaves street
3 Cranes in the Borough of Southwarke.
3 Cups in Holbourne.

D.
The Greene Dragon in Chepeside
Dragon in Pauls Churchyard.
Dragon in White Chappell
Dragon on St Lamberts hill, and in Thames street,
Dragon and Mermayde in Thames street, at the foot of Pauls hill

Dragon in Southwarke, neere Saint Giorge's Church
Dragon in Drury Lane
Dragon in White Friers.
Dog at Westminster
Dog in Drury Lane
Dog at Creede Lane end, neere Ludgate
Dog within Newgate
Dog in Chancery Lane.
Dolphin in Thames street neere Dowgate
Dolphin in Old-Fish street.
St. Dunstane.

E.
Spred Eagle in Grayes Inne Lane
Eagle in Cow Lane.

F.
Fountaine in Fleetstreet
Fountaine in East-Smithfield
Fountaine in Fanchurchstreet
Fountaine in the Old Bayly
Fountaine in the Strand neere the Savoy
Fountaine in Saint Annes Lane ueere [sic, i.e. neere] Aldersgate.
Fleece in Bedford-Berry, Alias, the Covent Garden
Fleece in Little Brittaine
Fleece in Cornhill, neere Birchin Lane end.
Faulcon on the Banke side
Fanlcon in Rosemary Lane.
Fortune in Drury Lane
Fortune in Golding Lane.
The Flower De Lices in Finch Lane neere Cornehill.
The Golden Field-Gate, at the upper end of Holborne.

G.
Globe in Fleetstreet
Globe in Shorditch
Globe in King street at Westminster.

Globe in the Woolstaple at Westminster.
The Globe in Thridneedle street
Globe in little Eastcheape
Globe neere Holbourne Barres.
Criphon [sic, i.e Griphon] in White Chappell.
George in Turnbull street
George in St Iohns streete
George in Fleet Lane
George within Aldgate
George in White Friers
Greyhound without Creeplegate
Greyhound in Bowlane
Greyhound in the Blacke Fryers
Greyhound in Fleetstreet
Greyhound in Knightrider street.
Greyhound in Southwarke, or the upper Ground.
Goate in Smithfield.
The Garter in Long Aker.
The Grashopper in Threedneedle street, neere Finch Lane end.

H.
The White Hart neere Charing Crosse.
Hart in Shoreditch
Hart in White Chappell
Hart in Smithfield
Hart in the Strand
Hart in Tothill street at Westminster
Hart at Hoxton in St Leonard Shoreditch Parish
Hart at Drury Lane end neere Holbourne
Hart without Bishopsgate.
The White Horse in Lumbard street
Horse in Old Fish street
Horse Flying in Woodstreet.
The Harrow in Charterhouse Lane
Harrow in Gracious street
Harrow in Little Woodstreet
The Horshoe in Drury Lane

The Hoope in Thame street, neere Saint Magnus Church
The Harts Hornes and Miter at the end of Carterlane, neere Black-friers
The Horne in Fleetstreet

I.
Saint Iohns of Ierusalem at Clerkenwell
The Saint Iohns Head in Chauncery lane
Iohns Head at Milkstreet end
Iohns Head neere Ludgate.

K.
The Kings head in Shoreditch
Kings head in Saint Iohn street
Kings head in Rose-mary lane, or King of Sweden
Kings head in King street, at Westminster
Kings head neere Leaden hall
Kings head within Bishopsgate
Kings head without Bishopsgate, neere the Spittle
Kings head at the end of Canning street, or Walbrooke
Kings head in Saint Clements lane neere Lumbardstreet
Kings head in Pudding lane
Kings head in new Fishstreet
Kings head in old Fishstreet
Kings head on Tower hill, or neere East-Smithfield.
Kings head in Drury Lane.
King of Swedens Head without Bishopsgate
Kings head in the Strand
Kings head in the Blacke Friers
Kings head in Fleetstreet, at Chancery Lane ende.
Kings head at Horsey Downe
Kings head in Holbourne
Kings head neere Alhallowes in Thamestreet
Kings head at the West end of the Covent Garden, or Bedford berry.
The Katherin Wheele at Saint Katherins
Katherin Wheele in Tothill street, at Westminster
The Kings Armes in Saint Martins lane, or Martins in the Fields
Kings Armes in Cateaten street at Ironmonger lane end

Kings Armes at Milford lane end, neere Saint Clements, Strand
Kings Armes in the Burrough of Southwarke
Kings Armes in Holbourne
Kings Armes in Thridneedle street, neere Broadstreet
Kings Armes in Saint Martins

L.
The Golden Lyon neere York-house or Buckingham-house
Lyon in Lincolnes Fields neere the Cockpit
Lyon at Westminster in King street
Lyon in Fetter Lane
Lyon in the Strand
Lyon in Silver street, neere Woodstreet
The White Lyon at the end of Tower street, neere to the Hill
Lyon in the Crottchet Friers
Lyon in Canning street
Lyon in Chancery Lane
Lyon at the Mill-bank at Westminster
The Red Lyon in Shoreditch
Lyon at Billingsgate
Lyon in Grasse street, or Gracious street
Lyon neere Saint Georges Church in Southwarke
Lyon at Saint Olaves Watergate in Southwarke.
The Lamb in Drury Lane

M.
The halfe Moone in White Chappell
Moone in the Minories
Moone in Saint Katherins
Moone in Aldersgate street
Moone in the Strand
The Man in the Moone in King street, at Westminster
Man in the Moone in Cheape-side
The Mouth at Bishopsgate
Mouth within Aldersgate.
The Saint Martin neere Charing-Crosse.
Mermayd in Shoe-lane

Mermayd at Billingsgate
Mermayd in Cornehill
Mermayd in Cheapside
Mermayd in Breadstreet
Mermayd neere Charing-Crosse
Mermayd in the Burrough of Southwarke
Mermayd in Watling street neere Bowlane
Mermayd in Pater-noster-Row
Mermayd at Aldersgate
The Miter in Saint Stevens Alley at Westminster
Miter neere Aldgate
Miter in Loathbury at the end of Bartholmew-lane
Miter in Fenchurch street
Miter at the lower end of Cheapside
Miter in Breadstreet
Miter in Woodstreet
Miter in the Strand, neere to Denmarke house
Miter and Castle in Fleetstreet
Miter in Saint Iohn street
The Maydenhead in Thames street, or Bushlane
Maydenhead and George in the upper ground in Surrey
Maydenhead at Saint Giles in the fields

N.
Nags head at Clerkenwell
Nags head in Saint Iohns street
Nags head at Westminster
Nags head at the corner, against Leadenhall
Nags head in Thames street neere the Customhouse
Nags head in Cheape side
Nags head neere Bassings hall
Nags head without Temple Bar.

P.
The Princes Armes at Hoxton
Princes Armes at Pauls Chaine
Princes Armes at Saint Martins lane

Princes Armes neere the Church at Westminster
Princes Armes neere the Bouling Alley at Westminster
Princes Armes over against Denmarkehouse
Princes Armes in Holborne
Princes Armes in West-Smithfield
The Popes head neere Smithfield Pens
Popes head in Moorefields
Popes head in Cornhill
Popes head in Chancery lane
The Pye at Aldgate
The Peacocke in Thames street neere the old Swan
Peacocke without Temple Bar
The Plough without Aldersgate
Pauls head at Pauls Chaine
The Phenix in Long Aker
The Pellican in Drury Lane

Q.
The Queenes head in West-smithfield
Queeenes head in East-smithfield
Queenes head againe in East-smithfield
Queenes head in Queene street
Queenes head in the Strand
Queenes head in Bishopsgate street
Queenes head in Thames street neere the Customhouse
Queene Elinor's head at Queene hithe
Queenes head in Pater-noster-row
Queenes head neere Holborne Conduit
Queenes head in Red-crossstreet
Queenes Armes in the Burrough of Southwarke
Queenes Armes at the end of Saint Nicholas Shambles

R.
The Rose at Fleet-bridge
Rose in the Covent Garden, or Bedfordberry
Rose in Saint Peters street at Westminster
Rose against Barking Church, at the end of Tower street

Rose at the Counter gate in the Powltry
Rose in Newgate Market
Rose in Shoreditch
Rose at Temple Bar
Rose in Thames street, neere the Tower dock
Rose at the upper end of Holborne
The Ram in Fleetstreet, at Ram Alley end
Rams head in Saint Olaves in Southwark

[S]
The Sun in Shoreditch
Sun in White-chappell
Sun in the Minories
Sun in Old Fishstreet
Sun in Sheere lane
Sun at Westminster
Sun neere Mooregate
Sun neere Cripplegate
Sun in Aldersgate street
Sun in New Fishstreet
Sun in Old street
Sun in the Strand
Sun in Holborne
Star in the Minories
Star at Chick lane end
Star at Saint Katherins
Star in Fenchurch street
Star in Little Eastcheap
Star in Cheap-side
Star in Coleman street
The 7 Stars by Smithfield Bars
The Ship in White-cross street
Ship at the Posterne gate neere the Tower
Ship at Saint Katherins
Ship at Bermondsey house, or the Armes of Bristow
Ship in the Dukes place neere London Wall
Ship neere Saint Mary Ax

Ship behind the Exchange
Ship in Long Alley, neere Moore Fields
Ship in Bishopsgate street
Ship in Fenchurch street
Ship neere Little Eastcheape at Rood lane end
Ship in Thames street, at Trinity lane end
Ship behind Old Fishstreet
Ship in the Old Baily
Ship in the Strand
Ship on the Bankside
The Swan in White-cross street
Swan in New Fishstreet
Swan at Westminster
Swan at Dowgate
Swan in Knightrider street
Swan in Old Fishstreet
Swan in the Strand
Swan at Saint Giles in the Fields
Swan in Holbourne
The Shepherd in East-smithfield
The Salutation in Tower street
Salutation neere Billingsgate
Salutation neere Mooregate, or London Wall
Salutation in the Strand
Salutation in Montague Close, in Southwarke
Salutation in Holbourne

T.
The 3 Tuns at Guild Hall gate
3 Tuns in Newgate Market
3 Tuns in Grass-street, or Gracious street
3 Tuns neere Charing-Crosse
3 Tuns in Fleetstreet
3 Tuns in Pauls Church-yard
3 Tuns in Smithfield
3 Tuns in Petticoat Lane
3 Tuns at the Tower Hill

3 Tuns at Westminster
3 Tuns at Saint Mary Hill, neere Billingsgate
3 Tuns at Garlick hithe
3 Tuns in the Burrough of Southwarke
3 Tuns at the lower end of Great Woodstreet
3 Tuns neere Holbourne Bridge
3 Tuns on the Bank-side
The Tun neere the Banke-end in Southwarke
The Tun in Thames street, against the Customhouse
Turnstile in Holbourne
A Taverne with a Bush and no Signe, under the new Burse
Taverne with a Bush and no Signe, in Milford lane
Two Tavernes in the Tower of London

V.
The Vineyard in Queenes street
Vintage neere the 3 Cranes in the Vintrey
Venice, the Signe neere Saint Clements without Temple-bar

W.
The two Wrastlers in Lincolns Inne Fields
The White Horse in Nicholas Shambles
The Windemill in Loathbury

Besides these Tavernes before mentioned, there are foure Houses in London that doe sell Rhennish Wine, inhabited onely by Dutchmen; namely,
The Stilliyard.
The Swan in Thames street
The Swan in Crooked lane
The Sun at Saint Mary Hill

Thus (Gentle Reader) I have ran a Course
That would have tyr'd (perhaps have kild) a Horse:
For if the winged Pegasus (like Mee)
Had watred been, h'had had no eyes to see:
Or if Bucephalus had trotted so,

Hee had been lam'd and founder'd long agoe.
Yet is my Task not done, for I must Play
A Second Part before I have my Pay:
Which Second Part shall to your view declare
The Tavernes in ten Shires, and where they are;
Within what County, in what Towne, what Signe,
Or else (if not what Signe) who sels the Wine.
The Counties are, Brave Barkshire, Hampshire, Essex,
Kent, Surrey, Hartford, Middlesex, and Sussex;
With Buckingham and Oxford; these are they
Which in my Second Part I must display.

FINIS.

THE HONORABLE AND MEMORABLE FOUNDATIONS

*T*he second part, or sequel, to Taylor's list of London and Westminster inns, is a very different work, in both its construction and its sources. Its subject, ten counties, embraces the whole of south-east England as far as Buckingham, Oxford and Christchurch, with descriptions of most significant towns and an apparently comprehensive list of all licensed taverns and tavern proprietors, almost 700 establishments.

The descriptions of places, unless well known to Taylor from visits or acquaintances, are derived from his usual sources, William Camden and John Speed (as he occasionally acknowledges), but he also displays a flair for the pithy summary – as perfected by Thomas Fuller in his Worthies of England more than two decades later – such as Portsmouth, which 'thrives better by war than by peace', or Romford, 'a sweet, savery, cleane and gainfull market for hoggs, and all other sorts of swine'. The barbs are generally good-humoured: Harwich is 'not only full of people, but honestly peopled for the most part of them', Burford 'is a good market towne, but beware of a Burfourd bayt [a local ale], for it may breed the staggers'; Maidenhead has three taverns – 'It may be one too many'.

His judgements, though derivative, are worth preserving. More valuable to the historian of individual places or of travel and hospitality are his lists of taverns. The distinction between taverns, inns and other drinking establishments has long been blurred, but in Taylor's day was real. A tavern was a premises licensed to sell wine, either on its own account, or as part of an inn, and it often also provided accommodation for travellers. It catered for a clientele of higher standing than that of an alehouse, and was originally associated with towns, although by Taylor's time many existed in villages. In his address to 'Mine Hosts' he draws a distinction between London taverns, which catered for the local drinking clientele and did not serve food, and these provincial taverns, which provided food, stabling and accommodation, and charged accordingly. Taylor clearly has derived his information from an official list (probably no longer extant), whether compiled by the Vintners Company or a government *agency, which gives his pamphlet an importance that has perhaps not generally been appreciated.*

In the text modern place names are appended [in square brackets] when Taylor's spelling is so different as to hinder identification.

THE HONORABLE AND MEMORABLE FOUNDATIONS, ERECTIONS, RAISINGS, AND RUINES, OF DIVERS CITIES, TOWNES, CASTLES, AND OTHER PIECES OF ANTIQUITIE, WITHIN TEN SHIRES AND COUNTIES OF THIS KINGDOME; Namely, Kent, Sussex, Hampshire, Surrey, Barkshire, Essex, Middlesex, Hartfordshire, Buckinghamshire, and Oxfordshire: With the Description of many famous Accidents that have happened, in divers places in the said counties. Also, a Relation of the Wine Tavernes either by their signes, or names of the persons that allow, or keepe them, in, and throughout the said severall Shires.
By John Taylor.
London, Printed by A. M. 1636.

To all the Good-Fellowes in generall, and particular, that do keep, inhabit, allow, or maintaine the wine tavernes, or inne tavernes in the ten Shires and counties before named.

MINE HOSTS,

I hope I am not much mistaken in calling you gentlemen, or kind friends; if you be either, it is as much as I looke for, or can deserve; you onely are the men that do truly merit the name and title of mine hosts, for alas, our citie tavernes have no other entertainment, but welcome gentlemen, a crust, and what wine will you drinke? But you, brave minded, and most joviall Sardanapalitans,[1] have power and prerogative (cum privilegio) to receive, lodge, feast, and feed both man and beast; you have the happinesse to boile, roast, broile and bake fish, flesh, and foule, whilst wee in London have scarse the command of a gull, a widgeon, or a woodcock; and for your further, and more high reputation, the most part of your customers come riding to your houses, where almost all our

---

[1] Sardanapalus, last king of the Assyrians, was renowned for decadence and self-indulgence.

guests are footmen; with you it is common for the master to drinke pintes or quarts out of pots, whilst his horse is eating of bottles.[1] besides, our citie tavernes are not troublesome to their clients with many various items, and reckonings; but briefly, so much for sack, clarret, or white; whilst you have the predominance to assault a man with a bill, and call him to a strait and strict account, not onely for himselfe, but for the doings of his horse; the jury is divided or woven into five parts, in the manner of linsey woolsey;[2] namely, the hostes, the drawer, the chamberlaine, the tapster, and the hostler. Who having view'd the bill of inditement, (they) being themselves, accusers, evidence, plaintiffe, jury, and judges; the finall sentence is pronounced at their owne bar of justice, where the delinquents conscience knowing all to bee justly laid to his charge, with patience and fortitude, suffers the irrevokeable doome to passe upon him, paies the reckoning, puts the bill out of all force and vertue, paying his fees, hee is discharged with a heartily welcome. Of all, or the most part of such accounts, actions, debts, or demands, our citie tavernes have a long time pleaded not guilty. They cannot bee tax'd with the deadly sin of gluttony, nor are they troubled with the harsh musick of trencher-scraping,[3] so that if I were to be transform'd, or metamorphos'd into a hogg, I would bee loath to dwell in one of our tavernes, because I should have such plenty of wash, and such scarcity of graines.

But gentlemen, though I am bold (a little) to play the (—)[4] with you, yet I assure you, I love you well; but for some more speciall love and favour that I beare to my selfe. I have written this my second booke of tavernes, I have not written epigrams here, as I did upon the former, because in city and country the signes and the wines are all alike.

Yet (to give all the respectfull content that I can to my honorable, worshipfull, and others of my good friends, that are to pay me money, upon the receiving, or this my publishing this small booke.) I have recorded (in stead of epigrams) some monuments of antiquity, which my hope is, will bee more profitable and delightfull; and gentlemen (I meane you that are ingaged unto mee) in your just payment to mee, you may worke a piece of a wonder, (which is, to make a rich poet;) but alas! that stile is as much too

1   Pun on 'bottle' meaning 'bundle' of hay.
2   A coarse fabric woven, as its name suggests, from linen and woollen yarn.
3   Trenchers were wooden plates or platters.
4   Presumably 'Devil' has been omitted, thus 'to make fun of you'.

high for mee, as I am too low for it, (that's a bull) so much the better; for almost all men are turn'd grasiers, and speake buls familiarly, and those are the Mounsier Momusses,[1] who have sold their wise akers before they have sowed their wilde oates;[2] and these will censure harshly, any thing they understand hardly, whose knowledge is as much in the validitie and measure of a verse, as the asse had that judg'd the cuckoo's song to bee sweeter than the nightingales.[3]

I have laid the foundation of this project my selfe, it is a vineyard of mine own planting, the grapes of mine owne pressing, the wine of mine owne vintage (or vantage) the tavernes of mine owne finding, and the vintoners my own friends, in lieu of which, I am not mine own man, but theirs, or yours, or his, or hers, that wisheth mee well, as far as my intentions and actions are just, lawfull, or laudable,

John Taylor

These tavernes (some of them) were mistaken in the first booke, and some of them have been set up since the said booke was printed; therfore, to give satisfaction, I have here inserted them.

Angell neere St. Clements Church.
Angell neere Creechurch, or Aldgate.
Bull within Bishopsgate
Bull without Bishopsgate.
Bull or Buffles Head at Charing-Crosse.
Bush in Buttolph lane.
Castle without Cripplegate.
3. Cranes neere the Customhouse.
Crowne neere Dowgate, that was the Dolphin.
The Raine-Deere without Temple Barre.
Dog, or Talbot in Long Lane.

[1] Momus was the Greek god of mockery and satire.
[2] A convoluted pun, associating graziers (who have given up their arable land - their acres - for pasture), wiseacres (people who appear clever), and wild oats (youthful indiscretions). The word 'wiseacre' has nothing to do with acres, but is derived from the Dutch for soothsayer.
[3] This fable circulated in the middle ages and occurs in songs. Taylor's contemporary, Edward Topsell, included it in his *Fowles of Heavene*.

Dog neere Bishopsgate.
Fountaine in Bloomesbury.
Hart in Basing lane.
Golden-fleece without Temple Bar.
Greene Dragon at Breadstreet hill, was the Castle.
Globe in Bedlam.
Hart in Little Moorefields.
Harrow in Southwarke.
Hoope in Purpoole lane neere Graysin-lane.
Horse neere the Bridge in Southwarke.
Kings head in Southwarke.
The golden Lyon in Fleetstreet.
Maydenhead in Pudding lane.
Mayden-head in Bush-Lane.
Mermayd in White Crosse street.
Princes Armes in Fleetstreet late the Fountaine
Princes Armes in St. John street.
Princes Armes in Finch Lane, was the 3 Flower de Lices.
Queenes Head neere the Wardrope.
Queenes Armes at Westminster.
Queenes Armes in St. Martins.
Rose in Turnbull street.
Sun in Thames street neere Dice Key.
Salutation in Bermondsey street.
Ship in Butolph lane.
Ship at Smithfield Pens.

A CATALOGUE OF TAVERNES IN TENNE SHIRES ABOUT LONDON.

KENT

For noblemen, knights, gentlemen, soldiers, mariners; vertuous and beauteous ladies, and women of meanest degrees, comely, pretty, proper, handsome, cleanely, neat, and honest. Stored with all sorts of artificers, and inhabited with painefull and profitable husbandmen; famous for two most ancient cities, (whereof one is the chiefe metropolitan seat of England.) It hath many faire market townes, impregnable castles, secure and safe havens and harbours for shipping, aboundance of rich villages and hamlets: So that by the almighties blessings, and the peoples Industry, this (old kingdome) county is for fruit, fowle, flesh, fish, cloth, corne, wood and cattle, or all or any thing that is for the use of man to maintain life and pleasure, Kent is, and hath bin renowned universally.

Deptford, or Deepefourd, so called by reason of the deepenesse of the fourd or River there, where ships of great burthen may safely ride at ankor, there is a faire and usefull docke for the building or mending of the kings ships, it hath also a goodly storehouse for provision for the said ships. Deptford is sometimes called East-Greenewich. This towne hath these taverne licences or inhabiters.

The Kings Head, The Mermayd, The Sunne, and the Ship: the parties that keepe or maintaine them are William Tyle, Richard Aileworth, Jeffrey Nixon, William Dring.

Eltham, where the king hath a faire sommer house, at the first it was founded by Anthony Beck Bishop of Durham, who gave it to Elinor, wife to king Edward the first, but since often re-edified by succeeding princes. It hath a taverne under the name of one Nathanael Mercer.

Greenewich, for scituation and prospect a paradice of pleasure, the pallace there was first built by Humphrey Duke of Glocester, in the Reigne of King Henry the 6. Since when it hath beene re-edified, and made more large and sumptuous by King Henry the 7. Which pallace also was begun to be enlarged by the late vertuous Queene Anne, but now finished by our gracious Queene Mary. This towne is most famous for the birth of that admired wonder of her sexe, Queene Elizabeth, who was borne there, in the yeare of grace 1533. September the 7.

Greenewich hath thes wine tavernes: The Beare, The Crowne. The Kings Armes The Princes Armes. The Rose. And (which I should have named first) the Ship. kept by Henry Noris. Also there is a taverne with a bush onely, kept by Gregory Martin, and the Kings Armes at Deptford bridge in Greenewich parish.

Darentfourd, so called because it is scituate on the River Darent, it is vulgarly named Dartfourd, there was once a nunnery built by King Edward the third, which after was made a house for King Henry the 8. Where he did sometimes keepe his court. Dartford hath these tavernes: At the Bull, George Hanger. At the Cocke, William Somers. At the White Hart, Elizabeth Glover.

Gravesend (as the Learned antiquary Master Camden writes) is so called, because it is the end of the Greve Reeve, or Port Greves government, or bounds. It is a towne famous for receipt of all Nations, having at any time more faire Lodgings, and provision for entertainment, then many townes hath that are thrice as great; It hath oftentimes lodged kings, princes, and forreigne ambassadors; it is divided into two parishes, namely, Gravesend and Milton. It hath these wine tavernes. William Vernon at the Angell, Richard Tucker at the Ship. Thomas Young at the Anker. William Diston at the Bull. The Christopher. Thomas Skilhorne at the Horne

Seavenoake so called, because seven great oakes growing thereabouts, it is a good market towne and a great thorow-fare, and hath these tavernes: The Crowne, the Cat, and the Bull; they are tavernes in the tuition (or by the licenses) of Margery Pocock. Debora Pocock. and William Petley.

Tunbridge, (or the towne of bridges) so called, by reason, it hath five stone bridges, for passage over the River; which River is devided there into so many severall branches; it is lately famous for a healthfull, approved, sweet, medicinable water, that cures, or eases many diseases: The tavernes there, are at the dispose of two women: namely, Martha Bartlet, and Elizabeth Frye.

Maydstone, a faire, spacious, sweet, pleasant, rich, and populous market towne, hath these taverns, or taverne keepers, John Taylor, Thomas Davis, and Agnes Shorey.

Rochester, is a fine neate citie, long since founded by a bishop named Hamo: it was destroyed by Atheldred, king of the Mercians, anno 676. it hath been oftentimes spoyled by the Danes; the castle there hath been a strong piece of defence, it was built by a bishop named Gundulph; it was raced, and spoyl'd in the barons wars, in King Henry the third's Raigne. The cathedrall church there was built by Aethelbert king of Kent: The goodly stone bridge there was built by Sir Robert Knowles, Knight, with such spoyles as hee had valliantly gotten from the French in the raigne of King Richard the second. Rochester hath these tavernes, Thomas Lovell at the Kings head, Dorothy Allen, or Thomas Mot, at the Bull, John Stone, or Ambrose Groome at the White-hart, and John Domelow, or John Philpot at the Crowne.

Queenburrough was built by King Edward the third, in the

honour of Queene Phillip his Wife: there is a tavern which serves for minster as well as for Queenburrough, it is at the dispose or keeping of James Jacob. This towne is famous for my arrivall there (from London thither) with a boat of browne paper, anno 1619.

Feversham, a good towne, it was sometimes the residence of Athelstane, king of Kent; where hee enacted lawes: it is also famous for a sumptuous abbey, built there by King Stephen, and there himselfe, Queene Mawd his wife, and his sonne Prince Eustace were sepulchred. It hath three tavernes: at the Ship, Walter Moyses, the other two belongs to Samuell Thurstone, and James Hudson.

At the towne of Ashfourd, there may be three tavernes, for Thomas Mascall may or doth keepe two, the other doth belong to Peter Colebrand.

At Chepsted [Chipstead] one, Anthony Fuller.
At Lenham one, Robert Tray.
At Egerton one, Elizabeth Faireway.
At Erith one, Giles Sidgwick.
At Kenthatch [Kent Hatch, Crockham Hill] one, Edmund Plomley.
At Gowthurst [Goudhurst] one, Thomas Cowchman.
At Ashe one, John Tompson.
At Bromley two, Toby Priest, John Halfepenny, the Bell, the Hart.
At Chattham, Francis Giles.
At Folkstone one, Elizabeth March.
At Ferningham [Farningham] one, John Radcliffe.
At Elam [Elham] two, Jane Cuntrey, Robert Fox.
At Crayford one, Ralph Meykins, at the Angell.
At Lamberhurst, Mary Astone.
At Greenehive [Greenhithe] one, Miles Croxton, the signe, Callice Sands.
At Leedes, one Edward Lloyde.

Canterbury, or the Kentish burough or citie, is ancient and renowned, it hath metropolitan dignitie, chiefe over England: Augustine the monke, about the 67 yeare of Christ, came into Britaine; and at Canterbury kept his residence, where by his doctrine, and good example of life, hee confirmed and established many in the Christian faith; causing it to spread and flourish by his painefull ministery, so that after a holy and lawdable life ended, hee dyed, and was buried in that honorable city. It hath these tavernes, Elizabeth Lockley, or William Terry at the Rose; Edward Den, at the White-hart, James Penn, or George B. at the Red- Lyon, Elizabeth Bridg, at the Sarazens head, Miles Bull, or Warham Jemut, at the Bull, William Mann Esquire hath also a taverne license, Robert or Susan Turner, alias Baker, at the Chequer; Peter Winn, or Christopher Baldwin, at the Sun, 8.

At Milton and Newington one, William Dickins.
At Staplehurst one, William Poynet.
At Wye one, Simon Allen.
At Strowd [Strood] one, Edward Monox.
At Lewsham one, Elizabeth Tarpley.
At Sandway one, John White.
At Marden one, Anthony Young.
At Yalding one, Richard Pix.
At Offham one, Thomas Tresse.
At New Romney, three, Susan Wood, Sara Wood, Smith Tookey.
At Hawkhurst one, Agnes Viney.
At Bersted [Bearsted] one, Thomas Holford.

Deale, where stands a strong defencible castle, built by King Henry the eight, the place is famous for repulsing Julius Caesar three times thence before hee could arrive there: it hath these three tavernes kept by Susan Woodland, Mary Countrey, and Judith Hudson.

At Crambrooke [Cranbrook] two, Joan Kirkham, and John Leigh.
At Charing one, Anthony Page.
At Appledore and Biddenden—William Poynit,

Sandwich, so called, by reason of too much sand, which, not onely makes shoales and flats in the sea, but also chokes up the haven there; it is a faire rich towne, and one of the Cinque Ports; it hath had the triall of sundry alterations; It hath been often distress'd by the Danes; it was sack'd, spoil'd and burnt by Lewis, the Daulphin of France in the reigne of King John. King Edward the first placed there a staple for wooll. King Edward the third did honour it with much princely favour, since when, it was againe burnt by the French in King Henry the sixt his raigne, since which time it hath been so repaired, that it flourisheth beautifully and bountifully: there doe inhabit many Dutch people, who doe inrich themselves, and are profitable to the towne, by making divers sorts of stuffes there. Sandwich hath these tavernes: John Seymer, Axne Peyton, Hugh Rodes, Jane Wood, Roger Paine, and Alice Barrell.

At Saint Lawrence one, Katherine Hudson.
At Stonecrutch [Stonecrouch] one, under William Campion Esquire.
At Ospring one, Peter Greenstreet.
At Redred [Riverhead?], Mary Oxonbridge.
At Penchurst [Penshurst] one, Thomas Sexton.
At Woolwich, John Sims at the Hart.
At Saint Mary Cray one, Edward Fleet.
At Woodsgate [Westgate?] one, John Burdet.
At Benenden one, William Leedes.
At Blenchdy [Brenchley] one, Elizabeth Clampard.
At Wingham one; Elizabeth Ashton.
At Sunbridge [Sundridge] one, Anne Cacot.

Tenterden is a good towne for cloathing, and so is Crambrooke (before named) Tenterden hath two tavernes: Mathew Outred, and James Glover.

At Rootham [Wrotham] and Norflect [Northfleet], Thomas Spencer, the Crowne.
At Westram [Westerham] and Aeton Bridge [Edenbridge], Anne Spencer.
At Mawlin [Malling], George Huntley, may keepe two tavernes.
At Margate, two, Averie Jenkinson, and Henry Culmer.
At Lid [Lydd], Godfrey Martin, and Thomas Tookey.
At Sutton Valience, Anne Usmer.
At Seale, Mabell Sandall.
At Herne, William Towlson.
At Highgate, William Watson.
At Bexley and Footsbray [Foots Cray] Nathaniel Mercer.
At Hyde [Hythe] Henry Hart, William Nut.
At Sittingborne, foure, Margaret Husbands, Anne Wood, Margaret

Lawe, Thomas Rochfourd.

To finish my collections of this famous countie; I, for my rellish to my narration, and as an excellent seale, or easterne limitation to the most excellent bounds of Kent, I close up all with

Dover, a brave towne, and one of the Cinque ports, the most commodicus place for passage too and fro betweene the mighty kingdomes of England and France. It hath a good and safe haven, which was at the first made by the command of King Henry the eight, at sixty three thousand pound charges, which is called, Dover Peere: but in time, all the cost being almost lost, and by the violence of the raging sea, decayed and broken, Queen Elizabeth (of blessed memorie) with much of her owne cost, and Parliamentarie authority, enacted that a toll upon tonnage should be paid for some yeares, for all manner of goods transported inward or outward.

There is also an impregnable castle, which is the strongest hold, and fortresse in England, commanding both by land and sea; it is supposed to have been built by Julius Caesar. Dover hath these tavernes, taverne keepers, or allowers. John Low, Judith Haines, Edward Waller, John Hugesson, Anthony Percivall, Trustram Stevens.

At Dover Peere be these, William Streeting, Elizabeth Alley, and William Bradshaw, to whom I dedicate these few lines:

Kind friend, as thou didst once the favour gaine,
Great Britaines mightie prince to entertaine;
So entertaine these verses I have penn'd,
As my remembrance unto thee my friend:
Thou knowst (by old experience) that I love thee;
And if thou lov'st mee, I will one day prove thee.

The county of Kent had, in King Henry the eight's raigne, at the suppression of monasteries, abbies, nunneries, priories, frieries, colleges, hospitals, and (as they termed them) religious houses, the number of fifty three.

Kent is divided into sixty foure hundreds, or divisions; namely, Black-heath hundred, Lesnes, Rooksley, Axtave, Broomley, Whitstaple, Milton, Toltingtroph, Hoo, Tencham, Shammell, Feversham, Blengate,

Bouton under Bleath, Kingslow, Petham, Westgate, Ham, Downhamford, Tenterden, Preston, Felborow, Oxney Ile hundred, Blackburne, Wye, Winham, Charte, Stowting Conilos, Longbridge, Bircholt, Franchils Calhill, Heane, Blewborough, Street, Selbright fenden, Folkstone, Worth, Eyhorne, Lovingborough, Roluinden, New-church, Maydstone, Barnesield, Kinghamford, Brinkley and Horse, Saint Martins, Chattham and Gillingham, Bredge, Langport, Twyford, Watheling stone, Larkfield, Loway and Tunbridge, Alloftbridge, Littlefield, Marden, Wortham, Barkley, Godsheath, Westram, Crambrooke and Somerden.

     Kent hath seventeene good market townes, three hundred ninety eight parishes, and one hundred thirty seven wine tavernes.

SUSSEX.
Sussex, or South-Saxony, so named when there was an heptarchy, or government of 7 kings at once in England; because this county was the best part of the Southsaxon kingdom. It is a rich county, plenteous in iron-mines, and much good ordnance are cast there, with other necessary iron works: also it is much inriched by Glass-making. It is scituate neere the Brittish Ocean, whereby it is plentifully stored with fish: also it is nobly rich with inhabitants, and all other commodities for life and maintenance.

     Arundell, a towne famous for a goodly castle there, belonging to the Earles of Arundell and Surrey. This towne hath two tavernes, held by Micheas Henning, and Elizabeth Freeman.

At Chilkington [East? Chiltington], Charles Johnson.
At Witham [Withyham], William Pigott.
At Forrest Roe [Forest Row], Edw. Woodman, the Antelop.
At Battle, Mathew Cowchman doth or may keepe two tavernes
At Marsfield [Maresfield], William Mowhurst.

     Chichester was built by Cissa, the second king of the Southsaxons, an. 586 The bishops see for the Diocesse of Sussex or Chichester, was kept and held at Selsey till the time of King William the Conquerour. Chichester hath these tavernes: Thomas Powsley, Anne Billet, Mary Billet, Thomas Billet, Thomas Ball, Mathew Ball.

At Fronte [Frant], John Giles.
At Ditchelling [Ditchling], James Dansey.
At Newshoreham, Richard Gold.
At Tarring, William Fletcher.
At Hay field [Heathfield?] and Seaford, Richard Meade.
At Haughton [Houghton], George Coles.

Petworth, a pretty market-towne, where the Earle of Northumberland hath a goodly house, and is an honourable and bounteous housekeeper. It hath these two tavernes, Anthony Goodman, and John Hall.

At Hartfield, Mary Shelton.
At Ticehurst, Joane Kipping.
At Micheing [Mitching, i.e. Newhaven], Samuell Towers.
At Cuck field, Thomas Tasker.

Horsham seemes to take derivation from Horsa the Saxon, the brother of Hengist, the first king of Kent: It hath the allowance of two tavernes under one M. Robert Deering.

At Staining [Steyning] 2. Richard Briant, and Tho. Oliver.
At Wadehurst [Wadhurst], one Francis Wilfourd.

Winchelsea was overwhelmed with the sea, an. 1250. in the reigne of King Henry the third; since when the towne is built higher out of the danger or fury of the oceans violence: but the haven is decayed, to the townes great hinderance, and for the commoditie and profit of the towne of Rye. Winchelsea hath one taverner, John Pettit.

The towne of Midhurst hath foure taverners, John Kelsey, Anne Carus, Mary Hudson, and Joan White.

Hastings is a good and profitable fisher-town, a nursery for mariners and saylors: It had a mint to coyne money in it, in the time of King Athelstan: and it is named the first of the Cinque Ports; it had these ports and towns belonging to it, namely, Seaford, Pemsey [Pevensey], Hodney [Hydney, now in Eastbourne], Bulverhith, Winchelsea and Rye: all which were at any time at command of the king to set out 21 serviceable ships, for the service of their prince and country (within forty dayes warning) and to beare all the charge of the sayd shipps for the space of fifteene dayes, and the king was to be at all the charges after the fifteene dayes were expired. Hastings hath two tavernes, John Phissenden, and Francis Wennell.

Lewis, a famous market towne, which had a mint in it, in King Athelstanes Reigne, for his coine of gold and silver, or other mettals. It hath 6. churches, and a goodly house belonging to the Earle of Dorset; a mighty memorable battle was fought there anno 1264. betwixt King Henry the third and Simon Montfort Earle of Leaster, where the Earle tooke the king, and the king of the Romanes prisoners. Lewis hath these taverns, or number of houses for the sale of wines. Agnes Thurgood, Thomas Oliver, Robert Carter, and William Peake may keep two tavernes if he will.

At Lingfield [Lindfield?] Beding [Beeding], and Bramborow [Bramber], Richard Meade.
At Billinghurst, John Agate.
At Uckfield, John Forde.
At Backesteed [Buxted], Thomas Oliver.
At Cliffe, Richard Meade, and William Peake.
At Crawley and Worth, John Peake.
At Brighthelmeson [Brighton], Alice Harding, and William Peake.
At Barreash [Burwash], Mayfield, Pemsey [Pevensey], and Westham, Thomas Oliver.
At Dallington, Henfield, and Abfreston [Alfriston?], Thomas Oliver.
At East-Greensteed [Grinstead], John Langridge, and Henry Baldwin: the signes at East Greensted, are the Crowne, and the Cat.

Rye, is a good towne, and was made strong by William of Ipres, (a valiant nobleman and Earle of Kent) It was walled in the undefensible and weakest places by King Edward the 3. Terrible stormes and tempests hath done more for them, then they could well have done for themselves: for the blustring raging winds hath formerly caused the violence of the sea to make them a good haven: but great pitty it is, for it is much decay'd. For Rye is a brave flourishing towne, and serves London and many other places with fish in aboundance: It hath these tavernes in name or number. Richard Pecote. John Halsey. Richard Thomas.

Sussex had at the suppression of abbyes, nunneries, priories, frieries, colledges and hospitalls 32. This county is devided into 6. devisions, or hundreds, called rapes, namely, Chichester, Arundell, Bramber, Lewis, Pemsey and Hastings. There are in Sussex 18 market townes, 312 parishes, and 61 tavernes.

MIDDLESEX.
MIddlesex doth (almost) round beguirt the two famous cities of London and Westminster: and although I have in my former booke made mention of many of the tavernes neere adjoyning to the sayd cities; yet to make this my second narration in the better forme and order, I haue named some of the said tavernes againe, because I would play the part of an honest true taylor, and put in all the stuffe.

At Chelsey, Richard Eeds the signe of the Dog.
At Fulham, Joseph Holden, Richard Parkes: the signes are, the Kings Armes, and the Nags head.
At Hammersmith, Alice Robinson, or Thomas Warner at the white Hart, and Thomas Holden at the Goat or Antelop.
At Chiswick, Valentine Smith at the Kings head.
At Acton, John Coothridge, and William Aldridg: their signes are the Cock, and the Bell.
At Old Brentford, and New Brentford, are these signes, the Three Pidgeons, the Halfe Moone, the Lyon, the Goat, the George the Swan.
The Garter neere Hammersmith in London way towards Brentford.
At Hownslow, Henry Needles, and Martha Warwick: the signes are, the Katherin Wheele, and the George.
At Edgworth [Edgeware], Henry Haley.
At Harrow hill, Peter Jones.
At Strangreene [Strand on the Green], Thomas Blithe.
At Northket [Northolt?], Katherin Awceter.
At Thistleworth [Isleworth], Anne Parks.
At Rayslip [Ruislip], Margaret Price.
At Kenzington, Annis Turbervill, at the Lyon.
At Knightsbridge, Richard Kellway, Elizabeth Sharpe, there are three taverne signes, Grave Maurice, the Swan and the Rose.

HONORABLE AND MEMORABLE FOUNDATIONS 407

Uxbridge is a faire long market towne, it hath many innes, and foure of them be tavernes, John Raynor, Edmund Morrice, Sara Hitchcock and Michael Web: The signes are, the Chequer, the George, the Crowne, and the White horse.

The Toy taverne at Hampton-Court needs no signe.
At Twickenham Anne Palmer.
At Paddington, Walter Whitlock.
At Kingsland, George Willis; the signe, the King, or Princes Armes.
At Newington [Stoke Newington], John Usher, at the Sun.
At Islington are these signes and tavernes: the Angell, the Globe, the Lyon, the Miter, the Nags-head, the Swan, and the Sarazens head.
At Kentish towne, the Rose, Gregory Machin.
At Whetstone [Wheatstone], the Lyon, and the Princes Armes, Samuell Augier, Richard Taylor.
At White-chappell, Habacuck Kirby.
At South Mimms, Thomas Avis, the Bell.
At Hillingdon, Katherin Taylor.
At Pinner, Margery Bateman.
At Saint Giles [St Giles-in-the-Fields], John Prince, William Pearpoynt.
At Kenton, William Bird.
At Tottenham Court, John Day.
At Tottenham-highcrosse, Mathew Beuning, at the Sun.
At Chiswell street, Samuell Taylor.
At Cow-crosse [in Clerkenwell], Robert Jordane.
At Edmonton, Stephen Goodyere.
At Highgate, at the Mermayd, Mary Sell.
At Budfont [Bedfont], Thomas Weldish.
At Hackney, William Gore, and William Cave: the signes are the Mermayd and the Rose.
At Engfield [Enfield], Elizabeth Kirby, and Mary Southwell.
At Hardington [Hartington? in Chiswick], Elizabeth Osbourne.
At Totnam street, Francis Key.
At Hayes, Mary Hill.
At Feltham, Robert Butler
At Holloway street, Ezechiel Catesby, the Bell.

At Black-wall, Zachary Gilby, the signe of the Armes of the East India Company.
The Crosse at Ratcliffe, the Dragon, the Kings head, the Mermayd, the Ship, the Queenes head, the Lyon, the ship at Dickshore [Duke Shore, Limehouse], and the Hoope, and the three Kings.
In Ratcliffe high-way, the Anker, the Garter, the Rose.
At Bow, the Flower de Lice, the George, and the Kings head.
At Mile end, the Nags-head.
At Lime-house, John Jennings.
At Wapping, James Bull: the Bull, the Angell, the Crosse, the Dragon, the Gunne, the Ship, the Popes-head, the Rose, and the Kings head.
At Popler, the Ship, the Lyon.
The Bull at Stepney, and the Bull-head.

These that follow hereafter named, are already in my former booke, because they are so neere to the cities of London and Westminster, but because they are in this county of Middlesex, I will name them once more.

Neere the Bowling Alley at Westminster, Henrie Normaville.
In Galley street, Daniel Hitche.
In Holborne, William Matthewes, Thomas Simcots.
In Saint John street, Margery Baines, and Mary Moisley.
In Saint Martins in the fields, Richard Jeyner, Anne Parks, and Gertred Swan.
In Silver street, John Thomas.
In Tuttle street, Jeffrey George.
In Savoy parish, Robert Amery, and Thomas Blunt.
In the Tower Liberties, Thomas Foster.

Stanes is famous for a meadow neere it called, Rennimead or Running mead [Runnymede], where in the twelfe or thirteenth yeare of the raigne of King John, the most part of the Lords, and great States of England met, and oppos'd the king in warlike manner, the Lords rebelliously to compell the king, and the king to defend his person, and royall prerogative; and at last (after much councell and debating) they forc'd the king to yield to such conditions as were never observ'd. Stanes is a good through fare, and hath these tavernes: Thomas Wilkins, John Shorter, and Margaret Venman; the signes are, the Bush, the Bell and the Lyon.

This county had of religious houses, as abbies, nunneries, priories, frieries, colleges and hospitalls, nine. London, within and without the walles and liberties, thirty one.

It hath these hundreds, or divisions; Edmonton, Gore, Finsbury and Wenulocks, Barne, Osulston, Elthorne, Istleworth, Spelthorne.

It hath seventy three parishes, three market townes, and a hundred and one wine tavernes.

ESSEX.
Essex, or East Saxony, is a good, a great, and a rich county, stored plentifully with wood, fish, flesh, butter, cheese, saffron, and as good calves as any other county, or countrey whatsoever; in a word, it is stored with any thing, or all things needfull.

Colchester stands neere the River Colne, it is a walled towne, with fifteene churches, and one other, a most stately building, now ruined with an old castle, which time hath brought into a consumption. This towne is famous for adtiquity [sic], it was built by Coylus, a good king of Britaine, it is said that this Coylus was father to Queen Hellen, who was borne, or brought up in this towne, she was the mother of Constantine the great Emperor, who built Constantinople. Colchester hath these seven wine tavernes: Francis Kitteridg, John Portkell, Lawrence Browne, Mary Spilesby, Mary Bloomfield, Elizabeth Wyles, Elizabeth Wade.

At Barking, Joan Gowen, or George Lilly at the Bull.
At Braintree two, John Sparhawke, and Ralph Burton.
At Manningtree, George Springet, and Robert Heywood.
At Abridge, Samuell Newbold.
At Sotfield [Southfield?], Anne Dae.
At Epping, John and Mary Archer at the Cock.
At Grayes, Thomas Farnell and Edward Knightly.
At Danbury, William Dickins.
At Harlow John Josceline.
At Rochfourd, Judith Rix.

At Orsed [Orsett] neere Graies, Anthony Web.
At Raynam [Rainham], John Slany.
At Wethersfield, John Aldridge.
At Sampford Magna [Great Sampford], Ireffrey [sic] Baker.
At Pritlewell, Thomas Wait.
At Thacksted [Thaxted], Edward Constable.
At Stork [Stock], Charles Newman.
At Woodham-feries [Woodham Ferrers], Oliver Higham.
At Springfield, Richard Smith.
At Thorpe, John Beriffe.
At Wivenhoe, John Parker.
At Purfleet, Dame Martha Harris.

 Brentwood, or Burntwood, is an ancient towne and had a market and a faire, allowed by King Stephen, and continued ever since. It hath these tavernes: the Crowne, the Angell; but there are three in all, kept or allowed by Richard Smith, Jane Taylor, and John Camper, the Angell.

At high Lasterne [High Easter?], Robert Plat.
At Dagnam [Dagenham], Joan Bird.
At Lexden, John Pottler.
At Leigh, James Hare.
At Southweald, Edward Woodford.
At Aveley, Lucy Ringsoll.
At Saint Ozith [St Osyth], Thomas Rand.
At Bardfield, John Rudland.
At South Ockenden, Elizabeth Wortley.
At Dedham John Wills.
At Hornden [Horndon on the Hill], Nicholas Richold.
At Upminster, Elizabeth Saward.
At Tarling, Dina Hasler.
At Blackmore, John Pechy.
At Little Waltham, Abel White.
At Eastcolne [Earls Colne], Samuell Burton.

 Ingarstone [Ingatestone], a good towne for market, and excellent neate entertainment for travellers, it hath these tavernes: Agnis White,

John Bond.

At Bocking, Joan Kent, Francis Fitch.
At Chippinganger [Chipping Ongar], Will. Stane, Katherin Stane.
At Waltham Abby, Tho: More, Mary Waterer.
At Walthamstow, Ralph Baker, Thomas Shaw.

 Rumford [Romford] is a sweet, savery, cleane and gainfull market for hoggs, and all other sorts of swine, and of what else is needfull for mans life. It hath these tavernes, the Angell, the Bell, the White Hart, and the Cocke.

At Rawleigh [Rayleigh], Rob. Luckin, and Tho Parker.
At Dunmow, George Deane, and Agnes Gynn.
At East Tilburly [Tilbury], John French.
At Boreham, John Lane.
At Halstead 3. William Thurstone, John Coe, Thomas Harvie.
At Hithe [Hythe] neere Colchester, Edward Legg, Francis Allen.
At Ilford, Francis Blanchard, the signe of the blew Boare.

 Wittam, or Whittam [Witham] is an ancient very faire throughfaire. It was built by King Edward the Elder, in the yeare 914; which was 154 yeares before the Norman Conquest, 722 yeares since: It hath two tavernes, William Nevell (alias) Smith, and John Alexander.

At Stratford Langthon two, Ralfe Keeling, and William Lovell.
At Low Laighton, or Laighton stone [Leytonstone], Roger Falkstone, the signe of the Huntsman.
At Burnham, Robert Rowdon.
At Hatfield Peverell, Abigail Lane.

 Hatfield Broadoake, so called, because a broad oake, being a goodly faire tree grew there, that spread a great compasse. It hath one taverne kept by or for one John Earle.
 Chelmsford, a faire goodly market-towne, hath these 4 taverns, Simon Wilmot, George Solme, Nicholas Sutton, and Tho. Freeman; the signes are, the three Tunnes, the Cock, the Black boy, and the Lyon.

At Bricksley [Brightlingsea] Roger Greene.
At Kelvadon, John Theedham.

 Harwich, hath an excellent good road for shipping. It is a good strong towne, well strengthened by naturall scituation, and artificiall fortresses: it is not only full of people, but honestly peopled for the most part of them. The River Stoure there divideth Essex from Suffolke. Harwich hath three tavernes, kept or allowed by Alice Farley, Will. Hart, and Margaret Moore.

At Brookstreet at the Bull, Agmondesham Pickayes.
At Chigwell one, allowed by Tho: Pennington
At Plashie [Pleshey] and St. Annes, Will. Chandler.
At Much Parindon [Great Parndon], Roger Worthington.

 Walden, or Saffron-walden, so called for the great quantitie of saffron that growes thereabouts. It hath had a faire castle, which is now ruinated. It is a very good market towne, and it hath a corporation, with large priviledges: It hath three tavernes allowed, or inhabited by Simon Willmott, Katherine Bates and Thomas Watton.

At Much [Great] Wakering, Mawd Goldingham.
At newport, John Sell.
At Little-baddo [Baddow], Abigail Lane.
At Much [Great] Waltham, Abell White.

 Maldon was a citie in the time of Calligula the Emperour, above fourty yeares after Christ, It was then called Camallodunum: It hath beene spoyled by the Danes, and since repayred by the Normans: but by the industry of the people there, it hath beene and is still a towne of great worth and reputation: it hath a good haven, and a taverne for a safe harbour kept or allowed by Ursula Edwards.
 This countie of Essex (in the Reigne of King Henry 8.) had at the suppression of monasteries, abbies, nunneries, priories, frieries, colledges and hospitals, 35. Essex is divided into 20 severall hundreds; namely, Ultford, Hinckford, Rorchford, Chelmesford, Chaford, Winstree,

Lexden, Dengie, Ougar [sic], Tendring, Thurstable, Barstable, Dunmow, Waltham, Freshwell, Harlow, Havering, Clavering, Becontree, Wittham.

Essex hath one and twenty market townes, foure hundred and fifteene parishes, and one hundred and seven tavernes.

HARTFORDSHIRE.

Hartfordshire, is a county that surpasseth all countries and counties for making the best malt; and for good cleane High-waies, conscionable short Miles, meat, drinke, lodging for travellers, kind men, women faire and honest, and with any thing that is necessary, this county is plentifully stored withall.

Barkhamstead [Berkhamsted] is a good market towne, and it had once a castle there of strength, the ruines of it are there yet to be seene; it hath been the habitation for kings and princes, for the most noble Prince Richard, brother to the king of England, dyed there: which Richard was king of the Romanes, and earle of Cornewall. This castle ruined, is also famous, for the residence there of that most illustrious royall spark, Edward the Black Prince: and lastly, it is memorable for being the birth-place of King Richard the third. Barkhamstead hath two tavernes allowed or kept by Stephen Besowth, and Francis Baker.

At Tring, William Blacknall.
At Stevenedge, John Nodes.
At Whethamstead [Wheathampstead], Thomas Stepping.
At Redburne [Redbourne], Prudence Miles.
At Sabridgeworth [Sawbridgeworth], John Burr.
At Walton [Watton-at-Stone?], George Honor.
At Colney or Coney [Colney Heath], William Tompson.

Barnet is a good market towne for sheepe and beasts, it is a great thorow-fare, and famous for the battle fought neere it (on Easter day, the 14th of Aprill, 1471) betwixt King Edward the 4 and the Earles of Warwick and Oxford, where Warwick was slaine, and with great slaughter of men on both sides, King Edward had a bloudy victory. Barnet hath these tavernes: John Brisco at the Antelop, Henry Owen at the red Lyon, Thomas Brisco at the Rose; the Crowne.

At Baldock 2, James Haiday and John Thurgood.
At Stevenledg [Stevenage], John Nodes.
At Stansted Abby, John Giver.
At the Bell at Richmonsworth [Rickmansworth], Sara Marsh.
At Bishops Hatfield, William Walker, and Elizabeth Barefoot.

  Hartford is the provinciall towne of this Shire; there is a castle (as some write) built by King Edward the first: this towne hath been much larger, and in greater prosperity and accompt, for it had 4 churches, namely, All-Saints, and Saint Andrews, which are now standing; the other 2 are decayed, or down, their names were Saint Maries, and Saint Michaels. Hartford hath these 3 tavernes: Will: Scant at the Bell, Anne Vinmunt, Tho: Noble, Henry Chalkley, and Henry Butler; these 4 persons last named, doe inhabit and allow, the other 2 tavernes there being the signes of the Glove, and the Angell

At [Hemel] Hempstead 2, Will: Smith, and Dorcas Goodwin.
At Hitchin three, George Haiday, Thomas Harding, Priscilla Warner.
At Hoddesden, John Sydes at the Black Lyon, and Francis Williams at the Chequer.
At Waltham Crosse two, Katherin Holt at the Bell, and Rosamond Hawton.
At Royston three, Leonard Hamond, Anne Crofts, and Thomas Hagger.
At Watford 2, Edward How, and Henry Gery.
At Markatstreet [Markyate], John Crane.
At Wellwin [Welwyn], Jesper Wilshire.
At Barkway, John Rawley, and Thomas Smith.

  Ware is a great thorow-fare, and hath many faire innes, with very large bedding, and one high and mighty bed, called the Great Bed of Ware: a man may seeke all England over, and not find a married couple that can fill it. Ware hath 3 tavernes: Wil: Cross, or Wil: Raste at the Crown, Shelton Amery, Christopher Robinson, widow Hall at the George, also she keepes a wine-seller at the Christopher.
At Bishops-starford [Stortford] two, George Hawkins, and John Cheyny.
At Buntingford two, Edward Bullen, and Anne Hensham.
At Wormeley, Rich: Bishop at the Black Lyon.

At Much-hadham, Edmund Rustat.
At Puckeridge two, Sir John Wats doth allow one, and the other is inhabited or allowed under one Will: Northage.

Saint Albanes is famous for antiquity, and for the death of our English proto-martyr St. Alban, hee was martyr'd there in the raigne of Dioclesian the emperor, ann. 268. After he had suffred many torments, lastly his head was struck off, and immediatly the executioner was struck blind. Offa king of the Mercians built the goodly abby church there, an. 795. and the said church was dedicated to Christ and St. Alban, from whom the town hath denomination. The brazen font in the church was brought out of Scotland by Sir Richard Lea Knight, an. 1543. in the 36 yeare of the raigne of K Henry the 8. This towne is also famous for two memorable bloody battels there betwixt K. Edward the 4. and K. Henry the 6. where both the kings had various fortunes: It hath these wine tavernes; the Blew Bore, the Lyon, the Kings Armes.

Kingslangley is also famous for being sometimes the residence of kings, Edmund of Langley, Son to K. Edward the third was borne there, and K. Richard the second was first buried there: It hath a tavern kept or allowed by Rose Deacon.

At Abbots Langley, one Nicholas Breakespeare was borne, who was afterwards Pope of Rome by the name of Hadrian the 4th, he died suddenly chok'd with a fly in his cup.

This county of Hartford, had, at the suppression of popery, 22 religious houses, as abbies, etc. It hath 8 divisions or hundreds; namely, Odsey, Caysho, Branghing, Hartford, Hiching, Edwinstree Broadwater, and Dacorum. This county hath 18 market townes; 120 parishes, and 52 tavernes.

HAMPSHIRE.
Hampshire, or Hantshire, is a goodly rich county, abounding in corne, wood, pasture, and much enriched with innumerable Commodities from the sea

Southampton is a faire, sweet and pleasant town, it hath had triall of both fortunes often, it was quite consumed by fire, in the raigne of K. Edward the 3. anno1337. since when it is better re-edified and much increased, well defenced with wals; turrets, a haven, and a strong castle built by K. Richard the second, it is rich in marchants and inhabitants, and by the grant of K. Henry the 6. it is a county of itselfe. It hath 8 wine tavernes, either allowed or inhabited by Thomas Miles, Tho: Stoner, Tho. Smith, Augustine Reignolds, Oliver Stoner, Elizabeth King, Eliz: Nevey, and Eliz: Elzey.

At Mew-church [Newchurch? IoWight], Benjamin Newland.
At Alton 3. Jo. Butler, Jo. Goldsbery, Basill Kemp.
At Basing-stoake three, Anne Cross, or Robert White at the Bell, Avis Tate, or Anthony Spittle at the Maydenhead, Thomasin Barrell, or Captaine Marlow at the George.

Ringwood is a very ancient towne, it was in estimation and prosperity more than 1100. yeares ago in the raigne of Cerdicus, K. of West Saxons, anno 508. it is now a good market town, and hath 2 taverners allowed by Will: Tarvar and John Wiseman.

At Petersfield two, Richard Goodwin, and Agnes Wood.
At Stokebridge [Stockbridge] one, Francis Leison.
At Havant, William Woolgar.
At Fareham, Anne Wilks.
At Alsford [Alresford] three, Anne Tinkeridg, Rachell Tinkeridg, Mary Williams.
At Buckland [now in Portsmouth], Henry Fabyn.

Tichfield [Titchfield], where K. Henry the sixt was married to the valiant Virago, Qu. Margaret, daughter to Reinard Earle of Anjou. and titularie king of Scicilia and Jerusalem. There is a goodly house, the chiefe seat and residence of the honorable Earle of Southhampton. Tichfield hath one tavern, Rich: Brown.

At Andover three, John Milier, John Hercy, and Mary Sowth.
At Hook, Bridget Woolfe, the signe of the Bell.
At Romsey three, Alexander Elver, William Bloys, and Dorothy Loade.

Christ-Church, by the Saxons, it had once a castle in it of a good strength; the towne was much repaired by one Ralph Flammard Bp. of

Durham, anno 1094. in the raign of K. Rufus, or William the 2. this bishop was deane of this Christ Church, and there he erected a fair monastery. This town hath one taverne, John Powson.

At Warnford [Warneford], Richard Woods, and Mabell Vinn.
At Limmington [Lymington], George Castle.
At Castbrooke [Carisbrooke], Margaret Hayles.
At Newport, in the Isle of Wight, one John James, may, or doth keepe three tavernes.
At Newtowne, Jarvice Taylor.
At Cowse three, Morgan Adams, Margaret Hayles, William Edwards.
At Yarmuth, Anne Garyre.

At Brading, John James. So there are nine taverns in the Ile of Wight. This iland to the county of Hampshire, is 20 miles in length and 12 miles in bredth in the broadest place; it is a most plentifull strong defencible countrey, sea, art and nature made so. It is peopled with valiant and warlike inhabitants, Henry Bewchamp Earle of Warwick was crowned king of the Ile of Wight, in the raigne of King Henry the sixt.

At Forthingbridg [Fordingbridge] one taverne, Richard Boen.
At Hambledon one, Christopher Organ.
At Bishops Waltham one, John Hawksworth.
At Eastincon [East Meon?] one, Jane Loving.
At Botley, Dorathy Doncastle.

Winchester is a very famous and ancient citty, it was the royall seat of the West Saxon kings; it had 6 houses in it for coining and minting mony in the raigne of King Athelstane; and long since that all the publike records and evidences of the whole kingdom of England were kept there. This citie hath been twice fired by sudden mis-fortunes; and in King Stephens raigne it was sack'd and spoil'd by rude soldiers that belong'd to the king, and Mawd the Empresse factions; but after it was much enrich'd by the royall favour of King Edward the 3, who caused a mart or staple of wooll and cloth to be kept there, but since (as times hath altred) this worthy city hath suffred many changes, yet still with fame and reputation she beares up her head. Winchester hath 4 tavernes Joan Prat, Anne Bud, Thomas Brexton, and Cornelius Brexton.

At Soake [Soke], neere Winchester three, William Pope, John Noake, and Walter Travers.
At Lippock [Liphook], Robert Palmer.
At Sutton Sconey [Scotney], Michaell Nicholas.
At Hartlerow [Hartley Row], Anthony Maynard, or John Wild at the George.

Portsmouth, so called, because it stands at the mouth of the port or haven; it is a strong towne and fortresse, with a garrison; and it thrives better by war than by peace: It hath 4 tavernes, Richard James, Owen Jennings, Dorothy Jennings, and William Haberley. Portsmouth liberties, one Anthony Haberly hath, or may keepe two tavernes.

At Gosport, neere Portsmouth two, Anne Clarke, and William Towerson.
At Hartford bridge, Thomas Bickton, or William Wild at the Swan.
At Milbrooke, Margery Strood.

Odiam [Odiham] is a pretty market towne, where sometimes David King of the Scots was kept prisoner, in King Eward [sic] the third's raigne; since when, the kings of England have, and do, now, and then lodge there in a royall mansion of their owne: there was a fortresse there in the raigne of King John, of such strength, that thirteene Englishmen, did hold it fifteen dayes against Lewis the Daulphin of France, who assaulted it with a mighty armie, yet could not win it from the said thirteen men. Odiam hath one taverne, kept by Bridget Dickenson, or one Mistrisse Keyes, at the George.

Hampshire had at the suppression of popery, of abbies, nunneries, priories, frieries, colleges, hospitals 30. This shire hath 18 market townes, parishes 253. It is divided into 40 hundreds, or divisions, as Crundon, Acton, Selburne, Odiam, Eastmean, Sutton, Bartenstacy, Finchdeane, Portsdown, Tichfield, Mansbridge, Meanstock, Fawley, Hambledon, Budlegate, Redbridge, Kings, Sombourne, Andover within, Andover without, Hornwell, Bosmere, Fareham, Averstock and Gosport, Waltham, Eringer, Pastrac, Kings Cleare, Thoragate, Overton, Basingstoake extra Holdshot, Christ-church, New-forrest, Ringwood,

Barmanspit, Forthingbridge, Buntsborough, Mainsborough, Chutesey, and Michell dever. Number of tavernes in this county seventy three.

BARKSHIRE.
Barkeshire is a rich and plentifull county, and a great helpe to her neighbour provinces for wood and corne; which necessary commodities are the cause that no other thing fitting for mans use is wanting in this countie.

Windsor is a daintie, faire, and spacious towne, with a royall castle, of such magnificent structure, and so scited and seated, that for prospect it is unparalleld, and deserves respect transcendent beyond all the princely fabricks in Great Brittain. That victorious Mars of men, King Edw. 3. was borne in Winsor, and he founded the said castle. He held prisoners King John of France, and David K. of Scots: since which time the castle was made more stately and conspicuous by King Edw. 4. and a noble Knight Sir Reignold Bray was at great charge in the augmenting of it; since when the famous and worthy memorable Queene Elizabeth, beautified it with the stone gallery, or walke towards the Thames. The right honourable Order of the Garter was first instituted by K. Edw 3. at Burdeaux in France, but since that time it hath bin continued at Winsor for that noble installation: and in the beautifull chappell there, are all the armes and hatchments of that noble fellowship, placed in their degrees. Also in this famous castle was borne that good and pious King Henry the 6 who founded Æton Colledge, and the worthy structure of Kings Colledge in Cambridge. Winsor hath these tavernes, the Crosskeyes, the George, the Garter, and the White Hart.

Wantage is a place of great antiquity, long before the Norman Conquest there was a house for the king, for Aelfred the 23 king of the West Saxons was borne there, who raigned, anno 872: there is or may be two tavernes kept by Edward Gallant at the signe of the Elephant.

At Buscot one, Adam Kirby.
At Twyford one, Henry Millward.
At Enborne one, Anne Plantin.
At Wareseile [Warfield?] one, Thomas Garson.

Abendun, Abbington, or Abinton [Abingdon], the name was

first derived from a famous abby built there by Cissa, one of the Saxon kings, which abby was throwne downe by the Danes, and after raised againe by king Edgar anno 995. since which time it grew to that state and greatnesse, that scarse any monastry in England could top it either for wealth or pomp; but there remaines little or nothing of it now but ruines and rubbish, as reliques of the greatnesse which once it had, from it the towne was called abby-town, now changed into the name Abington; it is a faire and sweet scituation, famous for a rare crosse in the market place, and for plenty of mault made and sold there: It hath but one taverne kept by one John Prince, who at his pleasure may keepe three tavernes there if he will.

At Theale one, John Bowyer.
At Winfield [Winkfield] one, John Hawkins.
At Binfield, Richard Williams.
At Thackham [Thatcham], Robert Humphrey.
At Farington [Faringdon] two, Simon Turner, and Margaret Handy.
At Okingham [Wokingham] two, Will: Hunt, and Rich: Thorp.
At Lamburne one, kept by one Daintree at the two neck'd Swan.
At Hungerford one, Thomas Smith.

Wallingford was a good towne in the raigne of K. Edward the Confessor. an. 1042. It hath been a walled towne, as appeares by the ruines of it, with a strong castle neere the river of Thames, which is now almost defac'd into fragments. King Stephen with all his force could not win it from the besieged empresse Mawd; In the raigne of K. Edw. 3. an 1334 this town was of such greatnesse that it had 12 churches, which now are demolished and diminished to 1, or scarce two; (such are the changes of transitory things) it is a good market town, and stands commodiously, having two tavernes under William Donnington and John Smith.

Newbery is a rich town for the trade of clothing, it sprang out of the consumption of an old towne, which is neere it, called Spene, or Spinhamlands; there are three tavernes, under John Greenoway, Thomas Howes, and Anthony Linch.

Spinhamland [Speenhamland] hath two tavernes under Richard Cox, and James Garroway.

Maydenhead is so called, as some say, of a maid's head that was cut off at Colleyne in Germany, which from thence was brought thither, and worshipped; the people supposing it to be the Head of one of the 1100 virgins (or maids) that suffred with Saint Ursula, how certaine it is I know not, but this I know, that there are good inns, lodging and entertainment, halfe of it being in the parish of Bray, having these taverns: the Beare, the Greyhound the Lyon, the White hart, the Sarazens head: It may be one too many.

Reading is the prime and principall town in this county of Barkshire, for faire buildings, large streets for cloathing and other blessings: King Henry the first, with his wife, and his daughter Mawd the empresse, were buried there. Reading hath these tavernes, kept or allowed by John Domelaw, Elizabeth Foster, John Bagley, Richard Alexander, John Skot, and George Duell at the George.

This shire had at suppression of monasteries, of abbies, nunneries, priories, frieries, colleges and hospitals, 14. It is divided into 20 devisions, or hundreds; namely, Hormer, Farington, Ganfield, Shrievenham, Kentbury, Oke, Braye, Wanting, Riplemore, Compton, Morton, Cookeham, Barnelth, Lamborne, Wargrove, Reading, Sunning, Theale, Charleton, and Fairecrosse.

Barkshire hath also 11 good market townes, 140 parishes, and 40 tavernes.

SURREY.

Surrey, or Southrey, because it lies south from the river of Thames, it is a rich county, and if the inhabitants do not want thankfulnesse to God, there is nothing wanting (either pleasant or profitable) for the life and maintainance of men.

Farnham is a fine towne in the rode betwixt London and Winchester, it hath a faire castle in it, which was built by Henry Earle of Bloys, brother to King Stephen; it stands lofty on a hill, seeming to overlooke the towne, as it overtops it; it was throwne downe by King Henry the third, in the barons wars; but the bishops of Winchester (who are the owners of it) hath from time to time rais'd and repaired it to that goodly structure. The town hath 3 tavernes inhabited or allowed under John Folder, Anne Hoore, and Anne Martin.

At Haselmere one, Robert Palmer.
At Cobham, John Perior.
At Godstone two, the Bell and the Greyhound.
At Peckham one, the Greyhound.
At Linyuill [Lyne Hill], Thomas Chapman.
At Lederhead, or Leatherhead two, John Rogers, Thomas Clark.
At Byfleet one, John Baily.
At Mowlsey [Molesey], Anthony Powell.

    Chertsey is a pretty little market towne neere the Thames, where there is a decayed left handed bridge over the river, I wish it mended, the people are for the most part very kind and honest. It hath or may have 2 taverns, Ellin Day, and John Stare.
At Croydon 2, the George and the Greyhound.

    Guilford [Guildford] is a good market towne where kings have kept their court as appeares by an old decaied house there to this day. Also, there are the ruines of an ancient castle to be seene neere the brooke: This towne hath very faire innes, and good entertainment, at the tavernes, the Angell, the Crowne, the White hart and the Lyon.

At Wimbleton, the two Lyons and Wheat-sheafe.
At Godalming (corruptly called Godlyman) are two, under Henry Westbrooke and George Bridger.
At Bagshot are two, the Bush, Scipio le Squire, or Mr. Anthill, and Robert Battin at the Lyon.
At Barnes, Richard Hill at the Beare.

    Rygate [Reigate] is anciently famous for affronting and repulsing the Danes neer there in Holensedale, neere which is a ruinated castle, called Holme Castle; the tavernes may be two, but William Pistor hath the command, the Hart.

At Little Monlesey [West Molesey?], Parnell Nitingale, White hart.
At Riple [Ripley], Anne Stanton at the Dog.
At Stretham [Streatham], William Lads at the Antelop.
At Barmestreet [Banstead?] one, Julian Haberley.
At Cashalton [Carshalton] one, Mary Rutleage at the White Lyon.

At Lambeth and Lambeth Marsh, the Faulcon, the Kings head, the White Lyon, the Three Squirrels, the Three Tuns, the Vine.
At Egham, the Kings head, and Katherin wheele, by Elizabeth Clarke, and Margaret Guy.
At Micham [Mitcham] one, William Holland.
At Tooting one, Elinor Serient.
At Mortlake two, Miles Bourne at the Princes Armes, and Phebe Tucker at the Maidenhead.
At Waddon one, Christian Weller.
At Camberwell, John Stratfield, and Jane Webb.
At Bleechingles [Blechingley], Anne Fince.
At Waybridge [Weybridge], Kate Williams.

Kinston [Kingston], a very commodious and good well govern'd towne, an excellent market (especially for corne.) In old time it had a faire castle belonging to the earls of Glocester. Three Saxon kings were crowned there on a Scaffold in the market place, namely, Edwin, Athelstane, and Etheldred, in memory of which there are the figures of those kings in the church. Before those kings were crowned there, the towne was called Mereford, and ever since those coronations, it hath bin called Kingston, or the kings towne. Parliaments have bin held there divers times: It hath many good innes, and these tavernes, the Castle, the Crane, the Kings head, the Saracens head, and the Hand in hand.

At Meistham [Merstham], Reignold Durkin.
At Battersea, Henry Norton, Anne Boswell, the Mermayd. At Darking, Toby Ridge, Edward Goodman, and John Comber.
At Ewell two, Katherin Umbrevile, and Francis Kendall: but one may serve that towne, and doth (as I think) which is the signe of the Popinjay.
At Newington, the Bull, and the Kings Armes.
At Putney 2. the white Lyon, and the red Lyon.
At Wandsworth, Mary Gibson, Sith Browne, and William Sherlocke.
At Cobham, the Lyon, the George.
The Golden Lyon neere old Paris Garden.
At Rederhith [Rotherhithe] three, the Mermayd, the Sun, and the Rose.

Richmond, was called Sheene before K. Henry the 7. built the stately palace there. There was a goodly house neere the said foundation in old time, for K. Edw. 3. died there: so likewise did Queen Anne the wife of K. Richard 2. King Henry 5. built much there, which being burnt by casuall misfortune, K. Henry 7. built upon the old ground-worke. In that Palace that now is, dyed the sayd royall founder of it, King Henry, and after that there died his grandchild Queen Elizabeth, both unmatchable princes for internall and externall endowments. There are two tavernes, the Lyon, and the Princes Armes.

This county of Surrey had at the suppression of monasteries, abbies, nunneries, priories, frieries, colledges and hospitalls, 14. It hath 8 market townes, and it is divided into thirteene hundreds, or Divisions, namely, Chertsey, Woking, Farnham, Emley Bridge, Darking, Croydon, Kingston, Blackheath, and Wooton, Capthome, and Effingham, Godalming, Tanridge, Reygate, Brixton and Wallington. It hath 140 parishes, and of tavernes 71.

BUCKINGHAMSHIRE.
Buckinghamshire is a rich and fat soyle, and by the bountie of heaven plentifully replenished with the fruits of the earth.

Marlow, was so named because it stands in chaulkie or marle ground: it is a good market towne, and hath one taverne under John Farmour.

At Winslow, Nicholas Brinsall.
At Chaffant, [Chalfont] Robert Ducke.
At Burnham, John Phipp.
At Oney [Olney], Lewis Ablestone.

Brill is so ancient, that King Edward the confessor had a house in it, and sometimes kept his court there. It hath bin formerly a market town; it is a place most fertill and fruitfull, and hath a brave, beautifull, and pleasant prospect. It hath one taverne, the Kings Armes, kept by Christopher Gregorie.

At Brickhill two, John Hutchinson, and Jane Holmes.
At Cheneis [Chenies], John Barefoot.
At Hanslap [Hanslope], Richard Perry.

At Newport Pagnell two, John Prestman, and Elizabeth White.
At Slowgh two, the Crowne, and the White Hart, John Checkley.
At Fenny streetford, John Kims.
At Ever [Iver], William Atkins.

    Alesbery [Aylesbury] (as some say) so called for brewing of most mighty capitoll ale, as browne as a berry; it is a good market town, and hath these tavernes, and signes, Joseph Sexton, Jeffrey Standley and Anne Goldsworth, the George, the Kings head, and the Bush.

At Amersham, John Cross, Edward Bayly, and Tobias Saunders.
At Challey [Chearsley?], Robert Paine.
At Marsh Gibbon, Mary Robins.
At Beconsfield [Beaconsfield], Richard Bentley, Sara Hayles, the Bell.

    East Wickham [Wycombe], or high Wickham is a faire town, and a maior town, with these tavernes, the Lyon, the Nagshead, and the Katherin Wheele; but Mr. George Wells may (if he please) keep one more.

At West-wickham [Wycombe], Mary Wells.
At Farnham Royall, William Baldwin.
At Chessham [Chesham], Daniell West, and Eliz: Wolfe.
At Æton [Eton] two, Francis Dickinson, and Peter Wiggot; the signes there, are the Christopher, and the Sun.
At Missenden two, William Harris, and Thomas Gardner.
At Whit-church, William Theed.
At Ivinghoe, Edward Anthony.
At Wendover two, Richard Rowell, and Ralph Hill, the Lyon.

    Stonystretford [Stony Stratford] is so named for the place where it stands, and much of the countrey neere it is very stony; there is a taverne there, the signe of the Cock, Lloyde.
At Amesford two, the Sarazens head, the Bush.
    Colebrooke [Colnbrook] is a great through-fare, and hath these taverns, the George, the Estrich, the Katherin wheel Thomas Meale, Thomas Charley, John Childe.

At Prince Resborow [Princes Risborough], William Hastlegrove.

Buckingham is the provinciall towne of this shire, and hath these tavernes, the Cock and the Bush: Alexander Stotusbury, and Elizabeth Pollard.

This county had at suppression of monasteries, abbies, nunneries, priories, frieries, colleges and hospitals 22. It hath 8 divisions, or hundreds, Assenden, Stock, Newport, Burnham, Buckingham, Disborough, Collstow, Alesbery. It hath 11 market townes, 185 parishes, and 47 tavernes.

OXFORDSHIRE.
Oxfordshire is scarce second to any county in England for plenty of corne and pasturage, wood and fruits of all sorts, that this kingdome yields. It is also excellently watred with fine sweet rivers, as Ouse, or Isis, which some doe call the Thames; and the little River Cherwell also glides into it, so that this shire is furnish'd in plenty with fresh river fish of sundry kinds.

Banbury is a goodly faire market towne, and (as the learned Cambden) it is famous for cakes, cheese and zeale: it hath three taverns kept by Martin Wright, Elizabeth Collins, and Mathew Alsop.

At Stoken Church, Augustine Belson, the signe the White Hart.
At Nettlebed two, John White and Joh. Crowch: the signes are the Bull, and the Lyon.
At Watlington, Elizabeth Colebrooke.
At Bampton, Simon Turner.

Burfourd [Burford] is a good market towne, but beware of a Burfourd bayt, for it may breed the staggers: there are 3 tavernes inhabited or allowed under Edmund Hening, Agnes Dalby, and Simon Hator.

At Chippingnorton two, Christopher Deane, and Henry Cornish.
At Witney, Tho. Brooke at the Kings Armes.

Dorchester was a faire and goodly citie 1000 yeares agoe, for in anno 642. Oswald king of Northumberland, was a Godfather to one

Cingilse, a king of the West Saxons, which king was converted from paganisme to Christianity, and was then and there baptized in this town of Dorchester. The Cuines [sic, i.e. ruines] whereof that are neere it, doe shew in part how far the ancient greatnesse extended, it is now but a little towne; the River of Tame doth fall into Isis hard by this towne: it hath one taverne, inhabited or allowed by Elizabeth Bernard.

At Stratton Awdley [Audley] there is one taverne, under the licence of John Burlace Esquire.
At Enstone, Richard Canning, and Mary Ayldworth.

  Thame is a good market towne, and is so named from the river of Tame or Thame that waters it; it hath two tavernes, Thomas Ballow, and Richard Kendall, the signes are the Red Lyon, and the Swan.
  At Benson one, Edward Snelling.
  Woodstocke house, or the kings pallace there was built by King Henry the 1. and the park there was also by him enclosed. This house was after made a pallace of private pleasure by King Henry the second, where hee injoyed his fading contentment with the faire Rosamond Clifford: The town is a pretty market towne, and chiefly famous for the breeding of the worthy Jeffrey Chaucer, the most ancient arch-Poet of England. Woodstocke hath sometimes but one taverne, and sometimes two, according to the pleasure of Mr. Tho: Rayer.

At Tatsworth [Tetsworth] two, John Poyner, and Elizabeth Tanner.
At Deddington two, Katherin Bennet, and Mary Baker.
At Islip two, Edward Stoakley, William Bradley, Kings head, Princes Armes.
At Wheatley two, John Smith, and Athaliah Robinson.

  Hendley or Henley is an excellent market town, with these tavernes, the White hart and the Elephant. Also, there is a taverne with a bush only, at the Bowling Green without the towne in Ox ford way. Robert Heyborne, Richard Pinder, and John Stevens.

OXFORD.
As the glorious beames of the resplendant sun cannot be made more

coruscant by the light of a silly taper, and as a drop of raine augments not the boundlesse ocean, so would any thing that should be spoken, or written by mee in the praise of this famous university and city be most needlesse or impertinent. The vigour of Hercules could not be encreased with the strength of a Pismire; it is high presumption to shew Apollo the grounds of poetry, or to teach the Muses (whose habitation is there) and there is the inexhausible magazin of all arts, Learning, and good littrature; therfore, with that little parcell of Latine which is translated out of Greeke, and spoken by Apelles the famous painter, Ne Sutor Ultra Crepidam, I will take leave of the university, and speake of the tavernes, which are five, Francis Harris, William Turner, Thomas Hallom, William Grice and Humphrey Budwit; the signes are the Mermayd, the Swan, the other three are onely bushes.

This shire had at the suppression of the Romish religion, of monasteries, abbies, nunneries, etc. 26. This county is devided into 14 hundreds or devisions; namely, Langtree, Bloxham, Tame, Banburie, Wootton, Binfield, Ewelme, Pitton, Chadlington, Bampton, Bullington, Plowghley, Dorchester, and Lewknor. Also Oxfordshire hath 11 market townes, 208 parishes, and 40 wine tavernes.

The totall of all the tavernes in all the ten shires and counties aforesaid, are 686, or thereabouts.

FINIS.

THE CARRIERS COSMOGRAPHIE

*T*HE THIRD COMPONENT *of Taylor's investigation of inns and taverns during 1636 was the most ambitious, the most troublesome to compile, and by far the most significant for historians.*[1] *That he saw it as a companion to the two preceding publications he makes clear in his preface, which also suggests that he contemplated revising it in future. Taylor, like any self-publicist, was fond of giving his pamphlets grandiose, eye-catching titles, so that one is inclined to overlook the significance of 'cosmographie'. Peter Heylyn's* Cosmographie *(1652), a kind of universal geography, was fifteen years in the future when Taylor wrote, but the word, and its simile 'chorography', had a scholarly, patrician ring about it, as employed by the early leisured antiquaries and topographers. Taylor translated it to the workaday, lowly activities of the common carrier and his associates, perhaps to show that they too, at their level, had devised a method for organising the world, and through their toil for making it run smoothly.*

Carriers in early modern England, and in many places until 1914, made inns at their urban destinations their depots, for dispatch and receipt of goods, for business of all kinds, and for accommodation for themselves and their horses. Taylor's pioneering directory of London carriers and their inns was therefore, as he intended, a useful directory, but it was also a demonstration that a network set to a regular timetable was in place to convey anything to anywhere in Britain and beyond. No-one, so far as is known, had attempted this before, although carriers had been plying their trade between the provinces and London for several centuries; nor was Taylor's survey repeated until 1681, by Thomas Delaune, and then in greater and more reliable detail.

The directory is arranged by letter of the alphabet (but not strictly alphabetically) of the places whence the carriers came. The main list is followed by a shorter account, arranged by inn, of the carriers from Kent,

---

[1] I am indebted to Dorian Gerhold, whose *London Carriers and Coaches 1637-1690* (2016) analyses and explains the work, and compares it with later listings.

Surrey and Sussex, whose practice was to lodge in Southwark, south of the river. Finally, there is useful information about the coastal and river trade, with details of the quays and wharves of embarkation.

Until a few decades before Taylor's list most carriers would have used packhorses, although some had two-wheeled vehicles known as wains. But by the 1620s four-wheeled waggons were also quite widely in use, and these occur infrequently in the Cosmographie, *along with coach-waggons (which were similar), footposts and a single higgler, or pedlar. Carriers worked to a fixed weekly cycle, journeying on set days between home town (or nearby village) and their London inn, so that listing them should have been straightforward. But two problems confronted Taylor. Since several carriers might travel together to nearby destinations and serve intermediate towns on their way, it was not always easily to distinguish between them. And because when he compiled his list there had been recent legislation restricting and ordering their activities, carriers were understandably suspicious of Taylor's motives, and so were reluctant to supply him with the information he required. Consequently the result should not be regarded as comprehensive nor entirely accurate, and cannot be used for statistical calculations.*

Setting aside these imperfections Taylor's Cosmography stands as a considerable achievement, and he deserves respect for his dedication in providing a useful directory for his contemporaries, and for later historians an invaluable window on a humble but necessary and well organised trade. In the following transcript original place-name spellings have been retained, and the modern form indicated [in square brackets] when identification is not obvious.

(Text derived from Huntington Library copy C23740 13692 (online at Historical Texts EEBO, from STC); and checked against a copy in the Hartlib Papers, University of Sheffield (online at: http://www.dhi.ac.uk/hartlib).)

THE CARRIERS COSMOGRAPHIE. or A Briefe Relation, of The Innes, Ordinaries, Hosteries, and other lodgings in, and neere London, where the Carriers, Waggons, Foote-posts and Higglers, doe usually come, from any parts, townes, shires and countries, of the Kingdomes of England, Principality of Wales, as also from the Kingdomes of Scotland and Ireland.

THE CARRIERS COSMOGRAPHIE

With nomination of what daies of the weeke they doe come to London, and on what daies they returne, whereby all sorts of people may finde direction how to receiue, or send, goods or letters, unto such places as their occasions may require.

As also, Where the Ships, Hoighs, Barkes, Tiltboats, Barges and wherries, do usually attend to Carry Passengers, and Goods to the coast Townes of England, Scotland, Ireland, or the Netherlands; and where the Barges and Boats are ordinarily to bee had that goe up the River of Thames westward from London.

By John Taylor.
London Printed by A. G. 1637.

To all Whom it may concerne, with my kinde remembrance to the Posts, Carriers, Waggoners and Higglers.

If any man or woman whomsoever hath either occasion or patience to Read this following description, it is no doubt but they shall find full satisfaction forasmuch as they laid out for the booke, if not, it is against my will, and my good intentions are lost and frustrate. I wrote it for three Causes, first for a generall and necessary good use for the whole Common-wealth, secondly to expresse my gratefull duty to all those who have honestly paid me my mony which they owed me for my Bookes of the collection of Tavernes, in London and Westminster, and tenne shires or Counties next round about London, and I doe also thanke all such as doe purpose to pay me heereafter: thirdly, (for the third sort) that can pay me and will not; I write this as a document: I am well pleased to leave them to the hangmans tuition (as being past any other mans mending) for I would have them to know, that I am sensible of the too much losse that I doe suffer by their pride or cousenage, their number being so many, and my charge so great, which I paid for paper and printing of those bookes, that the base dealing of those sharks is Insupportable; But the tedious Toyle that I had in this Collection, and the harsh and unsavoury answers that I was faine to take patiently, from Hostlers, Carriers, and Porters, may move any man that thinks himselfe mortall to pitty me.

A direction to the reader

In some places I was suspected for a proiector, or one that had devised some tricke to bring the Carriers under some new taxation; and sometimes I was held to have been a man taker, a Serieant or baylife to arrest or attach mens good or beasts; indeed I was scarce taken for an honest man amongst the most of them: all which suppositions I was inforced oftentimes to wash away, with two or three Jugges of Beere, at most of the Innes I came to; In some Innes or Hosteries, I could get no certaine Intelligence, so that I did take Instructions at the next Inne unto it, which I did oftentimes take upon trust though I doubted it was indirect and imperfect,

    Had the Carriers hostlers and others knowne my harmelesse and honest intendments, I doe thinke this following relation, had beene more large and usefull, but if there be any thing left out in this first Impression, it shall be with diligence inserted hereafter, when the Carriers and I shall bee more familiarly acquainted, and they, with the hostlers, shall be pleased in their ingenerosity, to afford me more Ample directions. In the meane space, I hope I shall give none of my Readers cause to curse the Carrier that brought me to towne.

    Some may object that the Carriers doe often change and shift from one Inne or lodging to another, whereby this following direction may be heereafter untrue, to them I answer, that I am not bound to binde them, or to stay them in any place, but if they doe remove, they may be enquired for at the place which they have left or forsaken, and it is an easie matter to finde them by the learned intelligence of some other Carrier, an hostler, or an understanding Porter.

    Others may obiect and say that I have not named all the townes and places that Carriers doe goe unto in England and Wales: To whom I yeeld, but yet I answer, that if a Carrier of Yorke hath a letter or goods to deliver at any towne in his way thither, he serves the turne well enough, and there are carriers and messengers from Yorke to carry such goods and letters as are to be past any waies north, broad and wide as farre or further than Barwicke [Berwick]: so he that sends to Lancaster, may from thence have what he sends conveyd to Kendall, or Cockermouth, and what a man sends to Hereford may from thence be passed to Saint

Davids in Wales, the Worster carriers can convey any thing as farre as Carmarthen, and those that goe to Chester may send to Carnarvan: the carriers or posts that goe to Exeter may send daily to Plimouth, or to the Mount in Cornewall, Maxfield [Marshfield], Chipnam, Hungerford, Newberry: and all those Townes betweene London and Bristow, the Bristow carriers doe carry letters unto them, so likewise all the townes and places are served, which are betwixt London and Lincolne, or Boston, Yarmouth, Oxford, Cambridge, Walsingham, Dover, Rye or any places of the Kings Dominions with safe and true carriage of goods and letters; as by this little bookes directions may be perceived. Besides, if a man at Constantinople or some other remote part or Region shall chance to send a letter to his parents, master, or friends that dwell at Nottingham, Derby, Shrewsbury, Exeter, or any other towne in England; then this booke will give instructions where the Carriers doe lodge that may convey the said letter, which could not easily be done without it: for there are not many that by hart or memory can tell suddenly where and when every carrier is to be found, I have (for the ease of the Reader and the speedier finding out of every townes name, to which any one would send, or from whence they would receive, set them downe by way of Alphabet; and thus Reader if thou beest pleased, I am satisfied, if thou beest contented, I am paid, if thou beest angry, I care not for it.

A speedy way to finde out all Carriers

A

The Carriers of Saint Albanes doe come every Friday to the signe of the Peacocke in Aldersgate street, on which daies also commeth a coach from Saint Albanes to the bell in the same street, the like coach is also there for the Carriage of passengers every Tuesday.

The Carriers of Abington doe lodge at the George in bred-street, they do come on Wednesdaies and goe away on Thursdaies.

The Carriers of Aylsbury, in Buckingham shire, doe lodge at the George neere Holborne bridge, and at the swan in the strand, and at the Angel behinde Saint Clements church, and at the bell in holborne, they are at one of these places every other day.

The Carriers of Asbur [Happisburgh, Norfolk?] doe lodge at the castle in great wood-street, they are to bee found there on Thursdaies, Fridaies and Saturdaies.

B

The Carriers of Blanvile [Blandford] in Dorcetshire, doe lodge at the chequer neere Charing crosse, they doe come thither every second Thursday, also there commeth carriers from Blandfourd, to the signe of the Rose neere Holbourne bridge.

The Carriers of Brayntree, and Bocking in Essex doe lodge at the signe of the Tabbard in Gracious street, (neere the conduit) they doe come on Thursdaies and goe away on Fridaies.

The Carriers of Bathe doe lodge at the three cups in bread street they come on Fridaies and goe on Saturdaies.

The Carriers of Bristow [Bristol] doe lodge at the three Cups in bred-street, and likewise from Bristow on Thursdaies a Carrier which lodgeth at the swan neere to holborne bridge,

The Carriers of Brewton [Bruton, Somerset] in Dorcetshire doe lodge at the Rose neere holborne bridge, they come on Thursdaies and goe away on frydaies.

The Carriers from divers parts of Buckinghamshire and Bedfordshire, are almost every day to bee had at the signe of the Saracens head without Newgate.

The Carriers of Broomsbury [Bromsberrow, Glos?], doe lodge at the signe of the Maidenhead in Cat-eatonstreet, neere the guildhall in London, they come on Thursdaies and goe away on Fridaies.

The Carriers of Bingham, in Nottinghamshire, doe lodge at the blacke bull in smithfield, they come on Fridaies.

The Carriers of Bramley [Abbots or Kings Bromley?] in Staffordshire, doe lodge at the castle neere smithfield barres, they come on Thursdaies and goe away on Fridaies or Saturdaies.

The Carriers of Burfoord in Oxfordshire, doe lodge at the bell in Friday street, they come on Thursdaies and goe away on Fridaies.

The Carriers of Buckhingham doe lodge at the kingshead in the old change, they come Wednesdaies and Thursdaies.

The Carrriers of Buckingham, doe lodge at the saracens head in carter lane, they come and goe Fridaies and Saturdaies.

The Carriers of Bewdley in Worcestershire, doe lodge at the castle in woodstreet, they come and goe Thursdaies, Fridaies and Saturdaies.

The Carriers of Buckingham, doe lodge at the George neere holborne bridge, they come and goe on Wednesdaies, Thursdaies and Fridaies.

The Carries [sic] of Brackley in Northamptonshire, doe lodge at the George neere holborne bridge, they come and goe on Wednesdaies Thursdaies and Fridaies.

The Carriers of Banbury in Oxfordshire doe lodge at the George neere holborne bridge, they goe and come Wednesdaies, Thursdaies and Fridaies.

The Carriers of Bedford doe lodge at the three horseshooes in in [sic] aldersgatestreet, they come on Thursdaies.

The Carriers of Bridge-north doe lodge at the Maidenhead in cat-eaton street, neere the guild-hall.

The Carriers of Bury (or saint Edmonds Bury) in Suffolke, doe lodge at the dolphin without bishopsgate, they come on Thursdaies.

The Waggons of Bury or Berry in Suffolke, doe come every Thursday to the signe of the foure swans in bishopsgate street.

A foote-post doth come from the said Berry every wedensday to the greene dragon in bishopsgate street, by whom letters may be conveyed to and fro.

The Carriers of Barstable in Devonshire, doe lodge at the starre in breadstreet, they come on Fridaies and returne on Saturdaies or mundaies.

The Carriers of Bampton doe lodge at the Mer-maid in carterlane: and there also lodge the Carriers of Buckland, they are there on Thursdaies and Fridaies.

The Carriers of Brill in Buckinghamshire, do lodge at the signe of Saint Pauls head in carterlane, they come on Tuesdaies and wedensdaies.

The Carriers of Bampton in Lancashire [Westmorland?], doe lodge at the beare at Bashingshaw, they are there to bee had on Thursdaies and Fridaies, also thither commeth Carriers from other parts in the said County of Lancashire.

The Carriers of Batcombe in Somersetshire, do lodge at the crowne (or Jarrets Hall) at the end of bassing lane neare bread street, they come every Friday.

The Carriers of Broughton, in Leicestershiere, doe lodge at the signe of the Axe in Aldermanbury; they are there every Friday.

C

The Carrier of Colchester do lodge at the crosse-keyes in Gracious street, they come on the Thursdaies and goe away on the Fridaies.

The Carrier of Chessam [Chesham] in Buckinghamshire, doth come twice every weeke to the signe of the white Hart in high Holborne at the end of Drury lane.

The Carrier of Cogshall [Coggeshall] in Suffolk doth lodge at the spread Eagle in Gracious streete, he comes and goes on Thursdaies and Fridaies.

The Waggons from Chippinganger [Chipping Ongar] in Essex, doe come every Wednesday to the crowne without Algate.

The Waggons from Chelmsford in Essex, come on Wednesdaies to the signe of the blew Boare without Algate.

The Carriers of Cheltenham in Glocestershire, doe lodge at the three cups in Bredstreet, they doe come on Fridaies and goe away on Saturdaies.

The Carriers of Cambden [Chipping Campden] in Glocestershire, and of Chippingnorton, doe lodge at the three Cups in Bredstreet, they come and goe Thursdaies, Fridaies, and Saturdaies.

The Carriers of Chester doe lodge at the castle in Woodstreete, they are there to be had on Thursd. Frid. and Saturdaies.

The Carriers of Chard in Dorsetshire [i.e. Somerset], do lodge at the Queenes Armes neere Holborne bridge, they are there to be had on Fridaies.

The Carriers of Chard doe lodge at the George in Bredstreet.

The Carriers of Chester do lodge at Blossomes (or Bosomes Inne) in Saint Laurence lane, neere Cheapside, every Thursday.

The Carrier of Coleashby [Cold Ashby] in Northamptonshire, doe lodge at the signe of the Ball in Smithfield; also there doe lodge Carriers of divers other parts of that country at the Bell in Smithfield, they do come on the Thursdaies.

The Carriers of Crawley in Bedfordshire [North Crawley, Bucks?], doe lodge at the Beare and ragged staffe in Smithfield, they come on the Thursdaies.

The Carriers of Coventry in Warwickeshire, doe lodge at the Ram in Smithfield, they come on Wednesdaies and Thursdaies.

There are other carriers from Coventry that doe on Thursdaies and Fridaies come to the Rose in Smithfield.

The Carrier of Creete in Leicestershire [Greetham, Rutland?], doe lodge at the Rose in Smithfield.

The Waggons or Coaches from Cambridge, doe come every Thursday and Friday to the blacke Bull in Bishopsgate street.

The Carriers of Coventry doe lodge at the signe of the Axe in St Mary Axe in Aldermanbury, they are there Thursdaies and Fridaies.

The Carriers of Cambridge, doe lodge at the Bell in Coleman streete, they come every Thursday.

The foot-post of Canterbury doth come every Wednesday and Saturday to the signe of the two neck'd Swanne at Sommers key, neere Billingsgate,

The Carriers of Crookehorne [Crewkerne, Somerset] in Devonshire, doe lodge at the Queens Armes neere Holborne bridge, they come on Thursdaies.

D

The Carriers of Dunmow in Essex, doe lodge at the Saracens head in Gracious street, they come and goe on Thursdaies and Fridaies.

The Waggons from Dunmow, doe come every Wednesday to the crowne without Algate.

The Carriers of Ditmarsh [Tidmarsh?] in Barkeshire, doe lodge at the

George in Bredstreet.

The Carriers of Doncaster in Yorkeshire, and many other parts in that country, doe lodge at the Bell, or Bell Savage without Ludgate, they do come on Fridaies, and goe away on Saturdaies or Mundaies.

The Carriers of Dorchester, doe lodge at the Rose neere Holborne bridge, they come and goe on Thursdaies and Fridaies.

The Carriers of Denbigh in Wales, doe lodge at Bosomes Inne every Thursday: also other carriers doe come to the said Inne from other parts of that country.

The Carrier of Daintree [Daventry], doth lodge every Friday night at the crosse keyes in St Johns street.

The Carrier from Duncehanger [Deanshanger], and other places neere Stony Stratford, doe lodge at the three cups in St Johns streete.

The Carriers of Derby, and other parts of Derbyshire, doe lodge at the Axe in St Mary Axe, neere Aldermanbury, they are to be heard of there on Fridaies.

The Carriers of Darby doe lodge at the castle in woodstreet every weeke, on Thursdaies or Fridaies.

E

The Carrier of Epping in Essex doe lodge at the Prince his Armes in Leadenhallstreet, he commeth on Thursdaies.

The Carriers of Exeter do lodge at the star in breadstreet, they come on Fridaies and goe away on Saturdaies or mundaies.

The Carriers of Exeter do lodge at the rose neere holbornebridge they come on Thursdaies.

The Carriers of Evesham in Worcestershire doe lodge at the castle in woodstreet, they come thither on Fridaies.

F

The Carriers of Feckingham [Feckenham]-forrest in Worcestershire doe lodge at the crowne in high holbourne, and at the Queenes head at Saint Giles in the fields, there is also another Carrier from the same place.

The Carrier of Faringdon in Barkeshire doe lodge at the Saint Pauls head in Carter lane, they come on Tuesdaies and goe away on wedensdaies.

G

Carriers from Grindon [Grendon] Underwood, in Buckinghamshire doe lodge at the Paul-head in carter lane, they are to bee found there on Tuesdaies and Wednesdaies.

The Carriers of Glocester doe come to the Saracens head without Newgate, on Fridaies.

The Carriers of Gloster doe lodge at the Saracens head in carter lane, they come on Fridaies.

Clothiers doe come every weeke out of divers parts of Glocestershire to the Saracens head in Friday street.

The Waines or Waggons doe come every weeke from sundry places in Glocestershire, and are to bee had at the swan neere holborne Bridge.

There are Carriers of some places in Glocestershire that doe lodge at the mer-maide in Carterlane.

H

Carriers from Hadley [Hadleigh] in Suffolk, doe lodge at the George in Lumbardstreet, they come on Thursdaies.

The Carriers of Huntingdon, doe lodge at the White Hinde without Cripplegate, they come upon Thursdaies and goe away on Fridaies.

The Carriers of Hereford, doe lodge at the Kings Head in the old change, they doe come on Fridaies and goe on Saturdaies.

The Carriers of Hallifax in Yorkeshire doe lodge at the Greyhound in smithfield, they doe come but once every moneth.

The Carriers of Hallifax are every Wednesday to be had at the Beare at Bashingshaw.

The Carriers of Hallifax doe likewise lodge at the Axe in Aldermanbury.

The Carriers of Hallifax doe likewise lodge at the white hart in Colemanstreet.

The Carrier of Hatfeild in Hartfordshire, doe lodge at the bell in Saint Johns street, they come on Thursdaies.

The Carriers of Harding [Harpenden] in Hartfordshire doe lodge at the Cocke in Aldersgatesteete, they come on Tuesdaies, Wednesdaies and Thursdaies.

The Carrier or waggon of Hadham, in Hartfourshire do lodge at the Bull in Bishopsgatestreet, they doe come and goe, on mundaies Tuesdaies, Fridaies and Saturdaies.

The Waggon, or Coach from Hartfourd Towne doth come every Friday to the foure swannes without Bishopsgate.

The Waggon or Coach of Hatfeild, doth come every Friday to the Bell in Aldersgate street.

I

The Carriers of Ipswich in Suffolke, doe lodge at the signe of the George in Lumbardstreet, they doe come on Thursdaies.

The Post of Ipswich, doth lodge at the crosse keyes in Gracious streete, he comes on Thursdaies, and goes on Fridaies.

The Waines of Ingarstone [Ingatestone] in Essex, doe come every Wednesday to the Kings Armes in Leadenhall street.

The Carriers of Ivell [Yeovil, Somerset] in Dorsershire, do lodge at Jarrets hall, or the crowne in Basing lane, neere Breasteeet.

K

The Carriers of Keinton [Kineton, Warwickshire] in Oxfordshire, doe lodge at the Bell in Friday street, they are there to be had on Thursdaies and Fridaies.

The Post of the Towne of Kingston upon Hull (commonly called Hull) doth lodge at the sign of the Bull over against Leadenhall.

L

The Carrier of Lincolne doth lodge at the white Horse without Cripplegate, he commeth every second Friday.

The Carriers of Laighton Beud sart [sic] (corruptly colled Laighton Buzzard) in Bedfordshire, doe lodge at the Harts Hornes in Smithfield, they come on Mundaies and Tuesdaies.

The Carriers of Leicester do lodge at the Saracens head without Newgate, they doe come on Thursdaies.

The Carriers of Leicester do also lodge at the castle neer Smithfield bars, they doe come on Thursdaies.

There be Carriers that do passe to and through sundry parts of

Leicestershire, which doe lodge at the Ram in Smithfield.

The like Carriers are weekely to be had at the Rose in Smithfild, that come and goe through other parts of Leicestershire.

The Carriers of Lewton [Luton, Bedfordshire] in Hartfordshire do lodge at the Cocke in Aldersgate street, they are there Tuesdaies and Wednesdaies.

The Carriers of Leeds in Yorkshire, doe lodge at the Beare in Bassinshaw, they come every Wednesday.

The Carriers of Leedes, doe also lodge at the Axe in Aldermanbury.

The Carrier of Leicester do lodge at the Axe in Aldermanbury.

The Carriers of Loughborough in Leicestershire, do lodge at the Axe in Aldermanbury: also other Carriers doe lodge there which do passe through Leicestershire, and through divers places of Lancashire.

M

The Carriers of Mawlden [Maldon] in Essex, do lodge at the crosse keyes in Gracious street, they come on Thursd. and go on Fridaies.

The Carriers of Monmouth, in Wales, and some other parts of Monmouthshire, do lodge at the Paul head in Carter lane, they do come to London on Fridaies.

The Carriers of Marlborough, doe lodge at the signe of the Swan neere Holborne bridge, they do come on Thursdaies.

There doth come from great Marlow in Buckinghamshire, some Higglers, or demie Carriers, they doe lodge at the Swanne in the Strand, and they come every Tuesday.

The Carriers of Manchester, doe lodge at the Beare in Bassingshaw, they doe come on Thursdaies or Fridaies.

The Carriers of Manchester, doe likewise lodge at the signe of the Axe in Aldermanbury.

The Carriers of Manchester, doe also lodge at the two neck'd Swan in Lad lane (betweene great Woodstreet, and Milk-street end) they come every second Thursday: also there do lodge Carriers that doe passe through divers other parts of Lancashire.

The Carriers of [Long] Melford in Suffolke, doe lodge at the spread-Eagle in Gracious street, they come and goe on Thursdaies aud [sic] Fridaies.

N

Carriers from New-elme [Ewelme, Oxon?] in Barkeshire doe lodge at the George in breadstreet they come on Wednesdaies and Thursdaies.

The Carriers of Netherley [Netherland?] in Staffordshire doe lodge at the Beare and ragged staffe in smithfield, they doe come on Thursdaies.

The Carriers of Northampton, and from other parts of that county and country there about, are almost every day in the weeke to be had, at the Ram in smithfield.

There doth come also Carriers to the Rose in smithfield, daily which doe passe to, or through many parts of Northamptonshire.

The Carriers of Nottingham, doe lodge at the crosse-keyes in Saint Johns street, he commeth every second Saturday.

There is also a footpost doth come every second Thursday from Nottingham, he lodgeth at the swan in Saint Johns street.

The Carriers of Norwich doe lodge at the Dolphin without Bishopsgate, they are to bee found there on mundaies and Tuesdaies.

The Carriers of Newport Pannel in Buckinghamshire, doe lodge at the Peacocke in Aldersgate street, they doe come on mundaies and Tuesdaies.

The Carriers of Nantwich in Chesshire, doe lodge at the Axe in aldermanbury, they are there Wednesdaies, Thursdaies and Fridaies.

The Carriers of Nuneaton in Warwickshire, doe lodge at the Axe in Aldermanbury, they come on Fridaies.

O

The Carriers of Oxfoord doe lodge at the Saracens head without Newgate (neere Saint sepulchers Church) they are there on Wednesdaies or almost any day.

The Carriers of Oney [Olney] in Buckinghamshire, doe lodge at the Cocke in Aldersgatestreet at long lane end, they doe come on mundaies, Tuesdaies and Wednesdaies.

P

The Carriers of Preston in Lancashire doe lodge at the Bell in Friday street, they are there on Fridayes.

R

The Carriers of Redding in Barkeshire doe lodge at the George in Breadstreet, they are there on Thursdaies and Fridaies.

The Carriers from Rutland, and Rutlandshire, and other parts of Yorkeshire, do lodge at the Ram in Smithfield, they come weekly, but their daies of Comming is not certaine.

S

The Carriers of Sudbury in Suffolke doe lodge at the Saracens Head in

Gracious street, they doe come and goe on Thursdaies and Fridaies.

The Carriers of Sabridgworth [Sawbridgeworth] in Hartfordshire do lodge at the Princes Armes in Leadenhall street, they come on Thursdaies.

The Waines from Stock in Essex, doe come every Wednesday to the Kings Armes in Leadenhall street.

The Carriers from Stroodwater [Stroud] in Glocestershire doe lodge at the Bell in Friday street, they doe come on Thursdaies and Fridaies.

The Carriers of Sisham [Syresham] in Northhamptonshire do lodge at the Saracens head in Carter-lane, they come on Friday, and returne on Saturday.

The Carriers from Sheffield, in Yorkeshire doth lodge at the Castle in Woodstreet, they are there to bee found on Thursdaies and Fridayes.

The Carriers from Salisbury doe lodge at the Queenes Armes neere Holbourne bridge, they come on Thursdayes.

The Carriers of Shrewsbury, doe lodge at the Mayden-head in Cateaton street, neere Guildhall, they come on Thursdaies.

The Carriers of Shrewsbury do also lodge at Bosomes Inne, they doe come on Thursdaies, and there doe lodge Carriers that doe travell divers parts of the County of Shropshire and places adioyning.

S

The Carrier from Stony-stratfourd doe lodge at the Rose and Crowne in Saint Johns street, he commeth every Tuesday.

There doth come from Saffron-Market [Swaffham], in Norfolke, a footpost who lodgeth at the chequer in Holbourne.

The Carriers of Stampfoord [Stamford], doe lodge at the Bell in

Aldersgatestreet, they doe come on Wednesdaies and Thursdaies.

The Waggon from Saffron Walden in Essex, doth come to the Bull in Bishopsgatestreet, it is to bee had there, on Tuesdaies and Wednesdaies.

The Carriers of Shaftsbury, and from Sherbourne in Dorcetshire doe lodge at the Crowne (or Jarrets Hall) in Baseing lane neere Breadstreet, they come on Fridaies.

The Carriers from Stopfoord [Stockport] in Chesshire do lodge at the Axe in Aldermanbury, also there are Carriers to other parts of Chesshire.

The Carriers of Staffoord, and other parts of that county, doe lodge at the swan with two necks, in Lad lane, they come on Thursdaies.

T

Carriers from Teuxbury [Tewkesbury] in Glocestershire doe lodge at the three Cups in Breadstreet, they come and goe on Fridaies and Saturdaies.

The Carriers of Tiverton in Devonshire, doe lodge at the starre in Breadstreet, they come on Fridaies and returne on Saturdaies or mundaies.

The Carriers of Tame [Thame], in Oxfoordshire, doe lodge at the Saracens head in carterlane, they come and goe Fridaies and Saturdaies.

The Carriers of Torceter [Towcester] in Northamptonshire, doe lodge at the Castle neere smithfield Barres, they come on Thursdaies.

V

Carriers from Vies, (or the De-Vises) [Devizes] in Wiltshire, doe lodge at the signe of the swan neere Holbourne Bridge, they come on Thursdaies and goe away on Fridaies.

W

The Carrier from Wendover in Buckinghamshire doth lodge at the blacke Swanne in Holborne, and is there every Tuesday and Wednesday.

The Carrier of Wittham in Essex doth lodge at the Crossekeyes in Gracious-street every Thursday and Friday.

The Carriers of Wallingfield [Waldingfield] in Suffolck doe lodge at the Spreadeagle in Gracious-street, they come and goe on Thursdayes and Fridayes.

The Carriers of Wallingford in Barkeshire doe lodge at the George in Breadstreet, their daies are Wednesdaies, Thursdaies, and Fridaies.

The Carriers of Winchcombe in Glocestershire doe lodge at the three Cups in Breadstreet, they come and goe on Fridaies and Saturdaies.

The Clothiers of sundry parts of Wiltshire doe weekely come and lodge at the Saracens head in Friday-street.

The Carriers of Warwick doe lodge at the Bell in Friday-street they are there on Thursdaies and Fridaies.

The Carriers of Woodstock in Oxfordshire doe lodge at the Mermaid in Carterlaine on Thursdaies and Fridaies.

The Carriers of Wantage in Berkshire doe lodge at the Mermaid in Carterlane, their daies are Thursday and Friday.

The Carriers of Worcester doe lodge at the Castle in Woodstreet, their daies are Fridaies and Saturdaies.

The Carriers of Winsloe [Winslow] in Buckinghamshire doe lodge at the Georg neere Holbornbridge, Wednesdaies, Thursdaies and Fridaies.

The Waggon from Watford in Middlesex doth come to the the Swan

THE CARRIERS COSMOGRAPHIE 449

neere Holbornebridge, on Thursdaies.

The Carriers from Wells in Sommersetshire doe lodge at the Rose neere Holbornebridge, they come on Thursdaies, and on Fridaies.

The Carriers from Witney in Oxfordshire doe lodge at the signe of the Sarasinshead without Newgate, they come on Wednesdaies.

Their commeth a Waggon from Winchester every Thursday to the Swan in the Strand, and some Carriers comes thither from divers parts of Buckinghamshire,but the daies of their comming are not certaine.

The Carriers of Worcester doe lodge at the Maydenhead in Cateatenstreet, neere Guildhall, they come on Thursdaies.

The Carriers from many parts of Worcestershire and Warwickshire doe lodge at the Rose and Crowne in high Holborne, but they keepe no certaine daies.

The Carriers of Warwicke doe come to the Queenes head neere St. Giles in the fields, on Thursdaies.

The Carrier of Walsingham in Norfolke doe lodge at the Chequer in Holborne, he commeth every second Thursday.

The Carriers of Wendover in Buckinghamshire do lodge at the Bell in Holborne.

There doth a Poste come every second Thursday from Walsingham to the Bell in Holborne.

The Carrier of Ware in Hartfordshire doth lodge at the Dolphin without Bishopsgate, and is there on mundaies and Tuesdaies.

There is a Footepost from Walsingham doth come to the Crossekeyes in Holborne every second Thursday.

There are Carriers from divers parts of Warwickeshire that doe come weekely to the Castle neere Smithfield barres, but their daies of comming are variable.

There is a Waggon from Ware at the Vine in Bishopsgatestreet every Friday and Saturday.

The Carriers of Wakefield in Yorkeshire doe lodge at the Beare in Bashinshaw, they do come on Wednesdaies.

The Carriers of Wells in Somersetshire, do lodge at the Crowne in Basing lane neere Breadstreet, they come and goe on Fridaies and Saturdaies.

The Carriers of Wakefield and some other parts of Yorkeshire doe lodge at the Axe in Aldermanbury, they are to be had there on Thursdaies.

The Carriers of Wakefield and some other parts of Yorkeshire doth also lodge at the Whitehart in Colemanstreet, they come every second Thursday.

Y

The Carriers of Yorke, (with some other parts neere Yorke, within that County) doe lodge at the signe of the Bell, or Bell salvage without Ludgate, they come every Fridaie, and goe away on Saturday or munday.

A Footepost from Yorke doth come every second Thursday to the Rose and Crowne in Saint Johns street.

For Scotland.

Those that will send any letter to Edenborough [Edinburgh], that so they may be conveyed to and fro to any parts of the Kingdome of Scotland, the Poste doth lodge at the signe of the Kings Armes (or the Cradle) at the upper end of Cheapside, from whence every Monday, any that have occasion may send.

THE CARRIERS COSMOGRAPHIE

The Innes and lodgings of the Carriers which come into the Burrough of Southwarke out of the Countries of Kent, Sussex, and Surrey.

A Carrier from Reygate [Reigate] in Surrey doth come every Thursday (or oftner) to the Falcon in Southwark.

The Carriers of Tunbridge, of Seavenoake, of Faut [Frant] and Staplehurst in Kent, doe lodge at the Katherinewheele, they doe come on Thursdaies and goe away on Fridaies: also on the same daies doe come thither the Carriers of Marden, and Penbree [Pembury], and from Warbleton in Sussex.

On Thursdaies the Carriers of Hanckhurst [Hawkhurst] and Blenchley [Brenchley] in Kent, and from Darking [Dorking] and Ledderhead [Leatherhead] in Surrey doe come to the Greyhound in Southwarke.

The Carriers of Tenterden and Penshurst in Kent, and the Carriers from Battell in Sussex doe lodge at the signe of the spurre in Southwarke, thy come on Thursdaies and goe away on Fridaies.

To the Queenes head in Southwarke doe come on Wednesdaies and Thursdaies, the Carriers from Portsmouth in Hampshire, and from Chichester, Havant, Arundell, Billinghurst, Rye, Lamberhurst, and Wadhurst, in Sussex, also from Godstone, and Linvill [Lingfield] in Surrey, they are there to be had Wednesdaies, Thursdaies and Fridaies.

The Carriers from Crambroke [Cranbrook] and Bevenden [Benenden] in Kent, and from Lewis, Petworth, Uckfield, and Cuckfield in Sussex, doe lodge at the Tabbard, or Talbot in Southwarke, they are there on Wednesdaies, Thursdaies, and Fridaies.

To the George in Southwarke come every Thursday the Carriers from Gilford [Guildford], Wanuish [Wonersh], Goudhurst, and Chiddington in Surrey, also thither come out of Sussex(on the same daies weekly) the Carriers of Battell, Sindrich [Sundridge], and Hastings,

The Carriers from these places undernamed out of Kent, Sussex and Surrey, are every weeke to bee had on Thursdaies at the White hart in the Borough of Southwarke; namely Dover, Sandwich, Canterbury, Biddenden, Mayfield, Eden (or Eaten Bridge) Hebsome [Epsom], Wimbleton, Godaliman, (corruptly called Godly man) [Godalming] Witherham [Withyham], Shoreham, Enfield [Henfield], Horsham, Haslemoore [Haslemere], and from many other places, farre and wide in the said Counties, Carriers are to be had almost daily at the said Inne, but especially on Thursdaies and Fridaies.

The Carriers from Chiltington, Westrum [Westerham], Penborough [Pembury] Slenge, Wrotham, and other parts of Kent, Sussex, and Surrey, doe lodge at the Kings head in Southwarke, they doe come on Thursdayes, and they goe on Fridayes.

Every weeke there commeth and goeth from Tunbridge in Kent a Carrier that lodgeth at the Greene Dragon in fowle Lane in Southwarke, neere the Meale-market.

Here followeth certaine directions for to find out Ships, Barkes, Hoyghs, and Passage Boats, that doe come to London, from the most parts and places by sea, within the Kings Dominions, either of England, Scotland or Ireland.

A Hoigh doth come from Colchester in Essex, to Smarts key, neere Billingsgate, by which goods may bee carried from London to Colchester weekly.

He that will send to Ipswich in Suffolk, or Linn [Kings Lynn] in Northfolke, let him goe to Dice key, and there his turne may be served.

The Ships from Kingston upon Hull (or Hull) in Yorkeshire do come to Raphs Key, and to Porters key.

At Galley key, passage for men, and Carriage for Goods may bee had from London to Barwicke [Berwick].

At Chesters key, shipping may be had from Ireland, from Poole from Plimouth, from Dartmouth and Weimouth.

At Sabbs Docke, a Hoigh or Barke is to be had from Sandwich or Dover in Kent.

A Hoigh from Rochester Margate in Kent, or Feversham and Maydston doth come to St Katherines Dock.

Shipping from Scotland are to bee found at the Armitage or Hermitage below St Katherines.

From Dunkirk at the custome house key.

From most parts of Holland or Zealand, Pinkes or shipping may be had at the Brewhouses in St Katherines.

At Lion key, twice (almost in every 24 houres, or continually are Tydeboats, or Wherries that passe to and fro betwixt London and the townes of Deptford, Greenwich, Woolwich, Erith, and Greenhith in Kent, and also boats are to be had that every Tyde doe carry goods and passengers betwixt London and Rainam [Rainham], Purfleet, and Grayes in Essex.

At Billinsgate, are every Tyde to be had Barges, lighthorsmen Tiltboats and Wherries, from London to the Townes of Gravesend and Milton in Kent, or to any other place within the said bounds, and (as weather and occasions may serve beyond, or further.

Passage Boates, and Wherries that do cary Passengers and goods from London, and back again thither East or West above London Bridge.

TO Bull Wharfe (neere Queenhithe) there doth come and goe great boats twice or thrice every weeke, which boats doe cary goods betwixt London and Kingston upon Thames, also thither doth often come a Boat from Colebrooke [Colnbrook], which serveth those parts for such purposes.

Great Boats that doe carry and Recarry Passengers and goods to and fro betwixt London and the Townes of Maydenhead, Windsor, Stanes, Chertsey, with other parts in the Counties of Surry, Barkeshire, Midlesex, and Buckingamshire, do come every Munday, and Thursday to Queenhith, and they doe goe away upon Tuesdayes and thusdaies.

The Redding [Reading] Boat is to be had at Queenhith weekly.

All those that will send letters to the most parts of the habitable world, or to any parts of our King of Great Britaines Dominions, let them repair to the Generall Post-Master Thomas Withering at his house in Sherburne Lane, neere Abchurch.

FINIS.

A BRIEF DIRECTOR

*T*his small eight-page pamphlet, undated and without imprint (but thought to be c.1642)[1] is at first sight merely an abridgement of the Carrier's Cosmographie. For the most part this is the case, and generally it follows the order of the entries in that work; but in his direction to the reader of the Cosmographie Taylor explained his difficulty in compiling it, and 'if there be any thing left out in this first Impression, it shall be with diligence inserted hereafter'. So this may be intended as a revised edition of the earlier work, or (since it is anonymous) it is possibly a pirated copy of his work, abridged and compiled by someone else.

      Comparison of the two works shows that, as well as abbreviating the Cosmographie entries in order to save space (and omitting a few – either deliberately or by mistake), Taylor or his plagiarist did indeed add entries. In fact about 26 places not listed in the Cosmographie were included for the first time, making this hitherto overlooked work more significant than at first it appears. Occasionally too mistakes were corrected, such as correctly assigning Kineton to Warwickshire, which in the Cosmographie had been placed in Oxfordshire. For the convenience of users I have emboldened the new entries that do not occur in the Cosmographie, but I have not repeated the modern spellings of place-names, except when they occur only in these additional entries.

(Text derived from Harvard University Library copy , T434aA (Wing 2nd ed.) online at Historical Texts EEBO)

A BRIEF DIRECTOR FOR THOSE THAT WOULD SEND THEIR LETTERS TO ANY PARTS OF ENGLAND, SCOTLAND, OR IRELAND. Or a List of all the Carriers, Waggoners, Coaches, Posts, Ships, Barks, Hoys, and Passage boats, that come to London, from the most parts and places, by Land & Sea.

---

1   If by Taylor it is unlikely to post-date March 1643, when Taylor fled from London to avoid arrest as a tax-defaulter.

A lphabetically Printed, so that none may pretend Ignorance, who would gladly send, but know not where to carry their Letters. With the dayes when they come, and when they return. And also to send Letters to the most habitable parts of the World, and to have an answer.

A. The Carriers of Abbington lodge at the George in Bred-street, come on Wednesday, and go on Thursday. Alisbury, Buckinghamshire, at the George at Holborn-Bridge, the Swan in the Strand, the Angel behind St. Clements Church, and the Bell in Holborn; every other day. St. Albans, on Friday, at the Peacock in Aldersgate-street; a Coach to the Bell there on Tuesday. Asbur at the Castle in Woodstreet, on Thursd. Frid. and Saturday.

B. Blanvile, Dorset. at the Chequer near Charing Crosse, every second Thursd. Blandford at the Rose at Holborn bridg. Braintree & Bocking in Essex, at the Talbot in Gracious street, com on Thursdays, and go on Fridays. Bathe at the Three Cups in Bred-street, on Fridays, and go on Saturdayes. Bristol there also, on Thursdays at the Swan neer Holborn Bridge. Brereton in Dorset: at the Rose near Holborn-Bridge, on Thursdays, & go on Fridays. **Blackburn in Lancashire at the Bell in Friday-street, on Wednesdayes and Fridays. Berre [Bury] in Lancashire, at the Ax in Alderman-bury on Wednesdayes and Fridayes.** From Buckinghamshire and Bedfordshire, at the Sarazens head without Newgate; and at the Queens Arms near Holborn-bridge, at the Windmill in St. Johns street. Broomsbury at the Mayden-head in Cateaten street, on Thursdays, and Fridays. Bingham, Notting. on Fridays, at the Bull in Smithfield-bars. Burford, Oxon, at the Bell in Friday-street, on Thursday. Buckingham at the Kings Head in the old Change, Wednesdayes and Thursdayes, and at the Sarazens-head in Carterlane, Fridays at the George near Holborn-bridge, on Wednesdays. Bewdley at the Castle in Woodstreet, Thursdays. Brackley at the George near Holborn-bridge, on Wednesdays. Banbury at the George near Holborn-bridge, Wednesdayes. Bedford at the Three Horshoes in Aldersgate street, on Thursdayes. Bridgenorth at the Maidenhead in Cateaten-street. Bury at the Dolphin without Bishopsgate, on Thursdayes. The Waggons of Bury come every Thursday to the Four Swans in Bishopsgate-street. A Foot-Post from the said Berry, on Wednesday, to the Green-Dragon in Bishopsgate-street. Barstable at the Star in Bredstreet, on Fridays. Bampton at the Mermaid in Carterlane, on Thursdayes. Brill at St. Pauls Head in Carterlane, on Tuesdayes. Bampton at the Bear at Basingshaw, on Tuesdayes. Balcomb [sic] at the Crown in Basinglane, on Fridayes. Broughton at the Ax in Aldermanbury, on Friday. **A Coach goes to Buk [?] from the Kings Arms at Leaden-hall.**

C. Colchester doe lodge at the Crosse-keys in Gracious-street, on Thursdayes. Chesham at the White heart in Holborn. Cogshall at the Spread-Eagle in Gracious-street, Thursdayes. Chippingonger in Essex, Wednesdayes, to the Crowne without Algate. Cheltenham in Glouc. Cambden, Chippin-Norton, Fridayes, at the three Cups in Bredstreet. Chester at Blossoms Inn, in St. Laurence lane, Fridayes and Saterdayes. **Congerton [Congleton] in Cheshire at the Ax in Aldermanbury, on Thursdayes and Fridayes.** Chard in Dorcetshire at the Queens Arms near Holborn-bridge, on Fridays, and at the George in Bred-street. Cole-Ashby in Northamp. at the Ball in Smithfield, Crawley in Bedfordsh: at the Bear and Ragged staffe in Smithfield, on Thursdayes. Coventry in Warwicksh. at the Ram in Smithfield, on Wednesdayes and Thursdayes. Creet in Leicestersh. at the Rose in Smithfield. Coaches from Cambridge, on Thursday and Friday at the black Bull in Bishopsgate-street. Coventry at the Ax in Aldermanbury, on Thursdayes. Cambridge at the Bell in Colemanstreet, on Thursday. Foot-post of Canterbury, every Wednesday and Saturday, to the Swan at Summers key. Crookhorn in Devonshire doe lodge at the Queens Arms near Holborn-bridge, on Tuesdayes. **Coln in Lancash. at the White horse at Cripple-gate, on Wednesday. Chesterfield in Derbish. at the Castle in Woodstreet, on Wednesday.**

D. Dunmow in Essex, at the Saracens-head in Gracious-street, Thursdayes and Fridayes. The Wagons lye at the Crown without Algate. Ditmarsh in Barksh. at the George in Bredstreet. Doncaster in Yorksh. at the Bell Savage without Ludgate, on Fridays and Mondayes. Dorchester at the Rose near Holborn-bridge, Thirsdayes. Denbigh in Wales, at Bosoms Inn every Thursday. Daintree, Friday, at the Crosse keys in St. Johns street. From Duncehanger at the three Cups in St. John street. Derby and Derbishire at the Ax in Aldermanbury, Fridays, and at the Castle in

Woodstreet Thursdays and Fridayes.

E. Epping in Essex, at the Princes Arms in Leadenhal-street Thursdayes. Exeter at the Star in Bredstreet on Fridayes, and at the Rose neer Holborn-bridge on Thursdayes. Evesham in Worcest. at the Castle in Woodstreet, Friday.

F. Feckingham Forest in Worcestersh. at the Crown in high Holborn; and at the Queens-Head in St. Giles in the Fields. Farington in Barkshire, at St. Pauls head in Carterlane, on Tuesdayes.

G. Grindon Underwood in Bucks. at St. Pauls head in Carterlane, on Tuesdayes. Gloucester at the Saracens head without Newgate, and at the Saracens head in Carterlane, on Fridayes. Waggons every week from Gloucestershire, at the Swan near Holborn Bridge.

H. Hadley in Suffolk, at the Kings Arms in Leadenhall-street, on Wednesdayes. Huntington at the white Hinde without Cripplegate, on Thursdayes. Hereford at the Kings Head in the Old Change, on Fridayes. Halifax at the Greyhound in Smithfield, and at the Bear in Basingshaw, likewise at the Ax in Aldermanbury, also at the White Hart in Coleman-street. Hatfield in Hertford at the Bell in St. John street, Thursdayes. Harding in Hertford. at the Cock in Aldersgate-street, on Tuesday. Waggon lies at the Bull in Bishopsgate street, Mondayes, &c. A Coach from Hartford every Friday to the Four Swans within Bishopsgate. A Coach from Hatfield every Friday, to the Bell in Aldersgate-street. **Highworth at the Rose at Holborn-bridge, on Saturday.**

I. Ipswich at the George in Lumbard street, Thursdays. The Post of Ipswich at the Crosse-keys in Gracious street, on Thursdayes. Ingerstone in Essex, on Wednesday, to the Kings Arms in Leadenhall street. Jewel in Dorcet, at Jarrets Hall. **Isle of Wight at the Bell-Savage, and Bell in Friday street, on Saturdayes.**

K. Keinton in Warwick. at the Bell in Friday-street, Fridayes. Kingston upon Hull, at the Bull in Leadenhall-street. **Kendall at the White Horse without Cripple-gate, on Thursday.**

L. Lincoln at the White Horse without Cripple-gate, on Friday. Laighten Beudesart, at the Harts-Horns in Smithfield, Mondayes. Leicester at the Saracens head without Newgate, and at the Castle near Smithfield-bars on Thursdayes. Lewton in Hertford. at the Cock in Aldersgate-street, Tuesd. Leeds in York. at the Bear in Basingshaw, wednesday, and at the Ax in Aldermanbury. Leicester at the Red Lyon in Aldersgate-street. Loughborough at the Ax in Aldermanbury.

M. Malden in Essex at the Cross-keys in Gracious-street, Thursdayes. Monmouth at St. Pauls head in Carter-lane. Marlborough at the Swan near Holborn-bridge, Thursdayes. Manchester at the Bear in Basingshaw, on Thursdayes. And at the Ax in Aldermanbury, and at the Two-necked Swan in Ladlane. **Mansfield in Nottingh. at the Castle in Woodstreet, Thursdayes. Maxfield in Cheshire, at the Ax in Aldermanbury, thursdayes. Middlewich at the Ax in Aldermanbury, on Fridayes.**

N. New Elm at the George in Bredstreet, wednesdayes. Netherly in Stafford, at the Bear and ragged Staff in Smithfield, thursday. Northampton and Nottingham at the Ram in Smithfield, Saturday. Norwich at the Dolphin without Bishopsgate, Mondayes. Nantwich in Cheshire, at the Ax in Aldermanbury, on wednesday. Nuneaton in Warwick. at the Ax in Aldermanbury, Friday. **Newbery at the Kings arms near Holborn-bridge, wednesdayes. Northwich in Cheshire, at the Ax in Aldermanbury, Thursday. From Newark in Notting. a Coach and Waggon on Saturdayes, at the Crosse keyes in Whitecrosse-street. Naylans [Nayland, Suffolk] at the four Swans in bishopsgate street.**

O. Oxford at the Saracens head without Newgate, and in Warwick lane. Oney in Bucks. at the Cock in Aldersgate-street, on Mondayes. Oundle in Northamp. at the Ram in Smithfield. **Ockingham [Wokingham, Berkshire] at the White Horse in Friday street, Fridayes.**

P. Preston in Lancash. at the Bell in Friday-street. **Pontefract in York. at the Bell in Basingshaw, on Wednesdayes.**

R. Redding in Berks. at the George in Bredstreet, Thursdayes. **Rochdel** in Lancash. at the Ax in Aldermanbury wednesday. Richmond in Yorksh. at the Bell in Basinghal-street, and Rippon, wednesday.

S. Sudbury in Suffolk, at the Saracens head in Gracious-street, on thursdayes. Sabridgeworth in Hertfordsh. and Stock in Essex. at the Kings arms in Leadenhall-street, thursdayes. Stroodwater in Glouc. at the Bell in Friday-street, Fridays. Soisam in Northamp. at the Saracens-head in Carter-lane, fridays. Sheffield in Yorksh. at the Castle in Woodstreet, thursdayes. **Swallowfield in Berks. at the black Bull in Holborn, thursdayes.** Salisbury at the Queens arms neer Holborn bridge on thursday. Shrewsbury at Bosoms Inn, on thursdays, **Skittlebrig [Skip Bridge, NW of York?] and Ferribrig [Ferrybridge] at the Bell at Basinghall, wednesdays.** Stoppard in Cheshire; at the Ax in Aldermanbury. Stonystretford at the Rose and Crown in St. Johns street, tuesday. From Saffron Market is a Foot-post at the Chequer in Holb. Stampford at the Bell in Aldersgate-street, wednesdayes. The Waggon from Saifren-Walden in Essex, at the Bull in Bishopsgate-street, tuesdayes. Shaftsbury and Sherborme, at Jarrets hall on Fridayes. Stopford in Cheshire at the Ax in Aldermanbury. Stafford at the Swan with two Necks in Ladlane, thursdayes. **Coach from Stanford [Stamford, Lincs?] in Leicst. to the Crosse-keys in Whitecrosse-street, saturdayes.**

T. Teuxbury in Glouc. at the three Cups in Bredstreet, fridayes. Tame in Oxon, at the Saracens head in Carter-lane, fridays. Tiverton in Devon, at the Star in Bredstreet, on fridays. Towceter in Northamp. at the Castle in Smithfield Thursdayes.

V. Vies, or Devises, at the Swan near Holborn-bridge, on Thursdayes.

W. Wendover in Bucks.at the black Swan in Holborn, Tuesday. Wittham in Essex at the Crosse-keys in Gracious-street, Thursdayes. Wallingfield in Suffolk, at the Spread-Eagle in Gracious-street, Thursdayes. Wallingford, Berks at the George in Bredstreet, wednesdayes. Winchcomb in Glouc. at the three Cups in Bredstreet, fridayes. Warwick at the Bell in Friday-street, fridayes. A Waggon from Ware at the Vine in Bishopsgate-street, fridayes. Woodstrck [sic] in Oxon. Wantage, Berks. at the Maremaid in Carterlane, Thursdayes. Worcester, at the Castle in Woodstreet, and at the Mouth at Aldersgate, on fridayes. Winsloe in Bucks. at the George neer Holborn-bridge, wednesday. Watford in Middlesex at the Swan near Holborn-bridge. Wells in Somers. at the Rose near Holborn-bridge, Thursdayes. Witney in Oxon. at the Saracens head without Newgate, wednesdayes. Winchester at the Rose at Holborn-bridge on Thursday. Worcester at the Maydenhead in Cateaton-street, Thursdayes. Worcest. and Warwick. at the Rose & Crown in High-Holborn. Walsingham in Norf. at the Chequer in Holborn, Thursday. Wendover in Bucks. at the Bell in Holborn. A Foot-post cometh to the Crosse keys in Holborn every second Thursday. Wakefield in Yorksh. at the Bear in Basingshaw, the Ax in Aldermanbury, and the White-hart in Coleman-street, on Thursdayes. **Warrington and Wiggon, at the Bell in Friday-street, wednesdayes.**

Y. York, at the Bell-Savage without Ludgate, on friday. A Foot-post from York to the Rose and Crown in St. Johns street, Thursday.

THE INNS AND LODGINGS OF THE CARRIERS WHICH COME INTO THE BURROUGH OF SOUTHWARK OUT OF THE COUNTIES OF KENT, SUSSEX, AND SURREY.

A Carrier from Rygate in Surrey, comes every Thursday to the Falcon in Southwark. Tunbridge, of Sevenoak, of Faut, and Staplehurst in Kent, at the Katherine Wheel on Thursdayes; also the Carriers of Marden, Penbree, and Warbleton in Sussex. On Thursdayes from Haukhurst and Bleneby in Kent; and from Darking and Ledderhead in Surrey, to the Greyhound in Southwark. Tenterden and Penshurst in Kent, and Battel in Sussex, at the Spur in Southwark, on Thursd. To the Queenshead in Southwark on wednesd. come from Portsmouth in Hantshire, and from Chichester, Havant, Arundel, Billinghurst, Rye, Lamberhurst, and Wadhurst, in Sussex, and from Godstone and Linvil in Surrey. Crambroke, Bevenden, in Kent, and from Lewis, Petworth, Uckfield and Cuckfield in Sussex, do lodge at the Talbot in Southwark, on wednesdayes. To the George in Southwark, on Thursdayes come from Gilford, Wanvish, Goudhurst, and Chiddington in Surrey. To the White Hart in the Burrough of Southwark, come from Dover, Centerbury, Sandwich, Biddenden, Mayfield, Edenbridge, Hebsome, Winbleton, Godalimen, Witherham, Shoreham, Enfield, Horsham, Hostmoor, on

Fridayes. From Cubington [?], Westrum, Peuborough, Slenge, Wrotham, to the Kingshead in Southwark, on Thursday. A Carrier from Tunbridge to the Green Dragon in Foul-lane, and Queens Head in Southwark, on Friday.

From Epsome Welis, cometh a Coach and Waggon to the Kings Head in Southwarke every other day.

CERTAIN DIRECTIONS FOR TO FIND OUT SHIPS, BARKS, AND HOIGHS THAT DOE COME TO LONDON.

A Hoigh from Colchester comes to Smarts Key weekly. From Ipswich or Lyn, to Dice key. From Barwick to Galley key. From Ireland, Pool, Plimouth, Dartmouth, Weymouth, to Chesters key.

From Sandwich or Dover in Kent, to Sibbs Dock. From Rochester, Marget, Feversham, and Maidstone, to Katherines Dock. From Scotland, at the Armitage. From Dunkirk at the Custome-house key. From Holland or Zealand, at the Brew-houses in St. Katherines.

At Lyon key Tide-boats passe between London and Deptford, Greenwich, Woolwich, Erith, Greenhith, Raynam, Turfleet, and Grayes.

At Billingsgate are Barges, Light-horsemen, Tilt boats, and Wherries, to Gravesend, Milton, or further.

Passage boats to carry Passengers either East or West, about London-bridge.

At Bull Wharf come boats twice a week, which carry Goods between London, and Kingston upon Thames, and Colebrook. Boats for Passengers and Goods, to Henly, Maidenhead, Windsor, Stanes, Chertsey, and Redding, at Queenhith.

All those that would send Letters to the most habitable parts of the world, or to any parts of Great Britain, either England, Scotland, or Ireland, let them repair to the Generall Post-Master at the Stocks by the Exchange.

INDEX OF PERSONS AND PLACES

This index includes most persons and places found in the introduction, texts and notes. Some mythological, fanciful, historical, Biblical and classical names are omitted. Places are entered under their current names, with variant spellings (even when the identification is uncertain) following in brackets and cross-referenced from their alphabetical place in the index. Hundred names (and other county divisions), however, are generally indexed under Taylor's spelling, which he derived from Camden. Most places in England and Wales are identified by their historic county, which means that many now regarded as falling within London are located to Essex, Kent, Middlesex or Surrey. Named streets and locations in London and Westminster are included in the main sequence, but the names of individual inns and taverns have not been indexed. Some county names have been abbreviated, as follows:

Beds: Bedfordshire; Berks: Berkshire; Bucks: Buckinghamshire; Caernarvons: Caernarvonshire; Cambs Cambridgeshire; Cardigans: Cardiganshire; Carmarthens: Carmarthenshire; Cumb: Cumberland; Derbs: Derbyshire; Glam Glamorganshire; Glos: Gloucestershire; Hants: Hampshire; Herefs: Herefordshire; Herts: Hertfordshire; Hunts: Huntingdonshire; Lancs: Lancashire; Leics: Leicestershire; Lincs: Lincolnshire; Merioneths: Merionethshire; Mon: Monmouthshire; Northants: Northamptonshire; Northumb: Northumberland; Notts: Nottinghamshire; Oxon: Oxfordshire; Pembs: Pembrokeshire; Salop: Shropshire; Som: Somerset; Staffs: Staffordshire; Warwicks: Warwickshire; Wilts: Wiltshire; Worcs: Worcestershire; Yorks: Yorkshire

Abbington *see* Abingdon
Abbots Bromley, Staffs, 435
Abbots Langley, Herts, 201, 415
Abchurch, London, 454
Abendun *see* Abingdon
Abercairny (Abercarny), Perth, 64, 70, 72
Aberconwy, Caernarvons, 335, 336
Aberdeen (Aberdeene), 62
Aberdovey (Aberdovy), Merioneths, 337
Aberistwith *see* Aberystwyth
Abersom *see* Atherstone
Aberystwyth (Aberistwith), 327, 338
Abfreston *see* Alfriston
Abingdon (Abbington, Abbendun, Abington, Abinton), Berks, 199, 204, 205, 223, 256, 257, 264, 291, 292, 331, 345, 419, 420, 433, 456
Ablestone, Lewis, 424
Abridge, Essex, 409
Acherson, James, 79
Acmooty (Acmootye), James, 79; John, 63, 79, 81

Acton, Hants, 418
Acton, Middlesex, 406
Adams, Morgan, 417
Adlington, Cheshire, 47
Adrian, John, 378
Aeton *see* Eton
Africa (Affrica, Affricke, Africke), 21, 42, 301, 303, 313
Agate, John, 405
Aileworth, Richard, 397
Albans, St *see* St Albans
Aldeburgh (Aldbrough), Suffolk, 133
Aldridg, William, 406
Aldridge, John, 410
Alesbery *see* Aylesbury
Alexander, John, 411; Richard, 421
Alfriston (Abfreston), Sussex, 405
Algiers (Argiere), 301
Alisbury *see* Aylesbury
Allaway *see* Alloa
Allde, Edward, 128, 160
Allen, Dorothy, 398; Francis, 411; Simon, 400

Allington, Devon, 298
Alloa (Allaway), Scotland, 69
Alloftbridge, Kent, 403
Alnwick (Anwick, Anwicke), Northumb, 81
Alresford (Alsford), 416
Alsleben (Ashleaven), Germany, 109
Alsop, Mathew, 426
Alton, Hants, 276, 283, 416
Altona (Altonagh), Germany, 8
America, 21, 162, 313
Amersham, Bucks, 425
Amery, Robert, 408; Shelton, 414
Amesford, Bucks, 425
Amsterdam, Netherlands, 105, 221, 317
Anandale *see* Annandale
Andersey Island, Berks, 205
Andover, Hants, 307, 416, 418
Anglesey, 328, 336
Ankerwycke (Ankerwike), Bucks, 211
Annan, River, Scotland, 57
Annandale (Anandale), Scotland, 55, 57
Anstruther, Sir Robert, 82
Anthill, Mr (of Bagshot), 422
Anthony, Edward, 425
Antwerp, Belgium, 289, 380
Anwick, Anwicke *see* Alnwick
Aperley, Master, 263
Apley Hall, Salop, 259
Appleby, Westmorland, 54
Appledore (Aplear), Devon, 298
Appledore, Kent, 400
Arabia, Arabian, 142, 186, 375
Archer, Mary, 409
Archbald, John, 69
Arnet, William, 80
Arundel (Arundell), Sussex, 306, 403, 406, 451, 461
Arundell, Earl of, 195
Asbur *see* Happisburgh
Aschersleben (Ashers Leaven), Germany, 109
Ashby, Cold (Coleashby), Northants, 437, 457
Ash (Ashe), Kent, 399
Ashers Leaven *see* Aschersleben
Ashford (Ashfourd), Kent, 399
Ashleaven *see* Alsleben
Ashton, Edmond, 263; Elizabeth, 401
Ashton Hall, Lancs, 51
Assenden, Bucks, 426
Astone, Mary, 399
Atherstone (Abersom), Warwicks, 237
Atholl, Earl of, 76
Atkins, Master, 318; William, 425
Atkinson, George, 82
Aubrey, John, 190, 215
Augier, Samuell, 407
Aveley, Essex, 410

Averstock, Hants, 418
Avis, Thomas, 407
Avon, River, Hants, vii, 159, 182, 258,
Avon, River, Monmouths, 258
Avon, River, Som, 249, 254, 258, 261, 264
Avon, River, Warwicks, 249, 263, 265, 267
Avonmouth, Glos, 261
Awbrey, John, 343
Awceter, Katherin, 406
Axminster (Axmister), Devon, 307
Axtave, Kent, 402
Ayldworth, Mary, 427
Aylesbury (Alesbery, Alisbury, Aylsbury), Bucks, 199, 203, 425, 426, 433, 456
Aylsham, Norfolk, 140, 322
Azores, Islands, 33, 63

Bablock Hithe (Bablack Hive), Oxon, 257
Bach, Johann S, 20
Bacharach, Germany, 98
Backesteed *see* Buxted
Bacon, Francis, 123; Roger, 242
Baddow (Baddo), Little, Essex, 412
Badenoch (Bagenoch), Scotland, 36, 76
Bagley, John, 421
Bagpuize *see* Kingston Bagpuize
Bagshot, Surrey, 276, 422
Baily, Old, London, 250, 389
Baily, John, 422
Baines, Margery, 408
Baker, Francis, 413; Ireffrey, 410; Mary, 427; Ralph, 411; Susan, 400;
Balcomb *see* Batcombe
Baldock, Herts, 325, 414
Baldwin, Christopher, 400; Henry, 405; William, 425
Ball, Mathew, 403
Ballater, Scotland, 71
Ballingham, Herefs, 264
Balloch (Ballo), Scotland, 76
Ballow, Thomas, 427
Bampton, Oxon, 426, 428, 436, 457
Bampton, Westmorland, 436, 457
Banbury (Banburie), Oxon, 199, 231, 426, 428, 435, 456
Banckside *see* Bankside
Banes, M., 191
Banffshire, Scotland, 77
Bangor, Caernarvons, 336
Banister, Thomas, 51
Bankside (Banckside, Banke side), London, 89, 256, 382, 389, 390
Banstead (Barmestreet), Surrey, 422
Barbican, London, 39
Bardfield, Essex, 410
Barkeshire *see* Berkshire

Barkhamstead *see* Berkhamsted
Barking, Essex, 202, 387, 409
Barkley, Kent, 403
Barksh, Barkshire, Bark-shire *see* Berkshire
Barkway, Herts, 414
Barmanspit, Hants, 419
Barmestreet *see* Banstead
Barmouth (Bermoth), Merioneths, 337
Barnard, John, 355
Barne, Middlesex, 409
Barnelth, Berks, 421
Barnes, Surrey, 422
Barnesield, Kent, 403
Barnet, Herts, 39, 325, 413
Barningham, North, Norfolk, 140
Barnsley, Glos, 327, 344, 345
Barnsley, Yorks, 232
Barnstaple (Barnstable, Barstable), Devon, 298, 413, 436, 457
Baron Hill, Anglesey, 336
Barreash *see* Burwash
Barstable *see* Barnstaple
Bartenstacy *see* Barton Stacey, 418
Bartholmew-lane, London, 386
Bartlet, Martha, 398
Barton Stacey (Bartenstacy), Hants, 418
Barton upon Humber, Lincs, 229
Barwick, Barwicke *see* Berwick
Baseing *see* Basing
Bashingshaw, Bashinshaw *see* Basingshaw
Basildon, Essex, 208
Basing (Baseing, Bassing) Lane, London, 396, 436, 442, 447, 450, 457
Basinghall
Basinghal-street, London, 460
Basingshaw (Bashingshaw, Bashinshaw, Bassings hall, Bassinshaw), London, 386, 436, 441, 443, 450, 457-59, 461
Basingstoke (Basingstoake), Hants, 416, 418
Bass Rock, Scotland, 79
Bassing *see* Basing
Bassings hall, Bassinshaw *see* Basingshaw
Bastable, Gregory, 159, 180
Batcombe (Balcomb), Som, 436, 457
Bateman, Margery, 407
Bates, Katherine, 412; Master, 82; Thomas, 250
Bath (Bathe), Som, 250, 254, 261, 262, 264, 282, 287, 290, 293, 301, 434, 456
Battel, Battell, *see* Battle
Battersea, Surrey, 423
Battin, Robert, 422
Battle (Battel, Battell), Sussex, 359, 403, 451, 461
Bavaria, Germany, 96, 358
Bawdsey, Suffolk, 133
Bawwaw *see* Blackwater

Baylie, James, 79
Bayly *see* Old Bailey
Baynham, Herefs, 264
Beachy [Head], Sussex, 173
Beaconsfield (Beconsfield), Bucks, 425
Beame, Beamer *see* Bohemia
Bearsted (Bersted), Kent, 400
Beauchamp (Bewchamp), Henry, 417
Beaumaris (Beumorris, Bewmaris), Anglesey, 336
Beck, Anthony, 397
Beconsfield *see* Beaconsfield
Becontree, Essex, 413
Bedfont (Budfont), Middlesex, 407
Bedford, Beds, 381, 384, 435, 456
Bedfordberry, London, 387, 382
Bedfordshire (Bedfordsh), 434, 437, 442, 443, 456, 457
Beding *see* Beeding
Bedlam, London, 396
Beeding (Beding), Sussex, 405
Belford, Northumb, 81
Belgrade, Serbia, 22
Bellinshurst *see* Billingshurst
Belson, Augustine, 426
Belvoir (Belvoyre, Bever) Castle, Leics, 225
Ben Avon (Benawne), Scotland, 71
Benenden (Bevenden), Kent, 401, 451, 461
Bennet, Katherin, 427
Benson, Oxon, 427
Bentley, Richard, 425
Beriffe, John, 410
Berkhamsted (Barkhamstead), Herts, 413
Berkshire (Barkeshire, Barksh, Barkshire, Berkeshire, Berks), 85, 199, 200, 208, 210, 223, 257, 291, 292, 328, 331, 391, 393, 419, 421 438, 440, 444, 445, 448, 454, 457-60
Bermondsey, Surrey, 379, 388, 396
Bermoth *see* Barmouth
Bernard, Elizabeth, 427
Berre *see* Bury
Berry *see* Bury St Edmunds
Bersted *see* Bearsted
Berwick on Tweed (Barwick, Barwicke), Northumb, 33, 79-81, 432, 452, 462
Besowth, Stephen, 413
Bessley *see* Bisley
Bethlen (Bethlem), Gabriel, 96
Beumorris *see* Beaumaris
Beuning, Mathew, 407
Bevenden *see* Benenden
Bever *see* Belvoir
Bewchamp *see* Beauchamp
Bewdley, Worcs, 259, 435, 456
Bewmaris *see* Beaumaris
Bexley, Kent, 401

Bicknor, Welsh, Herefs, 264
Bickton, Thomas, 418
Biddenden, Surrey, 400, 452, 461
Bideford, Devon, 298
Bigod (Bigot), Hugh, 320
Billet, Anne, 403; Mary, 403; Thomas, 403
Billinghurst see Billingshurst
Billingsgate (Billinsgate), London, 6, 385, 386, 389, 390, 438, 452, 453, 462
Billingshurst (Bellinshurst, Billinghurst, Billinshurst), Sussex, 347, 353, 354, 405, 451, 461
Billinsgate see Billingsgate
Billinshurst see Billingshurst
Binfield, Berks, 420
Binfield, Oxon, 428
Bingham, Notts, 434, 456
Birchin Lane, London, 382
Bircholt, Kent, 403
Bird, Joan, 410; Roger, 85, 86, 87, 89, 91; William, 407
Birdlip, Glos, 71
Bisham, Berks, 200, 210
Bishop, Richard, 414
Bishopsgate (street), London, 380, 383–85, 387, 389, 395, 396, 435, 436, 438, 441, 444, 447, 449, 450, 456, 457, 458, 459, 460
Bishops Hatfield, Herts, 414
Bishops Stortford (Starford), Herts, 202, 414
Bishopsthorpe, Yorks, 154
Bishops Waltham, Hants, 417
Bisley (Bessley), Glos, 257
Blackburn, Blackburne, Lancs, 403, 456
Black(e) Friars (Friers), London, 383, 384
Blackheath, Surrey, 402, 424
Blackmore, Essex, 410
Blacknall, William, 413
Blackney see Blakeney
Blackstone Edge, Lancs, 235
Blackwall, Essex, 202, 280, 408
Blackwater (Bawwaw), Hants, 131, 276
Blair Atholl, Scotland, 73
Blakeney, Glos, 261
Blakeney (Blackney), Norfolk, 127, 141, 142
Blanchard, Francis, 411
Blandford (Blandfourd, Blanvile) Forum, Dorset, 434, 456
Blechingley (Bleechingles), Surrey, 423
Blenchdy, Blenchley see Brenchley
Bleneby, Kent, 461
Blengate, Kent, 402
Blewborough, Kent, 403
Blisland (Blistland), Cornwall, 299
Blithe, Thomas, 406
Blithe Bridge see Blyth Bridge
Blois (Bloys), Henry, earl of, 421

Bloomesbury see Bloomsbury
Bloomfield, Mary, 409
Bloomsbury (Bloomesbury), London, 396
Bloxham, Oxon, 428
Bloys see Blois
Bloys, William, 416
Blundel, Master, 116
Blunt, Thomas, 408
Blyth (Blithe) Bridge, Scotland, 57
Bocking, Essex, 411, 434, 456
Bodleian Library, Oxford, xi, xiv, 160, 216
Bodmin (Bodman), Cornwall, 299
Boen, Richard, 417
Bognor, Sussex, 175
Bohemia (Beame, Beamer, Bohem, Böhmische), x, 92, 93, 95–98, 99, 107, 109, 110, 113, 114, 116, 118, 121, 122, 124, 125, 289
Bolingbroke, Henry of, 334
Bolters see Boulter's
Bonaventure, Charles, 96
Bond, John, 411
Boorne, see Borna
Bordeaux (Burdeaux), France, 67, 419
Boreham, Essex, 411
Borna (Boorne), Germany, 110
Bosmere, Hants, 418
Boston, Lincs, 127, 142, 143, 227, 433
Boswell, Anne, 423
Bosworth, Market (battle), Leics, 218, 221, 222, 266
Botley, Hants, 417
Boulter's (Bolters) Lock, Bucks, 211
Bourne see Eastbourne
Bourne, Miles, 423
Bourton (Burton) on the Water, Glos, 198
Bouton under Bleath, Kent, 403
Boveney, Bucks, 211
Bow, London, 408
Bow Bridge, Leics, 221
Bowlane, London, 383, 386
Bowser, Mistris, 258
Bowyer, John, 420; Sir William, 81
Boyse, Richard, 173
Brackley, Northants, 435, 456
Brading, Wight, 417
Bradley, William, 427
Bradshaw, William, 168, 402
Braemar, Scotland, 33, 70, 71
Brainford see Brentford
Braintree (Brayntree), Essex, 409, 434, 456
Bramber (Bramborow), Sussex, 405, 406
Bramley see Bromley
Brandenberge, Germany, 95
Branghing see Braughing
Branthwaite, Edmond, 53, 54

INDEX OF PERSONS AND PLACES 467

Brasserton, John, 317
Braughing (Branghing), Herts, 415
Braunschweig (Brunswick), Germany, 93, 105-7
Bray (Braye), Berks, 201, 211, 421
Bray, Arthur, 164; Sir Reignold, 419
Brayford (Brayfourd), Devon, 298
Brayntree, *see* Braintree
Breadstreet (Breasteeet, Bredstreet, Broadstreet), London, 381, 385, 386, 396, 433, 434, 436, 437, 439, 442, 444, 445, 447, 448, 450, 456–60
Breakespeare, Nicholas, 415
Breakneck *see* Brecknock
Breame *see* Bremen
Breamore (Breamer), Hants, 188
Brea of Marr(e), Scotland, 36, 70, 71, 74, 76
Breasteeet *see* Breadstreet
Brechin (Breckin, Breechin, Breekin), Scotland, 33, 70, 77, 78
Brecknock (Breakneck), Wales, 235
Bredge, Kent, 403
Bredstreet *see* Breadstreet
Breechin, Breekin *see* Brechin
Bremen (Breame), Germany, 24
Brenchley (Blenchdy, Blenchley), Surrey, 401, 451
Brent, River, 201
Brentford (Brainford, Brentfoord), Middlesex, 180, 192, 275, 291, 406
Brentwood (Burntwood), Essex, 202, 410
Brereton *see* Bruton
Breton, Nicholas, 290
Brewton *see* Bruton
Brexton, Thomas, 418
Brian, Mr (of Cambridge), 324, 325
Briant, Richard, 404
Brickhill, Bucks, 424
Bricksley *see* Brightlingsea
Bridg, Elizabeth, 400
Bridgenorth *see* Bridgnorth
Bridger, George, 422
Bridgewater *see* Bridgwater
Bridgnorth (Bridgenorth), 259, 435, 456
Bridgwater (Bridgewater), 287, 295, 340, 341
Brielle *see* Brill
Brighthelmeson *see* Brighton
Brightlingsea (Bricksley), Essex, 412
Brighton (Brighthelmeson), 405
Brill, Bucks, 424, 436, 457
Brill (Brielle), Germany, 105
Brinkley, Kent, 403
Brinsall, Nicholas, 424
Brisco, John, 413
Brisley (Brissley), Norfolk, 322
Bristol (Bristoll, Bristow, Brystow), 181, 249, 250, 254, 261, 262, 264, 266, 268, 282, 290, 388, 433-4, 456
Brixton, Surrey, 424
Broadwindsor (Broad Winsor), Dorset, 307
Broadoake, Hatfield, Essex, 411
Broadstreet *see* Breadstreet
Broadwater, Herts, 415
Brockhampton, Herefs, 264
Bromley (Broomley), Kent, 203, 399, 402, 435
Bromley (Bramley), Abbots, or Kings, Staffs, 435
Bromsberrow (Broomsbury), Glos, 434, 456
Brooke, Mr (of Glastonbury), 295; Thomas, 426
Brookstreet, Essex, 412
Broomes well *see* Brownswell
Broomley *see* Bromley
Broomsbury *see* Bromsberrow
Broughton, Leics, 436, 457
Broughton, Scotland, 57
Brown Richard, 416
Browne, Lawrence, 409; Sith, 423
Brownswell (Broomes well), Herts, 39
Bruce, David, 225; Sir George, 65, 66, 68
Brunswick, *see* Braunschweig
Brunswick-Wolfenbüttel, Germany, 106
Bruton (Brereton, Brewton), Som, 434, 456
Brystow *see* Bristol
Buchan (Bughan), James, earl of, 71, 77
Buckeburg (Buckaburgh, Buckaburghe), Germany, 26
Buckingham (Buckhingham, Buk), Bucks, 34, 203, 328, 381, 391, 392, 426, 433, 435, 456, 457
Buckingham-house, London, 385
Buckinghamshire (Bucks), 199, 201, 209–11, 256, 291, 331, 393, 424, 434, 436, 437, 440, 443, 445, 448, 449, 454, 456, 458–61
Buckland, Hants, 416, 436
Buckle, Sir Cuthbert, 379
Buckley *see* Bulkeley
Buckstahoo *see* Buxtehude
Bucquoy (Buquoy), Charles, count of, 96
Bud, Anne, 418
Bude, Cornwall, 298
Budfont *see* Bedfont
Budlegate, Hants, 418
Budwit, Humphrey, 428
Bughan *see* Buchan
Buk *see* Buckingham
Bulkeley (Buckley), Thomas, 336
Bull, James, 408; Miles, 400
Bullen, Edward, 414
Bullinbrook *see* Bolingbroke
Bullington, Oxon, 428
Bulverhith, Sussex, 404

Buntingford, Herts, 83, 414
Buntsborough, Hants, 419
Buquoy *see* Bucquoy
Burdeaux *see* Bordeaux
Burdet, John, 401
Burford (Burfoord, Burfourd), 198, 263, 264, 392, 426, 435, 456
Burg Dankwarderode, Germany, 106
Burgate, Hants, 188
Burlace, John, 427
Burnet-Iland *see* Burntisland
Burnham, Bucks, 424, 426
Burnham, Essex, 411
Burntisland (Burnet-Iland, Burnt-Iland), Scotland, 62, 63, 64, 78, 194
Burntwood *see* Brentwood
Burr, John, 413
Burton *see* Bourton; Kings Barton
Burton, Ralph, 409; Samuell, 410
Burwash (Barreash), Sussex, 405
Bury (Berre), Lancs, 456
Bury (Berry) St Edmunds, Suffolk, 435, 436, 457
Buscot, Berks, 419
Bush, Mr (of Lambourn), 85
Bushel, Captaine, 116
Bushell, Thomas, 338
Bush-lane, London, 375, 386, 396
Butler, Henry, 414; Jo., 416; Robert, 407,
Butolph (Buttolph) lane, London, 395, 396
Butter, Jonathan, 318
Buttolph *see* Butolph
Buxted (Backesteed), Sussex, 405
Buxtehude (Buckstahoo), Germany, 23, 24, 29
Buzzard, Leighton (Laighten, Laighton), Beds, 217, 442, 459
Byfleet, Surrey, 422

Cacot, Anne, 401
Caerleon (Carbean), Mon, 258, 344
Caermarden(shire) *see* Carmarthen(shire)
Caernarvon (Carnarvan), 225, 327, 328, 336, 337, 433
Cairn (Carny) o' Mount, Scotland, 77
Caister (Castor)-on-Sea, Norfolk, 134
Calais (Cales, Callice), France, 63, 266
Calhill, Kent, 403
Callice, *see* Calais
Calshot, Hants, 282
Camallodunum, 412
Cambden *see* Camden
Camberley, Surrey, 276
Camberwell, Surrey, 423
Camborne, Cornwall, 302
Cambridge, Cambs, viii, 107, 309, 311, 324, 325, 419, 433, 438, 457

Cambridgeshire, 324
Camden *see* Campden
Camden (Cambden), William, xi, xii, 36, 44, 133, 143, 147, 197, 202, 227, 252, 254, 265, 291, 294, 309, 319, 345, 355, 392, 398, 426
Camelford (Camelfourd), 299
Campden (Cambden, Camden), Chipping, Glos, 437, 457
Camper, John, 410
Campion, William, 401
Canning Street, London, 380, 384, 385
Canning, Richard, 427
Canterbury (Centerbury), Kent, 107, 186, 347, 362, 399, 438, 452, 457, 461
Capp, Bernard, vii, xv, 193, 347
Capthome, Surrey, 424
Caradoc, 334
Carbean *see* Caerleon
Carbery, earl of, 340
Cardiff(e), Glam, 344
Cardigan, Cardigans, 328, 336
Cardiganshire, 338
Carew, John, 304, 305; Richard, 305
Carey (Carow), Herefs, 264
Carisbrook(e) (Castbrooke), Wight, 281, 417
Carleton, Sir Dudley, 193, 195, 196, 253
Carlile *see* Carlisle
Carlin (Carling) Gill, Yorks, 53
Carlisle (Carlile), Cumb, 33, 54, 57
Carmarthen (Caermarden, Caermarthen), 327, 328, 338, 339, 433
Carmarthenshire (Caermardenshire), 339
Carnarvan *see* Caernarvon
Carny *see* Cairn
Carow *see* Carey
Carpenter, —, (weir owner), 205
Carshalton (Cashalton), Surrey, 422
Carter-lane (Carterlaine), London, 435, 436, 440, 443, 446, 448, 459, 460
Carter, Robert, 405, 435
Carus, Anne 404
Cary, Sir Henry, 195
Cashalton *see* Carshalton
Castbrooke *see* Carisbrook
Casterton, Cambs, 325
Castleton, Derbs, 216, 226
Castor *see* Caister
Cateaton (Cateaten) Street, London, 384, 434, 435, 446, 449, 456, 461
Catesby, Ezechiel, 407
Cave, William, 407
Caversham, Oxon, 208
Cawood (Cowood), Yorks, 229, 230
Caysho, Herts, 415
Cecil, Sir Edward, 195
Centerbury *see* Canterbury

INDEX OF PERSONS AND PLACES 469

Cerdicus, 416
Cervantes, Miguel de, 67, 232, 292
Chadlington, Oxon, 428
Chaffant *see* Chalfont
Chaford, Essex, 412
Chalfont (Chaffant), 424
Chalkley, Henry, 414
Challey *see* Chearsley
Chancery (Chauncery) lane, London, 384
Chandler, Will., 412
Chapman, Thomas, 422
Chard, Som, 437, 457
Charels *see* Charles
Charford (Chartford), Hants, 188
Charing, Kent, 400
Charing-Crosse, London, 381, 383, 385, 386, 389, 395, 434, 456
Charles I (Charels), king, 94, 266, 281, 283, 284, 288, 304, 353
Charles II, king, 19, 157, 357
Charleton, Berks, 421
Charley, Thomas, 425
Charte, Kent, 403
Charterhouse Lane, London, 383
Chartford *see* Charford
Charwell *see* Cherwell
Chatham (Chattham), Kent, 399, 403
Chaucer, Geoffrey, 278, 427
Chauncery *see* Chancery
Cheap(e)side, London, 223, 380, 386, 388, 437, 450
Cheapstow *see* Chepstow
Chearsley (Challey), Bucks, 425
Checkley, John, 425
Chelm(e)sford, Essex, 412
Chelsea (Chelsey), Middlesex, 406
Cheltenham, Glos, 198, 258, 437, 457
Chemnizt, Germany, 110
Chenies (Cheneis), Bucks, 424
Chepsted *see* Chipstead)
Chepstow (Cheapstow), Mon, 249, 262
Chertsey, Surrey, 201, 212, 422, 424, 454, 462
Cherwell (Charwell), River, 199, 426
Chesham, Bucks, 425, 436, 457
Cheshire (Chesshire), 46, 47, 235, 445, 447, 457, 459, 460
Chessam, Chessham *see* Chesham
Chesshire *see* Cheshire
Chester, Cheshire, x, 216, 235–37, 268, 289, 327–29, 333, 334, 433, 437, 457
Chesterfield, Derbs, 225, 457
Chesters key, London, 453, 462
Cheyny, John, 414
Chichester, Sussex, 176, 403, 406, 451, 461
Chick lane end, London, 388
Chiddington, Surrey, 451, 461

Chigwell, Essex, 412
Childe, John, 425
Chiltington (Chilkington), Sussex, 403, 452
Chippenham (Chipnam), 433
Chipping Ongar (Chippinganger), 411, 437
Chipping Campden (Cambden, Camden), Glos, 437, 457
Chipping (Chippin) Norton, Oxon, 426, 437, 457
Chipstead (Chepsted), Kent, 399
Chiswell street, London, 407
Chiswick(e), Middlesex, 201, 406, 407
Chlorus, Constantius, 231
Chomutov (Comoda), Bohemia, 111
Christchurch, Hants, vii, 159, 177, 178, 182, 392, 416, 417, 418
Churn, River, 198, 199, 257, 258
Chutesey, Hants. 419
Cicero, 184
Cicester, Ciciter *see* Cirencester
Cingilse, king, 427
Cinque ports, 168, 400, 402, 404
Cirencester (Cicester, Ciciter), Glos, 199, 249, 257, 290
Cissa, 403, 420
Citizen *see* Sittensen
Clackmannanshire, Scotland, 69
Clampard, Elizabeth, 401
Clare, Gilbert di, 266
Clark, John, 324; Thomas, 422
Clarke, Anne, 418; Captaine, 135, 141; Elizabeth, 423
Claudius, Emperor, 265
Clavering, Essex, 413
Clayton, —, (of Hastings), 173
Clearkenwell *see* Clerkenwell
Cleeve, Oxon, 207
Clements, St, London, 381, 384, 385, 390, 395, 433, 456
Clenennau (Clenennau), Caernarvons, 337
Clerkenwell (Clearkenwell), Middlesex, 40, 381, 384, 386, 407
Cliffe, Sussex, 405
Clifford, Rosamond, 427
Clift, Mathew, 262
Clifton Hampden, Oxon, 205
Climenie *see* Clenennau
Clowance, Cornwall, 302
Clydogau, Llanfair, Cardigans, 338
Cobbett, William, vii
Coberley, Glos, 198, 258
Coberspath, Scotland, 79, 80
Cobham, Surrey 283, 422, 423
Cockburnspath, Scotland, 79
Cockermouth, Cumb, 432
Coe, John, 411

Coggeshall (Cogshall), Essex, 437, 457
Colchester, Essex, 131, 409, 411, 436, 452, 457, 462
Cold Ashby (Coleashby), Northants, 437, 457
Coldfield, Sutton, Warwicks, 33, 44
Coleashby *see* Cold Ashby
Colebrand, Peter, 399
Colebrook(e) *see* Colnbrook
Colebrooke, Elizabeth, 426
Coleford, Glos, 262
Coleharbour, London, 380
Colemanstreet, London, 388, 438, 441, 450, 457, 458, 461
Coles, George, 404
Collein, Colleyne *see* Kolín
Collin *see* Cologne
Collins, Elizabeth, 426; Mr (of Winchelsea), 172
Collstow, Bucks, 426
Colne (Coln), Lancs, 457
Colnbrook (Colebrook(e), Bucks, 201, 291, 425, 453, 462
Colne, River, 131, 199, 201, 409
Colney (Coney) Heath, Herts, 156, 413
Cologne (Collin), Germany, 105
Colton, Master (of Goring), 207
Comber, John, 423
Comoda *see* Chomutov
Compostella, Jacomo, 21
Compton, Berks, 421
Coney *see* Colney
Congleton (Congerton), Cheshire, 457
Conilos, Kent, 403
Constantine, emperor, 409
Constantinople, 409, 433
Constantius, emperor, 231
Conway *see* Cwmann
Coobridge *see* Cowbridge
Cook(e)-Ruffian, 75
Cooke, —, (of Cirencester), 257
Cookham (Cookeham), Berks, 211
Coond(e)-lane-end *see* Coundlane
Cooras *see* Culross
Coothridge, John, 406
Corbet, Vincent, 334
Coriat *see* Coryat
Cornehill *see* Cornhill
Cornewall *see* Cornwall
Corney, Master (of Westmorland), 54; (of York), 231
Cornhill (Cornehill), London, 381, 382, 386, 387
Cornish, Henry, 426
Cornwall (Cornewall), 288, 289, 298–303, 305, 306, 315, 316, 413, 433
Coryat(e) (Coriat), Thomas, xii, 3, 4, 5, 34, 67, 108, 155, 291
Cotswolds (Coteswould, Cotswould), 198, 257
Coundlane (Coond(e)-lane-end), Salop, 260
Covent-Garden, London, 273, 325, 328, 348, 381, 382, 384, 387
Coventry, Warwicks, xi, 33, 44, 215, 216, 223, 224, 254, 265, 332, 438, 457
Covill, Master (of Lancaster), 52
Cow Lane, London, 382
Cowbridge (Coobridge), Glam, 343
Cow-crosse, Middlesex, 407
Cowes (Cowse), Wight, 176, 277–79, 417
Cowood *see* Cawood
Cowse *see* Cowes
Cox, Richard, 420
Cranbrook (Crambroke, Crambrooke), Kent, 400, 401, 403, 451, 461
Crane, John, 414
Cranz (Crants), Germany, 23
Crawley, Sussex, 405
Crawley, North, Bucks, 437, 457
Cray, St Mary, Kent, 401
Crayford, Kent, 399
Creechurch, London, 395
Creede Lane End, London, 382
Creeklad *see* Cricklade
Creeplegate *see* Cripplegate
Creet(e) *see* Greetham
Crewkerne (Crookehorn(e)), Som, 438, 457
Cricklade (Creeklad), Wilts, 257
Crighton, Master (of Dunfermline), 65
Cripplegate (Creeplegate, Criplegate), London, 46, 380, 383, 388, 395, 441, 442, 457–9
Crockern (Crockham) Pill, Som, 261, 399
Crofts, Anne, 414
Cromer, Norfolk, 127, 135, 138, 140, 159
Cromford Moor, Derbs, 225
Cromwell, Oliver, 283
Crookehorn(e) *see* Crewkerne
Cross, Anne, 416; John, 425; Wil. 414
Crowan (Crowen), Cornwall, 302
Crowch, Joh., 426
Crowen *see* Crowan
Crowmarsh Gifford, Oxon, 205
Croxton, Miles, 399
Croydon, Surrey, 201, 353, 422, 424
Crundon, Hants, 418
Cubington, Kent, 462
Cuckfield, Sussex, 404, 451, 461
Culham (Cullom), Oxon, 205
Culmer, Henry, 401
Culross (Cooras), Scotland, 65
Cumberland, 55, 114
Custom house (key), London, 85, 151, 268, 386, 387, 390, 395, 453, 462
Cwmann (Conway), Cardigans, 338

INDEX OF PERSONS AND PLACES 471

Czech Republic 16

Dacorum, Herts, 415
Dadlington, Leics, 215, 222, 237
Dae, Anne, 409
Dagenham (Dagnam), Essex, 410
Daintree *see* Daventry
Dalby, Agnes, 426
Dallington, Sussex, 405
Dalston (Dalstone), Sir George, 54; Sir John, 54
Dalwhinnie, Scotland, 76
Dam, —, 41
Damm, Jacob, 12
Dampier (Dampeier), Count of, 96
Danbury, Essex, 409
Dankwarderode, Burg (Germany), 106
Dansey, James, 404
Darbie, Darby *see* Derby
Dardesheim (Darsam), Germany, 107
Darent, River, 203, 397
Darentfourd. *see* Dartford
Darington *see* Darlington
Darking *see* Dorking
Darlington (Darington), Durham, 81
Darnaway (Tarnaway), Scotland, 76
Darsam *see* Dardesheim
Dartford (Darentfourd, Dartfourd), Kent, 203, 397
Dartmouth, Devon, 453, 462
Datchet, Bucks, 211
Daventry (Daintree), Beds, 33, 41, 42, 420, 439, 457
Davis, Thomas, 398
Day, Ellin, 422; John, 407
Deacon, Rose, 415
Deal (Deale), Kent, 166, 400
Dean (Deane), Forest, Glos, 261, 265
Deane, Christopher, 426; George, 411
Deanshanger, Northants, 439, 457
Deddington, Oxon, 427
Dedham, Essex, 410
Dee, River, 235
Deepefourd *see* Deptford
Deering, Robert, 404
Defoe, Daniel, vii, 325
Dekker, Thomas, 121
Delaune, Thomas, 429
Deloney, Thomas 23
Den Haag, Netherlands, 105,
Den, Edward, 400
Denbigh, Denbighshire, 328, 439, 457
Dengie, Essex, 170, 413
Denkte, Gross, Germany, 107
Denmark (Denmarke), 65, 386
Denmarkehouse, London, 387
Deptford (Deepefourd), Kent,164, 203, 397, 453, 462
Derby (Darbie, Darby), 83, 216, 225–6, 289, 433, 439, 457
Derby, Earl of, 83, 235
Derbyshire, x, 216, 225, 457
Dereham, Norfolk, 322
Devil's (Divells)Arse, Derbs, 215, 216, 226, 239, 289
Devizes (Devises, De-Vises, Vies), Wilts, 447, 460
Devon, Devonshire, 298, 303, 306, 307, 436, 438, 447, 457, 460
Dickenson, Briedget, 418
Dickins, William, 400, 409
Dickinson, Francis, 425
Dickshore *see* Duke Shore
Dike, Sir Thomas, 356
Disborough, Bucks, 426
Disert *see* Dysart
Distar Lane, London,380
Diston, William, 398
Ditchling (Ditchelling), Sussex, 404
Ditmarsh *see* Tidmarsh
Divoká, Bohemia, 111
Dix, Francis, 229
Döhren (Dorne), 26
Dolbenmaen, Caernarvons, 337
Domelaw (Domelow), John, 398, 421
Doncaster, Yorks, 82, 157, 439, 457
Doncastle, Dorathy, 417
Donnington, William, 420
Dorcet *see* Dorset
Dorchester, Dorset or Oxon, 439, 457
Dorchester, Oxon, 195–97, 199, 426–8,
Dorchester, Viscount, 195–7
Dore (Doyre), River, 252
Dorking (Darking), Surrey, 423, 424, 451, 461
Dorne *see* Döhren
Dorney, John, 252
Dorset (Dorcet), Dorsetshire, 281, 303, 307, 405, 434, 437, 442, 447, 456, 457, 458
Dorverden (Durfurne), Germany, 26
Douglas (Dowglasse), Alexander, 77
Dove Gang (Gany), Derbs, 225
Dover, Kent, 166–68, 347, 362, 402, 433, 452, 453, 461, 462
Dowgate, London, 382, 389, 395
Dowglasse *see* Douglas
Downes, John, 298
Downham Market, Norfolk, 229
Downhamford, Kent, 403
Downton, Wilts, 188
Doyre *see* Dore
Drake, Sir Francis, 138
Duke Shore (Dickshore), London, 408
Drayton, Michael, xii, 143, 194, 197, 254

Dresden, Germany, 118
Dring, William, 397
Drummond, David, 63, 81
Drury Lane, London, 382–85, 387, 437
Ducke, Robert, 424
Dudley, Lord, 3
Dudstone (Dunstone), Glos, 265
Dumbarton (Dumbritton), Scotland, 230
Dumfermline (Dunferming), 64, 65
Dumfriesshire, 57
Dunbar (Dunbarr), Scotland, 62, 79
Duncehanger see Deanshanger
dunce-stable see Dunstable
Dunchurch, Warwicks, 43
Duncombe, Sanders, 370
Dundalk(e), Baron, 188
Dundee, 62, 78
Dunfermline, 33, 65
Dungeness, Kent, 170
Dunkirk, France, 453, 462
Dunmow, Essex, 411, 413, 438, 457
Dunsmore, Warwicks, 43
Dunstable (dunce-stable), Beds, 40, 100
Dunster (Dunstar), Som, 297
Dunstone see Dudstone
Durfurne see Dorverden
Durham, 81, 397, 417
Durkin, Reignold, 423
Durley, Hants, 281
Duvall, Henry, 96
Dysart (Disert), Scotland, 62

Earle, John, 411
Earls Colne (Eastcolne), Essex, 410
Eastbourne (Bourne), Sussex, 347, 356, 358, 359, 363, 404
Eastcheap(e), London, 380, 388
Eastcolne see Earls Colne
Easter, Good or High (Esterford), Essex, 131, 410
East Gosford (Gasford), Scotland, 79
East Green(e)wich, Kent, 397
East Grinstead (Greensteed), Sussex, 405
East Haddington, Scotland, 79
Eastincon see East Meon
Eastington (Eston), Glos, 259
East Looe (Loo, Low), Cornwall, 305, 306
Eastman (Estman), Thomas 159, 180, 188
East Meon (Eastincon, Eastmean), 417, 418
East Molesey (Monlesey, Mowlsey), Surrey, 201, 422
East Wittering, Sussex, 176
Eaton, Norfolk, 319
Eaton see Eton
Eaton Bridge see Edenbridge
Ecclesgreig (Eggels Land), Scotland, 70

Edenborough see Edinburgh
Edenbridge (Eaton Bridge), 401, 452, 461
Edenthorpe (Streethorpe), Yorks, 157
Edgeware (Edgware, Edgworth), Middlesex, 331, 406
Edinburgh (Edenborough, Edinborough, Endenborough), Scotland, 33–36, 54, 58, 60–2, 69, 70, 76–78, 80, 117, 450
Edmonds, Sir Thomas, 195
Edmonton, Middlesex, 407, 409
Edward (kings): Elder, 411; Confessor, 73, 420, 424; I, 397, 400, 414; II, 225; III, 224, 225, 266, 378, 397, 398, 400, 405, 415, 417; IV, 124, 266, 320, 413, 415
Edwards, Alderman, 235; Ursula, 412, William, 417
Edwinstree, Herts, 415
Eeds, Richard, 406
Effingham, Surrey, 424
Egerton, Kent, 399
Egerton, Alice, 340
Eggels Land see Ecclesgreig
Egham, Surrey, 423
Elam see Elham
Elbe, River, 8, 16, 94, 118
Elgin (Elgen), Scotland, 76, 77
Elham (Elam), Kent, 399
Elizabeth (queen), 289, 351, 379, 402, 419, 424
Elland, Yorks, 148
Ellis, Henry, 251
Elmes, —, 208
Eltham, Kent, 397
Elthorne, Middlesex, 409
Elver, Alexander, 416
Ely (Elye), Cambs, 8, 95, 118, 324
Elzey, Elizabeth, 416
Emley Bridge, Surrey, 424
Enborne, Berks, 200, 419
Endenborough see Edinburgh
Enedor see St Enoder
Enfield (Engfield, Henfield), Middlesex, 407, 452, 461
Engie (Engye), Earl of, 71, 76, 77
Enoder (Enedor), St, Cornwall, 299
Enstone, Oxon, 427
Epping, Essex, 409, 439, 458
Epsom (Epsome, Hebsome), Surrey, 452, 461, 462
Eringer, Hants, 418
Erith, Kent, 164, 399, 453, 462
Ernst, Count, 26, 115
Erskin, James, 71; John, 71, 73, 77
Erzgebirge, Bohemia, 110
Esham see Evesham
Esk, River, 55, 57
Essex, 86, 89, 105, 130, 131, 164, 165, 202, 203,

INDEX OF PERSONS AND PLACES   473

317, 318, 391, 393, 409, 412, 413, 434, 437–39, 442, 443, 446–48, 452, 453, 456–60
Esterford *see* Easter
Estman *see* Eastman
Eston *see* Eastington
Eton (Aeton, Eaton), Bucks, 211, 401, 425
Evanowich, Gregory, 22
Evans, Thomas, 338
Evenlode (Yenload), River, 199
Ever *see* Iver
Evershot, Dorset, 307
Evesham (Esham, Evesholm), Worcs, 263, 265, 440, 458
Ewell, Surrey, 201, 423
Ewelme (New-elme), Oxon, 428, 444
Exeter, Devon, 288, 298, 306, 433, 439, 458
Exford, Som, 298
Exmouth, Devon, 298
Exton, Sir Piers of, 157
Eyhorne, Kent, 403
Eynsham, Oxon, 257

Fabyn, Henry, 416
Fairecrosse, Berks, 421
Faireway, Elizabeth, 399
Fairfax, Thomas, Lord, 283, 352
Fairlight (Fairlegh, Fairleigh), Sussex, 172
Fairy Cross (Ferry Crosse), Devon, 298
Fakenham, Norfolk, 322
Falkland, Henry, Viscount, 195
Falkstone, Roger, 411
Falmouth (Faymouth), Cornwall, 303
Falstaff, Sir John, 13
Fanchurchstreet *see* Fenchurch Street
Fareham, Hants, 416, 418
Faringdon (Farington), Berks, 288, 292, 420, 421, 440, 458
Farley, Alice, 412
Farmour, John, 424
Farndon, Cheshire, 235
Farneham *see* Farnham
Farnell, Thomas, 409
Farnham (Farneham), 192, 283, 421, 424, 425
Farningham (Ferningham), Kent, 399
Faseley *see* Fazeley
Faut *see* Frant
Faversham (Feversham), Kent, 399, 402, 453, 462
Fawley, Hants, 418
Fawley Court, Bucks, 209
Fawlkland *see* Falkland
Faymouth *see* Falmouth
Fazeley (Faseley), Staffs, 237
Feckenham (Feckingham), Worcs, 440, 458
Feirden *see* Verden an der Aller
Felborow, Kent, 403

Feltham, Middlesex, 407
Fen, Master, 229
Fenchurch (Fanchurch) Street, London, 382, 386, 388, 389
fenden, Selbright, Kent, 403
Fenny Stratford, Bucks, 425
Fensham *see* Fincham
Fenton, John, 64
Ferningham *see* Farningham
Ferribrig *see* Ferrybridge
Ferring, Sussex, 175
Ferry Crosse *see* Fairy Cross
Ferrybridge (Ferribrig), Yorks, 460
Fettercairn, Scotland, 77
Feversham *see* Faversham
Fiennes, Celia, vii
Fife, Scotland, 62, 65
Figge, Mathew, 177
Fince, Anne, 423
Finch Lane, London, 382, 383, 396
Fincham (Fensham), Norfolk, 229
Finchdeane, Hants, 418
Finchley, Middlesex, 39
Finsbury, Middlesex, 409
Finsbury-fields, London, 376, 380
Fisherton Bridge, Wilts, 188
Fishstreet, London, 46, 380, 384, 388, 389
Fist, Mr (of Billingshurst), 354
Fitch, Francis, 411
Flammard, Ralph, 416
Flanders, 212, 270
Fleet Dock, London, 317
Fleet Lane, London, 383
Fleet, Edward, 401
Fleetbridge, London, 380, 387
Fleetstreet, London, 381–84, 386, 388, 389, 396
Fletcher, William, 404
Flint, Flintshire, 194, 327, 328, 334
Flodden Field, Northumb, 69
Flotman, Newton, Norfolk, 319
Foane Hope *see* Fownhope
Folkestone (Folkstone. Folstone), Kent, 168, 399, 403
Foots Cray (Footsbray), Kent, 401
Forcedike *see* Fossdyke
Forde, John, 405
Fordingbridge (Forthingbridg), Hants, 187, 417, 419
Forest Row (Forrest Roe), Sussex, 403
Forfar (Forfard), Scotland, 78
Forres, Scotland, 76
Forrest Roe *see* Forest Row
Forrest, Thomas, 2
Forthingbridg *see* Fordingbridge
Fossdyke (Forcedike), 144

Foster, Elizabeth, 421; Thomas, 408
Foul-lane, Southwark, 462
Foulness (Fowlenesse), Essex, 131
Founehope see Fownhope
Fowey (Foye), Cornwall, 305
Fowlenesse see Foulness
Fownhope (Foane Hope, Founehope), 262, 264
Fox, Robert, 399
Foy, Herefs, 263
Foye see Fowey
Fraddon, Cornwall, 299
Frampton on Severn, Glos, 258
France, 62, 100, 230, 378, 379, 400, 402, 418, 419
Franchils, Kent, 403
Frant (Faut, Fronte), Sussex, 404, 451
Freeman, Elizabeth, 403; Tho. 411
Freezeland see Friesland
French, John, 411
Freshwell, Essex, 413
Friday-street, London, 448, 456, 458–61
Frier, - (of Norfolk), 227-8
Friesland (Freezeland), Netherlands, 7
Frinton, Essex, 131
Froburge see Fröhburg
Frogmill (Frogge-mill) Farm, Berks, 210
Fröhburg (Froburge), 110
Fromebridge (Froombridge), Glos, 258, 259
Fronte see Frant
Froombridge see Fromebridge
Fulham, Middlesex, 406
Fuller, Anthony, 399; Thomas, 264, 392
Fyfield, Berks, 292

Gads Hill, Kent, 71
Gage, Elizabeth, 281
Gainsborough (Gainsborowe), 144, 253
Galbreath, Ancient, 116
Galcombe see Gatcombe
Ganfield, Berks 421
Gardner, Thomas, 425
Garroway, James, 420
Garson, Thomas, 419
Garyre, Anne, 417
Gascoigne, George, 361
Gasford see Gosford
Gatcombe (Galcombe), Glos, 261, 268, 269
Gayton, Norfolk, 322, 323
Geary, Captain, 301
Geethe see Keith
Genoa, Italy, 96
George, Jeffrey, 408
Gerhold, Dorian, viii, 429
German, Germany, 3, 4, 8, 9–31, 33, 59, 69, 93–110, 113, 118–21, 122, 289, 421

Gertrude, Mrs (of Cornwall), 302
Gery, Henry, 414
Giant's Well, Cornwall, 301
Gibb, John 65
Gibbon, Marsh, 425
Gibson, Mary, 423
Gifford, Crowmarsh, Oxon, 205
Gilbert, Adrian, 160, 190, 191
Gilby, Zachary, 408
Giles-in-the-Fields, St, London, 275, 386, 389, 404, 407, 440, 449, 458
Giles, Francis, 399; John, 404
Gilford see Guildford
Gillingham, Kent, 403
Glamorganshire (Glomorganshire), 266, 328, 341
Glaneske see Glen Esk
Glastonbury (Glastenbury), Som, 288, 294, 295
Glen Esk, Scotland, 70
Glocester, Glocestershire see Gloucester, Gloucestershire
Glomorganshire see Glamorgamshire
Gloucester (Glocester), viii-x, 71, 160, 198, 203, 212, 249–52, 254, 258, 259–69, 290, 327, 328, 344, 397, 423, 440, 458
Gloucestershire (Glocestershire), 198, 265, 266, 327, 437, 440, 446–84, 457, 458 460
Glover, Elizabeth, 397; James, 401
Godalming, (Godaliman, Godalimen, Godlyman), Surrey, 422, 424, 452, 461
Godolphin House, Cornwall, 300–2
Godolphin, Anthony, 300; Francis, 300–2
Godsheath, Kent, 403
Godstone, Surrey, 422, 451, 461
Gogerddan, Plas, Cardigan, 338
Gold, Richard, 404
Goldingham, Mawd, 412
Goldsbery, Joseph, 416
Goldsworth, Anne, 425
Goodman, Anthony, 404; Edward, 423
Goodrich, Herefs, 264
Goodwin Sands, Kent, 166
Goodwin, Dorcas, 414; Richard, 416
Goodyere, Stephen 407
Gordon, George, 71, 77
Gore, Middlesex, 409
Gore, William, 407
Goreing see Goring
Gorges, Edward, Lord, 159, 188, 191
Goring (Goreing), Oxon, 159, 174, 207, 256
Gosford (Gasford), Scotland, 79
Gosport, Hants, 418
Gosson, Henry, 95
Gotham, Notts, 96, 138, 225, 284
Goudhurst (Gowthurst), Kent, 399, 451, 461

INDEX OF PERSONS AND PLACES 475

Gouries *see* Gowrie
Gowen, Joan, 409
Gowrie (Gourie), John, Earl of, 99
Gowthurst *see* Goudhurst
Gracious Grass) street, London, 389, 448, 457, 459, 460
Grain (Grane), Isle of, Kent, 165
Graies, *see* Grays
Grampian Mountains, Scotland, 70
Grane *see* Grain
Grantham, Lincs, 225
Graunt, Laird of, 76
Grave, - (of Hamburg), 12
Gravesend, Kent, 6, 7, 23, 88, 93, 94, 97, 100–5, 130, 164, 202, 311, 317, 362, 363, 398, 453, 462
Gray, Sir Andrew, 116
Gray(e)s (Graies), Essex, 409, 410, 453, 462
Grayes-Inne lane, London, 41, 382, 396
Great Parndon (Parindon), Essex, 412
Great Sampford, Essex, 410
Great Tew (Tue), Oxon, 331, 332
Great Wakering, Essex, 131, 412
Great Waltham, Essex, 412
Great Yarmouth, Norfolk, xii, 127, 133, 134, 433
Greece, 28, 108, 196
Greene, Robert, 323; Roger, 412
Greenehive *see* Greenhithe
Greenewich *see* Greenwich
Greenhithe (Greenehive, Greenhith), Kent, 399, 453, 462
Greenoway, John, 420
Greensted, Greensteed *see* Grinstead
Greenstreet, Peter, 401
Greenvill *see* Grenville
Greenwich (Greenewich, Greenwitch), Kent, 160, 164, 194, 453, 462
Green(e)wich, East, Kent, 397
Greetham (Creet(e)), Rutland, 438, 457
Gregorie, Christopher, 424
Gregory, Emperor, 22
Grendon (Grindon) Underwood, Bucks, 440, 458
Grenville (Greenvill), John, 301
Gretna, Scotland, 54
Grice, William, 428
Griffin, Edward, 4
Griffith, Edward, 334
Grimes, Lieut,116
Grindon *see* Grendon
Grinstead (Greensted, Greensteed), East, Sussex, 405
Gröningen (Groning), Germany, 94, 107, 109
Groome, Ambrose, 398
Gross Denkte (Rosondink), Germany, 107
Grove, Francis, 372

Grub-street, London, 376, 380
Guildford (Gilford, Guilford, Guldeford), Surrey, 201, 283, 361, 422, 451, 461
Guildhall, London, 434, 435, 446, 449
Guilford *see* Guildford
Guilliam, William, 262
Guinn, William, 339
Guldeford *see* Guildford
Gurwin, Sir Henry, 54
Guy, Margaret, 423
Gybbs, George, 4
Gynn, Agnes, 411

Haag (Hage), Den, Netherlands, 105
Haberley, Julian, 422; William, 418
Haberly, Anthony, 418
Hackney, Middlesex, 407; coaches, 123, 129, 367–73
Haddington, Scotland, 79
Hadham, Much, Herts, 415, 441
Hadleigh (Hadley), Suffolk, 440, 458
Hadnock (Hancocks), Mon, 264
Hage, Hague *see* Haag, Den
Hagger, Thomas, 414
Haiday, James, 414
Haines, Judith, 402
Hakluyt, Richard, xii
Halberstadt (Halverstadt), Germany, 107
Hale, Hants, 188
Haley, Henry 406
Halifax (Hallifax), Yorks, x, 148, 149, 214, 215, 216, 234–5, 289, 330, 441, 458
Hall, John, 404; widow, 414
Halle (Hall), Germany, 109
Hallom, Thomas, 428
Halsey, John, 406
Halstead, Essex, 411
Halton (Hatton), George, 128; Richard, 128
Halverstadt *see* Halberstadt
Ham, Kent, 403
Hambleden (Hambleton), Bucks, 210
Hambledon, Hants, 417, 418
Hambleton *see* Hambleden
Hamburg (Hambrogh, Hamburgh), viii, x, 2–4, 8–23, 25, 31, 33, 34, 93–5, 105, 107, 118, 121, 289
Hammersmith, Middlesex, 201, 406
Hammond, Colonel, 284
Hamon, Robert fitz, 266
Hamond, Leonard, 414
Hampden, Clifton, Oxon, 205
Hampshire (Hampshire, Hantshire), 176, 188, 192, 200, 281, 282, 391, 393, 415, 417, 418, 451, 461
Hampstead Hill, Middlesex, 71
Hampton-Court, Middlesex, 407

Hanckhurst *see* Hawkhurst
Hancocks *see* Hadnock
Handy, Margaret, 420
Hanger, George, 397
Hanham, Glos, 264
Hanslope (Hanslap), Bucks, 424
Hantshire *see* Hampshire
Happisburgh (Asbur), Norfolk 434, 456
Harding *see* Harpenden
Harding, Alice, 405; Thomas, 414
Hardington *see* Hartington
Hare, James, 410
Harlech (Harleck), Merioneths, 327, 337
Harley *see* Hurley
Harlow, Essex, 409, 413
Harmer, Jacob, 332
Harpenden (Harding), Herts, 441, 458,
Harries Passage, King, Cornwall, 303
Harris, Francis, 428; Martha, 410; William, 425
Harrison, John, 231; William, xi, xii, 149, 194, 197
Harrow, Middlesex, 383, 396, 406
Hart, Henry, 401; Will, 319-20, 412
Hartfield, Sussex, 404
Hartford, Hartfourd *see* Hertford
Hartfordshire, Hartfourshire *see* Hertfordshire
Hartington (Hardington), Middlesex, 407
Hartley Row (Hartlerow), Hants, 418
Harvey, William, 255
Harvie, Thomas, 411
Harwich, Essex, 127, 131–33, 311, 318, 392, 412
Haslemere (Haselmere, Haslemoore, Hostmoor), 422, 452, 461
Hasler, Dina, 410
Hastings, Sussex, 172, 173, 220, 348, 359, 404–6, 451
Hastlegrove, William, 426
Hatfield (Hatfeild), 157, 325, 411, 414, 441, 458
Hatfield Broadoake, Essex, 411
Hator, Simon, 426
Hatton *see* Halton
Haughton *see* Houghton
Haukhurst *see* Hawkhurst
Havant, Hants, 416, 451, 461
Havering, Essex, 202, 413
Haviland, John, 194
Hawkhurst (Hanckhurst, Haukhurst), Kent, 400, 451, 461
Hawkins, George, 414; John, 420
Hawksworth, John, 417
Hawton, Rosamond, 414
Hayes, Middlesex, 407
Hay field, *see* Heathfield
Hayle, Cornwall, 302
Hayles, Margaret, 417; Sara, 425

Heal, Felicity, viii
Heane, Kent, 403
Heathfield (Hay field), Sussex, 404
Hebsome *see* Epsom
Heidelberg (Heidelberge, Germany, 108, 118
Heldesheim *see* Hildesheim
Heligoland (Holy Land), 7
Helston, Cornwall, 302
Hemel Hempstead, Herts, 414
Hemsworth, Mr (of York), 156
Henderson, James, 78
Hendley *see* Henley
Henfield, Sussex, 405 *see also* Enfield
Hening, Edmund, 426
Henley (Hendley, Henly), Oxon, 194, 208–10, 291, 427, 462
Henning, Micheas, 403
Henry (kings), I, 421, 427; II, 219, 320, 427; III, 227, 266, 320, 378, 398, 404, 405, 421; IV, 334; V, 424; VI, 224, 397, 401, 415, 416, 417, 419; VII, 107, 334, 340, 378, 397, 423, 424; VIII, 69, 147, 223, 303, 340, 379, 397, 400, 402, 412, 415
Hensham, Anne, 414
Herbert, William, 189
Hercy, John, 416
Hereford, 249, 250, 262, 263, 265, 290, 432, 441, 458
Herne, Kent, 401
Herrick, Robert, 127
Hertford (Hartford, Hartfourd), 391, 414, 415, 418, 458, 459
Hertfordshire (Hartfordshire, Hartfourshire), 201, 393, 413, 441, 443, 446, 449
Hessen, Germany, 107
Heyborne, Robert, 427
Heyden, Margaret, 282
Heylyn, Peter, 429
Heywood, John, 314; Robert, 409
Hiching *see* Hitchin
Higham, Oliver, 410
Highgate, Kent, 401
Highgate, Middlesex, 407; Hill, 38, 71
High-Holborn, London, 461
Highworth (Hiworth), Wilts, 292, 458
Hildesheim (Heldesheim), Germany, 94, 105
Hill, Mary, 407; Ralph, 425; Richard, 422; Thomas, 259
Hillingdon, Middlesex, 407
Hilton, Andrew, 43; Nathaniel, 354
Hinckford, Essex, 412
Hinckley, Leics, 237
Hinde, Master (of Preston), 51
Hitchcock, Sara, 407
Hitche, Daniel, 408
Hitchin (Hiching), Herts, 414, 415

INDEX OF PERSONS AND PLACES 477

Hithe *see* Hythe, 411
Hiworth *see* Highworth
Hockcliffe (Hockley, Hockliffe, Hockly), Beds, 40, 41, 217
Hockley-in-the-hole, London, 40
Hockliffe, Hockly *see* Hockcliffe
Hoddesden, Herts, 414
Hodney *see* Hydney
Hohenlohe, Prince of, 115
Holborn (Holbourne), London, 275, 380–5, 387, 388–90, 408, 433–35, 437–40, 443, 446–9, 456–58, 460, 461; Bridge, 439, 448, 449, 456–61
Holden *see* Howden
Holdernesse, —, 211
Holdshot, Hants, 418
Holensedale, Surrey, 422
Holford, Thomas, 400
Holinshed (Hollinshead), Raphael, xi, xii, 156, 194, 197, 218, 230
Holland, Netherlands, 105, 212, 270, 453, 462
Holland, Master (of Puckeridge), 83; Philemon, xi, 44; William, 353, 423
Hollinshead *see* Holinshed
Hollock, Prince of, 115
Holloway (Hollywell), London, 38
Holloway Street, London, 407
Holme Castle, Surrey, 422
Holmes, Jane, 424
Holt, Castle, Wight, 281
Holt, Katherin, 414
Holyhead, Anglesey, 33
Holy Land *see* Heligoland
Holy-rood-House, Edinburgh, 60
Holywell, Flintshire, 334–5
Honing, Norfolk, 321
Honiton, Devon, 287, 306
Hoo, Kent, 402
Hook, Hants, 308, 416
Hooper, Master (of Gatcombe), 261
Hoore, Anne, 421
Horeham, Sussex, 356
Horgy, Krusné, Bohemia, 110
Hormer Berks, 421
Horncastle, Lincs, 227, 229
Horndon (Hornden) on the Hill, Essex, 410
Hornwell, Hants, 418
Horsey *see* Osea
Horsey Down, London, 384
Horsham, Sussex, 404, 452, 461
Hortones, Master (of Siddington), 257
Hostmoor *see* Haslemere
Houghton (Haughton), Sussex, 404
Houghton Regis, Beds, 40
Houn(d)sditch, London, 7
Hounslow (Hownslow), Middlesex, 406

Howard, Thomas, 195
Howden (Holden), Yorks, 229
Howes, Edmund, 373, 379; Thomas, 420
Hownslow *see* Hounslow
Hoxton, London, 381, 383, 386
Huddersfield, Yorks, 233
Hudson, Dr, 81; James, 399; Judith, 400; Katherine, 401; Mary, 404
Hugesson, John, 402
Hull, Yorks, 127, 137, 145–50, 152, 180, 214–16, 229, 253, 268, 289, 330, 442, 452, 458
Hulme, Lancs, 48
Humber, River 143–9, 153, 180, 229, 253
Humphrey, Duke, 420
Hungary, 96
Hungerford, Berks, 200, 420, 433
Hungroad, Glos, 261
Hunningham, Warwicks, 332
Hunt, Will, 420
Huntingdon (Huntington), 82, 83, 441, 458
Huntingdon Earl of, 178, 220; Henry of, 251
Huntingdonshire (Huntington-shire), 186, 324
Huntington Library, 34, 95, 309, 430
Huntley, George, 401; Marquess of, 71, 77
Huntly Castle, Scotland, 77
Hurley (Harley) Berks, 210
Hurst Castle, Hants, 176, 188, 281, 283
Hutchinson, John, 424; Sir Thomas, 224
Hyde *see* Hythe
Hydney (Hodney), Sussex, 404
Hythe (Hithe), Essex, 411
Hythe (Hyde), Kent, 169, 362, 401

Iffley, Oxon, 204
Ilford, Essex, 411
Inckson *see* Ingestone
India, 3, 42, 67, 408
Ingatestone (Ingarstone, Ingerstone), 410, 442, 458
Ingestone (Inckson, Inkson), Herefs, 263
Ingram, Sir Arthur, 230
Inkson *see* Ingestone
Inverness, 76
Ipswich, Suffolk, 309, 311, 318, 319, 442, 452, 458, 462
Ireland, 283, 340, 430, 431, 452, 453, 455, 462
Isis (Thames), River, 193–213, 252, 257, 258, 264, 273, 426, 427
Isleworth (Istleworth, Thistleworth), Middlesex, 406, 409
Islington, Middlesex, 34, 38, 83, 407
Islip, Oxon, 427
Istleworth *see* Isleworth
Italy, Italian, 3, 135, 251, 267, 305, 327, 333, 351
Ivell *see* Yeovil
Iver (Ever), Bucks, 425

Ives, St, Hunts, 186
Ivie (Ivy), John, 191
Ivinghoe, Bucks, 425
Ivy see Ivie

Jackman, W T, 367
Jacob, James, 399; Richard, 379; Sibella, 379
James, John, 417; Richard, 418
James (kings), I, 51, 56, 65, 93, 99, 105, 113, 116, 136, 176; IV (Scotland), 69; V (Scotland), 61; VI (Scotland), see James I
Jaques, Sir Roger, 231
Jeakes, Samuel, 347, 361
Jemut, Warham, 400
Jenkinson, Averie, 401
Jennings, John, 408; Owen, 418
Jerusalem, 384
Jeyner, Richard, 408
John (king), 162, 227, 266, 324, 378, 408, 418
Johnson, Charles, 403; see also Jonson
Johnston, St (Perth), 70
Jones, Peter, 406; Rice, 343; Thomas, 260; Mr, 302, 343, 406
Jonson (Johnson), Ben, 35, 78, 168, 228, 230, 317
Jordane, Robert, 407
Josceline, John, 409

Karbery, Earl of, 340
Katherine's, St, London, 384, 385, 388, 453, 461; Dock, 453; Hospital and Stairs, 161
Kayes, Mr (of York), 156
Keeling, Ralfe, 411
Keen (Skeene), Mt, Scotland, 71
Keinsham see Keynsham
Keinton see Kineton
Keith, (Geethe), Scot, 77
Kellway, Richard, 406
Kelsey, John, 404
Kelvedon (Kelvadon), Essex, 412
Kemp(e), Basill, 416; Robert, 139; Will, xii, 34, 85
Kendall, Westmorland, 423, 427, 432, 458
Kenisham see Keynsham
Kennet, River, 200
Kent, 86, 90, 97, 100, 130, 160, 164–66, 168, 170, 171, 203, 317, 318, 347, 348, 362, 391, 393, 396–99, 402–5, 411, 429, 451–53, 461, 462
Kentbury, Berks, 421
Kent Hatch, Kent, 399
Kentish Town, Middlesex, 407
Kenton, Middlesex, 407
Kensington (Kenzington), Middlesex, 406
Kepler, Johannes, 28
Ket(t), Robert, 320

Keverne, St, Cornwall, 305
Keynsham (Keinsham, Kenisham, Kinsham), Som, 264, 266
Kiddal (Kidell), Yorks, 231
Kidsgrove, Staffs, 46
Killegrew, Sir Peter, 283
Kimble, Captain, 135, 141
Kims, John, 425
Kincardineshire, Scotland, 77
Kinderne see Könnern
Kindrochet (Kindroghit) Lodge, Perthshire, 73
Kineton (Keinton), Warwicks, 442, 455
King, Elizabeth, 416
Kinghamford, Kent, 403
King Harries Passage, Cornwall, 303
Kinghorn(e), Scotland, 62, 78
Kingroad (Kingrode), Glos, 261, 262, 268
Kings Barton (Burton), Glos, 265
Kings Bromley (Bramley), Staffs, 435
Kings Langley, Herts, 415
Kingslow, Kent, 403
Kings Lynn (Lin, Linn(e), Lyn), Norfolk, x, 216, 227, 289, 309, 311, 319, 321, 324, 452, 462
Kings Sombourne, Hants, 418
Kingston, Sussex, 175
Kingston Bagpuize, Berks, 292
Kingston (Kinston) on Thames, Surrey, 283, 292, 423, 424, 453, 462
Kingston (Kingstone) upon Hull see Hull
Kingussie, Scotland, 76
Kinsham see Keynsham
Kinston see Kingston
Kipping, Joane, 404
Kirby, Adam, 419; Habacuck, 407
Kirkcaldy (Kirkady), Scotland, 62
Kirkham, Joan, 400
Kitteridg, Francis, 409
Knightly, Edward 409
Knightsbridge, Middlesex, 406
Knowles, Sir Robert, 398
Knox, John, 77
Koblenz, Germany, 98
Kolín (Collein, Colleyne), Czech Republic, 16, 421
Könnern (Kinderne), Germany, 109
Krusné Horgy, Bohemia, 110

Lad lane, London, 444, 447, 459, 460
Ladon (Loden), River, 252
Laechlad see Lechlade
Laighten see Leighton
Laighton see Leighton, Leyton
Laleham (Lallum), Middlesex, 212
Lamberhurst, Kent, 399, 451, 461
Lamberts hill, St, London, 381
Lambeth, Surrey, 164, 423

Lambourn (Lamborne, Lamburne), Berks, 85, 420, 421
Lampeter, Cardigans, 338
Lancashire (Lancash), 52, 337, 436, 443–45, 456, 457, 459, 460
Lancaster, Lancs, 46, 50–52, 432
Lancaster, duke of, 220
Lancelles, Vincent, 333
Lane, Abigail, 411, 412; John, 411
Langfoord, Langford see Longford
Langland, William, 182
Langley, Abbots, Herts, 201
Langley, Kings, Herts, 415
Langport, Som, 403
Langridge, John, 405
Langthon, Stratford, Essex, 411
Langtree, Oxon, 428
Langworth, Lieut, 116
Lanhydrock, Cornwall, 299
Larkfield, Kent, 403
Lasterne, High see High Easter
Laurence lane, St, London, 437, 457
Lawe, Margaret, 401-2
Lawrence, St, Kent, 401
Lea, River, 202
Lea, Sir Richard, 415; Robert, 104
Leadenhall (Leadenhal)-street, London, 381, 386, 439, 442, 446, 457, 458, 460
Leaster see Leicester
Leatherhead (Ledderhead, Lederhead), Surrey, 422, 451, 461
Leaven, Ashers see Aschersleben
Lechlade (Laechlad, Lechlad), Glos, 199, 257, 258
Ledderhead, Lederhead see Leatherhead
Lee see Leigh-on-Sea
Leech, River, 199
Leeds (Leedes), Kent, 399,
Leeds (Leedes), Yorks, 186, 215, 231, 232, 289, 401, 443, 459
Leedes, William, 401
Lee-on-the-Solent, Hants, 283
Leese (Leiz, Leize), Germany, 26, 28, 361
Leeth see Leith
Legg, Edward, 411
Legge, William, 306
Leghorn see Livorno
Legh see Leigh
Leicester (Leister), 215, 216, 218–25, 227, 237, 266, 289, 442, 443, 459
Leicester, earl of, 219, 405
Leicestershire (Leicestersh, Leicestershiere, Leicst), 222, 225, 227, 436, 438, 443, 457, 460
Leiden (Leyden), Netherlands, 105
Leigh (Legh), John, 400; Sir Urian, 47, 50, 164

Leigh-on-Sea (Lee), Essex, 89, 130, 164, 203, 410
Leighton (Laighten, Laighton), Buzzard, Beds, 217, 442, 459 Leipzig, Germany, 94, 109
Leison, Francis, 416
Leister, see Leicester
Leith (Leeth), Scotland, 61, 62, 78
Leiz, Leize see Leese
Leland, John, vii, xi-xiii, 194, 287, 301
Lenham, Kent, 399
Leogorne see Livorno
Leonard, St, London, 381, 383
Lesnes, Kent, 402
Leutmeritz see Litomerice
Levales, Mr (of Cornwall), 301
Levingston, Henry, 78
Lewerenz sin Kind, 12
Lewes (Lewis), Sussex, 347, 355, 356, 405, 406, 451, 461
Lewis, Sir Thomas, 343; see also Lewes, Louis
Lewknor, Oxon, 428
Lewisham (Lewsham), Kent, 400
Lewton see Luton
Lexden, Essex, 410, 413
Leyden see Leiden
Leyton (Leighton), 202, 411
Lichfield, Staffs, 44, 45, 216, 237, 333
Lid, see Lydd
Lidbrook see Lydbrook
Lilly, George, 409
Limehouse, London, 162, 408
Limestreet, London, 381
Limmington see Lymington
Lin see Lynn
Linch, Anthony, 420
Lincoln(e), 127, 143, 144, 233, 253, 332, 433, 442, 459
Lincoln(e)s Inn fields, London, 385, 390
Lincoln(e)shire (Lincs), 142, 227, 229, 253, 460
Lindfield (Lingfield), Sussex, 405
Lindsay, Barnard, 62
Lingfield (Linvil(l)), Surrey, 451, 461; see also Lindfield
Linn(e) see Lynn
Linvil(l) see Lingfield
Linyuill see Lyne Hill
Liphook (Lippock), Hants, 418
Little (Litle) Tintern, Mon, 262
Litomerice (Leutmeritz), Bohemia, 118
Little Baddow (Baddo), Essex, 412
Little Brittaine, London, 382,
Little Eastcheape, London, 383, 388, 389
Littlefield, Kent, 403
Littlehampton, Sussex, 175
Little Moorefields, London, 396
Little Stonham, Suffolk, 319

Little Waltham, Essex, 410
Little Woodstreet, London, 383
Livorno (Leghorn, Leogorne), Italy, 267
Llandeilo, Carmarthens, 339, 340
Llanfair Clydogau, Cardigans, 338
Llanidloes, Merioneths, 336
Llanrumney, Glam, 344
Llantrithyd (Llanstrithyott), Glam, 343
Lloyd(e), —,(of Caernarvon), 337; —,(of Stony Stratford), 425; Edward, 399; Humphrey, 328, 329; Randall, 187; Thomas, 259; Walter, 338
Loathbury, London, 386, 390
Lochaber (Loquhabor), Scotland, 72
Lockley, Elizabeth, 400
Loden see Ladon
Lombard (Lumbard) Street, London, 373, 383, 384, 440, 442, 458
London, vii, ix-xii, 3, 4, 9, 12, 23, 31, 33, 36–38, 40, 51, 57, 59, 66, 71, 79, 81, 83, 85, 86, 94, 95, 97, 107, 113, 115, 122, 123, 127, 128, 144, 148, 152, 154, 157, 158, 160, 161, 164, 180, 189, 192, 194, 199, 201, 202, 204, 211, 216, 222, 223, 230, 247, 250–53, 256, 258, 263, 267–69, 272–75, 280, 283, 288, 289, 291, 293–95, 300, 305, 306, 308, 309, 311, 312, 316, 317, 320, 325, 327–29, 331, 336, 345, 347, 353, 363, 367, 369, 370, 372–75, 378, 379, 388–90, 392, 393, 396, 399, 405, 406, 408, 409, 421, 429–31, 433, 434, 443, 452–55, 462; *and see streets and locations indexed by name*
London-bridge, London, 462
Long-Acre (Aker), London, 325, 348, 379, 383,
Long Alley, London, 389
Longbridge, Kent, 403
Longford, Wilts, 159, 188, 191
Longueval, count of, 96
Long Lane, London, 7, 381, 395, 445
Long Melford, Suffolk, 444
Long Wittenham, Oxon, 205
Looe (Loo, Low), East and West, Cornwall, 305, 306
Loquhabor see Lochaber
Loughborough, Leics, 443, 459
Louis (Lewis), dauphin of France, 400, 418
Lovell, Thomas, 398; William, 411
Lovingborough, Kent, 403
Low see Looe
Low Laighton see Leyton
Low, John, 402
Loway, Kent, 403
Lower Basildon, Berks, 208
Lower Lydbrook, Glos, 262
Lowestoft, Suffolk, 133
Lubeck, Germany, 14

Luckin, Rob., 411
Luckman, —, (of Shrewsbury), 260
Ludgate, London, 382, 384, 439, 450, 457, 461
Lugg(e), River, 252
Lumbard, Lumbardstreet see Lombard
Lüneburg (Luningburgh), Germany, 24
Luton (Lewton), Beds, 443, 459
Lydbrook (Lidbrook), Glos, 262, 263
Lydd (Lid), Kent, 171, 401
Lymington (Limmington), Hants, 177, 417
Lyn see Lynn
Lyne Hill (Linyuill), Surrey, 422
Lynn (Lin, Linn(e), Lyn), Kings, Norfolk, x, 216, 227, 289, 309, 311, 319, 321, 324, 452, 462

Maas, River, Netherlands, 105
Mabb, William, 301
Macclesfield (Macksfield), Cheshire, 47, 459
Machabeus, - (of Hull), 146
Machin, Gregory, 407
Mackay, Charles, 367
Macksfield see Macclesfield
McRae, Andrew, viii, xi
Magdalen College, Oxford, 199
Magdeburge, Germany, 95
Magnus, St, London, 384
Maidenhead (Maydenhead), Berks, 201, 211, 291, 392, 454 462
Maidstone (Maydston(e)), Kent, 398, 403, 453, 462
Mainsborough, Hants, 419
Mainz, Germany, 98
Maldon (Malden, Maulden, Mawlden), Essex, 131, 412, 443, 459
Malling (Mawlin), Kent, 401
Malmesbury (Malmsbury), Wilts, 249, 293
Malmesbury, William of, 294
Maltby (Maultby), William, 148
Malvern, Malvernes, Worcs, 71
Manchester (Manhester), Lancs, 33, 48–51, 215, 235, 443, 444, 459
Mandevill(e), Geoffrey de, 266; Sir John, 67;
Manhester see Manchester
Mann, William, 400
Manners, Francis, 176
Manningtree, Essex, 409
Mansbridge, Hants, 418
Mansfelt, Count, 115, 116
Mansfield, Notts, 459
Mapledurham (Maple Ducham), Oxon, 208
Marazion, Cornwall, 300, 301
Marble Arch, London, 12
Marden, Kent, 400, 403, 451, 461
Maresfield (Marsfield), Sussex, 403
Margaret, queen, 416
Margate (Marget), Kent, 401, 453, 462

Marienberg, Germany, 110
Market Bosworth, (battle), Leics, 218, 221, 222, 266
Markyate (Markatstreet), Herts, 414
Marlborough, Wilts, 200, 443, 459
Marlow, 200, 210, 256, 416, 424, 443
Marlow, Captain, 416
Marlowe, Christopher, 109
Marr(e), Brea of, Scotland, 36, 70, 71, 74, 76
Marr, Earl of, 64, 69–72, 75, 77
Marsfield *see* Maresfield
Marsh, Sara, 414
Marshfield (Maxfield), Glos, 433
Marsh Gibbon, Bucks, 425
Marsh locke, Oxon, 208, 414, 425
Marston, John, 304
Marsworth, Bucks, 199
Martin, Anne, 421; Edward, 320, 321; Godfrey, 401; Gregory, 397; Mrs (of Petworth), 54
Martins, St, London, ix, 347, 384–86, 396, 403, 408
Marylebone, London, 88, 275
Mascall, Thomas, 399
Mason, Thomas, 337
Mathew *see* Matthew
Mathewes, Joan, 282; William, 282
Matthew (Mathew), Tobias (Toby), 154
Matthewes, William, 408
Maude, empress, 266
Maulden *see* Maldon
Maultby *see* Maltby
Mawlden *see* Maldon
Mawlin *see* Malling
Maxfield *see* Marshfield
Maximilian, emperor, 358
Maxwell, John, 59, 78
Maydenhead *see* Maidenhead
Maydston(e) *see* Maidstone
Mayfield, Sussex, 405, 452, 461
Maynard, Anthony, 418
Meade, Richard, 404, 405
Meanstock, Hants, 418
Meaux Abbey, Yorks, 147, 180
Medmenham (Mednam), Bucks, 210
Medway, River, 195
Meeching *see* Miching
Meistham *see* Merstham
Melford, Long, Suffolk, 444
Meon, East, Hants, 417
Mercer, Nathanael, 397, 401
Mercia, 219, 398, 415
Mereford, Surrey, 423
Merionethshire, 328, 336, 337
Merlyn, 339
Merriman, Dr (of Neath), 343
Merstham (Meistham), Surrey, 423

Mevagissey (Mevageasie, Mevagesey), Cornwall, 287, 303-5
Mew, Master (of Eastington), 259
Mew-church *see* Newchurch
Meykins, Ralph, 399
Michaels Mount, St, Cornwall, 288, 289, 300, 301
Micham *see* Mitcham
Micheing *see* Miching
Michel(l)dever, Hants, 419
Miching (Meeching, Micheing, Mitching), Sussex, 173, 404
Middlesex (Midlesex), 39, 161, 201, 202, 212, 275, 291, 308, 328, 331, 391, 393, 406, 408, 448, 454, 461
Middleton Moor, Derbs, 225
Middleton-on-Sea, Sussex, 175
Middlewich, Cheshire, 459
Midhurst, Sussex, 404
Midlesex *see* Middlesex
Midleton *see* Middleton-on-Sea
Milan, Italy, 296
Millbrook (Milbrooke), Hants, 418
Milford Haven, Pembs, 340
Milford Lane, London, 385, 390
Milier, John, 416
Milk-street, London, 384, 444
Mill-bank, London, 385
Millent, Robert de, 266
Millward, Henry, 419
Milton, Kent, 317, 398, 400 402, 453, 462
Mimms, South, Herts, 217, 407
Minden, Germany, 3, 28
Minks, Mistris, 109
Minories, London, 379, 385, 388
Miserden, Glos, 257
Missenden, Bucks, 425
Mitcham (Micham), Surrey, 353, 423
Mitching *see* Miching
Moffat (Mophot), Scotland, 57
Moisley, Mary, 408
Moldau (Moldove), River, Bohemia, 113
Mole, River, 201
Molesey (Monlesey, Mowlsey), East and West, Surrey, 201, 422
Molton, South, Devon, 298
Mondevill, William de, 266
Mongewell, Oxon, 205
Monlesey *see* Molesey
Monmouth (Mounmouth), 250, 251, 262, 264, 265, 328, 344, 443, 459
Monmouth, Geoffrey of, 145, 156, 218, 230, 241, 251
Monmouthshire (Mon), 258, 262, 344, 443
Monnow, River, 252
Monox, Edward, 400

Montague Close, London, 389
Montague, viscount, 359
Montfort, Simon de, 405
Montrose, Scotland, 70
Moore, Margaret, 412; Sir William, 379
Moorefields, London, 387, 389, 396
Mooregate, 83, 388, 389
Mophot see Moffat
Moray (Morayshire), Scotland, 76, 77
More, Tho. 411
Morgan, Sir Thomas, 189, 191, 344
Morrell Green see Murrell Green
Morrice, Edmund, 407
Morrine, Thomas, 333
Mortimer, Roger de, 225
Mortlake, Surrey, 423
Morton, Berks, 421
Mosse, Master (of Lydbrook), 263
Mot, Thomas, 398
Mounmouth see Monmouth
Mount, St Michaels, Cornwall, 288, 290, 300, 301, 433
Mountfort, Almerick, 266
Mounthermer, Richard de 266
Mowhurst, William, 403
Mowlsey see Molesey
Moyses, Walter, 399
Much-Hadham, Herts, 415, 441
Murray, Capt, 63; Sir Patrick, 76; Sir William, 64, 70–72, 76–77
Murrell (Morrell), Green, Hants, 308

Nantwich, Cheshire, 237, 333, 445, 459
Naples, Italy, 137
Narborough (Narbury, Northbery), Norfolk, 227
Nashe, Thomas, xii, 58, 109, 133
Nasse see Naze
Nayland (Naylans), Suffolk, 459
Naze (Nasse), 131
Neale, Sir Paul, 230; see also Neile
Neath, Carmarthens 343
Neather-Stoy see Nether Stowey
Neile (Neale), Richard, 229
Neinburgh see Nienburg
Nether Stowey (Neather-Stoy), Som, 287, 295
Netherlands, 105, 212, 270, 320, 444
Netherl(e)y, Staffs, 444, 459
Nettlebed, Oxon, 426
Nevell, William, 411
Nevey, Eliz., 416
Neville, Tarring, Sussex, 356
Newark(e), Notts, 82, 158, 220, 459
Newberry, Newbery see Newbury
Newbery, John, 281
Newbold, Samuell, 409

Newbridge, Oxon, 264
Newbury, Berks, 200, 420, 433, 459
Newcastle, Northumb, 33, 46, 81
Newcastle under Lyme, 46
Newchurch (Mew-church), Wight, 416
New-church, Kent, 403
New-elme see Ewelme
New Forest (forrest), Hants, 181, 418
Newgate, London, 380–82, 388, 389, 434, 440, 442, 445, 449, 456, 458, 459, 461
Newhall, Warwicks, 44
Newhaven, Sussex, 173, 404
Newington, Kent, 400
Newington, Surrey, 423
Newland, Benjamin, 416
Newlocke, Berks, 210
Newman, Charles, 410
Newnham, Glos, 263 see also Nuneham
Newport, Bucks, 426
Newport, Essex, 412,
Newport, Mon, 258, 344,
Newport, Wight, 273, 277–79, 281, 282, 417
Newport Pagnell (Pannell), Bucks, 425, 445
Newquay, Cornwall, 299
New Romney, Kent, 400
Newshoreham, Sussex, 404
Newton Flotman, Norfolk, 319
Newtown(e), Wight, 417
New Winchelsea, Sussex, 360
New Windsor, Berks, 378
Nicholas, St, London, 373, 380, 387, 390
Nicholas, Michael, 418
Nienburg (Neinburgh), Germany, 26
Nitingale, Parnell, 422
Nixon, Anthony, 7; Jeffrey, 397
Noake, John, 418
Nodes, John, 413, 414
Nonsuch Palace, Surrey, 202
Norbury, Surrey, 201
Nore (Nowre), The, Kent/ Essex, 165
Norf see Norfolk
Norflect see Northfleet
Norfolk (Norf, Northfolke), 127, 140–42, 215, 216, 227, 229, 309, 318–21, 324, 434, 452, 461
Noris, Henry, 397
Normaville, Henrie, 408
Norris, William, 260
Northage, Will., 415
Northallerton, Yorks, 81
Northampton, 218, 444, 459
Northamptonshire (Northamp, Northhamptonshire), 435, 437, 444, 446, 447, 457, 459, 460
North Barningham Hall, Norfolk, 140
North Berwick, Scotland, 79

Northbery see Narborough
North Crawley, Bucks, 437
Northfleet (Norflect), Kent, 401
Northfolke see Norfolk
Northhamptonshire see Northamptonshire
Northolt (Northket), 406
North Stoke, Oxon, 205
Northumberland (Northumb), 64, 69, 80, 81
North Walsham, Norfolk, 321
Northwich, Cheshire, 459
North Wootton (Wooton), Norfolk, 227, 324
Norton, Chipping, Oxon, 331
Norton, Henry, 423
Norwich, Norfolk, xii, 229, 309, 311, 319–21, 444, 459
Notestein, Walter, vii
Nottingham, 96, 216, 224, 225, 433, 444, 459
Nottinghamshire (Notting, Notts), 138, 284, 434, 456, 459
Nowre see Nore
Nuneaton, Warwicks, 445, 459
Nuneham (Newnham) Courtenay, Oxon, 204

Oakley, Water, Berks, 211
Oakley, Mistris (of Carmarthen), 339
Oatlands, Surrey, 201, 256, 266
Ock, River, 199
Ockenden (Ockingdon), Essex, 202
Ockenden, South, Essex, 410
Ockingham see Wokingham
Odcombe, Som, 4, 5, 67, 155
Odiham (Odiam), Hants, 418
Odsey, Herts, 415
Offa, Mercian king, 415
Offham, Kent, 400
Ogilby, John, 33, 40
Oke, Berks, 421
Okes, Nicholas, 95
Okingham see Wokingham
Olaves, St, London, 379, 381, 385, 388
Old Baily (Bayly), London, 250, 381, 382, 389
Old Brentford, Middlesex, 406
Old Change, London, 441, 456, 458
Old Street, London, 388
Old Winchelsea, Sussex, 359
Old Windsor, Berks, 211, 378
Oliver, Thomas, 404, 405
Olney (Oney), Bucks, 424, 445, 459
Ongar (Ougar), Essex, 411, 413, 437
Ongar, Chipping (Chippinganger), 411, 437
Ore, Sussex, 172
Orford Ness (Nasse), Suffolk, 133
Organ, Christopher, 417
Orsett (Orsed), Essex, 410
Osbourne, Elizabeth, 407
Osea (Horsey) Island, Essex, 132

Ospring, Kent, 401
Osulston, Middlesex, 409
Oswald, Northumbrian king, 426
Osyth (Ozith), St, Essex, 410
Ougar see Ongar
Oundle, Northants, 459
Ouse (Owse), River, 143, 153, 154, 173, 186, 253, 426
Outred, Mathew, 401
Overton, Hants, 418
Owen, Henry, 413; Sir John, 337
Owse see Ouse
Oxford (Oxfoord), ix, 25, 47, 105, 193–95, 197–200, 204, 215, 233, 249, 250, 257, 264, 273, 290, 292, 334, 352, 378, 391, 392, 413, 427, 433, 445, 459; see also individual locations
Oxfordshire (Oxfoordshire, Oxfords, Oxon, Oxonia), 197, 200, 204, 205, 207, 208, 253, 257, 328, 331, 393, 426, 428, 435, 442, 444, 447, 448, 449, 455, 456, 460, 461
Oxnead (Oxnet), Norfolk, 309, 322
Oxney, Kent, 403
Oxon see Oxfordshire
Oxonbridge, Mary, 401
Oxonia see Oxfordshire
Ozith see Osyth

Paddington, Middlesex, 407
Page, Anthony, 400
Pagnell (Pannel), Newport, Bucks, 425, 445
Paine, Elizabeth, 282; Robert, 425; Roger, 401
Pal(l)atinate, German, 96, 105
Palgrave, Sir Austin, 139, 140
Pallatinate see Palatinate
Palmer, Anne, 407; Master (of Nottingham), 224; Robert, 418, 422
Pangbourne, Berks, 200
Pannel see Pagnell
Parindon see Parndon
Paris, France, 423
Parker, John, 410; Roger, 146, 153; Sir Thomas, 356; Thomas, 411
Park(e)s, Anne, 406, 408; Richard, 406
Parndon (Parindon), Great, Essex, 412
Parr, Thomas, 323
Paston, Sir William, 322
Pastrac, Hants, 418
Peak, The, Derbs, 215, 216, 225, 226, 239, 240, 289
Peake, William, 405
Pearpoynt, William, 407
Pechy, John, 410
Peckham, Surrey, 422
Pecote, Richard, 406
Peeblesshire, Scotland, 57

Pembroke (Pembrook(e)), 340
Pembrokeshire (Pembrookshire), 328, 340
Pembroke (Pembrook), earl and countess of, 189, 190, 307
Pembury (Penborough, Penbree, Peuborough), Kent, 451, 452, 461, 462
Pemsey *see* Pevesney
Penborough, Penbree *see* Pembury
Penchurst *see* Penshurst
Pendennis Castle, Cornwall, 287, 303
Pendragon, Uter (Uther), 241, 265
Peneus, River, 196
Penhale (Penhall), Cornwall, 299
Penigh *see* Penny
Penistone, Yorks, 232
Penllyn (Penline), Glam, 343
Penmaen (Penmen)-mawr, Caernarvons, 335
Penmark, Glam, 343
Penmen *see* Penmaen
Penn, James, 400
Pennell, Job, 128
Pennington, Tho., 412
Penny (Penigh), Germany, 110
Penny com quick, Cornwall, 303
Penrith, Cumb, 54
Penrudduck, Capt, 176; Sir Thomas, 188
Penshurst (Penchurst), Kent, 401, 451, 461
Penwarne, Cornwall, 304
Penzance, Cornwall, 301
Percivall, Anthony, 402
Percy, Algernon, 354
Perior, John, 422
Perry, Richard, 424
Pershore, Worcs, 263, 265
Perth, Scotland, 70, 99
Pescod, Capt, 135, 139, 141
Peterhaghen *see* Petershagen
Peters, St, London, 294, 387
Petersfield, Hants, 416
Petershagen (Peterhaghen), Germany, 28
Petham, Kent, 403
Petley, William, 398
Pettcarne, Patrick, 70
Pettit, John, 404
Petworth, Sussex, 347, 354, 355, 404, 451, 461
Peuborough *see* Pembury
Pevensey (Pemsey), Sussex, 359, 404–6
Peverell, Hatfield, Essex, 411
Peveril Castle, Derbs, 226
Peyton, Axne, 401
Phillip, queen, 399
Phillip's Marsh, St, Bristol, 261
Philpot, John, 398
Phineas, Thomas, 224
Phipp, John, 424
Phissenden, John, 405

Phoenix (Phoeniz) Alley, London, 325, 348
Picard, Sir Henry, 378
Pickayes, Agmondesham, 412
Piddock, John, 45
Pigott, William, 403
Pill, Som, 261
Pinner, Middlesex, 407
Pinners, John, 49
Pirna (Pirne), Germany, 118
Pinder, Richard, 427
Pisa, Italy, 267
Pistor, William, 422
Pitton, Oxon, 428
Pix, Richard, 400
Plantagenet, Humphrey, 266
Plantin, Anne, 419
Plas Gogerddan, Cardigans, 338
Plashie, *see* Pleshey
Plat, Robert, 410
Pleshey (Plashie), Essex, 412
Plimouth *see* Plymouth
Plimpton *see* Plympton
Plinnillimon *see* Plynlimon
Plomley, Edmund, 399
Plowghley, Oxon, 428
Ployden, Master, 208
Plymouth (Plimouth), Devon, 287, 303, 306, 433, 453, 46Plympton (Plimpton), Devon, 306
Plynlimon (Plinnillimon, Pumlumon), Cardigans, 336
Pocahontas, 280
Pocock, Margery, 398
Pollard, Elizabeth, 426
Pontefract (Pomfret), Yorks, 157, 459
Poole (Pool), Dorset, 181, 453, 462
Pope, William, 418
Poplar (Popler), London, 408
Porlock, Som, 298
Portkell, John, 409
Portsdown, Hants, 418
Portsmouth, Hants, 159, 176, 195, 392, 416, 418, 451, 461
Pottler, John, 410
Poultry (Powltry), London, 381, 388
Powell, Anthony, 422; David, 329; Master (of Usk), 344; Mistris (of Pembroke), 340
Powltry *see* Poultry
Powsley, Thomas, 403
Powson, John, 417
Poyner, John, 427
Poynet (Poynit), William, 400
Prague, Bohemia, viii, x, xiii, 3, 92–94, 97, 109, 111–16, 118, 121, 122
Prannell, Henry, 379
Prat, Joan, 418

INDEX OF PERSONS AND PLACES 485

Prestman, John, 425
Preston, Kent, 403
Preston, Lancs, 33, 51, 52, 445, 459
Prestwitch, Edmond, 48–51
Price, Aaron, 344; Sir Richard, 338
Priest, Toby, 399
Prince, John, 407, 420
Prince(s) Risborough (Resborow), Bucks, 426
Priors Thorns, Norfolk, 227
Prit(t)lewell, Essex, 410
Probus, emperor, 378
Puckeridge, Herts, 83, 415
Pumlumon *see* Plynlimon
Purfleet (Turfleet), Essex, 410, 453, 462
Purton, Wilts, 292
Putney, Surrey, 423

Queenborough (Queenburrough, Quinborough, Quinbroghs), Kent, 7, 85, 86, 89, 90, 398, 399
Queenhith(e), London, 453, 454, 462
Quinborough, Quinbroghs *see* Queenborough
Quintilian, 5

Radcliffe, John, 399
Radnorshire, 341
Rainham (Rainam, Raynam), Essex, 410, 453, 462
Ramsbury, Wilts, 200
Ramsey, Thomas, 187
Ramsgate, Kent, 165
Rand, Thomas, 410
Raphs key, London, 452
Raste, Wil., 414
Ratcliffe, London, 408
Ratcliffe, Thomas, 306
Ratton, Sussex, 356
Ravensburne, River, 203
Rawleigh *see* Rayleigh
Rawley, John, 414
Rayer, Tho., 427
Rayleigh (Rawleigh), Essex, 411
Raynam *see* Rainham
Raynor, John, 407
Rayslip *see* Ruislip
Reading, Berks, 200, 208, 421, 445, 454, 459, 462
Recorde, Robert, 43
Redbourne (Redburne), Herts, 413
Redbridge, Hants, 418
Redburne *see* Redbourne
Redcrosse street, London, 381, 387
Redding *see* Reading
Rederhith *see* Rotherhithe
Redmoor (Redmore), Leics, 222
Redred *see* Riverhead

Redruth (Redruith), Cornwall, 300
Reepham (Repham), Norfolk, 322
Reigate (Reygate, Rygate), Surrey, 201, 422, 424, 451, 461
Reignolds, Augustine, 416
Reinard, earl of Anjou, 416
Remlingen (Remling), Germany, 107
Rennimead *see* Runnymede
Repham *see* Reepham
Resborow *see* Risborough
Reygate *see* Reigate
Rhine, River, 96, 98, 114
Rhuddlan (Rudland), Denbighshire, 334, 335, 410
Rice, John, 356
Richard (kings), II, 157, 334, 379, 398, 415, 416, 424; III, 218, 221, 266, 413
Richardson, William, 134
Richmond, earl of, 340
Richmond, Surrey, 423
Richmond, Yorks, 460
Richmonsworth *see* Rickmansworth
Richold, Nicholas, 410
Rickmansworth (Richmonsworth), Herts, 414
Ridge, Toby, 423
Riggs, —, (of Stamford), 82
Ringsoll, Lucy, 410
Ringwood, Hants, 187, 416, 418
Riple *see* Ripley
Riplemore, Berks, 421
Ripley (Riple), Surrey, 422
Ripon (Rippon), Yorks, 460
Risborough (Resborow), Princes, Bucks, 426
Rislip *see* Ruislip
Riverhead (Redred), Kent, 401
Rix, Judith, 409
Robartes, Lord, 299
Robins, Mary, 425
Robinson, Adam, 54; Alice, 406; Athaliah, 427; Christopher, 414
Rochdale (Rochdel), Lancs, 235, 459
Rochester, Kent, 398, 453, 462
Rochford (Rochfourd, Rorchford), Essex, 409, 412
Rochfourd, Thomas, 402
Roding, River, 202
Rodonburgh *see* Rotenburg
Rogers, John, 422
Rollington (Rowlington), Wilts, 190
Roluinden, Kent, 403
Romford (Rumford), Essex, 392, 411
Romney (Rumney), Kent, 169, 171, 362, 400
Romsey, Hants, 416
Rood lane, London, 389
Rooksley, Kent, 402
Rootham *see* Wrotham

Roprecht the Robber, 16
Rorchford *see* Rochford
Roseland, Cornwall, 303
Rosemary lane, London, 382, 384
Rosondink *see* Gross Denkte
Ross (Rosse), Herefs, 262–64
Rotenburg (Rodonburgh), Germany, 24, 29
Roterdam *see* Rotterdam
Rotherhithe (Rederhith), Surrey, 162, 423
Ro(t)terdam, Netherlands, 94, 105
Rowdon, Robert, 411
Rowell, Richard, 425
Rowlington *see* Rollington
Rowse, Reignald, 344
Roxburgh(e), Scotland, 367
Royston, Herts, 414
Rudland *see* Rhuddlan
Rudles poole, Berks, 211
Rufus, William, king, 417
Rugby, Warwicks, 43
Ruislip (Rayslip, Rislip), Middlsex, 331, 406
Rumford *see* Romford
Rumney *see* Romney
Runnymede (Rennimead), 211, 408
Rupert (Rupertus), prince, 94, 114, 122
Rushington *see* Rustington
Rushworth, J., 367
Rustat, Edmund, 415
Rustington (Rushington), Sussex, 175
Ruthven, Scotland, 76
Ruthven, John, 99
Rutland, Rutlandshire, 176, 225, 324, 438, 445
Rutleage, Mary, 422
Rye, Sussex, 172, 347, 348, 360–62, 404, 405, 433, 451, 461
Rygate *see* Reigate
Ryve, Thomas, 341

Sabbs Dock, London, 453
Sabridgeworth, Sabridgworth *see* Sawbridgeworth
Sacheverell, Henry, 44
Sackville, Thomas, 107
Saffron-Market *see* Swaffham
Saffron (Saifren)-Walden, Essex, 412, 447, 460
St Albans (Alban, Albanes, Albons), 39, 57, 266, 415, 433, 456
St Allen, Cornwall, 303
St Andrews, Scotland, 62
St Clements, London, 381, 384, 385, 390, 395, 433, 456
St Davids, Pembs, 327, 340, 433
St Enoder (Enedor), Cornwall, 299
St Giles-in-the-Fields, London, 275, 386, 389, 404, 407, 440, 449, 458
St Ives, Hunts, 186

St Johnston, Scotland, 70
St Katherine's, London, 384, 385, 388, 453, 461; Dock, 453; Hospital and Stairs, 161
St Keverne, Cornwall, 305
St Lamberts hill, London, 381
St Laurence lane, London, 437, 457
St Lawrence, Kent, 401
St Leonard, London, 381, 383
St Magnus, London, 384
St Martins, London, ix, 347, 384–86, 396, 403, 408
St Mary Cray, Kent, 401
St Michaels Mount, Cornwall, 288, 289, 300, 301
St Neots, Hunts, 186
St Nicholas, London, 373, 380, 387, 390
St Olaves, London, 379, 381, 385, 388
St Osyth (Ozith), Essex, 410
St Peters, London, 294, 387
St Phillip's Marsh, Bristol, 261
St Stevens alley, London, 386
Salisbury (Salisburie, Salsberry, Sarum), Wilts, vii, x, 158–61, 179–81, 185, 187, 188, 191, 192, 249, 251, 253, 287, 289, 307, 446, 460
Salop *see* Shropshire
Salsberry *see* Salisbury
Sampford, Great, Essex, 410
Sandall, Mabell, 401
Sandford (Stanford) on Thames, Oxon, 204
Sandgate, Kent, 168
Sandiway (Sandy Lane end), Cheshire, 235
Sandway, Kent, 400
Sandwich, Kent, 160, 186, 400, 401, 452, 453, 461, 462
Sandy Lane end *see* Sandiway
Sanquhar, Lord, 82
Sapham, Sapharn *see* Swaffham
Saracoale, Mistress (of Manchester), 51
Sardanapalus, 77, 393
Sark, River, 54
Šárka, Divoka, Bohemia, 111
Sarum *see* Salisbury
Saunders, Tobias, 425
Savoy, London, 381, 382, 408
Saward, Elizabeth, 410
Sawbridgeworth (Sabridg(e)worth), Herts, 413, 446, 460
Saxony, Germany, viii, 3, 26, 95, 105, 106, 109, 110, 118, 202, 353, 409
Saxony-Anhalt, Germany, 107
Scarborough (Scarborow), 324
Schaumburg (Scomburgh, Shomburgh), Germany, 26, 27
Scicilia *see* Sicily
Scilly Isles, Cornwall, 301

INDEX OF PERSONS AND PLACES

Scoggin, John, 124
Scomburgh see Schaumburg
Sconey see Scotney
Scotland, x, xi, 33–36, 51, 54–80, 83, 85, 93, 99, 116, 127, 194, 215, 230, 235, 266, 289, 330, 379, 415, 430, 431, 450, 452, 453, 455, 462
Scotney (Sconey) Sutton, Hants, 418
Seaford, Sussex, 404
Seale, Kent, 401
Seavenoake see Sevenoaks
Seavern(e) see Severn
Sedbergh, Yorks, 53
Selbright, Kent, 403
Selburne, Hants, 418
Selby, Yorks, 154, 229
Sellindge (Slenge), Kent, 452, 462
Selsey, Sussex, 175, 403
Semmenstedt (Soclem), Germany, 107
Sennen (Sevin), Cornwall, 302
Sentabin, John, 302
Serient, Elinor, 423
Sevenoak(s) (Seavenoake), Kent, 398, 451, 461
Severn (Seavern(e), Severne), River, 249, 252, 254, 257–59, 261, 263–65, 267–9, 290
Severus, emperor, 231
Sevin see Sennen
Sexton, Joseph, 425; Thomas, 401
Seymer, John, 401
Shaftesbury (Shaftsbury), Dorset, 307, 447, 460
Shakespeare, William 65, 98, 113, 202, 218, 278, 290, 296
Shammell, Kent, 402
Sharpe, Elizabeth, 406
Shaw, Thomas, 411
Sheene, Surrey, 423
Sheepey, see Sheppey
Sheere Lane, London, 388
Sheffield, Yorks, 233, 430, 446, 460
Shelton, Mary, 404
Sheppey (Sheepey, Sheppeies) Island, Kent, 7, 85, 86, 165
Sherbin, Scotland, 266
Sherborne (Sherborme, Sherbourne), Dorset, 307, 447, 460
Sherburne Lane, London, 454
Sherlocke, William, 423
Shewesbury see Shrewsbury
Shillito, George, 157
Shiplake (Shiplocke), Oxon, 208
Shoeburyness (Shobury), Essex, 131, 165
Shoe-lane, London, 385
Shomburgh see Schaumburg
Shoreditch (Shorditch), London, 379, 381–5, 388
Shoreham, Sussex, 175, 452, 461

Shorey, Agnes, 398
Shorter, John, 409
Shrewsbury (Shewesbury, Shrewsbury, Shrewsbery, Shrosebury), Salop, 138, 249, 250, 260, 290 433, 446, 460
Shri(e)venham, Berks, 421
Shropshire (Salop), 260, 446
Shrosebury see Shrewsbury
Sibbs Dock, London, 462
Sicily (Scicilia), 135, 416
Siddington (Suddington), Glos, 257
Sidgwick, Giles, 399
Simcots, Thomas, 408
Sims, John, 401
Sindrich see Sundridge
Sisham see Syresham
Sittensen (Citizen), Germany, 24
Sittingbo(u)rne, Kent, 401
Skeene see Keen
Skelton, John, 58
Skidmore, Stephen, 379
Skilhorne, Thomas, 398
Skip Bridge (Skittlebrig), Yorks, 460
Skot, John, 421
Slany (Slowne), Bohemia, 111
Slany, John, 410
Slenge see Sellindge
Slough (Slowgh), Bucks, 201, 291, 425
Slowne see Slany
Smarts key, London, 452, 462
Smith, Jack, 167; John, 280, 420, 427; Richard, 410; Thomas, 414, 416, 420; Tom, 167; Valentine, 406; William, 411
Smithfield (Smithfild), London, 344, 379, 383, 387–89, 396, 435, 437, 438, 441–45, 447, 450, 456–60
Snelling, Edward, 427
Snowdon, Caernarvons, 336
Soclem see Semmenstedt
Soisam see Syresham
Soke (Soake), Hants, 418
Solent, 176
Solme, George, 411
Solomon, king, 230
Sombourne, Kings, Hants, 418
Somerden, Kent, 403
Somers, William, 397, 461
Somerset (Som, Somers, Somersetshire, Sommersetshire), 67, 261, 264, 282, 292, 295–8, 434, 436–8, 442, 449, 450, 461
Sommers key, London, 438
Sommersetshire see Somerset
Sonning (Sunning), Berks, 200, 208, 421
Sotfield see Southfield
South Mimms, Herts, 217, 407
South Molton, Devon, 298

South Ockenden, Essex, 410
Southampton (Southamton, Southhampton, Souththampton), Hants, 181, 268, 275–7, 281, 415, 416
South Bank, London, ix
Southend, Essex, 89, 130, 131, 164
Southey, Robert, 16
Southfield (Sotfield), Essex, 409
Southhampton *see* Southampton
Southrey *see* Surrey
Southsaxon *see* Sussex
Souththampton *see* Southampton
Southwark, London/ Surrey, 375, 376, 380–83, 385–88, 389, 390, 396, 429, 451, 452, 461, 462
Southweald, Essex, 410
Southwell, Mary, 407
Sowth, Mary, 416
Spain (Spaine), 59, 62, 63, 67, 73, 96, 100, 117, 147, 162, 305, 321
Sparhawke, John, 409
Sparta, Greece, 72
Speed (Speede), John, 36, 147, 156, 197, 227, 254, 291, 319, 345, 348, 392
Speenhamland (Spene, Spinhamland), Berks, 420
Spelthorne, Middlesex, 409
Spencer, Sir James, 379; Mr (of Aberconwy), 335; Thomas, 266, 401
Spene *see* Speenhamland
Speyside, Scotland, 76
Spilesby, Mary, 409
Spinaye *see* Spinye
Spinhamland *see* Speenhamland
Spinola, Ambrogio, 96, 98
Spinye (Spinaye), Scotland, 77
Spittle, London, 384
Spittle, Anthony, 416
Springet, George, 409
Springfield, Essex, 410
Squibb, Thomas, 191
Squire, Scipio le, 422
Stade (Stoad), Germany, 8, 31
Stafford (Staffoord), Staffs, 46, 328, 447, 459, 460
Staffordshire (Staffs), 33, 46, 237, 435, 444,
Staines (Stanes), Middlesex, 192–4, 201, 204, 211, 212, 256, 276, 308, 408, 454, 462
Staining *see* Steyning
Stamford (Stanford, Stampfoord, Stampford), Lincs, 33, 82, 158, 446, 460
Standley, Jeffrey, 425
Standlynch (Stonely(e)), Wilts, 188
Stane, Katherin, 411
Stanes *see* Staines
Stanford *see* Sandford, Stamford

Stanhum *see* Stonham
Stanley, William, 235
Stansted Abbey, Herts, 414
Stanton, Anne, 422
Staplehurst, Kent, 400, 451, 461
Starford *see* Stortford
Steevenedge *see* Stevenage
Steevens, Elizabeth, 281
Stenning *see* Steyning
Stephans, Nathaniell, 258
Stephen. king, 266, 399, 410, 417, 420, 421
Stephens, John, 258
Stepney, London, 408
Stepping, Thomas, 413
Sterling *see* Stirling
Sternburgh, Germany, 27
Stevenage (Steevenedge, Stevenedge, Stevenledg), Herts, 325, 413, 414
Stevens alley, St, London, 386
Stevens, John, 427; Trustram, 402
Steward, Mr (of Golden Grove, Llandeilo), 341
Steyning (Staining, Stenning), Sussex, 355, 404
Stirling (Sterling), Scotland, 64, 69, 70
Stoad *see* Stade
Stoakley, Edward, 427
Stock (Stork), Essex, 410, 446, 460
Stockbridge (Stokebridge), Hants, 416
Stocke, Richard, 187
Stockport (Stopfo(o)rd, Stoppard), Cheshire, 47, 447, 460
Stody, Sir John, 379
Stoke Newington, Middlesex, 407
Stokebridge *see* Stockbridge
Stokenchurch, Oxon, 331, 426
Stone, Staffs, 45, 237, 333
Stone, John, 322; Nicholas, 322
Stonecrouch (Stonecrutch), Kent, 401
Stonehouse, Glos, 258
Stonely(e) *see* Standlynch
Stoner, Thos, 416
Stonham (Stanhum), Little, Suffolk, 319
Stony Stratford (stratfourd, stretford), Bucks, 41, 45, 425, 439, 446, 460
Stopfo(o)rd, Stoppard *see* Stockport
Stork *see* Stock
Stortford (Starford), Bishops, Herts, 202, 414
Stotusbury, Alexander 426
Stourbridge (Sturbridge), Cambs, 309, 325
Stoure (Stowre), River, 202, 412
Stow on the Wold, Glos, 198
Stow, John, 373, 379
Stowd *see* Stroudwater
Stowey, Nether, Som, 287, 295
Stowmarket, Suffolk, 319
Stowre *see* Stoure
Stowting, Kent, 403

INDEX OF PERSONS AND PLACES 489

Strand, London, 380–89, 433, 443, 449, 456
Strand on the Green (Strangreene), 406
Stratfield, John, 423
Stratford Bow, Essex, 202
Stratford (Streetford), Fenny, Bucks, 425
Stratford Langthon, Essex, 411
Stratford (Stretford) on Avon, Warwicks, 249, 254, 265
Stratford, Stony, Bucks, 41, 45, 425, 439, 446, 460
Strathbogie (Stroboggy), Scotland, 77
Stratton (Stratten), Cornwall, 298, 299
Stratton Audley (Awdley), 427
Streatham (Stretham), Surrey, 422
Streatley, Berks, 85
Street, Kent, 403
Streetford see Stratford
Streethorpe see Edenthorpe
Streeting, William, 402
Stretford see Stratford
Stretham see Streatham
Stroboggy see Strathbogie
Strood (Strowd), Kent, 400
Strood, Margery, 418
Stroodwater see Stroudwater
Stroud, Glos, 249, 257, 258, 446
Stroudwater (Stowd, Stroodwater), River, 257, 446, 460
Strowd see Strood
Stuart, Elizabeth, 93, 113; James, 71; John, 78
Sturbridge see Stourbridge
Sudbury, Suffolk, 445, 460
Suddington see Siddington
Suetonius, 325
Suffolk (Suffolck, Suffolke), 133, 319, 412, 435–7, 440, 442, 44, 445, 448, 452, 458–60
Summers key, London, 457
Sunbridge see Sundridge
Sunbury, Surrey, 201
Sundridge (Sindrich, Sunbridge), Kent, 401, 451
Sunning see Sonning
Surrey (Southrey, Surey Surry), 161, 192, 195, 201, 202, 212, 266, 347, 353, 386, 391, 393, 403, 421, 424, 429, 451, 452, 454, 461
Sussex (Southsaxon), 172, 174, 347, 348, 353–56, 359, 361, 362, 391, 393, 403, 406, 429, 451, 452, 461
Sutton, Hants, 418
Sutton Coldfield (Coffill), Warwicks, 33, 44
Sutton Courtenay, Berks, 205
Sutton Scotney (Sconey) Sutton, Hants, 418
Sutton Valience, Kent, 401
Sutton, Nicholas, 411
Swaffham (Saffron-Market, Sapham, Sapharn), Norfolk, 227, 229, 446, 460

Swallowfield, Berks, 460
Swansea, Glam, 327, 341
Sweden, 384
Swift, Mr (of North Wootton), 324; Sir Robert, 157
Syresham (Sisham, Soisam), Northants, 446, 460

Tadcaster, Yorks, 231
Talbot, John, 138
Taliaris (Talliaris), Carmarthens, 339
Talke, Staffs, 46
Tame, River, 197–203, 252, 427, 428
Tame see Thame
Tanner, Elizabeth, 427
Tanridge, Surrey, 424
Taplow, Bucks, 201, 211
Tarling, Essex, 410
Tarnaway see Darnaway
Tarpley, Elizabeth, 400
Tarring, Sussex, 356, 404
Tarvar, Will., 416
Tasker, Thomas, 404
Tate, Avis, 416
Tatsworth see Tetsworth
Taylor, Jane, 410; Jarvice, 417; John (the author), passim; John (of Bristol), 261; John (of Gloucester), 344; John (of Maidstone), 398; Katherin, 407; Mr (of St Albans), 40; Richard, 407; Samuell, 407; Thomas, 358
Teme, River, 252
Temple (Bar), London, 180, 210, 380, 386–88, 390, 395, 396
Templeman, Mr (of Christchurch), 178
Tenby, Pembs, 340
Tencham, Kent, 402
Tendring, Essex, 413
Tenterden, Kent, 401, 403, 451, 461
Terry, William, 400
Tetbury, Glos, 199, 203
Tetsworth (Tatsworth), Oxon, 427
Teuxbury see Tewkesbury
Tew (Tue), Great, Oxon, 331, 332
Tewkesbury (Teuxbury, Tewxbury), Glos, 254, 259, 263, 265, 266, 447, 460
Thacker, Richard, 321
Thackham see Thatcham
Thacksted see Thaxted
Thame (Tame), Oxon, 193, 194, 197, 252, 384, 427, 428, 447, 460
Thames (Thamisis), River, ix, x, 7, 33, 66, 75, 85–87, 91, 97, 129, 130, 160, 161, 165, 180, 193–204, 208, 210–12, 249, 253, 254, 256–58, 264, 317, 324, 367, 373, 380–82, 386–90, 396, 419–22, 426, 431, 453, 462

Thamestreet, London, 384
Thamisis *see* Thames
Thatcham (Thackham), Berks, 420
Thaxted (Thacksted), Essex, 410
Theale, Berks, 420, 421
Theed, William, 425
Theedham, John, 4Thessaly, Greece, 196
Thistleworth *see* Isleworth
Thomas, Sir Anthony, 227; John, 408; Richard, 406; Walter, 342
Thom(p)son (Tompson), —, (Taylor's associate), 100–3; John, 337
Thorngate (Thoragate), Hants, 418
Thorp, Rich., 420
Thorpe, Essex, 410
Threedneedle (Thridneedle) Street, London, 383, 385
Thurgood, Agnes, 405; John, 414
Thurstable, Essex, 413
Thurstone, Samuell, 399; William, 411
Tiberius, emperor, 265
Ticehurst, Sussex, 404
Tichfield *see* Titchfield
Tidmarsh (Ditmarsh), Berks, 438
Tilbury (Tilbery, Tilburly), Essex, 93, 94, 105, 107, 108, 118, 121, 318, 411
Tillingham (Tittingham), Essex, 131
Tilly, John, 236
Timur the Lame, 168
Tinkeridg, Anne, 416
Tintern(e), Little (Litle), Mon, 262
Titchfield (Tichfield), Hants, 283, 416
Tittingham *see* Tillingham
Tiverton, Devon, 447, 460
Todrigg, George, 78
Toltingtroph, Kent, 402
Tompson, John, 399; William, 413; *see also* Thompson
Tonbridge (Tunbridge), Kent, 266, 398, 403, 451, 452, 461, 462
Tookey, Smith, 400; Thomas, 401
Tooting, Surrey, 423
Topcliffe, Yorks, 81
Topsell, Edward, 395
Torceter *see* Towcester
Tothill (Tuthill, Tuttle) street, London, 375, 379, 383, 384, 408
Tottenham (Totnam, Tottenham-highcrosse), Middlesex, 407
Towcester (Torceter, Toweter), Northants, 41, 447, 460
Tower dock, London, 388
Tower Gate, London, 379,
Tower hill, London, 384, 389
Tower (Towre) of London, 113, 161, 388, 390, 408

Tower street, London, 380, 385, 387, 389
Towers, Samuell, 404
Towerson, William, 418
Towlson, William, 401
Towre *see* Tower
Traherne, Phillip, 263
Transylvania, 96
Travers, Walter, 418
Tray, Robert, 399
Trent, River, 143–45, 253
Tresse, Thomas, 400
Treveneague (Trimineague, Trimiweagow), Cornwall, 300, 302
Tring, Herts, 199, 413
Trinity lane, London, 389
Trinovantes, tribe, 251
Tromp Trump), Martin van, 362
Truro, Cornwall, 299, 303
Tucker, Phebe, 423; Richard, 398
Tudor, Edmund, 340; Margaret, 69
Tue *see* Tew
Tunbridge *see* Tonbridge
Turbervill(e), Annis, 406; Anthony, 343
Turfleet *see* Purfleet
Turn(e)bull street, 383, 396
Turner, Simon, 420, 426; Susan, 400; William, 428
Tuthill, Tuttle *see* Tothill
Tweed, River, 80, 81
Twickenham, Middlesex, 407
Twyford, Berks, 419
Twyford, Kent, 403
Tyburn(e), London, 12, 88, 225, 275
Tyrie, Captain, 63

Uckfield, Sussex, 405, 451, 461
Ulrich, Frederick, 106
Ultford, Essex, 412
Umbrevile, Katherin, 423
Underhill, Thomas, 187
Underwood, Grendon, Bucks, 440, 458
Upminster, Essex, 410
Usher, John, 407
Usk(e), River, 258
Usk(e), Mon, 344
Usmer, Anne, 401
Uter (Uther) Pendragon, 241, 265
Uxbridge, Middlesex, 407

Valckenburgh, Johan van, 10
Valience, Sutton, Kent, 401
Vandenbrooke, Ancient, 116
van Tromp *see* Tromp
Vaughan, Henry, 327, 339, 341; Richard, 327, 340, 341
Veare *see* Vere

INDEX OF PERSONS AND PLACES 491

Venice, Italy, xii, 390
Venman, Margaret, 409
Venner, Master (of Warwick), 332
Verden (Feirden) an der Aller, Germany, 24
Vere (Veare), Sir Horace, 105
Vernon, William, 398
Vienna, Austria, 96
Vies *see* Devizes
Villiers (Villeirs), George, 34
Viney, Agnes, 400
Vinmunt, Anne, 414
Vinn, Mabell, 417
Vintrey, London, 390
Virgil, 123, 246
Virginia, 280
Vltava, River, 113
Vowte, Mr (of Norwich), 321

Waddon, Surrey, 423
Wade, Elizabeth, 409
Wadhurst (Wadehurst), Sussex, 404, 451, 461
Wakefield, Yorks, 232, 450, 461
Wakering, Great, Essex, 131, 412
Walbrooke, London 384
Walden, Saffron, Essex, 412, 447, 460
Waldingfield (Wallingfield), Suffolk, 448, 460
Wales, 176, 199, 235, 258, 264, 283, 290, 327–29, 334–44, 345, 347, 362, 379, 430, 432, 433, 439, 443, 457
Walker, William, 414
Waller, Edward, 402
Wallingfield *see* Waldingfield
Wallingford Berks, 194, 200, 205, 225, 420, 448, 460
Wallington, Surrey, 424
Walsham, North, Norfolk, 321
Walsingham, Norfolk 433, 449, 461
Waltham, Essex, 413
Waltham Abbey, Essex, 378, 411
Waltham, Bishops, Hants, 417, 418
Waltham Cross, Herts, 414
Waltham, Great, Essex, 412
Waltham, Little, Essex, 410
Walthamstow, Essex, 202, 378, 411
Walton *see* Watton
Walton on Thames, Surrey, 210
Wandle, River, 353
Wandsworth, Surrey, 201, 423
Wantage (Wanting), Berks, 419, 421, 448, 460
Wanuish, Wanvish *see* Wonnersh
Wapping, London, 12, 162, 408
Warbleton, Sussex, 451, 461
Ware, Herts, 83, 202, 414, 449, 450, 460
Warfield (Wareseile), Berks, 419
Wargrave (Wargrove), Berks, 421
Warn(e)ford, Hants, 283 417

Warner, Priscilla, 414; Thomas, 406
Warnford *see* Warneford
Warrington, Cheshire, 323, 461
Warrington, Sampson, 323
Warwick(e), 83, 267, 327, 328, 332, 413, 448, 449, 458–61
Warwick, earl of, 83, 417; Martha, 406
Warwick(e)shire (Warwicks, Warwicksh), 43, 44, 237, 254, 438, 442, 445, 449, 450, 455, 457
Washern, Wilts, 189
Waterer, Mary, 411
Watford, Herts, 414, 448, 461
Watheling stone, Kent, 403
Watling Street, London, 386
Watlington, Oxon, 426
Wats, Sir John, 415
Watson, William, 401
Watton, Thomas, 412
Watton-at-Stone (Walton), Herts, 413
Waybridge *see* Weybridge
Wealdstone (Wheatstone, Whetstone), Middlesex, 407
Weaveham, Cheshire, 235
Weazer *see* Weser
Web, Anthony, 410; Michael, 407
Webb, Jane, 423
Weimouth *see* Weymouth
Welbecks weare, Oxon, 208
Weldish, Thomas, 407
Weller, Christian, 423
Welles *see* Wells
Wells, Som, 288, 293, 449, 450, 461
Wells (Welles)-next-the-Sea, Norfolk, 142
Wells, George, 425; Mary, 425
Wellwin *see* Welwyn
Welsh Bicknor, Herefs, 264
Welwyn (Wellwin), Herts, 414
Wendover, Bucks, 425, 448, 449, 460, 461
Wennell, Francis, 405
Wenulocks, Middlesex, 409
Weser (Weazer), River, 28
West Looe, 305
West Molesey, Surrey, 201, 422
West Wittering, Sussex, 176
West Wycombe (wickham), Bucks, 425
Westbrooke, Henry, 422
Westerham (Westram, Westrum), Kent, 203, 401, 403, 452, 462
Westgate (Woodsgate), Kent, 401, 403
Westham, Sussex, 405
Westmerland *see* Westmorland
Westminster, London, 69, 107, 237, 238, 283, 294, 373–76, 379, 380, 382–90, 392, 396, 406, 408, 431
Westmorland (Westmerland), 53, 54, 436

Westram, Westrum *see* Westerham
Wethersfield, Essex, 410
Wey, River, 201
Weybridge (Waybridge), Surrey, 256, 423
Weymouth (Weimouth), Dorset, 453, 462
Whaddon, baron of, 34
Wharncliffe, Yorks, 215, 233
Wheately (Whately, Wheatley), Oxon, 200, 427
Wheatenhurst, Glos, 259
Wheathampstead (Whethamstead), Herts, 413
Wheatley *see* Wheately
Wheatstone *see* Wealdstone
Whethamstead *see* Wheathampstead
Whetstone *see* Wealdstone
Whitchurch, Bucks 425
Whitchurch, Oxon, 208
White Mountain, battle, 93, 113, 124
White, Abell, 412; Agnis, 410; Elizabeth, 425; Joan, 404; John, 400; robert, 416
Whitechappell, London, 382, 383, 388, 407
Whitecrosse-street, London, 381, 388, 389, 396, 459, 460
Whitefriars, London, 383
Whitelocke (Whitlock), Sir James, 194, 209, 210
Whitlock, Walter, 407
Whitminster (Whitmister), Glos, 259
Whitmore, Sir William, 259
Whitney, Master, 116
Whitstable (Whitstaple), Kent, 402
Whittam *see* Witham
Whitworth, Capt John, 334
Wickham, Hants, 283; *see also* Wycombe, High
Wigan (Wiggon), Lancs, 461
Wiggot, Peter, 425
Wight, Isle of, 94, 176, 253, 272–74, 277, 281, 282, 284, 290, 417, 458
Wigmor(e), earl of, 225
Wigston, Thomas, 220
Wike *see* Wyke
Wild, William, 418
Wilfourd, Francis, 404
Wilkins, Thomas, 409
Wilks, Anne, 416
Williams, Francis, 414; Kate, 423; Mary, 416; Mr (of Petworth), 354; Richard, 420
Willis, George, 407
Willmott (Wilmot), Simon, 411, 412
Wills, John, 410
Wilmot *see* Wilmot
Wilshire, Jesper, 414
Wilson, William, 357
Wilton, Herefs, 262, 264, 265
Wilton, Wilts, 160, 189, 251, 288, 307
Wiltshire (Wilts), 159, 161, 180, 182, 188, 200, 257, 292, 447, 448

Wimbledon (Wimbleton, Winbleton), Surrey, 195, 422, 452, 461
Wimborne (Winburne), Dorset, 281
Winbleton *see* Wimbledon
Winburne *see* Wimborne
Winchcomb(e), Glos, 460
Winchelsea (Winchelsey), Sussex, 172, 359, 360, 404
Winchester, Hants, 159, 192, 230, 281, 417, 418, 421, 449, 461
Windover, William, 191
Windrush, River, 198, 199, 263
Windsor (Winsor), Berks, 69, 180, 195, 201, 211, 378, 419, 454, 462
Winfield *see* Winkfield
Wingfield, Thomas, 260
Wingham (Winham), Kent, 401, 403
Winifred's (Winifrid's) Well, Flintshire, 194, 327, 334, 335
Winkfield (Winfield), Berks, 420
Winn, Peter, 400
Winslow (Winsloe), Bucks, 424, 448, 461
Winsor *see* Windsor
Winstree, Essex, 412
Wirksworth (Wortsworth), Derbs, 225, 226
Wiseman, Captain, 135, 141; John, 416
Witham (Whittam, Wittam, Wittham), Essex, 143, 411, 413, 448, 460; *see also* Withyham
Witherham *see* Withyham
Withering, Thomas, 454
Witherington, Sir Henry, 63, 64, 81
Withyham (Witherham, Witham), Sussex, 403, 452, 461
Witney, Oxon, 198, 426, 449, 461
Wittam *see* Witham
Wittenham, Long, Oxon, 205
Wittering, East and West, Sussex, 176
Wittham *see* Witham
Wivenhoe, Essex, 410
Woking, Surrey, 424
Wokingham (Ockingham, Okingham), Berks, 420, 459
Wolfe, Eliz., 425
Wolfenbüttel (Wolfunbuttle), Germany, 94, 106, 107
Wolsey, Thomas, 103, 319
Wonersh (Wanuish, Wanvish), Surrey, 451, 461
Wood, Agnes, 416; Jane, 401; Sara, 400; Susan, 400
Woodford, Edward, 410
Woodham Ferrers (feries), Essex, 410
Woodland, Susan, 400
Woodman, Edw., 403
Woods, Richard, 417
Woodsgate *see* Westgate
Woodstock(e) (Woodstrck), Oxon, 266, 427,

INDEX OF PERSONS AND PLACES 493

448, 460
Woodstreet(e), London, 381, 383, 385, 386, 390, 434, 435, 437, 439, 440, 444, 446, 448, 456–60
Woolfe, Bridget, 416
Woolgar, William, 416
Woolstaple, London, 383
Woolwich, Kent, 401, 453, 462
Wooton, Kent, 424; *see also* Wootton
Wootton, North, Norfolk, 227, 428
Worcester (Worster), 259, 260, 290, 357, 433, 448, 449, 460, 461
Worcestershire (Worcest, Worcestersh, Worcs), 263, 435, 440, 449, 458, 461
Wormeley, Herts, 414
Worstead (Worsted), Norfolk, 321
Worster *see* Worcester
Worth, Kent, 403
Worth, Sussex, 405
Wortham, Kent, 403
Worthing, Sussex, 159, 174
Worthington, Roger, 412
Wortley, Yorks, 232
Wortley, Elizabeth, 410; Sir Francis, 230, 232–4
Wortsworth *see* Wirksworth
Wright, Edward, 95; Martin, 426; Master (of Chester), 235
Wrotham (Rootham), Kent, 401, 452, 462

Wroughton, Wilts, 200
Wycombe (Wickham), High, Bucks, 201, 425
Wycombe (wickham), West, Bucks, 425
Wye, Kent, 400, 403
Wye, River, 249, 252, 254, 258, 262–64, 268, 290
Wyke (Wike)-upon-Hull, Yorks, 147
Wyles, Elizabeth, 409

Yalding, Kent, 400
Yarmouth (Yarmuth), Wight, 176, 417
Yarmouth, Great, Norfolk, xii, 127, 133, 134, 433
Yenload *see* Evenlode
Yeovil (Ivell), Som, 67, 442
York(e), x, xiii, 33, 81, 82, 126–9, 136, 143–6, 148, 154156, 157, 159, 214–16, 229–31, 233, 253, 289, 308, 347, 357, 381, 432, 450, 459–61
York-house, London, 385
York(e)shire (Yorkes, Yorksh), 81, 82, 137, 156, 157, 180, 186, 216, 439, 441, 443, 445, 446, 450, 452, 457, 460, 461
Young, Andrew, 400; Thomas, 398

Zchopau (Shop), Germany, 110
Zealand, 453, 462
Zouch(e), Edward la, 168

www.ingramcontent.com/pod-product-compliance
Lightning Source LLC
Chambersburg PA
CBHW070934180426
43192CB00039B/2177